SCI-FI
ON TAPE

A Complete Guide to Science Fiction and Fantasy on Video

JAMES O'NEILL

BillboardBooks
An imprint of Watson-Guptill Publications
New York

Senior Editor: Bob Nirkind
Editor: Amy Handy
Book and cover design: Jay Anning
Production Manager: Ellen Greene

Library of Congress Cataloging-in-Publication Data
O'Neill, James, 1956–
    Sci-fi on tape : a comprehensive guide to science fiction and
fantasy films on video / James O'Neill.
        p.   cm.
    ISBN 0-8230-7659-8
    1. Science fiction films—Catalogs. 2. Fantastic films—Catalogs.
3. Video recordings—Catalogs. I. Title.
PN1995.9.S26053   1997
016.79143'615—dc21   96-52599
                                                      CIP

Manufactured in the United States

First printing, 1997

1 2 3 4 5 6 7 8 9 / 99 98 97

INTRODUCTION

Perennially popular with audiences of all ages, science fiction and fantasy films make the impossible possible, the unimaginable into something that can be imagined and experienced over and over again like a favorite dream come true. Taking the viewer from the distant past far into the future, from the depths of space to the depths of the sea, these films embrace the imaginings of everyone from H. G. Wells and Jules Verne to George Lucas and Steven Spielberg.

Arranged alphabetically and conveniently cross-referenced with variant release titles, *Sci-Fi on Tape* presents a concise synopsis and review for each entry, along with the current distributor, year of release, Motion Picture Association of America rating, running time, director, and main cast, as well as a half- to four-star rating. In addition to films, a number of sci-fi television series available on video have been included—everything from the benchmark *Star Trek* series to cult favorites like *Doctor Who* and *The Prisoner*—with episode guides that are as up to date as possible.

The moviegoing public continues to exhibit a ceaseless fascination for fantastic films, from silents like *Metropolis* to the current smash *Independence Day*. *Sci-Fi on Tape* should provide a convenient, readable, and entertaining companion for these cinematic journeys into the world of the incredible.

STAR RATINGS

★★★★   Excellent

★★★☆   Very Good

★★★   Good

★★☆   Average

★★   Fair

★☆   Poor

★   Very Poor

☆   The Worst

MOTION PICTURE ASSOCIATION OF AMERICA (MPAA) RATINGS

G   General Audiences
All ages may be admitted for viewing.

PG   Parental Guidance Suggested
All ages may be admitted but parental guidance is suggested.

PG-13   Parental Guidance Suggested; Parents of Children Strongly Cautioned
All ages may be admitted but parental guidance is suggested, especially for children under 13.

R   Restricted
Admission is restricted to persons over a specified age (usually 17) unless accompanied by a parent or guardian.

NC-17   No One Under 17 Admitted
Admission is restricted to persons over 17 years of age.

X   No One Under 18 Admitted
Admission is restricted to persons over 18 years of age.

Where MPAA ratings were not applicable, the following designations were used:

NR   Not Rated
Films that were made prior to the establishment of the MPAA (in 1968), as well as many made-for-TV movies.

UR   Unrated
Films released without an MPAA rating, including many European-made films and re-releases containing additional or restored scenes of graphic violence or sex.

SCI-FI

ON TAPE

ABBOTT AND COSTELLO GO TO MARS

★☆ MCA/Universal, 1953, NR, 77 min. Dir: Charles Lamont. Cast: Bud Abbott, Lou Costello, Mari Blanchard, Robert Paige, Martha Hyer, Horace McMahon, Jack Kruschen, Anita Ekberg.

This mistitled mess may be Bud and Lou's worst film. After accidentally blasting off in a rocket, the boys first land in New Orleans during Mardi Gras, which they mistake for Mars, and are joined by crooks McMahon and Kruschen. Then it's on to Venus, where the sultry Blanchard holds court over a bunch of man-hungry Miss Universe contest winners. Good special FX are about all this lame fantasy-comedy has going for it.

ABBOTT AND COSTELLO MEET THE INVISIBLE MAN

★★★ MCA/Universal, 1951, NR 82 min. Dir: Charles Lamont. Cast: Bud Abbott, Lou Costello, Arthur Franz, Nancy Guild, Adele Jergens, Sheldon Leonard, William Frawley, Gavin Muir.

Boxer Franz, wrongly accused of his manager's murder, shoots up with Claude Rains's old invisibility formula to duck the cops and then turns to private eyes Bud and Lou to help clear himself. Probably A&C's best '50s film, this is helped tremendously by its great supporting cast and first-rate FX by (uncredited) veteran John P. Fulton. Funniest scene: Lou and the punching bag.

ABRAXAS, GUARDIAN OF THE UNIVERSE

★☆ Image Entertainment, 1990, R, 87 min. Dir: Damien Lee. Cast: Jesse Ventura, Marjorie Bransfield, Sven-Ole Thorsen, James Belushi.

Awful *Terminator 2* clone from the director of *Food of the Gods 2*. Former pro wrestler Ventura is the title guy, an outer space bounty hunter after a genetically altered madman (Thorsen) who's come to Earth to find the woman he assaulted and impregnated five years earlier.

Original ad art from Abbott and Costello Go to Mars *(1953).*

Pitiful, would-be actioner Ventura desperately tries to save.

ABSENT MINDED PROFESSOR, THE

★★★ Disney, 1961, NR, 97 min. Dir: Robert Stevenson. Cast: Fred MacMurray, Nancy Olson, Keenan Wynn, Tommy Kirk, Ed Wynn, Leon Ames.

One of Walt Disney's most popular '60s comedies with MacMurray as the title character: a high school science teacher who discovers "Flubber," an antigravity rubber. Little more than a TV sitcom expanded to feature length but as such a lot of fun with good FX and a game cast of veteran character actors—always the Disney comedy's greatest strength. By all means avoid the offensively ugly colorized version. Sequel: *Son of Flubber*.

ABYSS, THE

★★★ Fox, 1989, PG-13, 172 min. Dir: James Cameron. Cast: Ed Harris, Mary Elizabeth Mastrantonio, Michael Biehn, Leo Burmester, Todd Graff, Kimberly Scott.

Cameron's *Close Encounters* in the deep with Harris and Mastrontonio as estranged husband-and-wife engineers trying to raise a crippled nuclear sub and encountering aliens and their downed space craft. Cameron's much-sought-after director's cut finally makes it to video and, although thirty minutes longer than the theatrical version, is better paced with more substantial character development and the original, much better, ending. State-of-the-art morphing FX—a computer-generated bit of wizardry that's become a bit overused since—a great cast, and lots of tension and excitement help make this the best sci-fi blockbuster of the late '80s.

ADVENTURES IN DINOSAUR CITY

★★ Republic, 1991, PG, 88 min. Dir: Brett Thompson. Cast: Omri Katz, Shawn Hoffman, Tiffanie Poston, Pete Koch, Megan Hughes.

Three kids are transported to an alternate prehistoric universe inhabited by ultrahip dino teens. Bland kiddie fare, a bad cross between *Teenage Mutant Ninja Turtles* and *Jurassic Park*, with puppetry FX and annoyingly cute characters.

ADVENTURES OF A GNOME CALLED GNORM, THE

★★ Polygram, 1989, PG, 86 min. Dir: Stan Winston. Cast: Anthony Michael Hall, Claudia Christian, Jerry Orbach, Eli Danker, Mark Harelik, Robert Z'Dar.

Makeup FX whiz Winston's followup to his directorial debut, *Pumpkinhead*, rates as one of the weirdest movies ever to survive development hell. Hall is a young cop who teams up with the title character, recently arrived in L.A. from his underground lair, to track down a gang of diamond smugglers. Shelved for five years before its quickie '94 video release, this lunkheaded flick keeps daring you to like it but it's hard to warm up to. Still, despite surprisingly weak makeup FX, this is better than all those stupid *Leprechaun* movies. That's not much, but it's something. Original title: *A Gnome called Gnorm*.

ADVENTURES OF BARON MUNCHAUSEN, THE

★★★ RCA/Columbia, 1989, PG, 126 min. Dir: Terry Gilliam. Cast: John Neville, Sarah Polley, Eric Idle, Oliver Reed, Valentina Cortese, Jonathan Pryce, Charles McKeown, Uma Thurman, Sting, Robin Williams.

Monty Python's Gilliam followed up his cult favorites *Time Bandits* and *Brazil* with this underrated new interpretation of the exploits of the legendary liar. The Baron (Neville, also an excellent Sherlock Holmes in the underappreciated thriller *A Study in Terror*) sets out to save a fabled city from invading Turks and ends up encountering the world's fattest man, as well as the king of the moon (an uncredited Williams at his most manic), and is even swallowed by a sea monster. Wonderfully quaint special FX and a fabulous cast help make this box office disappointment worthy of video rediscovery. Italian horror director Michele Soavi (*The Church, Cemetery Man*) directed second unit and is credited by Gilliam as saving the film when it ran over schedule.

ADVENTURES OF BUCKAROO BANZAI, THE: ACROSS THE EIGHTH DIMENSION

★★★ Vestron, 1984, PG, 103 min. Dir: W. D. Richter. Cast: Peter Weller, Ellen Barkin, John Lithgow, Jeff Goldblum, Christopher Lloyd, Rosalind Cash.

Weller is Buckaroo, a rock singer/neurosurgeon/race-car driver who discovers that Orson Welles's famous 1938 *War of the Worlds* radio broadcast was real and that the U.S.A. has long been infiltrated by dastardly, shape-shifting aliens from the eighth dimension. Almost too smart-assed for its own good, this sci-fi comedy gets by thanks to some very funny ideas and a terrific cast, especially Lithgow (sounding like Bela Lugosi trying to read the St. Louis phone book) as the demented Dr. Emilio Lizardo. Aka *Buckaroo Banzai*.

ADVENTURES OF CAPTAIN MARVEL, THE

★★★ Nostalgia Merchant, 1941, NR, 240 min. Dirs: William Witney, John English. Cast: Tom Tyler, Frank Coghlan, Jr., Louise Currie, William Benedict, Robert Strange, George Pembroke.

Young Billy Batson (Coghlan) is given a secret word ("Shazam!") by the gods that transforms

Iulia Sointseva wins the Sigourney Weaver look-alike contest in Aelita, Queen of Mars *(1924).*

him into the heroic Captain Marvel (Tyler) who battles the dastardly villain the Scorpion (Benedict). A totally entertaining '40s serial with all those great hokey touches you know and love. The previous year Tyler played Kharis the mummy in the *Mummy's Hand.* Aka *The Return of Captain Marvel.*

ADVENTURES OF HERCULES, THE

★ MGM/UA, 1984, PG, 90 Min. Dir: Lewis Coates (Luigi Cozzi). Cast: Lou Ferrigno, Milly Carlucci, Sonia Viviani, William Berger, Carlotta Green, Claudio Cassinelli.

The muscle-bound Greek hero (the *Incredible Hulk's* Ferrigno) encounters various monsters and Amazons in this brain-dead followup to the 1983 *Herc* remake. Rock-bottom Italian stinker originally called *Hercules II.*

ADVENTURES OF STELLA STARR, THE

See: *Starcrash.*

ADVENTURES OF SUPERMAN, THE

★★★ Warner, 1953–57, NR, 50 min. per tape. Dirs: Thomas Carr, Lew Landers, Phil Ford, George Reeves, others. Cast: George Reeves, Phyllis Coates, Noel Neill, Jack Larsen, John Hamilton, Robert Shayne.

Episodes of the classic series released in two-shows-per-tape packages. Among the best: "Superman on Earth," the series pilot; "The Haunted Lighthouse," with Jimmy Olsen encountering a gang of smugglers; "Through the Time Barrier," with the cast projected into prehistoric times; "Great Caesar's Ghost," where Perry White is haunted by the title specter; and, my personal favorite, "The Wedding of Superman," where Lois Lane dreams that she and the Man of Steel get hitched.

AELITA, QUEEN OF MARS

★★☆ Sinister Cinema, 1924, NR, 77 min. Dir: Ikov Protanzanov. Cast: Igor Ilinski, Iulia Sointseva, Nokolai Tseretelli, Konstantin Eggert.

The first manned mission to Mars encounters a strange alien race in this rare Russian sci-fi silent. Visually imaginative but hard to navigate—it sports the original Russian title cards with no English translation. Aka *Revolt of the Robots.*

AFTERMATH, THE

★☆ Vestron, 1979, PG, 94 min. Dir: Steve Barkett. Cast: Steve Barkett, Lynne Margulies, Sid Haig, Larry Latham.

Dull, unimaginative direct-to-video cheapie (although actually made originally for theatrical distribution—hah!) about a pair of astronauts who return to Earth from a lengthy space mission and end up battling the mutant survivors of a nuclear war. The '50s camp classic *World Without End* handled a similar storyline with a lot more style and verve. Aka *Zombie Aftermath.*

AFTERSHOCK

★☆ Prism Entertainment, 1990, R, 90 min. Dir: Frank Harris. Cast: Christoper Mitchum, Elizabeth Kaitan, Hay Roberts, Jr., John Saxon, Richard Lynch, Russ Tamblyn, Michael Berryman, Chuck Jeffreys.

This cheap vid flick tries unsuccessfully to mix *The Day the Earth Stood Still* with *Mad Max* as an alien arrives on Earth to help mankind only to discover that we've already destroyed ourselves with the survivors living in a devastated wasteland. A great exploitation cast wasted on lackluster material.

AFTER THE FALL OF NEW YORK

★★ Vestron, 1983, R, 95 min. Dir: Martin Dolan (Sergio Martino). Cast: Michael Sopkiw, Anna Kanakis, Valentine Monnier, Roman Geer.

Enjoyably trashy Italian-made *Mad Max/Escape from New York* rip with Sopkiw as the two-fisted Mel Gibson-Kurt Russell clone searching the ruins of Manhattan for Kanakis, the last fertile woman left alive after the apocalypse. Lots of gory action keeps this derivative potboiler always on the move.

AGENCY

★★ Vestron, 1981, R, 93 Min. Dir: George Kaczender. Cast: Robert Mitchum, Lee Majors, Valerie Perrine, Saul Rubinek, Alexandra Stewart.

Slightly similar to David Cronenberg's *Videodrome*, this well-cast Canadian quickie has the *Six Million Dollar Man* himself as a corporate executive who discovers a dastardly plot engineered by Mitchum to rig a presidential election via subliminal TV messages. The good cast and interesting premise aren't particularly well handled but this has its moments. Aka *Mind Games*.

ALICE

★★★ Orion, 1990, PG-13, 106 min. Dir: Woody Allen. Cast: Mia Farrow, Alec Baldwin, William Hurt, Joe Mantegna, Blythe Danner, Cybill Shepherd, Bernadette Peters, Judy Davis, Keye Luke, Gwen Verdon, Patrick O'Neal, Julie Kavner, Elle MacPherson, Judith Ivey.

Unhappily married Farrow seeks a cure for her depression from Asian herbalist Luke (great in his last role). She becomes invisible so that she can spy on rotten husband Hurt, is visited by the ghost of dead first love Baldwin, is advised by muse Peters, and eventually finds true love with down-to-earth Mantegna. Critically drubbed upon release and not very popular at the box office, this Allen fantasy-comedy is actually pretty good; its look at how various societal conventions (like marriage and religion) restrict women is heavy-handed and

underdeveloped but the cast is perfect and this works a lot better as a fantasy about self-discovery and finding your heart than it does as a feminist rewrite of *Alice in Wonderland*.

ALICE IN WONDERLAND

★★☆ Warner, 1985, NR, 94 min. Dir: Harry Harris. Cast: Natalie Gregory, Telly Savalas, Shelley Winters, Roddy McDowall, Anthony Newley, Ringo Starr, Red Buttons, Sid Caesar, Imogene Coca, Sherman Hemsley, Robert Morley, Martha Raye, Sammy Davis, Jr., Arte Johnson, Donald O'Connor, Scott Baio.

Irwin Allen (who else?) produced this musical, all-star TV version of Lewis Carroll's fantasy about a little girl (Gregory) who falls down a rabbit hole and ends up in a wonderland populated by weird characters played by a cast better suited to a disaster movie. Originally shown in two parts, the second half of this mini-series is out on tape as *Alice Through the Looking Glass*. Personally, I'd rather see the old Paramount Pictures version from 1933 featuring big names like Cary Grant and Gary Cooper in makeup scary enough to pass muster in a horror film.

ALICE THROUGH THE LOOKING GLASS

★★☆ Warner, 1985, NR, 93 min. Dir: Harry Harris. Cast: Natalie Gregory, Steve Allen, Ernest Borgnine, Ann Jillian, Donna Mills, Patrick Duffy, Jonathan Winters, Carol Channing, Karl Malden, Lloyd Bridges, Harvey Korman, Steve Lawrence, Pat Morita, John Stamos, Sally Struthers, Beau Bridges, Jack Warden, Eydie Gorme.

The second half of *Alice in Wonderland* takes Gregory into an even weirder world on the other side of the mirror, where even more hard-up TV and movie stars await. Allen also wrote the songs for this bloated *Wizard of Oz* wannabe, which keeps you hooked just to see who'll pop up next.

ALIEN

★★★ Fox, 1979, R, 116 min. Dir: Ridley Scott. Cast: Sigourney Weaver, Tom Skerritt, Veronica Cartwright, Yaphet Kotto, John Hurt, Ian Holm, Harry Dean Stanton.

Friday the 13th meets *It! The Terror from Beyond Space* in this popular outer space thriller with Weaver and company coming face to, eh, teeth with the movies' most convincingly otherworldly monster. This embellishes its routine, predictable scenario—there are bits borrowed from any number of '50s and '60s B flicks—with a genuinely unnerving ambiance well sustained by director Scott (*Blade Runner, Thelma and Louise*), bizarre photography and set design, graphic violence, and a one-of-a-kind

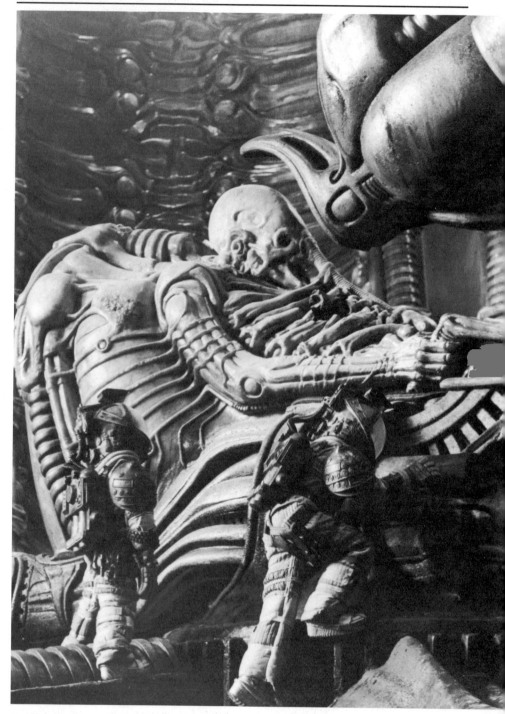

Earth astronauts examine an eerie extraterrestrial ectoskeleton in Alien *(1979).*

creature designed by Swiss surrealist painter H. R. Giger and executed by Italian FX master Carlo Rambaldi. Sequels: *Aliens, Alien 3,* and *Alien: The Reserrection.*

ALIENATOR

★★ Video Treasures, 1989, R, 92 min. Dir: Fred Olen Ray. Cast: Jan-Michael Vincent, John Phillip Law, Ross Hagen, Teagan, Dyann Ortelli, Jesse Dabson, P. J. Soles, Robert Quarry, Dawn Wildsmith, Robert Clarke, Leo Gordon, Richard Wiley.

Schlockmeister Ray does his own low-budget take on *The Terminator* with the statuesque Teagan as an unstoppable alien warrioress sent to Earth to find runaway alien Hagen. Pretty bad but the cast of familiar budget faces make it worth a look.

ALIEN CONTAMINATION

★★ Cannon, 1980, R, 88 min. Dir: Lewis Coates (Luigi Cozzi). Cast: Ian McCulloch, Louise Marleau, Marino Mase, Sigfried Rauch, Gisela Hahn, Carlo de Mejo.

Alien eggs that cause people to explode graphically when they get splashed with the eggs' slimy contents are featured in this hilariously over-the-top-and-into-your-lap Italian *Alien* sequel wannabe. Not a good movie but still hard to resist. Aka *Contamination* and *Toxic Spawn.*

ALIEN FACTOR, THE

★☆ United Entertainment, 1978 , PG, 82 min. Dir: Don Dohler. Cast: Don Leifert, Tom Griffith, Mary Mertens, Geroge Stover.

Alien monsters in a variety of shapes and sizes terrorize a Baltimore suburb in this semi-amateur effort. Some of the low-cost FX are surprisingly good but the acting is awful and the story and direction are almost nonexistent.

ALIEN FROM L.A.

★☆ Cannon, 1988, PG, 87 min. Dir: Albert Pyun. Cast: Kathy Ireland, Thom Mathews, William R. Moses, Linda Kerridge, Don Michael Paul, Richard Haines.

Laughable fantasy with covergirl Ireland as an archeologist's ditzy daughter who stumbles upon the lost civilization of Atlantis while searching for her missing dad. Kathy is easy on the eyes but her acting will make your teeth hurt.

ALIEN INTRUDER

★☆ PM Entertainment, 1992, R, 90 min. Dir: Ricardo Jacques Gale. Cast: Billy Dee Williams, Tracy Scoggins, Maxwell Caulfield, Stephen Davies.

Aliens meets *The Dirty Dozen* in this grade-C sci-fi/action filler about four condemned prisoners of some future society sent on a suicide mission to the dreaded G-sector of space to rescue a team of missing scientists. The pro cast helps, but not much.

ALIEN NATION

★★☆ CBS/Fox, 1988, R, 94 min. Dir: Graham Baker. Cast: James Caan, Mandy Patinkin, Terence Stamp, Leslie Bevins, Kevin Major Howard, Peter Jason.

In the near future, tough cop Caan is partnered with Mr.-Potato-Headed alien detective Patinkin in order to discover the identity of the brutal murderer targeting other alien "newcomers" as victims. Entertaining but heavyhanded in its antiprejudice message, this is basically just another buddy-cop movie with sci-fi trimmings. Jimmy and, especially, Mandy are good but there's a particularly absurd ending involving mutating alien bad guy Stamp. Later a TV series.

ALIEN NATION: DARK HORIZON

★★☆ Fox, 1995, PG, 90 min. Dir: Kenneth Johnson. Cast: Scott Patterson, Gary Graham, Eric Pierpont, Michele Searabelli, Terri Treas, Nina Foch.

In this sequel to the *Alien Nation* television series, evil humans and aliens conspire to send the "newcomers" back to their home world and sell them into slavery. Fans of the series should enjoy this thoughtful and well-acted if somewhat predictable spinoff.

ALIEN PREDATOR

★★ Video Treasures, 1984, R, 90 min. Dir: Deran Sarafian. Cast: Dennis Christopher, Lynn-Holly Johnson, Martin Hewitt, Luis Prendes, J. O. Basso.

College students touring rural Spain in an RV are terrorized by deadly creatures spawned by microbes brought to Earth by the downed Skylab space station. Cheapie sci-fi/horror salvaged by its likable leads and icky monsters, the latter showing up mainly at the end. Aka *Origins Unknown* and *The Falling.*

ALIENS

★★★★ Fox, 1986, R, 137 min. Dir: James Cameron. Cast: Sigourney Weaver, Michael Biehn, Lance Henriksen, Carrie Henn, Paul Reiser, Bill Paxton, Jenette Goldstein, William Hope.

After her rescue after fifty years in suspended animation, *Alien* survivor Weaver leads an elite team of marines back to the planet where her crew first encountered the alien monster. Upon their arrival our heroes discover the bodies of slaughtered colonists; a lone little girl survivor, whom Sigouney adopts as a surrogate daughter; and an entire army of shapeshifting monstrosities and their voracious queen. This sci-fi/horror/actioner just may be the best sequel of the sequel-glutted '80s in that it actually goes its original one better with superior characters, great dialogue ("Game over, man! Game over!" "Get away from her, you bitch!"), and pacy, suspenseful direction. The laser disc version contains crucial additional footage that, hopefully, will someday be included in a "Director's Cut" video edition.

ALIENS ARE COMING, THE

★★ Worldvision, 1980, NR 94 min. Dir: Harvey Hart. Cast: Max Gail, Tom Mason, Caroline McWilliams, Eric Braeden, Melinda Fee, Fawne Harriman, Matthew Laborteaux, Ed Harris.

Routine made-for-TV *Invasion of the Bodysnatchers* clone (with a touch or two of the TV series *The Invaders,* too) about evil aliens possessing humans in order to take over the Earth. No special FX to speak of (apart from a glowing-green-possessed-eyes effect) but a good cast of TV-friendly actors and a series-baiting "It's not over yet!" nonending.

ALIEN SEED

★ AIP, 1989, R, 88 min. Dir: Bob James. Cast: Eric Estrada, Heidi Payne, Steven Blade.

Fifth-rate video fodder about a government coverup of an alien visitation—now where have we heard that one before? Everything about this is strictly bottom-of-the-barrel; only the most diehard of Estrada groupies need apply.

ALIEN TERMINATOR

★☆ Cosmic, 1995, R, 95 min. Dir: Dave Payne. Cast: Maria Ford, Rodger Halston, Emile Levisetti, Casandra Leigh.

Paltry rerun of everything from *Alien* and *The Terminator* to *The Terror Within* about a genetically engineered mutant (which looks like an especially ugly Muppet) terrorizing scientists and the like in an underground complex. Yawn. Ford is good in a rare leading role; usually cast as a stripper or bimbo, pretty Maria really deserves better than she's gotten in the exploitation stakes.

ALIEN 3

★★☆ Fox, 1992, R, 114 min. Dir: David Fincher. Cast: Sigourney Weaver, Charles Dance, Charles S. Dutton, Lance Henricksen, Brian Glover, Paul McGann.

Nobody much likes this third, but not final, chapter in the *Alien* series but it's not *that* bad. Weaver crash lands on an all-male prison planet infected with lice (forcing her to shave her head) and later an all-new alien that goes on the usual killing spree. As ever, Sigourney

rises to the occasion with another tough-as-nails performance (this time laced with a touch of heartbreaking melancholy) and the downbeat ending is a shocker. Fincher next helmed the horrific box office hit *Se7en.*

ALIEN WITHIN, THE

See: *Origin Unknown.*

ALLAN QUARTERMAIN AND THE LOST CITY OF GOLD

★ Cannon, 1985, PG, 99 min. Dirs: Gary Nelson and Newt Arnold. Cast: Richard Chamberlain, Sharon Stone, James Earl Jones, Henry Silva, Robert Donner, Cassandra Peterson.

The unwanted sequel list grows with the addition of this followup to the shot-at-the-same time *Indiana Jones* wannabe *King Solomon's Mines* remake—and, believe it or not, this is even worse! Chamberlain and Stone search central Africa for Dick's long-lost adventurer brother and stumble across a savage tribe and their fabulous treasure. The flimsiest Tarzan B movie is a classic when compared to this tedious waste of time, a remake of the equally forgettable but a bit more fun *King Solomon's Treasure.*

ALL MONSTERS ATTACK

See: *Godzilla's Revenge.*

ALL OF ME

★★★ HBO, 1984, PG, 92 min. Dir: Carl Reiner. Cast: Steve Martin, Lily Tomlin, Victoria Tennant, Jason Bernard, Madolyn Smith, Dana Elcar.

Martin is hilarious in this surprisingly poignant fantasy-comedy about a lawyer forced to share his body with the soul of a recently deceased millionairess whose attempt at selective reincarnation goes rather amiss. Steve's inspired physical humor coupled with a fine performance, matched by Tomlin in a smaller but no less important role, and a smart script make this an underrated, often forgotten gem.

ALMOST AN ANGEL

★★ Paramount, 1990, PG, 95 min. Dir: John Cornell. Cast: Paul Hogan, Linda Kozlowski, Elias Koteas, Charlton Heston, Doreen Lang, Joe Dallesandro, David Alan Grier, Stephanie Hodge.

Hogan followed up his two *Crocodile Dundee* movies with this bland fantasy about a con man who's nearly killed by a car, has a vision of the Almighty (played by guess who?), and, believing that he's now an angel, tries to reform. Hogan's charisma is about all that carries this slight vehicle. Just the thought of Heston and Dallesandro together in the same movie makes my head hurt.

ALPHA INCIDENT, THE

★ Media, 1976, PG, 84 min. Dir: Bill Rebane. Cast: Ralph Meeker, John Goff, Irene Newell, Stafford Morgan.

Nobody asked him to, but the director of the infamous *Giant Spider Invasion* returns with yet another Wisconsin-lensed stinker, this one a bargain-basement *Andromedia Strain* about an alien disease altering the personalities and cell structures of a group of stranded travelers at a remote railway station. Although you do get to see a scenery-munching Meeker dissolve into a puddle of glop, that's still not reason enough to watch.

ALPHAVILLE

★★☆ Sinister Cinema, 1965, NR, 98 min. Dir: Jean-Luc Godard. Cast: Eddie Constantine, Anna Karina, Akim Tamiroff, Howard Vernon.

This '60s art house favorite was actually one of several films featuring expatriot American actor Constantine as secret agent Lemmy Caution but was the only one in the series to get a wide release outside of France. Caution trails missing fellow agent Tamiroff to the futurist city of Alphaville, where mad scientist Vernon is trying to dominate all with a powerful, mind-controlling computer. Beautifully photographed in glacial black and white but awfully slow going. Sinister's print is missing a brief, nonerotic instance of female nudity involving a lady in high heels displayed in a glass case.

ALTERED STATES

★★★ Warner, 1980, R, 102 min. Dir: Ken Russell. Cast: William Hurt, Blair Brown, Charles Haid, Bob Balaban, Thaao Penghilis, Drew Barymore.

Russell's controversial film version of Paddy Chyefsky's take on *Dr. Jekyll and Mr. Hyde* is like *The Monster on the Campus* on acid. Hurt traces the origins of man through racial memory and ends up transforming into a rampaging Neanderthal man and worse. Awesome Dick Smith makeup FX and some startling images help you overlook the dull characters and confusing continuity.

ALWAYS

★★ MCA/Universal, 1989, PG, 121 min. Dir: Steven Spielberg. Cast: Richard Dreyfuss, Holly Hunter, John Goodman, Brad Johnson, Audrey Hepburn, Marg Helenberger, Roberts Blossom, Keith David.

Spielberg's long-treasured attempt to remake the '40s fantasy *A Guy Named Joe* results in a heartfelt but contrived and corny misfire. Dreyfuss is the daring pilot who dies trying to put out a forest fire and is then guided back to Earth by angel Hepburn (in her last film) to help his grieving girlfriend, Hunter, find love with hunky Johnson. Considering its themes of life, love, and death, this is way too cute for its own good but the actors are good and it's all reasonably entertaining in the manner of *Ghost*.

AMAZING COLOSSAL MAN, THE

★★★ Columbia/Tri Star, 1957, NR, 79 min. Dir: Bert I. Gordon. Cast: Glenn Langan, Cathy Downs, William Hudson, Larry Thor, James Seay, Russ Bender.

Gordon's low-budget reversal of Jack Arnold's *The Incredible Shrinking Man* is, in its own way, just as good and certainly a lot funnier. Exposure to the blast of a plutonium bomb causes Lt. Colonel Glenn Manning (Langan, who's first-rate) to double in size every day until he goes crashing through Las Vegas and carries off fiancée Carol (Downs) to the top of Boulder Dam, King Kong-style. Most of the special FX are awful and it's too talky for its own good, yet despite this it still works. Once seen, the giant syringe impalement is a hard image to shake. Sequel: *War of the Colossal Beast*.

AMAZING MR. BLUNDEN, THE

★★★ Media, 1972, PG, 99 min. Dir: Lionel Jeffries. Cast: Laurence Naismith, Diana Dors, Garry Miller, Rosalyn Landor, Lynne Frederick, Marc Granger.

British character actor Jeffries directed this likable fantasy about a ghost called Mr. Blunden (Naismith) who takes a young girl and her little brother on a trip into the past to save two children from an evil governess (Dors in a terrific character role). Overcomplicated but well made; though aimed at kids, it never talks down or gets cute for its own sake, like many similar American movies of this type.

AMAZING SPIDERMAN, THE

★★ Fox, 1977, NR, 94 min. Dir: E. W. Swackhamer. Cast: Nicholas Hammond, Lisa Eilbacher, David White, Michael Pataki, Thayer David, Hilly Hicks.

Two episodes of the short-lived TV series, derived from Stan Lee's popular comic character, spun into feature length. Tracing Spidy's origin, this isn't as stolid and predictable as the same era's more popular *Incredible Hulk* show but is often just as unintentionally funny—the wall-crawling scenes look like a skinny guy in ski pajamas swinging on a clothesline.

AMAZING STORIES

★★ MCA/Universal, 1985–87, NR, 75 min. per tape. Dirs: Steven Spielberg, Martin Scorsese, Robert Zemeckis, Tim Burton, Paul Burtel, Danny DeVito, others. Cast: Kevin Costner, Christopher Lloyd, John

Lithgow, Patrick Swayze, Lea Thompson, Sam Waterston, Danny DeVito, Sondra Locke, Keifer Sutherland, Carrie Fisher, Sid Caesar, Andrew McCarthy, Rhea Perlman, Gregory Hines, Helen Shaver, Mary Stuart Masterson, Charlie Sheen, Casey Siemaszko, Leo Rossi, June Lockhart.

Spielberg's highly hyped marriage of Rod Serling to Walt Disney resulted in a watchable but never compelling anthology series. The main problem was that few of the stories dramatized were amazing enough to entertain in anything but the most superficial manner, not to mention a confusing change in tone from week to week from comedy to fantasy to science fiction to suspense to horror. A few of the episodes, however, are of note: "The Doll," starring Emmy-winning Lithgow; "The Wedding Ring," with real-life couple DeVito and Perlman; "Go to the Head of the Class," starring an especially manic Lloyd; "Mirror, Mirror," with Waterston and Shaver; and the clever animated "Family Dog," a pilot for a never developed spin-off series.

AMAZING TRANSPARENT MAN, THE

★ Sinister Cinema, 1960, NR, 58 min. Dir: Edgar G. Ulmer. Cast: Douglas Kennedy, Marguerite Chapman, James Griffith, Ivan Triesault, Read Morgan, Cormel Daniel.

Shot in Texas by B-movie auteur Ulmer, this cheapjack ripoff of The Invisible Man has to be one of the darkest, most depressing films ever made. Gangster Kennedy is busted out of prison by Chapman so that he can serve as the subject for scientist Triesault's invisibility experiments. Kennedy becomes a chuckling, transparent bank robber and general nuisance but the experiment has given him a fatal dose of radiation and he and most of the rest of the petty, bickering characters are eventually killed off in an atomic blast. Everything about this paltry production is the pits, from the awful FX (the "invisible" Kennedy is obviously shouting his lines at the other actors while just out of camera range) to the hammy acting and pompous dialogue. Ed Wood must have loved it.

AMAZONS

☆ Concorde, 1987, R, 77 min. Dir: Alex Sessa. Cast: Windsor Taylor Randolph, Penelope Reed, Joseph Whipp, Danitza Kingsley.

Pathetic, Argentina-shot sword and sorcery nonsense about buxom warrior women trying to save their village from the evil intents of sorcerer Whipp. Even the most ardent fan of big breasts and mindless violence will be quickly bored with this inept fantasy.

AMAZON WOMEN ON THE MOON

★★★ MCA/Universal, 1987, R, 84 min. Dirs: John Landis, Joe Dante, Peter Horton, Carl Gottlieb, Robert Weiss. Cast: Rosanna Arquette, Steve Guttenberg, Michelle Pfieffer, Ed Begley, Jr., Steve Forrest, Sybil Danning, Griffin Dunne, Arsenio Hall, Andrew Dice Clay, Paul Bartel, Lou Jacobi, Henry Silva, Carrie Fisher, Peter Horton, Ralph Bellamy, Monique Gabrielle, Phil Hartman, Henny Youngman, Russ Meyer, Forrest J. Ackerman.

This scattershot fantasy-comedy anthology, much in the manner of Landis's earlier Kentucky Fried Movie, has more hits than misses and is a lot of fun. Best segments: on-target B&W spoofs of The Invisible Man and old sex education films; a day in the life of playmate Gabrielle; the title parody of sci-fi cheapies like Queen of Outer Space; and all the abuse heaped upon poor Arsenio. Better than you'd think.

AMBUSHERS, THE

★☆ RCA/Columbia, 1968, NR, 102 min. Dir: Henry Levin. Cast: Dean Martin, Senta Berger, Janice Rule, James Gregory, Albert Salmi, Kurt Kastner, Beverly Adams.

Third in the Matt Helm spy series is probably the weakest, with Dino out to stop villain Salmi from sabotaging America's first flying saucer—America's first what? Since it's pretty obvious that Martin wasn't taking any of this seriously, no one watching should either.

AMERICAN CHRISTMAS CAROL, AN

★★ Goodtimes, 1979, NR, 95 min. Dir: Eric Till. Cast: Henry Winkler, David Wayne, Dorian Harewood, Susan Hogan, Chris Wiggins, R. H. Thompson.

The Fonz himself follows in the footsteps of everyone from Alastair Sim to Albert Finney in this pallid TV version updated to 1930s New England. I guess they decided to go with this when plans for an Anson Williams version of Nicholas Nickleby fell through. The old age Scrooge makeup is real phony-looking.

AMERICAN CYBORG: STEEL WARRIOR

★★ Warner, 1994, R, 95 min. Dir: Boaz Davidson. Cast: Joe Lara, Nicole Hansen, John P. Ryan.

TV Tarzan Lara stars in this ersatz Terminator about the last fertile woman left on Earth after a nuclear war being pursued by a killer android programmed to wipe out mankind's final hope for survival. Routine but not without interest.

AMPHIBIAN MAN, THE

★★ Sinister Cinema, 1962, NR, 99 min. Dirs: Gennadi Kazansky, Vladimir Chebotaryov. Cast:

Vladimir Korenev, Anastasia Vertinskaya, Mikhail Kizakov, Anatoly Smiranin.

Odd Soviet-made fantasy about a young man transformed into a water breather by his scientist father. When he falls in love with the daughter of a local fish peddlar our gilled-out hero (who likes to wear a *Creature from the Black Lagoon*-like suit to scare fishermen), finds his life suddenly complicated to no good end. Badly dubbed and hard to follow, this is still a lot more entertaining than the megabuck dud *Waterworld*.

ANDROID

★★★ Media, 1984, PG, 80 min. Dir: Aaron Lipstadt. Cast: Klaus Kinski, Don Opper, Brie Howard, Norbert Weisser, Crofton Hardester, Kendra Kirschner.

Nicely underplayed story about a gentle android (Opper) who discovers that his scientist-creator (Kinski, playing it close to the vest, for once) is about to replace him with a more advanced female model. When three escaped convicts arrive on Kinski's private space station home, Opper uses the opportunity to strike back at his master. Cheaply shot on sets left over from *Battle Beyond the Stars*, this is humorous without being forced and at times oddly charming.

ANDROID AFFAIR, THE

★★☆ MCA/Universal, 1995, PG-13, 90 min. Dir: Richard Kletter. Cast: Harley Jane Kozak, Griffin Dunne, Ossie Davis, Saul Rubinek.

Based on a story by Issac Asimov, this cable movie concerns a woman doctor (Kozak) who finds herself falling in love with the android (well played by Dunne) whose faulty heart she has been assigned to repair. A mild but sometimes emotionally involving sci-fi romance.

ANDROMEDA STRAIN, THE

★★★ MCA/Universal, 1971, PG, 130 min. Dir: Robert Wise. Cast: James Olson, Arthur Hill, David Wayne, Kate Reid, Paula Kelly, Ramon Bieri.

Low-keyed adaptation of Michael Crichton's novel about an alien virus that wipes out nearly the entire population of a tiny midwestern town (only the town drunk and a tiny baby survive!) and the team of doctors who try to contain the disease before it spreads across the globe. Overlong but with a great cast of character actors and a tense climax, this is far superior to the later, quite similar box office smash *Outbreak*.

ANGEL ON MY SHOULDER

★★★ Prism Entertainment, 1946, NR, 101 min. Dir: Archie Mayo. Cast: Paul Muni, Anne Baxter, Claude Rains, Onslow Stevens, George Cleveland.

Typical '40s fantasy with Muni in an atypical role as a murdered ganster reincarnated as a judge who at first sets out to take revenge on his killers but instead falls in love with the lovely Baxter. Rains is a delight as the devil and Muni and Baxter are also fine in this lightweight farce, which was remade for TV in 1980.

ANGEL ON MY SHOULDER

★★ HBO, 1980, NR, 96 min. Dir: John Berry. Cast: Peter Strauss, Barbara Hershey, Richard Kiley, Janis Page, Seymour Cassel, Murray Matheson.

Bland TV remake with Strauss as the executed hoodlum sent back to Earth by Satan in the form of a judge to do evil, though, of course, things don't quite work out that way when Strauss falls for the sexy Hershey. Kiley has fun in the old Claude Rains role but Strauss is too smug and smirky to engender much audience sympathy. If they did this movie again today, imagine Bruce Willis in the role and you'll see what I mean.

ANGELS IN THE OUTFIELD

★★★ MGM/UA, 1951, NR, 102 min. Dir: Clarence Brown. Cast: Paul Douglas, Janet Leigh, Keenan Wynn, Donna Corcoran, Spring Byington, Lewis Stone, Ellen Corby, Bruce Bennett, Bing Crosby, Ty Cobb, Joe DiMaggio, voice of James Whitmore.

Pleasent baseball fantasy about a rough-and-tumble team manager (the delightful Douglas) who promises an invisible angel (voiced by Whitmore) that he'll reform if the angel and his heavenly pals help Douglas's team overcome their losing streak. Only young Corcoran can see the angels in the outfield and she tells reporters Leigh and Wynn, who investigate. Sweet-natured and innocent, this is a lot more fun than the FX-tricked-up Disney remake.

ANGELS IN THE OUTFIELD

★★ Disney, 1994, PG, 103 min. Dir: William Dear. Cast: Danny Glover, Tony Danza, Christopher Lloyd, Brenda Fricker, Ben Johnson, Joseph Gordon-Levitt.

All the state-of-the-art special effects in the world can't help this well-cast but totally hollow remake obviously made to cash in on the success of *Field of Dreams* and other popular baseball films of the time. Glover is the team manager and Lloyd is (the now visible) guardian angel with the kid character changed from a girl to a boy (Gordon-Levitt from the new *Dark Shadows* and *Third Rock from the Sun*) who hopes that his favorite team's new winning ways is a sign that he will be reunited with his estranged dad. If anything, this is even cornier than the original.

ANGRY RED PLANET, THE

★★☆ HBO, 1959, NR, 83 min. Dir: Ib Melchior. Cast: Gerald Mohr, Nora Hayden, Les Tremayne, Jack Kruschen, Paul Hahn.

A woman survivor of the first manned mission to Mars narrates in flashback her expedition's various perils including carnivorous plants, a giant rat-spider monster, and a huge, pulsating blob of protoplasm. This tries to be visually imaginative by shooting the Mars sequences in "Cinemagic" (the footage is printed in negative and then tinted red), giving the movie a unique look but also producing a serious case of eye strain in the viewer. Still, this has enough nice little touches and solid acting to make it worth watching in small doses.

ANNA TO THE INFINITE POWER

★★☆ RCA/Columbia, 1983, NR, 101 min. Dir: Robert Weimer. Cast: Dina Merrill, Martha Byrne, Jack Gilford, Mark Patton, Donna Mitchell.

Kid-friendly sci-fi about a young girl (Byrne) suffering weird, psychic nightmares and later learning from her mom (Merrill) that she and many others are the result of an experiment in cloning. Byrne then begins a journey of discovery as she searches out her lookalike "sisters." Byrne and Merrill are good in this minor fare that often resembles an episode of TV's *Are You Afraid of the Dark?*

A*P*E

☆ Goodtimes, 1976, PG, 87 min. Dir: Paul Leder. Cast: Joanna De Varona (Joanna Kearns), Ros Arrants, Alex Nicol.

Rushed out to cash in on the '76 *King Kong* remake, this is by far the worst giant monster movie ever made. A stunt man in a ratty monkey costume kicks over cardboard houses, punches out a rubber shark, and flips the army the bird as he searches Korea for lady love De Varona (now known as TV actress Kearns, who I'll bet looks back on this as a career highlight). Originally released in 3-D, this is good for a couple of laughs but after about thirty minutes or so even that isn't enough. Do the *Mystery Science Theatre 3000* boys know about this thing? Aka *Attack of the Horny Gorilla*.

A.P.E.X.

★★★ Republic, 1994, R, 103 min. Dir: Phillip H. Roth. Cast: Lisa Ann Russell, Mitchell Cox, Marcus Aurelius, Robert Keats.

Above-average made-for-video flick about a futuristic robot probe sent into the past where it acidentally causes a plague that devastates the world and alters the future. Can Cox, the probe's creator, return to the past and make amends? An imaginative and well-made sleeper.

APOLLO 13

★★★ MCA/Universal, 1995, PG, 140 min. Dir: Ron Howard. Cast: Tom Hanks, Kevin Bacon, Bill Paxton, Ed Harris, Gary Sinise, Kathleen Quinlan, Clint Howard.

More science fact than science fiction, this detailed account of the infamous and near-fatal 1971 accident that befell the Apollo 13 moon mission and her crew is suspensful and well acted. Not as powerful as Philip Kaufman's *The Right Stuff* but entertaining nonetheless.

APPLEGATES, THE

★★★ Video Treasures, 1991, R, 90 min. Dir: Michael Lehman. Cast: Stockard Channing, Ed Begley, Jr., Dabney Coleman, Bobby Jacoby, Cami Cooper, Glenn Shadix.

Heathers director Lehman committed career suicide by following his popular high school angst-and-murder fest with this bizarre fantasy comedy about Brazilian cockroaches in human form who invade suburbia. The "Applegates" (Stockard, Ed, and clan) try to be the perfect white bread family but occasionally can't help indulging in a bit of people-munching with victims secreted away in the basement. This spoofs the phoniness of modern suburban life almost as effectively as *Heathers* did teen peer pressure and features a game cast going full tilt and very effective makeup and special effects. Original title: *Meet the Applegates*.

ARCADE

★★ Paramount, 1993, PG-13, 85 min. Dir: Albert Pyun. Cast: Megan Ward, Peter Billingsley, Seth Green, Sharon Farrell, John de Lancie.

Pyun (*The Sword and the Sorcerer*) directs this juvenile Charles Band-produced *Tron* ripoff about a video game that zaps its young players into an alternate universe. Ward is the teen heroine who sets out to save the kids, her brother among them, from this Sega system from hell. Likable actors but cheap FX; this much-delayed video fodder is mostly for undemanding kids with 85 minutes to kill.

ARENA

★★☆ Paramount, 1991, PG-13, 97 min. Dir: Peter Manoogian. Cast: Paul Satterfield, Claudia Christian, Marc Alaimo, Hamilton Camp.

Mild Empire Pics fare, a sort of sci-fi *Rocky* with Satterfield as a warrior involved in intergalactic gladitorial games who must fight against incredible odds to win back the championship for Mother Earth. Had this played up the comic aspects more it would have been one of Empire's best; as is, it's just minor beefcake and monsters fun.

AROUND THE WORLD UNDER THE SEA
★★ MGM/UA, 1966, NR, 117 min. Dir: Andrew Marton. Cast: Lloyd Bridges, Shirley Eaton, David McCallum, Brian Kelly, Gary Merrill, Keenan Wynn, Marshall Thompson, Celeste Yarnall.

TV producer Ivan (*Flipper*) Tors whipped up this well-made but dull undersea adventure flick to exploit a sub-full of familiar small-screen faces, not to mention Bond girl Eaton. Traveling the oceans of the world in an atomic submarine called the *Hydronaut*, scientists plant sonic devices to warn of seaquakes and have all the usual problems of disasters, sabotage, and romatic complications—obvious reason why Shirley's aboard, though they still could have . . . oh, never mind. The climactic attack by a gigantic electric eel helps but this is still little more than a well-cast sleeping pill.

ARRIVAL, THE
★★ Prism Entertainment, 1990, R, 103 min. Dir: David Schmoeller. Cast: Joseph Culp, Robin Frates, John Saxon, Robert Sampson, Michael J. Pollard.

Oldster Sampson is hit by a meteor fragment and begins turning younger, eventually devolving into good-looking Culp, but must drink blood to remain that way. Standard-issue direct-to-video sci-fi thriller with a good but wasted cast.

ARRIVAL, THE
★★★ LIVE, 1996, PG-13, 109 min. Dir: David Twohy. Cast: Charlie Sheen, Lindsay Crouse, Ron Silver, Teri Polo.

Released just before *Independence Day* and quickly forgotten, this directorial debut for screenwriter Twohy (*Waterworld*) is an impressive sci-fi paranoia thriller that holds up almost all the way through. A goateed Sheen seems initially miscast but rises above this by giving a good account of himself as a young scientist who discovers the coverup of an alien invasion and finds himself marked for extinction. Twohy builds tension nicely and by concentrating on characterization over FX, he has created one of only a handful of recent science fiction films (another being *The Puppetmasters*) where you actually come to care about the characters and their predicament rather than just coming to see some splashy special effects.

ASSASSIN
★★ Academy Entertainment, 1986, PG-13, 94 min. Dir: Sandor Stern. Cast: Robert Conrad, Karen Austin, Robert Webber, Jonathan Banks, Richard Young.

Run-of-the-mill TV movie with Conrad as an aging CIA agent called out of retirement to stop a deranged killer called Golem (Young) who turns out to be an amok cyborg. Conrad is in nimble form but he's about all this action flick has going for it.

ASSASSIN
★☆ Academy Entertainment, 1989, PG-13, 94 min. Dir: Sandor Stern. Cast: Robert Conrad, Karen Austin, Richard Young, Robert Webber, Jonathan Banks.

Golem, a killer cyborg created by a deranged scientist, runs amuck, and only retired CIA operative Conrad can stop it. Predictable direct-to-video vanity piece for the aging former *Wild, Wild West* star with little to offer apart from a few *Terminator*-like thrills.

ASSIGNMENT: OUTER SPACE
★★ Sinister Cinema, 1960, NR, 72 min. Dir: Anthony Dawson (Antonio Margheriti). Cast: Rik Von Nutter, Gaby Farinon, Archie Savage, Alain Dejon, Franco Fantasia, Aldo Pini.

When its computer mysteriously malfunctions, the first manned flight into space is driven off course and into danger. Poorly dubbed and saddled with annoying canned music, this Italian space movie still provides marginal interest thanks to some unusual touches for the time—the astronauts include a woman and a black man—and the visual flair provided by horror veteran Margheriti. Aka *Space Men*.

ASTOUNDING SHE MONSTER, THE
★ Sinister Cinema, 1958, NR, 60 min. Dir: Ronnie Ashcroft. Cast: Robert Clarke, Marilyn Harvey, Kenne Duncan, Jeane Tatum, Ewing Brown, Shirley Kilpatrick.

Kilpatrick (a popular nude model of the day) is a stacked alien in skin-tight silver lamé and heels whose fortuitous arrival disrupts the kidnapping of heiress Harvey by gangster Duncan and his gang. Ed Wood-style hilarity with a ponderous narrator on hand to explain the obvious and a musical score left over from *The Beast with a Million Eyes*. Aka *The Mysterious Invader*.

ATLANTIS, THE LOST CONTINENT
★★ MGM/UA, 1961, NR, 90 min. Dir: George Pal. Cast: Anthony Hall, Joyce Taylor, John Dall, Edward C. Platt, Frank de Kova, Jay Novello, Berry Kroeger, Edgar Stehli.

One of Pal's weakest fantasy films, this comes off like a poor man's Harryhausen as Greek fisherman Hall pursues lovely Atlantian princess Taylor back to her legendary island home. Stilted acting and too much stock footage (much of the fiery destruction at the end is lifted from the burning of Rome climax from *Quo Vadis*) but some of the FX are good, the photography colorful, and there's a weird, out-of-nowhere, *Island of Dr. Moreau*-like subplot involving mad surgeon Kroeger and his beast men.

ATLAS

★★ Sinister Cinema, 1960, NR, 80 min. Dir: Roger Corman. Cast: Michael Forest, Barboura Morris, Frank Wolff, Walter Maslow.

Quickie king Corman's contribution to the early '60s muscle man/fantasy genre, actually shot on location in Greece, with Forrest as the conspicuously unpumped title hero who faces various low-budget challenges before winning the heart of breathless heroine Morris. Laughs aplenty with a cast better-suited to *Goodfellas* and Corman himself filling in as an extra during one of the battle scenes.

ATLAS AGAINST THE CYCLOPS

See: *Atlas in the Land of the Cyclops.*

ATLAS IN THE LAND OF THE CYCLOPS

★★ Sinister Cinema, 1961, NR 98 min. Dir: Antonio Leonuiola. Cast: Gordon Mitchell, Chelo Alonso, Dante DePaolo, Vira Silenti.

Mitchell is Atlas (actually he's playing Maciste, but who pays attention to names?) and the cyclops lives in a labyrinth and is under the control of the evil Queen Capice (Alonso). Can our strong boy save the true heir to the throne from becoming Cyclops chow? For muscle-heads only.

ATOMIC BRAIN, THE

★ Sinister Cinema, 1964, NR, 70 min. Dir: Joseph Mascelli. Cast: Frank Gerstle, Erika Peters, Marjorie Eaton, Judy Bamber, Frank Fowler, Lisa Lang.

Originally titled *Monstrosity*, this movie under any name is one of the most inept ever made. Dying old lady millionaire Eaton backs the brain transplantation experiments of doctor Gerstle; in return, he's to put her brain into the shapely young body of Peters. Naturally things don't quite work out that way, and Marge's mind ends up trapped in a cat. Pathetic acting—everyone seems to have a completely unconvincing foreign accent—and unctuous narration (provided by an uncredited Bradford Dillman as a favor to his brother, coproducer Dean Dillman), but the photography (provided by director Mascelli, author of *The Cinematog-*

rapher's Handbook) is often pleasing in its unusual setups and composition.

ATOMIC KID, THE

★☆ Republic, 1954, NR, 86 min. Dir: Leslie H. Martinson. Cast: Mickey Rooney, Robert Strauss, Elaine Davis, Whit Bissell.

Blake Edwards wrote this painfully unfunny comedy with Rooney (on a career downslide) as a prospector who develops superpowers after being exposed to an atomic bomb blast. Aimed at kids, this pitiful attempt to make radiation poisoning seem fun in the era of "duck and cover" is almost shockingly naive and misinformed.

ATOMIC MAN, THE

★★ Sinister Cinema, 1956, NR, 78 min. Dir: Ken Hughes. Cast: Gene Nelson, Faith Domergue, Joseph Tomelty, Peter Arne, Vic Perry.

An intriguing but unsatisfying British-made sci-fi/espionage thriller. Reporter Nelson (a dancer from the musical *Oklahoma!*) and sultry girlfriend Domergue investigate the experiments that have caused a scientist to be projected seven and a half seconds into the future. Bland programmer that doesn't sufficiently develop its unique gimmick. Aka *Timeslip*.

ATOMIC RULERS OF THE WORLD

★★☆ Something Weird, 1956, NR, 83 min. Dirs: Teruo Ishi, Akira Mitsugi, Koreyoshi Akasaka. Cast: Ken Utsui, Minoru Takada, Junko Ikeuchi, Utako Mitsuya.

In 1956, the Shintoho Company of Japan created a series of nine short subjects starring Utsui as Starman (originally known as Supah Jaiyanto, or Super Giant), a flying superhero from the Emerald Planet. In this second of four reedited "features" released directly to U.S. TV—derived from episodes 2 and 3, *Kaisiji no Majyo* (*Invaders from the Planets*) and *Chi Kyo Metsuto Suzen* (*The Earth in Danger*)—our martial arts-expert alien hero battles U.S. gangsters out to destroy Japan with an atomic bomb. Lots of cheesy fun.

ATOMIC SPACESHIP

See: *Flash Gordon* (1936).

ATOMIC SUBMARINE, THE

★★ Sinister Cinema, 1960, NR, 72 min. Dir: Spencer G. Bennet. Cast: Arthur Franz, Dick Foran, Brett Halsey, Tom Conway, Joi Lansing, Bob Steele, Paul Dubov, Victor Varconi.

An experimental new submarine is sent to the North Pole to investigate a series of disasters and discovers that cyclopean aliens are melt-

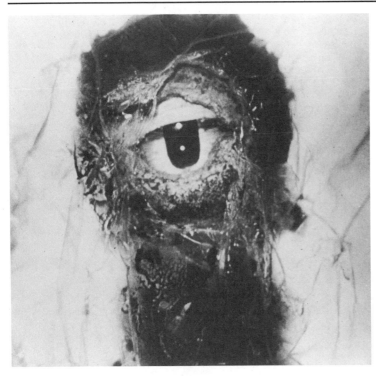

Peek-a-boo! It's the cyclopean hand puppet from space in The Atomic Submarine *(1959).*

ing the ice cap in order to flood the world. This Alex Gordon production is hampered by its low budget but has a terrific B-movie cast (the ever-glowering Franz, likable Foran, and suave Conway are best, though the platinum-tressed Lansing is wasted) and a pretty cool puppet-monster.

ATOM MAN VS. SUPERMAN

★★☆ Warner, 1950, NR, 150 min. Dir: Spencer G. Bennet. Cast: Kirk Alyn, Noel Neill, Lyle Talbot, Tommy Bond, Pierre Watkin, Jack Ingram.

Fun serial, the second and last to feature the Man of Steel before becoming a TV star, with Supe (Alyn) going up against archnemesis Lex Luthor (Talbot), who's using an atomic heat ray to hold the city of Metropolis hostage. Alyn is sincere and Talbot grandly hammy in this entertaining chapter play also released, in condensed form, as a feature.

ATOR, THE FIGHTING EAGLE

★ HBO, 1983, PG, 98 min. Dir: David Hills [Aristede Massacessi]. Cast: Miles O'Keeffe, Sabrina Siani, Ritza Brown, Edmund Purdom, Laura Gemser, Warren Hillman.

Low-grade Italian *Conan the Barbarian* clone with hard-bodied nonactor (and one-time

Tarzan) O'Keeffe as the titular hero battling a villainous tyrant known as the Spider. Comatose sword-and-sorcery wannabe followed by an equally lame sequel, *Blade Master.*

ATTACK FROM SPACE

★★☆ Something Weird, 1956, NR, 79 min. Dirs: Teruo Ishi, Akira Mitsugi, Koreyoshi Akasaka. Cast: Ken Utsui, Minoru Takada, Junko Ikeuchi, Utako Mitsuya, Kan Hayashi, Teruhisa Ikeda.

Super Giant parts 5 and 6—*Jinko Eisei to Jinrui no Hamatsu (The Sinister Spaceship)* and *Uchutei to Jinko Eisei no Gekitotsu (The Destruction of the Space Fleet)* form the basis of this adventure with our hero (Utsui) up against invaders from the Sapphire galaxy who use an Earth scientist in their plans for conquest. More fun stuff from Shintoho.

ATTACK OF THE EYE CREATURES

See: *The Eye Creatures.*

ATTACK OF THE 50-FOOT WOMAN

★★★ Fox, 1958, NR, 66 min. Dir: Nathan Hertz [Nathan Juran]. Cast: Allison Hayes, William Hudson, Yvette Vickers, Roy Gordon.

One-of-a-kind camp foolishness obviously made to grab off some of the success of *The*

Amazing Colossal Man. Hayes is great in her signature role as Nancy Archer, a neurotic, hard-drinking rich gal whose claims of seeing a flying saucer and its giant pilot are disbelieved until contact with the alien causes Nancy to grow into a towering Amazon with a blonde rise and bed-sheet bikini. Hudson is Nancy's smarmy, cheating husband and Vickers his vampy mistress in this low-brow masterpiece, surely one of the twenty five or so most famous titles in movie history.

ATTACK OF THE 50-FOOT WOMAN

★★ HBO, 1993, NR, 89 min. Dir: Christopher Guest. Cast: Daryl Hannah, Daniel Baldwin, William Windom, Paul Benedict.

Unnecessary comic made-for-cable remake directed by the real-life husband of Jamie Lee Curtis. This time Hannah, the neglected wife of rotter Baldwin (brother of Alec, Billy, and Steve), becomes both a giantess and a liberated woman. In today's politically correct climate, she merely lectures her husband's mistress rather than killing her, and in the end takes her unfaithful spouse away to an alien world where the little men serve the big women. Mildly amusing but the original is much funnier without even trying.

ATTACK OF THE 60-FOOT CENTERFOLD

★★ New Horizons, 1995, R, 83 min. Dir: Fred Olen Ray. Cast: J. J. North, Raelyn Saalman, Tim Abell, Russ Tamblyn, Tommy Kirk, Jay Richardson, Michelle Bauer, Tammy Parks, Nikki Fritz, Ted Monte.

The title says it all in this adolescent wet dream spoof of the '50s classic. Howard Stern favorite North is the sweet, ditzy bikini model transformed by an accidental exposure to a

William Hudson is Allison Hayes's main squeeze in Attack of the 50-Foot Woman *(1958).*

new growth hormone into an often topless she-giant who takes on archrival Saalman, after she takes the formula, in a grudge match that looks like the climax of *War of the Gargantuas* remade for the Playboy Channel. Knuckleheaded fun for both girl- and old B-movie-actor watchers alike.

ATTACK OF THE MONSTERS
See: *Gamera vs. Guiron.*

ATTACK OF THE PUPPET PEOPLE
See: *The Fantastic Puppet People.*

ATTACK OF THE ROBOTS
★★ Sinister Cinema, 1962, NR, 85 min. Dir: Jess [Jesus] Franco. Cast: Eddie Constantine, Sophie Hardy, Fernando Rey, François Brion.

Constantine is an Interpol agent (though not the same one he played in *Alphaville*) investigating a series of murders of prominent men where the killers turn out to be robots dressed all in black with dark glasses. The prolific Franco's contribution to the James Bond spy craze, this has some interesting things about it but is spoiled by the usual cardboard production values and dreadful dubbing. Aka *Cards on the Table.*

AT THE EARTH'S CORE
★★ Goodtimes, PG, 89 min. Dir: Kevin Connor. Cast: Doug McClure, Peter Cushing, Caroline Munro, Cy Grant.

Scientist Cushing and adventurer McClure use a huge cylindrical drilling machine called the Iron Mole to bore their way to the center of the Earth, where they find a strange world inhabited by various monsters and primitive human slaves including the curvy Munro. This Edgar Rice Burroughs fantasy was Amicus Pictures' followup to their success *The Land that Time Forgot* and is dumb but entertaining, with outlandish monsters and a funny performance by Cushing as the daffy professor.

AURORA ENCOUNTER, THE
★★ New World, 1986, PG, 90 min. Dir: Jim McCullough. Cast: Jack Elam, Peter Brown, Carol Bagdasarian, Spanky McFarland, Dottie West, Will Mitchell.

Cheap *E.T.*-inspired sci-fi aimed at kids. In the late 19th century a diminutive alien arrives in a small rural community, but since he can only be seen by children and one old coot (Elam, having fun), no one believes the close encounter really happened. Rather crassly, the tiny bald alien is played by a child with the very real genetic disorder Hutchinson Gilford

Syndrome (which causes children to age prematurely), giving this Texas-shot flick a rather distasteful air despite an overall atmosphere of earnestness.

AUTOMATIC
★★ Republic, 1994, R, 90 min. Dir: John Murlowski. Cast: Olivier Gruner, Daphne Ashbrook, John Glover, Jeff Kober, Dennis Lipscomb, Penny Johnson.

Yet another unwieldy combo of sci-fi and martial arts starring French kickboxer Gruner as an andriod who saves Ashbrook from rape, accidentally killing the attacker in the process and becoming marked for destruction. Well enough made and well acted by a manic Glover as a smarmy corporate exec, but when all is said and done this is no different than about a hundred other direct-to-video sci-fi entries, so why bother?

BABES IN TOYLAND
See: *March of the Wooden Soldiers.*

BABES IN TOYLAND
★★☆ Disney, 1961, NR, 105 min. Dir: Jack Donohue. Cast: Ray Bolger, Annette Funicello, Tommy Sands, Ed Wynn, Tommy Kirk, Henry Calvin, Gene Sheldon, Ann Jillian.

Disney tried to make their own variation on *The Wizard of Oz* (complete with erstwhile Scarecrow Bolger as the black-cloaked bad guy Barnaby) in this colorful but insincere version of the Victor Herbert operetta. Lots of splashy sets, costumes, and special effects as the evil Barnaby tries to take over Toyland, but despite some good casting (Funicello, Wynn, and Kirk come off best) this hasn't the heart to make it work, and lacks the spooky undercurrent that makes the Laurel and Hardy version (*March of the Wooden Soldiers*) so memorable.

BABES IN TOYLAND
★★ Orion, 1986, NR, 144 min. Dir: Clive Donner. Cast: Drew Barrymore, Keanu Reeves, Richard Mulligan, Eileen Brennan, Pat Morita, Jill Schoelen.

Drew and Keanu may be babes, all right

(depending on your preference, of course), but this overlong TV-version remake of the Victor Herbert musical fantasy cuts out most of the original songs and drags badly. Mulligan's enjoyable mugging as Barnaby is about the only thing that kept me watching.

BABY, SECRET OF THE LOST LEGEND
★★ Disney, 1985, PG, 95 min. Dir: B.W.L. Norton. Cast: William Katt, Sean Young, Patrick McGoohan, Julian Fellowes.

Bambi meets *Godzilla* in this minor Disney flick, with Katt and Young discovering a cute baby brontosaurus in Africa. McGoohan is the big game hunter out to exploit sweet li'l baby until the bronto's mom thunders in for the *Gorgo*-inspired climax. Sometimes amusing and with variable special FX, but after all the *E.T.*-style cuteness the violent ending makes you wonder just what audience this was shooting for. Aka *Dinosaur, Secret of the Lost Legend.*

BACKLASH: OBLIVION 2
★★☆ Paramount, 1996, R, 82 min. Dir: Sam Irvin. Cast: Richard Joseph Paul, Jackie Swanson, Andrew Divoff, Meg Foster, Isaac Hayes, Julie Newmar, George Takei, Maxwell Caulfield, Carel Struycken, Musetta Vander, Jimmie F. Skaggs, Brent Huff.

Better than *Oblivion*, this sequel seems more in control of both its story and its impressive cast of name-brand has-beens, most of whom are better served here than in part one. Caulfield (in one of his best performances since his stint as the deranged closet case in *The Boys Next Door*) is a bounty hunter after statuesque villainess Vander, and there are good turns from almost everyone else and humorous bits that are a lot less self-conscious and a lot funnier than those in the first film. The last-minute homage to the *Gamera* series (or maybe it's *One Million Years B.C.*) is out of place but a nice surprise.

BACK TO THE FUTURE
★★★MCA/Universal, 1985, PG, 116 min. Dir: Robert Zemeckis. Cast: Michael J. Fox, Christopher Lloyd, Lea Thompson, Crispin Glover, Thomas F. Wilson, Marc McClure, Wendie Jo Sperber, Claudia Wells, James Tolkan, Billy Zane.

Delightful fantasy comedy with Fox as an '80s teen who goes back in time to the '50s in inventor-friend Lloyd's time machine (fashioned from a DeLorean), where he meets his parents as high school seniors and accidentally prevents their meeting, thus nearly wiping out his own future existence! Cleverly written and played, this made a movie star of Fox—who replaced Eric Stoltz several weeks into production—and had a hit Huey Lewis soundtrack. It

was followed by two sequels of varying interest and a Saturday morning cartoon series.

BACK TO THE FUTURE PART II
★★ MCA/Universal, 1989, PG, 107 min. Dir: Robert Zemeckis. Cast: Michael J. Fox, Christopher Lloyd, Lea Thompson, Thomas F. Wilson, Elizabeth Shue, James Tolkan, Charles Fleischer, Joe Flaherty.

Picking up where Part I left off, Fox and Lloyd rocket into the future, where they discover old nemesis Wilson wreaking havoc after having learned the secret of time travel himself. In the end everyone must return to the '50s setting of the original to set things right. This dark, dreary sequel isn't nearly as much fun as the original but finally begins to percolate during its oddball parallel-time ending sequence with some standout special FX. Lovely Shue is wasted in the thankless role of Fox's girlfriend, while a frantic Michael J. plays everyone but the kitchen sink.

BACK TO THE FUTURE PART III
★★☆ MCA/UNIVERSAL, 1990, PG, 117 min. Dir: Robert Zemekis. Cast: Michael J. Fox, Christopher Lloyd, Mary Steenburgen, Lea Thompson, Thomas F. Wilson, Elisabeth Shue, James Tolkan, Richard Dysart, Pat Buttram, Dub Taylor.

The final film in the BTTF trilogy makes amends for the bleakness of Part II with this bright, breezy western spoof. Fox and Lloyd are now in the old West, where Mike battles an evil ancestor of Wilson while Lloyd falls in love with progressive school marm Steenburgen (practically repeating her role from *Time After Time*) and is fated to die in a shootout. Can history be changed to save him? High spirits all around help keep this from becoming just another soulless Hollywood FX machine but by now all this endless time-tripping has worn a bit thin.

BAD CHANNELS
★ Paramount, 1992, R, 86 min. Dir: Ted Nicolaou. Cast: Martha Quinn, Paul Hipp, Charlie Spradling, Aaron Lustig, Ian Patrick Williams, Melissa Behr.

Plotless video fodder about an alien working as a DJ and shrinking human women to tiny size for study. Charles Band's Empire Pictures has probably made worse movies but we've all got better things to do rather than trying to figure out which is which.

BAD GIRLS FROM MARS
★★ Vidmark Entertainment, 1990, R, 86 min. Dir: Fred Olen Ray. Cast: Edy Williams, Oliver Darrow, Brinke Stevens, Jay Richardson, Jeffrey Culver, Dana Bently.

Russ Meyer veteran Williams stars in this moderately amusing spoof of low-budget moviemaking. The shooting of the cheapie *Bad Girls from Mars* keeps getting disrupted by a mysterious killer who keeps knocking off any actress cast in the leading lady spot. Better at poking fun at the rigors of independent movie making than at lampooning cheapie sci-fi or horror pictures, this bears more than a passing resemblance to Joe Dante and Allan Arkush's *Hollywood Boulevard.*

BAMBOO SAUCER, THE

★★☆ Republic, 1968, PG, 100 min. Dir: Frank Telford. Cast: Dan Duryea, Lois Nettleton, John Ericson, Nan Leslie, Bob Hastings.

After a talky first half, this little sleeper starts to get good as competing U.S. and Soviet scientific teams head to Tibet in search of a downed flying saucer. Good performances, well-written dialogue, and solid direction make up for the dull beginning and some shoddy FX at the end. Aka *Collision Course.*

BARBARELLA

★★★ Paramount, 1968, PG, 98 min. Dir: Roger Vadim. Cast: Jane Fonda, John Phillip Law, Anita Pallenberg, Milo O'Shea, David Hemmings, Marcel Marceau, Claude Dauphin, Ugo Tognazzi.

This pop art film translation of the French comic strip perfectly casts Fonda, at the height of her sex kitten period, as the futuristic lady astronaut searching for a missing scientist on a weird planet ruled by sex-obsessed bitch-queen Pallenberg. This is so '60s that it hurts but it's still good fun, filled with weird visuals, strange characters, and a lot of sex talk and (mild) nudity for a PG-rated movie. Aka *Barbarella, Queen of the Universe.*

BARBARELLA, QUEEN OF THE UNIVERSE

See: *Barbarella.*

BARBARIAN QUEEN

★☆ Vestron, 1984, R, 85 min. Dir: Hector Olivera. Cast: Lana Clarkson, Katt Shea Ruben, Dawn Dunlap, Frank Zagarino, Susana Traverso, Victor Bo.

Shot in Argentina, this features the implant-perfect charms of Clarkson, who, as the lady of the title, leads her tribe of Playmate warrior women against a gang of murderous cut-throats. Another bogus pseudo-sword-and-sorcery excuse to watch naked women mud-wrestle. But hey, I'm not arguing with success.

BARBARIAN QUEEN II: THE EMPRESS STRIKES BACK

★ LIVE, 1989, R, 87 min. Dir: Joe Finley. Cast: Lana

Clarkson, Greg Wrangler, Rebecca Wood, Elizabeth Jaegen, Roger Cuday.

This unwanted followup brings back the boda-cious Clarkson once again to take on the evil males around her, in this case kingdom-stealing bad brother Wrangler (whose name sounds like it should belong to a gay porno star). Only for those who'd give the original a four-star rating.

BARBARIANS, THE

★★ Cannon, 1987, R, 87 min. Dir: Ruggero Deodato. Cast: David Paul, Peter Paul, Richard Lynch, Eva La Rue, Virginia Bryant, Michael Berryman.

Beefcake watchers will get their fill and then some in this mindless muscle epic starring real-life twin weightlifters the Paul Brothers. The boys play bumbling warriors who wear too much eye makeup but very little clothing as they face off against supreme bad guy Lynch and his low-budget monster to save a beautiful queen. This is a rather unusual offering to come from Italian movie violence king Deodato but it's not without its dopey charm.

BARB WIRE

★☆ Polygram, 1996, UR, 98 min. Dir: David Hogan. Cast: Pamela Anderson, Temuera Morrison, Victoria Rowell, Jack Noseworthy, Steve Railsback, Udo Kier, Xander Berkeley, Clint Howard.

Although not really silicon queen Anderson's first movie (as it was publicized), this futuristic comic book may very well be her last! Based on Chris Warner's Dark Horse comic, this features Pam (looking alarmingly like femme-impersonator RuPaul) as the big-busted Barb, who is asked by old love Morrison and his new gal Rowell to help them fight the evil "Congressional Directorate," which overthrew the U.S. government in the year 2017. Even with all the *Blade Runner/The Crow* atmospherics and oddball casting (thank you, Steve, Udo, and Clint) this never adds up to much more than a B-grade vanity production for a not especially interesting "star." The unrated video contains some graphic violence cut from the theatrical prints.

BARON MÜENCHHAUSEN

★★★ Video City, 1943, NR, 110 min. Dir: Josef von Baky. Cast: Hans Albers, Brigitte Horney, Wilhelm Bendow, Leo Slezak, Kaethe Kaack, Hermann Speelmans.

Produced by the Nazi party under the supervision of General Joseph Goebbels, this German fantasy follows the exploits of the good baron as he pursues harem girls and princesses from the earth to the moon. This elaborate fantasy is like a weird Euro-Disney film full of visual trickery and corny, often mildly sexual humor and isn't quite the total propaganda film you might expect.

BATMAN

★★ Fox, 1966, NR, 105 min. Dir: Leslie H. Martinson. Cast: Adam West, Burt Ward, Lee Meriwether, Cesar Romero, Burgess Meredith, Frank Gorshin, Alan Napier, Neil Hamilton, Stafford Repp, Madge Blake.

Rushed into production to cash in on the popularity of the TV series (and not actually made up of series episodes as often reported), this quickie theatrical spinoff of all that mid-'60s small screen Bat-mania is modest fun but never really cuts loose. Batman and Robin (the ever stoic West and Ward) have their hands full when their four greatest enemies—the Joker (Romero), Penguin (Meredith), Riddler (Gorshin), and Catwoman (Meriwether, subbing for an otherwise-occupied Julie Newmar)—team up and come into possession of a device that can dehydrate human beings into little piles of colored sand. Full of gimmicks and silly bits of deadpan comedy, this made a ton of money at kiddie matinees and is still probably best enjoyed by those who first saw it under those circumstances. Aka *Batman-The Movie.*

BATMAN

★★☆ Warner, 1989, PG-13, 126 min. Dir: Tim Burton. Cast: Michael Keaton, Jack Nicholson, Kim Basinger, Robert Wuhl, Billy Dee Williams, Jack Palance, Michael Gough, Pat Hingle, Jerry Hall, Tracey Walter.

Returning to the dark, brooding roots of the Bob Kane comic-strip character, this megabuck movie eschews the campiness of the old TV show in favor of angst galore. Keaton is the deeply disturbed Bruce Wayne who dons the Bat costume in order to deal out vigilante vengeance against the criminal element he holds responsible for the death of his parents. Nicholson, meanwhile, steals it in a proto-Jack performance as the toxin-scarred, totally bonkers Joker while Basinger is vapid and annoying as Batty's love interest Vicky Vale. Handsome production design, a fine score by Danny Elfman, and a solid supporting cast—especially horror movie veteran Gough as Alfred the butler—add to the effectiveness of this somber box office smash. Sequels: *Batman Returns, Batman Forever,* and *Batman and Robin.*

BATMAN FOREVER

★★ Warner, 1995, PG-13, 121 min. Dir: Joel Schumacher. Cast: Val Kilmer, Jim Carrey, Tommy Lee Jones, Nicole Kidman, Chris O'Donnell, Michael Gough, Pat Hingle, Drew Barrymore, Debi Maser, René Auberjonois.

Kilmer takes over for Keaton and Schumacher for Burton in this lighter, more colorful, but decidedly minor second sequel to the 1989 *Batman.* The caped crusader battles the psychotic Two Face (Jones) and the loony Riddler (Carrey) while gaining a new partner in former circus acrobat Robin (O'Donnell) and a new love interest in criminal psychologist Kidman. Jones overdoes it and Carrey basically is just playing the Mask all over again but O'Donnell brings some youthful bounce that helps make up for Kilmer's comatose Batman/Bruce Wayne double act. The plot is paper-thin and there's enough in the way of homoeroticism in the Batman-Robin relationship (not to mention the costuming) to make Robert Maplethorpe blush.

BATMAN RETURNS

★★★ Warner, 1992, PG-13, 125 min. Dir: Tim Burton. Cast: Michael Keaton, Danny De Vito, Michelle Pfeiffer, Christopher Walken, Michael Gough, Pat Hingle, Michael Murphy, Cristi Conway, Paul Reubens, Diane Salinger.

The second and best of the series, this plays more like a gothic horror film than an action-fantasy. De Vito, in makeup modeled after Lon Chaney in *London After Midnight,* is the Penguin, a grotesque criminal mastermind who's backed as a mayoral candidate by millionaire businessman Max Schreck (Walken, whose character is named for the German actor who starred in the silent *Nosferatu*). When Walken tries to murder mousey secretary Pfeiffer for knowing too much, she reemerges in the identity of the black-leather-clad Catwoman and falls for the perennially depressed Bruce Wayne. With its bleak atmosphere and air of sad hopelessness, this may be the most down-beat holiday-set movie since *Black Christmas* and is certainly one of the darkest recent Hollywood movies to become a major box office hit. Great performances all around and a melancholy Danny Elfman score.

BATMAN-THE MOVIE

See: *Batman* (1966).

BATTERIES NOT INCLUDED

★☆ MCA/Universal, 1987, PG, 106 min. Dir: Matthew Robbins. Cast: Hume Cronyn, Jessica Tandy, Elizabeth Pena, Frank McRae, Michael Carmine, Dennis Boutsikaris.

This Steven Spielberg production is so darn cute you want to kick it. Tiny, toylike alien spacecraft buzz about a Manhattan tenement set for demolition and help the stereotypical residents (including those Hallmark Hall of Fame darlings Cronyn and Tandy) out of various jams. Originally planned as an episode of *Amazing Stories,* at least on TV it would have been shorter—and shown free of charge.

BATTLE BENEATH THE EARTH
★★ MGM/UA, 1968, NR, 91 min. Dir: Montgomery Tully. Cast: Kerwin Mathews, Viviane Ventura, Peter Arne, Robert Ayres, Martin Benson, Al Murdock.

Low-grade thriller about a Communist Chinese plot to tunnel under the U.S. and plant atomic weapons. This pulp cross between James Bond and Fu Manchu has dull direction and cheap special FX but is just corny enough to provide an hour and a half of mindless tomfoolery.

BATTLE BEYOND THE STARS
See: *The Green Slime.*

BATTLE BEYOND THE STARS
★★★ Vestron, 1980, PG, 103 min. Dir: Jimmy T. Murakami. Cast: Richard Thomas, Darlanne Fleugel, George Peppard, Robert Vaughn, John Saxon, Sybil Danning, Sam Jaffe, Morgan Woodward, Marta Kristen, Julia Duffy.

An outer space remake of *The Magnificent Seven,* this above-average Roger Corman production is lots of fun. Thomas is the youth who gathers together a colorful group of warriors to battle space villain Saxon. Among them are space cowboy Peppard, busty Valkyrie Danning (in an outfit that had to be optically fogged when they showed this on NBC years ago), and original *Magnificent Seven* cast member Vaughn. The decent low-budget FX were reused by the ever-frugal Corman in later productions like *Galaxy of Terror, Forbidden World,* and *Android.*

BATTLE BEYOND THE SUN
★★ Sinister Cinema, 1963, NR, 75 min. Dirs: Alexander Kozyr, Thomas Colchart [Francis Ford Coppola]. Cast: Ed Perry, Arla Powell, Andy Stewart, Bruce Hunter.

In an infamous bit of restructuring, Roger Corman took a Soviet space movie called *Niebo Zowiet: The Heavens Call* and had Coppola refashion it into a typically American sci-fi cheapie with the insertion of some hastily shot monster

footage in which the battling beasties look suspiciously like a penis and vagina duking it out. The original footage still retains much of its eerie ambiance while the badly dubbed Russian cast is saddled with bogus American pseudonyms.

BATTLE FOR THE PLANET OF THE APES
★★ Fox, 1973, PG, 86 min. Dir: J. Lee Thompson. Cast: Roddy McDowall, Claude Akins, Natalie Trundey, Paul Williams, Lew Ayres, John Huston, Severn Darden, France Nuyen, Austin Stoker, Bobby Porter.

The fifth and final Apes movie is certainly the weakest ,with ape leader McDowall trying to bring peace between the apes and their human slaves despite interference from gorilla general Akins and mutant leader Darden. Fans of the series will like how this cleverly dovetails into the beginning of the first movie but a slow first hour and obviously low budget soon take their toll. Followed by two TV shows, one live action (with McDowall), the other animated.

Natalie Trundy, Roddy McDowall, and Bobby Porter pose for a family portrait in Battle for the Planet of the Apes *(1973).*

BATTLE OF THE WORLDS

★★☆ Sinister Cinema, 1961, NR, 84 min. Dir: Anthony Dawson [Antonio Margheriti]. Cast: Claude Rains, Bill Carter, Maya Brent, Umberto Orsini, Jacqueline Derval.

One wonders what was going through his mind while Rains was filming this silly but well-shot sci-fi cheapie in Italy. An aged but still spry Claude is a scientist who's discovered a rogue asteroid on a collision course with Earth. The asteroid turns out to be a spacecraft from a dead civilization and an expedition is dispatched to find out more about them. Margheriti brings strong atmosphere to a slight production.

BATTLESTAR GALACTICA

★★ MCA/Universal, 1979, PG, 125 min. Dir: Richard A. Colla. Cast: Lorne Greene, Dirk Benedict, Richard Hatch, Jane Seymour, Ray Milland, Maren Jensen, Patrick Macnee, Laurette Sprang, Lew Ayres, John Colicos.

Feature version of the premiere episode of the heavily hyped TV *Star Wars* clone, drastically edited and with a specially shot ending. Greene leads the survivors of a doomed planet in search of a new home; Benedict is the Han Solo clone and Hatch the Luke Skywalker wannabe. The John Dykstra FX and impressive robot aliens called Cylons are the best things about this routine space opera. A number of series episodes are available on the MCA/Universal label, most notably: *Mission Galactica: The Cylon Attack,* with a great guest role for Lloyd Bridges; *Baltar's Escape,* featuring the always amusing Colicos in the title role; and the *Enemy Mine*—like *Return of Starbuck,* the best segment of the thankfully short-lived *Galactica: 1980* series.

BATTLETRUCK

See: *Warlords of the 21st Century.*

BEAST FROM 20,000 FATHOMS, THE

★★★ Warner, 1953, NR 79 min. Dir: Eugene Lourie. Cast: Paul Christian, Paula Raymond, Cecil Kellaway, Kenneth Tobey, Donald Woods, Lee Van Cleef.

Atomic testing in the arctic unleashes a huge prehistoric monster from its icy tomb, the beast heading straight for New York City. This low-budget monster pic became one of the top box office hits of 1953 and established Ray Harryhausen as the master of inexpensive stop-motion wonders. When released in Japan, this film's success there served as the inspiration for Toho's *Godzilla* series and was itself pretty much remade by director Lourie as *The Giant Behemoth* and *Gorgo.* Best scene: the beast snacking on one of New York's finest.

BEASTMASTER, THE

★★★ MGM/UA, 1982, PG, 118 min. Dir: Don Coscarelli. Cast: Marc Singer, Tanya Roberts, Rip Torn, John Amos.

Coscarelli, who's spent most of his career endlessly remaking his first hit *Phantasm* to lesser and lesser effect, was basically just trying to do a quickie *Conan* ripoff here but ended up with a nice little B movie that's actually a lot better. Singer is the hunky hero who can handle a broadsword with the best of them and can also communicate with animals *Doctor Doolittle* style. Torn is the evil wizard Marc must fight to avenge his dad's death and Roberts, Charlie's most angelic Angel, is the sweet slave girl along for the ride. This fantasy adventure was only a minor hit but did well enough on video to develop a bit of a cult and inspired a couple of belated sequels.

BEASTMASTER 2: THROUGH THE PORTAL OF TIME

★★ Republic, 1990, PG-13, 107 min. Dir: Sylvio Tabet. Cast: Marc Singer, Kari Wuhrer, Wings Hauser, Sarah Douglas, James Avery, Robert Z'Dar, Arthur Malet, Michael Berryman.

This long-in-the-waiting sequel isn't nearly as good as the first but still provides minor action and laughs. Our loin-clothed hero (Singer) is in a new fight with a new nemesis (the always intense Hauser) when he's blasted through a time barrier into the modern world. When Hauser follows, Marc joins forces with perky Los Angeleno Wuhrer to defeat him. Amusing and/or exciting in fits and starts, this ignores much of what made the original so much fun and instead spends too much of its time routinely ripping off flicks like *Mad Max* and *The Terminator.*

BEASTMASTER 3: THE EYES OF BRAXUS

★★ MCA/Universal, 1995, PG, 92 min. Dir: Gabrielle Beaumont. Cast: Marc Singer, Tony Todd, Sandra Hess, Lesley-Anne Down, David Warner, Patrick Kilpatrick.

Beastmaster Singer returns for a third installment, this time aided by *Candyman's* Todd and trying to stop evil lord Warner from using a magical stone to resurrect some dark god called Braxus. Run-of-the-mill sword-and-sorcery nonsense that's another big comedown from the original film and wastes a talented cast, including Down as a seductive witch.

BEAST OF YUCCA FLATS, THE

★ Sinister Cinema, 1961, NR, 60 min. Dir: Coleman Francis. Cast: Tor Johnson, Douglas Mellor, Barbara Francis, Tony Cardoza.

Johnson is a Soviet scientist on the run from Russian agents who's exposed to an atomic bomb blast and turns into a "monster" who doesn't look much different than a preblast Tor. Our mountainous hero then wanders around the desert for fifty-odd—*very* odd—minutes while various stupid people keep blundering into his path and a narrator drones on about the obvious. One of no-budget auteur Francis's few excursions into sci-fi/horror, this brain cell-crushing motion picture (and I use the term loosely) makes Ed Wood's movies look like the work of Welles or Fellini—or both.

BEAUTY AND THE BEAST

★★★★ Nelson, 1946, NR, 90 min. Dir: Jean Cocteau. Cast: Jean Marais, Josette Day, Marcel André, Mila Parely, Nane German, Michel Auclair.

Exquisite French fantasy based on the popular story by Marie LePrine De Beaumont. When a merchant dares to pick a rose belonging to a half-human, half-lion beast (Marais), the merchant's daughter must pay the price by coming to live in the beast's castle. Unexpectedly, though, the beauty (Day) and the monster fall in love. Dreamily photographed in settings that seem literally to be alive (and were modeled on the drawings of Gustave Doré), this film's spell is so expertly woven that you hardly even notice that the actors aren't speaking English. Remade in 1963, as a TV movie in 1976, and as a popular Disney animated feature in 1990, not to mention the TV series, none have the ability to capture the imagination and feel of a fairy tale brought to life as does this definitive version.

BEAUTY AND THE BEAST

★★ Republic, 1987–89, NR, 50 min. per tape. Dirs: Richard Franklin, Victor Lobl, Peter Medak, Gabrielle Beaumont, others. Cast: Linda Hamilton, Ron Perlman, Roy Dotrice, Jay Acovone.

A New York City attorney (Hamilton) is viciously mugged and left for dead only to be rescued and nursed back to health by a sewer-dwelling beast man (Perlman) who falls hopelessly in love with her. A popular cult item in its day, this series has always seemed too sloppily sentimental for its own good. Still, the actors are sincere (a little *too* sincere considering the often ridiculous circumstances they find themselves in) and the baroque atmosphere of tragic love and impossible desire is occasionally affecting.

BEDAZZLED

★★★ CBS/Fox, 1968, PG, 107 min. Dir: Stanley Donen. Cast: Peter Cook, Dudley Moore, Raquel Welch, Eleanor Bron, Barry Humphries, Michael Bates.

The magic word is "Julie Andrews!" in this Faust updated for the Go-Go generation. Moore, a nebbishy short-order (get it?) cook hopelessly in love with Bron, is promised his heart's desire if he sells his soul to the devilish Cook. Guest star Welch is satanic temptress Lillian Lust. A very funny film, especially for those familiar with Moore's work only after he "went Hollywood," with stylish direction and bright dialogue.

BEDKNOBS AND BROOMSTICKS

★★★ Disney, 1971, G, 117 min. Dir: Robert Stevenson. Cast: Angela Lansbury, David Tomlinson, Roddy McDowall, Sam Jaffe, Roy Snart, Cindy O'Callaghan, Ian Weighill.

Delightful musical fantasy in the *Mary Poppins* vein with Lansbury as an amateur witch, taking a black magic correspondence course, who uses her powers to aid the British army during World War II. A solid blend of humor and special FX. Like *Poppins,* this features a lengthy animated sequence wherein the human cast hobnobs with a crew of talking cartoon animals.

BEGINNING OF THE END, THE

★☆ Goodtimes, 1957, NR, 73 min. Dir: Bert I. Gordon. Cast: Peter Graves, Peggie Castle, Morris Ankrum, Thomas B. Henry, Richard Benedict, Than Wyenn.

Back-projected grasshoppers rampage over photographs of the Chicago skyline in Gordon's almost-remake of *Them!* Radiation-contaminated grain consumed by the hoppers cause them to grow into monsters, and the devastation they cause is investigated by intrepid reporter Castle while scientist Graves and army guy Ankrum try to find a way to stop them. This has a surprisingly suspenseful first twenty minutes or so but once those badly matted-in buggers appear it never recovers. Amusingly, the big-budget film *The Swarm* stole its ending from this ten-day wonder.

BELL, BOOK AND CANDLE

★★★ Columbia/TriStar, 1958, NR, 103 min. Dir: Richard Quine. Cast: James Stewart, Kim Novak, Jack Lemmon, Ernie Kovacs, Hermione Gingold, Elsa Lanchester.

The stars of Hitchcock's *Vertigo* reunite for this frothy adaptation of the John Van Druten play about an engaged publisher (Stewart) put under a spell by a love-starved witch (Novak at her most smoldering). Solid, well-cast fantasy-comedy that may have been the inspiration for TV's *Bewitched* series and almost cries out for a Tom Hanks-Meg Ryan remake.

BENEATH THE PLANET OF THE APES
★★★ Fox, 1970, PG, 95 min. Dir: Ted Post. Cast: James Franciscus, Charlton Heston, Kim Hunter, Maurice Evans, Linda Harrison, James Gregory, Victor Buono, Paul Richards, Jeff Corey, Natalie Trundy.

Picking up exactly where the original *Apes* movie left off, this finds Heston stumbling into the dreaded "Forbidden Zone," where he ends up the captive of psychic, hideously disfigured human mutants who live in the ruins of New York City and worship an unexploded nuclear device. Franciscus is another astronaut from Earth's past sent into the future to find Chuck just as a gorilla army led by general Gregory invades the mutant stronghold and, in one of the most shocking endings ever, the entire world is destroyed when the bomb is touched off by a dying Heston. Economically reusing some standing sets on the Fox lot—some of them built for *Hello Dolly* (!)—this violent, fast-paced sequel was almost as popular as the first *Planet of the Apes*, making the all-out climax look like something of a misstep, but not one impossible to get around since they managed to come up with three more sequels after this. Incidentally, this is the one and only *Apes* flick without Roddy McDowall in the cast, though he does appear in some flashback footage at the beginning.

BEYOND ATLANTIS
★ United Entertainment, 1973, PG, 89 min. Dir: Eddie Romero. Cast: Patrick Wayne, John Ashley, Leigh Christian, George Nader, Lenore Stevens, Sid Haig.

Paltry adventure fantasy with Wayne (son of the Duke) and Haig (son of a couple named Haig, I guess) as pearl thieves who encounter an underwater civilization of water breathers living in the ruins of Atlantis (even though this takes place in the Pacific Ocean). Ashley is the scientist hero, Christian the curvaceous Atlantian heroine, and Nader a campy cult leader in this Filipino time waster that's so mild it doesn't even contain any of the action or topless females you'd ordinarily expect from this director and cast.

BEYOND THE TIME BARRIER
★★ Sinister Cinema, 1960, NR, 75 min. Dir: Edgar G. Ulmer. Cast: Robert Clarke, Darlene Tompkins, Arianne Arden, Vladimir Sokoloff, John Van Dreelen, Read Morgan.

Test pilot Clarke is projected into the year 2024 where he discovers the world recovering from nuclear devastation, with normal folk living underground and crazed mutants kept in cages. Shot back to back with *The Amazing Transparent Man,* this is something of an improvement, with some imaginative direction and solid acting to offset the corny dialogue and familiar situations. Like *Transparent Man,* though, this often bleak movie wears its nihilism on its sleeve.

BEYOND TOMORROW
★★ Hollywood Home Theatre, 1939, NR, 84 min. Dir: A Edward Sutherland. Cast: Richard Carlson, Jean Parker, Harry Carey, C. Aubrey Smith, Charles Winninger, Maria Ouspenskaya.

Old-fashion bit of Hollywood corn with a young couple (Carlson and Parker) brought together for the holidays by three old coots who turn out to be ghosts on a divine mission. The good cast makes palatable a syrupy fantasy.

BIG
★★★☆ Fox, 1988, PG, 102 min. Dir: Penny Marshall. Cast: Tom Hanks, Elizabeth Perkins, Robert Loggia, John Heard, Jared Rushton, Jon Lovitz, Mercedes Ruehl, David Moscow.

A twelve-year-old boy, frustrated by his youth and small stature, wishes he were big—and wakes up the next morning to discover that he has aged twenty years overnight! The best of several "body switching" fantasies from this period, this well-directed, perceptively written comedy is highlighted by Hanks's charming performance as the innocent little boy in a man's body who tries to come to grips with landing a job, finding a place to live, and dealing with the romantic interest of coworker Perkins. Contrived in places but still one of the best, most honest "feel-good" movies of the 1980s.

BIGFOOT AND THE HENDERSONS
See: *Harry and the Hendersons.*

BIGGLES
See: *Biggles: Adventures in Time.*

BIGGLES: ADVENTURES IN TIME
★★ Imperial Entertainment, 1986, PG, 108 min. Dir: John Hough. Cast: Neil Dickson, Alex Hyde-White, Peter Cushing, Fiona Hutchinson, Marcus Gilbert, William Hootkins.

Based on a British series of boys' books written by Captain W. E. Johns, this rather flat adventure fantasy casts Hyde-White as the modern hero sent back in time to World War I, where he aids the stalwart flyboy Biggles (Dickson) in his battles against the Germans. Sometimes amusing, and with a nice cameo by Cushing, but too uncertain as to whether it wants to be a comedy or a straight action pic really to work. Original title: *Biggles.*

BIG TROUBLE IN LITTLE CHINA
★★ Fox, 1986, PG-13, 99 min. Dir: John Carpenter. Cast: Kurt Russell, Kim Cattrall, James Hong, Victor Wong, Dennis Dun, Kate Burton.

Russell is a kinda stoopid, big-mouthed trucker who gets caught up in a Chinatown tong war while trying to rescue a friend's fiancée and eventually finds himself facing some powerful Chinese black magic. Carpenter's late-in-the-day *Raiders* provides minor fun, with good FX, music, and wide-screen photography, but keeps mistaking rampant stupidity for a genuine sense of humor. Not as annoying as *Indiana Jones and the Temple of Doom* but no *Escape from New York,* either.

BILL AND TED'S BOGUS JOURNEY
★★★ Orion, 1991, PG, 98 min. Dir: Peter Hewitt. Cast: Keanu Reeves, Alex Winter, William Sadler, Joss Ackland, George Carlin, Pam Grier, Amy Stock-Poynton, Sarah Trigger.

The boneheaded duo from *Bill and Ted's Excellent Adventure* returns for this even more bodacious sequel. When our dudes get bumped off by their robot doubles they must travel from Heaven to Hell and back, eventually being challenged by Death himself (veteran baddie Sadler in a funny change-of-pace role) to everything from chess to Twister. Full of great special FX and dumb-as-dirt humor, this unapologetically dopey movie is real brain candy.

BILL AND TED'S EXCELLENT ADVENTURE
★★☆ Nelson, 1989, PG, 89 min. Dir: Stephen Herek. Cast: Keanu Reeves, Alex Winter, George Carlin, Bernie Casey, Amy Stock-Poynton, Dan Shor, Tony Camilieri, Rod Loomis.

California surfer dudes Bill and Ted (Winter and Reeves in the roles they were born to play) are about to flunk history but think they've found the answer when a guy from the future (Carlin) visits them in his phone booth/time machine. The boys then take off into the past, where they round up various historical figures like Socrates, Joan of Arc, and Billy the Kid to ace that sucker. This pleasantly funny, oh-so-'80s comedy only starts to take off near the end but is helped along by its having-a-wonderful-time cast and often inventive script. Followed by *Bill and Ted's Bogus Journey* and an animated TV series.

BIOHAZARD
★☆ Cinema Group, 1984, R, 78 min. Dir: Fred Olen Ray. Cast: Aldo Ray, Angelique Pettyjohn, David Pearson, Richard Hench, Loren Crabtree, Carroll Borland.

Ray's cheap take on *E.T.* and *Alien* has a pint-sized monster—spawned by some NASA experiments trying to contact some other dimension—scampering about Los Angeles, and bumping off extras while the main cast members argue a lot. The late, great Pettyjohn (looking sadly faded) is our psychic heroine and there's a surprise ending that makes no sense at all. Worth sitting through just for the outtakes shown during the end credits. Followed by an in-name-only sequel and remade as *Deep Space.*

BIOHAZARD: THE ALIEN FORCE
★★ Vidmark Entertainment, 1995, R, 88 min. Dir: Steve Latshaw. Cast: Steve Zurk, Christopher Mitchum, Susan Fronsoe, Tom Ferguson, Patrick Moran, Katherine Culliver.

Shot in Florida, this Fred Olen Ray-backed semisequel to *Biohazard* is better made but just as predictably derivative. A genetically engineered mutant that lives off human spinal fluid escapes from a scientific complex and goes on a killing spree while hunted by the lab's security chief and an investigative reporter. Though it borrows much from other movies like *Sygenor,* this cheapie also shares plot similarities with the big budget *Species,* except this was made first.

BIONIC WOMAN, THE
★★☆ MCA/Universal, 1975, NR, 96 min. Dir: Richard Moder. Cast: Lindsay Wagner, Lee Majors, Richard Anderson, Alan Oppenheimer.

The two-part *Six Million Dollar Man* episode that introduced us to Jamie Sommers (Wagner), the world's first bionic woman, this is at once silly (how do you hurt your ear in a skydiving accident?) and earnest (thanks mainly to Lindsay's acting) but is still enjoyable for fans. And how many of you forgot that our heroine allegedly dies at the end of the story?

BISHOP'S WIFE, THE
★★★ Nelson, 1946, NR, 108 min. Dir: Henry Koster. Cast: Cary Grant, Loretta Young, David Niven, Monty Woolley, Gladys Cooper, Elsa Lanchester.

Sweet-natured Christmas fantasy about a charming angel (Grant) sent to Earth to help bishop Niven and wife Young raise money for a new church—only to fall in love with the neglected wife. One of Hollywood's many postwar fantasies full of angels and ghosts and one of the best with solid casting and a sentimental but well-written script. Remade as *The Preacher's Wife.*

BLACKBEARD'S GHOST
★★★ Disney, 1968, G, 107 min. Dir: Robert Stevenson. Cast: Peter Ustinov, Dean Jones, Suzanne Pleshette, Elsa Lanchester, Joby Baker, Elliott Reid, Richard Deacon, Kelly Thordsen.

Ustinov is a blast as the infamous pirate, cursed by his witch wife to walk the Earth forever, who helps Jones save his seaside home from being turned into a casino by gangsters. Formula Disney comedy given a lift via a trenchant script that gets most of its humor from good characters rather than the usual carload of hokey special FX.

BLACK HOLE, THE
★★ Disney, 1979, PG, 97 min. Dir: Gary Nelson. Cast: Maximilian Schell, Yvette Mimieux, Anthony Perkins, Robert Forster, Ernest Borgnine, Joseph Bottoms, voices of Roddy McDowall and Slim Pickens.

This Disney *Star Wars* cash-in opened the same day as *Star Trek: The Motion Picture* and like that movie is little more than a lot of big-budget FX in search of a story. Mostly just a remake of *20,000 Leagues Under the Sea* set in space, this features Schell as a half-mad scientist whose huge spacecraft is perched on the edge of a black hole, a mysterious space phenomenon he intends to study. When space travelers Mimieux, Perkins, Forster, Borgnine (this is starting to sound like the cast of a disaster movie), and Bottoms stumble upon him, Schell makes plans to drag them into the black hole as well. This has outstanding miniatures and matte paintings and a good score by John Barry

but can't seem to settle on the right approach, throwing in everything from stormtrooperish killer androids to comic-relief robots (voiced by McDowall and Pickens) to a confusing, *2001*-style ending. One scene, though, involving a fiery meteorite rolling down a corridor as our heroes flee across a bridge in front of it, will take your breath away.

BLACK SCORPION, THE
★★★ Warner, 1957, NR, 87 min. Dir: Edward Ludwig. Cast: Richard Denning, Mara Corday, Carlos Rivas, Mario Navarro.

Scientists Denning and Rivas investigate volcanic eruptions in Mexico as huge prehistoric scorpions are unleashed from their subterranean lair and begin to feast on the locals. Corday is the fiery ranch owner who catches Denning's eye. Pretty much a remake of *Them!* (even some of the same sound FX are utilized), this is given grit by its cheap but remarkable animation FX supervised by Willis (*King Kong*) O'Brien, including a scene where the monsters derail a passenger train and then hungrily pluck out all the survivors like someone digging out the raisins from a box of raisin bran.

BLACK SCORPION
★★ New Horizons, 1995, R, 92 min. Dir: Jonathan Winfrey. Cast: Joan Severance, Bruce Abbott, Garrett Morris, Rick Rossovich, Casey Siemazko, Rick Dean.

Severance is a female cop who takes the law into her own hands. After the murder of her father she dons a sexy costume to become the seductive crime fighter known as the Black

"I'm ready for my closeup, Mr. O'Brien!" The Black Scorpion *(1957).*

Scorpion. This Roger Corman-produced distaff *Batman* with cleavage, originally made for cable, copies ideas from *The Crow* and its title from a classic big bug flick of the '50s (which had the double advantage of Mara Corday and Willis O'Brien animation) but really isn't all that special; most of the humor it generates is strictly the unintentional kind. Followed by a sequel.

BLADE MASTER, THE

★ Media, 1984, PG, 92 min. Dir: David Hills [Aristede Massacessi]. Cast: Miles O'Keeffe, Lisa Foster, Charles Borromel, David Cain Haughton, Chen Wong.

Nobody asked for it but here comes the sequel to *Ator, the Fighting Eagle*. Once again we're presented with miles of Miles as he reminisces about past experiences (okay, okay, he has flashbacks of the first movie), fights more bad guys over the possession of some prehistoric explosive device, and, in a ludicrous ending, hang glides to the rescue! Lots of barbaric hilarity. TV title: *Cave Dwellers*.

BLADE RUNNER

★★★★ Warner, 1982, R, 117 min. Dir: Ridley Scott. Cast: Harrison Ford, Rutger Hauer, Sean Young, Edward James Olmos, Daryl Hannah, Joanna Cassidy, William Sanderson, Joe Turkel, M. Emmet Walsh, Brion James.

Based on Philip K. Dick's novel *Do Androids Dream of Electric Sheep?* this futuristic masterpiece stars Ford as a sullen (and possibly repressed homosexual) exterminator of "replicants," artificially created human beings used as slave labor on other planets. When a band of renegade replicants arrive in the hellish, rainlashed Los Angeles of the next century, Ford is assigned to hunt them down, only to learn the sad truth that he has been slowly losing his own humanity while his allegedly less-than-human quarry have been gaining theirs. Full of awe-inspiring, and much-imitated, FX by Douglas Trumboll, this blend of '40s *film noir* and science fiction is one of the most emotionally engaging movies of its kind and came as something of a

Rutger Hauer goes bobbing for Fords in Blade Runner *(1982).*

surprise to moviegoers of the time, who were obviously expecting another *Star Wars* or *Raiders* and left this to die on the vine. Ford has been better elsewhere but Hauer, Hannah, Sanderson, Cassidy, and Turkel are excellent, bringing to life a gallery of complex, screwed-up people who are a far cry from the scrubbed-face teens and cute robots of most '80s sci-fi. Originally released at 123 minutes, the film was first released on video in an uncut version with some violence reinserted and has since been reedited into this definitive "Director's Cut" edition minus the narration and the tacked-on "happy" ending-featuring shots lifted from *The Shining*!

BLAKE'S 7

★★☆ BFS Video, 1978–81, NR, 105 min per tape. Dirs: Vere Lorrimer, Pennant Roberts, Michael E. Briant, others. Cast: Gareth Thomas, Sally Knyvette, Paul Darrow, Jan Chappell, Michael Keating, David Jackson, Glyn Owen, Peter Tuddenham.

British TV series, created by *Doctor Who*'s Terry Nation and starring Thomas as Blake, the leader of a band of dissidents trying to escape the future Earth after it's been taken over by an evil totalitarian government. The episodes run the gamut from pulpy to thought-provoking, often resembling a cross between *Lost In Space* and *2001*.

BLANKMAN

★★ Columbia/TriStar, 1994, PG-13, 92 min. Dir: Mike Binder. Cast: Damon Wayans, David Alan Grier, Robin Givens, Jason Alexander, Christopher Lawford, Jon Polito.

Two of the stars of *In Living Color* team up for this silly superhero spoof about a nerdy inventor (Wayans) turned crime fighter. Blankman, though, has no superpowers and keeps getting both himself and his older brother (Grier) into trouble. Fans of the stars may find this amusing.

BLITHE SPIRIT

★★★ United American, 1945, NR, 96 min. Dir: David Lean. Cast: Rex Harrison, Constance Cummings, Kay Hammond, Margaret Rutherford, Hugh Wakefield, Joyce Carey.

Spirited filmization of the Noel Coward play about a newly married widower (Harrison) haunted by the playful ghost of his dead first wife. Breezy supernatural comedy with future Miss Jane Marple Rutherford stealing it as a wacky medium.

BLOB, THE

★★☆ Goodtimes, 1958, NR, 82 min. Dir: Irwin S. Yeaworth, Jr. Cast: Steve McQueen, Aneta Corseaut, Earl Rowe, Olin Howlin.

Fifties camp classic with McQueen (in his first starring role) as the overaged high school senior trying to stop the title monster: a flesh-eating, ever-expanding mass of space proto-plasm that invades supermarkets, diners, movie theaters, and other icons of '50s life in its search for human food. Not as good as you'd like it to be, with a slow pace and a stilted supporting cast, but that one-of-a-kind monster and catchy Burt Bacharach theme make it a watchable neo-classic of its era. Followed by the sequel *Son of Blob* and the 1988 remake.

BLOB, THE

★★★Columbia/TriStar, 1988, R, 92 min. Dir: Chuck Russell. Cast: Kevin Dillon, Shawnee Smith, Donovan Leitch, Candy Clark, Jeffrey DeMunn, Joe Seneca.

This lavish remake improves on the original in almost every respect; too bad the storyline is so old hat now. The blob is back, only now it's some sort of military superweapon gone wrong, Leitch has the Steve McQueen part but after being built up as the hero he goes the way of Janet Leigh in *Psycho*, leaving rebel-without-a-clue Dillon and homecoming queen-type Smith to fill the bill. The great special FX by Lyle Conway and a nicely tongue-in-cheek-but not insulting-approach do wonders for this old war horse. What a shame it flopped so badly at the box office.

BLOOD BEAST FROM OUTER SPACE

See: *Night Caller from Outer Space.*

BLUE BIRD, THE

★★☆ Fox, NR, 88 min. Dir: Walter Lang. Cast: Shirley Temple, Spring Byington, Nigel Bruce, Gale Sondergaard, Eddie Collins, Sybil Jason.

After losing out on the lead in *The Wizard of Oz*, twelve-year-old Shirley was shuttled by 20th Century-Fox into this lavishly technicolored cash-in. It did better in theaters than *Oz* but is all but forgotten today. Temple and her younger brother go off in pursuit of the Blue Bird of Happiness and end up in a magical land where their pets take on human form (the cat is played by Sondergaard who, incidentally, was originally to be in *Oz* too, as the Wicked Witch) and they meet Father Time and other fabulous characters. Good to look at but rather stiff and charmless, with a supporting cast better suited to a Hitchcock film. Remade in 1976.

BLUE THUNDER

★★★ Columbia/Tristar, 1983, R, 108 min. Dir: John Badham. Cast: Roy Scheider, Malcolm McDowell, Candy Clark, Daniel Stern, Warren Oates, Joe Santos.

Terrific sci-fi/action movie for fourteen-year-

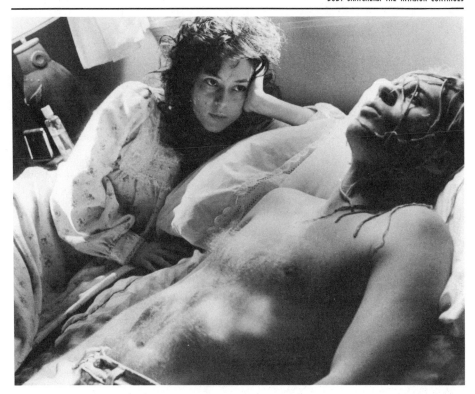

"I told you not to eat spaghetti in bed!" Meg Tilly in Body Snatchers: The Invasion Continues *(1993).*

old boys of all ages about an experimental futuristic helicopter stolen by desperate police pilot Scheider trying to save it from terrorists who want to use it to attack the summer Olympics in Los Angeles. Far from believable and McDowell cuts the ham thick in the first of a decade's worth of campy bad guy performances but with breathtaking stunts and solid performances by Scheider, Stern as his earnest young partner, and Clark as Roy's nutty girlfriend who apparently went to the Hal Needham school of defensive driving.

BLUE TORNADO

★★ Vidmark Entertainment, 1990, PG-13, 96 min. Dir: Tony Dobb. Cast: Dirk Benedict, Patsy Kensit, Ted McGinley, David Warner.

When his best friend is killed by a mysterious force while they are testing an experimental new aircraft, air force test pilot Benedict investigates and uncovers a government conspiracy to cover up an alien visitation. Unconvincing crossbreed of *Top Gun* and *Hangar 18,* this never catches fire despite the best efforts of its cast.

BODY SNATCHERS

See: *Body Snatchers: The Invasion Continues.*

BODY SNATCHERS: THE INVASION CONTINUES

★★★ Warner, 1993, R, 87 min. Dir: Abel Ferrara. Cast: Gabrielle Anwar, Billy Wirth, Meg Tilly, R. Lee Ermey, Forest Whitaker, Christine Elise, Terry Kinney, Reilly Murphy.

Action man Ferrara's gritty sequel/remake to the '78 *Invasion of the Body Snatchers,* this stars Anwar as a teenager who begins noticing strange behavior in her family after they relocate to a southern army base where dad is about to conduct some environmental testing. Assuming everyone saw the earlier *Body Snatcher* movies, this completely dispenses without any explanations about the pods and what they do and instead moves full throttle forward as our heroine desperately tries to escape from a terrifying, increasingly impossible situation. Several unexpectedly grim plot twists for a '90s movie and a brilliant performance by Tilly as Anwar's young stepmom add to the enjoyment. Aka *Body Snatchers.*

BORROWER, THE

★★☆ Cannon, 1989, R, 91 min. Dir: John McNaughton. Cast: Rae Dawn Chong, Don Gordon, Tom Towles, Antonio Fargas, Madchen Amick, Larry Pennell.

McNaughton's disappointing followup to *Henry, Portrait of a Serial Killer*, this tongue-in-cheek monster-from-outer-space flick follows the exploits of an alien criminal banished to Earth, where he possesses various individuals. Unfortunately the heads of those possessed have a nasty habit of exploding, forcing the alien to continually "borrow" heads from reluctant donors. A good cast and some knowing homages to B horror and sci-fi films of the past make this forgettable flick a harmless watch.

BOY AND HIS DOG, A

★★☆ Media, 1975, R, 87 min. Dir: L. Q. Jones. Cast: Don Johnson, Susanne Benton, Jason Robards, Alvy Moore, Helene Winston, Charles McGraw.

Some people find this low-budget adaptation of a famous Harlan Ellison story brilliant but it's always left me rather cold—and from what I've heard, Ellison doesn't like it much either. Johnson is a rather dopey teenager who's survived nuclear devastation with the help of his psychic dog, Blood. When Don stumbles upon an underground civilization of fellow survivors he falls in love, or something, with beautiful Benton but in the end must choose between the woman and his best friend. Grim but often funny, with Johnson hitting just the right note of postadolescent angst; the box covers of most sell-through video versions of this title like to feature shots of the older, sometimes bare-chested star from his *Miami Vice* days.

BOY WHO COULD FLY, THE

★★★ Lorimar, 1986, PG, 114 min. Dir: Nick Castle. Cast: Lucy Deakins, Jay Underwood, Bonnie Bedelia, Colleen Dewhurst, Fred Gwynne, Louise Fletcher, Mindy Cohn, Jason Priestley.

Sweet, Spielburgian fantasy concerns a teenage girl (Deakins) who becomes fascinated with the autistic boy-next-door (Underwood) who, she later discovers, can fly like a bird. Often looks a bit much like an extended *Afterschool Special* but the marvelous cast (the female characters are especially well drawn and well acted) and good flying FX make this work. Incidentally, director Castle got his show business start playing Michael Myers in the original *Halloween*. It's a funny business, isn't it?

BOY WITH GREEN HAIR, THE

★★☆ King of Video, 1948, NR, 82 min. Dir: Joseph Losey. Cast: Dean Stockwell, Robert Ryan, Barbara Hale, Pat O'Brien, Richard Lyon, Walter Catlett.

A well-intentioned but heavy-handed indictment of prejudice in all its forms, this stars the young Stockwell as the kid who wakes up one morning with green locks and and must then endure all manner of harassment and suspicion. Dated but well-acted fantasy; today, the kid would just dress all in black and join an alternative rock group.

BRAIN, THE

★★★ Sinister Cinema, 1962, NR, 83 min. Dir: Freddie Francis. Cast: Peter Van Eyck, Anne Heywood, Bernard Lee, Ellen Schweirs, Cecil Parker, Maxine Audley, Miles Malleson, Jack MacGowran.

Atmospheric remake of *Donovan's Brain*, with Van Eyck as the scientist whose mind is taken over by the disembodied brain of a powerful financier, driving the doc to solve the millionaire's murder. Well cast, this British-West German coproduction bogs down a bit in the middle when the mystery subplot starts to take over but its dark photography and stark set design often recalls the best of the silent German horror films. Aka *Ein Toter Sucht Seinen Morder (Over My Dead Body)* and *Vengeance*.

BRAIN, THE

★★ Avid Entertainment, 1988, R, 91 min. Dir: Edward Hunt. Cast: Tom Breznahan, Cyndy Preston, David Gale, George Buza, Brett Pearson, Christina Kossack.

I guess this funny-stupid Canadian-made flick is supposed to be some sort of homage to *The Brain from Planet Arous* or something with its big, balloonlike, brain-with-a-face monster floating around and strangling people with its spinal cord tail while it wills TV self-help guru Gale (who never gave an unenthusiastic performance) to use hypnosis over the airwaves to make everyone watching his slave. Really dumb but hard not to like, this rather resembles an episode of *The Monkees* but without the lip-synch singing.

BRAIN EATERS, THE

★★☆ Columbia/TriStar, 1958, 60 min. Dir: Bruno De Sota. Cast: Ed Nelson, Joanna Lee, Alan Frost, Jack Hill, Jody Fair, Leonard Nimoy.

Really loose adaptation of Robert Heinlein's *The Puppetmasters* about parasitic creatures from the center of the earth controlling the will of various civic leaders in Smalltown, U.S.A. Cheesy as all hell but with a certain crude creepiness. Since appearing in this, Nelson and Nimoy became big '60s TV stars, Lee a successful TV writer, and Hill a film director. Who says appearing in B movies never leads to anything?

BRAIN FROM PLANET AROUS, THE

★★☆ Rhino, 1957, NR, 70 min. Dir: Nathan Hertz [Nathan Juran]. Cast: John Agar, Joyce Meadows, Robert Fuller, Thomas B. Henry.

Agar gives perhaps his best performance in this wonderfully inane flick about a floating brain creature from outer space possessing geologist John and forcing him to paw girlfriend Meadows—oh, those alien hormones—and laugh maniacally while wearing uncomfortable-looking contact lens; meanwhile model airplanes blow up. Another fun B-minus '50s classic from Juran under his nom-de-cheap Hertz.

BRAINSTORM

★★★ MGM/UA, 1983, PG, 106 min. Dir: Douglas Trumbull. Cast: Christopher Walken, Natalie Wood, Louise Fletcher, Cliff Robertson, Joe Dorsey, Jordan Christopher.

Mostly filmed in 1981 and then completed two years later following the drowning death of star Wood, this special FX extravaganza about the nature of life and death concerns the research being conducted by scientists Walken and Fletcher. They construct a helmet that allows one person to experience another's thoughts and emotions; this comes in handy for reactivating Wood's long-dormant feelings for husband Walken or allowing Chris to experience the afterlife when Fletcher dies while wearing the device. Though the FX are great, fortunately they aren't the whole show thanks to excellent acting from a restrained Walken, a sadly affecting Wood, and a crusty Fletcher in her best role. The hokey "power of love" ending is borrowed wholesale from *Altered States*.

BRAINWAVES

★★ Embassy, 1982, R, 81 min. Dir: Ulli Lommel. Cast: Suzanna Love, Keir Dullea, Tony Curtis, Vera Miles, Percy Rodrigues, Eve Brent Ashe.

Love's life is saved when scientist Curtis reactivates her brain with the stored brainwaves of a murder victim—whose murder Suzanna then begins seeing in visions. Compact sci-fi/stalker movie; nothing exceptional but it's reasonably put together by art house horror meister Lommel and has a good cast—though Tony is alleged to have been too coked-up even to remember his lines!

BRAZIL

★★★ MCA/Universal, 1985, R, 131 min. Dir: Terry Gilliam. Cast: Jonathan Pryce, Kim Greist, Robert DeNiro, Katherine Helmond, Ian Holm, Bob Hoskins, Michael Palin, Ian Richardson.

Gilliam's followup to *Time Bandits* is set in a hopeless future world where ineffectual bureaucrat Pryce tries to cling to his innocent dreams and his hope of finding happiness with Greist. Stunning production design, inventive special FX, and lots of guest stars in this blend of fantasy and jet black comedy.

BRENDA STAR

★☆ Columbia/TriStar, 1986, PG, 87 min. Dir: Robert Ellis Miller. Cast: Brooke Shields, Tony Peck, Timothy Dalton, Diana Scarwid, Charles Durning, Eddie Albert, Jeffrey Tambor, Henry Gibson, Ed Nelson, Kathleen Wilhoite.

This expensive film version of the long-running comic strip by Dale Messick may have languised on the shelf longer than any other major studio film in the last several years. Completed in '86, it had a run outside the U.S. in 1989 but didn't show up on these shores until 1992, and it really wasn't worth the wait. Handsome Peck (son of Gregory) is the artist who enters his own comic strip to join creation Brenda (Brooke, who isn't bad) in her fight against Nazis, Communists, and other perils. Sumptuously photographed by Freddie Francis and generally well cast, it's the poor direction and undeveloped scripting that make this perhaps the worst live-action film adaptation of a comic book.

BREWSTER MCCLOUD

★★★ MGM/UA, 1970, R, 101 min. Dir: Robert Altman. Cast: Bud Cort, Sally Kellerman, Michael Murphy, Shelley Duvall, William Windom, René Auberjonois, Stacy Keach, Margaret Hamilton.

Cort is a weird, nerdish fellow who lives in the Houston Astrodome and dreams of flying like a bird. Kellerman is Bud's guardian angel (recently deprived of her wings) and Murphy is the hip cop who suspects our hero of a series of bizarre murders. Altman's first film after *M*A*S*H*, this odd fantasy/black comedy grows on you as it goes along with Hamilton in a funny *Wizard of Oz* in-joke and a downbeat ending they'd never go with today.

BRIGADOON

★★★ MGM/UA, 1954, NR, 108 min. Dir: Vincente Minelli. Cast: Gene Kelly, Van Johnson, Cyd Charisse, Elaine Stewart, Barry Jones, Hugh Laing.

Understated musical fantasy with Kelly and Johnson as American tourists who encounter an enchanted Scottish village where the inhabitants come alive one day every one hundred years. Not as splashy and gaudy as many of its contemporaries, this Lerner and Lowe adaptation is stagey but full of warmth and a melancholy charm all its own. Remade as *2,000 Maniacs*—just kidding, folks.

BRONX EXECUTIONERS, THE

★★ MGM/UA, 1986, R, 88 min. Dir: Bob Collins. Cast: Gabriel Gori, Chuck Valenti, Margie Newton, Bob Robinson.

If you thought the Bronx was a tough place to live now, according to this flick it will someday become the battleground between androids, robots, and humans, with sheriff Gori joining forces with a renegade android to save the city. Another mindless *Mad Max/Terminator* clone full of gratuitous violence and other fun stuff.

BRONX WARRIORS, THE

See: *1990: The Bronx Warriors.*

BROTHER FROM ANOTHER PLANET, THE

★★★ Key, 1984, NR, 104 min. Dir: John Sayles. Cast: Joe Morton, Darryl Edwards, Steve James, Leonard Jackson, Maggie Renzi, Rosette Le Noire, David Strathairn, John Sayles.

Writer-director Sayles's funny, thoughtful tale of a mute black alien (Morton) who comes to New York where everyone he meets is taken in by his brilliance even though he never says a word! Sometimes looks like a Spike Lee reworking of *Being There* and not all the subplots and story points work, but overall this is a nicely unpretentious and entertaining sleeper.

BUCK ROGERS

See: *Buck Rogers Conquers the Universe.*

BUCK ROGERS CONQUERS THE UNIVERSE

★★☆ CBS/Fox, 1939, NR, 91 min. Dirs: Ford Beebe and Saul Goodkind. Cast: Buster Crabbe, Constance Moore, Philip Ahn, Tom Steele, Roy Barcroft, Jackie Moran, Kenne Duncan, Henry Brandon.

Feature version of Universal's twelve-chapter *Buck Rogers* serial with our hero (Crabbe) awakening in the year 2,500 to battle the sinister Killer Kane and his army of zombie-like Zuggs. The editing makes this race along at breakneck speed and there are some clever touches but Buck Rogers was never as good as *Flash Gordon.* Aka *Buck Rogers: Planet Outlaws* and *Buck Rogers: Destination Saturn.*

BUCK ROGERS: DESTINATION SATURN

See: *Buck Rogers Conquers the Universe.*

BUCK ROGERS IN THE 25TH CENTURY

★★☆ MCA/Universal, 1979, PG, 89 min. Dir: Daniel Haller. Cast: Gil Gerard, Erin Gray, Pamela Hensley, Henry Silva, Tim O'Connor, Joseph Wiseman.

Pilot film for the TV series released as a theatrical feature. Buck (a relaxed Gerard) is an astronaut who awakens from suspended animation to find himself in the 25th century, where the evil Princess Ardala (Hensley in outfits that could melt the polar icecap) and her right-hand man Killer Kane (Silva) are out to conquer the earth. Modestly enjoyable in the *Battlestar Galactica* vein, at least this has the good sense not to take itself too seriously, with Mel Blanc as the voice of Twiki the robot. Several episodes of the series are also out on video, including my favorites *Space Vampire,* with an intergalactic Nosferatu after sultry Wilma Deering (Gray); *Ardala Returns,* featuring a welcome comeback for Hensley and her scanty wardrobe; the goofy gangster parody *Vegas in Space;* and the campy *Unchained Woman,* guest starring a young Jamie Lee Curtis.

BUCK ROGERS: PLANET OUTLAWS

See: *Buck Rogers Conquers the Universe.*

CABIN BOY

★★★ Touchstone, 1994, PG-13, 80 min. Dir: Adam Resnik. Cast: Chris Elliott, Melora Walters, Ritch Brinkley, Brian Doyle-Murray, James Gammon, Brion James, Andy Richter, Ann Magnuson, Russ Tamblyn, Ricki Lake, Bob Elliott, David Letterman.

Nobody seems to like this oddball mix of *Captains Courageous* and a Ray Harryhausen fantasy-adventure but I think it's pretty damn funny. Of course, I also loved Elliott's short-lived TV series *Get a Life,* so maybe that helps. Anyway, Chris plays a prissy, effeminate "fancy lad" who gets shanghied aboard the sailing vessel *The Filthy Whore* and has a variety of strange encounters with a huge ice monster, a half-man half-shark (Tamblyn), and the six-armed goddess Kali (Magnuson) to whom he loses his virginity—unless you count all those lasivious seamen on *The Filthy Whore.* So I liked it, so sue me.

CALLER, THE

★★☆ TransWorld Entertainment, 1987, R, 98 min. Dir: Arthur Alan Seidelman. Cast: Malcolm McDowell, Madolyn Smith.

Gentleman caller McDowell menaces woman-on-the-verge-of-a-nervous-breakdown Smith at a remote cabin. She keeps killing him but he keeps coming back. Starts out like *Repulsion* meets *Halloween* until a last act twist into *Terminator* science fiction territory. Good actors struggle with often frustrating material, but not without its rewards.

CANNIBAL WOMEN IN THE AVOCADO JUNGLE OF DEATH

★★☆ Prism Entertainment, 1988, PG-13, 90 min. Dir: A. D. Athens [J. F. Lawton]. Cast: Shannon Tweed, Bill Maher, Adrienne Barbeau, Barry Primus, Karen Mistal.

Fairly funny *Indiana Jones* spoof with *Playboy* playmate Tweed as a feminist college professor who goes with student Mistal and macho jerk guide Maher (from TV's *Politically Incorrect*) into the wilds of Southern California, where they encounter a cult of piranha women led by Barbeau. The PG-13 rating keeps this from being too sexy or bloody but Maher is good as the wisecracking hero and the ladies, in their loincloths and tooth necklaces, make this a fun throwback to grade-Z masterpieces like *Prehistoric Women*. Aka *Piranha Women*.

CANTERVILLE GHOST, THE

★★★ MGM/UA, 1944, NR, 95 min. Dir: Jules Dassin. Cast: Charles Laughton, Margaret O'Brien, Robert Young, William Gargan, Reginald Owen, Una O'Connor.

Laughton is well cast as a 17th-century ghost who must haunt his castle until he performs a heroic act. Young is his modern-day descendant and O'Brien the young girl he befriends in this pleasant comic fantasy, based on the story by Oscar Wilde. Quite similar to the recent *Casper* movie in many ways and much better. Remade twice for TV.

CANTERVILLE GHOST, THE

★★ Columbia/TriStar, 1986, NR, 96 min. Dir: Paul Bogart. Cast: John Gielgud, Ted Wass, Andrea Marcovicci, Alyssa Milano.

Routine TV remake with Gielgud as the ineffectual ghost trying to scare Wass and family out of his castle, eventually making friends with young Milano. Sir John's delightful capering helps considerably in wading through this by-the-numbers retrend.

CAPE CANAVERAL MONSTERS, THE

★ Sinister Cinema, 1960, NR, 69 min. Dir: Phil Tucker. Cast: Scott Peters, Linda Connell, Jason Johnson, Katherine Victor, Gary Travis.

The director of *Robot Monster* strikes again with this tale of formless aliens who possess the bodies of a pair of recently killed NASA scientists in order to thwart the U.S. space program. More coherent than *Robot M*, Tucker might've been able to make something of the *Invasion of the Body Snatchers*-like premise if he had the talent to pull it off. Bad acting—apart from Victor, who brings a nice touch of desperation to her role as the living-dead woman scientist—and a grating musical score dominate.

CAPRICORN ONE

★★★ Avid Entertainment, 1978, PG, 124 min. Dir: Peter Hyams. Cast: Elliott Gould, James Brolin, Hal Holbrook, Karen Black, Telly Savalas, Brenda Vaccaro, Sam Waterston, O. J. Simpson, Denise Nicholas, David Huddleston, Lee Bryant, David Doyle.

Gould, the movies' most unlikely action hero, is a reporter who discovers that NASA scientists have faked a failed Mars exploratory mission—in fear of losing government funding and public support—and now must murder the three astronauts who allegedly died when the mission ended in disaster. A big-budget, all-star, action-packed thrill ride of the post-Watergate '70s, this is packed with the sort of cynicism you just don't find in movies today. Though the plotting won't bear too close an examination, this moves along so quickly that you'll hardly notice the contrivances.

CAPTAIN AMERICA

★★☆ Nostalgia Merchant, 1944, NR, 240 min. Dirs: John English, Elmer Clifton. Cast: Dick Purcell, Lorna Gray, Lionel Atwill, Charles Trowbridge, Russell Hicks, Frank Reicher.

Republic Pictures' fifteen-chapter serial with Purcell as the titular captain (in a less than effective costume) battling bad guy supreme Atwill and his earth-shattering invention, the "Thunder Bolt." Not bad, especially when the neon-eyed Lionel takes center stage. Aka *The Return of Captain America.*

CAPTAIN AMERICA

★★ MCA/Universal, 1979, NR, 91 min. Dir: Rod Holcomb. Cast: Reb Brown, Heather Menzies, Steve Forrest, Len Birman, Robin Mattson, Joseph Ruskin.

Made-for-TV pilot for a proposed series starring the Captain, played by jut-jawed Brown. In this adventure, our hero must save the world from a madman threatening to blow up everyone and everything with a stolen nuclear device. Typically bland TV fare.

CAPTAIN AMERICA 2: DEATH TOO SOON

★☆ MCA/Universal, 1979, NR, 96 min. Dir: Ivan Nagy. Cast: Reb Brown, Connie Selleca, Christopher Lee, Len Birman, Lana Wood, Katherine Justice.

The first Captain America TV movie must've

scored a few ratings points because he was back a few months later in this even weaker followup effort. The plot involves our hero's attempt to stop terrorists who attempt to take over the world by using a drug that induces rapid aging. You'll feel like you've aged a lifetime while watching this lethargic tale unfold. Only the good supporting cast is worth a note.

CAPTAIN AMERICA

★☆ Columbia/TriStar, 1990, PG-13, 103 min. Dir: Albert Pyun. Cast: Matt Salinger, Melinda Dillon, Ronny Cox, Darren McGavin, Ned Beatty, Scott Paulin.

Filmed in '90 and then shelved for several years, this ill-advised *Batman* cash-in stars Salinger as the World War II-era superhero who's awakened from suspended animation in the 1990s to battle his old archnemesis the Red Skull (Paulin). The supporting cast of familiar character actors is capable but almost nothing else—from the gimmickry to the failed campy humor—works.

CAPTAIN SINBAD

★★ MGM/UA, 1963, NR, 85 min. Dir: Byron Haskin. Cast: Guy Williams, Heidi Bruhl, Pedro Armendariz, Abraham Sofaer, Bernie Hamilton, Geoffrey Toone.

The King brothers followed up their successful *Godzilla* imitation *Gorgo* with this unofficial sequel to *The Seventh Voyage of Sinbad.* Williams is well cast as the heroic sailor man, who here must rescue princess Bruhl from the clutches of evil wizard Armendariz, who can't be killed because he keeps his heart safely hidden in a tower at the edge of the world. The clunky but colorful FX include a cloak of invisibility, a huge mailed fist, and a many-headed dragon and I'm sure Harryhausen didn't lose any sleep over any of this. Stupid but fun.

CARNOSAUR

★★☆ New Horizons, 1993, R, 83 min. Dir: Adam Simon. Cast: Diane Ladd, Raphael Sbarge, Jennifer Runyon, Clint Howard.

While daughter Laura Dern was making the biggest-budget dinosaur movie of all time for Steven Spielberg, her mom (Ladd) was over at the Roger Corman lot slogging her way through this opportunistic but actually more fun *Jurassic* wannabe. Chicken eggs contaminated with dino DNA hatch out cute little puppets that'll rip your throat out, and women who ingest the eggs end up giving birth to bowling ball-sized reptile eggs that spawn saurians with near-human intelligence. It all has something to do with mad scientist Diane's attempt to replace mankind with a race of superdinosaurs,

but all these silly plot considerations take a back seat to a lot of gory death scenes, low-budget dino rampages, and overacting from Ladd—who you'd swear was channeling the spirit of Louise Fletcher if Fletcher weren't still alive—the likes of which you've rarely seen.

CARNOSAUR 2

★☆ New Horizons, 1994, R, 82 min. Dir: Louis Morneau. Cast: John Savage, Cliff De Young, Don Stroud, Rick Dean, Ryan Thomas Johnson, Arabella Holzbog, Miguel A. Nunez, Jr., Neith Hunter.

James Cameron should sue over this derivative sequel that not only swipes the entire plot (not to mention characters and dialogue) from *Aliens* but also bites bug chunks out of *Terminator 2* as well. A rescue team trying to discover what happened to the personnel at a military-run mining operation near Yucca Flats encounters flesh-munching dinosaurs hatched from eggs left over from the first *Carnosaur* and finds teen survivor Johnson. The FX are better here but the plot is mean-spirited and annoying with the most likable character dying first and a dragged-out climax that sets a whole new standard for dramatic ludicrousness.

CASINO ROYALE

★★★ Columbia/TriStar, 1967, NR, 130 min. Dirs: John Huston, Ken Hughes, Robert Parrish, Joe McGrath, Val Guest. Cast: David Niven, Peter Sellers, Ursula Andress, Orson Welles, Joanna Pettet, Woody Allen, Daliah LaVi, William Holden, Deborah Kerr, Charles Boyer, John Huston, Jean-Paul Belmondo, Kurt Kastner, Barbara Bouchet, Terence Cooper, Jacqueline Bisset.

Nobody much likes this big-bucks, out-of-control spoof of the James Bond series, based on the one novel Cubby Broccoli couldn't get the rights to, but I've always thought it a lot of fun ever since first catching it on TV in the early '70s. Niven is an aging Bond, brought out of retirement to battle the evil Dr. Noah's plot to unleash a virus on the world that will make all women beautiful and kill off all men over five feet tall. Sellers is an expert card player hired to impersonate 007 at the title casino, where he goes up against SMERSH operative Welles (try not to laugh when Orson accidentally dons a pair of bejeweled lady's eyeglasses in mistake for his X-ray ones). Andress is femme fatale Vespa Lind, Pettet is Bond's daughter by Mata Hari, Bouchet is Miss Moneypenny's daughter, and Bisset is Miss Goodthighs. With a flying saucer, Frankenstein's monster, an apocalyptic climax (where most of the huge cast is killed off), and Allen in funny scenes he mostly improvised himself ("Let's run amuck, or, if we get tired, let's walk amuck!").

CASPER

★★ MCA/Universal, 1995, PG, 100 min. Dir: Brad Silberling. Cast: Christina Ricci, Bill Pullman, Cathy Moriarty, Eric Idle, Amy Brenneman, Don Novello.

Joyless kiddie fantasy based on the popular old one-note cartoons about the ghost of a little boy searching for a friend. Widower parapsychologist Pullman and young teen daughter Ricci move into the spooky old house haunted by Casp and his rude, crude brothers the Ghostly Trio (who behave like spectral frat boys), while villains Moriarty and Idle search the place for hidden treasure. Like too many recent Hollywood "concept" movies, this tries to hide its basic hollowness behind a ton of razzle-dazzle FX; technically the film is great and Ricci and Pullman likable but an overall gloomy atmosphere of death and depression and some very misplaced humor (why is the preteen Casper so thrilled to have a girl in his bed?) result in one of the most misguided and annoying kid's movies in many a moon.

CAT FROM OUTER SPACE, THE

★★ Disney, 1978, G, 104 min. Dir: Norman Tokar. Cast: Ken Berry, Sandy Duncan, McLean Stevenson, Harry Morgan, Roddy McDowall, voice of Ronnie Schell.

Painless Disney sci-fi comedy about a friendly alien stranded on earth who just happens to look like a talking housecat. Like too many '70s Disney flicks this mostly looks like an overlong TV sitcom but there are a few laughs and a pleasant cast, including two M*A*S*H regulars who never actually met on the TV show. I wonder if the makers of E.T. ever saw this?

CAT WOMEN OF THE MOON

★★ Rhino, 1954, NR, 64 min. Dir: Arthur Hilton. Cast: Sonny Tufts, Marie Windsor, Victor Jory, William Phipps, Douglas Fowley, Carol Brewster.

Fifties camp classic with one of the great joke titles of all time. An expedition to the moon discovers a race of cat-suited babes with psychic powers, a hankering for our men, and a desire to take over our planet; lady astronaut Windsor almost falls under their influence. There's also a big puppet spider, as well as stilted acting galore from a once-in-a-lifetime cast. Originally released in 3-D, this was remade as *Missile to the Moon* and is also known as *Rocket to the Moon.*

CAVEMAN

★★☆ CBS/Fox, 1981, PG, 91 min. Dir: Carl Gottlieb. Cast: Ringo Starr, Barbara Bach, Dennis Quaid, Shelley Long, Jack Gilford, John Matusak.

Fun spoof of dinosaur epics like *One Million Years B.C.*, with bungling ex-Beatle Ringo, the curvaceous Bach, dorky Quaid, and a pre-*Cheers* Long just trying to get along while battling beefy behemoth Matusak and various Dave Allen-animated dinos. You won't laugh Jurassic off but it's a fun time waster.

CHANDU ON THE MAGIC ISLAND

See: *The Return of Chandu.*

CHARLEY AND THE ANGEL

★★☆ Disney, 1973, G, 93 min. Dir: Vincent McEveety. Cast: Fred MacMurray, Cloris Leachman, Harry Morgan, Kurt Russell, Kathleen Cody, Vincent Van Patten.

It's *My Three Sons* meets *Here Comes Mr. Jordan* with MacMurray as a hard-nosed family man given a chance to make peace with his family by angel Morgan before his upcoming demise. This period fantasy isn't as corny as some Disney films but it doesn't exactly break new ground either, though MacMurray plays a character not too far removed from his alleged real-life self. This was one of Russell's many Disney flicks during his teen idol phase, while pretty Cody was a regular during the final season of *Dark Shadows.*

CHARLY

★★★ CBS/Fox, 1968, PG, 103 min. Dir: Ralph Nelson. Cast: Cliff Robertson, Claire Bloom, Lilia Skala, Leon Janney, Dick Van Patten.

Robertson won an Oscar for his fine work here as the title character, a retarded man turned genius via scientific experimentation. This adaptation of Daniel Keyes's *Flowers for Algernon* is often needlessly arty but is well-served by the performances of Robertson and Bloom as a sympathetic teacher who falls in love with Charly.

CHERRY 2000

★★☆ Orion, 1986, PG-13, 93 min. Dir: Steve DeJarnatt. Cast: Melanie Griffith, David Andrews, Ben Johnson, Harry Carey, Jr., Pamela Gidley, Tim Thomerson.

A sort-of feminist *Mad Max* with a red-headed Griffith as the distaff Road Warrior leading Andrews on a search for replacement parts for Cherry (Gidley), David's robotic love doll. As they trek across the desert our heroes encounter hammy bad guy Thomerson, the grizzled and great Johnson, and—of course—fall in love. Shelved for three years, this futuristic adventure movie is no undiscovered classic but is better than it had any right to be, with Griffith in good form as the ballsy heroine.

CHILDREN OF THE DAMNED
★★★ MGM/UA, 1963, NR, 89 min. Dir: Anton M. Leader. Cast: Ian Hendry, Alan Badel, Barbara Ferris, Alfred Burke, Sheila Allen, Clive Powell, Patrick Wymark, Bessie Love.

Solid sequel to *Village of the Damned* with six supernaturally powered children from around the globe who hole up in a London church while scientist Hendry tries to save them from military assassination. Where the original was full of gothic mood and small-town quaintness, this takes the children into the world of international politics and prejudices, often looking like a low-key early Bond film. Good acting (especially Hendry and Badel as the subtly gay heroes who become divided over the children's fate when heroine Ferris takes an interest in Ian) and a nicely matter-of-fact downbeat ending too.

CHINA SYNDROME, THE
★★★★ Columbia/TriStar, 1979, PG, 122 min. Dir: James Bridges. Cast: Jane Fonda, Jack Lemmon, Michael Douglas, Scott Brady, James Hampton, Peter Donat, Wilford Brimley, James Karen.

Though slightly dated, this sci-fi-tinged disaster movie is still powerful and backed up by the best performances of Fonda's and Lemmon's careers—Douglas had to wait until *Wall Street* for his career pinnacle. Fonda, an L.A. TV news reporter, and Douglas, her cameraman, are alerted to a coverup of a near-catastrophic accident at a nuclear power plant by guilt-ridden supervisor Lemmon. When Jack is fired, he grabs a gun and takes the power plant personnel hostage until Jane and Mike can broadcast his story to the public. Intelligently written in a quiet, nonexploitive manner and building to a heart-stopping climax, this was released just before the real-life nuclear accident at Three Mile Island, Pennsylvania, and benefited enormously from the subsequent publicity.

CHITTY CHITTY BANG BANG
★★★ MGM/UA, 1968, G, 142 min. Dir: Ken Hughes. Cast: Dick Van Dyke, Sally Ann Howes, Lionel Jeffries, Gert Frobe, Anna Quayle, Benny Hill, Robert Helpmann, James Robertson Justice.

Lavish *Mary Poppins* wannabe adapted from the book by Ian Fleming is often more fun but suffers from overlength and a slow first half. Van Dyke is a widowed inventor in Edwardian England who turns an old race car into a

It's a small world after all, in Children of the Damned *(1963).*

fabulous flying machine that takes him, his two kids, and pretty Howes on an adventure to a mythical kingdom with a ban on children. Cheesy special FX but some of the songs (like *Me Ol' Bamboo* and *Doll on a Music Box*) are good. Frobe and Jeffries are funny (while Hill doesn't get to leer at even one bikini girl), and this was a bigger hit than other megaflop musicals of the time like *Doctor Doolittle*.

CHRISTMAS CAROL, A

★★★ MGM/UA, 1938, NR, 69 min. Dir: Edwin L. Marin. Cast: Reginald Owen, Gene Lockhart, Terry Kilburn, Kathleen Lockhart, Lynne Carver, Leo G. Carroll, Barry MacKay, Ann Rutherford, D'Arcy Corrigan, June Lockhart.

Solid MGM adaptation (and simplification) of the Charles Dickens classic, with glossy production values and a first-rate cast, featuring Owen as a nicely crotchety Scrooge. A typical Hollywood touch is the transformation of the Ghost of Christmas Past into a buxom Ziegfeld girl (Rutherford, later in *Gone with the Wind*). Like many classic black-and-white Christmas movies, this is also available in a colorized version.

CHRISTMAS CAROL, A

★★★★ Goodtimes, 1951, NR, 86 min. Dir: Brian Desmond Hurst. Cast: Alastair Sim, Jack Warner, Kathleen Harrison, Mervyn Johns, Hermione Baddeley, Michael Hordern, George Cole, Carol Marsh, Miles Malleson, Ernest Thesiger, Peter Bull, Rona Anderson, Clifford Mollison, Hattie Jacques, Patrick Macnee, Francis DeWolff.

The definitive Scrooge in this definitive version of the Dickens story, Sim is superb as the caustic, embittered businessman who has his humanity restored to him one Christmas Eve when he is visited by the ghost of his late partner (Hordern) and then three further spirits representing Christmases past, present, and yet to come. One of the great British films of the '50s, with a sterling cast of character actors, solid direction, and a nice sense of period authenticity.

CHRISTMAS CAROL, A

★★★ Fox, 1984, NR, 98 min. Dir: Clive Donner. Cast: George C. Scott, Nigel Davenport, Frank Finlay, Edward Woodward, Susannah York, David Warner, Lucy Gutteridge, Angela Pleasence, Roger Rees, Anthony Walters.

Of the (too) many TV versions of the Dickens classic, this is easily the best. Scott is in good form as Scrooge and the British supporting cast is well chosen, especially Woodward as a robust Ghost of Christmas Present and

Pleasence (Donald's daughter) as a wraithlike Ghost of Christmas Past. If the older versions of this famous story don't interest you, see this one instead.

CIRCUITRY MAN

★★ Columbia/TriStar, 1990, R, 85 min. Dir: Steven Lovy. Cast: Dana Wheeler-Nicholson, Jim Metzler, Dennis Christopher, Lu Leonard, Vernon Wells.

Wheeler-Nicholson is the beautiful bodyguard trying to smuggle computer chips in a futuristic world lorded over by the evil half-man, half-computer Plughead (Wells). Modest sci-fi/action flick with a good role for Christopher as desert scum, this was a popular enough video renter to inspire a slightly better-made sequel.

CIRCUITRY MAN II: PLUGHEAD REWIRED

★★☆ Columbia/TriStar, 1994, R, 97 min. Dirs: Robert Lovy, Steven Lovy. Cast: Deborah Shelton, Jim Metzler, Vernon Wells, Traci Lords, Dennis Christopher, Paul Wilson.

The sultry Shelton takes over the heroine spot as Plughead returns with world conquest on his mind. This better-cast sequel is smart enough not to take itself too seriously and that's always a help in navigating these direct-to-video action movies.

CITY LIMITS

★ Vestron, 1985, PG-13, 85 min. Dir: Aaron Lipstadt. Cast: John Stockwell, Kim Cattrall, Darrell Larson, Rae Dawn Chong, Robby Benson, James Earl Jones, John Diehl, Don Opper.

Whatever possessed Lipstadt to follow up his fun *Android* with this bleak and depressing postapocalyptic crap? An interesting cast is pretty much wasted in useless roles (Benson spends all his screen time sitting behind a desk in a room that looks like the manager's office at the local K-Mart) in this tale of bands of violent young people roaming the nuked-out future looking for—well just what they were looking for I could never figure out. Jones's phone book commercials provide him with more dignity.

CLAN OF THE CAVE BEAR

★★ CBS/Fox, 1986, R, 98 min. Dir: Michael Chapman. Cast: Daryl Hannah, James Remar, Pamela Reed, Tom Waites, John Doolittle, Curtis Armstrong.

Well-intentioned but unintentionally stupid film version of the Jean M. Auel bestseller, written by John Sayles, no less, with Hannah well cast as a pretty cavegal adopted by a tribe of Neanderthals and eventually raised to become their healer. *One Million Years B.C.* was a lot more fun but then that had animated dinosaurs and Raquel Welch in a doeskin bikini.

CLASH OF THE TITANS

★★★ MGM/UA, 1981, PG, 118 min. Dir: Desmond Davis. Cast: Harry Hamlin, Judi Bowker, Laurence Olivier, Maggie Smith, Burgess Meredith, Claire Bloom, Ursula Andress, Sian Phillips.

In ancient Greece, the valiant Perseus (Hamlin) must slay the dreaded snake-haired Medusa—whose glance can turn the living to stone—in order to use its severed head as a weapon to save the Princess Andromeda (Bowker) from sacrifice to a sea monster called the Kraken. Overlong and flatly directed, this can't hold a candle to earlier Ray Harryhausen fantasies like *The Seventh Voyage of Sinbad* and *Jason and the Argonauts* but is still entertaining, with top-notch stop motion (by Harryhausen, in his last film, and Jim Danforth), a good score by Laurence Rosenthal, playful acting from Olivier (as Zeus), Smith and Meredith, and Hamlin in a diaper. But that mechanical owl, Bubo, has got to go. Shooting title: *Perseus and the Gorgon's Head*.

CLASS OF 1999

★★★ LIVE, 1990, UR, 98 min. Dir: Mark L. Lester. Cast: Bradley Gregg, Traci Lind, Malcolm McDowell, Stacy Keach, Pam Grier, Patrick Kilpatrick, John Ryan, Joshua Miller.

Not really a sequel to Lester's controversial actioner *The Class of 1984*, this campy sci-fi followup is in its own way just as good. At the turn of the next century, inner-city high school troublemakers are kept in check by a trio of android teachers (Grier, Kilpatrick, and Ryan, all well cast) until a predictable malfunction turns them into unstoppable killing machines. Great, mindless fun borrowing from everything from *The Terminator* to the *Friday the 13th* series in its mixture of tongue-in-cheek thrills and gory violence. Also out in a cut R version.

CLASS OF 1999, PART II: THE SUBSTITUTE

★★ Vidmark Entertainment, 1994, R, 90 min. Dir: Spiro Razatos Cast: Sasha Mitchell, Nick Cassavetes, Caitlin Dulany, Jack Knight, Rick Hill.

A reprogrammed android teacher (Mitchell) is given another chance to do the *To Sir, With Love* bit at a tough high school but his love for Dulany screws up his programming and more mayhem erupts. The robotic Mitchell is well used (and gets to use both of his facial expressions) but this obvious, routine sequel hasn't much to offer that you haven't seen before—a lot of times before.

CLASS OF NUKE 'EM HIGH, THE

★★ Video Treasures, 1986, R, 81 min. Dirs: Richard W. Haines, Samuel Weil [Lloyd Kaufman]. Cast: Janelle Brady, Gilbert Brenton, Robert Prichard, R. L. Ryan.

Troma's attempt to cash in on the unexpected success of the much better *Toxic Avenger* resulted in this gore comedy about nuclear waste at Tromaville High turning students into mutants and unleashing a murderous creature in the basement. Almost dumb enough to work, but a little more talent might have yielded funnier results. At least it's better than its sequels.

CLASS OF NUKE 'EM HIGH, PART II: SUBHUMAN MELTDOWN, THE

★☆ Video Treasures, 1991, R, 95 min. Dir: Eric Louzil. Cast: Brick Bronsky, Lisa Gaye, Leesa Rowland, Michael Kurtz, Trinity Loren.

More mutant madness at Tromavill High as evil scientist Gaye plots to turn the students into mindless zombies—those not already mindless zombies, that is. Well, there's a cameo by porn harlot Loren and a good supporting role for Tromie the giant nuclear squirrel, but I don't think that even that is enough to justify wasting 95 minutes of your life on this.

CLEAN SLATE

★★ MGM/UA, 1994, PG-13, 107 min. Dir: Mick Johnson. Cast: Dana Carvey, Valeria Golina, James Earl Jones, Kevin Pollack, Michael Murphy, Olivia D'Abo.

Shameless ripoff of *Groundhog Day* with *Saturday Night Live* alumnus Carvey as a bumbling private eye who wakes up every morning with no memory of the previous day's experiences and has to relive them over and over again. The cast has talent and that dog is a piss; too bad the movie they're all in is so dull and unimaginative.

CLOCKWORK ORANGE, A

★★★★ WARNER, 1971, R, 137 min. Dir: Stanley Kubrick. Cast: Malcolm McDowell, Patrick Magee, Adrienne Corri, Aubrey Morris, Warren Clarke, Michael Bates, James Marcus, Margaret Tyzack, David Prowse, Virginia Wetherell.

Maybe Kubrick's best film, this controversial version of Anthony Burgess's novel stars McDowell in his signature role of Alex, the leader of a gang of "Droogs," violently antisocial young misfits of a future society. Jailed for a brutal rape-murder, Alex is "deprogrammed" of his violent ways with soothing bouts of torture and Beethoven but after his release his past quickly catches up with him. Banned in Britain (where it was made) and still popular today with young people not

Malcolm McDowell as Alex, the ultimate teen role model in A Clockwork Orange *(1971).*

even born during its rocky original release (when it was first rated X by the MPAA), this acerbically tongue-in-cheek head trip is one you're not likely to forget.

CLONES, THE

★★ LIVE, 1973, PG, 86 min. Dirs: Paul Hunt, Lamar Card. Cast: Michael Greene, Bruce Bennett, Gregory Sierra, Susan Hunt, Stanley Adams, John Drew Barrymore.

Moderately well-done low-budgeter about a sinister government cloning operation. First-rate performances and a terrific ending but overall too slow and static to really work; a bigger budget would have done wonders.

CLOSE ENCOUNTERS OF THE THIRD KIND

★★★☆ Columbia/TriStar, 1977, PG, 135 min. Dir: Steven Spielberg. Cast: Richard Dreyfuss, Francois Truffaut, Melinda Dillon, Teri Garr, Cary Guffey, Bob Balaban, Lance Henriksen, Roberts Blossom.

Electrician Dreyfuss and single mom Dillon have "close encounters" with UFOs leading them to a Wyoming mountain—the Devil's Tower—where the U.S. government is about to have its first meeting with beings from outer space. Originally Spielberg's best movie, full of childlike awe and wonder, this has been ever since compromised by the inclusion of additional climactic scenes for the so-called "special edition" released in 1980. The additional FX add nothing and really spoil much of the film's mystery, not to mention the perfectly timed-to-the-images John Williams music. This gentle movie is still the best all around sci-fi film of the '70s, with brilliant Douglas Trumbull special effects and emotional Williams music, but I've always felt that if at first you do succeed—stop.

CLUB EXTINCTION

★★ Prism Entertainment, 1990, R, 112 min. Dir: Claude Chabrol. Cast: Alan Bates, Jennifer Beals, Andrew McCarthy, Jan Niklas, Hans Zischler, Wolfgang Preiss.

Chabrol tries to update the old Dr. Mabuse series but the results aren't very good. In a futuristic Berlin, police inspector Niklas investigates a rash of mysterious suicides that he feels are actually murders. Is popular health clinician Bates behind it all? The title makes it sound like a slasher movie but it isn't that exciting. The main interest here comes in wondering how Bates, Beals, and McCarthy were persuaded to appear in this German-Italian misfire. Aka *Dr. M.*

COCOON

★★★ Fox, 1985, PG-13, 117 min. Dir: Ron Howard. Cast: Don Ameche, Wilford Brimley, Hume Cronyn, Steve Guttenberg, Tahnee Welch, Brian Dennehy, Jessica Tandy, Maureen Stapleton, Jack Gilford, Gwen Verdon, Linda Harrison, Barret Oliver.

Oldsters living in a Florida retirement home are rejuvenated by swimming in a pool containing strange alien cocoons. When the humanlike extraterrestrials (led by Dennehy) arrive to collect these cocoons, they offer the old folk a new lease on life on a brave new world—it's okay to use all these clichés when discussing a movie as corny as this. A wonderfully entertaining sci-fi comedy full of warmth and the joy of living, with a perfect cast led by a spry Ameche in his Oscar-winning performance.

COCOON: THE RETURN

★★ Fox, 1988, PG, 116 min. Dir: Daniel Petrie. Cast: Don Ameche, Wilford Brimley, Hume Cronyn, Steve Guttenberg, Tahnee Welch, Jessica Tandy, Jack Gilford, Maureen Stapleton, Gwen Verdon, Elaine Stritch, Courtney Cox, Brian Dennehy.

Totally unnecessary sequel, with Ameche and company returning to earth to rescue some damaged alien cocoons and save a captured extraterrestrial from scientific study. The stars' good spirits carry this tired followup a lot further than it deserves to go. Brings new meaning to the word *pointless.*

COLLISION COURSE

See: *Bamboo Saucer, The*

COLOSSUS: THE FORBIN PROJECT

★★★ MCA/UNIVERSAL, 1970, PG, 100 min. Dir: Joseph Sargent. Cast: Eric Braeden, Susan Clark, Gordon Pinsent, William Schallert, Robert Cornthwaite.

Scientist Braeden's new super computer begins to act independently, linking up with its Russian counterpart and gaining control of the entire U.S. defense system in order to blackmail mankind into submission. James Bridges wrote this intelligent adaptation of the novel *Colossus* by D. F. Jones with a good role for *Young and the Restless* stalwart Braeden and a nicely ambiguous ending. Aka *The Forbin Project.*

COMMUNION

★★☆ Virgin Vision, 1989, R, 107 min. Dir: Philippe Mora. Cast: Christopher Walken, Lindsay Crouse, Frances Sternhagen, Andreas Katsulas, Terri Hanouer, Joel Carlson.

Walken is writer Whitley Strieber (author of *Wolfen* and *The Hunger,* among others) in this adaptation of the autobiographical tale of Strieber's alleged abduction by aliens and how the experience has haunted his life. This fails to convince as docudrama but has some tense, scary alien sequences and a typically wigged-out performance from Walken to keep you watching.

COMPANION, THE

★★ MCA/Universal, 1995, R, 94 min. Dir: Gary Fleder. Cast: Kathryn Harrold, Bruce Greenwood, Talia Balsam, Brion James.

Novelist Harrold buys a robotic "companion" (Greenwood) she programs with the traits of her perfect fantasy man. Trouble sets in when the android begins taking his "feelings" for his owner too far and begins murdering those who come between them. Predictable made-for-cable sci-fi/horror thriller that may be worth seeing for the performances; otherwise, you've seen it all before.

COMPUTER WORE TENNIS SHOES, THE

★★☆ Disney, 1970, G, 90 min. Dir: Robert Butler. Cast: Kurt Russell, Cesar Romero, Joe Flynn, William Schallert, Alan Hewitt, Richard Bakalyan.

The first of four Disney comic fantasies for Russell; basically a retooling of the Merlin Jones films (*The Misadventures of Merlin Jones, The Monkey's Uncle*) for the flower generation. In this one, Kurt recieves a jolt from a computer and is transformed into a genius whose knowledge is then sought by gangster Romero. Pretty routine comedy remade for TV in 1995. Sequels: *The Barefoot Executive; Now You See Him, Now You Don't;* and *The Strongest Man in the World.*

CONAN THE BARBARIAN

★★ MCA/Universal, 1982, R, 129 min. Dir: John Milius. Cast: Arnold Schwarzenegger, Sandahl Bergman, James Earl Jones, Max von Sydow, Gerry Lopez, Mako, Valerie Quennessen, Ben Davidson, Cassandra Gaviola, William Smith.

The Robert E. Howard character was finally brought to the screen after years in the planning stage but the end result hardly seemed worth the wait. Schwarzenegger is perfectly cast (and for years would be typecast) as the muscle-bound hero out to avenge the slaughter of his village by snake cult leader Jones.

Bergman is the beautiful Amazon who joins him in his quest and there are a lot of other colorful characters too, but the muddled storyline keeps everyone and everything at such a distance you never really get involved. Still, this is much better than most of the myriad of European imitations it spawned over the years.

CONAN THE DESTROYER
★★☆ MCA/Universal, 1984, PG, 103 min. Dir: Richard Fleischer Cast: Arnold Schwarzenegger, Grace Jones, Wilt Chamberlain, Sarah Douglas, Mako, Olivia D'Abo, Tracey Walter, Jeff Corey.

Surprisingly bright sequel to the ponderous original done in the style of a Saturday morning cartoon show. Conan aids a young princess in fulfilling her destiny as the maiden who must find a sacred key used to bring an ancient deity back to life and along the way encounters various wizards, warriors, and monsters. Schwarzenegger makes Conan more likable this time and Douglas, as usual, makes for a smooth villainess, but the one to watch is Jones in her screen debut. Flashing a magnificent smile and dashing about with abandon, she handles her warrior women role with style and aplomb and alone is worth the price of admission.

CONDORMAN
★★ Disney, 1981, PG, 90 min. Dir: Charles Jarrott. Cast: Michael Crawford, Barbara Carrera, Oliver Reed, James Hampton, Jean-Pierre Kalfon, Dana Elcar.

Mild Disney fantasy comedy with a pre-*Phantom of the Opera* Crawford as a dorky cartoonist who takes on the persona of his character Condorman in order to help Soviet spy Carrera defect. Even with Reed chewing the scenery as the bad guy and Carrera's considerable beauty this superhero spoof hasn't much to offer.

CONEHEADS
★★★ Paramount, 1993, PG, 87 min. Dir: Steve Barron. Cast: Dan Aykroyd, Jane Curtin, Michelle Burke, Chris Farley, Michael McKean, Dave Thomas, Jason Alexander, David Spade, Michael Richards, Lisa Jane Persky, Laraine Newman, Garrett Morris, Phil Hartman, Adam Sandler, Chris Rock, Jan Hooks, Jon Lovitz, Sinbad.

The critics weren't kind and nobody went to see it, but this is actually one of the best (along with *The Blues Brothers* and *Wayne's World*) Saturday Night Live movie spinoffs. Aykroyd and Curtin are the married, pointy-headed invaders from the planet Remulak who pass themselves off as immigrants from France. The Coneheads settle in New Jersey, have a daughter (who grows into Burke; Newman, who played the part on TV, has a cameo), and end up loving life on Earth so much that they're eventually forced back to Remulak for a confrontation with their leader. What could have been just a one-joke story is well developed and fun, with a carload of *SNL* regulars in roles both large and small and some impressive FX at the end.

CONNECTICUT YANKEE, A
★★★ Fox, 1931, NR, 78 min. Dir: David Butler. Cast: Will Rogers, Maureen O'Sullivan, Myrna Loy, Frank Albertson, William Farnum.

An electrical shock sends Will back to the time of the Knights of the Round Table in this early talkie version of Mark Twain's *A Connecticut Yankee in King Arthur's Court*. Rogers is perfectly cast and a young O'Sullivan and Loy are lovely in this genial farce. Aka *A Connecticut Yankee in King Arthur's Court*.

CONNECTICUT YANKEE IN KING ARTHUR'S COURT, A
See: *Connecticut Yankee, A*

CONNECTICUT YANKEE IN KING ARTHUR'S COURT, A
★★★ MCA/Universal, 1949, NR, 106 min. Dir: Tay Garnett. Cast: Bing Crosby, Rhonda Fleming, William Bendix, Sir Cedric Hardwicke, Virginia Field, Henry Wilcoxon.

Crosby's easy charm propels this musical remake. Der Bingel is transported back to Merry Olde England, where his modern ways (not to mention all that singing) get him branded as a wizard but also win him the hand of the gorgeous Fleming. Good fun, with Bendix a standout as Bing's lackey. Remade as the Disney films *Unidentified Flying Oddball* and *A Kid in King Arthur's Court* and under the original title as a TV movie starring Cosby—not Crosby—kid Keisha Knight Pulliam.

CONNECTICUT YANKEE IN KING ARTHUR'S COURT, A
★★ Family Home Entertainment, 1989, NR, 95 min. Dir: Mel Damski. Cast: Keshia Knight Pulliam, Jean Marsh, René Auberjonois, Emma Samms, Whip Hubley, Michael Gross.

A ten-year-old modern lass is whisked back to Arthurian times in this mostly lame made-for-TV updated vehicle for *Cosby Show* star Pulliam. The classy supporting cast tries to add some weight to the proceedings but most of this fantasy is so cute you just want to strangle it. Mark Twain could not be reached for comment.

CONQUEST

★ Media, 1984, R, 98 min. Dir: Lucio Fulci. Cast: Jorge Rivero, Andrea Occhipinti, Sabrina Siani, Conrado San Martin, Violetta Cela, Maria Scola.

Italian gore god Fulci's entry in the Conan sword-and-sorcery sweepstakes is this mostly unwatchable drivel about evil sorceress Siani's attempts at stopping warriors Tivero and Occhipinti from freeing her kingdom from bondage. A little bondage, or any kind of excitement, could only help this slow, badly dubbed fantasy from the king of maggot-faced zombies and intestine-vomiting damsels.

CONQUEST OF SPACE

★★ Paramount/Gateway, 1955, NR, 80 min. Dir: Byron Haskin. Cast: Eric Fleming, William Hopper, Walter Brooke, Ross Martin, Mickey Shaughnessy, Joan Shawlee, Phil Foster, William Redfield, Benson Fong, Vito Scotti.

Budget cuts and dull casting are the culprits in this least interesting of producer George Pal's '50s sci-fi films. Man's first expedition to Mars is sabotaged by a deranged commander (Brooke) who feels that God would not approve of space travel—though in the end He shows who's side He's really on. The special effects are good but too much would-be comic relief and a really unbelievable ending make this film version of Werner von Braun's *The Mars Project* seem more dated than it really is.

CONQUEST OF THE PLANET OF THE APES

★★☆ Fox, 1972, PG, 87 min. Dir: J. Lee Thompson. Cast: Roddy McDowall, Don Murray, Ricardo Montalban, Natalie Trundy, Hari Rhodes, Severen Darden.

The fourth in the Apes saga takes place in the "future" of 1991 where a plague has wiped out all the dogs and cats, and people have taken in apes as pets. McDowall is Caesar, the grown son of Zira and Cornelius, who leads his fellow simians in revolt against their human masters. The series begins its downslide here with less convincing makeup and a talky, heavy-handed script salvaged by good acting by McDowall and Montalban and an exciting climax apparently inspired by the Watts riots in Los Angeles.

CONTAMINATION

See: *Alien Contamination*

COOL WORLD

★★ Paramount, 1992, PG-13, 101 min. Dir: Ralph Bakshi. Cast: Gabriel Byrne, Kim Basinger, Brad Pitt, Frank Sinatra, Jr.

Bakshi's take on *Who Framed Roger Rabbit?*, this stars a miscast Byrne as a cartoonist who discovers an alternate universe inhabited by living animated characters. When he has sex with the curvaceous Holli Would she turns into Basinger and enters the human world. A well-made but ridiculously unfocused fantasy that's neither cute enough for kids nor sexy enough for adults.

COSMIC MAN, THE

★★ Sinister Cinema, 1959, NR, 72 min. Dir: Herbert Greene. Cast: John Carradine, Bruce Bennett, Angela Greene, Paul Langton, Scotty Morrow.

A low-budget spaceman flick from the '50s starring Carradine as the alien sounds like fun but this talky *Day the Earth Stood Still* imitation is just competent enough to be boring. John has black skin and a white shadow, arrives on earth in a flying white beachball, and cures a dying little boy of his leukemia, but it's still not very exciting. For hardcore Carradine fans only.

COSMIC MONSTERS, THE

★☆ Rhino, 1958, NR, 75 min. Dir: Gilbert Gunn. Cast: Forrest Tucker, Gaby Andre, Martin Benson, Alec Mango, Patricia Sinclair, Hugh Latimer.

Originally called *The Strange World of Planet X*, this cheap British programmer stars Tucker as an American scientist in England whose experiments with the ionosphere create big spiders and insects who show up almost too late to save this movie version of a BBC-TV serial.

COSMOS—WAR OF THE PLANETS

★☆ King of Video, 1977, PG, 90 min. Dir: Al Bradley [Alfonso Brescia]. Cast: John Richardson, Yanti Somer, Katia Christine, West Buchanan, Max Karis, Percy Hogan.

Richardson leads earth astronauts in battle against an alien threat in this cheap Italian-made *Star Wars* ripoff. Directed with none of the style that makes similar films like *Battle of the Worlds* or *Planet of the Vampires* so enjoyable, this pancake-flat concoction never lives up the excitement of its title. Aka *War of the Planets*.

COUNTDOWN

★★★ WARNER, 1968, PG, 101 min. Dir: Robert Altman. Cast: James Caan, Robert Duvall, Joanna Moore Jordan, Charles Aidman, Michael Murphy, Barbara Baxley, Steve Ihnat, Ted Knight.

A fictional account of man's first landing on the moon, with NASA replacing military man-astronaut Duvall with younger scientist Caan in the hopes that the latter's knowledge will help them win the space race with the Russians. Though dated, this is more scientifically accurate than *Destination Moon* and benefits from its low-key presentation and realistic performances by Caan and Duvall.

CRASH AND BURN
★★ PARAMOUNT, 1990, R, 85 min. Dir: Charles Band. Cast: Paul Ganus, Megan Ward, Ralph Waite, Eva LaRue.

Shot with leftovers from *Robotjox,* this Charlie Band quickie concerns a desert-based TV station being stalked by a huge, murderous robot. A few good FX but mostly just a sci-fi version of a *Friday the 13th* flick with the robot coming off like a mechanized Jason.

CRASH OF THE MOONS
★★ Sinister Cinema, 1953, NR, 78 min. Dir: Hollingsworth Morse. Cast: Richard Crane, Sally Mansfield, Scotty Beckett, Robert Lyden.

One of a half-dozen or so "features" culled from episodes of the early sci-fi TV show *Rocky Jones, Space Ranger* in which guys in T-shirts and baseball caps save the universe in their cardboard spaceship. In this adventure, Rocky (Crane) must stop the collision of two planets

and the destruction of their respective civilizations. Primitive acting and special FX but still fun in a silly sort of way.

CRATER LAKE MONSTER, THE
★★ VCI, 1977, PG, 85 min. Dir: William Stromberg. Cast: Richard Cardella, Glen Roberts, Mark Siegel, Kacey Cobb, Bob Hyman, Richard Garrison.

The story goes that the producer of this very low-budget creature feature had come into an inheritance and wanted to use it to make a monster movie. The good news is that he hired Dave Allen to animate the title critter, a pleosaur, and it looks great. The bad news is that he seems to have hired everybody he ever met as "actors" who make you wish Allen could have animated *them,* too, since our hatched-from-a-dino-egg-at-the-bottom-of-a-lake-by-a-meteorite beastie acts them all off the screen.

CRAWLING EYE, THE
★★★ Sinister Cinema, 1958, NR, 83 min. Dir: Quentin Lawrence. Cast: Forrest Tucker, Laurence Payne, Janet Munro, Jennifer Jayne, Warren Mitchell, Frederick Schiller.

Based on the British TV serial *The Trollenberg*

Forrest Tucker saves a little kid from a rampaging mushroom, or something, in The Crawling Eye *(1958).*

Terror (also the film's original title), this movie tells of eyeball-shaped aliens living in a cloud above a Swiss village, occasionally beheading a mountain climber with a stray tentacle or mentally communicating with psychic heroine Munro. Well acted and full of suspense; better special FX would've made this a classic.

CRAWLING HAND, THE

★ Rhino, 1963, NR, 88 min. Dir: Herbert L. Strock. Cast: Rod Lauren, Sirry Steffen, Peter Breck, Kent Taylor, Allison Hayes, Alan Hale, Richard Arlen, Arline Judge.

The severed, radioactive hand and arm of a dead astronaut take over the mind of the very Frankie Avalonish Lauren while going on a very cost-conscious rampage. This sleazy ripoff of *The Beast with Five Fingers* and *First Man into Space* has pitiful special FX (the "severed" hand almost always looks like some guy reaching around a corner or from behind some obstruction) and Lauren is so intense you keep thinking that he's going to do himself an injury. To give this thing some credibility, luckily there is everybody's favorite skipper Hale as the town sheriff.

CRAZY RAY, THE

★★☆ Festival, 1923, NR, 60 min. Dir: René Clair. Cast: Henri Rollan, Madeleine Rodrique, Albert Préjan.

Originally called *Paris Qui Dort (Paris Who Sleeps)*, this engaging silent fantasy stars Rollan as an Eiffel Tower watchman who discovers that all of the City of Light has been frozen in time by an inventor's ray machine. This amusing little movie often has the gentle charm of a Charlie Chaplin film.

CREATION OF THE HUMANOIDS

★ Sinister Cinema, 1962, NR, 75 min. Dir: Wesley E. Barry. Cast: Don Megowan, Frances McCann, Erica Elliott, Don Doolittle.

In the postatomic future, scientist Megowan discovers a plot to replace the dwindling human population with androids—his own sister has even fallen in love with one. Some people like to point out this film's similarities to the later *Blade Runner* or mention that it was Andy Warhol's favorite movie. Me, I just like to think of its as one of the most lifeless, badly acted sci-fi films ever made and leave it at that.

CREATOR

★★ HBO, 1985, R, 107 min. Dir: Ivan Passer. Cast: Peter O'Toole, Mariel Hemingway, Vincent Spano, Virginia Madsen, David Ogden Stiers, John Dehner.

O'Toole is a charming college professor who wants to recreate his late wife via cloning;

Spano is his favorite student; and Hemingway is the sexy embryo doner who helps out. Trying to make a romantic tragicomedy out of a plot better suited to a Bela Lugosi movie doesn't work at all; only O'Toole's considerable charisma makes this adaptation of a novel by Jeremy Leven worth watching.

CREATURE

★★★ Media, 1985, R, 94 min. Dir: William Malone. Cast: Stan Ivar, Wendy Schaal, Klaus Kinski, Diane Salinger, Lyman Ward, Annette McCarthy.

An expedition to Saturn's moon Titan encounters a reptilian alien menace with the ability to raise and control the dead. The best of the many low-budget *Alien* knockoffs, this has above-average acting (with especially good performances by heroine Schaal and guest star Kinski as a lecherous German astronaut), photography, and special FX to make it work. It's a lot more imaginative than many films with four times this one's budget. Aka *The Titan Find*.

CREATURES THE WORLD FORGOT

★★ RCA/Columbia, 1971, PG, 95 min. Dir: Don Chaffey. Cast: Julie Ege, Tony Bonner, Brian O'Shaughnessy, Robert John.

Hammer Films' fourth, last, and worst prehistoric adventure movie traces the lives of feuding brothers Bonner and O'Shaughnessy and their love for frequently topless cavebabe Ege. Beautifully photographed in the Canary Islands but there are no dinosaurs and very little excitement.

CREATURE WASN'T NICE, THE

See: *Naked Space*.

CREEPING TERROR, THE

☆ United, 1963, NR, 75 min. Dir: Art J. Nelson. Cast: Vic Savage [Art J. Nelson], Shannon O'Neil, William Thourlby, John Cairson.

A man-eating carpet from outer space menaces Lake Tahoe while the police and the military waste time examining its phone-booth-sized spaceship and a narrator talks on and on about such unrelated subjects as the idea that men never really grow up until they get married. All this might be unintentionally funny if it weren't so damned depressing. Aka *Dangerous Charter*.

CREEPING UNKNOWN, THE

See: *The Quatermass Xperiment*.

CREEPOZOIDS

★☆ Urban Classics, 1987, R, 72 min. Dir: David De Coteau. Cast: Linnea Quigley, Richard Hawkins, Ken Abraham, Kim McKamy, Michael Aranda, Joi Wilson.

Mindless no-budget *Alien* clone in which five futuristic army deserters—including scream queen par excellence Quigley—are chased around a deserted factory by a genetically engineered monster that looks like it's made out of plastic. The film tries to trick you by not resorting to the usual lone-female-survivor plot device, but that still doesn't make it very noteworthy since it's dominated by mostly bad acting and a totally gratuitous (is there any other kind?) Quigley shower scene.

CREMATORS, THE
★★ WesternWorld, 1972, PG, 75 min. Dir: Harry Essex. Cast: Maria Di Aragon, Marvin C. Howard, Eric Allison.

Fifties screenwriter Essex (*It Came from Outer Space, Creature from the Black Lagoon*) followed up his truly awful directional debut picture *Octaman* with this somewhat better low-budget adaptation of the novel *The Dune Rollers* by J. C. May. A sphere from space lands in the desert and starts rolling across country, absorbing all life in its path. Not great but a big improvement on *Octaman,* with some similarities to the '50s sleeper *Kronos.*

CRIME ZONE
★★☆ MGM/UA, 1988, R, 96 min. Dir: Luis Llosa. Cast: David Carradine, Sherilyn Fenn, Peter Nelson, Michael Shaner.

Made in Peru, this futuristic action flick is better than many similar efforts. Carradine is in good form as a member of an elitist society who recruits "subgrades" Fenn and her beau to commit crimes for him. Well done, with a nice surprise ending.

CRITTERS
★★☆ Columbia/TriStar, 1986, PG-13, 86 min. Dir: Stephen Herek. Cast: Dee Wallace Stone, Billy Green Bush, M. Emmet Walsh, Scott Grimes, Nadine Van Der Velde, Don Opper, Terrence Mann, Billy Zane.

One of the better *Gremlins* cash-ins, with toothy little hairballs from space (whose snarls and growls are subtitled) followed by alien bounty hunters to the Kansas spread of the all-American Brown family. Good budget FX by the Chiodo Brothers (who would follow this up with the much more outrageous *Killer Klowns from Outer Space*) and a fun cast having a good time make this the best of its creatively limited series.

CRITTERS 2: THE MAIN COURSE
★★ Columbia/TriStar, 1988, PG-13, 85 min. Dir: Mick Garris. Cast: Scott Grimes, Liane Curtis, Don Opper, Barry Corbin, Terrence Mann, Sam Anderson, Herta Ware, Eddie Deezen.

Three years after their last rampage the critters return, with their eggs often mistaken for the Easter eggs hunted by the local children and, in the funniest scene, the critters getting their teeth into some boob dressed as Peter Cottontail. Even more juvenile than the original but still minor fun.

CRITTERS 3: YOU ARE WHAT THEY EAT
★★ New Line, 1992, PG-13, 84 min. Dir: Kristine Peterson. Cast: Aimee Brooks, John Calvin, Leonardo DiCaprio, Katherine Cortez, Geoffrey Blake, Diana Bellamy, Don Opper, Terrene Mann.

The *Critters* do their Bruce Willis imitation in this *Die Hard*-derived series entry set in an inner-city high rise populated by about six people—keeps the budget down, you see. Shot back to back with part 4, this ends abruptly with a setup for the next sequel and in retrospect is probably only noteworthy for the appearance of a young DiCaprio in his preteen heartthrob days.

CRITTERS 4: THEY'RE INVADING YOUR SPACE
★★ New Line, 1992, PG-13, 95 min. Dir: Rupert Harvey. Cast: Don Opper, Brad Dourif, Angela Bassett, Paul Witthorne, Anders Hove, Eric DaRae, Terrence Mann, voice of Martine Beswick.

Actually they're invading *Alien* territory in this most sci-fi-themed of the group, with Opper and a couple of critter eggs ending up on a space station and terrorizing the crew. In the grand tradition of Billy Zane and Leonardo DiCaprio once again we get an up-and-coming star in a *Critters* flick—in this case, Basset—but she acquits herself well in the clichéd Sigourney Weaver tough-heroine spot. No better or worse than its immediate predecessors.

CROW, THE
★★★ Miramax, 1994, R, 117 min. Dir: Alex Proyas. Cast: Brandon Lee, Ernie Hudson, Michael Wincott, David Patrick Kelly, Angel David, Rochelle Davis, Tony Todd, Jon Polito.

David Schow adapted James O'Bare's moody black-and-white comic book into this dark fantasy about a musician (Lee) who is brutally murdered, along with his fiancée, by a gang of thugs and rises from the dead as the supernatural crime fighter the Crow. Lee, who was accidentally killed during filming, is perfectly cast as the vengeful antihero and this film's bleak landscape of drug-riddled, death-obsessed characters caught on with teens in much the same way as the music of Marilyn Mason or the books of Anne Rice. An admirably downbeat and uncompromising film that deserves its success and unexpectedly spawned a sequel: *The Crow: City of Angels*.

CROW, THE: CITY OF ANGELS
★★☆ Miramax, 1996, R, 85 min. Dir: Tim Pope. Cast: Vincent Perez, Mia Kischner, Iggy Pop, Richard Brooks.

This sequel gets around the problem of the loss of the original *Crow* star Brandon Lee by starting from scratch with a new star (Perez) and a new Crow. After he and his father are brutally murdered by drug lords, cartoonist Perez rises up as the new Crow, who strikes out for revenge. If anything this is even more downbeat and melancholy than the first film, but it's haunted by a sense of déjà-vu that keeps it from being as fresh and interesting as its predecessor.

CYBER BANDITS
★★ Columbia/TriStar, 1995, R, 86 min. Dir: Eric Fleming. Cast: Martin Kemp, Alexandra Paul, Adam Ant, Grace Jones, Robert Hays, Henry Gibson.

When secret agent Kemp is tattooed with a design marked with vital government data, everyone in this exceedingly campy cast is after his skin. Apart from this glorious bunch, this dull futuristic thriller hasn't much going for it.

CYBER C.H.I.C.
★ AIP, 1990, PG-13, 90 min. Dir: Ed Hansen. Cast: Kathy Shower, Jack Carter, Burt Ward, Phil Proctor, Kip King.

What is it about movies with the word *Cyber* in the title and these off-the-wall casts? Anyway, this is a peepshow reworking of *The Terminator* films with a buxom, hard-bodied android-played by guess who?—after the madman who's holding the world nuclear hostage. For Burt Ward movie completists only.

CYBERNATOR
★ Vista, 1991, R, 84 min. Dir: Robert Rundle. Cast: Lonnie Schuyler, Christina Perlata, James K. Williams, William Smith.

Cyborg assassins created by the military go on a rampage and are battled by cop Schuyler in this bland video concoction. Even the presence of veteran movie bad guy Smith doesn't do much to relieve the tedium.

CYBER NINJA
★★ Orion, 1994, NR, 80 min. Dir: Keita Amemiya. Cast: Hanabei Kawai, Hiroki Ida, Eri Mirishita, Makoto Yokoyama.

A live-action, Anime-like Japanese fantasy about a princess captured by an evil galactic warlord and slated for sacrifice. Luckily for her, a crack squad of space mercenaries led by the mysterious Cyber Ninja are on the way. Not bad, but nothing special.

CYBORG
★ MGM/UA, 1989, R, 86 min. Dir: Albert Pyun. Cast: Jean-Claude Van Damme, Deborah Richter, Vincent Klyn, Alex Daniels, Dayle Haddon.

Every postapocalyptic cliché in the book is trotted out as the "Muscles from Brussels" stomps through the futuristic wastelands with female cyborg Richter in tow as they search for a cure for a world-decimating plague. Inexplicably popular in some quarters, this dud inspired a couple of direct-to-video sequels and a number of imitators, but frankly, I don't give a Van Damme.

CYBORG 2
★☆ Vidmark Entertainment, 1993, R, 99 min. Dir: Michael Schoeder. Cast: Jack Palance, Elias Koteas, Angelina Jolie, Billy Drago.

Jolie is the cyborg this time, a bad gal battled by hero Koteas and his android partner. Soap opera-ish complications arise when Elias falls in love with Angelina. The cast, especially Palance, makes this followup better than the first *Cyborg*—but not much.

CYBORG SOLDIER
★ New Line, 1993, R, 97 min. Dir: Sam Firstenberg. Cast: David Bradley, Morgan Hunter, Jill Pierce, Dale Cutts.

Renegade cop Bradley wipes out berserk cyborg slaves in another by-the-numbers action flick of the future. My future would be a helluva lot brighter if I didn't have to watch any more of these direct-to-video brain cell killers.

CYBORG: THE SIX MILLION DOLLAR MAN
See: *The Six Million Dollar Man*.

CYCLOPS, THE
★★ Sinister Cinema, 1957, NR, 75 min. Dir: Bert I. Gordon. Cast: Gloria Talbott, James Craig, Lon Chaney, Jr., Tom Drake, Vincent Padula, Dean Parkin.

Talbott leads the search for her missing fiancé to a radiation-infested Mexico valley where the animals have become gigantic and her missing beau a huge, hideously deformed one-eyed monster. Gordon's special FX are all thumbs but there's a bit of suspense in the early going and the seasoned cast tries to put this thing over the best they can. Much of this was later reworked as *War of the Colossal Beast* with Parkin once again playing the monster.

and Mell his sultry mistress. There are lots of imaginative sets and colorful lighting, and a great score by Ennio Morricone. Not a box office hit, this should have given Bava's career the shot in the arm it always deserved and is certainly one of the all-time great pop-culture time capsules of the 1960s, with gimmicks and gadgets galore. Aka *Diabolik*.

DAGORA, THE SPACE MONSTER
★★ Sinister Cinema, 1963, NR, 80 min. Dir: Inoshiro [Ishiro] Honda. Cast: Yosuke Natsuki, Kiroshi Koizumi, Yoko Fujiyama, Akiko Wakabiyashi.

Japanese gangsters steal a cache of diamonds stolen from them by the title creature, a gigantic jellyfish from outer space. Like *The H Man,* this tries to combine sci-fi and crime drama but the results aren't nearly as good. But some of the special FX, with Dagora seizing buildings and bridges in its twisting tentacles, are good. Aka *Uchu Daikaiju Dogora (Space Monster Dogora).*

DALEKS—INVASION EARTH 2150 A.D.
★★★ Republic, 1966, NR, 84 min. Dir: Gordon Flemyng. Cast: Peter Cushing, Bernard Cribbins, Jill Curzon, Roberta Tovey, Andrew Keir, Ray Brooks.

The improved sequel to *Dr. Who and the Daleks* finds the Doctor (Cushing), his two granddaughters, and a London bobby transported into the twenty-second century where London comes under seize by an army of invading daleks in a huge war ship. Good fun with cheap but imaginative special FX and a great ending.

DAMNATION ALLEY
★★ CBS/Fox, 1977, PG, 87 min. Dir: Jack Smight. Cast: George Peppard, Jan-Michael Vincent, Dominique Sanda, Paul Winfield, Jackie Earl Haley.

Dull version of the Roger Zelazny novel of five survivors of a nuclear holocaust traversing a desert landscape in a customized RV (a typical '70s touch) in a search for the last remains of civilization. Pretty silly stuff, although Vincent and Sanda are attacked by a giant scorpion and Winfield is devoured by mutant cockroaches so it's not a total loss.

DANGER: DIABOLIK
★★★ Paramount/Gateway, 1967, NR, 88 min. Dir: Mario Bava. Cast: John Phillip Law, Marisa Mell, Adolfo Celi, Terry Thomas, Michel Piccoli, Claudio Gora.

Dino De Laurentiis produced this Italian-French coproduction based on a popular Euro-comic strip. Law is the supercriminal Diabolik

DANGEROUS CHARTER
See: *The Creeping Terror.*

DARBY O'GILL AND THE LITTLE PEOPLE
★★★ Disney, 1959, NR, 90 min. Dir: Robert Stevenson. Cast: Albert Sharpe, Janet Munro, Sean Connery, Jimmy O'Dea, Kieron Moore, Estelle Winwood.

Thoroughly entertaining, and even a bit scary, this Disney fantasy features a great Sharpe as the professional prevaricator who can't get anyone to believe him when he is befriended by the King of the Leprechauns. Good songs (Connery, in his first big movie role, even sings!) and great special FX in this slice of Irish whimsy.

DARK, THE
★★ Media, 1978, R, 92 min. Dir: John "Bud" Cardos. Cast: William Devane, Cathy Lee Crosby, Richard Jaeckel, Keenan Wynn, Vivian Blaine, Biff Elliot, Jacqueline Hyde, Casey Kasem, Warren Kemmerling, Philip Michael Thomas, Angelo Rossitto, John Bloom.

An alien head ripper terrorizes Los Angeles, stalked by writer Devane, reporter Crosby, and police detective Jaeckel. Originally a horror movie about a murderous walking corpse to be directed by Tobe Hooper, Hooper was replaced by Cardos and the film restructured in the editing by the producers (one of whom was Dick Clark!) into a sci-fi thriller meant to rip off *Alien.* The result is a confusing, nearly senseless melange of shooting stars, laser beams, and spooky occult music; it's not good but it's certainly watchable with its dynamite exploitation cast.

DARK CRYSTAL, THE
★★★ HBO, 1983, PG, 94 min. Dirs: Jim Henson, Frank Oz. Voices: Stephen Carlick, Lisa Maxwell, Billie Whitelaw, Perry Edwards, Jim Henson, Frank Oz.

Mystical sword-and-sorcery fantasy from Muppet kingpin Henson. The all-puppet cast tells the tale of two elfin innocents trying to save their world from villains out to control the all-powerful "Dark Crystal." Might be too much for the kid audience it was intended for and the story drags a bit, but once you get into it you find yourself forgetting that the cast is made up of felt-covered armatures and start relating to them as real people—an astonishing accomplishment.

DARKMAN

★★★ MCA/Universal, 1990, R, 96 min. Dir: Sam Raimi. Cast: Liam Neeson, Frances McDormand, Larry Drake, Colin Friels, Nelson Mashita, Nicholas Worth, Ted Raimi, Jenny Agutter.

Evil Dead auteur Raimi's take on the superhero genre with Neeson as a hideously disfigured scientist who uses the synthetic skin he's developed to make temporary faces he uses in a revenge plot against the gangsters who maimed him. Great makeup and camerawork help hide the fact that this is a far from original set of circumstances, borrowing from everything from *Doctor X* to *Batman,* but it's such a well-acted, exhilarating ride it's hard not to like it. Followed by a pair of direct-to-video sequels.

DARKMAN II: THE RETURN OF DURANT

★★ MCA/Universal, 1994, R, 93 min. Dir: Bradford May. Cast: Arnold Vosloo, Larry Drake, Kim Delaney, Renee O'Connor.

In the grand tradition of horror movie villains who won't die no matter what you do to them, Darkman's nemesis Durant (Drake) returns from a seemingly definitive demise to plague our hero anew. This routine sequel-for-video presents us with a new Darkman (Vosloo, replacing a too-big-now-for-this-sort-of-nonsense Liam Neeson) but the same old superhero antics.

DARKMAN III: DIE DARKMAN, DIE

★★☆ MCA/Universal, 1994, R, 87 min. Dir: Bradford May. Cast: Arnold Vosloo, Jeff Fahey, Darlanne Fluegel, Roxanne Biggs-Dawson, Alicia Panetta, Nigel Bennett.

This third in the series (actually shot back-to-back with II but held up for two years) has Fahey as the crime boss who uses mistress Biggs-Dawson to lure Darkman into a trap in order to learn his face-changing secrets. A lot better than II and almost as fun as the original, this is the most outrageously tongue-in-cheek of the series and is all the better for it, with Fahey really lettin' 'er rip.

DARK SIDE OF THE MOON, THE

★★☆ Vidmark Entertainment, 1989, R, 91 min. Dir: D. J. Webster. Cast: Will Bledsoe, Wendy MacDonald, Joe Turkel, Robert Sampson.

Futuristic astronauts discover an abandoned space shuttle containing a devil-possessed corpse in this sci-fi/horror hybrid. Not bad, with good acting and a few plot surprises, but hampered by a very low budget.

DARK STAR

★★☆ VCI, 1974, G, 83 min. Dir: John Carpenter. Cast: Brian Narelle, Andreijah Pahich, Dan O'Bannon, Cal Kuniholm, Joe Sanders.

Four lonely, bored astronauts find their mission to destroy unstable asteroids disrupted by an annoying, beachball-like alien. Carpenter's first film, begun as a UCLA student project and picked up for completion and distribution by Jack Harris, this is an often amateurish but entertaining spoof of films like *2001* and *Silent Running* and in some ways looks forward to cowriter-actor O'Bannon's later *Alien* screenplay.

D.A.R.Y.L.

★★☆ Paramount, 1985, PG, 99 min. Dir: Simon Wincer. Cast: Mary Beth Hurt, Michael McKean, Barret Oliver, Coleen Camp, Kathryn Walker, Josef Sommer.

Hurt and McKean adopt intelligent young Oliver and are shocked to learn that he is actually a robot in human form. A decent premise gets a bland, Disney-fied treatment that makes for a well acted but colorless fantasy.

DATE WITH AN ANGEL

★☆ HBO, 1987, PG, 105 min. Dir: Tom McLoughlin. Cast: Michael E. Knight, Emmanuelle Beart, Phoebe Cates, David Dukes, Phil Brock, Albert Macklin.

Shameless ripoff of *Splash* with Knight as an unhappily engaged musician who falls in love with beautiful angel Beart, who, quite literally, has dropped into his life. Painful-to-endure romantic fantasy-comedy from the man who brought you *Friday the 13th, Part VI.*

DAY AFTER, THE

★★★ Embassy, 1983, NR, 126 min. Dir: Nicholas Meyer. Cast: Jason Robards, JoBeth Williams, Steve Guttenberg, John Lithgow, Bibi Besch, Amy Madigan, Lori Lethin, Jeff East.

When Lawrence, Kansas, is destroyed by a Soviet missile, the people living in the general area soon succumb to radiation sickness and the general breakdown of society. An overwrought but bravely grim TV movie with good acting from Robards, Williams, and Lithgow and few pulled punches.

DAY IT CAME TO EARTH, THE

★★ King of Video, 1978, PG, 88 min. Dir: Harry Thomason. Cast: George Gobel, Wink Roberts, Roger Manning, Delight DeBruinne.

Janette Scott is victimized by some vegetation in The Day of the Triffids *(1963).*

A meteor falls into a bog and revives a recently rubbed-out Mafia hit man, who terrorizes teenagers at a sleep over. *Designing Women* co-creator Thomason's tribute to the tacky teen sci-fi flicks of the '50s, this is slow and badly acted (except for Lonesome George as a science teacher) but certainly captures the feel of the corny old movies it tries to emulate.

DAY OF THE DOLPHIN, THE

★★☆ Nelson, 1973, PG, 104 min. Dir: Mike Nichols. Cast: George C. Scott, Trish Van Devere, Paul Sorvino, Fritz Weaver, Jon Korkes, Edward Herrmann.

Scientist Scott discovers that the dolphins he has trained to understand human speech—and which can talk!—are being used in a plot to assassinate the president. An earnest but often ridiculous sci-fi thriller with a good cast and beautiful photography but an approach that often makes it look like a Disney film for adults.

DAY OF THE TRIFFIDS, THE

★★☆ Goodtimes, 1963, NR, 93 min. Dirs: Steve Sekely, Freddie Francis. Cast: Howard Keel, Nicole Maurey, Janette Scott, Kieron Moore, Mervyn Johns, Janina Faye.

A meteor shower blinds most of the people of the world and brings to Earth a plague of man-killing plants in this cheap-looking but well acted and scored adaptation of the John Wyndham novel. Sekely's original cut was too short so an uncredited Francis added several sequences set in a lighthouse, with Scott contributing some ear-splitting screams and Moore some sexiness. The main plot has '50s musical star Keel leading a handful of sighted survivors from England to Spain as they try to escape the triffids. Remade in New Zealand as a TV miniseries in 1981; this, and not *Village of the Dammed,* just cries out for a big-budget Hollywood redo.

DAY THE EARTH CAUGHT FIRE, THE

★★★ Republic, 1962, NR, 99 min. Dir: Val Guest. Cast: Edward Judd, Janet Munro, Leo McKern, Michael Goodliffe.

In this low-key British sci-fi drama, atomic testing causes a subtle shift in the Earth's orbit, sending it closer to the sun and causing temperatures to rise to dangerous levels. Judd is the cynical newspaper reporter covering the story who learns to love life (and costar Munro) just as the world is coming to an end. Well done, with few special FX and a nicely ambiguous ending. Look for Michael Caine as a traffic cop.

DAY THE EARTH FROZE, THE

★★ Sinister Cinema, 1959, NR, 67 min. Dir: Gregg Sebelious. Cast: Nina Anderson, Jon Powers, Peter Sorenson, voice of Marvin Miller.

Originally titled *Sampo,* this Finnish/Soviet coproduction concerns a witch who steals the sun and causes the world to freeze. Quaint special FX and colorful photography but the dubbed dialogue and songs will make your head hurt.

DAY THE EARTH STOOD STILL, THE

★★★★ Fox, 1951, NR, 91 min. Dir: Robert Wise. Cast: Michael Rennie, Patricia Neal, Hugh Marlowe, Sam Jaffe, Billy Gray, Frances Bavier, James Seay, Lock Martin.

Time has not dimmed the glow of this '50s classic about Klaatu (Rennie), an alien who arrives on Earth to warn its people not to spread their destructive ways to the stars under penalty of total destruction. Considered un-American by Richard Nixon, this slightly veiled story of the life of Christ (I know it's a stretch but it's there if you look for it) has excellent performances by Rennie, Neal (as the young widow who befriends him), Jaffe (as the Einstein-like scientist), and Gray (as Neal's nicely normal and unstereotypical kid); refined direction from Wise; and an understated electronic score by Bernard Herrmann. Edmund North adapted the story *Farewell to the Master* by Harry Bates complete with the chilling twist ending where it is the robot Gort (Martin) and *not* Klaatu who is in charge—maybe that was the un-American part.

DAY THE SKY EXPLODED, THE

★★ Sinister Cinema, 1958, NR, 80 min. Dir: William De Lane [Paolo Heusch]. Cast: Paul Hubschmid, Fiorella Mari, Madeleine Fisher, Ivo Garrani, Sam Galter, Giacomo Rossi-Stuart.

Horror great Mario Bava provided the imaginative photography for this otherwise dull French-Italian flick about a rocket sent crashing into the sun, causing asteroids to start falling to Earth and causing a wave of catastrophes. Sounds a lot more exciting than it actually is, with lousy dubbing and pathetic special FX. Original title: *La Morte Viene Dalla Spazio (Death Comes from Space).*

DAY THE WORLD ENDED, THE

★★☆ RCA/Columbia, 1955, NR, 78 min. Dir: Roger Corman. Cast: Richard Denning, Lori Nelson, Mike [Touch] Connors, Adele Jergens, Paul Birch, Paul Blaisdell.

Corman's first sci-fi film, this modest-budget widescreen feature involves a group of survivors of a devastating atomic blast bickering over who's in charge in a remote mountain house. Meanwhile, flesh-eating three-eyed mutants are on the prowl, one of whom (Blaisdell) is what's left of heroine Nelson's missing fiancé. With such typical '50s touches (not to mention Touch Connors) as a gangster and his moll among the survivors, lots of sexual innuendo, and a cool jazz score by Ronald Stein. Remade as *In the Year 2889.*

DAY TIME ENDED, THE

★★ Media, 1980, PG, 79 min. Dir: John "Bud" Cardos. Cast: Jim Davis, Dorothy Malone, Chris Mitchum, Marcy Lafferty, Natasha Ryan, Scott Kolden.

Good stop-motion FX distinguish this confusing cheapie about a family's desert home caught in the middle of a shift in the time-space continuum and invaded by strange monsters and aliens. Shot over a period of several years, this never makes any sense but is short enough not to outstay its welcome.

DEAD-END DRIVE-IN

★★ New World, 1986, R, 87 min. Dir: Brian Trenchard-Smith. Cast: Ned Manning, Natalie McCurry, Peter Witford, Wilbur Wilde.

In the Australia of the next century, unruly teens are imprisoned in an old abandoned drive-in theater until tough punk Manning decides to bust outta there. Violent and funny but not too original, this Aussie actioner borrows its look from *Escape from New York* and the *Mad Max* movies but has little of their style.

DEADLOCK

★★★ Video Treasures, 1991, R, 95 min. Dir: Lewis Teague. Cast: Rutger Hauer, Mimi Rogers, Joan Chen, James Remar.

Teague (director of such above-average creature features as *Alligator* and *Cujo*) ably handles this sci-fi updating of *The Defiant Ones.*

Lock Martin, Patricia Neal, and Michael Rennie star in the classic The Day the Earth Stood Still *(1951).*

The Manhattan parking problem is solved in a big way by The Deadly Mantis *(1957).*

The always great Hauer and Rogers are criminals outfitted with metallic collars that force them to stay together at all times—otherwise the collars are activated and their heads are detonated! This might sound silly but a smart script, solid direction, and a sharp cast turn this into something of a sleeper. Followed by a sequel. TV title: *Wedlock.*

DEADLY MANTIS, THE

★★ MCA/Universal, 1957, NR, 78 min. Dir: Nathan Juran. Cast: Craig Stevens, William Hopper, Alix Talton, Donald Randolph.

Routine '50s monster movie about a huge prehistoric preying mantis released from arctic ice by atomic testing (just like the dinosaur in *The Beast from 20,000 Fathoms*). It attacks a North Pole army base (just like *The Thing*) and peers in a window at heroine Talton (just like *Tarantula*) before flying to Washington, D.C., and menacing the Washington Monument (like the saucers in *Earth vs. the Flying Saucers*) and then moving on to New York City, where it dies in the Holland Tunnel (like the sewer-nesting ants in *Them!*). The special FX are wobbly and the cast bored (Talton replaced Mara Corday, who walked out on this as filming began); though it's efficiently directed by Juran it gets bogged down in places and boasts almost as much stock footage as *Plan 9 from Outer Space*.

DEADLY SPAWN, THE

★★☆ Arrow Entertainment, 1983, R, 79 min. Dir: Douglas McKeown. Cast: Charles George Hildebrandt, Tom De Franco, Richard Lee Porter, Jean Tafler, Karen Tigne, Elissa Neil.

During a torrential rainstorm, a house in New Jersey is infested by thousands of toothy alien tadpoles in a variety of sizes and it's up to kid hero Hildebrandt to stop them. A gory semi-amateur effort that's short on production values and acting talent but long on imagination and twisted charm. The Grandma Bunny party scene is a hoot. Aka *Return of the Aliens: The Deadly Spawn.*

DEADLY WEAPON

★☆ TransWorld Entertainment, 1989, PG-13, 90 min. Dir: Michael Miner. Cast: Rodney Eastman, Kim Walker, Gary Frank, Michael Horse.

Screwed-up teen (is there any other kind?) Eastman gets his hand on a powerful new weapon after it's lost in a train wreck and uses it to avenge himself on those he feels have wronged him. This one-note sci-fi actioner keeps taking itself way too seriously to work; it's like *Laserblast* without the tacky charm.

DEAD MAN WALKING

★★ Republic, 1987, R, 90 min. Dir: Gregory Brown.

Cast: Wings Hauser, Brion James, Jeffrey Combs, Pamela Ludwig.

Bounty hunter of the future Hauser is hired to find kidnapped heiress Ludwig and searches a plague-ravaged landscape in his quest. Another fill-in-the-blanks after-the-holocaust thriller with lots of brutal violence but not much else, though somewhat redeemed by that killer cast.

DEAD SPACE
★☆ RCA/Columbia, 1990, R, 72 min. Dir: Fred Gallo. Cast: Marc Singer, Laura Tate, Judith Chapman, Bryan Cranston.

Slickly done but wholly unnecessary why—bother remake of the splattery bad taste classic *Forbidden World*. Space jockey Singer (looking very haggard) and his robot companion arrive at a space station just as it's being terrorized by a shape-shifting killer mutant. Predictable and dull, with an anonymous supporting cast and none of the sick-pup touches that so distinguish the original.

DEATH COMES FROM SPACE
See: *The Day the Sky Exploded.*

DEATH OF THE INCREDIBLE HULK
★★ Rhino, 1990, NR, 96 min. Dir: Bill Bixby. Cast: Bill Bixby, Lou Ferrigno, Elizabeth Gracen, Philip Sterling, Andreas Katsulas, Barbara Tarbuck.

David Banner (Bixby) and an international spy ring are both after a formula that could free Banner from his alter ego the Hulk (Ferrigno) forever in this TV movie sequel to the popular series. Bill and Lou are both beginning to look a bit old for this nonsense but, as ever, Bixby's sincerity makes this worth watching for fans.

DEATH RACE 2000
★★★ New Horizons, 1975, R, 78 min. Dir: Paul Bartel. Cast: David Carradine, Simone Griffith, Sylvester Stallone, Mary Woronov, Louisa Moritz, Martin Kove, Joyce Jameson, Fred Grandy, Harriet White Medin, Don Steele.

Bartel's outrageous spoof of '70s car crash movies involves an auto race of the future where extra points are scored for the number of innocent pedestrians you run down—the very young and very old net the highest score. Maybe a bit too gory for its own good (producer Roger Corman allegedly added more blood after director Bartel completed his cut) but also screamingly funny in spots, with one of the greatest exploitation casts of the 1970s. Stallone is a piss in his last pre-Rocky role as hot-headed Machine Gun Joe. Sort-of sequel: *Deathsport.*

DEATH RAY OF DR. MABUSE, THE
★★ Sinister Cinema, 1964, NR, 90 min. Dir: Hugo Fregonese. Cast: Wolfgang Preiss, Peter Van Eyck, Yvonne Furneaux, Yoko Tani, Leo Genn, Werner Peters.

The power-mad Dr. Mabuse (Preiss) threatens the world with a destructive death ray while police inspector Van Eyck tries to stop him. The last of six West German-produced *Mabuse* films made in the early to mid '60s, this is far from the best but has a great cast and a few thrills. Aka *The Secret of Dr. Mabuse.*

DEATH RAY 2000
★★ Republic, 1981, NR, 96 min. Dir: Lee H. Katzin. Cast: Robert Logan, Ann Turkel, Dan O'Herlihy, Clive Revill.

Routine movie for TV with Logan as a secret agent out to foil terrorists from using a powerful superbomb to assassinate a world disarmament council. Flat direction and pat situations defeat a pretty good cast in this small-screen James Bond wannabe.

DEATHSPORT
★★ Warner, 1978, R, 83 min. Dirs: Henry Suso, Allan Arkush. Cast: David Carradine, Claudia Jennings, Richard Lynch, William Smithers.

Carradine returns (as a different character) in this sequel-in-name-only to *Death Race 2000*. In the year 3000, Dave and Playmate Jennings are amongst those involved in life-or-death gladitorial combat. Not nearly as much fun as *Death Race* despite the presence of the likable Jennings and premiere budget bad guy Lynch.

DEATHSTALKER
★★ Vestron, 1983, R, 80 min. Dir: John Watson. Cast: Richard Hill, Barbie Benton, Richard Brooker, Lana Clarkson, Bernard Erhard.

Muscleman hero Hill uses his mighty "sword of justice" to overcome villainous magician Erhard in this cheap but watchable Conan cash-in. One time Hugh Hefner squeeze Benton is the damsel in distress and Brooker (who played Jason in *Friday the 13th Part 3*) is a mountainous mutant in this first of an inexplicably popular sword-and-sorcery series.

DEATHSTALKER II: DUEL OF THE TITANS
★★ LIVE, 1987, R, 77 min. Dir: Jim Wynorski. Cast: John Terlesky, Monique Gabrielle, John La Zar, Toni Naples.

Goofed-out sequel with hunky Terlesky taking over the title role as our no-necked hero tries to save the kingdom of beauteous Princess Gabrielle, who's been replaced on the throne by an evil twin. Since none of this is played straight it's okay to laugh. Maybe the best (!?) of the series.

DEATHSTALKER III: WARRIORS FROM HELL

★★ LIVE, 1988, R, 85 min. Dir: Alfonso Corona. Cast: John Allen Nelson, Carla Herd, Terri Treas, Thom Christopher.

This time our hero is on a quest to find three magical stones promising world power and along the way makes nice-nice with lovely heroine Herd. Nelson (star of the aptly named *Hunk* and *Killer Klowns from Outer Space*) is probably the best actor to tackle the role of Deathstalker (Tom Hanks and Hugh Grant were otherwise engaged) and his spirited good humor makes this silly flick minor fun.

DEATHSTALKER IV: MATCH OF THE TITANS

★☆ New Horizons, 1992, R, 87 min. Dir: Howard R. Cohen. Cast: Rick Hill, Maria Ford, Michelle Moffett, Brett Clark.

Hill is back as Deathstalker but that's not much of a recommendation. This time our boy finds himself, and various other warriors, involved in dangerous gladitorial contests staged by bitch queen Ford. The last, thus far, and certainly least of the series, but at least it doesn't take itself too seriously.

DEATHWATCH

★★★ New Line, 1982, R, 117 min. Dir: Bertrand Tavernier. Cast: Romy Schneider, Harvey Keitel, Harry Dean Stanton, Max von Sydow.

Intriguing futuristic melodrama about a dying woman (brilliantly played by Schneider) whose last days are unknowingly being filmed by Keitel, who has a video camera implanted in his brain. A well-written and -directed satire (with serious undertones) on the right to privacy and the nature of media in our day-to-day lives. Filmed in West Berlin and Paris.

DEEP RED

★★ MCA/Universal, 1994, NR, 96 min. Dir: Craig R. Baxley. Cast: Michael Biehn, Joanna Pacula, Michael Des Barres, John De Lancie.

Not to be confused with the (much better) horror film by Dario Argento, this made-for-cable sci-fi thriller (first shown on the Sci-Fi Channel) stars Biehn and Pacula as estranged husband-and-wife private eyes protecting a little girl whose rare blood can heal the sick and wounded and even reverse aging. De Lancie is the evil alien scientist but even he can't bring much excitement to this too-serious-for-its-own-good affair.

DEEP SIX, THE

See: *Deepstar Six*.

DEEP SPACE

★★ TransWorld Entertainment, 1987, R, 90 min. Dir: Fred Olen Ray. Cast: Charles Napier, Ann Turkel, Bo Svenson, Ron Glass, Julie Newmar, James Booth, Norman Burton, Anthony Eisley, Peter Palmer, Elisabeth Brooks.

Ray remakes his cheapie *Biohazard* as a (slightly) bigger budgeted sci-fi/horror *Alien*-type monster movie. Napier and Turkel are the cops on the trail of a monster that's described as a giant roach but actually looks like an H. R. Giger reject. Nothing special but the veteran cast has fun and it's nice to see character actor Napier get a lead for a change. Despite the title, *none* of this takes place in outer space—even the monster was created on Earth.

DEEPSTAR SIX

★★ Avid Entertainment, 1989, R, 89 min. Dir: Sean S. Cunningham. Cast: Greg Evigan, Nancy Everhard, Cindy Pickett, Taurean Blacque, Miguel Ferrer, Nia Peeples, Marius Weyers, Matt McCoy.

Undersea workers building a government missile silo are attacked by a huge prehistoric crustacean unleashed by an underwater earthquake. Evigan is stalwart, Everhard is supportive, Ferrrer acts like a bonehead, and Peeples looks good dripping wet in this routine *Alien* in the ocean made to cash in on *The Abyss*. The ending is a direct steal from Cunningham's earlier *Friday the 13th* (itself stolen from *Carrie*) and was used again in the very similar *Leviathan*. Shooting title: *The Deep Six*.

DEF-CON 4

★★ New World, 1985, R, 88 min. Dir: Paul Donovan. Cast: Lenore Zann, Tim Choate, Maury Chaykin, Kate Lynch, Kevin King, John Walsch.

Shot-in-Canada low-budgeter about a trio of astronauts who return from a space mission to discover the Earth in ruins following the outbreak of World War III. When one of the astronauts is killed, the survivors (Zann and Choate) journey to supposed safety in Central America. Routine futuristic thriller in the *Logan's Run/Damnation Alley* mold without the money or the imagination to bring its story off.

DELUGE

★★ Sinister Cinema, 1933, NR, 70 min. Dir: Felix Feist. Cast: Peggy Shannon, Sidney Blackmer, Lois Wilson, Matt Moore, Edward Van Sloan, Samuel S. Hunds.

A handful of survivors struggle to stay alive after New York City is obliterated by a massive tidal wave. Once thought lost, this protodisaster film has interesting (if dated) special FX (much of which turned up in various serials and features over the next twenty-five years) but is bogged down by melodramatic acting and a dull love story subplot that takes center stage too much of the time.

DEMOLITIONIST, THE

★★☆ A-Pix, 1995, R, 91 min. Dir: Robert Kurtzman. Cast: Nicole Eggert, Bruce Abbott, Richard Grieco, Heather Langenkamp, Susan Tyrell, Peter Jason, Reggie Bannister, Tom Savini.

Although overly derivative (of *Robocop, Eve of Destruction,* and many more) this Roger Corman production is almost good, thanks mainly to an exceptional exploitation cast and a nice (if not consistant) sense of humor. Cop Eggert (of *Baywatch* fame) is rubbed out by minions of underworld kingpin Grieco (in a nice change-of-image role) and resurrected by scientist Abbott (in a parody of his role in the *Re-Animator* movies) as a bionic superheroine out for revenge. With Langenkamp as a perky TV reporter, Tyrell as the town mayor (!), and Bannister as a prison warden who gets fried in his own electric chair; this hasn't an original bone in its body but is a lot more fun than some other, quite similar films. Director Kurtzman is one of the founders of the KNB FX special makeup effects group.

DEMOLITION MAN

★★★ Warner, 1993, R, 115 min. Dir: Marco Brambilla. Cast: Sylvester Stallone, Wesley Snipes, Sandra Bullock, Nigel Hawthorne, Denis Leary, Rob Schneider, Benjamin Bratt, Glenn Shadix.

High-tech brain-candy with Sly as an ex-cop awakened after thirty-six years in suspended animation to battle recently resurrected foe Snipes (in a blonde do) in the futuristic city of "San Angeles." Plays better as a comedy than an actioner, with amusing swipes at political correctness, health food and fitness, and other easy targets. Stallone and Snipes are well matched and Bullock is typically likable as Sly's nonviolent-until-the-chips-are-down partner.

DEMON PLANET, THE

See: *Planet of the Vampires.*

DEMON SEED

★★★ MGM/UA, 1977, R, 94 min. Dir: Donald Cammell. Cast: Julie Christie, Fritz Weaver, Garrit Graham, Berry Kroeger, Lisa Lu, voice of Robert Vaughn.

First-rate film version of an early Dean R. Koontz novel about the wife (Christie) of a famous inventor (Weaver) whose superbrain computer Proteus IV (voiced with silky aplomb by Vaughn) decides to imprison Christie in her mechanized house until she agrees to be inseminated with his (its?) child—you don't want to know how. A tasteful, suspenseful handling of an adult subject done with enough wit to keep it from becoming disturbingly misogynistic, and a chilling twist ending. Christie gives one of her all-time best performances.

DEMONWARP

★ Vidmark Entertainment, 1987, R, 91 min. Dir: Emmett Alston. Cast: George Kennedy, David Michael O'Neill, Pamela Gilbert, Billy Jacoby, Colleen McDermott, Michelle Bauer.

It's cheesy T&A monster movie time again as young folk searching some woods for the legendary Bigfoot discover the hairy guy is actually a dodge to hide the corpse-raising activities of Satan-worshipping alien cannibals! And if that's not enough for you, Bauer is asked to expose her breasts gratuitously, Kennedy is a vengeful forest ranger hunting Bigfoot, and there's a ripoff *Carrie* shock ending. Almost jaw-dropping in its outrageous stupidity.

DESERT WARRIOR

★ Prism Entertainment, 1988, R, 89 min. Dir: Jim Goldman. Cast: Lou Ferrigno, Shari Sattuck, Tony East, Michael Monty.

Another bad *Mad Max* rip with the incredible Lou as one of the last survivors of a nuclear war struggling to stay alive in a contaminated world. Just struggling to get through this movie was such a chore that I guess I could handle the apocalypse without too much trouble.

DESTINATION MOON

★★☆ Nostalgia Merchant, 1950, NR, 91 min. Dir: Irving Pichel. Cast: John Archer, Warner Anderson, Tom Powers, Dick Wesson, Erin O'Brien-Moore.

Produced by George Pal and directed by former character actor Pichel (*Dracula's Daughter*), this was Hollywood's first serious science fiction film of its era—too bad it's not very good. The first manned mission to the moon encounters the usual problems (weightlessness, asteroids, et cetera) before landing on the surface of the moon (which looks like a dried lakebed) to plant the American flag. Coscripted by Robert Heinlein (from his story *Rocket Ship Galileo*), this has colorful photography, imaginative (if somewhat scientifically inacurate) settings, and decent special FX but is mired by a slow pace and the world's dullest cast. Most TV prints cut the special guest appearance by Woody Woodpecker.

DESTINATION MOONBASE ALPHA
★★ CBS/Fox, 1976, G, 93 min. Dir: Gerry Anderson. Cast: Martin Landau, Barbara Bain, Barry Morse, Catherine Schell.

In this patchwork "feature" cobbled together from two episodes of the briefly popular TV series *Space: 1999* (see episode guide), moonbase commander Landau (during the anything-goes period of his career) contends with a rogue planet and a deadly space disease. Fans of the show may want to check this out.

DESTROY ALL PLANETS
★★ Something Weird, 1968, NR, 85 min. Dir: Noriaka Yuasa. Cast: Kojiro Honga, Toru Takatsuka, Carl Clay, Peter Williams, Michiko Yaegaki, Mari Atsumi.

The fourth Gamera movie is certainly one of the dullest, with lots of stock footage to keep down the budget. Our colossal hero helps a couple of boy scouts battle squidlike invaders

from the planet Varas who, in the climax, mutate into one huge creature to take Gamera on mano-à-mano. Originally titled *Gamera tai Viras (Gamera vs. Viras)*; followed by *Gamera vs. Monster X.*

DEVIL GIRL FROM MARS
★★ Nostalgia Merchant, 1954, NR, 76 min. Dir: David MacDonald. Cast: Patricia Laffan, Hazel Court, Hugh McDermott, Adrienne Corri, Peter Reynolds, Joseph Tomelty.

Campy British low-budget imitation of a Hollywood sci-fi film with the formidable Laffan as the title gal. In a reversal of the usual cliché, Pat is an alien searching Earth for a husband. She sets down in the Scottish highlands (like *The Man from Planet X*) with her clunky robot and singles out McDermott as her man. You'll be Laffan throughout this almost absurdly serious tale that's distinguished by some especially pretty actresses, including future scream queens Court and Corri.

DIAMONDS ARE FOREVER
★★★ MGM/UA, 1971, PG, 119 min. Dir: Guy Hamilton. Cast: Sean Connery, Jill St. John, Charles Gray, Lana Wood, Jimmy Dean, Bruce Cabot, Bernard Lee, Lois Maxwell, Desmond Llewelyn, Bruce Glover, Putter Smith, Laurence Naismith.

After the relative failure of the deadly serious non-Connery *On Her Majesty's Secret Service*, Sean was paid a donated-to-charity cool million to reprise 007 once again in this fun, cartoonlike adventure. After allegedly disposing of nemesis Blofeld (now played by Gray) in revenge for the murder of his bride at the conclusion of *Secret Service*, Bond is off to Amsterdam and then Las Vegas, where his investigation of an international diamond smuggling ring eventually uncovers a plot by the resurrected Blofeld to control the world with a laser beam mounted on an orbiting satellite. Highlights include Wood's turn as bubbly Plenty O'Toole ("Hi, I'm Plenty!"), Glover and Smith as a pair of campy gay assassins, a *Bullitt*-inspired car chase through the streets of Vegas (check out the scene where 007 upends his car on two wheels to navigate a narrow alley and comes out of the alley on the opposite two wheels!), and the *great* Shirley Bassey theme song.

Patricia Laffan wears English Leather in Devil Girl from Mars *(1954).*

DICK TRACY

★★★ Sinister Cinema. 1937, NR, 150 min. Dirs: Ray Taylor and Alan James. Cast: Ralph Byrd, Kay Hughes, Smiley Burnette, Lee Van Atta, Francis X. Bushman, Byron Foulger.

A great serial based on the Chester Gould comic strip character. Byrd, the definitive screen Tracy, tries to stop a madman's plans to conquer the world with a destructive ray beamed from an airplane in flight. One gloriously absurd situation (and character) after another.

DICK TRACY (1945)

See: *Dick Tracy, Detective.*

DICK TRACY

★★★ Touchstone, 1990, PG, 104 min. Dir: Warren Beatty. Cast: Warren Beatty, Madonna, Al Pacino, Glenne Headley, Charlie Korsmo, Dustin Hoffman, James Caan, Mandy Patinkin, Dick Van Dyke, Charles Durning, Kathy Bates, Michael J. Pollard, Estelle Parsons, James Tolkan, Catherine O'Hara, R. G. Armstrong.

Obviously made to cash in on the mania surrounding the release of Tim Burton's *Batman,* this turned out much better than you'd expect for a Warren Beatty vanity production. Beatty is surprisingly good in the title role and Madonna adds some unexpected spice for a movie made by Disney. The plot involving Dick's befriending of kid Korsmo is unnecessary and doesn't work at all but the colorful set and costume design and Oscar-winning makeup used to bring a gallery of gruesome Tracy villains (played by an impressive array of guest stars, particularly Pacino) to life make this a blast.

DICK TRACY, DETECTIVE

★★ Sinister Cinema, 1945, NR, 62 min. Dir: William Berke. Cast: Morgan Conway, Anne Jeffreys, Mike Mazurki, Jane Greer.

Tracy battles a psychotic crook called Splitface (played by seasoned heavy Mazurki) in this slightly below-average '40s programmer. Ralph Byrd is sorely missed. Aka *Dick Tracy.*

DICK TRACY MEETS GRUESOME

★★☆ Sinister Cinema, 1947, NR, 65 min. Dir: John Rawlins. Cast: Boris Karloff, Ralph Byrd, Anne Gwynne, Lyle Latell.

This quickie RKO feature is pretty silly but has the advantage of Byrd as Tracy and Karloff as Gruesome—what more could you want? Boris is after Dr. A. Tomic's formula for a gas that can freeze people in place (perfect for robberies) and the blunt-jawed Ralph is out to

stop him. Lovely Gwynne is a pert Tess Trueheart. Aka *Dick Tracy's Amazing Adventure.*

DICK TRACY RETURNS

★★★ Nostalgia Merchant, 1938, NR, 150 min. Dirs: William Witney, John English. Cast: Ralph Byrd, Lynne Roberts, Charles Middleton, David Sharpe, Jerry Tucker, Ned Glass.

It's Tracy versus the murderous Stark gang (headed by Middleton, Ming the Merciless himself) in this hard-hitting serial. Byrd's second appearance as the consumate Dick and one of his best.

DICK TRACY'S AMAZING ADVENTURE

See: *Dick Tracy Meets Gruesome.*

DICK TRACY'S DILEMMA

★★ Goodtimes, 1947, NR, 60 min. Dir: John Rawlins. Cast: Ralph Byrd, Kay Christopher, Lyle Latell, Jack Lambert, Ian Keith.

Routine series entry has our Dick (Byrd, perfection as always) battling evil hook-handed killer Lambert. Forgettable but with fast-paced thrills; probably the weakest of the Byrd *Tracy's.*

DICK TRACY'S G-MEN

★★★ Nostalgia Merchant, 1939, NR, 150 min. Dirs: William Witney, John English. Cast: Ralph Byrd, Jennifer Jones, Irving Pichel, Ted Pearson, Walter Miller, Phyllis Isley.

The evil Zarnoff (Pichel) is the head of a spy ring being investigated by Tracy and his men. Zarnoff is captured, tried, and executed but experimental drugs restore him to life and send him on a rampage of revenge aimed at Dick. An above-average Tracy serial with a supernatural/horror twist.

DICK TRACY VS. CRIME, INC.

★★☆ Nostalgia Merchant, 1941, NR, 150 min. Dirs: William Witney, John English. Cast: Ralph Byrd, Ralph Morgan, Jan Wiley, Michael Owen, John Davidson, Robert Fraser.

Solid serial with Tracy up against the "Ghost," a masked mastermind with the power of invisibility who's behind a series of murders targeting underworld figures. Entertaining chapter play from those masters of the medium Witney and English.

DICK TRACY VS. CUEBALL

★★ Sinister Cinema, 1946, NR, 62 min. Dir: Gordon Douglas. Cast: Morgan Conway, Anne Jeffreys, Lyle Latell, Rita Corday, Dick Wessel.

Wessel is Cueball, a bald strangler pursued by Dick in this modest RKO programmer. Okay thrills, but Conway was always a poor substitution for the great Ralph Byrd.

DIGBY—THE BIGGEST DOG IN THE WORLD

★ Prism Entertainment, 1974, G, 88 min. Dir: Joseph McGrath. Cast: Jim Dale, Spike Milligan, Milo O'Shea, Angela Douglas.

Lame Brit imitation Disney movie about a sheepdog called Digby turned gigantic by some experimental growth serum called Protein X. Cheap gags and cheaper special FX.

DINOSAUR ISLAND

★★ New Line, 1993, R, 85 min. Dirs: Jim Wynorski, Fred Olen Ray. Cast: Ross Hagen, Richard Gabi, Antonia Dorian, Toni Naples, Michelle Bauer, Becky LeBeau, Steve Barkett.

Wynorski and Ray (a marriage made in exploitation movie Hell) team up for a breast-filled fantasy, a horny updating of movies like *Prehistoric Women* and *One Million Years B.C.* and mainly inspired by the '50s anticlassic *Untamed Women*. Seemingly designed for sex-starved teenage boys who don't know how to meet any real women, this features Hagen leading a bunch of military pinheads trapped on an island overrun with desirable women who drop their loinclothes like clockwork. Also present are the dinosaur prop from *Carnosaur*, a well-animated tricerotops, and some badly done puppet dinosaurs. Entertaining in its own small way, this is dirt-dumb enough not to seem as exploitive and sexist as you might think and is actually mildly enjoyable—like the comedy *Caveman* remade for the *Playboy* channel. The laser disc version contains the longer director's cut.

DINOSAUR, SECRET OF THE LOST LEGEND

See: *Baby, Secret of the Lost Legend.*

DINOSAURUS!

★★☆ Goodtimes, 1960, NR, 83 min. Dir: Irvin S. Yeaworth, Jr. Cast: Ward Ramsey, Kristina Hansen, Paul Lukather, Gregg Martell.

The creators of *The Blob* strike back with their most entertaining monster movie. Undersea construction work near an island in the Caribbean unearths a tyrannosaur, a brontosaur, and a cave man later revived by lightning. It's *Jurassic Park* without the overhead and the hype, with much of this played for comedy (especially the scenes involving cave guy Martell) and variable puppet FX by Tim Barr, Wah Chang, Marcel Delgado, and Gene Warren.

DOC SAVAGE: THE MAN OF BRONZE

★★ Warner, 1975, G, 100 min. Dir: Michael Anderson.

Cast: Ron Ely, Darrell Zwerling, Michael Miller, Pamela Hensley, Paul Wexler, Robyn Hilton, William Lucking, Paul Gleason, Eldon Quick, Michael Berryman.

Producer George Pal's last film, this big screen version of Kenneth Robeson's pulp hero has Doc (a well-cast Ely) and his followers, dubbed the Fantastic Five, battling the evil Captain Seas (Wexler). Sold as camp in the TV *Batman* style but actually a straight-faced action fantasy more in keeping with the later *Indiana Jones* movies, this has its moments, like an exciting opening chase sequence over the rooftops of Manhattan, but is too flatly constructed to make it work. And that G rating doesn't help at all.

DOCTOR DOOLITTLE

★★ Fox, 1967, NR, 144 min. Dir: Richard Fleischer. Cast: Rex Harrison, Samantha Eggar, Anthony Newley, Richard Attenborough, William Dix, Geoffrey Holder.

This titanic *Mary Poppins*-inspired musical-fantasy almost sank 20th Century-Fox without a trace when it became the biggest box office bust of the decade. Based on the famous stories by Hugh Lofting, this *does* have a well-cast Harrison as Doolittle, one great song ("Talk to the Animals"), and some impressive FX (both the song and special FX won Oscars) but it's too long for its slight storyline (something to do with the doc about to be committed for his insistence that he can speak with our four-legged friends) and has the crippling disadvantage of having the obnoxious Newley in the cast. Originally 152 minutes but cut after the premiere, this is being remade as an Eddie Murphy vehicle—*Beverly Hills Veterinarian?*

DOCTOR MORDRID

★★☆ Paramount, 1992, R, 89 min. Dirs: Albert and Charles Band. Cast: Jeffrey Combs, Yvette Niper, Brian Thompson, Jay Acovone.

Combs is good in this tailor-made vehicle combining elements of sci-fi, horror, and fantasy. Niper is a New York policewoman who discovers that her mysterious landlord (Combs) is actually a sorcerer charged with saving the world from evil magician Thompson. The climactic battle between a pair of animated dinosaur skeletons is a highlight.

DOIN' TIME ON PLANET EARTH

★★☆ Warner, 1988, PG, 83 min. Dir: Charles Matthau. Cast: Nicholas Strouse, Andrea Thompson, Hugh Gillin, Adam West, Candice Azzara, Hugh O'Brian, Roddy McDowall, Maureen Stapleton.

Walter Matthau's son directed this pleasant-enough comedy about an alienated teen (Strouse) convinced by his oddball dad and mom (a cast-to-perfection West and Azzara) that he's *literally* an alien from space, sent to lead a chosen number of humans to the stars. Not entirely successful but never less than interesting, with a nicely eclectic cast.

DOLLMAN

★★☆ Paramount, 1991, R, 86 min. Dir: Albert Pyun. Cast: Tim Thomerson, Jackie Earle Haley, Kamala Lopez, Humberto Ortiz, Nicholas Guest, Judd Omen.

Weirdly imaginative, tongue-in-cheek filler from producer Charles Band with Thomerson as a diminutive alien private eye after an evil flying head (no kiddin'!) hiding out in the barrio of an unnamed city on Earth. Thomerson has the right stuff as our tough little hero but inadequate production values and uneven FX occasionally hold him down.

DOLLMAN VS. DEMONIC TOYS

☆ Paramount, 1993, R, 64 min. Dir: Charles Band. Cast: Tim Thomerson, Tracy Scoggins, Melissa Behr, Phil Fondacaro.

Maybe the most needless sequel in the history of sequels, this catch-penny followup to *Dollman, Demonic Toys,* and *Bad Channels* plunges to new depths of desperation as our small-in-stature-but-big-in-nerve (and mouth) hero (the ever wry Thomerson) battles evil playthings to save Behr, shrunken by the nasty alien from *Channels.* The foul-mouthed, sexually abusive baby doll character was evidently meant to be funny (aka *Child's Play's* Chucky), but instead appears gross and disturbing.

DONOVAN'S BRAIN

★★★ MGM/UA, 1953, NR, 83 min. Dir: Felix Feist. Cast: Lew Ayres, Nancy Davis, Gene Evans, Steve Brodie, Lisa K. Howard, Tom Power.

Starkly faithful adaptation of the Curt Siodmak novel about a doctor (Ayres) illegally experimenting on the brain of a dead millionaire and who ends up becoming a pawn in the murdered man's revenge from beyond the grave against his crooked family and business associates. Well directed, and well acted by Ayres, Davis (aka former First Lady Nancy Reagan), and Evans. Previously filmed as *The Lady and the Monster* and remade as *The Brain.*

DOOMSDAY MACHINE, THE

★ Sinister Cinema, 1967, PG, 80 min. Dirs: Lee Sholem, Harry Hope. Cast: Denny Miller, Mala Powers, Bobby Van, Ruta Lee, Grant Williams, Henry Wilcoxon.

Unreleased until 1972, this supercheap talkfest involves a group of scientists on a space mission who escape the destruction of Earth (a toy globe is set on fire) and then spend the rest of the movie arguing about what they're going to do now. The cast of veterans includes *Incredible Shrinking Man* Williams cast against type as a lecherous creep.

DOOMWATCH

★★★ Embassy, 1972, PG, 92 min. Dir: Peter Sasdy. Cast: Ian Bannen, Judy Geeson, George Sanders, Geoffrey Keen.

Based on a British TV series, this taut ecological sci-fi/horror film involves scientist Bannen's investigation of an outbreak of the disfiguring disease acromegaly on a tiny island. With the help of school teacher Geeson he discovers that toxic dumping in the near by waters has contaminated the fish the locals catch. Well done on a budget, with good acting and makeup.

DOUBLE DRAGON

★★ MCA/Universal, 1994, PG-13, 96 min. Dir: James Yukich. Cast: Mark Dacascos, Scott Wolf, Alyssa Milano, Robert Patrick, Julia Nickson, Kristina Malandro Wagner, Leon Russom, John Mallory Asher, Al Leong, Vanna White, George Hamilton, Gilbert Gottfried.

Veteran rock video helmer Yukich directd this nonhit big screen expansion of the popular video game series. Dacascos and Wolf (the latter from the TV series *Party of Five*) are the cute young brothers who battle villain Koga Shuko (Patrick), who is out to complete the powerful tailsman of the double dragon—he has half of it and the boys the other. Set in a postapocalyptic Hollywood, this is well cast and designed but lacks a decent story and involving characters.

DOWN TO EARTH

★★☆ Columbia/TriStar, 1947, NR, 101 min. Dir: Alexander Hall. Cast: Rita Hayworth, Larry Parks, Marc Platt, Roland Culver, James Gleason, Edward Everett Horton, George Macready, Adele Jergens.

A semisequel to *Here Comes Mr. Jordan* with songs, this musical fantasy stars Hayworth as the goddess Terpsichore, who comes to Earth to help playwright Parks put on a show. Meanwhile, Gleason and Horton recreate their roles from *Mr. Jordan* and Culver has the old Claude Rains role. Hayworth's beauty and the lush Technicolor are the main attractions. Remade as *Xanadu.*

DRAGONHEART

★★☆ MCA/Universal, 1996, PG-13, 103 min. Dir: Rob Cohen. Cast: Dennis Quaid, Dina Meyer, David Thewlis, Pete Postlewaite, Julie Christie, voice of Sean Connery.

Quaid is good as a disillusioned Arthurian knight who's pressed into service to destroy a talking dragon (voiced by Connery) he ends up befriending instead. Politically corrected updating of *Dragonslayer* with smooth but cartoony ILM FX, this often flimsy fantasy is held together by the performances of Quaid and Connery (who makes Draco the Dragon a lot less cute and cuddly and a lot more likable than say, Robin Williams, would) and good atmosphere.

DRAGONSLAYER

★★★ Paramount, 1981, PG, 108 min. Dir: Matthew Robbins. Cast: Peter MacNicol, Caitlin Clarke, Ralph Richardson, John Hallam, Peter Eyre, Albert Salmi.

Sorcerer's apprentice MacNicol takes over for his murdered master Richardson when the magician is asked to dispose of a princess-devouring dragon that's been terrorizing the countryside. An effective medieval fantasy with great ILM dragon FX and some surprisingly grim and frightening moments (not to mention some gore and brief male nudity) for a PG-rated movie cofinanced by Disney.

DRAGONWORLD

★★★ Paramount, 1994, PG, 84 min. Dir: Ted Nicolaoi. Cast: Sam Mackenzie, Brittney Powell, John Calvin, Lila Kaye, John Woodvine, Andrew Keir.

Young American Mackenzie befriends a baby dragon living near the Scottish castle he's inherited and years later begins to regret the way the now fully grown creature is being exploited as a cheap tourist attraction. An entertaining direct-to-video semi-remake of *Mighty Joe Young* with decent FX and a likable cast.

DR. ALIEN

★★ Paramount, 1988, R, 87 min. Dir: David DeCoteau. Cast: Judy Landers, Billy Jacoby, Olivia Barash, Linnea Quigley, Troy Donahue, Ginger Lynn Allen, Edy Williams, Arlene Golonka, Stuart Fratkin, Raymond O'Connor.

A great schlock cast highlights this soft-core foolishness. Landers, as an alien in the guise of a sexy college professor (the sort of college professor that exists only in movies like this), transforms adoring geek student Jacoby into the superstud of her dreams. Nothing special but with a roster of stars like these there's certainly entertainment—not to mention bare breasts—to spare.

DR. CYCLOPS

★★☆ MCA/Universal, 1940, NR, 75 min. Dir: Ernest B. Schoedsack. Cast: Albert Dekker, Janice Logan, Thomas Coley, Victor Killiam, Charles Halton, Frank Yaconelli.

Decent special FX and gorgeous color photography (rare for a sci-fi/horror film of this period) distinguish this otherwise routine mad doctor movie. Dekker is the title doc, a myopic scientist who's perfected a shrinking machine he uses on visitors to his South American jungle laboratory. Okay thriller from the codirector of the original *King Kong*.

DREAM A LITTLE DREAM

★☆ Vestron, 1989, PG-13, 99 min. Dir: Marc Rocco. Cast: Corey Feldman, Corey Haim, Meredith Salenger, Jason Robards, Piper Laurie, Harry Dean Stanton, William McNamara, Susan Blakely, Victoria Jackson, Alex Rocco.

Probably the weakest of the "body switch" movies churned out like sausages after the success of *Big*, this stars Feldman and Salenger as teens imbued with the spirits of elderly neighbors Robards and Laurie. Once possessed, the kids learn the true meaning of life, or something. Robards and Laurie are fine but the kids are as annoying as ever and director Rocco (son of familiar character actor Alex Rocco, who also appears) is another of those filmmakers who mistakenly believes that flooding the soundtrack with golden oldies results in an atmosphere of instant nostalgia.

DREAM A LITTLE DREAM 2

★ Columbia/TriStar, 1994, PG-13, 90 min. Dir: James Lemmo. Cast: Corey Haim, Corey Feldman, Robyn Lively, Stacie Randall, Michael Nicolosi.

The sequel-nobody-asked-for list gets topped again by this needless fantasy about a pair of magical sunglasses, a beautiful spy, and still more psychic shenanigans. Only for the most desperate fans of the Corey & Corey show.

DREAMCHILD

★★★ Warner, 1985, PG, 94 min. Dir: Gavin Millar. Cast: Coral Browne, Ian Holm, Peter Gallagher, Caris Corfman, Nicola Cowper, Jane Asher.

Browne (Vincent Price's last wife) gives a bravura performance as an aged child psychologist who comes to a literary convention to celebrate the centennial of Lewis Carroll, author of *Alice in Wonderland*, only to be assaulted by repressed memories and fantasies involving Carroll's fictional creations. Complex and not always successful, this look at the dark side of childhood and children's fiction suffers from unconvincing period atmosphere (it's set in the 1930s) but has good and often quite creepy creature FX by Jim Henson's Creature Shop.

Albert Dekker is the myopic madman in Dr. Cyclops *(1940).*

DREAMSCAPE
★★★ HBO, 1984, PG-13, 95 min. Dir: Joseph Ruben. Cast: Dennis Quaid, Kate Capshaw, Eddie Albert, Christopher Plummer, Max von Sydow, David Patrick Kelly.

Ruben (*The Stepfather* and *The Good Son*) directed this suspenseful sci-fi/horror thriller about a devil-may-care psychic (Quaid) pressed into service by the U.S. government in order to save the president (a well-cast Albert) from assassination in his dreams. Imaginative low-budgeter with an excellent cast and impressive small-scale FX.

DR. GOLDFOOT AND THE BIKINI MACHINE
★★☆ Orion, 1965, NR, 90 min. Dir: Norman Taurog. Cast: Vincent Price, Frankie Avalon, Dwayne Hickman, Susan Hart, Fred Clark, Jack Mullaney, Milton Frome, Deborah Walley, Harvey Lembeck, Annette Funicello.

AIP's answer to TV's *Get Smart!* this silly but watchable comedy has Price as the title medico, an effete madman out to control the world's wealthiest men by marrying them off to his squadron of curvaceous robots. Hart is the android hooked up with rich nitwit Hickman and Avalon is the secret agent out to foil Goldfoot's scheme. Originally a musical, all the songs (apart from the title tune) were cut out before release (!), leaving a dumb but fun Bond spoof. With a *Pit and the Pendulum* in-joke and lots of Beach Party guest stars.

DR. GOLDFOOT AND THE GIRL BOMBS
★★ Orion, 1966, NR, 80 min. Dir: Mario Bava. Cast: Vincent Price, Fabian, Laura Antonelli, Franco Franchi, Ciccio Ingrassia, Moana Tahi.

It's got a good director, an interesting (to state the obvious) cast, and some funny bits, but this *Dr. Goldfoot* sequel is still pretty lame. This time the doc has constructed nuclear devices in the shape of beautiful women—women programmed to go off while having sex with various world officials. In Italy, where this was made, this was actually sold as a vehicle for comedians Franchi and Ingrassia, a comedy team almost as funny as Allen and Rossi—well, almost. Price can make anything worth seeing but here he's really got his work cut out for him. Look for Bava's cameo as an angel.

DR. M

See: *Club Extinction.*

DR. MABUSE VS. SCOTLAND YARD

★★☆ Sinister Cinema, 1963, NR, 90 min. Dir: Peter May. Cast: Peter Van Eyck, Wolfgang Preiss, Sabine Bethmann, Klaus Kinski, Walter Rilla, Dieter Borsche.

Good entry in the *Dr. Mabuse* series, with the doctor's spirit possessing the body of a psychiatrist and forcing him to continue Mabuse's wave of crime. Atmospheric direction and a solid cast in this West German thriller with sci-fi and horror overtones.

DR. NO

★★★ MGM/UA, 1962, NR, 111 min. Dir: Terence Young. Cast: Sean Connery, Ursula Andress, Joseph Wiseman, Jack Lord, Anthony Dawson, Zena Marshall, Bernard Lee, Lois Maxwell.

The first big-screen James Bond adventure is one of the simplest and best. Connery is lean and mean in his first go-round as 007, and the statuesque Andress sets the standard for all the Bond women to come. Wiseman is the title character, a Fu Manchu-like villain disrupting U.S. rocket launches from his island hideout in Jamaica, and *Hawaii Five-O*'s Lord is Felix Leiter. Shot for under a million dollars and emerging as one of the top box office hits of the year, this is virtually gadget-free (though it does have a mechanical dragon), and lacks a theme song.

DR. STRANGELOVE, OR HOW I LEARNED TO STOP WORRYING AND LOVE THE BOMB

★★★★ Columbia/TriStar, 1964, NR, 93 min. Dir: Stanley Kubrick. Cast: Peter Sellers, George C. Scott, Sterling Hayden, Slim Pickens, Keenan Wynn, Peter Bull, James Earl Jones, Tracey Reed.

Perfect black comedy with Sellers in a triple role as the U.S. president, a British army officer, and the title doc—the inventor of a powerful bomb dropped on the Russians by a renegade U.S. Army general. Hilarious stuff that's hardly dated a bit, even in these post-Cold War times, with a magnificent cast, trenchant dialogue, and a shocking ending. Sellers's phone call to the Kremlin is a classic movie moment.

DR. WHO AND THE DALEKS

★★☆ Republic, 1965, NR, 85 min. Dir: Gordon Flemyng. Cast: Peter Cushing, Roy Castle, Jennie Linden, Roberta Tovey, Barrie Ingham, Geoffrey Toone.

The first of a pair of theatrical spin-off quickies produced by Britain's Amicus Productions (best known for anthology horror movies like *Tales from the Crypt* and *Asylum*), starring Cushing as the beloved Time Lord. The doctor, his two granddaughters, and the elder girl's boyfriend are transported by the Tardis to a distant planet inhabited by a gentle race lorded over by the Daleks, aliens who travel about in rolling mechanical bodies like miniature tanks. Inexpensive but fun; originally released in the U.S. as the support feature for the original *Night of the Living Dead.*

DROP DEAD FRED

★☆ IVE, 1991, PG-13, 98 min. Dir: Ate De Jong. Cast: Phoebe Cates, Ric Mayall, Marsha Mason, Carrie Fisher, Tim Matheson, Bridget Fonda, Keith Charles, Ron Eldard.

Cates is very good as an unhappy divorcee living back home with mom Mason who suddenly finds herself visited by her imaginary childhood friend Drop Dead Fred (Mayall of *The Young Ones* TV series). This crude comic fantasy has a (surprising) following but really isn't very clever or funny and is worth watching only for a chance to see Phoebe in top form, but even she can't make a silk purse out of this sow's ear of a movie.

DUEL OF THE SPACE MONSTERS

See: *Frankenstein Meets the Space Monster.*

DUNE

★★ MCA/Universal, 1984, PG-13, 140 min. Dir: David Lynch. Cast: Kyle MacLachlan, Sean Young, Sting, Dean Stockwell, Max von Sydow, Virginia Madsen, Patrick Stewart, Brad Dourif, Francesca Annis, Jose Ferrer, Jurgen Prochnow, Linda Hunt, Kenneth McMillan, Freddie Jones, Richard Jordan, Silvano Mangano.

I have to admit that I've never really been a fan of Frank Herbert's mammoth novel, a '60s collegiate favorite; consequently I really don't think too much of the film version either. In the year 10,991 everyone is after water, drugs, and ultimate power on the desert planet Dune. There's a great cast, impressive special FX and photography, and every now and again things threaten to become interesting, but confusing narration (used to help pave over some glaring story holes) and general overlength help make this Lynch's most disappointing movie. The TV version (often shown on the Sci-Fi Channel) is expanded with outtakes and unused footage and actually plays better, but it was cobbled together without the director's participation and is credited to "Allen Smithee." If things can be worked out, perhaps this version will be released to video at some point as well.

DUNGEONMASTER, THE

★★ Vestron, 1985, PG-13, 74 min. Dirs: Rose Marie Turko, John Carl Buechler, Charles Band, David Allen, Steve Ford, Peter Manoogian, Ted Nicolaou. Cast: Jeffrey Byron, Leslie Wing, Richard Moll, Danny Dick.

There were more directors than cast members involved in the making of this sword-and-sorcery quickie about an evil wizard (Moll, chewing the scenery like licorice) who kidnaps a maiden (Wing), forcing her lover (Byron) to overcome seven challenges to rescue her. With more ups and downs than a seesaw, this has a couple of good segments (the ones directed by Allen and Buechler stand out) and modest FX but Byron's acting makes Steven Seagal look like John Malkovich.

DUPLICATES

★★ Paramount, 1992, PG-13, 91 min. Dir: Sandor Stern. Cast: Gregory Harrison, Kim Greist, Cicely Tyson, Kevin McCarthy, Lane Smith, William Lucking.

Medium telemovie with Harrison and Greist searching for their missing son and eventually discovering him in a mysterious clinic in upstate New York where he has become a guinea pig in the cloning experiments of scientist McCarthy. There are echoes of *Invasion of the Body Snatchers, Coma,* and others, a decent cast, and a fair amount of suspense until the contrivances start to show.

EARTH GIRLS ARE EASY

★★★ Avid Entertainment, 1989, PG, 100 min. Dir: Julien Temple. Cast: Geena Davis, Jeff Goldblum, Jim Carrey, Damon Wayans, Julie Brown, Michael McKean, Charles Rocket, Larry Linville.

California beautician Davis breaks up with jerk-of-a-boyfriend Rocket but doesn't have time to sing the blues when a teamful of friendly aliens land in her swimming pool and she and friend Brown decide to transform them into Valley dudes. What could have been another sci-fi comedy misfire (à la *My Stepmother Is an Alien* or *Spaceballs*) instead emerges as a genuinely infectious delight, with Davis in her signature role and a great supporting cast, including Brown singing her anthem "'Cause I'm a Blonde."

EARTHQUAKE

★★☆ MCA/Universal, 1974, PG, 121 min. Dir: Mark Robson. Cast: Charlton Heston, Ava Gardner, George Kennedy, Genevieve Bujold, Lorne Greene, Richard Roundtree, Marjoe Gortner, Victoria Principal, Barry Sullivan, Lloyd Nolan, Walter Matthau, Monica Lewis, John Randolph, Gabriel Dell.

Los Angeles is rocked by the big one in this elaborate but goofy disaster movie. Heston is the architect trying to save both bitchy wife Gardner and dishy girlfriend Bujold as L.A. crumbles in Sensurround. Kennedy is the tough cop trying to hold things together, Gortner is a nutso national guardsman, Roundtree is an Evel Knievel-like daredevil, and Principal wears a 'fro that would make Pam Grier proud. The Oscar-winning special FX hold up well but this plays better as a comedy than a serious drama, with hilariously overwrought acting and lots of bad '70s fashions. One thing though—not all the characters you expect to survive do, something that would never happen were this remade today.

EARTH VS. THE FLYING SAUCERS

★★☆ Columbia/Tristar, 1956, NR, 82 min. Dir: Fred F. Sears. Cast: Hugh Marlowe, Joan Taylor, Donald Curtis, Morris Ankrum, Thomas B. Henry.

After a frankly dull and talky first half this Ray Harryhausen vehicle really comes to life as withered aliens in robotlike protective suits lay waste to the world capitals, with Washington, D.C., taking a particularly spectacular beating. Harryhausen's simply amazing low-budget FX work features smoothly animated flying saucers and miraculously detailed miniatures of the capital building, the Washington monument, and other attractions being blasted to smithereens. One of the obvious inspirations behind the megahit *Independence Day.*

EARTH VS. THE SPIDER

★★ RCA/Columbia, 1958, NR, 72 min. Dir: Bert I. Gordon. Cast: Ed Kemmer, June Kenney, Gene Perrson, Sally Fraser.

Thirtysomething high school kids are menaced by an industrial-sized spider in this catch-penny Gordon version of *Tarantula.* The special FX aren't bad for Bert but this peaks during the spider's rampage through town and that only occurs halfway through the movie, leaving the last half hour feeling pretty anticlimactic. Aka *The Spider.*

EBIRAH, HORROR OF THE DEEP
See: *Godzilla vs. the Sea Monsters.*

EDWARD SCISSORHANDS
★★★ Fox, 1990, PG, 98 min. Dir: Tim Burton. Cast: Johnny Depp, Winona Ryder, Dianne Weist, Anthony Michael Hall, Alan Arkin, Vincent Price, Kathy Baker, Conchata Ferrell.

Haunting fantasy with horror and fairy-tale overtones about an artificial human being (Depp in his best performance) with huge scissors for hands who's taken in by a friendly Avon lady (the ebullient Weist) when his father-creator (Price in his last big-screen role) dies. Edward's ability to cut hair and sculpt fantastic forms from garden hedges make him a popular neighborhood attraction but his shears get in the way of his budding relationship with Weist's daughter (Ryder)—and just how *does* he go to the bathroom? Weird but touching relationship movie from *Batman* auteur Burton.

18 AGAIN!
★★ Starmaker, 1988, PG, 100 min. Dir: Paul Flaherty. Cast: George Burns, Charlie Schlatter, Tony Roberts, Anita Morris, Red Buttons, Jennifer Runyon.

An eighty-one-year-old millionaire (the actually ninety-two-year-old Burns) makes a birthday wish to be eighteen years old; a head injury grants the wish as his personality takes over college boy grandson Schlatter. Yet another tired body-switch comedy gets a slight lift from Schlatter's uncanny impression of all the trademark Burns mannerisms and the invigorating presence of ol' George himself, though he really isn't in this very much.

ELECTRIC DREAMS
★★ MGM/UA, 1984, PG, 96 min. Dir: Steve Barron. Cast: Lenny Von Dohlen, Virginia Madsen, Maxell Caulfield, voice of Bud Cort.

Nerdy Von Dohlen gets romantic advice from his computer on how to win gorgeous neighbor Madsen away from good-looking dullard Caulfield. Problems arise when the computer (voiced by Cort) develops feelings for the lady himself. Routine fantasy-comedy that never really expands on its premise. Lots of Culture Club tunes on the track including the pretty ballad "Love is Love." Almost like a polite version of *Demon Seed.*

ELECTRONIC MONSTER, THE
★★ Sinister Cinema, 1957, NR, 72 min. Dir: Montgomery Tully. Cast: Rod Cameron, Mary Murphy, Meredith Edwards, Peter Illing, Carl Jaffe.

Dull British programmer about mind control

experiments in a private clinic. Cameron is a detective investigating the death of a woman who may have been driven to it by her nightmares. Some imaginatively directed sequences bolster a tired plot. Aka *Escapement.*

ELIMINATORS
★★ CBS/Fox, 1986, PG, 96 min. Dir: Peter Manoogian. Cast: Patrick Reynolds, Denise Crosby, Andrew Prine, Conan Lee, Roy Dotrice.

A pre-*Next Generation* Crosby is a scientist who teams up with adventurer Reynolds, cyborg Prine, and ninja Lee to stop bad guy industrialist (is there any other kind of industrialist in the movies?) Dotrice from taking over the world. Low-grade *Raiders* clone hurt by Reynolds's awful acting but helped by Prine's self-deprecating turn as the cyborg.

EMBRYO
★★ Starmaker, 1976, R, 104 min. Dir: Ralph Nelson. Cast: Rock Hudson, Barbara Carrera, Diane Ladd, Roddy McDowall, Anne Schedeen, John Elrich, Jack Colvin, Dr. Joyce Brothers.

Nelson, who drove the movie *Charly*, directs this almost fascinatingly awful sci-fi/horror romp. Hudson is a researcher who grows the stolen fetus of a pregnant suicide victim in his laboratory. In record time the baby grows into the beautiful Carrera, a seductive superbrain with the bad habit of aging rapidly unless she can shoot up with fluid taken from a living human embryo. Funny and sickening in about equal proportions, with amusing cameos by McDowall and Dr. Brothers and an ending that's almost jaw-droppingly gross for an A-level Hollywood movie.

EMPIRE OF THE ANTS
★★ Embassy, 1977, PG, 89 min. Dir: Bert I. Gordon. Cast: Joan Collins, Robert Lansing, John David Carson, Jacqueline Scott, Pamela Shoop, Albert Salmi, Robert Pine, Brooke Palance.

Them! meets *Smokey and the Bandit* as Joanie lures a boatload of suckers to a phony real estate development in the Florida swamplands where everybody is set upon by gigantic, mutated ants. Collins remembers this as maybe the most difficult film she ever worked on—was it all that sloging through leech-infested swamps or that tacky K-Mart wardrobe?—but it's certainly fun to watch as she and her costars try to keep straight faces while battling puppet ants as they're smeared with stage blood or tackling a plot (allegedly based on H. G. Wells) that has the ants controlling an entire town through hypnosis.

EMPIRE STRIKES BACK, THE

★★★☆ Fox, 1980, PG, 124 min. Dir: Irvin Kershner. Cast: Mark Hamill, Harrison Ford, Carrie Fisher, Billy Dee Williams, Anthony Daniels, David Prowse, Peter Mayhew, Kenny Baker, Alec Guinness, Clive Revill, voices of James Earl Jones and Frank Oz.

The second and best film in the *Star Wars* trilogy finds Luke Skywalker (Hamill) being trained in the ways of the Jedi Knight by diminutive wizard Yoda (voiced by Oz) while Han Solo (Ford) and Princess Leia (Fisher) form an alliance with smuggler Lando Calrissian (Williams, cast in a token attempt to bring color to the *Star Wars* universe) to stop the empire and Darth Vader (played by Prowse but voiced by Jones). Darker and more mature than the first *Wars,* this develops the characters and plays down cuteness in favor of twisted relationships and startling revelations. The (naturally) great FX won an Oscar.

ENCHANTED COTTAGE, THE

★★★ Turner, 1945, NR, 91 min. Dir: John Cromwell. Cast: Dorothy McGuire, Robert Young, Herbert Marshall, Mildred Natwick, Spring Byington, Hillary Brooke.

Gentle fantasy with plain McGuire and disfigured war veteran Young finding love in a New England cottage where they magically are made beautiful—or maybe it's just the power of their love blinding their eyes. Delicate, understated adaptation of a play by Arthur Pinero, with McGuire and Young in good form and the sultry Brooke impressive as Bob's two-faced fiancée.

ENCINO MAN

★★ Hollywood Pictures, 1992, PG, 89 min. Dir: Les Mayfield. Cast: Sean Astin, Pauly Shore, Brendan Fraser, Megan Ward, Robin Tunney, Rick Ducommun, Mariette Hartley, Richard Masur.

California teens Astin and Shore discover a frozen Cro-Magnon man (Fraser) buried in Sean's backyard and after giving him a makeover try to pass him off as the new kid in school. This awkward vehicle for annoying MTV dude Shore is (I guess) a comic take-off on *Iceman* but I kept hoping it would turn into a remake of *Return of the Apeman,* with Fraser finally strangling his jerky costar. Despite its many faults, Fraser shines in the title role.

ENCOUNTER AT RAVEN'S GATE

★★☆ Hemdale, 1988, R, 85 min. Dir: Rolf Deheer. Cast: Ritchie Singer, Steven Vidler, Vincent Gil, Saturday Rosenberg.

Are all the weird goings-on in the tiny Australian town of Raven's Gate the result of

an alien invasion? A slow but well-made Aussie sci-fi thriller with some suspense and action but the concentration is mostly on mood and character.

ENCOUNTER WITH THE UNKNOWN

★★☆ United Entertainment, 1973, PG, 87 min. Dir: Harry Thomason. Cast: Rosie Holotik, Gene Ross, Gary Brockette, voice of Rod Serling.

Cheapo Texas-made anthology mixing up stories of sci-fi and the supernatural involving a curse, a female ghost, and a flying saucer. Made a few bucks at the drive-in when Serling was called in to add the *Twilight Zone*-ish narration but it's still an awkward waste of time.

ENDGAME

★★ Media, 1983, R, 96 min. Dir: Steven Benson. Cast: Al Cliver, Moira Chen [Laura Gemser], George Eastman, Gordon Mitchell.

It's postapocalyptic time again as Clive (a frequent actor in the gore films of Lucio Fulci) becomes a warrior in a series of life-or-death gladitorial bouts. This Italian film is strikingly similar to the later *Mad Max: Beyond Thunderdome* and is enjoyable in its own minor way, with bad guys dressed like Nazis, mind-reading mutants, and all the usual end-of-the-world accoutrements.

ENDLESS DESCENT

★☆ LIVE, 1989, R, 79 min. Dir: Juan Piquer Simon. Cast: Jack Scalia, Deborah Adair, Ray Wise, R. Lee Ermey, Ely Pouget, Edmond Purdom.

An experimental submarine disappears into a newly formed canyon in the ocean floor and is followed by a rescue mission commanded by hunky Scalia, who encounters a shoal of mutant sea monsters. Well cast for a cheapie (Adair as Scalia's ex-wife, Ermey as his usual military hard-ass) but sunk by flat direction and unimpressive FX. Aka *The Rift.*

END OF THE WORLD

★☆ Media, 1977, PG, 86 min. Dir: John Hayes. Cast: Christopher Lee, Sue Lyon, Kirk Scott, Lew Ayres, Macdonald Carey, Dean Jagger.

Aliens who are out to destroy the earth disguise themselves as a priest (Lee) and a conventful of nuns in order to carry out their dastardly plan. How so many well-known actors (even Kirk Scott!) were snookered into appearing in this no-budget wonder remains a true mystery, with our stars at odds throughout with bad writing, dull direction, and chintzy special FX.

ENEMY FROM SPACE
★★★ Corinth, 1957, NR, 84 min. Dir: Val Guest. Cast: Brian Donlevy, Sidney James, Bryan Forbes, Vera Day, William Franklyn, Michael Ripper, John Longden, John Van Eyssen.

Originally titled *Quatermass II* (surely the first instance of a sequel outfitted with Roman numerals in the title), this followup to *The Quatermass Xperiment* is better, with professor Quatermass (the ever-stern Donlevy) discovering that a secret government project actually masks an alien invasion. Eerily atmospheric and well scripted by director Guest and Nigel Kneale from Kneale's British TV play, this has echoes of *Invasion of the Body Snatchers,* a solid supporting cast (including future director Forbes), and some genuine chills. Aka *Quatermass II: Enemy from Space.*

ENEMY MINE
★★★ CBS/Fox, 1985, PG-13, 108 min. Dir: Wolfgang Peterson. Cast: Dennis Quaid, Louis Gossett, Jr., Brion James, Richard Marcus, Carolyn McCormick.

An outer space remake of *Hell in the Pacific* with human Quaid and alien Gossett (the latter—in excellent Chris Walas makeup—in one of his warmest roles) stranded on a desolate planet where the mortal enemies must work together to survive. Predictable but entertaining, with outstanding production design. Best scene: Dennis's reaction when he learns that Lou is pregnant!

ERIK THE VIKING
★☆ Orion, 1989, PG-13, 104 min. Dir: Terry Jones. Cast: Tim Robbins, Mickey Rooney, Eartha Kitt, Terry Jones, Imogen Stubbs, John Cleese, Antony Sher, Freddie Jones.

Flatly put together fantasy from several Monty Python regulars. Robbins, in the title role, travels to the ends of the earth and the pits of hell to discover the meaning of life. Well cast but almost hurtfully unfunny.

ESCAPE FROM L.A.
★★☆ Paramount, 1996, R, 115 min. Dir: John

"Look, can't we just get along?" Lou Gossett and Dennis Quaid in Enemy Mine *(1985).*

"No, I am not Captain Ron!" Kurt Russell in Escape from New York *(1981).*

Carpenter. Cast: Kurt Russell, Cliff Robertston, Stacy Keach, Valeria Golina, Bruce Campbell, Pam Grier, Steve Buscemi, George Corraface.

This may be the longest-in-development sequel since *Psycho II* and Carpenter takes no chances by simply remaking his original *Escape from New York* in a slightly different setting on a somewhat bigger budget. Russell is back as Snake Plissken, who this time is sent into the ruins of Los Angeles (turned into an isolated island by a devastating earthquake) to rescue the president's daughter. Among those he encounters are a heavily made-up Campbell as the "plastic surgeon general of Beverly Hills," the formidable Grier as a tough she-male, and the deranged Buscemi as a peddler of maps to the star's homes. Certainly watchable and Kurt is in trim, fightin' form, but a palpable atmosphere of déjà vu hangs over the film, making it seem almost as needless as Carpenter's *Village of the Damned* remake.

ESCAPE FROM NEW YORK
★★★ Nelson, 1981, R, 99 min. Dir: John Carpenter. Cast: Kurt Russell, Donald Pleasence, Adrienne Barbeau, Ernest Borgnine, Lee Van Cleef, Harry Dean Stanton, Isaac Hayes, Season Hubley, Tom Atkins, Charles Cyphers.

Carpenter followed up his horror hits *Halloween* and *The Fog* with this darkly humorous cult classic. Russell (doing Clint Eastwood better than Clint himself has in years) is great as eye-patched antihero Snake Plissken ("Snake Plissken? I thought you were dead!" everyone seems to say when they meet him), who is sent into the walled-off ruins of Manhattan (in the future, a high-security prison) to save U.S. president Pleasence when Air Force One crashes. Great casting and tense direction make this ahead-of-its-time thriller a genuine sleeper in the Carpenter oeuvre. Followed—after a 16-year delay—by *Escape from L.A.*

ESCAPE FROM THE BRONX

★ Media, 1985, R, 89 min. Dir: Enzo G. Castellari. Cast: Henry Silva, Verie d'Obici, Mark Gregory, Timothy Brent, Paolo Malco.

I can't imagine anybody wanting one, but they made this sequel to *1990: The Bronx Warriors* anyway and boy, is it bad. Silva brings what campy intensity he can to his role as the villain out to stop all the futuristic gang violence in Italy's favorite New York borough by killing everyone off. Too bad he didn't include the filmmakers on his hit list. For postapocalypse completists only.

ESCAPE FROM THE PLANET OF THE APES

★★★☆ Fox, 1971, PG, 98 min. Dir: Don Taylor. Cast: Roddy McDowall, Kim Hunter, Bradford Dillman, Natalie Trundy, Eric Braeden, Ricardo Montalban, Sal Mineo, William Windom, Albert Salmi, Jason Evers.

This ingenious sequel to *Beneath the Planet of the Apes* begins with ape scientist McDowall, Hunter, and Mineo rocketing into the past in Charlton Heston's salvaged spaceship in order to escape earth's destruction. Splashing down into the 1970s, our heroes are at first imprisoned in the Los Angeles zoo (where Sal is accidentally killed by an amorous gorilla) but Roddy and Kim eventually become popular celebrities—until scientific advisor to the president Braeden discovers that Kim is pregnant and that her son will grow into the ape leader who will bring about the fall of mankind. This moves from comedy to action to tragedy without ever missing a beat, and—though obviously shot on a restrictive budget—remains the cleverest, best-written, and best-cast sequel in the *Apes* series.

ESCAPEMENT

See: *The Electronic Monster.*

ESCAPES

★☆ Prism Entertainment, 1986, PG, 70 min. Dir: David Steensman. Cast: Vincent Price, John Mitchum, Shirley O'Kay, Todd Fulton.

Awful anthology of fantasy tales running the gamut from E.C. Comics-type horror to old lady O'Kay's encounter with a UFO. Price appears in the linking segment as a postman—surely one of the most demeaning roles in his long and colorful career.

ESCAPE TO WITCH MOUNTAIN

★★★ Disney, 1975, PG, 97 min. Dir: John Hough. Cast: Eddie Albert, Ray Milland, Donald Pleasence, Kim Richards, Ike Eisenmann, Denver Pyle.

Crabby millionaire Milland wants control of psychic preteens Richards and Eisenmann. Ray puts toady Pleasence on their tail and the kids take up with crusty but lovable Albert—who discovers that Kim and Ike are actually aliens. Entertaining thriller for kids with elements of sci-fi, mystery, and horror that was popular enough to inspire a sequel: *Return from Witch Mountain.*

ESCAPE 2000

★★ Nelson, 1981, R, 92 min. Dir: Brian Trenchard-Smith. Cast: Steve Railsback, Olivia Hussey, Michael Craig, Carmen Duncan.

This futuristic variation on *The Most Dangerous Game* stars Craig as the warden of a prison where inmates (like Railsback and Hussey) are given a chance at freedom if they survive the "Turkey Shoot," where prisoners are hunted like animals. I've been in love with Hussey ever since *Romeo and Juliet,* but even she can't help this violent and inept thriller, Olivia, Steve, and the most head explosions since *Scanners* give this Australian flick its only life. Aka *Turkey Shoot.*

E.T. THE EXTRA-TERRESTRIAL

★★★★ MCA/Universal, 1982, PG, 115 min. Dir: Steven Spielberg. Cast: Henry Thomas, Dee Wallace, Peter Coyote, Drew Barrymore, Robert MacNaughton, K. C. Martel, Sean Frye, C. Thomas Howell.

Fatherless suburban kid Thomas finds a stranded alien in his garage and takes in the gentle E.T. (actually an otherworldly scientist). The boy hides the alien in his bedroom closet and feeds him a steady diet of Reese's Pieces candy until mom (Wallace) and later the U.S. government discover the truth. For years the most popular film in history, Spielberg's greatest achievement here is that he makes E.T. (a Carlo Rambaldi creation that's part mechanical, part little-person-in-a-suit, and allegedly voiced by Debra Winger!) the most fully realized character in the film. Warm and true to life (especially in the characterization of the kids, who, today, would be little more than trendily dressed, wise-cracking little creeps), with an exhilarating John Williams score and a sensitive performance by Thomas.

EVE OF DESTRUCTION

★★☆ Orion, 1991, R, 98 min. Dir: Duncan Gibbons. Cast: Gregory Hines, Renee Soutendijk, Michael Greene, Kurt Fuller, John M. Jackson, Kevin McCarthy.

A great premise gets only a fair shake in this action thriller of the *Terminator* school. Popular Dutch actress Soutendijk made her U.S. movie debut as both a lady scientist and the android she has created in her own likeness: a nuclear device in human form that has been violently living out Renee's hatred of men ever since being abused by father McCarthy. Hines is nimble but badly cast as a police terrorism expert assigned the job of stopping the android's rampage. Some well-directed sequences but this never fulfills its promise.

EVIL BRAIN FROM OUTER SPACE, THE

★★ Something Weird, 1956, NR, 85 min. Dirs: Teruo Ishi, Akira Mitsugi, Koreyoshi Akasaka. Cast: Ken Utsui, Reiko Seto, Junko Ikeuchi, Terumi Hoshi.

The last of the Super Giant "movies"—derived from episodes 7, 8, and 9, *Uchu Kaijin Shutsugen (The Earthly Invaders)*, *Akuma no Keshiin (The Devil Incarnate)*, and *Dokuga Okoku (Kingdom of Poison Moth)*—is the silliest and most chaotic, with an evil alien genius keeping his mind alive *Donovan's Brain* style in one last-ditch attempt to stop the meddling of our hero Starman (Utsui). Lots of horror movie touches but the confused plot and awful dubbing quickly wear you down.

EVILS OF THE NIGHT

☆ Lightning, 1983, R, 85 min. Dir: Mardi Rustam. Cast: Neville Brand, Aldo Ray, Tina Louise, Julie Newmar, John Carradine, Karrie Emerson.

Crappy ripoff of *Without Warning* about vampire aliens, played by Carradine, Newmar, and Louise (Dracula, Catwoman, and Ginger— what a combo!), using hicks Brand and Ray to lure a gaggle of *Friday the 13th*-type teen victims into their clutches. Watching this movie is like watching five careers self-destruct all at once—not a pleasant experience if you have fond memories for any of those involved.

EVOLVER

★★ Vidmark Entertainment, 1994, R, 90 min. Dir: Mark Rosman. Cast: Ethan Randall, Cindy Pickett, John DeLancie, Paul Dooley, Cassidy Rae, Nassira Nicola.

Teen Randall wins a small robot by getting a perfect score in the video game Evolver (yeah, right; in real life he'd win a T-shirt). At first the little guy provides harmless fun for the whole family but, true to his name, Evolver moves beyond play violence into the real thing and the body count begins. Little more than a slasher movie with a robot in place of the usual masked killer, this is illogical and yet utterly predictable, salvaged by some decent direction and FX and a good cast.

EWOK ADVENTURE, THE

★★ MGM/UA, 1984, NR, 96 min. Dir: John Korty. Cast: Eric Walker, Warwick Davis, Fionnula Flanagan, Guy Boyd, Debbie Carrington, voice of Burl Ives.

A made-for-TV followup (produced by George Lucas) to *The Return of the Jedi* with the furry, teddy bear-like ewoks helping a pair of young kids, lost on the ewoks' world, find their way home. Okay kiddie fare for those who can stomach it; narrated by Ives ("Jimmy Crack Corn and I Don't Care").

EWOKS: THE BATTLE FOR ENDOR

★★ MGM/UA, 1985, NR, 95 min. Dirs: Ken Wheat, Jim Wheat. Cast: Wilford Brimley, Warwick Davis, Eric Walker, Aubree Miller, Sian Phillips, Carel Struycken.

Second and last ewok TV movie, with Brimley as a crusty but lovable hermit (what else?) who aids young Miller in her struggles against evil witch Phillips. The ewoks have less to do here, which is just as well since they wore out their welcome for me about halfway through *Return of the Jedi*—I'd rather see a cute teleflick starring Jabba the Hutt.

EXCALIBUR

★★★ Warner, 1981, R, 140 min. Dir: John Boorman. Cast: Nicol Williamson, Nigel Terry, Helen Mirren, Nicholas Clay, Cherie Lunghi, Corin Redgrave, Patrick Stewart, Liam Neeson.

Boorman's (*Zardoz; Exorcist II: The Heretic*) take on the Arthurian legend, this stylish, gritty fantasy traces the king's life from his brutal conceived-in-rape origin through to his battle-to-the-death with son Mordred, the offspring of Arthur and his witchy half-sister Morgana. Williamson adds a needed touch of lightness as Merlin the Magician and there are beautiful Irish locations and breathtaking costumes and special FX. Avoid the heavily doctored TV version, which eliminates most of the gore and sexuality so pivotal to the story. With this edition you're better off watching Disney's *The Sword and the Stone*.

EXPLORERS

★★☆ Paramount, 1985, PG, 107 min. Dir: Joe Dante. Cast: Ethan Hawke, River Phoenix, Jason Presson, Amanda Peterson, Dick Miller, Robert Picardo, Dana Ivey, Mary Kay Place.

Mild Dante fantasy with Hawke as a junior high sci-fi buff whose dream of reaching the stars is realized by genius friend Phoenix. Then things start to get really stupid as they encounter intergalactic adolescents hooked on Earth TV. Fans of the young dreamboat stars should enjoy the first half and sweet ending but all that supposed high-concept comedy in between is enough to make you retch. Good role for Miller, though. Originally 109 minutes, Dante recut the film slightly for TV and home video. Hey, Joe, whatever it takes.

EXTERMINATORS OF THE YEAR 3000
★ HBO, 1983, R, 101 min. Dir: Jules Harrison. Cast: Robert Jannucci, Alicia Moro, Alan Collins, Fred Harris, Beryl Cunningham, Luca Venantini.

Italian *Mad Max* clone that's so close to the original you keep expecting Mel Gibson to amble by at any moment. Instead of Mel, though, we get Bob, who rather stoically wades through all the violence and predictability on hand.

EYE CREATURES, THE
★ Sinister Cinema, 1965, NR, 80 min. Dir: Larry Buchanan. Cast: John Ashley, Cynthia Hull, Chet Davis, Bill Peck, Warren Hammack, Shirley McLine.

Totally awful Buchanan remake of *Invasion of the Saucer Men,* with Ashley and Hull as teen (yeah, sure) lovers out to foil an invasion of their small town's lovers' lane by alien monsters covered in eyeballs. Actually, the budget would allow only one of the aliens to be completely covered; the rest wear black body stockings with eyes on their hands and head. Too tedious to be as funny as you keep wanting it to be. TV title: *Attack of the Eye Creatures*—in truth, the actual onscreen title is *Attack of the the Eye Creatures,* but why nitpick when *everything* is so screwed up.

FABULOUS ADVENTURES OF BARON MUNCHAUSEN, THE
★★☆ Sinister Cinema, 1961, NR, 84 min. Dir: Karel Zeman. Cast: Milos Kopecky, Jana Brejchova, Rudolph Jelinek, Jan Werich.

Visually impressive but slow and uninvolving Czech fantasy, with the baron (Kopecky) involved in his usual capering, whether in the belly of a whale or on the surface of the moon. Aka *The Original Fabulous Adventures of Baron Muchausen*—whatever the hell that's supposed to mean.

FABULOUS WORLD OF JULES VERNE, THE
★★☆ Sinister Cinema, 1958, NR, 83 min. Dir: Karel Zeman. Cast: Lubor Tolos, Arnost Navratil, Miroslav Holub, Zatloukalova.

Beautiful-to-look-at but hard-to-follow (or hard-to-want-to-follow) fantasy involving several Verne stories, including *Twenty Thousand Leagues Under the Sea* and *Journey to the Center of the Earth.* Czech director Zeman imaginatively gives this the look of old book engravings come to life; too bad he didn't direct a good movie to go along with the photography and design.

FAHRENHEIT 451
★★★ MCA/Universal, 1967, NR, 111 min. Dir: Francois Truffaut. Cast: Julie Christie, Oskar Werner, Cyril Cussack, Anton Diffring, Jeremy Spenser, Bee Duffell, Alex Scott, Anna Palk, Ann Bell, Mark Lester.

Appropriately sterile adaptation of the classic Ray Bradbury novel about a totalitarian future society where all reading material is banned. Werner is an unhappily married fireman (who in this world must *set* fires rather than put them out) whose life is forever changed when he meets dissident Christie (who, in a double role, also plays Werner's wife), one of a group of radicals whose mission is to memorize books before they're all destroyed. Truffaut's only English-language feature, this is languid but eloquent, with a dreamy score by Bernard Herrmann and a haunting ending scene. The title refers to the temperature at which paper will burn.

FAIL SAFE
★★★ Columbia/TriStar, 1964, NR, 111 min. Dir: Sidney Lumet. Cast: Henry Fonda, Walter Matthau, Fritz Weaver, Dan O'Herlihy, Larry Hagman, Dom DeLuise.

Devastating film version of the book by Eugene Burdick and Harvey Wheeler. Fonda is in top form as the conscience-stricken U.S. president trying to deal with the aftermath of the accidental nuking of Moscow. Almost like a serious version of *Dr. Strangelove,* released at about the same time, with much suspense and an unforgettable downbeat ending.

FALLING, THE
See: *Alien Predator.*

FANTASTIC PLANET
★★ United, 1973, PG, 72 min. Dir: René Laloux. Voices: Barry Bostwick, Marvin Miller, Nora Heflin, Olan Soule, Cynthia Adler, Hal Smith.

Arty French-Czech animated feature about the suppression of a tiny alien race called Oms by a society of giants. A sort of pop art *Gulliver's Travels,* this is on the dull side (even with the rare-for-its time animated sex and nudity), with the U.S. version overdubbed by a crew of familiar voices. Interesting animation, though.

A miniaturized submarine takes a trip through the human body in Fantastic Voyage *(1965).*

FANTASTIC PUPPET PEOPLE, THE

★★ Sinister Cinema, 1958, NR, 78 min. Dir: Bert I. Gordon. Cast: John Hoyt, John Agar, June Kenney, Scott Peters, Laurie Mitchell, Ken Miller, Marlene Willis, Susan Gordon.

Better known as *Attack of the Puppet People*, this is one of Gordon's best-remembered but lesser sci-fi films. Hoyt is excellent in a rare leading role as a lonely dollmaker who shrinks the people he becomes attached to (like secretary Kenney and her boyfriend Agar) to doll size (with some ray machine of unknown origin) so that they can never leave him. Amusing but far too ambitious for its ultra-low budget. Look for a scene from *The Amazing Colossal Man* at a drive-in.

FANTASTIC VOYAGE

★★★★ Fox, 1966, NR, 100 min. Dir: Richard Fleischer. Cast: Stephen Boyd, Raquel Welch, Donald Pleasence, Edmond O'Brien, Arthur Kennedy, William Redfield, Arthur O'Connell, Jean Del Val, Barry Coe, James Brolin.

When Soviet defector Del Val is injured in an attempt on his life by Russian agents, U.S. government man Boyd is assigned the job of leading a miniaturized surgical team (traveling through the man's body in an experimental submarine) to Del Val's brain, where they can safely destroy with lasers an otherwise inoperable blood clot. Though some of its special FX have become dated, this is one of the most visually imaginative films ever made and has lost none of its power to awe the viewer, thanks to the literally fantastic set designs for the body interiors by Jack Martin Smith and Dale Hennesy and the suspenseful direction by Fleischer. Welch's first big film role (later that same year she'd become a star with *One Million Years B.C.*), her best scene has her tightly wetsuited form attacked by seaweed-like antibodies. David Duncan adapted the script from a story co-authored by Otto Klement and Jerome Bixby.

FANTASY ISLAND

★★☆ Video Treasures, 1977, NR, 96 min. Dir: Richard Lang. Cast: Ricardo Montalban, Bill Bixby, Hugh O'Brian, Eleanor Parker, Sandra Dee, Carol Lynley, Victoria Principal, Peter Lawford, Dick Sargent, Hervé Villechaize.

"Welcome to Fantasy Island!" Fans of this popular bit of '70s corn may be surprised at how serious and downbeat this first pilot film for the series can be. Guests pay the devious Mr. Roarke (Montalban) handsome sums to have their hearts broken and dreams crushed when their fantasies are brought to life. A big game hunter (O'Brian) wants to know what it feels like to be hunted like an animal; an aging World War II vet (Bixby) wants to go back in time to find a lost love (Dee); and a female tycoon (Parker) fakes her own funeral to discover which of her relatives is after her money. Followed by *Return to Fantasy Island*.

FIELD OF DREAMS

★★★ MCA/Universal, 1989, PG, 106 min. Dir: Phil Aldren Robinson. Cast: Kevin Costner, Amy Madigan, James Earl Jones, Burt Lancaster, Ray Liotta, Timothy Busfield, Dwier Brown, Gaby Hoffman.

Costner is a nice guy Iowa farmer inspired by a mystical voice to build a baseball diamond in his corn field. Everybody thinks he's crazy but the act resurrects the spirit of Black Sox scandal victim Shoeless Joe Jackson (Liotta) and others for one final game. An earnest, beautifully crafted fantasy with Costner good as a sort of latter-day Jimmy Stewart (a persona he might think of reviving), a hand-picked supporting cast, and a lovingly wrought atmosphere of hope and redemption that puts other baseball fantasies—like *Angels in the Outfield*—to shame.

FIEND WITHOUT A FACE

★★★ Republic, 1957, NR, 74 min. Dir: Arthur Crabtree. Cast: Marshall Thompson, Kim Parker, Kynaston Reeves, Terence Kilburn.

Well-remembered '50s monster flick with Reeves as an elderly scientist whose experiments with the power of thought coupled with atomic radiation result in the creation of invisible, spinal-fluid-sucking brain creatures. Talky and dull for its first two-thirds, this kicks into high gear in a big way when the monsters suddenly materialize and

"No, please, I'm not a hugger!" Kim Parker in Fiend Without a Face *(1957).*

lay siege to a boarded-up house *Night of the Living Dead*-style, with outrageous FX (filmed on the cheap in Austria) and surprising blasts of gore. Shot in England but set in Canada, a remake has been rumored for years and would most certainly be welcome.

FINAL COUNTDOWN, THE
★★★ Vestron, 1980, PG, 103 min. Dir: Don Taylor. Cast: Kirk Douglas, Martin Sheen, Katharine Ross, James Farentino, Ron O'Neal, Charles Durning.

A time warp sends the naval aircraft carrier U.S.S. Nimitz back in time to Pearl Harbor just before the Japanese air strike. Should commander Douglas use his modern weaponry to join in the battle and change history? Thoroughly entertaining if somewhat simplistic time travel yarn, this poses more questions than it convincingly answers but is well enough acted and directed to make this only a minor caveat.

FINAL PROGRAMME, THE
★★★ Thorn/EMI, 1973, R, 87 min. Dir: Robert Fuest. Cast: Jon Finch, Jenny Runacre, Sterling Hayden, Patrick Magee, Julie Ege, Hugh Griffith, Harry Andrews, Sarah Douglas, George Coulouris, Ronald Lacey.

The director of Vincent Price's *Dr. Phibes* movies helms this uneven but still worthwhile British fantasy based on Michael Moorcock's "Jerry Cornelius" stories. Finch is good as Cornelius, a sort of more intellectual version of James Bond, who discovers that a team of mad scientists (headed by the magnificent Runacre) are trying to rebuild civilization through the creation of a genetically engineered new Messiah—an amalgamation of both Finch's and Runacre's best qualities. Admired in some quarters and hated in others (it was a major flop on both sides of the Atlantic), this stylish concoction (kind of like the old *Batman* TV show on angel dust) is one of the strangest movies of the '70s and well worth seeing—but not in the heavily edited U.S. theatrical version retitled *The Last Days of Man on Earth*.

FIRE AND ICE
★★ Columbia/TriStar, 1983, PG, 80 min. Dir: Ralph Bakshi. Voices: Susan Tyrell, Maggie Roswell, William Ostrander, Stephen Mendel, Randy Norton, Leo Gordon.

Animator Bakshi's contribution to the early '80s sword-and-sorcery craze, this involves a beautiful princess, a hard-bodied warrior, and warring tribes from a mythical land of fire and ice. The Frank Frazetta production and character designs are great but the rotoscoped animation (traced from live action) leaves something to be desired.

FIREFOX
★★ Warner, 1982, PG, 124 min. Dir: Clint Eastwood. Cast: Clint Eastwood, Freddie Jones, David Huffman, Warren Clarke, Ronald Lacey.

Disappointing sci-fi-tinged actioner with Clint as a former flying ace (haunted by the usual flashbacks of wartime tragedies) sent behind Soviet lines to steal their latest weapon: a supersonic jet powered by psychic waves from the brain of its pilot. A shorter running time and a younger, more vital leading man (sorry, Clint) might have made this a lot more exciting in the vein of, say, *Blue Thunder*. As is, it's a long, angst-ridden wait until the spectacular aerial climax.

FIRE IN THE SKY
★★ Paramount, 1993, PG-13, 107 min. Dir: Robert Lieberman. Cast: D. B. Sweeney, Robert Patrick, Craig Sheffer, Peter Berg, James Garner, Henry Thomas, Kathleen Wilhoite, Noble Willingham.

Tracy Torme adapted Travis Wilson's book *The Walton Experience*, the supposedly true story of his abduction by aliens. The always likable Sweeney is good as Wilson and there's a telling cameo by a rock-solid Garner, but how much you warm up to this rather tepid sci-fi drama will depend entirely on how much of it you're willing to believe.

FIRE MAIDENS FROM OUTER SPACE
★ Sinister Cinema, 1955, NR, 80 min. Dir: Cy Roth. Cast: Anthony Dexter, Susan Shaw, Paul Carpenter, Harry Fowler, Sydney Tafler, Jacqueline Curtis.

In the grand tradition of *Devil Girl from Mars* comes this British slice of tripe about earth explorers sent to Jupiter's moon Ganymede, where they discover a race of beautiful women descended from the last survivors of Atlantis (!) who spend most of their time dancing to Borodin and running from a monster played by some guy in a black leotard with a burlap bag over his head. Who said only the Americans and Japanese were capable of making bad sci-fi films?

FIRE MONSTERS AGAINST THE SON OF HERCULES
★★ Sinister Cinema, 1962, NR, 82 min. Dir: Guido Malatesta. Cast: Reg Lewis, Margaret Lee, Andrea Aureli.

Herc's buffed boy takes on cavemen, a sea monster, and a many-headed Hydra wannabe in this routine muscle epic. Original title: *Maciste Contro I Mostri (Maciste Conquers the Monsters)*.

FIREWALKER
★☆ Media, 1986, PG, 104 min. Dir: J. Lee
Thompson. Cast: Chuck Norris, Louis Gossett, Jr.,
Melody Anderson, Will Sampson, Sonny Landham,
John Rhys-Davies.

Bottom-of-the-barrel *Raiders* clone with Chuck,
Lou, and Melody after an Aztec treasure in
Mexico. This alleged comedy-adventure is professionally directed by Thompson but isn't
particularly funny or exciting, with Norris
about as convincing in his first "light" role as
Adam Sandler would be playing Rambo.

FIRST MAN INTO SPACE
★★☆ Rhino, 1958, NR, 77 min. Dir: Robert Day.
Cast: Marshall Thompson, Marla Landi, Bill Edwards,
Robert Ayres.

The *Fiend Without a Face* producers strike again
with this somewhat less successful but still
pretty creepy sci-fi/horror hybrid. Edwards is
a hotshot test pilot transformed into a glittery,
one-eyed, blood-drinking monster after a sub-
orbital flight is bombarded by radioactive
space dust. Like *Fiend,* this starts slow but
builds to some really scary moments, like
when the monster is pulled over by the cops
for speeding (don't ask) and comes roaring out
of the car to tear apart the policemen, leaving
behind the bloody body of a woman in the
passenger seat. Aka *Satellite of Blood.*

FIRST MEN IN THE MOON
★★★ Columbia/TriStar, 1964, NR, 103 min. Dir:
Nathan Juran. Cast: Edward Judd, Martha Hyer,
Lionel Jeffries, Erik Chitty, Betty McDowall, Miles
Malleson, Marne Maitland, Peter Finch.

In the year 1899, eccentric British inventor Jeffries develops an antigravity paint to use on a
metal sphere that carries him, Judd, and Hyer
to the moon. There they encounter an underground insectoid race bent on conquering the
Earth. Quaintly old-fashioned science fiction
from the Jules Verne novel, featuring well-
done Ray Harryhausen FX (with only a few
stop-motion critters) and impressive wide-
screen photography (somewhat spoiled by
unletterboxed tapes). Jeffries has a ball and a
heavily made-up Finch cameos as a delivery
man. Amusingly, NASA used footage from
this film on TV during one of the moon shots
to explain a lunar landing!

FIRST SPACESHIP ON VENUS, THE
★★☆ Sinister Cinema, 1960, NR, 78 min. Dir: Kurt
Maetzig. Cast: Yoko Tani, Oldrich Lukes, Igancy
Machowski, Julius Ongewe, Gunther Simon, Kurt
Rackelman.

In this imaginative but slow-moving Polish-
East German flick (based on a book called *Planet of Death* by Stanislas Lem), a racially and sexually mixed team of astronauts is dispatched to
Venus, where they discover hordes of tiny,
insectlike creatures and the ruins of a vast civilization destroyed by nuclear war. Visually
impressive but understandably disjointed, the
U.S. version suffers from bad dubbing and the
cutting of nearly a half hour of footage.

FIVE
★★☆ Sinister Cinema, 1951, NR, 93 min. Dir: Arch
Oboler. Cast: William Phipps, Susan Douglas, James
Anderson, Charles Lampkin, Earl Lee.

Radio fantasist Oboler produced, wrote, and
directed this first of the '50s end-of-the-world
movies. The Big Bang devastates mankind,
(seemingly) leaving only five people, including
a pregnant widow (Douglas), a platitude-
spouting idealist (Anderson), and—in an
unusual touch for the time—a gentle black
doorman (Lee). Oboler's radio experience is
the obvious reason why there's more talk than
action and the happy ending is a flimsy com-
promise, but this cheapie is frequently well-
directed and -photographed and was very
influential.

5,000 FINGERS OF DR. T., THE
★★★ MGM/UA, 1953, NR, 88 min. Dir: Roy
Rowland. Cast: Peter Lind Hayes, Mary Healy, Tommy
Rettig, Hans Conreid.

Rettig is a young boy who dreads his weekly
piano lessons so much that he begins to dream
that his piano teacher (Conreid) is actually a
madman out to enslave the children of the
world at a gigantic keyboard. Written by none
other than Dr. Seuss, this imaginative fantasy
was ignored in its day but has since developed
a cult following, much in the tradition of *Willie
Wonka and the Chocolate Factory.*

FIVE WEEKS IN A BALLOON
★★★ Fox, 1962, NR, 101 min. Dir: Irwin Allen. Cast:
Sir Cedric Hardwicke, Red Buttons, Barbara Eden,
Peter Lorre, Fabian, Barbara Luna, Richard Haydn,
Herbert Marshall, Billy Gilbert, Henry Daniell, Mike
Mazurki, Raymond Bailey.

In the late nineteenth century, inventor
Hardwicke and a motley crew take an
experimental balloon across Africa to claim an
unexplored section of the continent before it is
taken over by vicious slave traders. This Allen
fantasy-comedy (based on the Jules Verne book
and filmed at a time when Verne was as hot a
ticket seller as Stephen King or Jane Austen is
now) relies on his usual formula of packing an
all-star cast into one misadventure after

another, with a comic relief chimp and Fabian (Fabian? Ahhh!) singing the catchy theme song.

FLASH, THE
★★★ Warner, 1990, NR, 94 min. Dir: Robert Iscove. Cast: John Wesley Shipp, Amanda Pays, Michael Nader, Tim Thomerson, Alex Desert.

The pilot movie for the short-lived TV series has Shipp well cast as Barry Allen, criminologist by day; tight-suited, high-speed superhero by night. In this adventure, our hero tries to avenge his brother's death by bringing the biker gang responsible to justice. Well done, with lots of action for the kids and Shipp and Pays for the adults.

FLASH II: REVENGE OF THE TRICKSTER, THE
★★ Warner, 1991, NR, 92 min. Dir: Danny Bilson. Cast: John Wesley Shipp, Amanda Pays, Mark Hamill, Alex Desert.

Two episodes of *The Flash* TV series edited into a feature, with Hamill on a hammy tear (and you wonder why Harrison Ford and not he became the big star) as the Trickster: a one-time magician turned criminal mastermind out to eliminate the Flash. Okay TV thrills.

FLASH GORDON
See: *Flash Gordon: Rocketship*

FLASH GORDON
★★☆ MCA/Universal, 1980, PG, 110 min. Dir: Mike Hodges. Cast: Sam Jones, Melody Anderson, Chaim Topol, Max von Sydow, Timothy Dalton, Ornella Muti, Brian Blessed, Mariangela Melato.

Splashy updated version of Alex Raymond's sci-fi hero scripted with broad, *Batman*-like strokes by Lorenzo Semple, Jr. The handsome but wooden Jones (whose previous claims to fame include being a *Playgirl* centerfold and appearing on TV's *The Dating Game*) is Flash, a studly football player who, along with girlfriend Dale Arden (sweet, dopey Anderson) is reluctantly flown by the cracked Dr. Zarkov (Topol, giving the film's funniest performance) to the planet Mongo, where Ming the Merciless (von Sydow, a long way from his Bergman days) and his sexy daughter Aura (Muti, who could almost turn Harvey Fierstein straight) hold sway. Lots of flashy camerawork, pop art set design, and a very loud score by Queen almost make this the *Barbarella* of the '80s, but it's too slow and self-consciously campy to be of more than mild interest.

FLASH GORDON CONQUERS THE UNIVERSE
★★☆ Sinister Cinema, 1940, NR, 120 min. Dirs: Ray Taylor, Ford Beebe. Cast: Buster Crabbe, Carol

Hughes, Charles Middleton, Frank Shannon, Anne Gwynne, Roland Drew.

Third and final Flash Gordon serial. Buster and the crew discover Emperor Ming's (Middleton) latest plan to conquer Earth with a death ray. Not as much fun as earlier adventures but still worth seeing. Also available from Sinister Cinema in a condensed feature version.

FLASH GORDON: MARS ATTACKS THE WORLD
★★ Sinister Cinema, 1938, NR, 99 min. Dirs: Ford Beebe and Robert Hill. Cast: Buster Crabbe, Jean Rogers, Charles Middleton, Frank Shannon, Donald Kerr, Beatrice Roberts.

Bland reediting of the second Flash serial (*Flash Gordon's Trip to Mars*) into a feature. Flash, Dale, and Zarkov travel to Mars to investigate a strange force directed at Earth and discover Ming up to his old activities. Mildly watchable but the drastic editing makes it hard to follow. Aka *The Deadly Ray from Mars*.

FLASH GORDON: ROCKETSHIP
★★★ Sinister Cinema, 1936, NR, 97 min. Dir: Frederick Stephani. Cast: Buster Crabbe, Jean Rogers, Charles Middleton, Frank Shannon, Priscilla Lawson, Richard Alexander.

Feature cut down from the first and best serial based on the Alex Raymond character. Flash (Crabbe at his most invigorating), Dale Arden (Rogers), and Dr. Zarkov (Shannon) travel in a cut-rate rocket to the planet Mongo, where the dreaded Ming the merciless (Middleton in the role of a lifetime) dominates all. With werewolflike beast men, a huge lobster monster, an undersea city, a city in the sky, stock music from *Bride of Frankenstein*, and enough entertainment value to survive such blunt editing as here. Aka *Spaceship to the Unknown*.

FLESH GORDON
★★★ Hen's Tooth, 1972, X, 80 min. Dirs: Michael Benveniste, Howard Ziehm. Cast: Jason Williams, Suzanne Fields, William Hunt, Joseph Hudgins, John Hoyt, Candy Samples.

A porno version of *Flash Gordon* doesn't sound like too hot an idea, but this turns out far better than you'd imagine thanks to above average FX. Flesh (Williams), his girl Dale Ardor (Fields), and Dr. Jerkoff (Hudgins) fly a penis-shaped rocket to the planet of Emperor Wang (Hunt), who's been bombarding the Earth with an impotence ray. Great stop-motion work by Dave Allen and Jim Danforth (the latter with his name spelled backward in the credits!)

include a sword-wielding bettleman, one-eyed penisaurus, and the great god Porno, who carries off Dale King Kong-style but looks like a mutant Richard Nixon! Originally a hard-core flick, most of the sex and frontal male nudity were later edited out for a wider R-rated release, but these scenes have recently been restored for this X-rated director's cut.

FLESH GORDON MEETS THE COSMIC CHEERLEADERS

★☆ New Horizons, 1989, R, 85 min. Dir: Howard Ziehm. Cast: Vince Murdocco, Robyn Kelly, William Hunt, Morgan Fox, Bruce Scott, Stevie-Lyn Ray, Blair Kashino, Sharon Rowley.

This long-in-development sequel is almost a total waste of time. Flesh (now played by Murdocco) gets fired off a movie where he's playing himself and is later kidnapped along with gal pal Dale (Kelly) by a trio of outer space cheerleaders who need help in defeating the reactivated impotence ray of Emperor Wang (Hunt, reprising his role from the original). The restrictive R rating makes this little more than a tired collection of preadolescent sex and bodily function jokes with an occasional good special effect.

FLIGHT OF THE NAVIGATOR

★★☆ Disney, 1986, PG, 88 min. Dir: Randal Kleiser. Cast: Joey Cramer, Cliff DeYoung, Veronica Cartwright, Sarah Jessica Parker, Matt Adler, Howard Hesseman.

A twelve-year-old boy (Cramer) is abducted by an alien spacecraft to act as its navigator. Eight years later the kid is returned to his parents—but he's still twelve! Modest Disney fantasy with an above average cast for this sort of thing and okay special FX. An unbilled Paul Reubens (aka Pee-Wee Herman) provides the voice of the obligatorily cute robot.

FLIGHT TO MARS

★★ Fries, 1951, NR, 71 min. Dir: Lesley Selander. Cast: Cameron Mitchell, Marguerite Chapman, Arthur Franz, Morris Ankrum, Virginia Huston, John Litel.

Veteran B-movie studio Monogram Pictures produced this somewhat imaginative but hopelessly cheap cash-in on *Destination Moon* and *Rocketship X-M.* Mitchell leads the first manned mission to Mars, where the dastardly Martians (who live in vast underground cities) plan to steal our rocket designs and launch an invasion. Unexpectedly shot in color, this has a few nice matte paintings but all the usual clichés as well, including Chapman as a friendly Martian girl who betrays her people when she falls for hero Mitchell.

FLINTSTONES, THE

★★ MCA/Universal, 1994, PG, 92 min. Dir: Brian Levant. Cast: John Goodman, Rick Moranis, Elizabeth Perkins, Rosie O'Donnell, Elizabeth Taylor, Kyle MacLachlan, Hallie Berry, Jonathan Winters, Richard Moll, voice of Harvey Korman.

Not exactly a Yabba Dabba Doo time, this live-action, big-bucks version of the classic '60s prehistoric cartoon show has expensive production values and good Jim Henson FX wasted on a trite storyline that's little more than a series of lame vignettes strung together—not surprising since more than thirty writers worked on this thing. Goodman is well cast as Fred Flintstone; Moranis is even better as Barney Rubble; Perkins and O'Donnell are perfect as Wilma and Betty—but whatever possessed Taylor to get involved in a big-screen comeback here as Wilma's mom? A few stray chuckles but its nonsuccess has probably spared us both a sequel and a live version of *The Jetsons* as well—thus far.

FLUKE

★★☆ MGM/UA, 1995, PG, 95 min. Dir: Carlo Carlei. Cast: Matthew Modine, Nancy Travis, Eric Stoltz, Jon Polito.

Based on a novel by James Herbert, this reincarnation fantasy is like a serious version of *Oh Heavenly Dog.* Yuppie businessman Modine is killed in a car crash and returned to Earth as a mutt who must both look after his former family and solve the mystery of his "accidental" death. Too heavy for kids and too silly for adults, this is well cast and sincere but hard to figure out just what audience it was made for.

FLY, THE

★★★ Fox, 1958, NR, 94 min. Dir: Kurt Neumann. Cast: David Hedison, Patricia Owens, Vincent Price, Herbert Marshall, Charles Herbert, Kathleen Freeman.

Canadian scientist Hedison tinkers with a matter teleportation device that eventually mixes his atoms with those of a fly, turning him into a bug-headed monster. Once you overlook the utter illogic of some of its story points this classic '50s monster flick—adapted by James Clavell from the story by George Langelaan—becomes a lot of fun, with glossy production values and wide-screen photography (rare for a monster movie of this vintage) and committed acting from all the principals (particularly the underrated Owens in what is really the lead role as Hedison's distraught wife). Followed by *Return of the Fly* and *Curse of the Fly* and the 1986 remake.

Jeff Goldblum takes a matter transmitter trip in The Fly *(1986).*

FLY, THE

★★★★ Fox, 1986, R, 97 min. Dir: David Cronenberg. Cast: Jeff Goldblum, Geena Davis, John Getz, Joy Boushel, Les Carlson.

This should be used as a guide for filmmakers on how to handle the remake of a classic film. Instead of simply redoing the same story, Cronenberg does a variation using much of the same material but in startlingly different ways. Goldblum and Davis (who were married for a while after making this) are both excellent as the matter-transmitting scientist and the concerned woman who loves him. The teleportation accident this time leads to Goldblum ingesting the fly's DNA and ultimately transforming into an icky insectlike monster. A sizable hit even though some viewers had problems with the large amount of gore and slime used to offset the love story, this is still Cronenberg's best film and a shining example of why he should abandon his higher aspirations and return to the sci-fi/horror genre posthaste.

FLY II, THE

★★ Fox, 1989, R, 104 min. Dir: Chris Walas. Cast: Eric Stoltz, Daphne Zuniga, Lee Richardson, John Getz, Harley Cross.

Routine, predictable sequel directed by Oscar-winning makeup man Walas. Almost a remake of *Return of the Fly*, this casts Stoltz as the son of Jeff Goldblum's and Geena Davis's characters who ages five times normal speed and eventually evolves into a particularly nasty and murderous fly creature. Even gorier than the original and with a funny cameo by Getz, but the happy ending is totally forced and unjustified.

FLYING SAUCER, THE

★☆ Rhino, 1950, NR, 69 min. Dir: Mikel Conrad. Cast: Mikel Conrad, Pat Garrison, Russell Hicks, Denver Pyle.

The first film of the '50s science fiction craze to deal with a flying saucer, this is actually a dated, tame espionage thriller with agent Conrad discovering that the UFO that's landed in Alaska is really part of a Russian invasion force. I guess they'd believe anything back then.

FOOD OF THE GODS

★★ Vestron, 1976, PG, 88 min. Dir: Bert I. Gordon. Cast: Marjoe Gortner, Pamela Franklin, Ida Lupino, Ralph Meeker, Jon Cypher, Belinda Belaski.

Gordon's second go at the H. G. Wells novel (the first was *Village of the Giants*—nufsaid?) takes place on a picturesque island off the coast of Canada, where the oatmeal-like gunk spurting out of the ground on Lupino's farm turns harmless animals and insects into dangerous monsters. The climax has most of the small cast trapped in Ida's farmhouse by a plague of jumbo rats who keep getting blasted in the head by realistic rifle shots that could cause a roomful of PETA members to pass out. Awful but funny, with over-the-top thesping on a grand scale and a lot of blood for a PG movie.

FOOD OF THE GODS PART 2

★☆ Avid Entertainment, 1988, R, 86 min. Dir: Damian Lee. Cast: Paul Coufos, Lisa Schrage, Michael Copeman, Jackie Burroughs.

Originally to be directed by Bert I. Gordon, this followup to his 1976 hit (believe it or not, it was a hit) has more giant rats on the attack at a college in upstate New York. Even funnier than part one, if that's possible, but overall not as much fun. Aka *Gnaw: Food of the Gods II*.

FORBIDDEN MOON

★★ Sinister Cinema, 1953, NR, 78 min. Dir: Hollingsworth Morse. Cast: Richard Crane, Sally Mansfield, Scotty Beckett, Robert Lyden.

More *Rocky Jones* adventures as our hero is dispatched to stop a dangerous planetoid on a collision course with Earth. The usual nonsense.

FORBIDDEN PLANET

★★★ MGM/UA, 1956, NR, 98 min. Dir: Fred McLeod Wilcox. Cast: Walter Pidgeon, Anne Francis, Leslie Nielsen, Warren Stevens, Earl Holliman, Jack Kelly, James Drury, Richard Anderson.

Shakespeare's *The Tempest* provided the basis for this tale of spaceship commander Nielsen and his crew landing on the planet Altair 4 to check on the well-being of a group of

Original poster art from Forbidden Planet *(1956).*

colonists. They find that only scientist Pidgeon and his daughter Francis are still alive and soon members of Nielsen's company are being attacked by a huge, invisible monster. Not one of my favorites, this is still influential (I can't believe Gene Roddenberry wasn't partly inspired by this while formulating *Star Trek*), with a solid cast and sleek MGM production values, but Wilcox's heavy-handed direction and an annoying electronic musical score often make it a chore to sit through. The letterboxed videocassette is the only way to see it though. Many props from this film (not to mention Robby the Robot) turned up later on TV shows like *The Twilight Zone* and *Lost in Space*.

FORBIDDEN WORLD

★★ Embassy, 1982, R, 77 min. Dir: Allan Holzman. Cast: Jesse Vint, Dawn Dunlap, June Chadwick, Linden Chiles.

This even cheaper followup to *Galaxy of Terror* costars a sweaty, wise-cracking Vint and the infamous vomit monster, the Gigeresque mutant biting a big chunk out of a very small cast until it ingests a cancerous liver and pukes itself to death. With so much gratuitous gore and female nudity, it's no wonder the remake (*Dead Space*) was forced to really clean up its act for these more politically correct times. Aka *Mutant*.

FORBIDDEN ZONE, THE

★★ Media, 1980, R, 75 min. Dir: Richard Elfman. Cast: Susan Tyrell, Herve Villechaize, Marie-Pascale Elfman, Toshiro Boloney, Viva.

Oingo Boingo member Elfman (brother of Danny) directs this bizarre musical fantasy that's so very weird it almost dares you not to like it. Marie-Pascal is carried off to the sixth dimension, where tiny pervert king Villechaize rules with leather gal queen Tyrell (whose acting here makes her psychotic turn in *Night Warning* seem restrained). Has its following and does offer some flashes of *Eraserhead*-like imagination, but not an easy film to embrace.

FORBIN PROJECT, THE

See: *Colossus: The Forbin Project*

FOREVER YOUNG

★★☆, Warner, 1992, PG, 102 min. Dir: Steve Miner. Cast: Mel Gibson, Jamie Lee Curtis, Elijah Wood, Isabel Glasser, George Wendt, Joe Morton.

Formula romantic fantasy about a 1930s test pilot who volunteers for an experiment in cryogenics and is accidentally revived more than fifty years later. Still a young man, he becomes involved with troubled young Wood and single-mom Curtis. Often moving but so squeaky clean I kept wondering if Jamie and director Miner ever discussed their earlier cinematic efforts like *Prom Night* or *Friday the 13th Part 2*.

FORTRESS

★★ Live, 1993, R, 95 min. Dir: Stuart Gordon. Cast: Christopher Lambert, Loryn Locklin, Kurtwood Smith, Lincoln Kilpatrick, Jeffrey Combs.

In a future where only one child per couple is allowed, Lambert and pregnant wife Locklin (who've lost their first child) attempt to flee their oppressive society only to be captured and imprisoned in the title model, where Chris undergoes tortures galore. Horror director Gordon scored a minor hit with this thriller. It's competently done but more than slightly similar to the 1971 TV movie *The Last Child* with Michael Cole, Janet Margolin, and Ed Asner in the roles essayed here by Lambert, Locklin, and Smith.

4-D MAN, THE

★★ New World, 1959, NR, 85 min. Dir: Irwin S. Yeaworth, Jr. Cast: Robert Lansing, Lee Meriwether, Robert Strauss, Patty Duke.

Lansing is typically good in this minor fare from the makers of *The Blob*, shot on some of the same Pennsylvania locations. Bob discovers a way to pass through solid objects but everyone he knows seems hell-bent on stealing his idea. The experiments begin to age him prematurely, forcing him to drain the life-force of others to stay young. Good special FX and acting help sustain this slack low-budgeter.

FOUR-SIDED TRIANGLE, THE

★★ Sinister Cinema, 1953, NR, 81 min. Dir: Terence Fisher. Cast: Barbara Payton, James Hayter, Stephen Murray, John Van Eyssen.

An early Hammer film for Fisher (with horror overtones) about a scientist (Hayter) who creates a duplication machine. In love with Payton, who is in turn in love with Murray, Hayter creates a double of the busty girl for himself but—big surprise—she loves Murray as well. Nothing much, and with poor acting from Payton in both roles, but the fiery climax looks like a dry run for one of Fisher's later Frankenstein movies.

F.P. I

See: *F.P. 1 Doesn't Answer*

F.P. I DOESN'T ANSWER

★★☆ Sinister Cinema, 1932, NR, 90 min. Dir: Karl Hartl. Cast: Conrad Veidt, Jill Esmond, Leslie Fenton, George Merritt, Donald Calthrop, Francis L. Sullivan.

Very early science fiction about sabotage and intrigue aboard a huge floating platform used for landing planes in the mid-Atlantic. Melodramatic but with some impressive special effects, this British-German-French coproduction was shot simultaneously with four different casts in four different languages (English, French, German, and Spanish). The other casts include Charles Boyer, Peter Lorre, Sybille Schmitz, and Pierre Brasseur.

FRANCIS

See: *Francis, the Talking Mule*

FRANCIS COVERS THE BIG TOWN

★★ MCA/Universal, 1953, NR, 86 min. Dir: Arthur Lubin. Cast: Donald O'Connor, Nancy Guild, Yvette Dugay, Gene Lockhart, William Harrigan, Gale Gordon.

Typical entry in the talking mule series. O'Connor becomes a cub reporter on a big-city newspaper and he and Francis (voiced by Chill Wills) become involved in a murder case. Mostly for fans of the series.

FRANCIS GOES TO THE RACES

★★☆ MCA/Universal, 1951, NR, 88 min. Dir: Arthur Lubin. Cast: Donald O'Connor, Piper Laurie, Cecil Kellaway, Jesse White, Barry Kelley, Hayden Rourke.

Pretty funny *Francis* comedy, with the mule coaching a race horse in how to be a winner and O'Connor falling for Laurie, daughter of horsebreeder Kellaway. Slightly better than usual entry.

FRANCIS GOES TO WEST POINT

★★☆ MCA/Universal, 1952, NR, 81 min. Dir: Arthur Lubin. Cast: Donald O'Connor, Lori Nelson, Alice Kelley, William Reynolds, Gregg Palmer, James Best, David Janssen, Les Tremayne.

An above-average cast helps this one as Francis helps Don get through basic training at the military academy. Look for Leonard Nimoy as one of the cadets.

FRANCIS IN THE HAUNTED HOUSE

★☆ MCA/Universal, 1956, NR, 80 min. Dir: Charles Lamont. Cast: Mickey Rooney, Virginia Welles, James Flavin, Paul Cavanagh, Mary Ellen Kaye, David Janssen, Richard Deacon, Timothy Carey.

The last and weakest *Francis* film has a new lead (Rooney), a new director (Lamont), a new voice for Francis (Paul Frees), and all the same old haunted house jokes as Mick and the mule caper about a set that looks like it was left over from some old Abbott and Costello movie—and probably was. Good supporting cast, though.

FRANCIS IN THE NAVY

★★☆ MCA/Universal, 1955, NR, 80 min. Dir: Arthur Lubin. Cast: Donald O'Connor, Martha Hyer, Richard Erdman, Jim Backus, David Janssen, Clint Eastwood, Martin Milner, Paul Burke.

O'Connor's last appearance in the series (and Lubin's last as director) finds Don in a dual role and all the usual service comedy carryings-on. Eastwood makes his second screen appearance in a small role.

FRANCIS JOINS THE WACS

★★★ MCA/Universal, 1954, NR, 94 min. Dir: Arthur Lubin. Cast: Donald O'Connor, Julie Adams, Mamie Van Doren, Lynn Bari, Allison Hayes, Mara Corday, ZaSu Pitts, Chill Wills.

The best and funniest *Francis* comedy has a military foul up sending O'Connor and Francis to a WAC base just blossoming with a full bouquet of Universal '50s starlets. Wills, the voice of Francis, has an on-screen acting role here as well.

FRANCIS, THE TALKING MULE

★★☆ MCA/Universal, 1949, NR, 91 min. Dir: Arthur Lubin. Cast: Donald O'Connor, Patricia Medina, ZaSu Pitts, Ray Collins, John McIntire, Tony Curtis.

The first in the series pretty much plays as they all do. O'Connor is a bumbling army screwup who becomes a hero thanks to his friendship with Francis, a garrulous army mule who talks like Chill Wills. Of course, every time Don tries to tell someone about this they think he's crazy. Harmless fun; years later director Lubin would take this idea to TV for the very similar *Mr. Ed* series. Original title: *Francis*.

FRANKENSTEIN MEETS THE SPACE MONSTER

★ Prism Entertainment, 1965, NR, 78 min. Dir: Robert Gaffney. Cast: Robert Reilly, James Karen, Nancy Marshall, Marilyn Hanold.

Effeminate aliens ruled by sexy bad actress Hanold land in Puerto Rico to kidnap bathing beauties as part of a plan to repopulate their dying world. The Frankenstein character is actually a NASA robot called Frank (Reilly) whose face is disfigured by a ray gun blast and who takes on Hanold's pet monster, Mull, to rescue heroine Marshall at the climax. One of the worst movies ever made (but, oddly, not the worst *Frankenstein* movie ever made), with

"I told you this would happen if you sneezed in your oatmeal!" Nancy Marshall and Robert Reilly in Frankenstein Meets the Space Monster *(1965).*

horrendous overacting, cheesy makeup, and lots of stock footage of rockets and Puerto Rican landmarks to pad the running time. Bruce Glover (Crispin's dad) can be seen as one of the aliens. Aka *Mars Attacks Puerto Rico* and *Duel of the Space Monsters*.

FREAKY FRIDAY

★★★ Disney, 1977, G, 95 min. Dir: Gary Nelson. Cast: Barbara Harris, Jodie Foster, John Astin, Patsy Kelly, Dick Van Patten, Sorrell Booke, Marie Windsor, Charlene Tilton.

When mother and daughter Harris and Foster magically exchange bodies for a day, each learns more about the other in the process. Fine performances by the two leads (you can see Jodie already beginning to develop into a real movie star) and a perceptive script (that does, admittedly, get a bit formula-bound in places) put this vastly underrated Disney comedy head and shoulders over the flood of very similar "body-switch" movies that proliferated about a decade later in the wake of *Big*.

FREEJACK

★★ Warner, 1992, R, 108 min. Dir: Geoff Murphy. Cast: Emilio Estevez, Rene Russo, Mick Jagger, Anthony Hopkins, Jonathan Banks, David Johansen, Amanda Plummer, Frankie Faison.

Race car driver Estevez is projected twenty years into the future, where he is pursued by bounty hunter Jagger, employed to bring Emilio back so that the dying Hopkins may take over his body. Flashy but senseless sci-fi

thriller tries to ape *Repo Man, Total Recall,* and others but never really comes off. Jagger overdoes it in his first acting role since the '70s but Hopkins (as usual) lights up the screen for his few scenes.

FROM THE EARTH TO THE MOON

★★☆ United Entertainment, 1958, NR, 100 min. Dir: Byron Haskin. Cast: Joseph Cotten, George Sanders, Debra Paget, Don Dubbins, Patric Knowles, Henry Daniell, Morris Ankrum, Carl Esmond.

Shortly after the conclusion of the Civil War, munitions maker Cotten and inventor Sanders construct a rocket fueled by something called "Power X." Cotten, Sanders, and Cotten's assistant Dubbins take off for the moon but stowaway Paget (Sander's concerned daughter) throws the rocket off course. Great cast and story are somewhat hampered by an obviously low budget with some rather paltry special effects. Esmond appears in the film as Jules Verne, upon whose novel this is based.

FUTURE COP

See: *Trancers*

FUTURE HUNTERS

★☆ Vestron, 1989, R, 100 min. Dir: Cirio H. Santiago. Cast: Robert Patrick, Linda Carol, Ed Crick, Richard Norton.

Cheap Filipino action fantasy with Norton as a kung fu fighter from the twenty-first century who goes back to the 1980s to help Patrick and Carol stop mad scientist Crick from altering the future. Ultra-inexpensive mix of *The Terminator* (interestingly, Patrick would later play the android in *T2*) and your standard-issue Steven Seagal/Jean Claude Van Damme martial arts epic.

FUTURE-KILL

★ Vestron, 1985, R, 85 min. Dir: Ronald Moore. Cast: Marilyn Burns, Edwin Neal, Doug Davis.

Two cast members from the original *Texas Chainsaw Massacre* (Burns and Neal) reteamed for this poorly done sci-fi/horror hybrid about a futuristic mutant killer called Splatter (Neal) killing the smarmy frat boys who earlier ridiculed him. Burns is a tough hooker who tries to stop Splatter. Grim little mess. Aka *Splatter.*

FUTUREWORLD

★★★ Goodtimes, 1976, PG, 104 min. Dir: Richard T. Heffron. Cast: Peter Fonda, Blythe Danner, Arthur Hill, John Ryan, Stuart Margolin, Yul Brynner.

In this first-rate sequel to *Westworld,* reporters Fonda and Danner investigate the newly reopened adult theme park and stumble upon a plan to replace world leaders with robot duplicates. Highlighting character over action, the film has a nicely well matched pair of leads in Fonda and Danner, with Brynner (the original *Westworld*'s gunslinger) turning up for an eerie, erotic dream sequence. Derivative of *Invasion of the Body Snatchers* but still well done.

GALACTIC GIGOLO

★ Urban Classics, 1987, R, 80 min. Dir: Gorman Bechard. Cast: Carmine Capobianco, Debi Thibeault, Ruth Collins, Angela Nicholas, Frank Steward.

Capobianco, coming on like a *very* poor man's Andrew Dice Clay, is an oversexed alien looking for easy Earth girls and running into sleazy gangsters instead. Cheesy sci-fi comedy with carloads of T&A but a few laughs; from the director of *Psychos in Love.*

GALAXINA

★★ Goodtimes, 1980, R, 95 min. Dir: William Sachs. Cast: Dorothy Stratton, Stephen Macht, James David Hilton, Avery Schreiber.

Murdered *Playboy* playmate Stratton gives an appropriately robotic performance as a desirable femme android in this cheap star vehicle. Sachs (*The Incredible Melting Man*) directs without flair and all the male cast members are so busy leering at Dorothy that she actually ends up doing the best acting in the film! For centerfold movie vehicle completists only.

GALAXIS

★☆ Turner, 1995, R, 91 min. Dir: William Mesa. Cast: Brigitte Nielsen, Richard Moll, John H. Brennan, Craig Fairbrass.

Nielsen is well cast as an Amazon warrior woman (no thespic stretch there, boy) in this otherwise humdrum no-brainer about Brigitte's search for a power source that will free her planet from the domination of evil demon Moll. The usual complications ensue.

GALAXY INVADER

★ VCI, 1985, PG, 80 min. Dir: Don Dohler. Cast: Richard Ruxton, Faye Tilles, George Stover, Greg Dohler, Anne Frith, Glenn Barnes.

Another Dohler semi-home movie passed off as a professional feature, with Barnes as an immobily masked alien going on a laser-wielding rampage in the Baltimore suburbs. At least Dohler's *Nightbeast* had a better monster costume and a bit of gore to relieve the tedium; this one has nothing.

GALAXY OF TERROR

★★★ Nelson, 1981, R, 81 min. Dir: Bruce D. Clark. Cast: Edward Albert, Erin Moran, Ray Walston, Zalman King, Grace Zabriske, Robert Englund, Sid Haig, Taffee O'Connell.

Outrageous rip-off of *Alien* (not to mention *Forbidden Planet* and *The Empire Strikes Back,*) with Albert leading a rescue team to a strange planet searching for a missing ship and encountering violent death in the form of their worst fears come true. O'Connell is raped by a gigantic maggot (a scene you're not likely to forget); Haig is stabbed to death by his own severed arm; *Twin Peaks'* Zabriske bursts into flames; *Red Shoe Diaries* maven King is mauled by an H. R. Giger reject; and *Happy Days'* own Moran is disemboweled before her head graphically bursts apart! Prerelease editing leaves the plot virtually incomprehensible and the ending is a disappointment, but this Roger Corman production still comes highly recommended for fans of the terminally weird.

GAMERA

★★☆ Celebrity, 1965, NR, 79 min. Dir: Moriaki Yuasa. Cast: Eiji Funakoshi, Michiko Sugata, Harumi Kieitachi, Junichiro Yamashita, Yoshiro Uchida.

The first and best of the long-running giant turtle series, this is Daiei Studios' answer to Toho's popular Godzilla. Gamera is awakened from arctic ice by a nuclear bomb blast and heads for Japan. There he proves indestructible as he stomps through Tokyo, forcing the army to come up with an ingenious plan to dispose of him. Originally released in the U.S. as *Gammera the Invincible* with new scenes featuring Brian Donlevy, Albert Dekker, John Baragrey, Diane Findlay, Dick O'Neill, and others. It's interesting to note that in the Japanese version (released in dubbed form here by Celebrity) it's the error of an American pilot that revives Gamera; in the U.S. version it's routine nuclear testing that does the deed, and a team of NATO military and scientist types (headed by Donlevy) who come up with the plan to defeat the monster (in the original version the Japanese figure it out all by themselves, thank you). Followed by nine sequels, beginning with *Gamera vs. Barugon.*

"So, are you Michelangelo, Leonardo, or what?"
Gamera *(1965).*

GAMERA VS. BARUGON
★★ Celebrity, 1966, NR, 101 min. Dir: Shigeo Tanaka. Cast: Kojiro Hongo, Kyoko Enami, Akira Natsuki, Koiji Fujiyama.

Accidentally released from his space capsule prison, Gamera returns to battle Barugon, a big-horned dinosaur that emits a rainbow freeze ray. The most "adult" oriented of the early Gamera movies, with a culture clash romantic subplot involving an innocent native girl (who adapts to miniskirts quite readily) and a modern Japanese man and no kids in sight. TV title: *War of the Monsters*.

GAMERA VS. GAOS
★★ Celebrity, 1967, NR, 87 min. Dir: Noriaki Yuasa. Cast: Kojiro Hongo, Kichijiro Ueda, Hisayuki Abe, Reiko Kashahara.

This time Gamera is pitted against Gaos, a gigantic batlike flying creature with destructive laser breath and a taste for humans (whom he tastes with a frequency quite alarming for a movie aimed at kids). The Rodan-like Gaos must have been pretty popular because he returned for a cameo in *Gamera vs. Guiron* and was a major threat again in *Gamera, Guardian of the Universe*. Aka *Gamera vs. Gyaos* and *Return of the Giant Monsters*.

GAMERA VS. GUIRON
★☆ Celebrity, 1969, G, 83 min. Dir: Noriaki Yuasa. Cast: Nobuhiro Kajima, Christopher Murphy, Miyuki Akiyama, Yuko Hamada.

Gamera flies into space to take on a pair of bodacious alien tootsies who've kidnapped a couple of annoying Earth boys to chow down on their brains. Will our titanic turtle stop the gals and their knife-headed watch-monster Guiron? This one *really* flies off the goofy meter with its acrobatic Gamera stunts, evil brain-munching villainesses, and the unforgettable Gamera theme sung in Japanese. TV title: *Attack of the Monsters*.

GAMERA VS. GYAOS
See: *Gamera vs. Gaos*.

GAMERA VS. ZIGRA
★☆ Celebrity, 1971, G, 91 min. Dir: Noriaki Yuasa. Cast: Eiko Yamani, Reiko Kashara, Mikiko Tsubouchi, Arlene Zoellner.

A beautiful female alien (played by Kashahara, the native girl from *Gamera vs. Barugon*) tries to take over the world with Zigra, a huge flying shark monster—but not if Gamera can help it. Overlong and overly complicated, but see it for the scene where Gamera does his Laurie Partridge impression using Zigra as a keyboard.

GAMMA PEOPLE, THE
★★ Columbia/TriStar, 1956, NR, 78 min. Dir: John Gilling. Cast: Paul Douglas, Eva Bartok, Leslie Phillips, Walter Rilla, Martin Miller, Rosalie Crutchley.

Oddball Brit sci-fi thriller with reporter Douglas and photographer Phillips ending up in the mythical country of Gudavia, where scientist Rilla has developed a mind-bending device that can turn people into either geniuses or imbeciles. Gilling went on to direct some diverting B-budget '60s horror films like *Shadow of the Cat* and *Plague of the Zombies*, but here he brings little panache to an interesting but poorly developed story.

GAMMERA THE INVINCIBLE
See: *Gamera*.

GAPPA THE TRIPHIBIAN MONSTER
See: *Monster from a Prehistoric Planet*.

GANJASAURUS REX
★ Rhino, 1987, NR, 100 min. Dir: Ursi Reynolds. Cast: Paul Bassis, Dave Fresh, Rosie Jones.

Cheap pro-drug monster movie (huh?) about a plastic prehistoric monster awakened from eons of sleep when the Man begins burning the marijuana fields above its resting place. Tries to be hip, clever, and funny but fails at all three. Just say no.

GAS-S-S-S!
★★★ Vestron, 1970, PG, 79 min. Dir: Roger Corman. Cast: Bud Cort, Cindy Williams, Robert Corff, Ben Vereen, Talia Shire, Elaine Giftos, Marshall McLuhan, Country Joe and the Fish.

A mysterious gas is unleashed from a defense plant in Alaska and everyone in the world over thirty dies from its effects. Can the young people of the Earth then unite to save civilization? Corman's black comic take on the end-of-the-world genre has some great moments and a terrific cast (many of them only a few years shy of stardom) but heavy reediting by AIP against Corman's wishes leaves the film feeling curiously unfinished and compromised. Still worth seeing, though. Aka *Gas-s-s-s!*, or *It May Become Necessary to Destroy the World in Order to Save It*.

GAS-S-S-S!, OR IT MAY BECOME NECESSARY TO DESTROY THE WORLD IN ORDER TO SAVE IT
See: *Gas-s-s-s!*

GHIDRAH, THE THREE-HEADED MONSTER
★★★ Interglobal, 1964, NR, 85 min. Dir: Inoshiro Honda. Cast: Yosuke Natsuki, Yuriko Hoshi, Hiroshi Koizumi, Akiko Wakabayasi, Emi Ito, Yumi Ito.

Ghidrah, a three-headed, twin-tailed flying dragon from space ravages the world until Godzilla, Mothra, and Rodan team up to stop him. One of Toho's most entertaining monster mashes, this mixes in secret agents, foreign spies, political intrigue, and other subplots with the usual monster battles and has a nicely tongue-in-cheek rather than insultingly flat-out comic approach that does it wonders. Original title: *Chikyo Saidaino Kessen (The Greatest Battle on Earth)*.

GHOST

★★★ Paramount, 1990, PG-13, 122 min. Dir: Jerry Zucker. Cast: Patrick Swayze, Demi Moore, Whoopi Goldberg, Tony Goldwyn, Rick Aviles, Vincent Schiavelli, Gail Boggs, Phil Leeds.

After he is murdered, Swayze discovers that he was the target of a hit and his ghost—with the help of psychic Goldberg—tries to warn girlfriend Moore that she too is in danger. Overlong and inconsistant (Swayze longs to touch Moore but can't; yet he can still slug a bad guy for a crowd-pleasing response), I kept getting the feeling that this started life as a straight horror movie but became a romantic fantasy (with a touch of comedy) as it went along. The stars are miscast (Demi is far too tough a gal for me to buy her vulnerable heroine act) but Whoopi won an Oscar for her fun turn and Schiavelli should have for his haunting performance as the subway ghost. A huge box office hit, this inspired Hollywood to churn out other big-budget fantasy films and made a chart-buster of the Righteous Brothers classic "Unchained Melody" all over again.

GHOST AND MRS. MUIR, THE

★★★ Fox, 1947, NR, 104 min. Dir: Joseph L. Mankiewicz. Cast: Gene Tierney, Rex Harrison, George Sanders, Edna Best, Anna Lee, Natalie Wood.

Romantic fantasy adapted from the novel by R. A. Dick about an independent young widow (the lovely Tierney) who discovers that her cottage on the English coast is haunted by the ghost of a woman-hating sea captain (Harrison). The plot is fairly routine but sensitive handling, good acting, and a lovely Bernard Herrmann musical score make this work. Later a TV series with Hope Lange and Edward Mulhare in the Tierney-Harrison roles.

GHOST DAD

★☆ MCA/Universal, 1990, PG, 84 min. Dir: Sidney Pointer. Cast: Bill Cosby, Kimberly Russell, Denise Nicholas, Ian Bannen, Christine Ebersole, Barry Corbin, Dana Ashbrook, Salim Grant, Brooke Fontaine, Dakin Matthews.

Everyone is wasting their time in this flop Cosby comedy (made while he was kicking ratings ass as the king of NBC-TV) about a widower killed in a car crash who returns in spirit form to help his orphaned kids. Sounds hilarious so far, right? Probably made to cash in on the success of *Ghost,* this is far too strained a premise to provide many laughs or tears.

GHOST GOES WEST, THE

★★☆ Nelson, 1936, NR, 82 min. Dir: Rene Clair. Cast: Robert Donat, Jean Parker, Eugene Pallette, Elsa Lanchester, Everly Gregg, Hay Petrie.

Strained but watchable farce with Donat as both an ancient Scottish ghost and his modern descendant who end up in Florida with the transplanted family castle and get involved in the usual ghost house comedy situations. The cast is good but this has almost a Disney-like blandness to it that makes it hard to get involved.

GHOSTS CAN'T DO IT

★ Columbia/TriStar, 1989, R, 95 min. Dir: John Derek. Cast: Bo Derek, Anthony Quinn, Leo Damian, Don Murray, Julie Newmar, Donald Trump.

And Bo can't act, but that's another story. In this yawn-inducing vanity fare, our perfect 10 runs around endlessly trying to fund a hunky body for the soul of deceased hubby Quinn (photographed through mosquito netting or something to make him appear reasonably younger) but still finds the time to strip off whenever director-hubby John thinks it's appropriate—like in every other scene. Even appearances by Newmar as a guardian angel and the Donald as, well, the Donald do little to relieve the tedium of this lame fantasy-comedy-sex film.

GIANT CLAW, THE

★☆ Goodtimes, 1957, NR, 74 min. Dir: Fred F. Sears. Cast: Jeff Morrow, Mara Corday, Morris Andrum, Robert Shayne.

"It's just a bird, a big bird!" Shayne keeps shouting but even Cookie Monster would be scarier than the hilariously inept buzzard marionette they parade before us in this nickel-and-dime '50s big-beast flick. Lots of stock footage from better films (like *Earth vs. the Flying Saucers* and *The Beast from 20,000 Fathoms*) and an all-pro cast (including *Playboy* doll and monster movie vet Corday) acting with so much sincerity that it hurts are utterly wasted on this cinematic lost cause about a gigantic vulture from the stars on a globe-trotting rampage. The New York City-trashing climax is pathetic.

GIANT GILA MONSTER, THE

★☆ Rhino, 1959, NR, 74 min. Dir: Ray Kellogg. Cast: Don Sullivan, Lisa Simone, Shug Fisher, Ken Graham.

A five-and-ten-cent-store pet gila monster smashes up toy cars and trains and snacks on lovers' lane smoochers while Sullivan comes on like a low-budget Elvis in this cheesy '50s monster movie. Shot in Texas by the team who brought you the slightly better *The Killer Shrews*, this has a few laughs but is too dull and drawn out to be worth sitting through to find them.

GIANT OF METROPOLIS, THE

★★ Sinister Cinema, 1961, NR, 92 min. Dir: Umberto Scarpelli. Cast: Gordon Mitchell, Bella Cortez, Liana Orfei, Furio Meniconi.

Muscular hero Mitchell leads an expedition to the city of Metropolis, a scientifically advanced burg where mind control is used to create an army of zombie slaves. Italian rip-off of *Atlantis, the Lost Continent* that's actually more watchable; muddled script and direction but colorful settings and photography.

GIANT SPIDER INVASION, THE

☆ VCL, 1975, PG, 82 min. Dir: Bill Rebane. Cast: Steve Brodie, Barbara Hale, Leslie Parrish, Alan Hale, Robert Easton, Bill Williams.

It's scary to think that I actually saw this no-budget wonder in a theater back in '75 but I did and I still can't get over it. Gigantic spiders spill out of a black hole into Wisconsin (I know, I know) and terrorize a cast of semifamiliar faces who probably looked upon this as an acceptable alternative to standing in the welfare line. This makes *Earth vs. the Spider* look like *Jurassic Park*.

GIANTS OF THESSALY, THE

★★☆ Sinister Cinema, 1960, NR, 86 min. Dir: Riccardo Freda. Cast: Roland Carey, Ziva Rodann, Massimo Girotti, Alberto Farnese, Moira Orfei.

Freda adds some colorful touches to this version of Jason and the Golden Fleece. Jason (Carey) encounters monsters and an evil queen (the sultry Rodann) in his quest for the fabulous treasure. Watchable sword-and-sandal fantasy with a grand musical score by Carlo Rustichelli.

GIGANTIS, THE FIRE MONSTER

See: *Godzilla Raids Again!*

GIRL IN HIS POCKET

★★ Sinister Cinema, 1957, NR, 82 min. Dir: Pierre Kast. Cast: Jean Marais, Genevieve Page, Jean-Claude Brialy, Agnes Laurent.

Minor French spoof of *The Incredible Shrinking Man*. Biology teacher Marais (of *Beauty and the Beast* fame) invents a shrinking potion that causes complications for everyone in this silly comedy. Aka *Un Amour de Poche (Love in the Pocket)* and *Nude in His Pocket*.

GIRL IN THE MOON

See: *Woman in the Moon.*

GLEN AND RANDA

★★★ United Entertainment, 1970 R, 94 min. Dir: Jim McBride. Cast: Steven Curry, Shelley Plimpton, Woodrow Chambliss, Garry Goodrow.

This underrated sci-fi drama (with black comic touches) is an Age of Aquarius variation on any number of old '50s B movies and *Twilight Zone* episodes. Curry is Glen, a post-Armageddon innocent who thinks that an old *Wonder Woman* comic is his key to salvation. Plimpton is Randa, the lass he meets in his travels and who joins Glen in his search for life in a nuclear-devastated landscape. Thoughtful low-budgeter with many interesting touches.

GNAW: FOOD OF THE GODS II

See: *Food of the Gods Part 2.*

GNOME CALLED GNORM, A

See: *The Adventures of a Gnome Called Gnorm.*

GNOME-MOBILE, THE

★★★ Disney, 1967, NR, 90 min. Dir: Robert Stevenson. Cast: Walter Brennan, Tom Lowell, Karen Dotrice, Matthew Garber, Ed Wynn, Richard Deacon.

Above-average Disney fantasy from a novel by Upton Sinclair. Brennan brings his usual twinkle to the dual role of a wealthy northern California lumberman and the gnome king who lives with his followers beneath an ancient redwood on the millionaire's property. Standard complications are enlivened by some unexpectedly harsh touches (the tycoon locked away in a madhouse and the gnome imprisoned in a freak show) and some excellent special effects.

GODZILLA AND SON

See: *Son of Godzilla.*

GODZILLA, KING OF THE MONSTERS

★★★★ Paramount/Gateway, 1954, NR, 79 min. Dirs: Inoshiro Honda, Terry Morse. Cast: Raymond Burr, Takashi Shimura, Momoko Kochi, Akira Takarada.

Tokyo is reduced to rubble for the first time in the original Godzilla film. Scenes shot in the U.S. with Burr and added to the reedited original work quite well and the moody monochrome night photography and pounding Akira Ifukube music (featuring the classic Godzilla theme) add to the undiminished luster of this monster classic. Favorite moments: Godzilla's first appearance, rising over the crest of an island hill; Kochi's shocked reaction to a demonstration of the "Oxygen Destroyer"; and a haunting shot of the bellowing monster as seen through a huge Tokyo aviary alive with terrified birds.

GODZILLA 1984
See: *Godzilla 1985.*

GODZILLA 1985
★★ Starmaker, 1984, PG, 88 min. Dirs: Koji Hoshimoto, R. J. Kizer. Cast: Raymond Burr, Ken Tanaka, Shin Takuma, Yasuko Sawaguchi.

After a decade of slumber, the Big G was back on the big screen to stomp Tokyo once again in this big-budget but rather hollow return engagement. The American version also brings back Burr (now almost as big as Godzilla) and

his presence adds a welcome touch of sobriety to a bad re-edit offering tacked on humorous elements (none of them very funny) and an overall muddling of the film's serious intentions, with our guy Zilla now seen as a big green metaphor for nuclear devastation. Originally called *Godzilla 1984*, this was a huge hit in Japan (and a minor one in the states) and inspired a whole new series of updated Godzilla movies.

GODZILLA ON MONSTER ISLAND
See: *Godzilla vs. Gigan.*

GODZILLA RAIDS AGAIN!
★★ Goodtimes, 1955, NR, 78 min. Dir: Motoyoshi Odo. Cast: Hiroshi Koizumi, Setsuko Wakayama, Mindru Chiaki, Takashi Shimura.

Originally called *Gojira no Gyaskushu (Godzilla's Counterattack)* and first released stateside by Warner Brothers as *Gigantis, the Fire Monster* when they couldn't get the rights to the Godzilla name, this feeble first followup to the

The WWF hits Japan in Godzilla Raids Again *(1955).*

The new, improved Godzilla takes a stroll through Osaka in Godzilla vs. Biollante *(1989).*

original *Godzilla* is one of the weakest entries. A new Godzilla and another monster called Anguris smash Osaka and each other until Anguris is bumped off and Godzilla is frozen alive in a glacier. Cheesy FX and a dull love triangle between a pair of jet pilots and the girl they both adore make this a bore.

GODZILLA'S COUNTERATTACK

See: *Godzilla Raids Again!*

GODZILLA'S REVENGE

★★☆ Paramount/Gateway, 1969, G, 69 min. Dir: Inoshiro Honda. Cast: Kenji Sahara, Tomonori Yazaki, Machiko Naka, Sachio Sakai.

The Godzilla series tries to emulate the Gamera films with this fantasy about a lonely kid who dreams of Monster Island and imagines a friendship with Godzilla's son Minya, who can even talk here! An odd mix of the serious and

the silly; I'd bet real money that John Hughes saw this before he wrote his *Home Alone* movies. Aka *Ord Kaiju Daishingeki (All Monsters Attack).*

GODZILLA VS. BIOLLANTE

★★★ HBO, 1989, PG, 104 min. Dir: Kazuki Omori. Cast: Kunihiko Mitamura, Yoshiko Tanaka, Masanobu Takashima, Megumi Odaka.

Godzilla survives his fall into the volcano at Mt. Mihara from the end of *Godzilla 1985* and lays waste to Osaka before taking on the enormous plant monster Biollante, an amalgamation of DNA from Godzilla, a rose petal, and the murdered daughter of a famous scientist. One of the most serious and downbeat of the entire *Godzilla* series, this is full of poetic images, melancholy music, and has a new foe for Godzilla clearly inspired by Audrey II from the *Little Shop of Horrors* movie musical.

GODZILLA VS. GIGAN

★★ Starmaker, 1972, PG, 89 min. Dir: Jun Fukuda. Cast: Hiroshi Ishikawa, Yuriko Hishimi, Tomoko Umeda, Minoru Takashima.

Godzilla and friend Angillus (the former Angurus from *Godzilla Raids Again!*) are given voice by an alien device in this colorful but dumb '70s Zilla flick. The aliens look like rejects from *Joe's Apartment* but disguise themselves as a teen student and his teacher-mentor (we won't get into that relationship) and plot the takeover of the world from an amusement park called Children's Land, complete with Godzilla-shaped office tower. Eventually, Godzilla and Angillus take on a robotic bird (with a circular saw in his belly) called Gigan and a rather plastic-looking new version of Ghidrah, who comes complete with stock footage of the old Ghidrah from a variety of earlier encounters. Routine fun for fans. Aka *Godzilla on Monster Island.*

GODZILLA VS. HEDORAH

See: *Godzilla vs. the Smog Monster.*

GODZILLA VS. KING GHIDORAH

★★★☆ Manga Entertainment, 1991, PG, 99 min. Dir: Kazuki Omori. Cast: Kiwako Hawada, Anna Nakagawa, Yoshio Tsuchiya, Megumi Odaka, Robert Scottfield, Kenji Sahara.

Toho really hit a home run with this elaborate followup to *Godzilla vs. Biollante.* It's an amazingly exciting tale of people from the future who take some 1990s companions on a trip back to the 1940s to prevent the atomic birth of Godzilla. History is changed but a whole new, far more destructive monster called King Ghidorah (a reinvention of the dragonlike Ghidrah, the Three-Headed Monster) is birthed, all part of a plan by the future people to prevent Japan from becoming the dominant world power in the twenty-first century. Somewhat derivative of movies like *Back to the Future* and *The Terminator* (Scottfield plays a Robert Patrick-like android) but so exhilarating that this hardy matters, with state-of-the-art man-in-a-suit monsters, a cleverly twisty plot (Godzilla is ultimately re-created as a pitiless, nuclear-powered death machine), and a pulse-pounding score by maestro Akira Ifukube. When first released in Japan, this caused a bit of a controversy due to its depiction of the U.S. military as a pack of bumbling cowards (this dubbed version goes the image one better by voicing them all as dirt-dumb rednecks and don't-ask-don't-tell types) but this being a *Godzilla* movie, after all, makes all this alleged subversion seem a bit of a stretch. One of the series' finest hours.

GODZILLA VS. MECHAGODZILLA

★★☆ Starmaker, 1974, PG, 84 min. Dir: Jun Fukuda. Cast: Masauki Daimon, Kazuya Aoyama, Reiko Tajima, Barbara Lynn.

Godzilla battles *Planet of the Apes*-reject aliens and their robot Zilla front man in this colorful episode. Made to celebrate Godzilla's twentieth anniversary, this is more elaborate than most '70s series entries with a healthier budget and more expansive plot than usual. Aka *Godzilla vs. the Cosmic Monster* and *Godzilla vs. the Bionic Monster.*

GODZILLA VS. MEGALON

★☆ Goodtimes, 1973, PG, 78 min. Dir: Jun Fukuda. Cast: Katshuhiko Saski, Hiroyuki Kawase, Yutaka Hayashi, Robert Dunham.

Godzilla and a robot called Jet Jaguar beat up on Megalon (a big beetle with drill arms) and guest star Gigan. The very worst of the *Godzilla* series, with minimal FX and awful dubbing. U.S. posters for this atrocity actually depicted Zilla and Megalon coming to blows atop New York's World Trade Center to cash in on the '76 *King Kong* remake.

GODZILLA VS. MONSTER ZERO

★★ Paramount/Gateway, 1965, PG, 93 min. Dir: Inoshiro Honda. Cast: Nick Adams, Akira Takarada, Kumi Mizuno, Akira Kubo, Keiko Sawai, Jun Tazaki.

The special effects (when not leaning on stock footage) aren't bad and the alien invasion plot (rehashed to greater effect in *Destroy All Monsters*) holds promise, but this ultimately routine entry is worth seeing mostly for Adams's totally out-of-control acting as heroic astronaut Glen. Nick is so intense you expect his head to blow off at any moment; even the big G would back down from this boy. Aka *Kaiju Kaisenso (Monster Zero).*

GODZILLA VS. MOTHRA

★★★☆ Paramount/Gateway, 1963, NR, 87 min. Dir: Inoshiro Honda. Cast: Akira Takarada, Yuriko Hoshi, Hiroshi Koizumi, Kenji Sahara, Emi Ito, Ymi Ito.

The second best of the series is an immediate followup to the more comic *King Kong vs. Godzilla.* A typhoon blows a comatose Godzilla and Mothra's huge egg ashore in Japan. Godzilla goes on his usual destructive tear and Mothra dies protecting the egg, which hatches out a pair of larvae that spin Zilla into a mammoth cocoon. Humorous without being corny, with solid FX photography and a personable cast (including the Ito sisters as those talking-in-unison tiny Mothra guardians). First released in the U.S. by AIP as *Godzilla vs.*

the Thing (they apparently couldn't get the rights to the Mothra name—if you listen carefully, you'll notice that everyone refers to the huge moth as Moedra).

GODZILLA VS. MOTHRA
★★☆ Manga Entertainment, 1992, PG, 97 min. Dir: Takao Okawara. Cast: Tatsuya Bessho, Satomi Kobayashi, Takehiro Murata, Shinjo Kobayashi, Keiko Imamura, Sayaka Osawa.

A semi-remake of the '63 version, this finds Godzilla up against both Mothra and its evil counterpart Battra. Bessho is the Indiana Jones-type hero hired by the Japanese government to retrieve Mothra's egg while the revived Godzilla is kept on the sidelines for the most part until a spectacular battle in a seaside Yokahama amusement park with the flying Mothra and Battra. Imamura and Osawa are Mothra's tiny twin princesses. An enormous success in Japan, this is fun but probably the least effective of the new Godzilla films I've seen. The dubbing job on the Manga tape is horrible, like an episode of *Johnny Soko*. Aka *Godzilla vs. Queen Mothra*.

GODZILLA VS. QUEEN MOTHRA
See: *Godzilla vs. Mothra* (1992).

GODZILLA VS. THE BIONIC MONSTER
See: *Godzilla vs. Mechagodzilla*.

GODZILLA VS. THE COSMIC MONSTER
See: *Godzilla vs. Mechagodzilla*.

GODZILLA VS. THE SEA MONSTER
★★☆ Goodtimes, 1966, NR, 83 min. Dir: Jun Fukuda. Cast: Akira Takarada, Kumi Mizuno, Toru Watanabe, Hideo Sunazuka, Emi Ito, Yumi Ito.

Bank robber Takarada and several others are shipwrecked on an uncharted island where they encounter native girl Mizuno (looking really hot), an evil organization known as the Red Bamboo, a huge shrimp known as Ebirah, and, of course, Godzilla. Though it takes a while to get going, this entertaining entry in the series eschews the usual city stomping for the flavor of the islands and is all the better for it. Also featuring a giant buzzard, a nuclear explosion, guest star Mothra, and the Ito sisters. Aka *Nankai No dai Ketto (Big Duel in the North Sea)* and *Ebirah, Horror of the Deep*.

GODZILLA VS. THE SMOG MONSTER
★★☆ Warner, 1971, G, 84 min. Dir: Yoshimitu Bano. Cast: Akira Yamuchi, Hiroyuki Kawase, Toshie Kimura, Toshio Shubaki, Keiko Mari.

In one of the weirdest *Godzilla* movies ever,

our outsized reptilian hero goes up against Hedorah, a creature made of sludge and pollution (*hedora* means "pollution" in Japanese). Director Bano goes all arty with animated inserts, multiple screens, and an ecological theme—not to mention the theme song "Save the Earth." For a film aimed at kids this has some surprisingly grisly touches—the teenage hero and a number of others are reduced to slimy bones by Hedorah's poisonous spillage. Aka *Godzilla vs. Hedorah*.

GODZILLA VS. THE THING
See: *Godzilla vs. Mothra* (1963).

GOKE, BODY SNATCHER FROM HELL
★★☆ Sinister Cinema, 1968, R, 84 min. Dir: Haijime Sato. Cast: Hideo Ko, Teruo Yoshida, Tomoni Sato, Masaya Takahashi.

Plane crash survivors are attacked by a dead man possessed by an alien force that transforms him into a bloodthirsty vampirelike monster. This decidedly off-the-wall Japanese movie is like a cross between *Alive* and *The Thing* and, though badly dubbed, has moments of odd visual beauty and some surprisingly gory touches. Aka *Body Snatcher from Hell* and *G the Vampire*.

GOLDEN CHILD, THE
★☆ Paramount, 1986, PG-13, 94 min. Dir: Michael Ritchie. Cast: Eddie Murphy, Charlotte Lewis, Charles Dance, Victor Wong, James Hong, J. L. Reate.

Dire action-comedy-fantasy with Murphy as a finder of lost children (oh sure) hired by beautiful Lewis to locate Reate, a supposedly mystical boy sought by demon-in-human-form Dance. Some of the FX (like a room falling away to expose the pits of hell) are good, Lewis is stunning, and Dance properly slimy, but this is first and foremost a Murphy vehicle and it lets both Eddie and his audience down in a big way. Murphy's character makes no sense, the attempts at humor are strained, and the alleged dare-doing makes this look like an Indiana Jones script Harrison Ford turned down for being too preposterous—which, given that this was made by Paramount, is a distinct possibility. Worse than *Beverly Hills Cop 3*.

GOLDENEYE
★★☆ MGM/UA, 1995, PG-13, 129 min. Dir: Martin Campbell. Cast: Pierce Brosnan, Izabella Scorpuco, Sean Bean, Famke Janssen, Joe Don Baker, Judi Dench, Desmond Llewelyn, Samantha Bond.

After an unprecedented six-year gap, the James Bond series resumed with this slight but watchable thriller introducing erstwhile *Rem-*

ington Steele Brosnan in the 007 role. Saddled with the almost impossible task of deconstructing (and even spoofing) the Bond image while trying to continue on with the grand traditions of the series, this new Bond is full of curious contradictions and strained attempts to be postmodern and politically correct but is only at its best while carrying on in the style of the old films. This time Bond is after a powerful space weapon that's fallen into the hands of a mystery villain who turns out to be the supposedly dead 006 (Bean), who hopes to use this "Goldeneye" device to restart the Cold War by bringing Russia back under Soviet control. Brosnan is a relaxed and confident 007; too bad he really doesn't seem to have the fire for the role yet. On the other hand, Scorpuco (as a Russian computer expert) is a likable, believable leading lady and Janssen is a scene-stealer as the villainous Xenia Onatopp (Pussy Galore, eat your heart out) who kills her lovers by crushing them with her thighs. And the show-stopping teaser sequence puts the openings of nearly all the other Bond movies to shame.

GOLDENGIRL
★★ Nelson, 1979, PG 104 min. Dir: Joseph Sargent. Cast: Susan Anton, Robert Culp, Curt Jurgens, Leslie Caron, Harry Guardino, Jessica Walter.

Big, blonde Anton and a more-or-less all-star supporting cast try to make some dramatic sense out of this corny *Bionic Woman*-type tale of Olympic hopeful Susan turned into a robotic superwoman by mad doctor Jurgens. Too silly to take seriously but the cast tries.

GOLDEN VOYAGE OF SINBAD, THE
★★★ Columbia/TriStar, 1973, G, 104 min. Dir: Gordon Hessler. Cast: John Phillip Law, Caroline Munro, Tom Baker, Douglas Wilmer, Kurt Christian, Martin Shaw, John David Garfield, Robert Shaw.

The second in Ray Harryhausen's *Sinbad* trilogy is flatly directed by Hessler and flatly acted by Law in the lead but still has a lot going for it. This time Sinbad helps a horribly disfigured Grand Wizier (Wilmer) stop a black magician (Baker) from gaining control of the fabulous Fountain of Destiny and the gifts it grants. Munro is incredibly sexy as a bewitching slave girl whose tattooed palm marks her as a sacrifice to an enormous cyclopean centaur. Also features a living wooden statue; a sword-wielding, six-armed kali figure; a golden griffin that battles the centaur at the climax; and a rousing score by Miklos Rozsa. Baker makes for a surprisingly sympathetic and human villain and *Jaws* star Shaw has an uncredited cameo in heavy makeup as a helpful oracle. Aka *Sinbad's Golden Voyage.*

GOLDEN YEARS, THE
★★ Worldvision, 1991, NR, 232 min. Dir: Josef Anderson. Cast: Keith Szarabajka, Felicity Huffman, Frances Sternhagen, Ed Lauter.

A condensed version (with a tacked on ending) of the short-lived Stephen King TV series about an elderly janitor (Szarabajka in bad makeup) exposed to radiation at a research lab. Soon afterward he begins to grow younger, taking up with pretty young Huffman and abandoning wife Sternhagen while being pursued by a mysterious government agency. A sometimes effective but overall uninvolving tribute to TV shows like *The Outer Limits* and *The Immortal* done damage by an unsympathetic lead character and insufficient explanations. Aka *Stephen King's Golden Years.*

GOLDFINGER
★★★★ MGM/UA, 1964, NR, 111 min. Dir: Guy Hamilton. Cast: Sean Connery, Honor Blackman, Gert Frobe, Shirley Eaton, Harold Sakata, Tania Mallett, Bernard Lee, Lois Maxwell, Desmond Llewelyn, Nadja Regin.

The quintessential James Bond movie with Connery in top form as 007, this time after gold-obsessed madman Frobe, who's out to gain control of the world's gold supply by contaminating the contents of Fort Knox with nuclear radiation. Blackman is man-hating Pussy Galore; Eaton is painted gold and suffocates; Sakata is Oddjob, the henchman with the lethal bowler hat; Shirley Bassey sings the classic title tune; and Connery is nearly castrated by a laser beam. Now that's entertainment.

GOLIATH AGAINST THE GIANTS
★★ Sinister Cinema, 1961, NR, 90 min. Dir: Guido Malatesta. Cast: Brad Harris, Gloria Milland, Fernando Rey, Barbara Carrol.

Yet another B-grade muscle fantasy with Harris as Goliath/Maciste battling a soggy sea monster and beautiful Amazons in his quest to ... well, to tell you the truth, I forgot. Run-of-the-mill sweat and swordplay.

GOLIATH AND THE DRAGON
★★☆ Sinister Cinema, 1960, NR, 90 min. Dir: Vittorio Vottafavi. Cast: Mark Forest, Broderick Crawford, Eleanora Ruffo, Gaby Andre, Phillipe Hersent.

This is one of those movies that's enjoyable for all the wrong reasons. An elaborate but totally unconvincing fantasy with Crawford as a corrupt political bigwig (picture Willy Stark in a toga) trying to take over an ancient kingdom. Forest (a real stiff) is the hero who must defeat a female wind demon, a triple-headed dog, a huge bat creature, and, of course, a dragon in order to save both wife and country from Brod's pudgy grasp. A regular riot, this low-brow Italian Harryhausen wannabe has ultra-chintzy special effects, inept dubbing, and a brassy Les Baxter score to keep you coming back for more.

GOONIES, THE

★★☆ Warner, 1985, PG, 114 min. Dir: Richard Donner. Cast: Sean Astin, Josh Brolin, Corey Feldman, Martha Plimpton, Jeff Cohen, Kerri Green, Ke Huy Quan, John Matusak, Anne Ramsey, Joe Pantoliano, Robert Davi.

Loud, frantic kid's action-fantasy about a group of twelve- to fifteen-year-olds who discover a treasure map leading to the underground ruins of a legendary pirate ship. Overlong and often incomprehensible but the young cast is likable and Donner keeps things moving. The family of villains (headed by Ramsey and including Matuszak as a deformed son who looks like Jason Voorhees on Prozac) seem like they belong in another movie entirely.

GOR

★☆ Warner, 1988, PG, 95 min. Dir: Fritz Kiersch. Cast: Urbano Barbarini, Oliver Reed, Jack Palance, Rebecca Ferratti, Larry Taylor, Arthur Vosloo, Paul L. Smith, Grahame Clarke.

Annoyingly bad tongue-in-cheek sword-and-sorcery flick with Barbarini as a handsome nerd whisked away to another dimension where he finds himself thought of as a hero by the locals who want him to dispose of despotic ruler Reed. Barbarini, a former male model and frequent fixture in late '80s Italian horror films, is good-looking (as we're constantly reminded) but has all the acting skills of a tub of margarine. Reed does his usual I-was-probably-drunk-during-all-the-filming bit and Palance turns up late in the action to set up the sequel: *Outlaw of Gor*. Even *Al Gore* would be more exciting than this.

GORATH

★★ Columbia/TriStar, 1962, NR, 77 min. Dir: Inoshiro Honda. Cast: Ryo Ikebe, Jun Tazaki, Akihiko Hirata, Yumi Shirakawa, Takashi Shimura, Kumi Mizuno.

A sort of Japanese *When Worlds Collide*, this takes place in futuristic 1980 when the rogue planet Gorath was on a collision course with Earth—you remember, don't you? Talky and not nearly as exciting as some of Honda's other sci-fi/horror films. The U.S. release version, cut from the original 89-minute Japanese print, completely omits the climactic

rampage of a huge walrus unleashed from the melting polar ice cap due to Gorath's approach. It might have helped.

GORGO

★★★ VCI, 1960, NR, 75 min. Dir: Eugene Lourie. Cast: Bill Travers, William Sylvester, Vincent Winter, Martin Benson.

Travers and Sylvester discover a baby dinosaur (a mere 65 feet tall) off the Irish coast and take it to London for display. When Junior's 200-foot-tall mama comes crashing into town, you get to witness some of the coolest man-in-a-monster suit mass destruction ever filmed west of Tokyo. Lourie's third go at virtually the same story (filmed previously as *The Beast From 20,000 Fathoms* and *The Giant Behemoth*), this is so streamlined that it dispenses completely with any romantic subplot (though there's no denying the homoerotic subtext in the Bill and Bill relationship) and just gets to the city smashin' it knows everyone came to see. Aka *The Night the World Shook*.

GRAND TOUR: DISASTER IN TIME

★★☆ Academy Entertainment, 1991, PG-13, 99 min. Dir: David N. Twohy. Cast: Jeff Daniels, Ariana Richards, Emilia Crow, Jim Haynie, Nicholas Guest, Marilyn Lightstone.

Daniels is his usual likable self in this offbeat fantasy about the owner of a bed-and-breakfast who comes to believe that a group of unexpected guests are actually travelers from the future who've come back in time for some sinister purpose. Doesn't always work but a solid cast and low-key presentation make this version of Lawrence O'Donnell and L. C. Moore's novella *Vintage Season* worth noting.

GREATEST BATTLE ON EARTH, THE

See: *Ghidrah, the Three-Headed Monster*.

GREEN HORNET, THE

★★☆ VCI, 1940, NR, 130 min. Dirs: Ford Beebe, Ray Taylor. Cast: Kenneth Harlan, Anne Nagel, Keye Luke, Ann Doran, Joseph Crehan, Wade Boteler, Gordon Jones, Alan Ladd.

Not-bad serial adapted from the popular radio character created by George W. Trendle. Harlan is Britt Reed, alias masked crime fighter the Green Hornet and Luke is his trusty assistant Kato. Played surprisingly straight and fairly well done on a tight budget. Followed by *The Green Hornet Strikes Again* and the '60s TV series.

GREEN HORNET, THE
★★ Goodtimes, 1966, NR, 75 min. Dirs: Norman Foster, Jerry Douglas. Cast: Van Williams, Bruce Lee, Wende Wagner, Walter Brooke.

Three episodes of the TV series (a one-season wonder rushed into production in order to cash in on *Batman*) clumsily reedited into a "feature" released to theaters in the early '70s to trade on Lee's popularity as a martial arts star. The plots involve a madman hunting gangsters *Most Dangerous Game*-style, a tong war, and a phony alien invasion. More serious in tone than *Batman* but not as much fun either.

GREEN HORNET STRIKES AGAIN, THE
★★ VCI, 1940, NR, 150 min. Dirs: Ford Beebe, John Rawlins. Cast: Warren Hull, Anne Nagel, Keye Luke, C. Montague Shaw, Nestor Paiva, Wade Boteler, Eddie Acuff, James Seay, Pierre Watkin, Roy Barcroft.

Hull takes over for Kenneth Harlan in this followup to the original *Green Hornet* serial with the Hornet and Kato (Luke) protecting a powerful new bomb from foreign agents. Routine chapter play.

GREEN SLIME, THE
★★ MGM/UA, 1968, G, 88 min. Dir: Kinji Fukasaku. Cast: Robert Horton, Luciana Paluzzi, Richard Jaeckel, Bud Windom.

A coproduction between Japan's Toei Studios and Hollywood's MGM, this hilarious *Alien* predecessor involves tentacled, one-eyed slimy monsters overrunning an Earth-orbiting space station. Will commander Horton stop the slime and win back poured-into-her-costumes Paluzzi from former pal Jaeckel before 88 minutes are up? What do you think? Tacky but fun with laughable special effects and a theme song that'll haunt you for weeks. Aka *Battle Beyond the Stars*.

GROUNDHOG DAY
★★★ Columbia/TriStar, 1993, PG, 103 min. Dir: Harold Ramis. Cast: Bill Murray, Andie MacDowell, Chris Elliott, Stephen Tobolowsky, Brian Doyle-Murray, Marita Geraghty, Rick Ducommun, Robin Duke.

One of Murray's best vehicles casts him as an acerbic TV weatherman who travels to Punxsutawney, Pennsylvania, to film the annual Groundhog Day ceremony. He becomes stuck in time, reliving the same day over and over. Although it runs a bit long, this fantasy-comedy is never predictable (which it easily could have become) and remains consistently on the mark. Elliott nearly steals it as Bill's long-suffering cameraman.

GROUNDSTAR CONSPIRACY, THE
★★☆ MCA/Universal, 1972, PG, 95 min. Dir: Lamont Johnson. Cast: George Peppard, Michael Sarrazin, Christine Belford, Cliff Potts, James Olson, James McEachin.

Sarrazin, the lone survivor of a bomb blast at a space research center, is hounded by agent Peppard, who feels that his survival was no accident. Shot in Canada, this sci-fi-tinged thriller is like a cross between *Columbo* and *The Fugitive* and, although the plot doesn't always stand up, the solid cast carries it through.

G THE VAMPIRE
See: *Goke, Body Snatcher from Hell.*

GULLIVER'S TRAVELS
★☆ United Entertainment, 1977, G, 80 min. Dir: Peter Hunt. Cast: Richard Harris, Catherine Schell, Norman Shelly, Meredith Edwards.

Mediocre half-animated/half-live action adaptation of the Jonathan Swift tale. Harris, looking like he just wandered in from the set of *Orca*, is Gulliver, shipwrecked on an uncharted island inhabited by tiny animated people who like to sing bad songs by Michael Legrand. Cheesy British-Belgian Disney wannabe.

GULLIVER'S TRAVELS
★★☆ Hallmark, 1995, PG, 187 min. Dir: Charles Sturridge. Cast: Ted Danson, Mary Steenburgen, John Gielgud, Peter O'Toole, Omar Sharif, Geraldine Chaplin, Edward Fox, Ned Beatty, Edward Woodward, Alfre Woodard, James Fox, Robert Hardy.

Overstuffed and rather overblown retelling of the Jonathan Swift story as a vehicle for Danson. Ted (in a wig that makes him look rather like the Cowardly Lion) stumbles from a land of little people to a world of giants in a quest of self-discovery, occasionally running into an Irwin Allen-type special guest star. Good FX by Jim Henson's Muppet guys but a less-bloated running time might have picked up the pace.

GUY NAMED JOE, A
★★☆ MGM/UA, 1943, NR, 120 min. Dir: Victor Fleming. Cast: Spencer Tracy, Irene Dunne, Van Johnson, Ward Bond, Esther Williams, Lionel Barrymore, James Gleason, Barry Nelson, Don DeFore, Blake Edwards.

Popular in its day, this World War II-era fantasy falls a bit flat when seen today. Tracy is a pilot killed in action who's allowed to return to Earth to see that girlfriend Dunne finds happiness with Johnson. Tracy can do no wrong but this rather wrong-headed attempt by Hollywood to try and help the American public deal with the tragic loss of loved ones in the war is too contrived to really work, especially with its absurd finale. Remade as *Always*.

GUYVER, THE

★★☆ New Line, 1992, PG-13, 92 min. Dirs: Screaming Mad George, Steve Wang. Cast: Mark Hamill, Vivian Wu, Jack Armstrong, David Gale, Jimmie Walker, Michael Berryman, Jeffrey Combs, Linnea Quigley.

This live-action comic book gets an A for effort but doesn't really come off. Armstrong becomes infected by an alien device that transforms him into iron-plated superhero the Guyver; top-billed Hamill is an evil CIA agent who turns into a cockroach and a typically wigged-out Gale (in his final role) is a mutant-creating mad scientist. Lots of FX and cast for the fans but overall this works better in animated form. Aka *Mutronics*.

GUYVER 2: DARK HERO

★★ Columbia/TriStar, 1994, R, 127 min. Dir: Steve Wang. Cast: David Hayter, Kathy Christopherson, Christopher Michael.

Wang alone helms this followup with the Guyver (now played by Hayter) returning to battle more monsters. Good makeup and well-handled action but the slim storyline isn't helped by a two-hour-plus running time.

GYPSY MOON

★★ Sinister Cinema, 1953, NR, 78 min. Dir: Hollingsworth Morse. Cast: Richard Crane, Sally Mansfield, Scotty Beckett, Robert Lyden.

One of the better *Rocky Jones* "movies," with our hero stranded on one of a pair of warring moons and trying to help the people find peace. Slightly more serious in tone than most other entries in this cheapie series.

HALF HUMAN

★★ Rhino, 1955, NR, 70 min. Dirs: Inoshiro Honda and Kenneth C. Crane. Cast: John Carradine, Morris Ankrum, Akira Takarada, Momoko Kochi, Kenji Kasashara, Akemi Negishi, Russ Thorson, Robert Karns.

Honda's first post-*Godzilla* monster film gets butchered big time in this all-thumbs reedit. Carradine narrates the (mostly undubbed) original story of an expedition finding an ape man and its child living in the snowy mountains of northern Japan. The original footage has a great deal of atmosphere but the new scenes are nothing but talk, talk, talk. Original title: *Jujin Yuki-Otoko (The Monster Snowman)*.

HANDMAID'S TALE, THE

★★★ HBO, 1990, R, 109 min. Dir: Volker Schlondorff. Cast: Natasha Richardson, Robert Duvall, Faye Dunaway, Aidan Quinn, Elizabeth McGovern, Victoria Tennant, Traci Lind, David Dukes.

Harold Pinter (of all people) adapted Margaret Atwood's novel about a future society where healthy young woman are brainwashed into becoming breeders for a new, "perfect" generation. Richardson is good as the "handmaid" chosen to bear industrialist Duvall's child while Dunaway does a *Mommie Dearest* turn as Bob's jealous wife. Rambling but well cast and thought-provoking.

HANDS OF STEEL

★☆ Vestron, 1986, R, 94 min. Dir: Martin Dolman [Sergio Martino]. Cast: Daniel Greene, Janet Agren, John Saxon, George Eastman.

Mostly dull Neapolitan actioner with Greene as an android who helps Agren flee bad guys in the Arizona desert. This silly movie starts out like *Over the Top* and ends up like *The Terminator* and is a waste of time either way.

HANGAR 18

★★ Worldvision, 1980, PG, 93 min. Dir: James L. Conway. Cast: Darren McGavin, Robert Vaughn, Gary Collins, Pamela Bellwood, Joseph Campanella, Philip Abbott, Steven Keats, James Hampton, Tom Hallick, William Schallert.

Well cast but tedious "based on a true case" sci-fi thriller about an alleged U.S. government coverup of a long-ago alien landing with the spaceship and extraterrestrial corpses hidden away in the dreaded Hangar 18. You can't knock a cast like this but the plotting is about as believable as an episode of *The Lost Saucer*. Shown on TV as *Invasion Force* with a whole new, and frankly ludicrous, ending.

HARDWARE

★★★☆ HBO, 1990, R, 92 min. Dir: Richard Stanley. Cast: Stacy Travis, Dylan McDermott, John Lynch, Iggy Pop, William Hootkins, Mark Northover.

Stanley's impressive feature debut was this tense sci-fi/horror/actioner about an android on a murderous rampage in the apartment of

"I knew this thing would rust in here!" Stacy Travis and Dylan McDermott in Hardware *(1990).*

pretty, resourceful Travis. McDermott is her hunky but useless boyfriend (with a robotic arm) and Hootkins is memorable as a peeping Tom neighbor who has his eyes gouged out. Somewhat reminiscent of earlier works like *Demon Seed* and *Trilogy of Terror* but strong enough to stand on its own, with grueling violence that earned this an X rating before cuts.

HARRY AND THE HENDERSONS

★★☆ MCA/Universal, 1987, PG, 110 min. Dir: William Dear. Cast: John Lithgow, Melinda Dillon, Kevin Peter Hall, Don Ameche, Lainie Kazan, Margaret Langrick, Joshua Rudoy, David Suchet.

The *E.T.* formula gets dusted off yet again in this amiable if predictable comedy of a family accidentally running down Bigfoot with their station wagon while camping in the north woods. They take the big guy home and all the expected comic complications ensue. Too long and too obvious but Lithgow makes almost anything worth watching and the Oscar-winning Rick Baker makeup (worn by Hall) is first-rate. Aka *Bigfoot and the Hendersons* and followed by a brief TV series that ended with the death of star Hall.

HARVEY

★★★☆ MCA/Universal, 1950, NR, 104 min. Dir: Henry Koster. Cast: James Stewart, Josephine Hull, Peggy Dow, Charles Drake, Cecil Kellaway, Victoria Horne, Jesse White, Wallace Ford.

In one of his best roles Stewart is great as Elwood P. Dowd, an amiable drunk whose dearest companion is a six-foot-three-inch invisible rabbit called Harvey. A solid adaptation of the Broadway hit written by Mary Chase. Hull won a best supporting actress Oscar for her re-creation of her stage role as Elwood's concerned sister. Remade for TV in 1996 with Harry Anderson in the Stewart role.

HAVE ROCKET WILL TRAVEL

★★☆ Columbia/TriStar, 1959, NR, 76 min. Dir: David Lowell Rich. Cast: Moe Howard, Larry Fine, Joe DeRita, Jerome Cowan, Anna Lisa, Robert Colbert.

After twenty years under contract, Columbia Pictures released the Three Stooges just months before their short subjects were unleashed on TV, creating a whole new generation of young fans. Knowing a good thing when they saw it, Columbia quickly rehired the boys (with DeRita standing in as the third stooge) for a series of quickie low-budget features. The first was this entertaining sci-fi spoof in which the Stooges accidentally travel via rocket to a strange planet inhabited by a

talking unicorn and a flame-spitting giant spider. To the surprise of everyone—save the Stooges' legions of fans—this became one of the top box office hits of 1959!

HAWK THE SLAYER

★★ IVE, 1980, PG, 93 min. Dir: Terry Marcel. Cast: John Terry, Jack Palance, Bernard Bresslaw, Harry Andrews, Roy Kinnear, Ferdy Mayne.

Terry and Palance are laughably cast as brothers in this well-directed but labored sword-and-sorcery tale. Handsome young John is the nice bro and craggy ol' Jack is (natch) the bad one as they vie for a sword with magical powers. Silly Brit programmer enlivened by its colorful supporting cast.

HEART AND SOULS

★★★ MCA/Universal, 1993, PG-13, 104 min. Dir: Ron Underwood. Cast: Robert Downey, Jr., Charles Grodin, Alfre Woodard, Kyra Sedgwick, Tom Sizemore, Elisabeth Shue.

A really complicated but rewarding variation on the overworked body-switch genre with an above-average cast and plot. In 1959, four people (Grodin, Woodard, Sedgwick, and Sizemore) are killed in a bus crash and their spirits enter a newborn who grows up to be banker Downey. Discovering that their only way into Heaven is to complete unfinished business in each of their lives, each spirit takes over Bob in turn to find salvation—and, of course, make the heartless Downey a better person in the bargain. Predictable but offbeat, with a talented, likable cast (the possessed Downey puts Steve Martin in *All of Me* to shame) and solid direction by Underwood.

HEARTBEEPS

★☆ MCA/Universal, 1981, PG, 79 min. Dir: Allan Arkush. Cast: Andy Kaufman, Bernadette Peters, Randy Quaid, Melanie Mayron, Kenneth McMillan, Christopher Guest, Dick Miller, voice of Jack Carter.

Stan Winston's special makeup is about the only good thing in this total muck-up about a pair of robots (Kaufman and Peters) that fall in love. A box office disaster, this nearly killed the careers of almost everyone involved and was obviously heavily reedited and cut back before release.

HEAVEN CAN WAIT

★★★ Fox, 1943, NR, 112 min. Dir: Ernst Lubitsch. Cast: Don Ameche, Gene Tierney, Laird Cregar, Charles Coburn, Marjorie Main, Spring Byington, Allyn Joslyn, Eugene Pallette.

Another fine '40s fantasy with Ameche at his best as a deceased womanizer who demands entrance to Hell for his wicked ways. The devil (a surprisingly dashing Cregar) examines Ameche's life in flashback only to discover Don's true love for beautiful Tierney. A beautifully cast supernatural comedy not to be confused with the Warren Beatty film of the same name.

HEAVEN CAN WAIT

★★☆ Paramount, 1978, PG, 100 min. Dirs: Warren Beatty, Buck Henry. Cast: Warren Beatty, Julie Christie, James Mason, Dyan Cannon, Charles Grodin, Jack Warden, Vincent Gardenia, Buck Henry.

Not a remake of the previous entry but an updated retelling of *Here Comes Mr. Jordan*. Beatty is a nice but dumb football player who dies before his time and is reincarnated in the body of a murdered millionaire. Beatty and Elaine May wrote the script as a chance to soften Beatty's image as a jerky skirt-chaser; it must have worked since this predictable fantasy raked in a bundle. Best performances come from Mason as Warren's cultured guardian angel and Cannon as the dead rich man's ditzy wife.

HEAVENLY KID, THE

★☆ HBO, 1985, PG-13, 87 min. Dir: Cary Medoway. Cast: Lewis Smith, Jason Gedrick, Jane Kaczmarek, Richard Mulligan.

Pathetic "comic" fantasy, one of dozens from this period, with Smith as a cocky early '60s greaser who dies in a drag race but can only get into Heaven if he helps straighten out the life of screwed-up nerd Gedrick. In a totally unlikely climax, we discover that Lewis is really Jason's dad, but that would make junior well into his twenties, not the teen depicted here. Oh, never mind. *Here Comes Mr. Jordan* this ain't.

HEAVENS CALL, THE

See: *Battle Beyond the Sun*.

HEAVY METAL

★★★ Columbia/TriStar, 1981, R, 90 min. Dir: Gerald Potterton. Voices: John Candy, Richard Romanus, Joe Flaherty, John Vernon, Eugene Levy, Jackie Burroughs, Don Francks, Alice Playden, Harold Ramis, Marilyn Lightstone.

Episodic animated feature adapted from the popular adult comic book and set to a full plate of appropriate music from various bands. Best tales are the first, about a futuristic cabby called Harry Canyon; the second, with Candy voicing the adventures of a nerdy teen who becomes a muscular warrior; and the fourth, a horror tale about a fighter pilot attacked by the zombies of his fellow crew

members. Full of sex, nudity, violence, and humor, this is very much an ancestor of today's popular Anime films from Japan and originally had to be cut to avoid an X rating—losing some graphic gore and full frontal male nudity along the way.

HELL COMES TO FROGTOWN

★★ New World, 1987, R, 86 min. Dirs: R. J. Kizer and Donald G. Jackson. Cast: Roddy Piper, Sandahl Bergman, Rory Calhoun, William Smith, Nicholas Worth, Cec Verrill.

Silly but watchable spoof of *Planet of the Apes* with "Rowdy" Roddy as the last fertile man on Earth out to rescue Amazon Bergman from a tribe of mutant frogmen—not the skindiving kind, but talking reptilian mutants. Cheap but amusing, with a well-chosen cast and decent frog FX. Sequel: *Return to Frogtown*.

HELL CREATURES

See: *Invasion of the Saucer Men*.

HERBIE GOES BANANAS

★★ Disney, 1980, G, 100 min. Dir: Vincent McEveety. Cast: Charlie Martin Smith, Elyssa Davalos, Steven W. Burns, Cloris Leachman, Harvey Korman, John Vernon, Richard Jaeckel, Alex Rocco.

Fourth and last of the *Love Bug* movies takes Herbie the intelligent Volkswagon and his new owners south of the border for a race in Brazil with all the usual "zany" complications. Plays like a TV movie, with the flat leads made up for by an impressive supporting cast.

HERBIE GOES TO MONTE CARLO

★★★ Disney, 1977, G, 91 min. Dir: Vincent McEveety. Cast: Dean Jones, Julie Sommers, Don Knotts, Eric Braeden, Roy Kinnear, Jacques Martin.

In the third *Love Bug* movie—the best of the sequels—Herbie gets back his original owner (Jones) and becomes an unwitting diamond smuggler while racing in Europe. Slickly done and funny almost in spite of Knotts's constant mugging.

HERBIE RIDES AGAIN

★★☆ Disney, 1974, G, 88 min. Dir: Robert Stevenson. Cast: Helen Hayes, Ken Berry, Stefanie Powers, Keenan Wynn, John McIntire, Huntz Hall.

Pleasant first sequel has Herbie now owned by Hayes and helping her stop Wynn from demolishing her quaint home (an abandoned firehouse) in order to build the world's tallest building. Berry, Powers, and Wynn seem quite at home in a Disney fantasy but seeing the First Lady of the Theater in such surroundings is indeed surprising—until you remember she won her Oscar for appearing in *Airport*. I guess after that, anything's possible.

HERCULES

★★☆ Goodtimes, 1957, NR, 107 min. Dir: Pietro Francisci. Cast: Steve Reeves, Sylva Koscina, Gianna Maria Canale, Fabrizio Mioni, Ivo Garrani, Luciana Paluzzi.

Joseph E. Levine made a mint by dubbing and exporting this Italian muscleman epic to U.S. theaters in 1959. Reeves is the definitive movie Hercules, all oiled up and ready to take on any and all obstacles so he can be united with the beautiful Koscina. Lots of fun, with colorful photography by Mario Bava, but, personally, I prefer the even campier sequel: *Hercules Unchained*.

HERCULES

★☆ MGM/UA, 1983, PG, 98 min. Dir: Lewis Coates [Luigi Cozzi]. Cast: Lou Ferrigno, Mirella D'Angelo, Sybil Danning, William Berger, Ingrid Anderson, Rosanna Podesta.

Flat-footed remake borrowing from both the Steve Reeves original and any number of Ray Harryhausen movies as well. Designed as a starring vehicle for erstwhile *Incredible Hulk* Ferrigno, this sees Herc trying to save kidnapped princess Anderson while battling a horde of cheapie mechanical monsters. Far too ambitious for its meager budget. Sequel: *The Adventures of Hercules*.

HERCULES AGAINST THE MOON MEN

★★☆ Goodtimes, 1964, NR, 88 min. Dir: Giacomo Gentilomo. Cast: Alan Steel, Jany Clair, Anna-Maria Polani, Nando Tamberlani.

In one of his strangest adventures, Herc (Steel) must save a princess from becoming the life force used to revive a moon goddess worshipped by a horde of rock men who look like they're left over from *Missile to the Moon*. Steel is not one of the best actors to don Herc's loincloth, but the odd plot (full of blatant sci-fi and horror film touches) and some imaginative direction make this worth watching. Aka *Hercules vs. the Moon Men*.

HERCULES AND THE CAPTIVE WOMEN

★★ Sinister Cinema, 1961, NR, 87 min. Dir: Vittorio Cottafavi. Cast: Reg Park, Fay Spain, Ettore Manni, Marlo Petri, Ivo Garrani, Gian Maria Volonte.

Initially promising but ultimately routine peblum (the Italian phrase for all these muscle flicks) with Herc (Park) going up against the super hot queen of Alantis (Spain, chewing the scenery like Joan Crawford on speed). Good color and some nice sets but not up to some of

the others in the *Hercules* canon.

HERCULES AT THE CENTER OF THE EARTH

See: *Hercules in the Haunted World*.

HERCULES IN THE HAUNTED WORLD

★★★ Sinister Cinema, 1961, NR, 83 min. Dir: Mario Bava. Cast: Reg Park, Christopher Lee, Leonora Ruffo, Giorgio Ardisson, Ida Galli.

Bava's directional abilities help to make this an above-average peblum. Herc (Park) travels to Hades in order to find a talisman to revive his comatose love (Ruffo). Along the way he battles rampaging rock creatures and Lee as a vampirelike villain. Bava's color schemes and camerawork really make the difference in this mix of fantasy, horror, and biceps. Aka *Hercules at the Center of the Earth*.

HERCULES, PRISONER OF EVIL

★★ Sinister Cinema, 1964, NR, 80 min. Dir: Anthony Dawson [Antonio Margheriti]. Cast: Reg Park, Mirelle Granelli, Ettore Manni, Maria Teresa Orsini.

Yet another Hercules adventure with horror movie overtones. This time our beefy boy encounters various monsters and a witch who transforms her victims into werewolves. A few effective moments.

HERCULES UNCHAINED

★★★ Goodtimes, 1959, NR, 101 min. Dir: Pietro Francisci. Cast: Steve Reeves, Sylva Koscina, Sylvia Lopez, Primo Carnera, Sergio Fantoni.

The second and best of the *Hercules* movies, with Reeves spending much of the movie as the hypnotized boy toy of eye-makeup-overkill-queen Lopez. Good fun, with one-time heavyweight champ Carnera in a cameo as a combative giant who gains strength from the Earth and is helpless when dunked in water.

HERCULES VS. THE MOON MEN

See: *Hercules Against the Moon Men*.

HERE COMES MR. JORDAN

★★★ Columbia/TriStar, 1941, NR, 93 min. Dir: Alexander Hall. Cast: Robert Montgomery, Evelyn Keyes, Claude Raines, Rita Johnson, James Gleason, Edward Everett Horton.

Boxer Montgomery dies too soon and is returned to Earth in the body of a millionaire marked for death by scheming wife Johnson. Delightful fantasy-comedy with excellent performances by Montgomery, Rains (as Bob's erudite guardian angel), and Gleason (as the boxer's flustered manager). Remade with Warren Beatty as *Heaven Can Wait*.

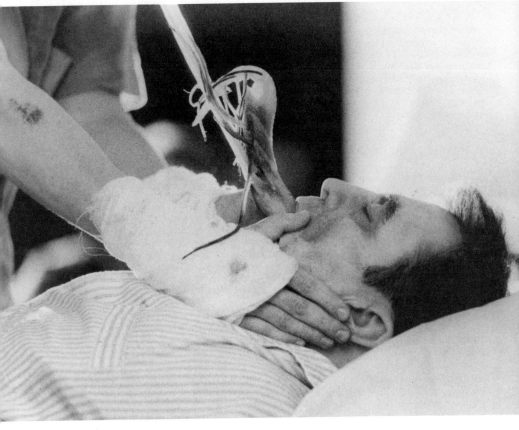

"Say Ahhhh!" The Hidden *(1987).*

HIDDEN, THE

★★★ Video Treasures, 1987, R, 97 min. Dir: Jack Sholder. Cast: Kyle MacLachlan, Michael Nouri, Clu Gulager, Claudia Christian, Ed O'Ross, Chris Mulkey.

Lethal Weapon meets *The Thing* in this slick, fast-paced sci-fi action flick. A parasitic alien possesses a variety of earthlings, driving each host to increasingly violent antisocial behavior while being hunted by cop Nouri and weird FBI guy MacLachlan (in, more or less, a warmup for his Agent Cooper role on *Twin Peaks*). Derivative but still one-of-a-kind thriller designed for speed and excitement, not logic or sense.

HIDDEN II, THE

★★ New Line, 1993, R, 89 min. Dir: Seth Pinsker. Cast: Raphael Sbarge, Kate Hodge, Jovin Montanaro, Christopher Murphy.

Needless sequel with Sbarge as an alien bounty hunter on Earth who teams with Hodge (daughter of the Michael Nouri character from the original, now grown up) to stop another outbreak of hidden creatures at an L.A. dance club. Colorlessly acted and directed; the alien parasite looks like a prop left over from *Jason Goes to Hell*—and probably was.

HIGH DESERT KILL

★★☆ MCA/Universal, 1989, NR, 96 min. Dir: Harry Falk. Cast: Chuck Connors, Anthony Geary, Marc Singer, Micah Grant, Deborah Anne Mansey, Lori Birdsong.

Mountain man Connors leads city slickers Geary, Singer, and Grant on a hunting trip that turns to terror when they are attacked and possessed by an alien entity that hunts them down one by one. Efficient made-for-cable movie with effective echoes of *Predator, Deliverance,* and *The Thing.*

HIGHLANDER

★★★ HBO, 1986, R, 116 min. Dir: Russell Mulcahy. Cast: Christopher Lambert, Sean Connery, Roxanne

Hart, Clancy Brown, Beatie Edney, Alan North.

Lambert is a mystical, ageless Scottish warrior who fights archenemy Brown from the sixteenth century to modern America. Bloody, stylish fantasy adventure; this was badly cut during its initial U.S. release but has recently been restored to its full length for this director's cut video. Connery lights up the screen in a brief but important role as Lambert's mentor. Followed by a pair of sequels and a TV series.

HIGHLANDER 2: THE QUICKENING

★★ Hemdale, 1991, R, 90 min. Dir: Russell Mulcahy. Cast: Christopher Lambert, Sean Connery, Virginia Madsen, Michael Ironside, John C. McGinley, Allan Rich.

In a routine sequel, Lambert trys to save the world from the protective shield he earlier installed for our protection. Along the way we learn that he and Connery (in another small role) are actually aliens, just one of the problems with this flashy but empty followup. Originally released at 88 minutes, 2 minutes worth of extra violence has been restored for this director's cut edition.

HIGHLANDER: THE GATHERING

★★ Hemdale, 1992, PG-13, 98 min. Dirs: Thomas J. Wright, Ray Austin. Cast: Christopher Lambert, Adrian Paul, Alexandra Vandernoot, Vanity, Richard Moll, Stan Kirsch.

The third entry in the series is actually two episodes of the *Highlander* TV series (including the pilot) edited together. Lambert and Paul battle immortal beings and save the world with boring regularity. Well cast but predictable and uninvolving.

HIGHLANDER: THE FINAL DIMENSION

★★ Miramax, 1994, R, 90 min. Dir: Andy Morahan. Cast: Christopher Lambert, Mario Van Peebles, Deborah Unger, Mako, Marc Neufield, Raul Trujillo.

Third (and presumably last) of the theatrical *Highlanders* with Lambert going at it this time with an ancient sorcerer (Van Peebles, camping it up to beat the band) discovered in a Japanese lake by archeologist Unger. Pretty dull stuff, not even enlivened by a totally gratuitous sex scene added back in for this director's cut video version.

HIGH SPIRITS

★★ Video Treasures, 1988, PG-13, 97 min. Dir: Neil Jordan. Cast: Peter O'Toole, Daryl Hannah, Steve Guttenberg, Beverly D'Angelo, Liam Neeson, Jennifer Tilly, Peter Gallagher, Ray McAnally, Connie Booth, Donal McCann.

Jordan followed up his art house reinterpretations of the horror (*The Company of Wolves*) and gangster (*Mona Lisa*) genres with this flop fantasy, though it's not that bad. O'Toole runs an Irish castle-hotel haunted by the ghosts of newlyweds (Hannah and Neeson) who died on their honeymoon. Predictably, unhappily married Guttenberg (who played the same role far too often in far too many late '80s movies) falls for Hannah and tries to find a way to restore her to life. Heavily cut and restructured by the distributor, this never makes up its mind whether to play for comedy, fantasy, horror, or romance and mainly just rambles on from set-piece to set-piece—some of them funny, most not. Best of all is O'Toole, who plays drunk and seems to be having a good time; his best moment occurs after his guests attempt a disastrous escape from the haunted castle and fail. Everyone drags themselves sullenly back inside, where an ebullient Peter proclaims: "Ah, here we are together again. One big happy family."

HITCHHIKER'S GUIDE TO THE GALAXY, THE

★★★ CBS/Fox, 1985, NR, 194 min. Dir: Alan Bell. Cast: Simon Jones, David Dixon, Joe Melia, Martin Benson.

After bad-tempered aliens destroy the Earth, the nebbishy sole survivor (Simon Jones, perfectly cast) spends his time bumming around the universe having close encounters with various strange life forms. This BBC-TV adaptation of Douglas Adams's cult radio serial (and book) is lots of fun—sort of like *Monty Python* meets *Doctor Who*.

H-MAN, THE

★★★ Columbia/TriStar, 1958, NR, 79 min. Dir: Inoshiro Honda. Cast: Kenji Sahara, Yumi Shirakawa, Akihito Hirata, Koreya Senda, Mitsuri Sato, Eitaro Ozawa.

Toho's answer to *The Blob* was this genuinely eerie, tensely atmospheric mixture of sci-fi, horror, and crime drama. Police are baffled by a series of mysterious disappearances, which they initially blame on underworld hitmen but which ultimately turn out to be the work of a mass of flesh-consuming, radioactive liquid. Slow to start but this eventually builds suspense until its show-stopping FX of melting, liquefied victims of the H-Man, courtesy of *Godzilla* man Eiji Tsurabaya. Even the usual lousy dubbing doesn't detract from this movie's effectively melancholy mood.

HOMEWRECKER

★★ Paramount, 1992, PG-13, 88 min. Dir: Fred

Walton. Cast: Robby Benson, Sydney Walsh, Sarah Rose Karr, voice of Kate Jackson.

A low-rent, sex-change variation on *Demon Seed*. Benson is miscast as a scientist who develops a computer (voiced to raspy perfection by Jackson) with human feelings. Not unexpectedly, the computer falls in love with its creator, takes over his house, and begins making attempts on the lives of his wife (Walsh) and daughter (Karr). Predictable made-for-cable sci-fi/horror quickie.

HONEY, I BLEW UP THE KID

★★☆ Disney, 1992, PG, 89 min. Dir: Randal Kleiser. Cast: Rick Moranis, Marcia Strassman, Robert Oliveri, Keri Russell, Lloyd Bridges, John Shea, Gregory Sierra, Kenneth Tobey, Julia Sweeney, Daniel Shalikar, Joshua Shalikar.

This inevitable followup to *Honey, I Shrunk the Kids* was smart enough not to repeat the first film's situations and (literally) go in a different direction—but who knew it would turn into a ripoff of *The Amazing Colossal Man*. Inventor Moranis accidentally enlarges his two-year-old son (played by the Shalikar twins) into a giant who eventually grows to over a hundred feet tall and carries off his teen babysitter (Russell) through the streets of Las Vegas. Good special effects but the thin plot begins to wear. I liked the last minute homage to *Attack of the 50-Foot Woman*, though.

HONEY, I SHRUNK THE KIDS

★★★ Disney, 1989, PG, 93 min. Dir: Joe Johnston. Cast: Rick Moranis, Marcia Strassman, Matt Frewer, Kristine Sutherland, Thomas Brown, Jared Rushton, Amy O'Neill, Robert Oliveri.

One of the best Disney comic fantasies in years, this concerns a group of neighbor kids (teenage and younger) accidentally shrunk to microscopic size by absentminded professor Moranis's new ray device. An entertaining reworking of the classic *Fantastic Voyage* for a modern youth audience (originally to be called *The Teeny-Weenies* and to be directed by *Re-Animator* man Stuart Gordon, who copenned the story with Robert Yuzna), with fine stop-motion FX by Phil Tippet and Dave Allen depicting various enlarged denizens of the kids' backyard, and a few interestingly harsh touches for a Disney flick (including the heroic death of the kids' giant ant protector). Sequels: *Honey, I Blew Up the Kid* and *Honey, We Shrunk Ourselves*.

HOOK

★☆ Columbia/TriStar, 1991, PG, 144 min. Dir: Steven Spielberg. Cast: Robin Williams, Dustin Hoffman, Julia Roberts, Bob Hoskins, Maggie Smith, Caroline Goodall, Charlie Korsmo, Amber Scott, Phil Collins, Arthur Malet.

Spielberg's worst film to date, this botched updating of the Peter Pan legend is almost fascinatingly awful. Williams (well cast) is the now middle-aged Pan, a heartless corporate bigwig forced to rediscover the joys of childhood and his magical heritage when his son and daughter are kidnapped by Captian Hook (Hoffman, in a career-killing act of campy desperation). About as bland and unsatisfying as a carload of McDonald's Happy Meals, with wasted appearances by Roberts as Tinker Bell and Smith in an embarrassing cameo as an aged Wendy. Makes *Doctor Doolittle* look like *The Wizard of Oz*.

HORROR OF THE BLOOD MONSTERS

★ VidAmerica, 1970, PG, 85 min. Dir: Al Adamson. Cast: John Carradine, Robert Dix, Vicki Volante, Joey Benson, Jennifer Bishop, Britt Semand.

Adamson pays tribute to Ed Wood (or something) with this cut-and-paste potboiler. Carradine leads an expedition to an alien world to investigate the source of a vampire plague ravaging the Earth. So cheap, John never leaves the ship and the planet is represented by tinted footage from and old Filipino cave man epic. Look for Al as a vampire during the opening montage. Aka *Vampire Men of the Lost Planet* and about a half dozen other equally absurd titles.

HORROR PLANET

★★ Nelson, 1980, R, 92 min. Dir: Norman J. Warren. Cast: Judy Geeson, Robin Clarke, Jennifer Ashley, Stephanie Beacham, Steven Grieves, Victoria Tennant.

Grisly British *Alien* clone with Geeson as an astronaut raped by a slimy monster in a cave on a hostile planet. Judy then turns into Betsy Palmer from *Friday the 13th* as she gruesomely kills off almost all her fellow space explorers before giving painful birth to a pair of mutant twins. Imaginative in its tasteless extremes, this manages simultaneously to put women in a position of power (Ashley is the group's female commander) and to be terribly misogynistic. Geeson, ironically enough, emerges as the most sympathetic character in the movie even after she slaughters and devours half the cast! Released to U.S. theaters in a cut version but restored for video. Original title: *Inseminoid*.

HORRORS OF THE RED PLANET

See: *The Wizard of Mars*.

HOWARD THE DUCK

☆ MCA/Universal, 1986, PG, 110 min. Dir: Willard Huyck. Cast: Lea Thompson, Jeffrey Jones, Tim Robbins, Paul Guilfoyle.

Many box office bombs don't really deserve their laughingstock reputation but, guess what? This one does—and then some! Steve Gerber's acerbic comic strip character becomes another big-screen animatronic waste of space as Howard, a ducklike alien from outer space, lands in Cleveland and is befriended by rocker wannabe Thompson—whose part as shark bait in *Jaws 3D* had more class. Jones adds a few mildly funny moments but this George Lucas-produced drek is still one of the worst—if not *the* worst—big-studio Hollywood production of the 1980s.

HUMAN DUPLICATORS, THE

★☆ LIVE, 1964, NR, 80 min. Dir: Hugo Grimaldi. Cast: George Nader, Barbara Nichols, George Macready, Dolores Faith, Richard Kiel, Hugh Beaumont, Richard Arlen, Tommy Leonetti.

Kiel is a very tall alien invader (speaking so slowly you could finish a three-course meal before he even finishes a sentence) who involves himself in scientist Macready's experiments in android creation. Nader (a one-time boyfriend of Rock Hudson) is the secret agent out to stop them, Nichols is the stereotypical dumb blonde secretary, *Beaver* dad Beaumont is the FBI chief, and Faith is Macready's blind daughter, who waltzes around the family mansion in dresses you won't believe. A tacky unintentional comedy that's, sadly, too slow and drawn out to be fun in the *Plan 9* manner. Italian horror buffs should look for the tinted stock shot from *Castle of Blood*. Aka *Jaws of the Alien*—guess why.

HUMAN VAPOR, THE

★★ Prism Entertainment, 1960, NR, 80 min. Dir: Inoshiro Honda. Cast: Tatsuya Mihashi, Kaoru Yachigusa, Yoshio Tsuchiya.

Toho cashes in on their own *H-Man* hit with this similar effort. Tsuchiya is a convict who can vaporize at will and uses this power to escape jail and rob banks and jewelry stores. Tired dramatically but with decent special effects.

HYPER SAPIAN: PEOPLE FROM ANOTHER STAR

★☆ Warner, 1986, PG, 95 min. Dir: Peter R. Hunt. Cast: Ricky Paull Goldin, Sydney Penny, Keenan Wynn, Gail Strickland, Peter Jason.

Terminal cuteness as runaway teen couple (Goldin and Penny) from outer space try to find freedom and peace in Wyoming. So sweet you want to smack it.

ICEMAN

★★★★ MCA/Universal, 1984, PG, 99 min. Dir: Fred Schepisi. Cast: Timothy Hutton, Lindsay Crouse, John Lone, Josef Sommer, David Strathairn, Danny Glover.

An almost overwhelmingly moving fantasy that takes a basically hackneyed horror concept (remember Bela Lugosi's *Return of the Ape Man*?) and breathes new life into it by treating its monster as a character rather than a threat. Lone is unforgettable as the gentle prehistoric man thawed from arctic ice who just wants to die and be with his lost loved ones. Hutton is equally fine as the only one of the scientific team that discovered Lone to relate to the "Iceman" as a man rather than a specimen. The scene where they sit together and sing "Heart of Gold" is heartbreakingly real rather than the cloyingly "cute" scene it might have become in some other movie. The sweeping glacial photography and atmospheric musical score add to the majesty of one of the most underrated films of the 1980s.

ICE PIRATES, THE

★★ MGM/UA, 1984, PG, 91 min. Dir: Stewart Raffill. Cast: Robert Urich, Mary Crosby, Michael D. Roberts, John Matuzak, Angelica Houston, John Carradine, Ron Perlman, Robert Symonds.

Forgettable science fiction comedy in the *Star Wars* mold. Urich mugs his way through as the leader of a band of intergalactic swashbucklers after the most valuable commodity in the universe—water—who ends up helping beautiful-but-annoying princess Crosby regain her throne. Sometimes funny, often silly and stupid, with low-budget FX but a decent supporting cast.

I COME IN PEACE

★★☆, Video Treasures, 1990, R, 92 min. Dir: Craig R. Baxley. Cast: Dolph Lundgren, Brian Benben, Betsy Brantley, Matthias Hues, David Ackroyd, Michael J. Pollard.

Lundgren and Benben (the unlikeliest movie partnership since Neil Diamond and Laurence Olivier) are a tough street cop and nerdy FBI agent (you know the type) after a murderous alien in this surprisingly watchable ripoff of *The Hidden*. Not much in the way of FX but plenty of car chases and explosions in this goofy if unimaginative movie.

ILLUSTRATED MAN, THE

★★☆, Warner, 1969, PG, 103 min. Dir: Jack Smight. Cast: Rod Steiger, Clare Bloom, Robert Drivas, Don Dobbins, Jason Evers, Tim Weldon, Christie Matchett.

Three-part anthology based on the stories of Ray Bradbury. Children murder their parents in a magical playroom that recreates the African veldt, complete with hungry lions; astronauts are driven mad on the planet Venus, where it's always raining; and a couple agonize over what to do to save their children from Earth's imminent destruction. This big-studio, big-star concoction had a lot of potential but blew it with pretentious direction and dialogue and a groovy '60s atmosphere that must have dated it six months after it came out. Still the actors are good, some of the sets nice, and the framing story (a weirdly homoerotic piece with Steiger as the tattooed title character alternately seducing and frightening young wanderer Drivas) is often more interesting than the tales it bridges.

Here comes the groom in I Married a Monster from Outer Space *(1958).*

I MARRIED A MONSTER FROM OUTER SPACE

★★★ Paramount, 1958, NR, 78 min. Dir: Gene Fowler, Jr. Cast: Tom Tryon, Gloria Talbott, Ken Lynch, John Eldredge.

Talbott begins to suspect the worst when new groom Tryon refuses to have sex with her and starts hanging around an all-male bar. But since this is the '50s they don't go on *Ricki*

Lake; in fact, Glo does a little PI work and discovers her man has been replaced by an icky alien from an (implied) gay race who've come to Earth to find human brides to carry on their dead-end species. Imaginative lighting and special effects and on-target acting carry this above-average sci-fi quickie from the director of *I was a Teenage Werewolf*.

I MARRIED A WITCH

★★★ MGM/UA, 1942, NR, 76 min. Dir: Rene Clair. Cast: Fredric March, Veronica Lake, Robert Benchley, Susan Hayward, Cecil Kellaway, Elizabeth Patterson.

Frothy Clair comedy with March as a politico whose life is turned upside down when a reincarnated witch (Lake), who was originally burned at the stake during the Salem witch trials (though no witches were actually burned there—but that's another story), enters his life and romances him away from pretty but uptight Hayward. Delightful fantasy adapted from a story by *Topper* author Thorne Smith. And like *Bell, Book, and Candle*, this is another obvious ancestor of TV's *Bewitched*.

INCREDIBLE HULK, THE

★★☆ MCA/Universal, 1977, NR, 96 min. Dir: Kenneth Johnson. Cast: Bill Bixby, Lou Ferrigno, Susan Sullivan, Jack Colvin, Susan Batson, Charles Siebert.

The made-for-TV movie that started the ball rolling for Bixby as Dr. David Bruce Banner, a scientist whose atomic experiments bring out the monster within and transform him into the mean, green hulk (Ferrigno). Like the subsequent series, this is rather somber and downbeat for a story aimed at kids even with the occasional bit of unintentional humor. Followed by a quickie sequel, *Return of the Hulk*, the long-running series, and several TV movie follow-ups.

INCREDIBLE HULK RETURNS, THE

★★ Goodtimes, 1988, NR, 96 min. Dir: Nicholas Corea. Cast: Bill Bixby, Lou Ferrigno, Jack Colvin, Lee Purcell, Charles Napier, Steve Levitt.

After several years in TV limbo, Bixby and Ferrigno were back in harness again for this silly followup telemovie. The hulk battles a resurrected superstrong Viking called Thor (an idea pinched from the cheapie horror flick *Giant from the Unknown*), who's played for laughs just as much as for thrills. Series fans might like it but this is more a vehicle for Marvel Comics' Thor character (I think they were definitely thinking series here) than for Banner or ol' green jeans.

INCREDIBLE MELTING MAN THE

★★ Orion, 1977, R, 85 min. Dir: William Sachs. Cast: Alex Rebar, Burr DeBenning, Myron Healy, Ann Sweeney, Michael Aldredge, Lislie Wilson, Rainbeaux Smith, Janis Blythe.

Cheeseball semi-rerun of *The First Man into Space*, with Rebar as an astronaut who returns from a trip to Saturn with a disease that causes him to dribble away into a pile of goo. DeBenning is the dull-as-dishwater hero who wanders around in circles while Alex bumps off nearly the entire cast until a downbeat ending that's as shocking as it is inept. Thankfully the Rick Baker makeup FX are pretty good for such a low-budget movie and then you've got Rainbeaux as a model who squeals as if she'd seen a mouse when she stumbles across the decapitated body of one of Melt's victims. Note: Most video and TV prints are missing the final few seconds, in which a janitor shovels our monster's remains into an ashcan before throwing his hands up in disgust and walking away.

INCREDIBLE MR. LIMPET, THE

★★ Warner, 1964, NR, 102 min. Dir: Arthur Lubin. Cast: Don Knotts, Carol Cook, Jack Weston, Andrew Duggan, Larry Keating, voice of Elizabeth McRae.

Knotts is an unhappily married nebbish who loves fish more than people and actually becomes (an animated) one when he accidentally drowns. In fish form, Don helps the Navy win World War II and finds true love with a girl fish (voiced by McRae). Popular in some circles, this "kiddie" movie is fairly depressing and actually sort of creepy when you think about it. The cartoon effects are at best fair.

INCREDIBLE PETRIFIED WORLD, THE

★ Sinister Cinema, 1958, NR, 70 min. Dir: Jerry Warren. Cast: John Carradine, Phyllis Coates, Robert Clarke, Sheila Noonan, Allen Windsor, Lloyd Nelson, George Skaff, Harry Raven.

Four people take a diving bell to the bottom of the ocean and end up trapped in a warren of unexplored caverns beneath the sea bed. A dull, talky no-budgeter wasting an interesting B cast on one of the most uneventful plots in movie history. There originally *was* a monster to be encountered somewhere along the line but it was so crappy-looking even Warren wouldn't use it and cut it out of the picture.

INCREDIBLE SHRINKING MAN, THE

★★★☆ MCA/Universal, 1957, 81 min. Dir: Jack Arnold. Cast: Grant Williams, Randy Stuart, April Kent, Paul Langton, William Schallert, Raymond Bailey.

Richard Matheson adapted his novel *The Shrinking Man* to the screen for this classic '50s sci-fi movie. Grant is exposed to a strange radioactive cloud and begins to grow smaller. His wife (Stuart) begins treating him like a child, he has a short-lived (pun intended) affair with circus midget Kent, and is eventually given up for dead after a house cat and a spider in the cellar become mammoth menaces. Williams is too much the glamour puss to really pull off his role and things get needlessly pious toward the end but Arnold directs with all his usual professionalism, the FX hold up pretty well, and at least this doesn't cop out with a contrived it's-gonna-be-all-right happy ending. A sequel, *The Fantastic Little Girl*, was never made (probably because the title sounded too much like a Shirley Temple movie) but the original was given a sex change for the remake *The Incredible Shrinking Woman*.

INCREDIBLE SHRINKING WOMAN, THE
★★★ Goodtimes, 1981, PG, 88 min. Dir: Joel Schumacher. Cast: Lily Tomlin, Charles Grodin, Ned Beatty, Henry Gibson, Elizabeth Wilson, Mark Blankfield, Rick Baker, Pamela Bellwood, John Glover, Mike Douglas.

Underrated serio-comic remake with Tomlin as a suburban housewife (not to mention consumer activist Judith Brasley and a cameo as Ernestine the telephone operator) whose exposure to various untested household products (brought home by advertising exec husband Grodin) causes her to shrink. Lily becomes a media celebrity but eventually ends up held prisoner by mad scientists Gibson and Wilson. The pastel color schemes and soft-focus photography often make the special effects seem less impressive than they are but the humor is mostly on target and Baker is great as a lab ape called Sidney who falls for Lily *King Kong*-style and rescues her at the climax. Look for Sally Kirkland as a supermarket cashier and love that "Galaxy Glue" theme music.

INDEPENDENCE DAY
★★★ Fox, 1996, PG-13, 135 min. Dir: Roland Emmerich. Cast: Bill Paxton, Jeff Goldblum, Will Smith, Margaret Colin, Mary McDonnell, Judd Hirsch, Randy Quaid, Harry Connick, Jr., Robert Loggia, Harvey Fierstein, Brent Spiner, Vivica Fox, Adam Baldwin, James Rebhorn, Raphael Sbarge.

The biggest box office smash in years, this tells of the invasion of Earth by merciless aliens who blast the major cities of the world to smithereens and plan to drain all our energy and natural resources until a courageous band of military men and civilians take the invaders on in a fight to the finish. Really little more

than a blending of *The War of the Worlds*, *Aliens*, and *Earthquake*, this is full of logic loopholes and ridiculously contrived crowd-pleasing bits of business, yet despite all this it really works beautifully well. From the opening shot of the alien mothership passing over the moon, with the vibration wiping out Neil Armstrong's footprints, to the closing shot of the survivors standing in the shadow of the ruined alien warship, Emmerich milks every scene (no matter how corny) for maximum effect. Most of the cast are just disaster-movie-type faces-in-the-crowd but Smith shows easy charm as the fly boy who loses a friend yet gains a wife and child and Loggia is his usual powerhouse self as the no-nonsense military chief of staff. Critics in general weren't very kind to this from-out-of-nowhere cash cow but I liked it fine—just please, spare us a sequel. Please.

INDIANA JONES AND THE LAST CRUSADE
★★☆ Paramount, 1989, PG-13, 127 min. Dir: Steven Spielberg. Cast: Harrison Ford, Sean Connery, Allison Doody, River Phoenix, Denholm Elliott, John Rhys-Davies, Julian Glover, Michael Byrne, Alex Hyde-White, Richard Young.

Third (but probably not last) entry in the *Indy* series with Professor Jones (Ford) teaming up with his estranged father (a delightful Connery) to find the legendary Holy Grail before the Nazis get their hands on it. Harry and Sean make a terrific team and the precredits sequence showing the young Indy (Phoenix) in an early adventure is a nice touch but this really doesn't cover any ground not already explored in the first *Raiders*. Doody's presentation as a greedy Nazi bitch is just as misogynistic as Kate Capshaw's shrieking bimbo bit in *Temple of Doom*. Where's Karen Allen when we really need her?

INDIANA JONES AND THE TEMPLE OF DOOM
★★ Paramount, 1984, PG, 118 min. Dir: Steven Spielberg. Cast: Harrison Ford, Kate Capshaw, Ke Huy Quan, Amrish Puri, Roshan Seth, Dan Aykroyd.

Prequel to *Raiders of the Lost Ark* has Indy in India—along with whining chanteuse Capshaw and annoying brat Quan—where they attempt to free the children of an impoverished village from slavery. This does boast some eye-popping stunts and special effects, and Ford is at his best as a leaner, meaner Indy than before. But the film keeps mistaking crudeness for humor and everything-but-the-kitchen-sink plotting for genuine invention, causing it to work only in fits and starts, unlike the nonstop roller coaster ride that was *Raiders*. The not-especially-bloody heart-rip-

Harrison Ford points the way to adventure in Indiana Jones and the Temple of Doom *(1984).*

ping sacrifice scenes were one of the main reasons the MPAA established the new PG-13 rating later that year.

INFRA-MAN

★★★ Goodtimes, 1976, PG, 92 min. Dir: Hua-Shan. Cast: Li Hsiu-hsien, Wang Hsieh, Yan Man-tzu, Terry Liu, Tsen Shy-yi, Huang Chien-lung.

Infra-man (Hsiu-hsien) a sort of low-grade Ultra Man, battles the evil Princess Dragon Mom (Liu) and her monstrous minions in this too-dumb-to-be-true Hong Kong sci-fi action flick. The special effects wouldn't cut it on the *Mighty Morphin' Power Rangers* TV show but totally off-the-wall plotting and absurd dubbing up-the-wazoo make this a sure bet for fans of the so-bad-it's-good school of genre B movies.

IN LIKE FLINT

★★☆ CBS/Fox, 1967, NR, 114 min. Dir: Gordon Douglas. Cast: James Coburn, Jean Hale, Lee H. Cobb, Andrew Duggan, Anna Lee, Yvonne Craig, Steve Ihnat, Herb Edelman.

Routine sequel to *Our Man Flint,* with Coburn back in action, this time up against an evil organization headed by Lee that's using brainwashing cosmetics to gain control of an experimental space station. As you can tell, no one could take a plot like this seriously and no one does here, either. Good cast, though, and lots of mod costumes and set design. The last of the series unless you count *The President's Analyst*—and some do.

INNERSPACE

★★☆ Warner, 1987, PG, 120 min. Dir: Joe Dante. Cast: Dennis Quaid, Martin Short, Meg Ryan, Kevin McCarthy, Fiona Lewis, Vernon Wells, Robert Picardo, Wendy Schaal, William Schallert, Henry Gibson, Orson Bean, Kathleen Freeman, Dick Miller, Kenneth Tobey.

Quaid is a cocky Navy test pilot who is miniaturized and accidentally injected into Short, causing each of them to vie for control of the same body. *Fantastic Voyage* meets *All of Me* in this derivative but watchable sci-fi comedy with a hand-picked Dante cast and some great, Oscar-winning special effects. Too bad it's so long and has a supposedly "happy" ending that follows Hollywood convention and ends up being completely unsatisfying.

INSEMINOID

See: *Horror Planet.*

IN SEARCH OF THE CASTAWAYS

★★★ Disney, 1962, NR, 100 min. Dir: Robert Stevenson. Cast: Hayley Mills, Maurice Chevalier, George Sanders, Wilfrid Hyde-White, Michael Anderson, Jr., Keith Hamshire.

Tongue-in-cheek Disney fantasy-adventure based on the Jules Verne novel. Teenage Mills and younger brother Hamshire, along with family friend Chevalier, persuade wealthy adventurer Hyde-White and his son Anderson to help them find Hayley's missing dad, lost somewhere in South America. This starts off like gangbusters and has a terrific avalanche-earthquake sequence before things begin to peter out later on. Hayley is good in one of her first "grown-up" roles (and even gets to be romanced by Anderson) and Sanders enlivens the ending as a double-crossing smuggler.

IN THE YEAR 2889

★★ Sinister Cinema, 1968, NR, 80 min. Dir: Larry Buchanan. Cast: Paul Peterson, Charla Doherty, Quinn O'Hara, Hugh Fegin, Billy Thurman.

Not-bad Buchanan remake of *Day the World Ended.* Survivors of a nuclear holocaust hide out in a mountain retreat where they bicker and bitch until a crusty-faced mutant shows up to carry off Doherty. Better acted and photographed than most of Larry's buck-and-a-half AIP remakes; this actually improves on the Corman original in a couple of instances, with an especially dramatic ending. Aka *Year 2889.*

INTRUDERS

★★★ Fox, 1992, NR, 163 min. Dir: Dan Curtis. Cast: Richard Crenna, Mare Winningham, Susan Blakely, Daphne Ashbrook, Ben Vereen, Roslind Chao, G. D. Spradin, Steven Berkoff.

Hypnotic regression reveals that sisters Winningham and Ashbrook were abducted by aliens years earlier. Or does it? Surprisingly suspenseful despite its length, Curtis directs this like one of the horror quickies from his heyday as king of the made-for-TV thriller, with plenty of moody atmosphere, blaring music, and cheap shocks. And damned if it doesn't work. Good performances from all concerned, too.

INTRUDER WITHIN, THE

★★☆ TransWorld Entertainment, 1981, NR, 91 min. Dir: Peter Carter. Cast: Chad Everett, Jennifer Warren, Joseph Bottoms, Rochne Tarkington.

It's *Alien* on a oil derrick as long-dormant eggs dredged from the bottom of the sea hatch shape-shifting monsters with big teeth that snack on the terrified workers. Well cast and with surprisingly elaborate monster design; too bad so little of it is shown. Aka *Panic Offshore* and *The Lucifer Rig.*

INVADERS, THE

★★☆ Republic, 1995, NR, 180 min. Dir: Paul Shapiro. Cast: Scott Bakula, Elizabeth Pena, Roy Thinnes, Richard Thomas, Richard Belzer.

A sequel to the popular '60s cult series (see episode guide) has Thinnes reprising his role as David Vincent, who passes his diary detailing the invaders' activities on to one Nolan Wood (Bakula, basically playing his *Quantum Leap* character all over again). Too politically correct and *X-Files*-influenced to work the way the old series did but still fairly diverting. Thinnes, in what little screen time he's allotted, is in good form as the understandably paranoid Vincent.

INVADERS FROM MARS

★★★ Nostalgia Merchant, 1953, NR, 78 min. Dir: William Cameron Menzies. Cast: Jimmy Hunt, Helena Carter, Arthur Franz, Leif Erickson, Hillary Brooke, Morris Ankrum.

A '50s almost-classic of preteen paranoia. Hunt

is the UFO-obsessed kid who can't get anyone to believe him when he sees a flying saucer land in his backyard. His parents and the local cops become Martian-controlled zombies but a sympathetic child psychologist (the stunning Carter in heels to die for) comes to the rescue. Director Menzies (production designer on *Gone With the Wind*) masks the tiny budget with brilliantly conceived shots of forced perspective and nightmarish landscapes full of sandpits and bubbling, melting spaceship and cave walls. The unforgettable shot of an unconscious Carter lying on a glass operating table with a jeweled alien control device spinning toward her tender neck is enough to even make you ignore the zips up the Martians' backs—one reason they usually back away from the camera. Some prints are missing the *Dead of Night*-inspired double twist at the end. Remade in 1986.

INVADERS FROM MARS

★★ Video Treasures, 1986, PG, 93 min. Dir: Tobe Hooper. Cast: Hunter Carson, Karen Black, Louise Fletcher, Timothy Bottoms, Laraine Newman, James Karen.

Big-budget remake of the ultra-cheap original directed by Hooper during his depressing post-*Poltergeist* slump. Carson (real life son of costar Black) is okay as the kid who witnesses the alien invasion, but the adults all act like they're in some *Saturday Night Live* sci-fi movie sketch (no wonder Newman's in this). An awful lot of very expensive FX work does little to hide the fact that this was all done a lot better and a lot more cheaply more than forty years earlier. Video Treasures letterboxed tape, though, transferred from the laser disc, is the only way to see it. Look for Jimmy Hunt in a cameo as a cop.

INVADERS FROM SPACE

★★☆ Something Weird, 1956, NR, 83 min. Dirs: Teruo Ishi, Akira Mitsugi, Koreyoshi Akasaka. Cast: Ken Utsui, Minoru Takada, Junko Ikeuchi, Utako Mitsuya.

The original Starman adventure-derived from episodes 1 and 2 of the Shintoho serial *Supah Jaiyanto (Super Giant)*—with our hero sent by the people of the Emerald Planet to save us from an impending invasion by the evil Salamander Men. A surrealistic blend of martial arts, bizarre special FX (just wait til you see the Salamander Men), and pathetic dubbing from our good friends at the Shintoho Company.

INVASION FORCE

See *Hanger 18*

INVASION OF THE ANIMAL PEOPLE

★ Sinister Cinema, 1960, NR, 73 min. Dirs: Virgil Vogel, Jerry Warren. Cast: John Carradine, Barbara Wilson, Robert Burton, Sten Gester.

The original footage of this Swedish sci-fi/horror flick, about a bigfoot-type monster sent on the prowl by alien invaders, has genuine atmosphere that is often strikingly effective. The new Warren scenes, though, offer the usual boredom, with Carradine on a cramped set talking out the action and generally getting in the way. Perhaps someday the original version, called *Terror in the Midnight Sun,* will become available so that we can evaluate this film on fairer terms.

INVASION OF THE BEE GIRLS

★★★ Nelson, 1973, R, 85 min. Dir: Denis Sanders. Cast: William Smith, Anitra Ford, Victoria Vetri, Cliff Osmond.

Ford (an original *Price Is Right* model), a human queen bee, transforms drab housewives into glamorous bee babes who exhaust their men to death during sex. An enjoyable tongue-in-cheek B thriller penned by pre-*Star Trek II* Nicholas Meyer and featuring a perfect cast of low-budget stalwarts. Aka *Graveyard Tramps.*

INVASION OF THE BODY SNATCHERS

★★★★ Republic, 1955, NR, 80 min. Dir: Don Siegel. Cast: Kevin McCarthy, Dana Wynter, Larry Gates, Carolyn Jones, King Donovan, Virginia Christine.

One of the greatest sci-fi/horror films ever made, based on the novel *The Body Snatchers* by Jack Finney. Paranoia sweeps through the California town of Santa Mira as people begin to claim that their friends and relatives are no longer their friends and relatives at all but sinister duplicates. Town doctor McCarthy and recently returned old flame Wynter discover that alien seed pods are birthing exact replicas of human beings and then absorbing their minds and memories so that the originals are "reborn" as emotionless extraterrestrials. Whether you take it as a subtle swipe at the '50s "commies under the bed" red scare, an attack on conformity, or just a straight thriller, this influential movie—one of the dozen or so best sci-fi films ever made—can't be beat. Remade in 1978 and as *Body Snatchers: The Invasion Continues* in 1993; some reissue prints are missing the "happy ending" wrap-up forced on director Siegel by distributor Allied Artists.

INVASION OF THE BODY SNATCHERS

★★★☆ MGM/UA, 1978, PG, 115 min. Dir: Phillip Kaufman. Cast: Donald Sutherland, Brooke Adams,

On-set drug abuse gets a little out of hand in Invasion of the Body Snatchers *(1955).*

Leonard Nimoy, Jeff Goldblum, Veronica Cartwright, Art Hindle, Lelia Goldoni, Kevin McCarthy.

The pods are back but in the aftermath of the Age of Aquarius it isn't the red baiters but the Me-generation types who get the satirical treatment here. Sutherland is a San Francisco health inspector who tries fruitlessly to stop the invasion. The great supporting cast includes Goldblum and Cartwright as behind-the-times hippies who run a mud bath and McCarthy in an alarming cameo, still running and shouting, "You're next!" until finally put out of his misery. The birth of each new replicant and the disintegration of the original, only suggested in the first film, are here made explicit through Tom Burman's special effects. Spooky twist ending, too.

INVASION OF THE SAUCER MEN.

★★☆ Columbia/TriStar, 1957, NR, 68 min. Dir: Edward L. Cahn. Cast: Steve Terrell, Gloria Castillo, Frank Gorshin, Lyn Osborn, Raymond Hatton, Russ Bender.

A small town lovers' lane is invaded by little green men with huge craniums and alcohol blood in this enjoyable AIP cheapie. Never really takes itself too seriously and that helps a lot. Great alien design by Paul Blaisdell, reminiscent of old sci-fi pulp magazine illustrations. Aka *Hell Creatures* and remade as *The Eye Creatures.*

INVASION OF THE SPACE PREACHERS

★★★ Rhino, 1990, R, 100 min. Dir: Daniel Boyd. Cast: Jim Wolfe, Guy Nelson, Eliska Hahn, Johnny Angel, Jimmy Walker.

I know the title makes this sound awful but this really is a pretty funny sci-fi spoof shot in West Virginia by Boyd, whose first film was the impressive low-budget horror anthology *Chillers.* Two buddies from the city (Wolfe and Nelson) head for a country retreat and find a crashed spaceship whose lizardlike pilot transforms into a beautiful blonde woman (Hahn). The guys then aid her in stopping an evil alien "Preacher," who uses mind control on his helpless human followers. There's an impressive title sequence and a lot of very good bits in this modest little movie that deserves more recognition. Aka *The Strangest Dreams.*

INVASION U.S.A.

★★ Sinister Cinema, 1952, NR, 74 min. Dir: Alfred E. Green. Cast: Peggie Castle, Gerald Mohr, Dan O'Herlihy, Robert Bice, Tom Kennedy, Phyllis Coates, Edward G. Robinson, Jr., Noel Neill.

An unnamed foreign power (but you know who they are) invade a complacent, unprepared America and blow it to smithereens in this daffy anti-Communist semi-sci-fi thriller. Great B cast (including *two* Lois Lanes!) and odd shocking plot twist, but the ridiculous surprise ending and enough stock footage for three Ed Wood movies made it tough to navigate.

INVISIBLE AGENT

★★ MCA/Universal, 1942, NR, 80 min. Dir: Edwin L. Marin. Cast: Jon Hall, Ilona Massey, Peter Lorre, Sir Cedric Hardwicke, J. Edward Bromberg, Albert Basserman.

In the dullest entry in Universal's *Invisible Man* series, Hall uses his invisibility formula to spy behind German lines during World War II. About as realistic a portrayal of wartime activities as any given episode of *Hogan's Heros,* somewhat redeemed by an above-average cast (with Lorre in his only Universal monster movie role). Surprisingly, the mediocre special effects (probably the result of a rushed shooting schedule) were nominated for an Oscar.

INVISIBLE AVENGER

★★ Sinister Cinema, 1958, NR, 60 min. Dir: James Wong Howe. Cast: Richard Derr, Mark Daniels, Helen Westcott, Jeanne Neher.

Veteran cinematographer Howe adds a few visual flourishes to this low-budgeter with Lamont Cranston (Derr), aka the Shadow, using his powers to investigate the murder of a New Orleans jazz musician. Occasionally imaginative but hampered by its lack of resources and a dull lead actor.

INVISIBLE BOY, THE

★★ MGM/UA, 1957, NR, 85 min. Dir: Herman Hoffman. Cast: Richard Eyer, Diane Brewster, Philip Abbott, Harold J. Stone, Robert H. Harris, Michael Miller.

Slickly done but weakly directed and written tale of a computer trying to take over the world (a new idea at the time) with young Eyer and friend Robby the Robot (of *Forbidden Planet* fame) out to stop it. Never really strikes the right balance between the suspenseful and the cute but not without interest.

INVISIBLE DR. MABUSE, THE

★★☆ Sinister Cinema, 1962, NR, 89 min. Dir: Harold Reinl. Cast: Lex Barker, Karin Dor, Werner Peters, Wolfgang Preiss, Sigfried Lowitz, Alan Dijon.

The bad doctor (Preiss) gets his hands on an invisibility machine and predictably uses it to try to take over the world. Well directed, fairly lively West German *Mabuse* sequel, with an above-average cast that includes the gorgeous Dor, then-wife of director Reinl. Aka *The Invisible Horror.*

INVISIBLE HORROR, THE

See: *The Invisible Mr. Mabuse.*

INVISIBLE INVADERS

★★ MGM/UA, 1959, NR, 66 min. Dir: Edward L. Cahn. Cast: John Agar, Jean Byron, Robert Hutton, John Carradine, Philip Tonge, Hal Torey.

Disembodied invaders from the moon inhabit the bodies of the recently dead in a plot to take over the Earth. This has some striking similarities to the later horror classic *Night of the Living Dead* (not to mention the sequel *Day of the Dead*) but an uninvolved cast (Agar looks cranky throughout) and dull direction make this sci-fi/horror hybrid a dull watch.

INVISIBLE KID, THE

★☆ Media, 1987, PG, 96 min. Dir: Avery Crouse. Cast: Jay Underwood, Karen Black, Wally Ward, Chynna Phillips, Brother Theodore.

Underwood uses his newfound invisibility powers for some *Porky's*-style low-jinks in this not very amusing supernatural comedy. Jay is likable enough but Black has one of her worst roles, as his annoying mom.

INVISIBLE MAN, THE

★★★★ MCA/Universal, 1933, NR, 71 min. Dir: James Whale. Cast: Claude Rains, Gloria Stuart, William Harrigan, Henry Travers, Una O'Connor, Forrester Harvey.

Whale's classic black comic adaptation of the

H. G. Wells book stars Rains as the chemist made invisible by an experimental drug called monocaine. Driven mad by his treatments, Rains becomes a madman who strangles policemen, wrecks trains, and robs banks (and laughs a lot), until a fortuitous snowstorm helps the authorities to track him down. John Fulton's special effects and Rains's magnificent vocal acting make this '30s classic a must.

INVISIBLE MAN RETURNS, THE

★★★ MCA/Universal, 1940, NR, 80 min. Dir: Joe May. Cast: Vincent Price, Nan Grey, Sir Cedric Hardwicke, John Sutton, Cecil Kellaway, Alan Napier.

Solid sequel with first-rate casting and FX. On the eve of his execution for the murder of his brother, Price uses the invisibility formula to escape prison and hunt down the real killer. Remade as *The New Invisible Man*.

INVISIBLE MAN'S REVENGE, THE

★★☆ MCA/Universal, 1944, NR, 77 min. Dir: Ford Beebe. Cast: Jon Hall, Evelyn Ankers, Alan Curtis, John Carradine, Gale Sondergaard, Leon Errol, Lester Matthews, Ian Wolfe.

Hall is a madman experimented on by dottering but not mad scientist Carradine with

"No, I don't want to pretend like we're the Jerky Boys!" John Carradine and Jon Hall in The Invisible Man's Revenge *(1944).*

an invisibility drug he uses to avenge himself on a wealthy family for imagined wrongs. Hall was previously seen in *Invisible Agent* but this really isn't a sequel; though the story is slow to develop the cast is good and the comic relief subplot (involving Errol) actually works and adds a bright touch to an otherwise dark plotline.

INVISIBLE RAY, THE

★★★ MCA/Universal, 1936, NR, 78 min. Dir: Lambert Hillyer. Cast: Boris Karloff, Bela Lugosi, Frances Drake, Frank Lawton, Beulah Bondi, Walter Kingsford.

Universal brings a touch of sci-fi to their usual mad doctor proceedings in this well-directed and photographed Karloff-Lugosi vehicle. It all starts in the usual windswept Balkan castle, where Karloff uses his private planetarium to chart the centuries-ago arrival on Earth of a meteor containing a rare element that eventually gives Boris a radioactive touch. Lugosi is good in a reasonably straight role as a fellow scientist. Even though the plot drags a bit, Western/serial expert Hillyer gives this a fine atmosphere aided by first-rate John Fulton FX.

INVISIBLE: THE CHRONICLES OF BENJAMIN KNIGHT

★☆ Paramount, 1994, R, 80 min. Dir: Jack Ersgard. Cast: Michael Dellafemina, Jennifer Nash, Brian Cousins, Curt Lowens, Alan Oppenheimer, Aharon Ipale.

Needless followup to *Mandroid* from Charles Band's Full Moon boys. Dellafemina becomes the invisible hero who tries to rescue heroine Nash from madman Lowens (in a metal mask) and his gang of rapists—with the rape angle played for comedy! Truly witless and annoying but with the occasionally nice special effect.

INVISIBLE WOMAN, THE

★★★ MCA/Universal, 1940, NR, 72 min. Dir: A. Edward Sutherland. Cast: Virginia Bruce, John Barrymore, John Howard, Charlie Ruggles, Oscar Homolka, Margaret Hamilton, Edward Brophy, Shemp Howard.

Delightful comedy with Barrymore as an absent-minded professor who invents an invisibility machine he uses on sharp-tongued fashion model Bruce. Homolka is the gangster who sends bumbling Brophy and Howard (in his pre-Stooges days) after the invention. Good fun with an outstanding cast and clever special effects.

IRON WARRIOR, THE

★ Media, 1987, PG-13, 82 min. Dir: Al Bradley. Cast: Miles O'Keeffe, Savina Gersak, Iris Peynado, Elizabeth Kaza, Tim Lane.

O'Keefe really stretches himself in a dual role as twin warriors raised by good and evil mothers who are driven to do battle. Miles fans might like it, but everyone else will find this Italian beef-cake-on-the-hoof a bore.

ISLAND AT THE TOP OF THE WORLD, THE

★★ Disney, 1974, G, 93 min. Dir: Robert Stevenson. Cast: David Hartman, Donald Sinden, Jacques Marin, Mako, Agneta Eckemyr, David Gwillim.

Hartman and Sinden travel to the arctic in search of the latter's missing son and discover a lost civilization of Vikings. Okay Disney fantasy-adventure suffers from a dull cast and a slow story but it gets better as it goes along, with solid special effects and imaginative production design.

ISLAND OF DR. MOREAU, THE

★★ Goodtimes, 1977, PG, 98 min. Dir: Don Taylor. Cast: Burt Lancaster, Michael York, Barbara Carrera, Nigel Davenport, Richard Basehart.

Nothing seemed to go right in this slick remake of *Island of Lost Souls,* based on the book by H. G. Wells. Shipwrecked York ends up on the island where Lancaster is advancing evolution through radical surgery. In one nice twist, York is himself de-evolutionized into a beastman until the predictable wrapup. Plastic makeup FX and a general misuse of glamorous Carrera—whose true identity was removed during the reediting of the ending even though her woman-to-leopard transformation remained a central image of the advertising artwork!—make this little more than a glossy missed opportunity.

ISLAND OF DR. MOREAU, THE

★★☆ New Line, 1996, PG-13, 114 min. Dir: John Frankenheimer. Cast: Marlon Brando, Val Kilmer, David Thewlis, Fairuza Balk, Ron Perlman.

Diplomat Thewlis, planewrecked at sea, is picked up by fey oddball Kilmer and transported to a private island, where scientist Brando is tinkering with animal DNA and creating a horde of quasi-human beast creatures. Originally to be directed by Richard Stanley, with Rob Morrow in the Thewlis role and Barbara Steele in a cameo as Brando's wife, this newest version of the H. G. Wells story has its moments but never really comes close to working. Marlon is, of course, just plain Marlon but still manages to give an interesting performance rife with subtleties. Val is anything but subtle as he sashays about in a sarong, imitates Brando, makes eyes at Thewlis, and generally makes a hilarious nuisance of himself—I can't tell if he's acting or not but he's certainly interesting to watch. Balk is an effectively feline presence as Brando's "daughter" and the Stan Winston makeups are pretty good, but this still suffers from a disappointing nonending and an overlying atmosphere of ennui it finds hard to shake.

ISLAND OF LOST SOULS

★★★★ MCA/Universal, 1932, NR, 69 min. Dir: Erle C. Kenton. Cast: Charles Laughton, Bela Lugosi, Richard Arlen, Lelia Hyams, Kathleen Burke, Arthur Hohl.

First and best film version of *The Island of Dr. Moreau* stars Laughton as the smarmy vivisectionist turning lions and tigers and bears into suffering "manimals" on his hellish Pacific paradise. Arlen is the shipwrecked "man from sea" who raises the temperature of sexy cat girl Burke (a beauty contest winner giving an amazingly feral and appealing debut performance), while Lugosi has a small but commanding role as the werewolf-like "Sayer of the Law": "Are we not men?" H. G. Wells hated it, but don't let that keep you away.

ISLAND OF TERROR

★★★ MCA/Universal, 1966, NR, 87 min. Dir: Terence Fisher. Cast: Peter Cushing, Edward Judd, Carole Gray, Niall MacGinnis.

Doctors Cushing and Judd and wealthy playgirl Gray are trapped on an island off the Irish coast being terrorized by tentacled, turtlelike creatures that suck the bone marrow from their victims. Well acted and quite scary in spots, even though the special effects are a bit of a letdown—when the monsters divide in two, they spew what looks like several gallons of runny macaroni and cheese in the process.

ISLAND OF THE BURNING DOOMED

★★☆ New Star, 1967, PG, 94 min. Dir: Terence Fisher. Cast: Christopher Lee, Peter Cushing, Patrick Allen, Sarah Lawson, Jane Merrow, William Lucas.

Underplayed sci-fi thriller with Lee and Cushing among the residents of a tiny island where unseen alien invaders are conducting climactic experiments to raise the Earth's temperature to match that of their home world. Nicely underplayed, if a bit slow. British title: *Night of the Big Heat*; released in the U.S. in 1971 as *Island of the Burning Damned* before the title was changed for TV.

IT CAME FROM BENEATH THE SEA

★★☆ Columbia/TriStar, 1955, NR, 78 min. Dir: Robert Gordon. Cast: Kenneth Tobey, Faith Domergue, Donald Curtis, Ian Keith.

Atomic testing revives an enormous prehistoric octopus (missing a tentacle or two for budgetary reasons) that's hunted by submarine commander Tobey. Eventually it ends up in San Francisco, where it wrecks the Golden Gate Bridge and much of Market Street. Practically a remake of Ray Harryhausen's previous hit, *The Beast from 20,000 Fathoms*, with a slight change in locale and creature, this is too talky for its own good (the early women's lib subplot is amusing but out of place) but every time one of those slimy tentacles rises into view (there's something about those groping, undulating tentacles that's eerily sexual) this Harryhausen flick finally kicks into gear.

IT CAME FROM OUTER SPACE

★★☆ MCA/Universal, 1953, NR, 81 min. Dir: Jack Arnold. Cast: Richard Carlson, Barbara Rush, Charles Drake, Russell Johnson, Kathleen Hughes, Dave Willock, Joe Swayer, George Eldredge.

When alien spacecraft crashes in the Arizona desert, the shape-shifting extraterrestrials disguise themselves as local townspeople in order to effect repairs. Arnold's first big 3-D sci-fi hit, based on a story by Ray Bradbury, is a bit of a disappointment when seen today. The spooky desert atmosphere is well caught and some of the special effects still hold up, but unfortunately the actors all have a tough time with their dull and/or pompous dialogue and the story seems needlessly padded. Still worthwhile, but mainly for fans of classic '50s science fiction. Followed by a made-for-cable sequel.

IT CAME FROM OUTER SPACE II

★★ MCA/Universal, 1995, PG-13, 85 min. Dir: Roger Duchowny. Cast: Brian Kerwin, Elizabeth Peña, Jonathan Carrasco, Bill McKinney, Howard Morris, Lauren Tewes.

This made-for-the-Sci-Fi-Channel sequel is actually a remake with another spaceship-load of shape-shifting aliens crashing in the desert and copying the appearance of locals who they've kidnapped as a cheap labor source to repair their ship. Pretty pointless; this has improved FX but is wholly lacking the creepy atmosphere Jack Arnold was able to bring to the original.

IT CONQUERED THE WORLD

★★☆ RCA/Columbia, 1956, NR, 68 min. Dir: Roger Corman. Cast: Peter Graves, Beverly Garland, Lee Van Cleef, Sally Fraser, Russ Bender, Paul Blaisdell.

One of Corman's most intelligent and down-beat '50s quickies, this features the infamous cucumber creature (designed and played by Blaisdell) from Venus who hitches a ride to Earth on an experimental rocket. The monster then uses scientist Van Cleef (a decade away from his success as a spaghetti Western star) to try and take over a rocket base with mind-controlling batlike minions. Graves is expendable as a pretty useless hero (who mainly functions as the film's moral conscience) but Garland is great as Lee's tough-talkin' wife who gets throttled by the monster in a surprisingly nightmarish moment. Remade as *Zontar, the Thing from Venus*.

IT'S A WONDERFUL LIFE

★★★★ Republic, 1946, NR, 129 min. Dir: Frank Capra. Cast: James Stewart, Donna Reed, Lionel Barrymore, Thomas Mitchell, Henry Travers, Beulah Bondi, Ward Bond, Gloria Grahame, Frank Faylen, H. B. Warner, Frank Albertson, Samuel S. Hinds.

On Christmas Eve, with his life falling apart, Stewart contemplates suicide but changes his mind after angel Travers shows him what the world would have been like had he never been born. I'm not much for sentimental Christmas movies but I must admit that this one really hits the spot. It's quaint without ever getting too corny and tough (even harsh) when it has to be. Stewart is perfection in his best-remembered role but Travers steals it as the wingless angel Clarence. Remade as the TV movie *It Happened One Christmas* (with Marlo Thomas as Stewart and Wayne Rogers as Donna Reed!) and ripped off by so many other TV dramas and situation comedies you'd need a whole other book to catalog them.

IT! THE TERROR FROM BEYOND SPACE

★★★ MGM/UA, 1958, NR, 68 min. Dir: Edward L. Cahn. Cast: Marshall Thompson, Shawn Smith, Kim Spalding, Ann Doran, Dabbs Greer, Ray "Crash" Corrigan.

Marshall is suspected in the deaths of all his fellow crewmen on the first manned Mars mission but the real killer (former serial star Corrigan in an ill-fitting monster suit) stows away on the rescue rocket for another murder spree. From the stilted performances to the cardboard sets to the chintzy special effects, this movie should have nothing going for it; yet low-key photography, fast cutting, and nicely bombastic music make this one of the most notable sci-fi B flicks of the '50s. *Alien*'s indebtedness to this film is so apparent that the producers of the later film tried to have this one banned from TV so that audiences wouldn't guess the source of all their ideas.

JABBERWOCKY

★★★ RCA/Columbia, 1977, R, 100 min. Dir: Terry Gilliam. Cast: Michael Palin, Max Wall, Deborah Fallender, John Le Mesurier, Annette Badland, Terry Jones.

Gilliam and Palin's follow-up to *Monty Python and the Holy Grail*, with Palin as a medieval moron who is ordered to slay the dreaded dragon Jabberwocky so that he can marry rotund princess Fallender—even though he's really in love with maiden Badland. Python fans should enjoy this but the more casual viewer may be alarmed by this comedy's excessive bloodshed.

JACK

★★ Hollywood Pictures, 1996, PG-13, 113 min. Dir: Francis Ford Coppola. Cast: Robin Williams, Diane Lane, Brian Kerwin, Bill Cosby, Fran Drescher, Jennifer Lopez.

Coppola (of all directors) helms this strange comedy-drama about a ten-year-old boy (Williams) suffering from a rare disease that causes him to age four times normal speed. Basically just a long-after-the-fact ripoff of *Big*, Williams revitalizes all those old childlike Mork mannerisms while everyone around him cries and frets and bemoans the fact that this poor kid hasn't long to live. It's basically just a sci-fi-tinged disease-of-the-week TV movie far beneath the talents of nearly all those involved. A box office flop, the ads advised viewers to "See Jack grow" and "See Jack smile" but I think this must've flown out of theaters before you had a chance to see Jack do much of anything.

JACK AND THE BEANSTALK

★★☆ Goodtimes, 1952, NR, 78 min. Dir: Jean Yarbrough. Cast: Bud Abbott, Lou Costello, Buddy Baer, Dorothy Ford, Shay Cogan, James Alexander, Barbara Brown, William Farnum.

While babysitting an annoying, effete little brat, Costello dreams that he is Jack (the sepia-toned film then changing to color in best *Wizard of Oz* tradition), climbing the beanstalk with butcher Abbott to the land of the giants, where they rescue princess Cogan and prince Alexander. This musical fantasy isn't bad, a

Todd Armstrong battles Ray Harryhausen's skeleton crew in Jason and the Argonauts *(1963).*

couple of the songs are pretty memorable and Baer makes for a formidable giant. Unfortunately the production values are fairly low, with cheap sets and crummy color processing, and Cogan and Alexander are about the most unappealing young lovers ever found in an A&C movie—or a Three Stooges, Ritz Brothers, Brown and Carney, or Wheeler and Woolsey movie, for that matter.

JACK THE GIANT KILLER
★★★ MGM/UA, 1962, NR, 94 min. Dir: Nathan Juran. Cast: Kerwin Mathews, Judi Meredith, Torin Thatcher, Walter Burke, Don Beddoe, Roger Mobley, Anna Lee, Tudor Owen.

After turning down the chance to produce Ray Harryhausen's *The Seventh Voyage of Sinbad* and then watching it rake in millions, Edward Small decided to make his own version by hiring *Sinbad*'s director, hero, and villain. Harryhausen was otherwise engaged so a young Jim Danforth headed up the FX team here, bringing to life a horned giant that carries off a

princess (Meredith); a two-headed giant that battles a sea monster with the head of a crocodile and the body of an octopus; and a winged gargoyle into which evil wizard Thatcher transforms himself at the climax. The animation is smooth but, unfortunately, the models aren't very well detailed, which is a shame since this is in some ways a better film than *Sinbad*, with a more colorful supporting cast and more interesting characters. Beware the reissue version, which was redubbed into an ersatz musical!

JASON AND THE ARGONAUTS
★★★★ Columbia/TriStar, 1963, NR, 104 min. Dir: Don Chaffey. Cast: Todd Armstrong, Nancy Kovack, Gary Raymond, Honor Blackman, Laurence Naismith, Nigel Green, Niall MacGinnis, Patrick Troughton.

Ray Harryhausen's finest achievement: a beautifully mounted, well-written, and beautifully scored (by Bernard Herrmann) mythical fantasy. Jason (Armstrong, cutting a fine figure even with the obviously dubbed voice) travels to the ends of the Earth in search of the fabled golden fleece. Along the way he meets up with Hercules (played with infectious gusto by Green) and encounters the huge living bronze statue Talos, the winged harpies, the many-headed dragon known as the Hydra, and an army of sword-wielding skeletons. After the original *King Kong,* this is probably the best-stop motion movie ever made, with an excellent cast and well-paced direction by Chaffey. Sequel: *Clash of the Titans.*

JAWS OF THE ALIEN
See: *The Human Duplicators.*

JOHNNY MNEMONIC
★★ Columbia/TriStar, 1995, R, 98 min. Dir: Robert Longo. Cast: Keanu Reeves, Dolph Lundgren, Dina Meyer, Takeshi Kitano, Ice-T, Henry Rollins, Denis Akiyama, Udo Kier.

Futuristic misfire with Reeves as a smuggler of vital information who keeps said information in a computer chip in his head (it's nice to know that there's *something* going on behind those soulful Keanu eyes). If he succeeds in his mission, our hero will have his memory and true identity restored to him. Flashy but uncompelling; still, any movie with Keanu, Dolph, Henry, and Udo in the same cast has got to be worth a look for kitsch value alone.

JONATHAN LIVINGSTON SEAGULL
★★ Paramount, 1973, G, 115 min. Dir: Hall Bartlett. Voices: James Franciscus, Juliet Mills, Hal Holbrook, Richard Crenna, Dorothy McGuire.

The world's first—and presumably last—movie about a talking, existential seagull, based on the peculiar best-seller by Richard Bach. Franciscus is Jonathan, who spends all his time pondering the meaning of life while the rest of his flock feast on garbage—including a copy of this movie's pompous script, I would hope. Awful songs by Neil Diamond are made endurable by some breathtaking aerial photography.

JOURNEY BENEATH THE DESERT
★★ Sinister Cinema, 1961, NR, 95 min. Dir: Edgar G. Ulmer. Cast: Haya Harareet, Rod Fulton, Georges Riviere, Jean Louis Tritgnant, Gabriele Tinti, Gian Maria Volonte.

A pair of adventurers discover the lost continent of Atlantis and its evil queen (Harareet, one of the stars of *Ben Hur*) beneath the Sahara desert. Ulmer manages to bring some stylish touches to this otherwise ponderous low-budget sci-fi/adventure. Aka *Antinea, L'Amante della Citta Sepolta (Atlantis, City Beneath the Desert).*

JOURNEY TO THE CENTER OF THE EARTH
★★★★ Fox, 1959, NR, 132 min. Dir: Henry Levin. Cast: James Mason, Arlene Dahl, Pat Boone, Diane Baker, Thayer David, Alan Napier, Peter Ronson, Alan Caillou.

Entertaining Jules Verne adaptation just jam-packed with thrills and excitement. Scottish geology professor Mason and favorite student Boone travel to Iceland, where they discover a path to the Earth's center beginning at the crater of a volcano. Accompanied by guide Ronson (who speaks no English), beautiful Dahl (whose late husband was the first to find the pathway), and a pet duck, they encounter various perils—including earthquakes, rock slides, bad guy David, and even dinosaurs—before they stumble upon the ruins of the lost city of Atlantis. One of the best sci-fi movies of the '50s, with good performances (even the out-of-place Boone isn't bad), suspenseful direction, imaginative set design, and great special effects. If you ever wondered where Spielberg got the rolling boulder scene in *Raiders of the Lost Ark,* look no further. Another fine Bernard Herrmann score, too. Followed by a 1960s cartoon show and remade as *Where Time Began.*

JOURNEY TO THE CENTER OF TIME
★★★ Academy Entertainment, 1967, NR, 82 min. Dir: David L. Hewitt. Cast: Scott Brady, Gigi Perreau, Anthony Eisley, Abraham Sofaer, Poupee Gamin, Lyle Waggoner.

This was always one of my favorite movies when I watched it on TV as a kid so please take that into consideration when you regard the rating. Brady stars as the jerky son of a millionaire industrialist who's been backing a series of time-travel experiments conducted by scientists Sofaer, Eisley, and Perreau. An accident sends everyone millions of years into the future (where they meet bald alien lady Gamin) and then millions of years into the past (where they encounter the least impressive dime-store pet lizard/dinosaur you've ever seen). Derivative of *The Time Travelers* and shot on a budget that wouldn't pay for the honeywagon on a studio film today, this gets by on the sheer strength of its imaginative story and solid performances from a good cast (including a pre-*Carol Burnett Show* Waggoner). And love that loop-the-loop-through-time ending.

JOURNEY TO THE FAR SIDE OF THE SUN
★★☆ MCA/Universal, 1969, PG, 99 min. Dir: Robert Parrish. Cast: Roy Thinnes, Ian Hendry, Lyn Loring, Patrick Wymark, Herbert Lom, Loni von Friedl.

TV puppet show kingpins Gerry and Sylvia Anderson produced this imaginative but rather dry tale about astronauts sent to a newly discovered twin of Earth on the other side of the sun. The spaceship crashes and lone survivor Thinnes awakens in a hospital back home— or is he? Good acting (especially Wymark) and FX but Parrish's direction is flat and the story somewhat confusing— though I like the ending where just about the entire cast is heartlessly killed off. Aka *Doppelganger*.

JOURNEY TO THE SEVENTH PLANET
★★★ HBO, 1961, NR, 83 min. Dir: Sidney Pink. Cast: John Agar, Greta Thyssen, Ann Smymer, Mimi Heinrich, Carl Ottosen, Ove Sprogoe.

Earth astronauts investigating Uranus run afoul of an alien brain creature that brings their fantasies—both good and bad—to life. Imaginative Denmark-made low-budget sci-fi has Agar leading a rather befuddled-looking Danish cast (with the gorgeous women all figments of the male astronauts imagination), but some clever photography and special effects keep things humming. A lot better than Pink's previous sci-fi extravaganza, *Reptilicus*. More or less remade as *Galaxy of Terror*.

JUDEX
★★★ Sinister Cinema, 1963, NR, 96 min. Dir: George Franju. Cast: Channing Pollock, Francine Berge, Edith Scob, Sylva Koscina, Michel Vitold.

Franju, director of the horror classic *The Horror Chamber of Dr. Faustus*, brings a beautiful sense of style and texture to this superhero film about Judex (Pollock), a master of disguise out to avenge himself on the criminal responsible for the death of his father. Lots of cool gadgets and imaginative gimmicks.

JUDGE DREDD
★★ Hollywood Pictures, 1995, R, 96 min. Dir: Danny Cannon. Cast: Sylvester Stallone, Armand Assante, Diane Lane, Max von Sydow, Jurgen Prochnow, Joan Chen, Rob Schneider, Balthazar Getty, Joanna Miles, Mitchell Ryan.

Sly is the title lawman, a respected judge by day (yeah, sure) and a helmeted supervigilante by night who's less interested in quoting criminals the law than in quoting their epitaphs. Another big-budget comic book fiasco, this has killer production design and a varied cast (did you ever think you'd see Max von Sydow and Rob Schneider costarring in the same movie?) but never really goes anywhere. Like so many similar films, this was probably aimed at kids but ended up being rated R anyway.

JULIA AND JULIA
★★☆ Fox, 1987, R, 97 min. Dir: Peter Del Monte. Cast: Kathleen Turner, Sting, Gabriel Byrne, Gabriele Ferzetti, Angela Goodwin.

Turner is excellent in this otherwise confusing parallel-time tale. Kathleen comes home one day to find long-dead husband Byrne alive and well and soon comes to realize that she's been mysteriously transported to a different reality where she may have a second chance with Gabe and escape brutish lover Sting. Fans of the star should see this but everyone else might find this Italian flick too annoyingly aloof.

JUMANJI
★★ Columbia/TriStar, 1995, PG, 104 min. Dir: Joe Johnston. Cast: Robin Williams, Bonnie Hunt, David Alan Grier, Kirsten Dunst, Bradley Pierce, Bebe Neuwirth.

After being trapped for twenty-six years inside a magical board game called Jumanji, Williams returns to the real world, but a strange dimensional flux keeps bringing various jungle animals and other creatures back to plague him. This elaborate fantasy was a surprise box office hit (Williams's second in a row after *Mrs. Doubtfire*) but despite state-of-the-art computer FX and a good cast it's kind of hard to warm up to.

JUNGLE, THE
★☆ Sinister Cinema, 1952, NR, 74 min. Dir: William Berke. Cast: Rod Cameron, Cesar Romero, Marie Windsor, Sulchana.

A semisequel to *The Lost Continent* (like it deserved one), with Cameron and Romero as adventurers in India who discover a lost tribe headed by Windsor and a herd of prehistoric mammoths (obviously played by elephants in fur coats). Shot on location, this often has flavor but overall will leave a bad taste in your mouth.

JURASSIC PARK
★★☆ MCA/Universal, 1993, PG-13, 126 min. Dir: Steven Spielberg. Cast: Sam Neill, Laura Dern, Jeff Goldblum, Richard Attenborough, Ariana Richards, Joseph Mazzello, Samuel L. Jackson, Wayne Knight.

Spielberg's homogenized film version of Michael Crichton's terrific best-seller about genetically engineered dinosaurs going on a rampage. One of the most popular films of all time, this *could* have been one of the best films of its kind, too, had Steven and company not decided to make a monster movie easily tied in with toy and Happy Meal sales. The FX are by and large outstanding

Sam Neill and Ariana Richards look good enough to eat to one prehistoric costar of Jurassic Park *(1993).*

but the whole thing has an antiseptic, untouched-by-human-hands feel to it that'll never put it in the same league with monster classics like the original *King Kong* or even *Godzilla*. Followed by *The Lost World*.

KID IN KING ARTHUR'S COURT, A
★★ Disney, 1995, PG, 90 min. Dir: Michael Gottlieb. Cast: Thomas Ian Nicholas, Joss Ackland, Art Malik, Paloma Buega, Ron Moody, Kate Winslet.

Why can't Disney leave *A Connecticut Yankee in King Arthur's Court* alone? Here, they remake their own *Unidentified Flying Oddball* version as yet another '90s baseball-themed fantasy for young boys. Nicholas is a fourteen-year-old little leaguer from California who falls down a hole in the outfield (yeah, right, whatever) and ends up back in Camelot, where he introduces the Arthurian crew to modern slang, ballplaying, and roller-blading. More cookie-cutter "family" fare from the kings of corporate kiddie mind control.

KILLER KLOWNS FROM OUTER SPACE
★★★ Media, 1988, PG-13, 86 min. Dir: Stephen Chiodo. Cast: Grant Cramer, Suzanne Snyder, John Vernon, Royal Dano, John Allen Nelson.

This imaginative spoof of *The Blob* is hoot and a half. Cannibalistic aliens who look like clowns take over a small town and transform its citizens into cotton candy-like substance. Great makeup work by the Chiodo Brothers and a cool theme song by the Dickies.

KILLERS FROM SPACE
★☆ Goodtimes, 1953, NR, 71 min. Dir: W. Lee Wilder. Cast: Peter Graves, Barbara Bestar, James Seay, Frank Gerstle, Steve Pendleton, John Merrick.

Literally bug-eyed aliens save the life of test pilot Graves so that he can help them take over the Earth with their army of gigantic animals and insects. Cheap alien invasion film salvaged from the junkheap by its unintended hilarity thanks to unconvincing makeup and

pathetic special effects. The operating scene, with Peter's flightsuit open a bit too much, gives the odd impression that our hero is being fondled by his Pingpong-ball-eyed captors.

KING DINOSAUR
★ Sinister Cinema, 1955, NR, 63 min. Dir: Bert I. Gordon. Cast: William Bryant, Wanda Curtis, Douglas Henderson, Patricia Gallagher, voice of Marvin Miller.

Mr. B.I.G.'s first and worst monster movie begins with a boring lecture (by Miller) about astronomy and space flight (to pad out the thin running time) until we settle down for the tale of how astronauts Bryant, Curtis, Henderson, and Gallagher discover prehistoric life on the planet Nova. Gordon's back-projected special effects are at their worst (and cheapest) here; this makes *The Cyclops* look like *Independence Day*. At least Joey the lemur enlivens things a bit.

KING KONG
★★★★ Turner, 1933, NR, 100 min. Dirs: Merian C. Cooper, Ernest B. Schoedsack. Cast: Fay Wray, Robert Armstrong, Bruce Cabot, Frank Reicher, Noble Johnson, James Flavin.

What more can be said about this most classic and influential of all monster movies? A labor of love for documentary filmmakers Cooper and Schoedsack and special effects maestro Willis O'Brien, their care and attention to detail can be seen in almost every frame of the film, from the nightmarish Gustave Doré-like backdrops of the jungles on Kong's island to the amazing details of scattering crowds, people peering out of buildings, and falling out of the wrecked el car in the climactic New York rampage. Max Steiner's music is probably the best, most emphatic score ever written for a 1930s movie. Followed by *Son of Kong* and remade in 1976 and 1997.

KING KONG
★★ Paramount, 1976, PG, 134 min. Dir: John Guillermin. Cast: Jessica Lange, Jeff Bridges, Charles Grodin, René Auberjonois, Ed Lauter, Rick Baker.

I'll never understand how someone could take over $20 million and still make such a botch job of the classic tale of beauty and the beast. Maybe it's the insulting, just-kiddin'-folks screenplay by Lorenzo Semple, Jr., or the rush-job special effects. Maybe it's the dazed and confusing '70s touches like women's lib, horoscopes, and *Deep Throat*. Or maybe it's just simply that when something works perfectly the first time around you should leave well enough alone. In any case, Lange is good

Fay Wray meets the gorilla of her dreams in King Kong *(1933).*

enough here to transcend her goofy character and awful dialogue to create someone you actually find yourself liking, and the John Barry musical score is just as good in its own way as was Max Steiner's music for the original. Don't blink or you'll miss the highly publicized giant Kong robot completely; Baker actually plays the part throughout most of the film.

KING KONG LIVES!

★ Goodtimes, 1986, PG-13, 104 min. Dir: John Guillermin. Cast: Linda Hamilton, Brian Kerwin, John Ashton, Peter Michael Goetz.

But can he live down this horrendous sequel to the *Kong* remake that starts to look surprisingly good by comparison? A female Kong, a heart transplant for the King, a beastly blessed event, and lots of laughable attempts at drama and tragedy are featured in maybe the worst sequel since *Breakin' 2: Electric Boogaloo.*

KING KONG VS. GODZILLA

★★★ Goodtimes, 1963, NR, 90 min. Dirs: Inoshiro Honda and Thomas Montgomery. Cast: Michael Keith, James Yagi, Tadao Takashima, Mie Hama.

The two monsters slug it out in this corny but fun Japanese creature feature, with new scenes (most of them pretty boring) added for U.S. release. Okay special effects but the ratty ape suit used for Kong could definitely use a major-league makeover.

KING OF KONG ISLAND

★ Sinister Cinema, 1968, R, 92 min. Dir: Robert Morris. Cast: Brad Harris, Esmeralda Barros, Marc Lawrence, Adrianna Alben, Mark Farran.

Obviously made to rip off *Planet of the Apes,* this Spanish cheapie went unreleased in the U.S. until 1977, when it was put out to rip off the *King Kong* remake. Mad scientists use radio brain implants to control a tribe of island-dwelling gorillas and turn them into an army of gorilla fighters. Not even as much fun as it sounds, with Barros featured in some gratuitous topless moments. Aka *Kong Island.*

KING OF THE ROCKET MEN
★★☆ Republic, 1949, NR, 240 min. Dir: Fred C. Brannon. Cast: Tristram Coffin, Mae Clarke, Don Haggerty, House Peters, Jr., James Craven, I. Stanford Jolley.

Coffin is the all-American scientist Dr. King, who invents a fabulous flying suit he uses to battle the sinister Dr. Vulcan, a madman with the usual world conquest on his mind. Originally released as *Lost Planet Airman,* this sci-fi serial is fun but long and drawn out and the obvious inspiration for *The Rocketeer.*

KING SOLOMON'S MINES
★★ MGM/UA, 1985, PG-13, 100 min. Dir: J. Lee Thompson. Cast: Richard Chamberlain, Sharon Stone, Herbert Lom, John Rhys-Davies, Ken Gampu, Shai K. Ophir.

H. Rider Haggard's classic adventure yarn is transformed into a lame *Raiders of the Lost Ark* ripoff. Chamberlain, in a butch mood as adventurer Allan Quartermain, tries to help Stone (doing a Kate Chapshaw impression) locate her missing father, who vanished in cannibal country while searching for a legendary diamond mine. Some good action and nice locations but the actors are all awful, making this a real patience tester. Sequel: *Allan Quartermain and the Lost City of Gold.*

KING SOLOMON'S TREASURE
★☆ VCI, 1976, PG, 89 min. Dir: Alvin Rakoff. Cast: David McCallum, Britt Ekland, Patrick Macnee, John Colicos, Hugh Rose, Wilfrid Hyde-White, Yvon Dufour, Ken Gampu.

McCallum searches the wilds of Canada for an African treasure guarded by barbarian queen Ekland. Preposterous H. Rider Haggard spin-off, with some familiar faces struggling through and an outlandish plot that throws in everything from cannibals to dinosaurs to keep you distracted. Actor Gampu should get some sort of endurance award for appearing in both this *and* the 1985 *King Solomon's Mines* remake.

KNIGHTS
★★ Paramount, 1992, R, 89 min. Dir: Albert Pyun. Cast: Kathy Long, Kris Kristofferson, Lance Henriksen, Scott Paulin, Gary Daniels.

In a future where vampire cyborgs prey on the human race, robot Kristofferson (giving an appropriately mechanical performance) trains five-time kickboxing champ Long for battle. In other words, it's *The Next Karate Kid* and *Buffy*

the Vampire Slayer meet *The Terminator.* Pretty bland for such an unusual premise and the climactic fight scene is ineptly staged, but there are a few laughs to be had.

KRONOS
★★☆ Nostalgia Merchant, 1957, NR, 78 min. Dir: Kurt Neumann. Cast: Jeff Morrow, Barbara Lawrence, John Emery, George O'Hanlon, Morris Ankrum, Robert Shayne.

A year before he directed *The Fly,* Neumann helmed this nearly as odd little movie. Aliens drop a huge, refrigeratorlike robot (dubbed Kronos) in the Mexican desert. Scientists Morrow and Lawrence investigate (little realizing that superior Emery is under alien control) as the huge machine begins to rampage across the countryside, absorbing all energy (including an atomic bomb) in its path. Marred by cheap special effects and a pace that progresses from too slow to too fast, this is a flawed but not unworthy variation on the usual '50s giant-monster-on-the-loose film.

KRULL
★★ Columbia/TriStar, 1983, PG, 117 min. Dir: Peter Yates. Cast: Ken Marshall, Lysette Anthony, Freddie Jones, Francesca Annis, Liam Neeson, Robbie Coltrane, David Battley, Bernard Bresslaw.

A weird blending of *Excalibur* and *Star Wars,* featuring Marshall as the handsome hero who must rescue kidnapped princess Anthony with a magical talisman. Interesting production design and special effects and amusing performances from Annis (as a witch) and Bresslaw (as a helpful Cyclops), but too plodding to build any real excitement.

LABYRINTH
★★★ Nelson, 1986, PG, 101 min. Dir: Jim Henson. Cast: David Bowie, Jennifer Connelly, Toby Froud, Shelly Thompson, Christopher Malcolm, Natalie Finland.

Monty Python's Terry Jones wrote and *Star Wars'* George Lucas was the executive producer on this curious modern-day retelling of *Alice in Wonderland* crossed with *The Wizard of Oz*. Beautiful Connelly is a teenager who resents having to babysit little brother Froud but later proves her love for him by risking her life when the brat is kidnapped by minions of Goblin King Bowie. Like Alice, Jennifer finds herself being sucked into an underground world of mystery and fantasy and like Dorothy, she must team up with some supernatural friends to succeed in her quest. Sometimes looks like the Muppets meet Ziggy Stardust, but clever special FX and Connelly's pleasing presence make this worth seeing.

LADYHAWKE

★★★★ Warner, 1985, PG-13, 101 min. Dir: Richard Donner. Cast: Matthew Broderick, Rutget Hauer, Michelle Pfeiffer, Leo McKern, John Wood, Alfred Molina.

Once you get past the casting of Broderick (*Ferris Bueller's Medieval Day Off?*) in the lead, you are easily caught up in the majesty of this beautiful fantasy—the best of the myriad mid-'80s sword-and-sorcery movies. Matthew is a young scalawag of the thirteenth century who, along with mentor McKern, aids a pair of cursed, star-crossed lovers. Hauer is the knight who each night turns into a wolf and Pfeiffer is his princess who each day becomes the hawk of the title. Heartbreaking mixture of romance, swashbuckling adventure, comedy, and the supernatural, with sweeping location photography, nicely understated acting, and a beautiful score by Andrew Powell.

LAND THAT TIME FORGOT, THE

★★ Goodtimes, 1974, PG, 90 min. Dir: Kevin Connor. Cast: Doug McClure, Susan Penhaligon, John McEnery, Keith Barron.

Plastic adaptation of the Edgar Rice Burroughs story about a German submarine (circa World War I) transporting American-British shipwreck survivors into custody that instead ends up on a lost continent of dinosaurs and cavemen. The original story held a lot of promise but the simplification of some of its most interesting ideas (like evolution on the continent advancing the further inland you go) and lousy monster mockups make this mostly a waste. Still, it did well enough in ticket sales to warrant a sequel: *The People That Time Forgot*.

LAND UNKNOWN, THE

★★ MCA/Universal, 1957, NR, 78 min. Dir: Virgil Vogel. Cast: Jock Mahoney, Shawn Smith, William Reynolds, Henry Brandon, Phil Harvey.

Originally to have been directed by Jack Arnold, this lethargic lost world movie could have used his directorial sense of urgency. A navy helicopter discovers a prehistoric valley near the South Pole inhabited by big plaster dinosaurs and stranded madman Brandon, who gets the hots for female reporter Smith. Imaginatively photographed in widescreen on some impressively designed sets, but this is so dull and uneventful it becomes a real chore to sit through. The only suspense comes from wondering how Smith—not to mention the even prettier Reynolds—manages to keep her hair and makeup so immaculate after months in a prehistoric rain forest.

LASERBLAST

★☆ Media, 1977, PG, 85 min. Dir: Michael Raye. Cast: Kim Milford, Cheryl Smith, Roddy McDowall, Keenan Wynn, Gianni Russo, Ron Masak, Dennis Burkley, Eddie Deezen.

Dull, poorly made sci-fi variation on *Carrie*. Milford is a pouty, bleach-blonde dweeb who finds an alien laser cannon in the desert near his home and begins transforming into a monster when he uses the weapon to avenge himself on his tormentors. Worth seeing only for sweet Cheryl (aka Rainbeaux) Smith and some Dave Allen animated alien critters who show up at the beginning and the end of the movie. You know a movie isn't working when *Eddie Deezen* is cast as a bullying cool guy!

LAST ACTION HERO

★☆ Columbia/TriStar, 1993, PG-13, 130 min. Dir: John McTiernan. Cast: Arnold Schwarzenegger, Austin O'Brien, Mercedes Ruehl, Anthony Quinn, Art Carney, Ian McKellen, Charles Dance, Tina Turner, F. Murray Abraham, Robert Prosky, Joan Plowright, Tom Noonan.

This wrong-headed vanity pic almost ruined its studio and trashed Arnold's career for good—and it's not even good for many laughs. O'Brien is kinda appealing as a lonely kid who's whisked into the motion picture screen by a magical ticket stub that puts him right along side his idol Jack Slater (played by guess who?). Eventually they both reemerge into the real world for some lame *Purple Rose of Cairo*-type tomfoolery. Where Schwarzenegger ever got the idea that his ideal costar would be an eleven-year-old boy is beyond me (the whole situation just bubbles with homoerotic NAMBLA overtones), while this whole movie is so smug and self-reverential you just want to smack it. Some good stunts and spot-the-star cameos help-but not much.

LAST CHASE, THE

★☆ Vestron, 1980, PG, 101 min. Dir: Martin Burke. Cast: Lee Majors, Burgess Meredith, Chris Makepeace, Alexandra Stewart, Ben Gordon.

The early '80s were not a good time for former bionic men and has-been penguins, as demonstrated by this hackneyed Canadian yawner. In the year 2000, the oil shortage has resulted in a twenty-year ban on all motor travel. Majors is a one-time auto racer who teams up with young Makepeace (star of *Meatballs*) to restore his classic Porsche for one final ride. This laughable relic of an earlier era is as tedious as it sounds.

LAST DAYS OF MAN ON EARTH, THE

See: *The Final Programme.*

LAST DAYS OF PLANET EARTH, THE

★★ Paramount/Gateway, 1974, PG, 90 min. Dir: Toshio Masuda. Cast: Tesuro Tamba, Toshio Kurosaw, So Yamamura, Kaoru Yumi, Kenju Kobayashi, Hiroshi Fujioka.

A big hit in Japan but released directly to U.S. TV, this is one of the most depressing disaster movies of the era. Nuclear contamination from bombs dropped around the world pollutes the atmosphere and oceans; people wear gas masks, have hallucinations, go mad, and commit suicide; and the sky turns into a gigantic mirror. Some of the special effects are imaginative and well done but the characters are cardboard (and the actors badly dubbed) and the plot little more than a string of nasty vignettes. Aka *Catastrophe 1999: The Prophecies of Nostradamus.*

LAST DINOSAUR, THE

★★ Edde Entertainment, 1976, NR, 93 min. Dirs: Alex Grassoff, Tom Kotani. Cast Richard Boone, Joan Van Ark, Steven Keats, Luther Rackley.

Millionaire sportsman Boone leads an expedition to a newly discovered prehistoric world beneath the North Pole so that he can hunt a tyrannosaurus. Fairly routine U.S.-Japanese coproduction, this seems to be aimed at kids (Boone's ultra-mild cussing is an obvious tipoff) but has no problem gruesomely dispatching the supporting cast—if they'd only bump off annoying "hero" Keats as well. If I ever meet Van Ark in person, I've got to remember to ask her about this movie—oh, and *Frogs* too. Might as well add insult to injury.

LAST MAN ON EARTH, THE

★★☆ Sinister Cinema, 1963, NR, 86 min. Dir: Sidney Salkow. Cast: Vincent Price, Franca Bettoia, Emma Danieli, Giacomo Rossi Stuart.

The first and better version of Richard Matheson's seminal vampire novel *I Am Legend* finds Price as the seeming sole survivor after a vampire plague ravages the world. Price is miscast and the film tends to be rather slow, but the atmospheric scenes of deserted cities, bodies burning on bonfires, and Vince warding off the grasping undead in his boarded-up home *Night of the Living Dead*-style have an unnerving impact. Remade as *The Omega Man.*

LAST STARFIGHTER, THE

★★★ MCA/Universal, 1984, PG, 100 min. Dir: Nick Castle. Cast: Lance Guest, Robert Preston, Dan O'Herlihy, Catherine Mary Stewart, Barbara Bosson, Chris Hebert, Cameron Dye, Wil Wheaton.

Unpretentious and entertaining mixture of *Star Wars* and *Wargames* about a teenage video game wiz (Guest) recruited by an alien race to help them battle an intergalactic empire bent on universal conquest. The characters are all refreshingly human—even the aliens—and a heavily made-up O'Herlihy and a jovial Preston (in his final role as a sort-of spaced-out *Music Man*) really stand out. A notable effort playing up people over FX, something you don't often see these days.

LAST WOMAN ON EARTH, THE

★★☆ Sinister Cinema, 1960, NR, 71 min. Dir: Roger Corman. Cast: Betsy Jones-Moreland, Anthony Carbone, Edward Wain [Robert Towne].

Corman's buck-and-a-half version of *The World, the Flesh, and the Devil* minus the racial issues but with gangsters and cool jazz instead. Underworld figure Carbone, sexy wife Jones-Moreland, and lawyer Wain (aka screenwriter Robert Towne) survive the apocalypse while scuba diving in Puerto Rico and then spend the next hour bickering about who's gonna date who (Tony and Ed never make eyes at each other, but you never know) and the expected violence erupts. Filmed on the sly while Rog was shooting *Creature from the Haunted Sea*, this clearly has rush job written all over it but in its own small way is quite interesting.

LATE FOR DINNER

★★ Columbia/TriStar, 1991, PG, 99 min. Dir: W. D. Richter. Cast: Brian Wimmer, Peter Berg, Marcia Gay Harden, Peter Gallagher, Colleen Flynn, Kyle Secor.

Offbeat but uneven sci-fi-comedy-drama about two guys on the run (Wimmer and Berg) who are frozen in a cryogenics experiment and revived three decades later. Can they restart their lives in a world where everything has changed (including friends and loved ones) but they haven't aged a day? Well acted and certainly heartfelt, but it keeps switching gears so often you never quite know how to react.

LAWLESS LAND, THE

★ MGM/UA, 1988, R, 78 min. Dir: Jon Hess. Cast: Nick Corri, Amanda Peterson, Leon, Xander Berkeley, Patricia Bunston, Walter Kliche.

In the not too distant future, teen lovers Corri and Peterson are chased down by bounty hunters sicced on them by her dad (Kliche). Cheap, unimaginative *Romeo and Juliet* meets *Mad Max* Roger Corman production shot in Chile.

LAWNMOWER MAN, THE

★★ New Line, 1992, R, 140 min. Dir: Brett Leonard. Cast: Jeff Fahey, Pierce Brosnan, Jenny Wright, Mark Bringleson, Geoffrey Lewis, Jeremy Slate.

A gruesome Stephen King short story about a guy who falls victim to a psychotic lawn-care guy who worships the Great God Pan gets turned into a flashy but empty ripoff of *Charly*. Brosnan is a scientist who experiments on retarded lawnmower man Fahey (in a hoot of a blonde wig), turning him into a murderous supergenius with world conquest on his mind. Leonard's initial film, *Dead Pit*, was an imagi-native variation on the usual post-*Dawn of the Dead* zombie movie, but this movie, despite a good performance from Bond-to-be Brosnan and a well-done "virtual reality" climax, is a bore. The 105-minute theatrical edition is practically incomprehensible; this longer director's cut edition makes more sense but still isn't very good.

LAWNMOWER MAN 2: JOBE'S WAR

★☆ New Line, 1996, R, 93 min. Dir: Farhad Mann. Cast: Patrick Bergin, Matt Frewer, Austin O'Brien, Ely Pouget, Camille Cooper, Kevin Conway.

Another in a recent string of totally needless sequels, this takes place in the bombed-out future where *Last Action Hero* alumnus O'Brien tries to convince scientist Bergin (in the old Pierce Brosnan role) to help bring about the downfall of the God-like Jobe (Frewer, in the old Jeff Fahey role). That this thing could snag a theatrical release while other, better films languish on the studio shelf is just one more proof that Hollywood is about to go right into the tank. Bergin and Pouget (as his lost love) are good but otherwise this cynical followup is an almost complete waste of celluloid.

LEGEND

★★☆ MCA/Universal, 1985, PG, 89 min. Dir: Ridley

Tim Curry in magnificent Rob Bottin makeup as the demon of Legend *(1985).*

Scott. Cast: Tom Cruise, Mia Sara, Tim Curry, David Bennet, Alice Playten, Billy Barty.

Scott's follow-up to *Blade Runner,* this beautifully crafted fairy tale suffers from a bland lead, inappropriate music (with a Tangerine Dream track used in place of the original Jerry Goldsmith score), and blunt editing (the 110-minute European version works much better). Curry is magnificent in chilling makeup as the devilish villain (he looks like a demon straight out of *Fantasia*) who wishes to gain control over a pair of unicorns; he kidnaps and attempts to corrupt a beautiful princess (Sara) to that end. Cruise, looking like he's auditioning for the role of Tinker Bell in *Hook,* is woefully out of his element as an innocent woodland boy who loves and tries to rescue Sara (you keep expecting him to start bopping through the forest in his underwear and a pair of dark glasses). Despite its many flaws, though, this is well worth a look for its gorgeous atmosphere and beautifully textured photography and set design.

LEGEND OF THE DINOSAURS

★★ Celebrity, 1977, PG, 89 min. Dir: Junji Kurata. Cast: Tsunehiko Watase, Nobiko Sawa, Tomoko Kiyoshima, Shotaro Hayashi.

This opens promisingly with an eerie scene of a girl tourist falling into a deep cavern at the base of Mt. Fuji filled with an icy blue mist and hatching dinosaur eggs. After that it quickly becomes just another nature-runs-amok thriller-a *Godzilla*-type Japanese monster flick retooled for the post-*Jaws* era. Plastic special FX but some really odd touches—including a shockingly inconclusive ending—make this of minor interest. Aka *Legend of the Dinosaurs and Monster Birds.*

LEGEND OF THE DINOSAURS AND MONSTER BIRDS

See: *Legend of the Dinosaurs.*

LEVIATHAN

★★☆ MGM/UA, 1989, R, 97 min. Dir: George P. Cosmatos. Cast: Peter Weller, Richard Crenna, Amanda Pays, Daniel Stern, Lisa Eilbacher, Ernie Hudson, Hector Elizondo, Meg Foster.

Undersea miners are mutated into monsters by contaminated vodka from a derelict Russian submarine called *Leviathan.* One of several similar films released at about the same time—*The Abyss, Deep Star Six, Lords of the Deep,* and so on—this is actually a fairly tense and effective, if predictable, variation on *The Thing.* The capable cast and direction help make up for its rather muddled storyline.

LIFEFORCE

★★ MGM/UA, 1985, R, 116 min. Dir: Tobe Hooper. Cast: Steve Railsback, Peter Firth, Frank Finlay, Mathilda May, Patrick Stewart, Michael Gothard.

Colin Wilson's pulpy novel *Space Vampires* gets turned into one of the biggest-budgeted exploitation movies of the '80s. A derelict alien spacecraft containing naked humanoid soul-suckers is discovered in the tail of Halley's comet and soon the alien queen (May) has half the population of London transformed into rampaging zombies. Released to theaters at 101 minutes, this video version makes a tad more sense but this really isn't the sort of movie you want to think about too much. A stray thought though: Isn't it interesting that the female space vampire always gets to parade around full frontal while her male counterparts are continually standing where various obstructions can conveniently block out their naughty bits?

LIFEPOD

★★☆ Cabin Fever, 1993, NR, 90 min. Dir: Ron Silver. Cast: Robert Loggia, Ron Silver, Jessica Tuck, Stan Shaw, Adam Storke, C.C.H. Pounder, Kelli Williams, Ed Gale.

This made-for-cable sci-fi remake of Hitchcock's *Lifeboat* finds a group of survivors stranded in space after their ship explodes in the year 2169. The group bickers and fights while reporter Tuck (in the old Tallulah Bankhead role) videotapes everything and various members of the group die. Even if you're not familiar with the original there isn't very much suspense here, but it's well enough acted and directed to keep you watching.

LIFESPAN

★★ Vestron, 1974, R, 85 min. Dir: Alexander Whitelaw. Cast: Klaus Kinski, Tina Aumont, Hiram Keller, Fons Radenmakers.

Odd European sci-fi about a scientist (Keller) trying to discover the secret immortality formula of colleague Kinski. Atmospheric but more concerned with sex and nudity than building a good plot. As always, Kinski's intensity is almost reason enough to sit through anything.

LIGHT AT THE EDGE OF THE WORLD, THE

★☆ Ace, 1971, PG, 119 min. Dir: Kevin Billington. Cast: Kirk Douglas, Yul Brynner, Samantha Eggar, Jean-Claude Drouot, Fernando Rey, Renato Salvatori.

Brynner and his pirates douse a powerful, futuristic lighthouse in order to wreck ships and plunder their cargo. Douglas is the lighthouse keeper who tries to stop Yul and rescue shipwreck survivor Eggar from rape at the hands of the lascivious pirates. This Spanish Jules Verne adaptation is so relentlessly tacky and downbeat that it defeats the talents of even such charismatic stars as Douglas and Brynner and is pretty violent and sexist for a film originally aimed at kids.

LIGHTNING BOLT

★★ Sinister Cinema, 1966, NR, 96 min. Dir: Anthony Dawson [Antonio Margheriti]. Cast: Anthony Eisley, Wandisa Leigh, Diana Lorys, Fulco Lulli, Ursula Parker.

An Italian James Bond imitation has Eisley (with Lucille Ball red rinse) as the secret agent out to stop a madman from taking over the world with a laser beam. Cheap but watchable sub-007 guns, gals, and guffaws. Aka *Operazione Goldman (Operation Goldman)*.

LIGHT YEARS

★★ Vidmark Entertainment, 1988, PG, 89 min. Dir: René Laloux. Voices: Glenn Close, Jennifer Grey, Christopher Plummer, John Shea, Penn Jillette, David Johansen.

A pastoral planet of innocent aliens is invaded by mutants who turn the inhabitants to stone. The queen (voiced by Close) sends a secret agent (voiced by Shea) out into space to find out what's going on. Issac Asimov wrote the English version of this ambitious but hard-to-follow French animated feature, somewhat similar in tone to *Fantastic Planet* but less oblique.

LIKE FATHER, LIKE SON

★ RCA/Columbia, 1987, PG-13, 98 min. Dir: Rod Daniel. Cast: Dudley Moore, Kirk Cameron, Margaret Colin, Catherine Hicks, Patrick O'Neal, Sean Astin.

Moore and Cameron (maybe the least likely father-and-child team since Lorne Greene and Ava Gardner in *Earthquake)* accidentally switch personalities thanks to an ancient Indian drug. This feeble ripoff of *Freaky Friday* got the drop on the rest of the body-switch comedies that followed the mega-successful *Big* and is by far the worst of the bunch—even *Dream a Little Dream* is better!—thanks to unfunny situations and Moore's endless mugging.

LIQUID SKY

★★☆ Media, 1983, R, 112 min. Dir: Slava Tsukerman. Cast: Anne Carlisle, Paula Sheppard, Susan Doukas, Otto Von Wernherr, Bob Brady, Elaine Grove.

Cultish New York-lensed low-budgeter about aliens seeking a powerful druglike substance released in the human bloodstream following orgasm. Carlisle is the beautiful lesbian model the aliens use to lure sex-crazed idiots into their clutches. Somewhat dated by its New Wave trappings but amazingly contemporary in its ambisexual, black-clad attitude, this is marred by its lack of production values and mostly catatonic performances but captures the New York club scene amazingly well.

LOBSTER MAN FROM MARS

★★ IVE, 1988, PG, 84 min. Dir: Stanley Sheff. Cast: Tony Curtis, Deborah Foreman, Patrick Macnee, Billy Barty, Tommy Sledge, Anthony Hickox.

Silly spoof with Curtis as a Hollywood mogul who decides to make a sure-fire hit starring the title alien, who's currently terrorizing the Southwest United States. The cast is game and the basic idea is clever but this hit-or-miss comedy never really comes off.

LOGAN'S RUN

★★☆ MGM/UA, 1976, PG, 119 min. Dir: Michael Anderson. Cast: Michael York, Jenny Agutter, Peter Ustinov, Richard Jordan, Farrah Fawcett, Roscoe Lee Browne.

The William F. Nolan and George Clayton Johnson novel (about a hedonisitc futuristic world where everyone must die at age twenty-one) gets the glossy studio treatment here. York and Jordan are cops in the year 2274 who pursue runners: people who refuse to take part in a spectacular ceremony that ends all life at age thirty. With his own time running out, Logan (York) decides to take off with comely Agutter and they eventually come across an aged Ustinov living in the ruins of Washington, D.C. The first half of this movie isn't bad but then things start to get silly, with a cat fight for Jenny and Farrah, Browne as a robot who looks like he's covered in Reynolds Wrap, and Ustinov babbling on and on as if he's ad-libbing until somebody locates his copy of the script. Watchable, but the Oscar-winning special FX seem pretty mediocre in these more computer-generated days. Followed by a TV series with Gregory Harrison and Heather Menzies in the York and Agutter roles.

LOOKER

★★ Warner, 1981, PG, 90 min. Dir: Michael Crichton. Cast: Albert Finney, Susan Dey, James Coburn, Leigh Taylor-Young, Dorian Harewood, Darryl Hickman.

Absurd thriller mixing elements of horror and sci-fi in this tale of a Beverly Hills plastic surgeon whose beautiful model-patients are being murdered and replaced by computer-created clones. Originally intended as a comedy before reediting changed it into a straight thriller,

Jenny Agutter and Farrah Fawcett reenact the second Ali-Fraser fight in Logan's Run *(1976).*

none of this makes sense (why are the models being killed and why frame Finney for the murders?) but it's still fairly funny, with Finney giving another of his grouchy, falling-off-the-wagon performances and Dey featured in a legendary brief nude scene—surprising for a PG-rated movie.

LORD OF THE RINGS, THE
★★☆ HBO, 1978, PG, 133 min. Dir: Ralph Bakshi. Voices: Christopher Guard, William Squire, John Hurt, Michael Sholes.

Ambitious but seriously flawed animated feature based on the first half of J.R.R. Tolkien's three-part epic about the various fabulous characters of Middle Earth competing for the all-powerful rings. Some good moments but Bakshi's modernist animated technique really isn't suited for this sort of storytelling.

LORDS OF THE DEEP
★☆ MGM/UA, 1989, PG-13, 79 min. Dir: Mary Ann Fisher. Cast: Bradford Dillman, Priscilla Barnes, Daryl Haney, Melody Ryane, Eb Lottimer, Stephen Davies.

Roger Corman's rock-bottom entry in *The Abyss* cash-in stakes. Dillman really goes over the top as a manic submarine commander whose coed vessel encounters an underwater flying saucer and its jellyfishlike occupants. *Three's Company* star Barnes is amazingly earnest considering the circumstances but otherwise this cheapie has almost nothing going for it. Corman appears briefly on a video monitor.

LOST CITY, THE
★ Sinister Cinema, 1935, NR, 120 min. Dir: Harry Revier. Cast: Kane Richmond, William "Stage" Boyd, Claudia Dell, Ralph Lewis.

Ludicrous serial about a mad scientist living in a ruined African city where he turns the locals into mindless zombies and constructs a powerful ray he wants to use for the usual world-conquering purposes. Ineptly acted, written, and directed jungle nonsense; could Ed Wood have seen and been inspired by this as a kid?

Also available in a shortened feature version.

LOST CONTINENT, THE

★★ Sinister Cinema, 1951, NR, 83 min. Dir: Sam Newfield. Cast: Cesar Romero, Hillary Brooke, Hugh Beaumont, John Hoyt, Whit Bissell, Acquanetta.

Even with a dream B-movie cast like this, this flatly directed lost-world epic is still a real ordeal to get through. A crashed rocket is traced to an island with a mountain inhabited by Augie Lohman-animated dinosaurs and some *One Million Years B.C.* stock footage. Half the movie seems to be Romero and company climbing the same plaster of paris rocks over and over again.

LOST EMPIRE, THE

★ Vestron, 1983, R, 86 min. Dir: Jim Wynorski. Cast: Melanie Vincz, Angela Aames, Raven de la Croix, Paul Coufos, Bob Tessier, Angus Scrimm.

Soft-porn spoof of old B movies and serials, with Vincz leading a bevy of near-naked warrior women against the cult of sinister Scrimm. Little more than a cheap excuse to get as many undressed, undertalented actresses as possible before the cameras, this artless pseudo-comedy isn't clever enough to work on any but the most sophomoric of levels.

LOST HORIZON

★★★★ Columbia/TriStar, 1937, NR, 132 min. Dir: Frank Capra. Cast: Ronald Colman, Jane Wyatt, John Howard, Edward Everett Horton, Margo, Sam Jaffe, Isabel Jewell, Thomas Mitchell.

Capra's classic version of James Hilton's novel about plane crash survivors in Tibet taken to the magical valley of Shangri-La, where there is peace and happiness and no one ever grows old. When Colman, younger brother Howard, and native girl Margo try to escape back to civilization, tragedy results. Beautifully filmed with imaginative set design and a perfect cast; this was shown in a cut reissue version for years but was finally restored to its original length for video and cable TV. The hilariously bad musical remake from 1973, with Peter Finch, Liv Ullmann, George Kennedy, Olivia Hussey, Sally Kellerman, and many more, is available on laser disc but as of this writing isn't out yet on cassette.

LOST MISSILE, THE

★★★ Sinister Cinema, 1958, NR, 70 min. Dir: Lester Berke. Cast: Robert Loggia, Ellen Parker, Larry Kerr, Philip Pine, Marilee Earle, Fred Engleberg.

Loggia is excellent in an early starring role in this underrated '50s B flick. A mysterious missile of unknown origin begins circling the globe and cuts a deadly radioactive path in its wake. When the city of Ottawa, Canada, is destroyed, scientists fear New York City will be next. Often too ambitious for its meager budget but surprisingly downbeat and honest for its time.

LOST PLANET, THE

★★ Republic, 1953, NR, 150 min. Dir: Spencer G. Bennet. Cast: Judd Holdren, Vivian Mason, Ted Thorpe, Forrest Taylor, Michael Fox, Gene Roth.

Second-rate serial with chapter-play stalwart Holdren as a reporter who uncovers an insidious invasion plot from the planet Ergro. Mostly just a lot of running around.

LOST PLANET AIRMEN

See: *King of the Rocket Men.*

LOST WOMEN

See: *Mesa of Lost Women.*

LOST WORLD, THE

★★★ Goodtimes, 1925, NR, 60 min. Dirs: Harry O. Hoyt, William Dowling. Cast: Wallace Beery, Bessie Love, Lewis Stone, Lloyd Hughes, Arthur Hoyt, Bull Montana.

Willis O'Brien's special FX are still the main reason to see this silent version of Arthur Conan Doyle's story about a plateau of dinosaurs discovered in South America. Beery is fun as blustery Professor Challenger, but most of the live-action nonmonster scenes (directed by Dowling) are cut from the most widely circulated prints of this prototypical monster movie. Remade in 1960 and 1992.

LOST WORLD, THE

★ Worldvision, 1992, PG, 99 min. Dir: Timothy Bond. Cast: David Warner, John Rhys-Davies, Eric McCormack, Tamara Gorski, Nathania Stanford.

Veteran sleaze merchant Harry Alan Towers wrote and produced this tacky new version of the Conan Doyle tale reset in Africa (where this was filmed). Apparently aimed at kids, this features cuddly rubber dinosaurs and little conflict or excitement. A simultaneously shot sequel, *Return to the Lost World,* is also out. I'd much rather see the 1960 Jill St. John version myself.

LOVE BUG, THE

★★★☆ Disney, 1969, G, 107 min. Dir: Robert Stevenson. Cast: Dean Jones, Michele Lee, Buddy Hackett, David Tomlinson, Joe Flynn, Benson Fong.

The first and best of four Herbie the Love Bug comedies about an intelligent Volkswagen Beetle and how it turns aging has-been stock car racer Jones into a winner. Overlong but full of bouncy charm and with an infectious theme song you'll be humming for days. Look for veteran actress Iris Adrian in an hilarious bit as an overaged car hop. Sequels: *Herbie Rides Again, Herbie Goes to Monte Carlo,* and *Herbie Goes Bananas.*

LOVE FACTOR, THE
★★ Sinister Cinema, 1969, R, 82 min. Dir: Michael Cort. Cast: Robin Hawdon, Dawn Addams, James Robertson Justice, Anna Gael, Valerie Leon, Yutte Stensgaard.

Originally titled *Zeta One,* this infamous British sexploitation flick, based on a story from the soft-core sci-fi magazine *Zeta,* stars Hawdon (of *When Dinosaurs Ruled the Earth*) as a Bond-like secret agent out to thwart the invasion of Earth by a race of extraterrestrial Amazons led by Addams. About as sexually enlightened as a *Hustler* comic strip but often quite amusing, it features a bevy of Brit horror and sci-fi starlets in various stages of undress.

LOVE IN THE POCKET, THE
See: *Girl in His Pocket.*

LUCIFER COMPLEX, THE
☆ VCL, 1976, R, 90 min. Dirs: David L. Hewitt, Kenneth Hartford. Cast: Robert Vaughn, Aldo Ray, Keenan Wynn, Merrie Lynn Ross, William Lanning, Victoria Carroll.

A really bad clone movie started by Hewitt and finished by Hartford. Vaughn is a secret agent who discovers a Florida-based cloning operation backed by an aged Adolf Hitler (played by a guy in awful makeup). I guess the producers were trying to recapture the flavor of the old *Man From U.N.C.L.E.* TV show but this looks more like a Jess Franco movie.

MAC AND ME
★ Orion, 1988, PG, 93 min. Dir: Stewart Raffill. Cast: Jade Calegory, Christine Ebersole, Jonathan Ward, Katrina Caspary, Lauren Stanley.

Disabled kid Calegory befriends alien baby Mac (short for Mysterious Alien Creature) he finds hiding in the basement of his California

home. Before you can say "E.T., phone lawyer!" they become the best of friends and heart-burning—I mean heart-warming—hilarity begins. This blatant Spielberg ripoff is cynical and unimaginative and full of cheap product plugs for McDonald's—Ronald even shows up at one point.

MACISTE CONQUERS THE MONSTERS
See: *Fire Monsters Against the Son of Hercules.*

MADAME SIN
★★★ Fox, 1972, NR, 73 min. Dir: David Greene. Cast: Bette Davis, Robert Wagner, Denholm Elliott, Catherine Schell, Roy Kinnear, Gordon Jackson.

Davis is an evil female Fu Manchu with world conquest in mind who easily manipulates CIA operative Wagner and all others around her. A theatrical release in Europe, this was shown only on TV in the States and isn't bad, with colorful acting from Bette, a solid supporting cast, and a wholly unexpected downbeat ending.

MADE IN HEAVEN
★★☆ Warner, 1987, PG, 101 min. Dir: Alan Rudolph. Cast: Timothy Hutton, Kelly McGillis, Maureen Stapleton, Don Murray, Amanda Plummer, Mare Winningham, Tim Daly, Ann Wedgeworth, Marj Dusay, Debra Winger, Ellen Barkin, Tom Petty, Neil Young, Ric Ocasek.

The always quirky Rudolph's idea of a mainstream Hollywood romantic fantasy, this has Hutton as a heroic chap who drowns saving a child and encounters the angelic McGillis up in Heaven. It's love at first sight but after they're reborn on Earth, will they ever find each other again? Heartfelt but weird, this has lots of cameos including Tim's then husband, I mean wife, Winger as a *male* guardian angel. No comment.

MAD MAX
★★★ Video Treasures, 1979, R, 93 min. Dir: George Miller. Cast: Mel Gibson, Joanne Samuel, Hugh Keays-Byrne, Steve Bisley, Tim Burns, Roger Ward.

The movie that made Gibson a star, this tough Australian sci-fi actioner is like a futuristic Western with its simple plot, simple characters, and straight-ahead direction. Mel is Max, a policeman charged with keeping the highways safe from violent speed-demon punks. When some of these punks cause the deaths of Max's wife and child, he goes on a vengeful rampage. Redubbed with American accents (even Mel!) and dumped on the drive-in circuit, this developed into a bonafide cult film in the wake of its widely popular first sequel.

Breathtaking stunts and breakneck pacing; followed by *The Road Warrior* and *Mad Max: Beyond Thunderdome.*

MAD MAX 2
See: *The Road Warrior.*

MAD MAX: BEYOND THUNDERDOME
★★☆ Warner, 1985, PG-13, 106 min. Dirs: George Miller, George Ogilvie. Cast: Mel Gibson, Tina Turner, Angelo Rossitto, Helen Buday, Rod Zuanic, Frank Thring.

As Tina sings, "We don't need another hero." Well, we really didn't need this third in the *Max* series but here it is anyway. Max (Gibson) stumbles upon the desert stronghold of Bartertown where Turner holds sway over a pack of feral children and teens and warriors battle to the death in the dreaded Thunderdome. Some good moments, and a nice role for veteran dwarf actor Rossitto, but this lacks the energy and pace of the first two MM adventures.

MAGIC SERPENT, THE
★★★ Something Weird, 1966, NR, 86 min. Dir: Tetsuya Yamauchi. Cast: Hiroki Matsukata, Tomoko Ogawa, Ryutaro Otomo, Bin Amatsu.

Ever since I first saw this Japanese fantasy on TV as a kid I've been haunted by it. Maybe it's because of the surprisingly grotesque violence (when people are decapitated the blood spurts profusely); maybe it's the ninja warriors appearing in a film years before they would become really popular; or maybe it's the fact that our sorcerer's apprentice hero and the wizard villain transform into a gigantic frog and dragon to battle it out over an elaborate miniature of the wizard's castle at the end. Yeah, that must be it. Well worth seeing for this ending alone. Aka *Froggo and Droggo* and *Grand Duel in Magic.*

MAGIC SWORD, THE
★★★ MGM/UA, 1962, NR, 80 min. Dir: Bert I. Gordon. Cast: Gary Lockwood, Anne Helm, Basil Rathbone, Estelle Winwood, Liam Sullivan, Jacques Gallo, Vampira, Angelo Rossitto.

Along with *The Amazing Colossal Man*, this is easily Gordon's best film, a colorful Sinbad rip with elements of action, fantasy, and horror. Rathbone really outdoes himself as a powerful warlock called Lodoc who kidnaps princess Helm and plans to feed her to his two-headed dragon unless some hero can withstand seven curses in order to reach her. Lockwood is likable and earnest as a young knight who has loved Helm from afar and risks his life against an ogre, a vampire woman, evil spirits, and a

deadly swamp to rescue her. Nice color photography and some pretty good special FX too. Aka *St. George and the Seven Curses.*

MAGIC VOYAGE OF SINBAD, THE
★★☆ Sinister Cinema, 1946, 79 min. Dir: Alexandre Ptouchko. Cast: Edward Stolar, Anna Larion, Lawrence Astan.

A Russian adaptation of an opera called *Sadko* by Rimsky-Korsakoff, this lavish fantasy was ineptly dubbed and edited for a 1960s release by Film group/AIP. The American title tries to make it sound like another Harryhausen ripoff but it's actually a beautifully crafted fairy tale about a hero (renamed Sinbad in the U.S. version) who travels to the land of a beautiful phoenix bird-woman in order to break her spell against his kingdom. Original title: *Sadko.*

MAGNETIC MONSTER, THE
★★☆ Sinister Cinema, 1953, NR, 76 min. Dir: Curt Siodmak. Cast: Richard Carlson, Jean Byron, King Donovan, Byron Foulger, Harry Ellerbe, Leo Britt.

Slow and talky for its first half, this builds in intensity as it reaches its climax. Carlson is a scientist who invents a new element that uses magnetism to draw energy from all sources and eventually grows into a dangerous mass that could destroy the world. The exciting ending borrows some special FX footage from the German silent film *Gold* and there are good performances from Carlson, Byron (later the mom on *The Patty Duke Show*), and Donovan.

MAKING MR. RIGHT
★★ HBO, 1987, PG-13, 95 min. Dir: Susan Seidelman. Cast: John Malkovich, Ann Magnuson, Glenne Headly, Ben Masters, Laurie Metcalf, Polly Bergen, Hart Bochner, Susan Anton.

PR person Magnuson is assigned the task of introducing android Malkovich (made in its creator's image) to the public and eventually falls in love with it. Seidelman's attempt at sci-fi romantic comedy falls a bit flat thanks to an overall lack of conviction but it's well acted and occasionally touching. Malkovich in a blonde wig, though, is a hard sight to take.

MAN BEAST
★★ Sinister Cinema, 1956, NR, 72 min. Dir: Jerry Warren. Cast: Rock Madison, Virginia Maynor, Lloyd Nelson, George Skaff.

Z-movie auteur Warren's best movie, this abominable snowman thriller has bad acting and a slow pace but excellent atmosphere and some startling plot twists. Originally cobbled with *Godzilla, King of the Monsters.*

MANDROID

★★ Paramount, 1993, R, 81 min. Dir: Jack Ersgard. Cast: Brian Cousins, Janette Allyson Caldwell, Michael Dellafemina, Curt Lowens.

The metal-masked, evil Dr. Drago (Lowens) gains control of the title robot and is opposed by a hero (Cousins) who can make himself invisible. An anything-goes direct-to-video sci-fi thriller from Charles Band's Full Moon Productions; this has some good action and gimmicks but never really comes off. Sequel: *Invisible: The Chronicles of Benjamin Knight*.

MAN FROM ATLANTIS, THE

★★☆ MCA/Universal, 1977, NR, 96 min. Dir: Lee H. Katzin. Cast: Patrick Duffy, Belinda J. Montgomery, Victor Buono, Lawrence Pressman, Art Lund, Dean Santoro.

Pilot film for the well-remembered but short-lived TV series, with the likable Duffy as the legendary undersea kingdom's last survivor (complete with webbed fingers and toes), who teams with pretty marine biologist Montgomery to defeat villain Buono. Good fun.

MANHUNT IN SPACE

★★ Sinister Cinema, 1953, NR, 70 min. Dir: Hollingsworth Morse. Cast: Richard Crane, Sally Mansfield, Scotty Beckett, Robert Lyden.

One of the better *Rocky Jones* adventures pits Rocky and company against space pirates from the Prah. The pirates use an invisibility cloak (later stolen by the Romulans, I suppose) in their raids and Rocky must find a way to disable it.

MANHUNT OF MYSTERY ISLAND

★★☆ Republic, 1945, NR, 160 min. Dirs: Spencer G. Bennet, Wallace Grissell, Yakima Canutt. Cast: Richard Bailey, Linda Stirling, Roy Barcroft, Kenne Duncan, Forrest Taylor, Jack Ingram, Tom Steele, Dale Van Sickel.

All the ingredients are here for a truly great serial but somehow this never rises above the routine. Barcroft, a reincarnation of the sinister Mephisto, employs his "Transformation Chair" to control the minds of gang members he uses to steal an experimental device called a "Radioatomic Power Transmitter." Some great stunts, obviously supervised by legendary stuntman Canutt, but too disjointed to really work. Also available in shortened feature form as *Captain Mephisto and the Transformation Machine*.

MANNEQUIN

★ Video Treasures, 1987, PG, 89 min. Dir: Michael Gottlieb. Cast: Andrew McCarthy, Kim Cattrall, James Spader, Estelle Getty, G. W. Bailey, Meshach Taylor.

Awful semi-remake of *One Touch of Venus* with Cattrall as an ancient Egyptian spirit housed in a Philadelphia department store mannequin. McCarthy is the store employee who is the only one who can see her come to life, resulting in painfully unfunny hilarity. Taylor's performance as a stereotypically flamboyant gay window dresser is especially insulting and annoying. Good Starship theme song, though, "Nothin's Gonna Stop Us Now."

MANNEQUIN TWO: ON THE MOVE

★ LIVE, 1991, PG, 95 min. Dir: Stuart Raffill. Cast: Kristy Swanson, William Ragsdale, Meshach Taylor, Terry Kiser, Stuart Pankin, Cynthia Harris.

This time it's Ragsdale as the window dresser and Swanson as the mannequin who comes alive (she's a peasant girl suffering from an ancient curse) in this "nobody asked for it" sequel to one of the most inept comedies of the '80s. Thank God for Kiser, though. If it wasn't for him, I think I would have bailed out of this crummy movie about ten minutes in. Then again, Terry, thanks for nothin'!

MAN WHO COULD WORK MIRACLES

★★★ Nelson, 1937, NR, 82 min. Dir: Lothar Mendes. Cast: Roland Young, Ralph Richardson, Joan Gardner, Ernest Thesiger, George Zucco, Joan Hickson, George Sanders, Torin Thatcher.

Dated but entertaining fantasy based on a story by H. G. Wells. Young is well-cast as a mousey department store clerk given magical powers; sadly, though, he never really gets what he wants. Typical British film of the period, with a super supporting cast of familiar faces.

MAN WHO FELL TO EARTH, THE

★★★ RCA/Columbia, 1976, R, 140 min. Dir: Nicolas Roeg. Cast: David Bowie, Rip Torn, Candy Clark, Buck Henry, Bernie Casey, Jackson D. Kane.

Imaginatively directed and photographed version of Walter Tevis's novel about a cat-eyed alien (Bowie) in the guise of a powerful corporate executive who's actually on Earth to find water for his home planet. Originally released in the U.S. at 114 minutes but later restored to its full length, this British sci-fi drama is offbeat and well acted throughout but starts to peter out as it reaches its conclusion. Needlessly remade as a TV movie in 1987.

MAN WHO WASN'T THERE, THE

★ Paramount, 1983, R, 111 min. Dir: Bruce Malmuth. Cast: Steve Guttenberg, Lisa Langlois, Jeffrey Tambor, Art Hindle, Morgan Hart, Bill Forsythe.

Strained spoof of old *Invisible Man* movies features Guttenberg as a government employee turned transparent by an experimental serum sought by foreign spies. Originally released in 3-D, this is so unfunny that it hurts, with lots of snide sexual humor.

MAN WITH THE GOLDEN GUN, THE

★★ MGM/UA, 1974, PG, 125 min. Dir: Guy Hamilton. Cast: Roger Moore, Britt Ekland, Christopher Lee, Maud Adams, Herve Villechaize, Clifton James, Richard Loo, Bernard Lee, Lois Maxwell, Desmond Llewellyn.

Moore's second James Bond romp is one of the weakest, with million-dollar-a-job hitman Lee hired to rub out 007, who's searching Hong Kong for a stolen solar-energy cannon. Ekland is sexy but her role as goofy female agent Mary Goodnight is positively demeaning, and bringing back James as the redneck sheriff from *Live and Let Die* makes this look like a big-budget *Smokey and the Bandit* movie. Lee is good, though. LuLu sings the forgettable theme song.

MARCH OF THE WOODEN SOLDIERS

★★★☆ Goodtimes, 1934, NR, 73 min. Dir: Gus Meins and Charles R. Rogers. Cast: Stan Laurel, Oliver Hardy, Charlotte Henry, Johnny Downs, Henry Brandon, Marie Wilson, Felix Knight, Jane Darling, Dick Alexander, Angelo Rossitto.

The first film version of Victor Herbert's fantasy operetta *Babes in Toyland* is a good vehicle for Stan and Ollie as bungling toymakers who accidentally create a squadron of six-foot (rather than six-inch) toy soldiers. Luckily these soldiers come in handy when Toyland is invaded by the evil Barnaby (Brandon, billed here as Henry Kleinbach) and his monstrous bogeymen. Like many '30s kid movies, this isn't afraid to throw a little horror into the brew (the bogeymen look like werewolves) and this mixture of scariness, fantasy, comedy, and songs comes off remarkably well and seems a lot fresher than many more recent children's fantasies. Originally released as *Babes in Toyland,* the title was changed with the advent of the 1961 Disney remake, which itself was remade again for TV in 1986.

MAROONED

★★ Columbia/TriStar, 1969, PG, 134 min. Dir: John Sturges. Cast: Gregory Peck, Richard Crenna, James Franciscus, David Janssen, Gene Hackman, Lee Grant, Nancy Kovack, Mariette Hartley, Scott Brady, Walter Brooke.

There's a stellar cast, Oscar-winning special FX, and top-notch production values. So how come this movie is so damn dull? Blame Sturges's turgid direction or the crippling running time, but dull this is. Astronauts Crenna, Franciscus, and Hackman are stranded in space due to a capsule malfunction and everybody argues and snipes until the awesomely pat and unlikely climax. TV title: *Space Travelers.*

MARS NEEDS WOMEN

★★★ Orion, 1964, NR, 80 min. Dir: Larry Buchanan. Cast: Tommy Kirk, Yvonne Craig, Byron Lord, Roger Ready, Warren Hammack, Anthony Houston.

Now calm down. I know this is one of Texas Z-movie director Buchanan's made-for-AIP-TV cheapies and that they're mostly a mess. Still, there's something almost quaint about this flatly directed and written but spiritedly acted foolishness about Martians who come to Earth seeking brides. Kirk, whose career is clearly on a downward spiral, more or less re-creates his character from *Pajama Party* while Craig, just a few years away from playing Batgirl, is sweet and sincere as an expert in space genetics. At least this isn't just a predictable remake of some '50s B movie.

MARTIAN CHRONICLES, THE

★★☆ Starmaker, 1979, NR, 320 min. Dir: Michael Anderson. Cast: Rock Hudson, Darren McGavin, Roddy McDowall, Bernadette Peters, Fritz Weaver, Gayle Hunnicutt, Bernie Casey, Nicholas Hammond, Jon Finch, Maria Schell, Richard Masur, Joyce Van Patten.

An elaborate but unconvincing made-for-TV miniseries based on the stories of Ray Bradbury. Hudson holds things together as the commander of the first Earth base on Mars; the best stories are "And the Moon Be Still as Bright" with Casey, "The Five Balloons" with McDowall and Weaver, and "The Off Season" with McGavin. Well acted but dull and unimaginative, with a teleplay by Bradbury himself.

MARTIANS GO HOME

★☆ Touchstone, 1990, PG-13, 89 min. Dir: David Odell. Cast: Randy Quaid, Margaret Colin, Anita Morris, Barry Sobel, Ronny Cox, Gerrit Graham, Vic Dunlop, John Philbin.

Pathetic movie based on Fredric Brown's humorous novel, with Quaid as a songwriter whose music accidentally summons hordes of little green men to Earth for many none-too-funny misadventures. Bad in the way only a high-concept studio product can be, wasting a pleasing performance from Quaid.

MARY POPPINS

★★★☆ Disney, 1964, NR, 140 min. Dir: Robert

"Wetsuits and headphones! Are you guys sure you're Martians?" Tommy Kirk and company in Mars Needs Women *(1964).*

Stevenson. Cast: Julie Andrews, Dick Van Dyke, David Tomlinson, Glynis Johns, Ed Wynn, Hermione Baddeley, Karen Dotrice, Matthew Garber, Arthur Treacher, Jane Darwell.

One of Disney's most popular films, this lush adaptation of the P. L. Travers's childrens book features Andrews in her most famous role, as the magical nanny who turns an Edwardian London household upside down with her fabulous ways. Great songs, a perfect cast, and a marvelous animated sequence help you overlook the film's general overlength and some uneven-but Oscar-winning-special FX. Van Dyke is great, but he really should have spent a little time at Berlitz before trying to tackle that cockney accent!

MASK, THE
★★★ New Line, 1994, PG-13, 101 min. Dir: Chuck Russell. Cast: Jim Carrey, Cameron Diaz, Peter Riegert, Amy Yasbeck, Peter Greene, Richard Jeni.

Maybe Carrey's best vehicle to date, here he stars as a timid bank clerk transformed by an ancient Norse mask into a green-faced, zoot-suited, wisecracking comic demon. In this new form Carrey can do magical acts, transform himself at will, and wins bombshell nightclub singer Diaz. The FX are great and most of the humor on-target in this adaptation of a Dark Horse comic that's also an unofficial remake of a 1961 horror movie, where the possesed mask was played for scares rather than laughs—if you doubt me, see both versions and note the

obvious parallels. Followed by a cartoon TV series and probably a sequel somewhere down the line. Director Russell also helmed the 1988 remake *The Blob*.

MASTER OF THE WORLD
★★★ Orion, 1961, NR, 104 min. Dir: William Witney. Cast: Vincent Price, Charles Bronson, Mary Webster, Henry Hull, David Frankham, Vito Scotti.

Richard Matheson scripted this fun but very low-budget adaptation of two Jules Verne novels (*Master of the World* and *Robur the Conqueror*). Price is a nineteenth-century pacifist who travels the world in his experimental flying machine, threatening various nations with destruction unless they give up their warring ways. Bronson is good but miscast as the hero who tries to stop him. Well directed by serial veteran Witney, but cheap production values and too much stock footage weigh this down. As always, Price is a treat.

MASTERS OF THE UNIVERSE
★★☆ Warner, 1987, PG, 106 min. Dir: Gary Goddard. Cast: Dolph Lundgren, Frank Langella, Courtney Cox, Meg Foster, James Tolkan, Billy Barty, Christina Pickles, Jon Cypher.

Fun live-action version of the cartoon series (based on a then-popular line of Mattel toys). Lundgren is well cast as muscular hero He-Man who comes to Earth to stop his nemesis Skeletor (Langella in effective makeup) from gaining control of a magical key that will give him power over the entire universe. *Friends* star Cox is the Earth teen who tries to help. Better than you'd expect, with a colorful cast and special FX.

MAX HEADROOM
★★★ Lorimar, 1987, NR, 60 min. Dirs: Rocky Morton, Annabel Jenke. Cast: Matt Frewer, Amanda Pays, Nickolas Grace, Hilary Tindall, Morgan Shepherd.

The original, British-made TV show (later expanded into a series in the U.S.) about a murdered television newsman who is reborn as a computer-generated image dubbed Max Headroom. Thought-provoking and visually stunning if a bit aloof, with good work from Frewer in the title role.

MAXIE
★★ Goodtimes, 1985, PG, 90 min. Dir: Paul Aaron. Cast: Glenn Close, Mandy Patinkin, Ruth Gordon, Barnard Hughes, Harry Hamlin, Valerie Curtin, Googy Gress, Leeza Gibbons.

Minor comic fantasy with Close as a San Francisco housewife possessed by the spirit of a 1920s flapper who wants to realize her dream of becoming a big movie star by forcing Glenn to audition for the lead in a remake of *Cleopatra*. The cast is better than their stale material, with Gordon in her last role (as an old friend of Maxie's who sees the truth) and old clips of Carole Lombard "playing" Maxie in some silent film footage.

MEDUSA AGAINST THE SON OF HERCULES
★★☆ Sinister Cinema, 1962, NR, 90 min. Dir: Alberto de Martino. Cast: Richard Harrison, Anna Ranalli, Arturo Dominici, Elisa Cegani, Leo Anchoriz.

Grandly absurd peblum has Perseus (referred to here as Hercules's son and played by Harrison) out to stop the dreaded gorgon Medusa, who isn't the usual witch with snakes in her hair but is instead played by a malevolent walking tree stump! Great fun almost in spite of itself. Aka *Persée L'Invincible (Perseus the Invincible)* and *Medusa vs. the Son of Hercules.*

MEDUSA VS. THE SON OF HERCULES
See: *Medusa Against the Son of Hercules.*

MEET THE APPLEGATES
See: *The Applegates.*

MEGAFORCE
★☆ CBS/Fox, 1982, PG, 99 min. Dir: Hal Needham. Cast: Barry Bostwick, Persis Khambatta, Michael Beck, Edward Mulhare, Henry Silva, George Furth.

Car crash specialist Needham directed this absurd, laughable action-fantasy about Ace Hunter (Bostwick, as miscast here as any actor in the history of motion pictures), a futuristic cop who heads up an elite squadron of crime fighters. Just one look at Barry in his spandex fightin' gear and you'll be laughing so hard you'll forget what the rest of the movie was about—just like me.

MEGAVILLE
★★ LIVE, 1990, R, 96 min. Dir: Peter Lehner. Cast: Billy Zane, Daniel H. Travanti, Grace Zabriskie, J. C. Quinn, Kristen Cloke, Stefan Gierasch.

A well-cast but mediocre futuristic movie about a time when all media has become controlled by the government; secret agent Zane (in a very unflattering haircut) investigates the underground TV broadcasts emanating from the title location. This mixes *Videodrome* with a standard chase story but never really gels.

MEMOIRS OF AN INVISIBLE MAN
★★☆ Warner, 1991, PG-13, 98 min. Dir: John Carpenter. Cast: Chevy Chase, Daryl Hannah, Sam Neill, Michael McKean, Stephen Tobolowsky, Rosalind Chao, Jim Norton, Patricia Heaton.

An industrial accident turns a stock broker invisible, forcing him to take it on the lam from secret agents. A box office flop, this was erroneously advertised as a comedy (it's not) but is actually a fairly amusing action-fantasy (with touches of humor, horror, and romance). Chase is in good form as the transparent hero (who we can sometimes see when the camera takes his character's point-of-view, which is confusing) and powerhouse ILM FX.

MENACE FROM OUTER SPACE
★★ Sinister Cinema, 1953, NR, 75 min. Dir: Hollingsworth Morse. Cast: Richard Crane, Sally Mansfield, Scotty Beckett, Robert Lyden, Maurice Cass.

It's Rocky Jones to the rescue once again when Earth is threatened by a rampaging rogue comet. About par for this low-budget course.

MERLIN AND THE SWORD
★★ Goodtimes, 1985, NR, 94 min. Dir: Clive Donner. Cast: Malcolm McDowell, Candice Bergen, Dyan Cannon, Edward Woodward, Rupert Everett, Liam Neeson, Lucy Gutteridge, Michael Gough, Maryam D'Abo, Terry Torday.

TV movie originally shown as *Arthur the King* at 150 minutes. Cannon tumbles down a hole à la *Alice in Wonderland* and ends up in Camelot, where she encounters King Arthur (McDowell), Merlin the Magician (Woodward), and evil witch Mogana (Bergen). Surprisingly mediocre considering the cast and director.

MESA OF LOST WOMEN

☆ Sinister Cinema, 1952, NR, 69 min. Dirs: Herbert Tevos, Ron Ormond. Cast: Jackie Coogan, Richard Travis, Mary Hill, Tandra Quinn, Angelo Rossitto, Allan Nixon, Katherine Victor, Dolores Fuller.

One of the most absurd movies ever made, this Ed Wood-quality epic concerns a mad scientist (Coogan in a toupee of Shatneresque proportions) creating long-nailed spider women for some obscure reason on a desert-bound mesa. Even a cast like this can't make this dud very interesting. Aka *Lost Women* and *Lost Women of Zarpa*.

METALSTORM: THE DESTRUCTION OF JARED-SYN

★ MCA/Universal, 1983, PG, 84 min. Dir: Charles Band. Cast: Jeffrey Byron, Kelly Preston, Tim Thomerson, Richard Moll, Mike Preston, R. David Smith.

The box-office success of his film *Parasite* is probably the only reason a big studio like Universal would back Band on this flat, unattractive 3-D *Mad Max* clone. Byron is the Mel hand-me-down out to stop the evil Jared-Syn (Mike Preston) from taking over the desert mining planet Lemuria. The ending threatens a sequel; thankfully it was never made.

METAMORPHOSIS

★★ Imperial Entertainment, 1990, R, 96 min. Dir: G. L. Edwards. Cast: Gene LeBrock, Catherine Baranov, Harry Cason, David Wicker.

Mediocre ripoff of Cronenberg's *Fly* remake stars LeBrock as a scientist whose experiments with immortality transform him into a prehistoric reptile monster. Some decent makeup FX but poor acting and unimaginative scripting override them.

METEOR

★★ Goodtimes, 1979, PG, 103 min. Dir: Ronald Neame. Cast: Sean Connery, Natalie Wood, Karl Malden, Henry Fonda, Brian Keith, Martin Landau, Trevor Howard, Richard Dysart, Joseph Campenella, Sybil Danning.

It's got an all-star cast, a lavish budget, and a talented director who helmed the disaster classic *The Poseidon Adventure*—and it's still awful! An enormous hunk of rock tumbles toward Earth, fragments break off and destroy Hong Kong (stock footage from *Tidal Wave*), the Alps (stock footage from *Avalanche*), and Manhattan (new footage that cribs alot from *Poseidon*). Connery is good as the astronomer who calculates the meteor's path but Keith steals it with a hilarious, atypical performance as a Russian scientist whose only knowledge of English is,

"Fuck the Dodgers!" The special FX are mediocre at best in one of the last disaster films of the '70s.

METEOR MAN

★★ MGM/UA, 1993, PG, 100 min. Dir: Robert Townsend. Cast: Robert Townsend, Marla Gibbs, Robert Guillaume, James Earl Jones, Bill Cosby, Stephanie Williams, Sinbad, Nancy Wilson, Frank Gorshin, Eddie Griffin.

Townsend (*Hollywood Shuffle*) wrote, directed, and stars in this slight superhero spoof as a meek Washington, D.C., schoolteacher who gets a few superpowers from a meteor. Deciding to use his limited abilities to fight inner-city crime, he takes to the streets in the costume sewn for him by his loving mom (Gibbs, of *The Jeffersons* and *227*). There's a great cast and some funny moments but the movie made to cash in on this one (*Blankman*) is actually a bit better.

METEOR MONSTER

★☆ Sinister Cinema, 1957, NR, 65 min. Dir: Jacques Marquette. Cast: Anne Gwynne, Gloria Castillo, Stuart Wade, Gilbert Perkins.

Veteran B movie photographer Marquette directs this cheesy Western-set monster movie with Perkins as the werewolf-like son of lady rancher Gwynne. Although clearly played by a middle-aged actor, the allegedly teenage monster got this way by being hit by a meteor fragment as a boy and, like most monsters from this period, has little on his mind but sex. He's is easily manipulated by tease Castillo (who had a role in the suspense-horror classic *Night of the Hunter* the previous year). Fairly abysmal, this is played too solemnly to be really funny. Aka *Teenage Monster* and *Monster on the Hill*.

METROPOLIS

★★★★ Goodtimes, 1926, NR, 120 min. Dir: Fritz Lang. Cast: Brigitte Helm, Alfred Abel, Gustav Froelich, Rudolf Klein-Rogge, Fritz Rasp, Heinrich George.

Classic German sci-fi silent about a magnificent futuristic city where the upper classes live in unimagined luxury provided by machines run by slavelike workers. Helm is the common girl loved by rich boy Froelich, who is duplicated as a robot by mad scientist Klein-Rogge. The robot Helm then tries to put down the very worker uprising the real Brigitte began. Impressive sets, photography, and special FX make this seventy-year-old film still seem surprisingly fresh. In the mid '80s it was cut slightly and had color tints and a Giorgio

Brigitte Helm wins the coveted Miss Universe 3000 title in Metropolis *(1926).*

Moroder musical score added for a surprising-ly theatrical reissue.

MIAMI GOLEM
See: *Miami Horror.*

MIAMI HORROR
★ Panther, 1985, R, 90 min. Dir: Martin Herbert [Alberto de Martino]. Cast: David Warbeck, John Ireland, Laura Trotter, Lawrence Loddi.

A pretty awful *Alien*-type Italian movie shot on location in Florida. Reporter Warbeck investigates scientist Ireland's plot to take over the world with an alien fetus kept in a big jar—don't ask how this helps you take over the world but John thinks it helps a lot. Bad dubbing and pathetic FX. Aka *Miami Golem.*

MIGHTY JOE YOUNG
★★★ Turner, 1949, NR, 94 min. Dir: Ernest B. Schoedsack. Cast: Terry Moore, Ben Johnson, Robert Armstrong, Frank McHugh.

Teenager Moore lives on an African ranch with her ten-foot gorilla, Joe. Showman Armstrong shows up and fast-talks Terry into bringing Joe to Hollywood for a humiliating night club act where the ape dresses like an organ grinder's monkey and plays tug-of-war with a team of pro wrestlers. When Joe gets drunk and wrecks the club, courts order him destroyed, but he is redeemed when he carries Terry and a little girl to safety during a spectacular orphanage fire. A seriocomic *King Kong* copy aimed at kids, this has great stop-motion by Willis O'Brien and a young Ray Harryhausen, plus Armstrong in great form in a parody of his *Kong* role. A remake is currently in development; many of this movie's basic situations reemerged in *Dragonworld.*

MIGHTY MORPHIN' POWER RANGERS: THE MOVIE

★★☆ Fox, 1995, PG, 93 min. Dir: Bryan Spicer. Cast: Karen Ashley, Jason David Frank, David Yost, Steve Cardenas, Amy Jo Johnson, Johnny Young Bosch, Paul Freeman, Gabrielle Fitzpatrick, Paul Schrier, Jason Narvy.

Not bad big-screen spin-off of the megapopular mid-'90s kid show about powerful high school ninja warriors (played mostly by actors pushing thirty) with the ability to morph into gigantic fighting robotic creatures who battle an evil alien wizard (played with relish by a heavily made-up Freeman). Lots of computer-generated FX and sophomoric comedy; this includes homages to *The Wizard of Oz,* various *Godzilla* movies, and even *One Million Years B.C.* (in the person of sexily clad warrior woman Fitzpatrick).

MILLENNIUM

★★ Avid Entertainment, 1989, PG-13, 108 min. Dir: Michael Anderson. Cast: Kris Kristofferson, Cheryl Ladd, Daniel J. Travanti, Robert Joy, Brent Carver, Lloyd Bochner.

Time travelers from the future, including ex-Angel Ladd in a really unflattering hairdo, kidnap airplane passengers to save them from crashes; investigator Kristofferson learns the truth when he and Cheryl become involved in an affair. Scripter John Varley based this on his story "Air Raid," but the interesting premise is bungled by general miscasting and Anderson's flat direction.

MILLION DOLLAR DUCK, THE

★★☆ Disney, 1971, G, 92 min. Dir: Vincent McEveety. Cast: Dean Jones, Sandy Duncan, Tony Roberts, Joe Flynn, James Gregory, Lee H. Montgomery.

Routine Disney comedy with Jones and Duncan discovering that son Montgomery's pet duck has the ability to lay golden eggs. Great cast (especially Flynn as a grouchy neighbor) but much of the slapstick is forced.

MIND GAMES

See: *Agency.*

MINDWARP

★★ Columbia/TriStar, 1991, R, 91 min. Dir: Steve Barnett. Cast: Bruce Campbell, Angus Scrimm, Elizabeth Kent, Maya McLaughlin.

The first of a trio of movies backed by *Fangoria* magazine, this gory *Mad Max*-like thriller takes place in the postnuke future where hero Campbell takes on sadistic villain Scrimm in a dank underground world. Gratuitously violent (in one scene, Scrimm grounds a girl to a pulp and then drinks her blood) and overly derivative, but Bruce and Angus are good.

MIRACLE MILE

★★★☆ HBO, 1988, R, 87 min. Dir: Steve DeJarnatt. Cast: Anthony Edwards, Mare Winningham, John Agar, Denise Crosby, Lou Hancock, Mykel T. Williamson, Brian Thompson, Kelly Jo Minter, Kurt Fuller, Robert Doqui.

A great, underrated end-of-the-world movie featuring Edwards as a musician beginning a relationship with waitress Winningham, who picks up a ringing payphone and learns that World War III is about to begin. At first no one believes him but then everybody begins to panic and Los Angeles starts to fall apart. The film starts to fall apart itself near the end but has a solid cast (Edwards and Winningham have you pulling for them all the way and Thompson has a great role as a macho gay helicopter pilot) and really knows how to build tension and suspense much in the manner of Ray Milland's *Panic in the Year Zero.*

MIRACLE ON 34TH STREET

★★★☆ Fox, 1947, NR, 96 min. Dir: George Seaton. Cast: Maureen O'Hara, John Payne, Edmund Gwenn, Natalie Wood, Gene Lockhart, Porter Hall, William Frawley, Thelma Ritter.

O'Hara is an executive at Macy's department store in New York who comes to realize that the jovial man called Kris Kringle (Gwenn) she hired to play Santa Claus is the genuine article. Kris is thought crazy by the courts but eventually proves his true identity to both the authorities and Maureen's cynical little daughter Wood. Gwenn and writer-director Seaton both won Oscars (as did Valentine Davies, who wrote the original story) but Ritter steals everyone's thunder in her screen debut as a trenchant Macy's customer. Remade for TV in 1973 and again for the big screen in 1994, but neither version can hold a candle to this original version of the holiday classic.

MIRACLE ON 34TH STREET

★★☆ Fox, 1994, PG, 114 min. Dir: Les Mayfield. Cast: Richard Attenborough, Elizabeth Perkins, Dylan McDermott, Mara Wilson, J. T. Walsh, James Remar, William Windom, Robert Prosky.

Lavish but routine remake has Attenborough sparkling in the role of department store Santa Claus Kris Kringle whose claims to be the real thing get him slammed into the nuthouse. Perkins is the store executive with the daughter (Wilson) who doesn't believe in Santa and McDermott is the lawyer who takes Kringle's case. If anything, this is even cornier than the original and that's the problem: the 1947 version was smart enough to play off the increasing cynicism of the postwar '40s honestly, whereas this one wants to be all cute and cuddly and is utterly plastic and uninvolving in comparison. When they say that they don't make movies like they used to they sure aren't kiddin'.

MISFITS OF SCIENCE

★★ MCA/Universal, 1986, NR, 96 min. Dir: James D. Parriott. Cast: Dean Paul Martin, Courtney Cox, Mark Thomas Miller, Kevin Peter Hall.

Pilot film for the short-lived TV series about teenagers with supernormal abilities, brought together by Martin to combine their powers for the good of mankind. Lots of cut-rate special FX and actors with three names.

MISSILE TO THE MOON

★☆ Rhino, 1958, NR, 78 min. Dir: Richard Cunha. Cast: Richard Travis, Cathy Downs, K. T. Stevens, Tommy Cook, Gary Clarke, Laurie Mitchell, Michael Whalen, Tania Velia.

Needing a cofeature for his *Frankenstein's Daughter,* Cunha slapped together this even sillier remake of *Cat Women of the Moon.* This new version includes juvenile delinquents, rock men, and a big spider prop left over from *Tarantula* but is too slow and lackluster to be as funny or as much fun as you keep wanting it to be.

MISSION MARS

★☆ Unicorn, 1968, NR, 95 min. Dir: Nick Webster. Cast: Darren McGavin, Nick Adams, George DeVries, Heather Hewitt, Shirley Parker, Michael De Beausset.

Three astronauts fly to Mars, where they discover a frozen Soviet cosmonaut who beat

A leftover prop from Tarantula *menaces a Barbara Eden wannabe in* Missile to the Moon *(1958).*

them there. Microbudgeted shot-in-Florida sci-fi/drama, this spends its first half dealing with the love lives of its heroes before it cuts to some NASA stock footage and then to some cheapie Martian sets where the astronauts wear motorcycle helmets. Too dull to be much fun; Adams died of a drug overdose before this was released.

MISSION STARDUST
★★ Rhino, 1968, G, 95 min. Dir: Primo Zeglio. Cast: Essy Persson, Lang Jeffries, John Karelsen, Pinkas Braun, Gianni Russo, Luis Davila.

This Italian adaptation of a book from the popular *Perry Rhodan* series has astronauts landing on the moon for the first time and discovering aliens (including Persson in a platinum Beatle wig) suffering from a deadly disease that may now spread to Earth. Full of great Mod sets and costumes but still not all that good, with lumpy dubbing and a weak plot.

MISTRESS OF THE WORLD
★★ Sinister Cinema, 1960, NR, 98 min. Dir: William Dieterle. Cast: Martha Hyer, Carlos Thompson, Micheline Presle, Gino Cervi, Sabu, Lino Ventura, Wolfgang Preiss, Georges Riviére, Hans Nielsen, Charles Regnier.

Hacked-down version of a two-part 190-minute sci-fi/adventure about a scientist who develops a machine that can disrupt the Earth's magnetic fields and the evil woman (Hyer) who wants to use this invention to rule the world. Impressive cast and good direction by veteran Dieterle, but the disjointed nature of the U.S. version of this French-German-Italian coproduction makes it understandably difficult to get into.

MOLE MEN AGAINST THE SON OF HERCULES
★★ Sinister Cinema, 1961, NR, 97 min. Dir: Antonio Leonviola. Cast: Mark Forest, Moira Orfei, Paul Wynter, Raffaella Carra, Gianni Garko, Graziella Granata.

Maciste (Forest) discovers a strange underground world of albino mutants and monsters in this Italian muscleman ripoff of *The Mole People*. Some fun to be had amidst all the grunting and sweating. Aka *Maciste, L'Uomo Piu Forte del Mondo (Maciste, Strongest Man in the World)* and *Molemen vs. the Son of Hercules.*

MOLEMEN VS. THE SON OF HERCULES
See: *Molemen Against the Son of Hercules.*

MOLE PEOPLE, THE
★★ MCA/Universal, 1956, NR, 76 min. Dir: Virgil Vogel. Cast: John Agar, Cynthia Patrick, Hugh

Beaumont, Alan Napier.

Scientists Agar and Beaumont discover an underground race of mole men monster slaves. One of Universal's weakest monster movies, this has interesting makeup and a potentially exciting story marred by Vogel's pedestrian direction and too much stock footage. The annoying downbeat ending was actually added at the last minute in postproduction.

MOM AND DAD SAVE THE WORLD
★☆ HBO, 1992, PG, 88 min. Dir: Greg Beeman. Cast: Teri Garr, Jeffrey Jones, Jon Lovitz, Eric Idle, Dwier Brown, Kathy Ireland, Thalmus Rasulala, Wallace Shawn.

Shelved for several years, this sci-fi comedy isn't very funny but it has flashes of imagination and is far from the worst thing you've ever seen. Alien leader Lovitz makes plans to destroy the Earth until he gets the hots for suburban housewife Garr and spirits both her and her husband Jones to his home world, where men are part dog and women are part fish. This has some good FX and a cast full of veteran farciers but still doesn't add up to very much more than a curious misfire.

MONOLITH
★★ MCA/Universal, 1993, R, 96 min. Dir: John Eyres. Cast: Bill Paxton, Lindsay Frost, John Hurt, Lou Gossett, Jr.

Clichés run riot in this action/sci-fi flick about a constantly bickering male-female cop team (Paxton and Frost) on the hunt for a murderous, body-switching alien on a rampage in Los Angeles. This well-produced but hollow movie borrows from many other (much better) movies without adding anything new and has an especially absurd climax.

MONOLITH MONSTERS, THE
★★☆ MCA/Universal, 1957, NR, 77 min. Dir: John Sherwood. Cast: Grant Williams, Lola Albright, Les Tremayne, Phil Harvey, Trevor Bardette, William Schallert.

This '50s B movie earns an extra half star for its uniqueness but it's still not really successful. A meteorite splinters into black crystalline rock formations that grow into towering monoliths that keep toppling over and growing into more and more monoliths whose touch can turn humans to stone. This borrows from *It Came from Outer Space, Them!*, and others and in some way anticipates the disaster movies of the '70s but the uneven special FX and some silly plot twists weigh it down.

Tremayne has a good role as a small-town newspaper editor who sees the monolith story as his ticket to success.

MONSTER A-GO-GO

☆ United Entertainment, 1965, NR, 70 min. Dirs: Bill Rebane, Sheldon Seymour [Herschell Gordon Lewis]. Cast: Phil Morton, June Travis, Lois Brooks, Henry Hite.

In one of the most unwatchable movies ever made, NASA scientists search for a missing astronaut transformed into a towering, zombielike monster (Hite, the "Tallest Man in the World"). Started by Rebane and then salvaged for release with new footage shot by gore king Lewis, this anticipates parts of *The Incredible Melting Man* but is still one of the most lifeless, badly acted movies ever. Even *Mystery Science Theatre 3000* couldn't make this enjoyable. Aka *Terror at Halfday*.

MONSTER BARAN, THE

See: *Varan the Unbelievable.*

MONSTER FROM A PREHISTORIC PLANET

★★ Orion, 1967, NR, 90 min. Dir: Haruyasu Moguchi. Cast: Tamio Kawaji, Yoko Yamamoto, Yuji Okata, Koji Wada.

There's no prehistoric planet in this okay Japanese *Gorgo* copy; instead there are explorers on an island finding a baby bird-billed dinosaur and taking it back to Tokyo for study. Soon, mom and dad are on a rampage to get their captive kid. Aka *Daikyaju Gappa (The Monster Gappa)* and *Gappa-the Triphibian Monster.*

MONSTER FROM GREEN HELL

★ Rhino, 1957, NR, 71 min. Dir: Kenneth Crane. Cast: Jim Davis, Barbara Turner, Eduardo Cianelli, Vladimir Sokoloff.

The codirector of the surrealist horror classic *The Manster* helmed this mostly worthless '50s Big Bug movie in which radiation from a crashed rocket turns wasps into huge monsters played by big phony mockups and briefly shown animated models. The only reason this cheapie is set in Africa is so that it can make liberal usage of stock footage from *Stanley and Livingstone,* which, by the way, contained no gigantic, man-eating insects to speak of.

MONSTER FROM MARS

See: *Robot Monster.*

MONSTER FROM THE OCEAN FLOOR

★☆ Vidmark Entertainment, 1954, NR, 64 min. Dir: Wyott Ordung. Cast: Anne Kimball, Stuart Wade, Dick Pinner, Jonathan Haze.

Roger Corman's first production was this very cheap monster flick featuring Kimball as a lady scientist searching for a sea monster along the Mexican coast. The monster turns out to be a big octopuslike critter with a light bulb on its head. Not very good but worth a few laughs; in the best Corman tradition, the eerie video box art bears absolutely no resemblance to the movie's contents.

MONSTER GAPPA, THE

See: *Monster from a Prehistoric Planet.*

MONSTER ON THE HILL

See: *Meteor Monster.*

MONSTER THAT CHALLENGED THE WORLD, THE

★★☆ MGM/UA, 1957, NR, 82 min. Dir: Arnold Laven. Cast: Tim Holt, Audrey Dalton, Hans Conreid, Casey Adams.

Gigantic prehistoric mollesks rampage in California's Salton Sea in this slow but well-made imitation of *Them!* A somewhat portly Holt is the two-fisted naval hero; the full-scale model monster FX are pretty well done for their time, with several unexpectedly grisly touches.

MONSTER YONGKARI, THE

See: *Yongary, Monster from the Deep.*

MONSTER ZERO

See: *The Atomic Brain.*

MONTY PYTHON AND THE HOLY GRAIL

★★★ Columbia/TriStar, 1974, PG, 90 min. Dirs: Terry Gilliam, Terry Jones. Cast: Graham Chapman, John Cleese, Terry Gilliam, Eric Idle, Terry Jones, Michael Palin, Carol Cleveland, Connie Booth.

The Python's second feature, after the compilation *And Now For Something Completely Different* (1972), is a very funny but also very uneven fantasy-comedy spoofing movies like *Camelot, Knights of the Round Table,* and even *The Magic Sword.* A cartoon-cutout animated God commands King Arthur (Chapman) to gather together the bravest knights in the land and along the way we encounter a cartoon dragon, a man-eating bunny rabbit, a castle of sirens, and the black knight, who refuses to give up the battle even after he's been chopped to bits like Udo Kier in *Andy Warhol's Dracula.* It doesn't always work but it's rarely dull and has enough blood to qualify for an R rating had it been released new to theaters today. My, how times have changed.

MONTY PYTHON'S THE MEANING OF LIFE

★★ MCA/Universal, 1983, R, 103 min. Dir: Terry Jones. Cast: Graham Chapman, John Cleese, Terry Gilliam, Eric Idle, Terry Jones, Michael Palin, Carol Cleveland, Simon Jones.

Wildly inconsistent sketch comedy involving everything from a musical production number about sperm to the world's fattest man (he graphically throws up his guts and then explodes) to a dinner party of dense society types visited by the Grim Reaper himself. More concerned with being offensive at all costs than being truly funny, this is mostly for hardcore Python fans.

MOON 44

★★ LIVE, 1990, R, 102 min. Dir: Roland Emmerich. Cast: Michael Paré, Lisa Eichhorn, Malcolm McDowell, Brian Thompson, Stephen Geoffreys, Roscoe Lee Browne.

There are good special FX and an interesting cast in this otherwise ponderous futuristic flick, with Paré investigating corporate intrigue at a mining colony on a distant alien moon. Emmerich would do better later with films like *Stargate* and *Independence Day.*

MOON PILOT

★★☆ Disney, 1962, NR, 98 min. Dir: James Neilson. Cast: Tom Tryon, Dany Saval, Brian Keith, Edmond O'Brien, Tommy Kirk, Kent Smith.

Technically outdated but still fairly pleasant Disney comedy has Tryon as an astronaut romanced by a beautiful alien girl (Saval) on the eve of his first space mission. The good cast helps what sometimes looks like one of the inspirations for the *I Dream of Jeannie* TV series.

MOONRAKER

★★ MGM/UA, 1979, PG, 126 min. Dir: Lewis Gilbert. Cast: Roger Moore, Lois Chiles, Michael Lonsdale, Corinne Clery, Richard Kiel, Emily Bolton, Blanche Ravalek, Bernard Lee, Lois Maxwell, Desmond Llewellyn, Geoffrey Keen, Walter Gotell.

The weakest entry in the long-running James Bond series (with *A View to a Kill* a close second), this is also the second-biggest moneymaker in the series and the most science fiction oriented. Practically a remake of *The Spy Who Loved Me,* this has Bond (Moore) and lady scientist Chiles investigating the activities of madman Lonsdale (one of the least impressive of the Bond villains), who plans to kill off the entire population of Earth and repopulate it with a beautiful master race he has relocated to an orbiting space station. Kiel returns from *The Spy Who Loved Me* as indestructible hitman Jaws but he's played

here as more of a cartoon than a threat; Lee makes his last appearance as M. Great special FX and a heartstopping opening stunt sequence but overall a bust, with a totally unmemorable theme song sung by Shirley Bassey.

MOONTRAP

★★☆ Image Entertainment, 1989, R, 92 min. Dir: Robert Duke. Cast: Bruce Campbell, Walter Koenig, Leigh Lombardi, Robert Kurcz.

A very cheap but well-written and -acted sci-fi thriller, starring *Evil Dead*'s Campbell and *Star Trek*'s Koenig as moon-shuttle pilots who accidentally reactivate an alien robot that goes on a lunar rampage. Better than you'd imagine, with interesting plot details and solid FX work.

MORONS FROM OUTER SPACE

★★★ Cannon, 1985, PG-13, 87 min. Dir: Mike Hodges. Cast: Griff Rhys Jones, Mel Smith, James B. Sikking, Dinsdale Landen, Jimmy Nail, Joanne Pearce.

Utterly dumb and utterly hilarious Brit sci-fi comedy about an accidental invasion by totally stoopid humanoid aliens whose spaceship crashes on Earth. A lot funnier than many bigger-budgeted and better-known sci-fi comedies.

MORTAL KOMBAT—THE MOVIE

★★ New Line, 1995, PG-13, 101 min. Dir: Paul Anderson. Cast: Christopher Lambert, Talisa Soto, Lyndon Ashby, Bridgette Wilson, Robin Shou, Cary Hiroyuki-Tagawa.

Three warriors (Sonya Blade, Jonny Cage, and Lui Kang) battle the servants of evil sorcerer Shang Tsung to determine the fate of the world in this flashy but empty big-screen version of the popular—and infamous for its violence—video game. Lots of morphing, special makeup, and loud music but literally nothing in the acting or story departments to hang your hat on.

MOTHRA

★★★ Columbia/TriStar, 1961, NR, 90 min. Dir: Inoshiro Honda. Cast: Franky Sakai, Kyoko Kagawa, Ken Uehara, Hiroshi Koizumi, Emi Ito, Yumi Ito.

An expedition to a radiation-beset South Seas island discovers a pair of tiny singing princesses (the Ito sisters), who are taken back to Tokyo and exploited as a TV attraction. Eventually the girls are rescued by Mothra, an enormous caterpillar that trashes Tokyo, spins a cocoon around the wreckage of Tokyo Tower, and ultimately emerges from it as a

Butterflies are free as the winged behemoth attacks in Mothra *(1961).*

titanic butterfly. One of the most poetic and beautifully crafted of the Toho monster movies, the miniatures aren't very realistic but the characters are likable and scenes of Mothra flying at the end have an odd sort of grace. Sequel: *Godzilla vs. Mothra* (1963).

MR. DESTINY

★★ Touchstone, 1990, PG-13, 110 min. Dir: James Orr. Cast: James Belushi, Linda Hamilton, Michael Caine, Jon Lovitz, Hart Bochner, Rene Russo, Courtney Cox, Kathy Ireland.

Routine *It's a Wonderful Life* wannabe, with Belushi as a shlub given a second chance at life by magical Caine (the best thing about the movie) who transports Jim back in time to a key turning point in his life at a high school baseball game. This fantasy for frustrated middle-aged men isn't awful but really doesn't go anywhere that dozens of other similar, and better, films have before or since.

MR. INVISIBLE

See: *Mr. Superinvisible.*

MR. PEABODY AND THE MERMAID

★★★ Republic, 1948, NR, 89 min. Dir: Irving Pichel. Cast: William Powell, Ann Blyth, Irene Hervey, Andrea King, Fred Clark, Clinton Sundberg.

Powell is spritely as a middle-aged fisherman who hooks gorgeous mermaid Blyth and brings her home to his bathtub, much to the chagrin of wife Hervey. Basically a ripoff of a British film called *Miranda,* with Glynis Johns as a mermaid, this comedy often falls flat but is bouyed by Powell's good spirits and Blyth's beauty and was clearly the major inspiration for *Splash.*

MR. SUPERINVISIBLE

★ Simitar Entertainment, 1970, G, 90 min. Dir: Anthony M. Dawson [Antonio Margheriti]. Cast: Dean Jones, Ingeborg Schoener, Gastone Moschin, Rafael Alonso, Peter Carsten, Philippe Leroy.

Scientist Jones, experimenting in curing the common cold, is turned invisible by a strange serum from India. Just thinking about a German-Spanish-Italian Disney ripoff kiddie comedy starring Jones and directed by Italian horror man Margheriti gives me a headache. Aka *Mr. Invisible.*

MULTIPLICITY

★★ Columbia/TriStar, 1995, PG-13, 117 min. Dir: Harold Ramis. Cast: Michael Keaton, Andie MacDowell, Harris Yulin, Eugene Levy.

Harried Keaton decides that there isn't enough of him to go around so he decides to have himself cloned. Alleged hijinks ensue as more and more Michaels show up to complicate the life of our hero and his confused wife MacDowell. Great state-of-the-art FX seem to be the main reason this slight fantasy was made and they remain the main reason to watch this—unless you just can't get enough Keaton, who made this weak fantasy-comedy rather than the third *Batman* movie.

MURDER BY MOONLIGHT

★★ Cineglobe, 1989, PG-13, 96 min. Dir: Michael Lindsay-Hogg. Cast: Julian Sands, Brigitte Nielsen, Gerald McRaney, Brian Cox.

Uninvolving TV movie with Nielsen as a NASA security agent sent to a moonbase in the year 2105 to investigate a series of murders. This unimaginative sci-fi whodunit also stars Sands as a Russian agent who helps our white-haired heroine.

MURDER BY TELEVISION

★★ Sinister Cinema, 1935, NR, 60 min. Dir: Clifford Sandforth. Cast: Bela Lugosi, June Collyer, Huntley Gordon, George Meeker, Claire McDowell, Hattie McDaniel.

Lugosi (who else?) is the chief suspect when an inventor who's perfected an early form of television is murdered. Cheap as can be but with a dash of imagination, good work from Bela, and a fun but ridiculous surprise ending.

MURDERERS' ROW

★★ RCA/Columbia, 1966, NR, 108 min. Dir: Henry Levin. Cast: Dean Martin, Ann-Margret, Karl Malden, Camilla Sparv, James Gregory, Beverly Adams.

The second Matt Helm film is one of the funniest, with Dino trying to save Washington, D.C., from madman Malden (whose acting here makes his eyeball-rolling turn in *Phantom of the Rue Morgue* look subdued), who plans to melt it with a laser beam. A mini-skirted Annie also figures in things as the daughter of a kidnapped scientist. This has more laughs than in both *Top Secret* and *Spy Hard* combined. Followed by *The Ambushers*.

MURDER IN SPACE

★★ Vidmark Entertainment, 1985, NR, 89 min. Dir: Steven Hilliard Stern. Cast: Wilford Brimley, Arthur Hill, Martin Balsam, Michael Ironside, Alberta Watson, Cathie Shirriff, Damir Andrei, Tom Butler.

Another outer space murder mystery, with the crew of a flight to Mars menaced on the return trip by a killer. It's well cast, but this made-for-cable flick looks mainly like a bad cross between episodes of *Buck Rogers* and *Murder, She Wrote*.

MUTANT

See: *Forbidden World.*

MUTANT HUNT

★☆ Wizard, 1986, R, 90 min. Dir: Tim Kincaid. Cast: Rick Gianasi, Mary-Anne Fahey, Joel von Ornsteiner.

Cheesy made-in-New York futuristic time waster has Gianasi as the hunky hero after killer cyborgs in twenty-first-century Manhattan. Pretty funny (most of it unintentional), with gory makeups by Ed French.

MUTANT ON THE BOUNTY

★★ Southgate, 1988, PG-13, 93 min. Dir: Robert Torrence. Cast: John Roarke, Deborah Benson, John Furey, Fox Harris, Kyle T. Heffner.

Obviously they came up with the title first, but this mild sci-fi comedy isn't all bad. Roarke is an android on a spaceship trying to discover which of the other passengers is a psychotic killer. A few laughs and a few thrills on a very low budget.

MUTANT SPECIES

★★ LIVE, 1995, R, 100 min. Dir: David A. Prior. Cast: Denise Crosby, Leo Rossi, Ted Prior, Powers Booth, Wilford Brimley.

Rossi is an astronaut who transforms into a big reptile monster that rips off people's heads and is battled by Crosby and soldier Prior. Routine but well acted (except for Prior, brother of the director) direct-to-video monster flick shot in Alabama but set in Texas. Sometimes plays like a somewhat better-cast remake of *The Incredible Melting Man*.

MUTATOR

★☆ Prism Entertainment, 1989, R, 87 min. Dir: John R. Bowey. Cast: Brion James, Carolyn Ann Clark, Milton Raphael Murill.

Veteran screen baddie James is badly miscast as a hero in this derivative, South Africa-shot potboiler about people trapped in a locked building with a murderous monster. You rarely see the monster but when you do it has a big cat face like one of the creatures in the Stephen King movie *Sleepwalkers* and really isn't much of a menace. Aka *Time of the Beast*.

MUTRONICS

See: *The Guyver.*

MY SCIENCE PROJECT

★★☆ Touchstone, 1985, PG, 94 min. Dir: Jonathan Betuel. Cast: John Stockwell, Danielle Von Zerneck, Fisher Stevens, Raphael Sbarge, Dennis Hopper, Barry Corbin, Ann Wedgeworth, Richard Masur, Michael Berryman, Pamela Springsteen.

Hit-or-miss teen comedy (from Disney) about high schoolers who discover and reactivate a time warp device that conjures up everything from mutants from the future to a Tyrannosaurus Rex. Good FX and Hopper (in something of a mini-comeback role) is great as an aging hippie science teacher, but this widely uneven fantasy never quite comes off.

MY STEPMOTHER IS AN ALIEN

★☆ RCA/Columbia, 1988, PG-13, 108 min. Dir: Richard Benjamin. Cast: Dan Aykroyd, Kim Basinger, Alyson Hannigan, Jon Lovitz, Joseph Maher, Seth Green, voices of Ann Prentiss, Harry Shearer.

Some talented people totally waste their time in this *Splash*-inspired dud about a beautiful alien woman (Basinger) who marries a nerdy Earth scientist (Aykroyd). Though aimed at kids, this almost laughless comedy contains a scene where Kim watches a porno movie (not shown) in order to learn how to have sex with hubby Dan—who hasn't had a hit since *Ghostbusters*.

MYSTERIANS, THE

★★★ United Entertainment, 1957, NR, 85 min. Dir: Inoshiro Honda. Cast: Kenji Sahara, Yumi Shirakawa, Momoko Kochi, Akihiko Hirata.

Top-notch Japanese sci-fi about a race of aliens from the dead world of Mysteriod who come to Earth with their towering robotic guardian (a token *Godzilla*-like touch) to kidnap women as mates. In other words, the Mysterians need women! One of the best films to come from the Toho Studios, with a breakneck pace and great Eiji Tsuburaya special FX.

MYSTERIOUS DR. SATAN, THE

★★☆ Nostalgia Merchant, 1940, NR, 250 min. Dirs: William Witney, John English. Cast: Eduardo Cianelli, Robert Wilcox, C. Montague Shaw, William Newell, Ella Neal, Charles Trowbridge.

Ciannelli is a hoot as the mad Dr. Satan who tries to take over the world with his prototype robot (it looks like a walking water heater) but is thwarted by masked hero Copperhead (Wilcox). Not bad serial later reedited into the feature *Doctor Satan's Robot*.

MYSTERIOUS INVADER, THE

See: *The Astounding She Monster*.

MYSTERIOUS ISLAND

★★★ Columbia/TriStar, 1961, NR, 100 min. Dir: Cy Endfield. Cast: Michael Craig, Joan Greenwood, Gary Merrill, Michael Callan, Beth Rogan, Herbert Lom.

Ray Harryhausen's special FX sparkle in this followup to *Twenty Thousand Leagues Under the Sea*. Near the close of the Civil War, northern prisoners escaping a southern army base are carried off by a balloon and after many days land on a Pacific island, where they encounter gigantic animals (most notably a crab, a chicken, and a swarm of bees), shipwrecked women, pirates, and the infamous Captain Nemo (Lom in an excellent cameo). Solid fantasy, with a dynamite musical score by Bernard Herrmann.

MYSTERIOUS TWO, THE

★☆ Star Classics, 1982, NR, 96 min. Dir: Gary Sherman. Cast: John Forsythe, Priscilla Pointer, James Stephens, Karen Werner, Robert Pine, Vic Tayback, Noah Beery, Robert Englund.

Feeble TV movie in which Stephens (from the *Paper Chase* TV show) discovers that charismatic evangelists Forsythe and Pointer are actually brainwashing aliens. A pilot for a never-developed series, luckily for John, who landed in the popular *Dynasty* next. Sherman also directed *Dead & Buried* and *Poltergeist III*.

MYSTERY SCIENCE THEATER 3000

★★★★ RHINO, 1990–93, NR, 91 min. per tape. Dirs: Jim Mallon, Trace Beaulieu, Kevin Murphy. Cast: Joel Hodgson, Michael J. Nelson, Trace Beaulieu, Frank Conniff, Kevin Murphy, Jim Mallon.

One of the funniest, cleverest TV shows ever made, this features the simple premise of a likable guy (original series creator Hodgson and later head writer Nelson) trapped on an orbiting satellite, where a mad scientist (Beaulieu) out to take over the world forces him to watch the world's worst movies. Each week our hero and his robot pals, Tom Servo and Crow T. Robot, sit in silhouette and quip away as some of the most God-awful (and most hilarious) films in history unspool. Three of the best shows have already been released on tape: *The Amazing Colossal Man* ("You look like Mr. Clean, Glenn. The Proctor and Gamble people are on the phone"); Hodgson's last show, *Mitchell* (they really rip into star Joe Don Baker); and Nelson's first episode, *The Brain that Wouldn't Die* ("Shannon Dougherty, no!" Crow shouts when a stripper cat fight begins). Let's hope that future releases will include some of my other favorites, including *Bride of the Monster* ("Ed Wood's wardrobe by Mrs. Wood"); *Godzilla vs. Megalon* ("Godzilla's back, and someone's got to pay!"); and *Kitten with a Whip* ("I am one whipped kitten").

MYSTERY SCIENCE THEATER 3000—THE MOVIE

★★☆ MCA/Universal, 1996, PG-13, 74 min. Dir: Jim Mallon. Cast: Michael J. Nelson, Trace Beaulieu, Kevin Murphy, Jim Mallon.

"Quick, call Frank Perdue!" Mysterious Island *(1961).*

A surprisingly uninspired big-screen version of the TV show, this has better production values and special FX but lacks the (admittedly rehearsed) off-the-cuff spontaneity of the television version. Another problem is that the movie they trash, *This Island Earth*, may be hoaky and dated but it's hardly *that* bad. Still, it's mildly amusing, especially for those not overly familiar to the show, but I only laughed out loud once, when Tom Servo compared the Faith Domergue-molesting mutant to an out-of-control Senator Ted Kennedy.

NAKED LUNCH
★★★ Fox, 1991, R, 115 min. Dir: David Cronenberg. Cast: Peter Weller, Judy Davis, Ian Holm, Julian Sands, Roy Scheider, Monique Mercure, Nicholas Campbell, Robert Silverman.

Few people understood, or wanted to understand, this filmization of William S. Burroughs's semi-autobiographical book. Weller is a would-be writer whose search for missing drug-addict wife Davis (who's brilliant in a double role) drags him into the drug-tinged underbelly of '50s New York City. Who else but Cronenberg could handle this story with such aplomb, mixing a powerhouse cast with some of the weirdest images in film history (Chris Walas created the various hallucinations, including a talking typewriter and mutants called mugwumps). Some Burroughs purists were unhappy with the watering down of the novel's gay sex angle, but what did they expect from a mainstream movie, even a weird one like this?

NAKED SPACE
★★ Edde Entertainment, 1981, PG, 88 min. Dir: Bruce Kimmel. Cast: Cindy Williams, Leslie Nielsen, Patrick Macnee, Gerrit Graham, Bruce Kimmel, Ron Kurowski.

Originally called *The Creature Wasn't Nice* and retitled (twice) for video, this modest spoof of *Alien* is about a spacecraft that picks up a monstrous alien lifeform that eats humans—and likes to sing, too. The cast is game but their material really isn't up to par; a few scattered laughs, especially from Nielsen as the dense-as-a-plank mission commander. Aka *Spaceship*.

NAVIGATOR: A MEDIEVAL ODYSSEY, THE

See: *The Navigator: An Odyssey Across Time.*

NAVIGATOR: AN ODYSSEY ACROSS TIME, THE

★★★ Trylon, 1988, PG, 92 min. Dir: Vincent Ward. Cast: Bruce Lyons, Chris Haywood, Hamish MacFarlane, Marshall Napier, Noel Appleby, Paul Livingston.

In the year 1348, young MacFarlane's kingdom is ravaged by the plague and a prophetic dream convinces him to dig a tunnel to a magical place where a cure will be found. Aided by brother Lyons, the tunnel is dug and the brothers end up in modern New Zealand, where people are dying from a new plague called AIDS. This provocative fantasy is well directed and often interesting but may be a bit too downbeat for the young audience it's aimed at. Aka *The Navigator: A Medieval Odyssey.*

NAVY VS. THE NIGHT MONSTERS, THE

★ Paragon, 1966, NR, 87 min. Dir: Michael A. Hoey. Cast: Mamie Van Doren, Anthony Eisley, Bobby Van, Pamela Mason, Phillip Terry, Bill Gray.

Cardboard ripoff of *The Day of the Triffids*, with Mamie et al. menaced by man-eating trees at a surprisingly tropical Antarctic naval base. A top exploitation cast tries to take all this seriously but there are still laughs galore. The ending features the most air force stock footage and cheesiest special FX since *The Crawling Eye*. Aka *The Night Crawlers*.

NEMESIS

★★★ Imperial Entertainment, 1992, R, 92 min. Dir: Albert Pyun. Cast: Olivier Gruner, Deborah Shelton, Tim Thomerson, Brion James, Merle Kennedy, Cary-Hiroyuki Tagawa, Yuji Okumoto, Marjorie Monaghan, Nicholas Guest, Jackie Earle Haley.

This futuristic thriller has direct-to-video written all over it but was actually put into some theaters and is a lot better than expected. Gruner is an android hunter with a bomb planted in his heart (he's part cyborg himself) and only three days to complete his globe-hopping mission before he explodes. This *Blade Runner/Terminator/Escape from New York* mix is well done on a budget, with Shelton as a seductive bad girl and Thomerson as a villain who turns into an animated metallic skeleton.

NEON CITY

★★★ Vidmark Entertainment, 1991, R, 107 min. Dir: Monte Markham. Cast: Vanity, Michael Ironside, Lyle Alzado, Richard Sanders, Valerie Wildman, Juliet Landau.

Familiar TV actor Markham directed this effective but bleak sci-fi road movie that finds Vanity, Ironside, and Alzado traveling across the nuked future wastelands of America on their way to the fabulous title metropolis. Well acted but very plain, with *WKRP* star Sanders (remember Les Nessman?) as a distributor of poison for suicidal, badly mutated nuclear war survivors.

NEPTUNE DISASTER, THE

See: *The Neptune Factor.*

NEPTUNE FACTOR, THE

★★ Fox, 1973, G, 97 min. Dir: Daniel Petrie. Cast: Ben Gazzara, Yvette Mimieux, Walter Pidgeon, Ernest Borgnine, Chris Wiggins, Donnelly Rhodes.

A first-rate, very disaster-film-like cast is about the only really worthwhile thing in this well-made but dull sci-fi thriller that resembles *Around the World Under the Sea* and *Marooned*. Gazzara commands a rescue sub trying to save three men trapped in an underwater laboratory by an earthquake. There are also some "sea monsters" played by blown-up photography of ordinary fish. The G rating helps keep things as bland and predictable as possible. Aka *The Neptune Disaster* and *Underwater Odyssey.*

NEUTRON AGAINST THE DEATH ROBOTS

See: *Neutron vs. the Death Robots.*

NEUTRON AND THE BLACK MASK

★★ Sinister Cinema, 1961, NR, 80 min. Dir: Federico Curiel. Cast: Wolf Rubinski, Armando Silvestre, Rosita Arenas, Claudio Brook.

One of several Mexican sci-fi adventures featuring Rubinski as the black masked wrestler/atomic superman Neutron (don't ask); here he battles Silvestre and his criminal band, who are after atomic secrets. Similar in concept to the even more popular Santo wrestling-horror films from South of the border and recommended for fans of the truly bizarre. Aka *Neutron, El Enmascarado Negro (Neutron, The Black Masked).*

NEUTRON AND THE COSMIC BOMB

See: *Neutron vs. the Maniac.*

NEUTRON, THE BLACK MASKED

See: *Neutron and the Black Mask.*

NEUTRON VS. THE AMAZING DR. CARONTE

★★☆ Sinister Cinema, 1960, NR, 83 min. Dir: Federico Curiel. Cast: Wolf Rubinski, Julio Aleman, Rosita Arenas, Armando Silvestre.

The first (I think) and one of the best of the Neutron films finds our masked hero up against Silvestre's army of hypnotized monster men. Dumb but fun.

NEUTRON VS. THE DEATH ROBOTS

★★★ Sinister Cinema, 1961, NR, 80 min. Dir: Federico Curiel. Cast: Wolf Rubinski, Rosita Arenas, Julio Aleman, Armando Silvestre, Claudio Brook, Beto el Boticario.

The best (in my who-cares opinion, anyway) Neutron movie finds the evil Dr. Caronte (Silvestre) experimenting with a powerful, disembodied superbrain created by grafting together the brains of three dead scientists. Great fun, this is like a WCW remake of *Donovan's Brain* crossed with a Republic serial. Aka *Neutron Against the Death Robots.*

NEUTRON VS. THE MANIAC

★★☆ Sinister Cinema, 1962, NR, 81 min. Dir: Federico Curiel. Cast: Wolf Rubinski, Gina Romand, Rudolfo Landa, Armando Silvestre.

Neutron and Dr. Caronte, searching for secret papers, end up in an asylum where a mad strangler is on the loose. The series takes a slight horror-whodunit turn here, with lots of spooky atmosphere and a surprise ending. Aka *Neutron and the Cosmic Bomb.*

NEVERENDING STORY, THE

★★★ Warner, 1984, PG, 92 min. Dir: Wolfgang Peterson. Cast: Noah Hathaway, Barrett Oliver, Tami Stronach, Moses Gunn, Patricia Hayes, Gerald McRaney, Sidney Bromley, voice of Alan Oppenheimer.

German director Peterson's (*Das Boot*) first English-language film was this visually imaginative fantasy about a young boy (Oliver) reading a book about a brave boy warrior (Hathaway) in a fantastical kingdom that's brought to life. Amazing special FX and a nice pro-reading stance make this kid's film far superior to the very similar Hollywood product *The Pagemaster* and its own live-action and animated sequels.

NEVERENDING STORY II: THE NEXT CHAPTER, THE

★★ Warner, 1990, PG, 89 min. Dir: George Miller. Cast: Jonathan Brandis, Kenny Morrison, Clarissa Burt, John Wesley Shipp, Martin Umbach, Alexandra Johnes.

Mad Max man Miller directed this more Americanized but who-needs-it followup, with Brandis as the coverboy kid hero who enters a magical book to aid (creepily sexy) girl empress Burt. This copies the look and general feel of the first film but is forced and phony and has none of its charm.

NEW EDEN

★★☆ MCA/Universal, 1994, R, 89 min. Dir: Alan Metzger. Cast: Stephen Baldwin, Lisa Bonet, Tobin Bell, Michael Bowen, Jane Hubert Whitten, Nicholas Worth.

Another postnuke adventure, this one done with a bit of wit. Baldwin (brother of Alec, Billy, etc., etc.) is the hero who goes from slave to warrior while falling for ex-*Cosby* kid Bonet as a desert scavenger. Despite the R rating this is pretty mild stuff, but is so obviously not taking itself seriously that it actually comes off a lot better than had its clichéd storyline been played straight.

NEW GLADIATORS, THE

★★ Media, 1983, UR, 90 min. Dir: Lucio Fulci. Cast: Jared Martin, Fred Williamson, Claudio Cassinelli, Al Cliver, Haruiko Yamanouchi.

Condemned prisoners are set against each other in televised gladiatorial combat in this Italian film that bears a certain similarity to *The Running Man*—except that this was made first. Lots of action and gore in this routine import. Aka *Rome 2072, The New Gladiators: 2072,* and *2020: New Barbarians.*

NEW GLADIATORS: 2072, THE

See: *The New Gladiators.*

NEW INVISIBLE MAN, THE

★★ Sinister Cinema, 1957, NR, 94 min. Dir: Alfredo B. Cravenna. Cast: Arturo de Cordova, Ana Luisa Peluffo, Augusto Benedico, Raul Meraz.

Unofficial remake of *The Invisible Man Returns,* with de Cordova using an invisibility formula to try to clear himself of a false murder charge. Unimpressive special FX but at least this one doesn't cop out with a phony happy ending. Aka *H. G. Wells's New Invisible Man* and *The Invisible Man in Mexico.*

NEXT ONE, THE

★★ Vestron, 1981, NR, 105 min. Dir: Nico Mastorakis. Cast: Keir Dullea, Adrienne Barbeau, Jeremy Licht, Peter Hobbs.

On an island off the coast of Greece, widow Barbeau and son Licht encounter strange Dullea, who at first appears to be an alien but later claims to be the brother of Christ. Weird sci-fi/romance with a confused storyline but beautiful locations and one of Barbeau's best performances.

NIGHT BEAST

★★ Paragon, 1982, R, 85 min. Dir: Don Dohler. Cast: Tom Griffith, Jamie Zemarel, Karin Kardian, George Stover, Don Leifert, Eleanor Herman.

Backyard reworking of *Alien* with a violent extraterrestrial in an immobile, *Rawhead Rex*-like mask gruesomely dispatching locals in the Baltimore area. This shot-on-a-shoestring semi-amateur effort is badly acted but has good gore and some laughs.

NIGHT CALLER

See: *Night Caller from Outer Space*.

NIGHT CALLER FROM OUTER SPACE

★★ Sony, 1965, NR, 84 min. Dir: John Gilling. Cast: John Saxon, Patricia Haines, Maurice Denham, Alfred Burke, Jack Watson, Barbara French, Aubrey Morris, Robert Crewsden.

A horribly disfigured alien (Crewsden) from the planet Ganymeade kidnaps women answering a personal ad in *Bikini Girl* magazine as part of a plot to bring fresh breeding stock to his dying world. This straightforward rehashing of a very campy plot is played too close to the vest to be as fun as it should be, but the black-and-white photography is effective and the final fate of heroine Haines is genuinely shocking. Aka *Night Caller* and *Blood Beast from Outer Space*.

NIGHT CRAWLERS, THE

See: *The Navy vs. the Night Monsters*.

NIGHTFALL

★☆ MGM/UA, 1988, PG-13, 83 min. Dir: Paul Mayersberg. Cast: David Birney, Sarah Douglas, Starr Andreeff, Andra Millian.

An ambitious but flat and utterly uninvolving low-budget adaptation of an Isaac Asimov short story. Birney, the ruler of a land where night falls only once every thousand years, tries to stop the panic that overtakes his people as the darkness grows. Douglas rips out her

own eyes rather than see the night in this surprisingly bloody but lifeless PG-13 release from Roger Corman's Concorde Pictures.

NIGHTFLYERS

★☆ IVE, 1987, R, 89 min. Dir: T. C. Blake [Robert Collector]. Cast: Catherine Mary Stewart, Michael Praed, Lisa Blount, John Standing, Michael Des Barres, Héléne Udy.

Future astronauts investigating some space phenomenon are killed off by their own spaceship, which has been imbued with the lifeforce of the commander's evil mother. Bland version of a story by George R. R. Martin, with an interesting cast but an absurd story that combines elements of *Alien* with the haunted house flick *Burnt Offerings*.

NIGHT OF THE BLOOD BEAST

★★ Sinister Cinema, 1958, NR, 65 min. Dir: Bernard L. Kowalski. Cast: Michael Emmet, Angela Greene, Ed Nelson, Georgianna Carter.

Years before *Junior*, Emmet played the world's *real* first pregnant man as an astronaut impregnated by a male alien (which looks like a moldy parrot) with its shrimplike spawn.

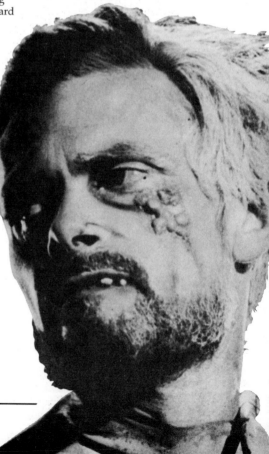

"Okay, who hid my Clearasil?" Night Caller from Outer Space (1965).

Everybody in this movie looks very dour and serious but this is still a howl, with (an often shirtless) Emmet going way over the top as the defiled hero whose obsessive relationship with the monster makes this look like the first Hollywood movie about a gay couple.

NIGHT OF THE COMET

★★☆ Video Treasurers, 1984, PG-13, 94 min. Dir: Thom Eberhardt. Cast: Catherine Mary Stewart, Kelli Maroney, Robert Beltran, Geoffrey Lewis, Mary Woronov, Sharon Farrell.

Pretty good semi-spoof sci-fi/horror thriller about a comet that causes most of the population of the world to disintegrate into piles of dust. Valley girl survivor sisters Stewart and Maroney fight over hunky fellow survivor Beltran while battling zombies and evil scientists Lewis and Woronov. Lots of in-joke references to other movies like *The Day of the Triffids, Dawn of the Dead,* and even *The Wizard of Oz.*

NIGHT THE WORLD SHOOK, THE

See: *Gorgo.*

NIGHT THEY SAVED CHRISTMAS, THE

★★ Cabin Fever, 1984, NR, 95 min. Dir: Jackie Cooper. Cast: Jaclyn Smith, Paul LeMat, Art Carney, June Lockhart, Paul Williams, Mason Adams.

Another interchangable made-for-TV Christmas fantasy with the lovely Smith and her kids trying to save Santa's workshop from destruction when it stands in the way of some oil pipeline construction. Carney (as Claus) and Williams (as a sarcastic elf) are well cast but this is still too routine to stand out from the rest of the holiday pack.

NIGHTWISH

★☆ Vidmark Entertainment, 1988, UR, 92 min. Dir: Bruce R. Cook. Cast: Clayton Rohner, Alisha Das, Elizabeth Kaitan, Jack Starrett, Bob Tessier, Brian Thompson.

Confused tale of four college students who take part in a professor's dream research project only to discover that they've been set up as victims of some alien breeding experiments. This makes almost no sense but has a good cast and some gruesome special FX.

1984

★★★☆ IVE, 1984, R, 115 min. Dir: Michael Radford. Cast: John Hurt, Richard Burton, Suzanna Hamilton, Cyril Cusack, Phyllis Logan, Gregor Fisher.

Just in time for the real 1984 came this almost perfect, and very oppressive, film version of George Orwell's classic novel. Hurt is well cast as Winston Smith, who works at rewriting history every day and disobeys party rules by falling in love with the bewitching Hamilton. Burton is restrained and chilling as O'Brien, the party official who punishes those who break Big Brother's rules by placing a rat cage on their faces. Full of grim, claustrophobic atmosphere and downbeat Eurythmics music, this is far superior to the 1955 version with Edmond O'Brien (which substituted a different, "upbeat" ending) and was Burton's last film.

1990: THE BRONX WARRIORS

★★ Media, 1982, R, 84 min. Dir: Enzo G. Castellari. Cast: Vic Morrow, Fred Williamson, Christopher Connelly, Mark Gregory, Stefania Giorlami, George Eastman.

Passable Italian imitation of *Mad Max* and *Escape from New York* with Morrow, in his penultimate role, as a corrupt cop after kidnapped heiress Giorlami in the postnuke Bronx. Williamson and Gregory are rival gang leaders (the latter playing "Trash") who band together to rescue her. Lots of violence and scenery chewing. Aka *I Guerrieri del Bronx (The Bronx Warriors)*; sequel: *Escape from the Bronx.*

NO ESCAPE

★★★ HBO, 1994, R, 118 min. Dir: Martin Campbell. Cast: Ray Liotta, Lance Henriksen, Kevin Dillon, Ernie Hudson, Stuart Wilson, Michael Lerner.

This very homoerotic action flick was a box office flop but it's actually pretty good. In the year 2022, Liotta is an ex-marine who escapes from a sadistic island prison with young Dillon and hides out in the jungle with Henriksen and his band of survivalists until recaptured by the minions of warden Lerner. With lots of gory violence and first-rate acting, this filmed-in-Australia version of the novel *The Penal Colony* by Richard Herley has a lot more going on below the surface than your more run-of-the-mill *Mad Max* clone.

NORMAN'S AWESOME EXPERIENCE

★☆ Southgate, 1987, NR, 98 min. Dir: Paul Donovan. Cast: Tom McCamus, Laurie Paton, Jacques Lussier.

Drab shot-in-Canada time travel farce about a nerdy computer geek called Norman who accidentally transports himself, a beautiful model, and her photographer back to ancient Rome. *The Three Stooges Meet Hercules* handled a very similar plot a helluva lot better than this cheesy *Bill and Ted* ripoff. Aka *A Switch in Time.*

NO SURVIVORS, PLEASE

★★☆ Sinister Cinema, 1963, NR, 95 min. Dirs: Hans

Albin, Peter Berneis. Cast: Maria Perschy, Robert Cunningham, Uwe Friedrichsen, Gustavo Rojo.

Not bad West German sci-fi about formless aliens taking over the bodies of world dignitaries in order to force various countries into a nuclear war that will destroy the world. The dubbing hurts but this has its moments.

NOT OF THIS EARTH
★★ MGM/UA, 1988, R, 80 min. Dir: Jim Wynorski. Cast: Traci Lords, Arthur Roberts, Roger Lodge, Ace Mask.

Opportunistic remake of the semiclassic 1956 Roger Corman original (Rog produced this one) presenting former underaged porno queen Lords in her first "legit" movie role as a nurse looking after alien vampire Roberts, who's come to Earth in search of human blood. Lots of breasts (big surprise) and clips from earlier Corman productions to pad out the slim, predictable storyline. Remade again for cable in 1996.

NOT OF THIS EARTH
★★☆ New Horizons, 1996, R, 88 min. Dir: Terence H. Winkless. Cast: Michael York, Parker Stevenson, Elizabeth Barondes, Richard Belzer, Mason Adams, Bob McFarland.

How many times are they gonna remake this before Roger Corman feels they got it right? Actually, this made-for-cable redo is a big step up from the previous Traci Lords version and almost on par with the original. Now it's York as the space vampire and Barondes as the nurse unknowingly supplying him with life-sustaining plasma. Easily the best of several "Roger Corman Presents" remakes of some of his earlier works (others include updatings of *The Wasp Woman, A Bucket of Blood,* and *Humanoids from the Deep*), with good casting, a noncampy approach to the scripting, and solid direction to offset that feeling of déjà-vu.

NOW YOU SEE HIM, NOW YOU DON'T
★★ Disney, 1972, G, 85 min. Dir: Robert Butler. Cast: Kurt Russell, Cesar Romero, Joe Flynn, Jim Backus, William Windom, Michael McGreevey, Joyce Menges, Edward Andrews, Mike Evans, Ed Begley, Jr.

Okay sequel to *The Computer Wore Tennis Shoes,* with brainy Russell inventing an invisibility spray sought by gangster Romero. Routine Disney comedy has the usual fine cast of seasoned character actors backing up the bland younger stars and some fun special effects.

NUDE IN HIS POCKET
See: *Girl in His Pocket.*

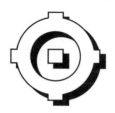

OBLIVION
★★ Paramount, 1994, PG-13, 94 min. Dir: Sam Irvin. Cast: Richard Joseph Paul, Jackie Swanson, Meg Foster, Issac Hayes, Julie Newmar, George Takei, Jimmie Skaggs, Carel Struycken, Musetta Vander, Irwin Keyes.

This shot-in-Romania outer space Western isn't especially good but it is mildly interesting and has a very strange cast. Paul is the hero, the son of a murdered sheriff in the dusty alien frontier town of Oblivion, up against Dave Allen-animated giant scorpions and Vander as a whip-wielding villainess. Takei (who isn't very funny) and Newmar (who is) trade off their *Star Trek/Batman* associations and Foster is good in an odd role as an android deputy. *Backlash: Oblivion II* is the improved sequel. Filmed as *Welcome to Oblivion.*

OFFICIAL DENIAL
★★☆ Paramount, 1993, NR, 96 min. Dir: Brian Trenchard-Smith. Cast: Parker Stevenson, Erin Gray, Dirk Benedict, Chad Everett, Michael Paré.

Shot in Australia, this made-for-cable sci-fi thriller (first shown on the Sci-Fi Channel) isn't bad. Stevenson (who goes through much of this with a shaved head), due to his claims of having been kidnapped and examined by aliens years before, is called upon by the military to try to communicate with a stranded extraterrestrial. Thoughtful little film from a director whose other films include sequels to *Leprechaun* and *Night of the Demons.*

OH GOD!
★★★ Warner, 1977, PG, 104 min. Dir: Carl Reiner. Cast: George Burns, John Denver, Teri Garr, Paul Sorvino, Ralph Bellamy, Barnard Hughes, David Ogden Stiers, George Furth.

Burns scored his biggest latter-day hit with this fantasy-comedy in which the Big Man upstairs comes to Earth, where he chooses supermarket worker Denver to spread the word that He's alive and well. Pretty funny, with George in top form (making up for the bland casting of Mr. Rocky Mountain High) and Garr practically reprising her disbelieving wife role from *Close Encounters of the Third Kind.*

OH GOD! BOOK II

★★ Warner, 1980, PG, 94 min. Dir: Gilbert Cates. Cast: George Burns, Suzanne Pleshette, David Birney, Louanne, Howard Duff, Hans Conreid, Wilfrid Hyde-White, Conrad Janis.

This bland sequel is virtually a remake of the original. This time Burns uses a little girl (for greater cuteness effect) to remind the world that He's still around. You may not still be around for the length of this contrived followup that has a capering Burns and not much else.

OH GOD! YOU DEVIL

★★☆ Warner, 1984, PG, 96 min. Dir: Paul Bogart. Cast: George Burns, Ted Wass, Ron Silver, Roxanne Hart, Eugene Roche, Robert Desiderio.

This not-bad third in the trilogy brings back Burns as both God *and* Satan, with Wass as a songwriter who sells his soul and is caught between the two Georges. Watchable fantasy-comedy from that period of '80s cinema when Hollywood was trying to sell TV star Wass (*Soap, Blossom*) as the next Chevy Chase—though he wasn't even the next Robert Hays.

OH, HEAVENLY DOG!

★★ CBS/Fox, 1980, PG, 103 min. Dir: Joe Camp. Cast: Chevy Chase, Jane Seymour, Omar Sharif, Robert Morley, Donnelly Rhodes, Benji.

A major box-office dud, this fantasy is more a vehicle for Benji than Chevy as the Chaseman plays an American private eye in London who's murdered and reincarnated as a dog to avenge the killing. Mildly entertaining but for a movie aimed at kids this is surprisingly violent and has uncomfortable scenes of Benji ogling the lovely Seymour. The same premise was more or less reworked as *Fluke*.

OMEGA MAN, THE

★★ Warner, 1971, PG, 98 min. Dir: Boris Sagal. Cast: Charlton Heston, Rosalind Cash, Anthony Zerbe, Paul Koslo.

Trendy-for-the-time remake of *The Last Man on Earth*, based on Richard Matheson's *I Am Legend*, plays down the horror elements in favor of lots of gun play and action. Heston is the rock-jawed survivor of a worldwide plague that's either killed off nearly everyone else or transformed them into light-sensitive zombies. Great scenes of Chuck tooling about the deserted streets of L.A. and lots of unintentional comedy.

ON BORROWED TIME

★★★ MGM/UA, 1939, NR, 99 min. Dir: Harold S. Bucquet. Cast: Lionel Barrymore, Sir Cedric Hardwicke, Bobs Watson, Beulah Bondi, Una Merkel, Ian Wolfe, Philip Terry, Eily Malyon.

When Death personified (Hardwicke) comes to claim elderly grandpa (Barrymore), the feisty old gent traps Death up a tree so that he can spend some more time with fatherless grandson Watson. Solid MGM adaptation of the play by Lawrence Edward Watkin mixes fantasy, humor, sentiment, and a touch of horror, with fine acting from Sir Cedric and Lionel. Although the ending is downbeat, it's curiously uplifting and satisfying.

ONE MAGIC CHRISTMAS

★★★ Disney, 1985, G, 88 min. Dir: Phillip Borsos. Cast: Mary Steenburgen, Harry Dean Stanton, Arthur Hill, Jan Rubes, Elizabeth Harnois, Gary Basaraba, Robbie Magwood, Elias Koteas.

This fairly routine Disney holiday movie gets a few extra points for being one of the most depressing "family" movies the studio ever turned out. Steenbergen is a suicidal mom at Christmas given new hope when daughter Harnois presses Santa (Rubes) and a guardian angel (Stanton) into service. (Stanton as a guardian angel? The angel of death, maybe.) The good cast is in top form but don't expect a lot of sweetness and light. Me? I thought it was great, the best Christmas flick since *Silent Night, Bloody Night*.

ONE MILLION B.C.

★★☆ Nostalgia Merchant, 1940, NR, 80 min. Dirs: Hal Roach, Hal Roach, Jr., D. W. Griffith. Cast: Victor Mature, Carole Landis, Lon Chaney, Jr., John Hubbard.

More people have probably seen the stock footage of battling lizards and crocodiles from this movie than have seen the actual movie itself. A big hit in its day, this features Mature and Landis as a Stone Age Romeo and Juliet involved with warring tribes, dinosaurs, and an active volcano. Slow but fun, with a modern-day framing device and a classic moment when a cave girl suddenly disappears beneath a carpet of steaming lava. Remade as *One Million Years B.C.*

ONE MILLION YEARS B.C.

★★★ Fox, 1966, NR, 91 min. Dir: Don Chaffey. Cast: Raquel Welch, John Richardson, Percy Herbert, Robert Brown, Martine Beswick, Jean Waldon.

The biggest hit ever for British horror film specialists Hammer Films, this also boosted the sex symbol image of star Welch. Raquel is first rate as the perky cavebabe Loana, who falls for brutish Richardson, has a cat fight with sexy rival Beswick, and battles a Ray Harryhausen-animated giant sea turtle before being carried off by a hungry teradon. Raquel's doeskin bikini, Harryhausen's FX, and Mario Nascimbene's evocative musical score are the highlights. This video print, taken from the original U.S. theatrical version, is missing about nine minutes of footage from the original British print, including some violence and a seductive Beswick dance number. Sequels: *Prehistoric Women, When Dinosaurs Ruled the Earth,* and *Creatures the World Forgot.*

ONE TOUCH OF VENUS

★★★ Republic, 1948, NR, 81 min. Dir: William A. Seiter. Cast: Ava Gardner, Robert Walker, Dick Haymes, Eve Arden, Olga San Juan, Tom Conway.

The gorgeous Gardner is perfectly cast as a department store statue of Venus come to life in this musical fantasy based on a popular Broadway hit. Walker is the smitten guy Ava sets her sights on and Arden offers her usual trenchant comic relief. Sort of remade as *Mannequin.*

ON THE BEACH

★★★☆ MGM/UA, 1959, NR, 133 min. Dir: Stanley Kramer. Cast: Gregory Peck, Ava Gardner, Fred Astaire, Anthony Perkins, Donna Anderson, Guy Doleman.

Devastating end-of-the-world drama from a novel by Nevil Shute. Peck is a U.S. submarine commander who arrives in Australia, the last inhabited place on Earth, as nuclear fallout wipes out the world's population. Greg falls for the lovely Ava but their affair is doomed as a cloud of nuclear death heads their way. Astaire, in his first dramatic role, is especially good as a retired race car driver. The fresh-faced Anderson (as Tony Perkins's wife) later carved a niche for herself in '70s exploitation as both Donna Anders and D. J. Anderson.

Raquel Welch in one of her breast— I mean best—roles in One Million Years B.C. *(1966).*

OPERATION GOLDMAN
See: *Lightning Bolt.*

ORIGINAL FABULOUS ADVENTURES OF BARON MUNCHAUSEN, THE,
See: *The Fabulous Adventures of Baron Munchausen.*

ORIGIN UNKNOWN
See: *Alien Predator.*

OUR MAN FLINT
★★★ CBS/Fox, 1966, NR, 107 min. Dir: Daniel Mann. Cast: James Coburn, Gila Golan, Lee J. Cobb, Edward Mulhare, Benson Fong, Gianna Serra, Sigrid Valdis, Shelby Grant, Rhys Williams, Russ Conway.

Coburn brings his usual wry charm to this secret agent spoof, filled with all the mid-'60s touches you've come to expect. Derek Flint (Coburn), the man from Z.O.W.I.E., is sent by his organization to stop a trio of mad meteorologists from taking over the world with their weather-control device. Much better than the somewhat similar Matt Helm films, this was popular enough to inspire a sequel (*In Like Flint*) and a later TV remake with Ray Danton in the Coburn role.

OUTBREAK
★★★ Warner, 1995, R, 127 min. Dir: Wolfgang Peterson. Cast: Dustin Hoffman, Rene Russo, Donald Sutherland, Cuba Gooding, Jr., Morgan Freeman, Kevin Spacey, Patrick Dempsey, Zakes Mokae.

This multimillion-dollar B movie works better than you'd expect and was a surprise box-office hit. Hoffman (miscast but trying) is an Army medical researcher out to stop a deadly new disease from spreading through a small California town and ultimately the entire country—maybe even the world. The disease is brought to the states by an annoyingly cute little monkey, who was also a regular on the TV show *Friends* (no, not Matt LeBlanc). During the crisis Hoffman is predictably reunited with estranged wife Russo (a plot device borrowed from *The Abyss*). Despite some drawbacks (including an unlikely action movie climax), this is very well acted and surprisingly intense for a mainstream Hollywood movie of the '90s, with echoes of *The Andromeda Strain* and *The Crazies* and some pretty shocking scenes that take this into horror film territory as well.

OUTER LIMITS: THE SAND KINGS, THE
★★ MGM/UA, 1995, NR, 96 min. Dir: Stuart Gillard. Cast: Beau Bridges, Helen Shaver, Lloyd Bridges, Kim Coates, Dylan Bridges, Craig Nicotero.

The feature-length pilot for the new Showtime *Outer Limits* series, this features Beau as a scientist studying some Martian soil in his home laboratory. Tiny, scorpionlike aliens hatch from the soil and begin to effect the scientist's life. Based on a story by George R. R. Martin, this is derivative of earlier *Limits* shows like *Wolf 359* and *The Zanti Misfits* but, like the subsequent new series, isn't nearly as good.

OUTLAND
★★★ Warner, 1981, R, 109 min. Dir: Peter Hyams. Cast: Sean Connery, Peter Boyle, Frances Sternhagen, James B. Sikking, Kika Markham, Clarke Peters, John Ratzenberger, Steven Berkoff.

This winning outer space remake of *High Noon* has a tough Connery performance as a marshal on Jupiter's Moon trying to clean up corruption in a mining town run by shady Boyle. Sternhagen is great as the crusty lady doctor who helps out our hero, and there's a race-against-the-clock climax and a *Scanners*-inspired exploding head scene.

OUTLAW
See: *Outlaw of Gor.*

OUTLAW OF GOR
★ Warner, 1987, PG-13, 89 min. Dir: John "Bud" Cardos. Cast: Urbano Barberini, Jack Palance, Rebecca Ferrati, Donna Denton, Nigel Chipps, Russel Savadier.

Nobody wanted a sequel to *Gor* but since this was shot back to back with the first one we're stuck with it anyway. Handsome mannequin Barberini is back as our hero, Denton is an evil queen, and Palance adds moments of wheezy hilarity as her priestly advisor in this *Conan*-esque rockgut that's already played on *Mystery Science Theater 3000* as simply *Outlaw*.

OVER MY DEAD BODY
See: *The Brain.* (1963)

PAGEMASTER, THE
★★ Fox, 1994, G, 75 min. Dirs: Joe Johnston, Maurice Hunt. Cast: Macaulay Culkin, Christopher

Lloyd, Mel Harris, Ed Begley, Jr., voices of Whoopi Goldberg, Patrick Stewart, Leonard Nimoy, Phil Hartman.

A lonely little kid (Culkin) is sent by a magical librarian (Lloyd, in yet another variation on his *Back to the Future* role) into a cartoon world filled with literary characters who all talk with familiar-sounding celebrity voices. Culkin's scenes were shot nearly two years before the animation and although fairly pleasant this pro-reading kids movie (similar to but not as good as *The Phantom Tollbooth*) was not a hit, crowding the shelves of various video and toy stores with a lot of unwanted tie-in merchandise.

PAJAMA PARTY

★★ Embassy, 1964, NR, 85 min. Dir: Don Weis. Cast: Annette Funicello, Tommy Kirk, Dorothy Lamour, Harvey Lembeck, Elsa Lanchester, Buster Keaton, Jody McCrea, Susan Hart, Donna Loren, Jesse White, Frankie Avalon, Don Rickles.

Fourth in the *Beach Party* series from AIP, this relegates Frankie to a cameo role and changes venue as an indoor PJ party is crashed by an alien (Kirk, in one of his first post-Disney, out-of-the-closet roles) studying "typical" Earth teens—who just happen to be played by actors pushing thirty. Not as much fun as earlier entries but still a nice '60s time capsule, with the usual roster of talented veterans to help things along. Tommy played virtually the same role later that year in *Mars Needs Women*. Look for a very young Teri Garr.

PANIC IN YEAR ZERO

★★★☆ Orion, 1962, NR, 93 min. Dir: Ray Milland. Cast: Ray Milland, Jean Hagen, Frankie Avalon, Mary Mitchell, Joan Freeman, Richard Garland, Scott Peters, Russ Bender, Richard Bakalyan, O. Z. Whitehead.

Milland directs himself in one of the best end-of-the-world movies. Ray is head of the Baldwin clan, who depart on a fishing trip the same morning the Big One is dropped on L.A. Chaos immediately sets in but Mr. Baldwin is determined to hold his family together even though wimpy son Avalon isn't much help and practically every other male survivor they encounter wants to rape hot daughter Mitchell—atomic fallout means some sort of heretofore unknown aphrodisiac or something. By concentrating on the human rather than the special-effects aspects of the story, this manages to impress on its obviously small budget, with assured direction by Milland and solid acting all the way down the line. If only Les Baxter's typically brassy music could have

been replaced with a more sedate, melodic score—by Ronald Stein, for instance. Aka *End of the World*.

PANIC OFFSHORE
See: *The Intruder Within.*

PARASITE

★☆ Paramount, 1982, R, 85 min. Dir: Charles Band. Cast: Robert Glaudini, Demi Moore, Vivian Blaine, Luca Bercovici.

Moore made an inauspicious big-screen debut in this gory, pointless clone of *Alien* and *Mad Max*. Scientist Glaudini (who possesses all the charisma of a pound of liverwurst) experiments with flesh-eating parasites in a desert town where various ancillary characters are chewed up and *Guys and Dolls* star Blaine's head explodes. This made money thanks to some clever 3-D FX not present on the tape, but still isn't very good.

PARIS WHO SLEEPS
See: *The Crazy Ray.*

PEACEMAKER

★★ Fries, 1990, R, 90 min. Dir: Kevin S. Tenny. Cast: Robert Forster, Lance Edwards, Hilary Shepard, Robert Davi, Bert Remsen.

Tenney (*Witchboard*) directs his own low-budget variation on *The Hidden*, with Forster and Edwards as an alien cop and criminal fighting it out on Earth—but which is which? A few novel twists and good acting from Forster but this movie's attempt at sparkling comic dialogue falls painfully flat.

PEANUT BUTTER SOLUTION, THE

★★☆ New World, 1986, PG, 91 min. Dir: Michael Rubbo. Cast: Mathew Mackay, Siluck Saysanasy, Alison Podbrey, Michael Hogan, Michel Maillot, Helen Hughes.

Weirdly likable kid's film in which Mackay gets so scared at a carnival haunted house ride that all his hair falls out. Real ghosts try to help him with a formula derived from peanut butter but this solution only causes more trouble. Imaginative and funny, this Canadian fantasy isn't nearly as cutesy and cloying as many of its American cousins.

PEE-WEE'S BIG ADVENTURE

★★★ Warner, 1985, PG, 90 min. Dir: Tim Burton. Cast: Pee-wee Herman [Paul Reubens], Elizabeth Daily, Mark Holton, Diane Salinger, Tony Bill, Cassandra Peterson, Jan Hooks, Ed Herlihy, Phil Hartman, Monte Landis, Alice Nunn, Professor Toru Tanaka, James Brolin, Morgan Fairchild, Twisted Sister.

Hilarious fantasy road movie stars Pee-wee (a childlike adult) going off in search of his missing bike and encountering various wild adventures. Burton's first feature-length, live-action film, this is highlighted by Pee-wee's big shoe dance to *Tequila,* his encounter with "Large Marge" (Nunn), and a funny spoof at the end on how Hollywood twists "reality" into a more romantic version of the truth. This movie's popularity lead Burton to *Beetlejuice, Edward Scissorhands,* and other kid's films for grown-ups, while Reubens brought Pee-wee to Saturday morning TV for a popular series that was ultimately canceled following the star's arrest for indecent exposure at a porno theater—try making sense out of *that* one.

PEGGY SUE GOT MARRIED

★★★★ Fox, 1986, PG-13, 104 min. Dir: Francis Ford Coppola. Cast: Kathleen Turner, Nicolas Cage, Catherine Hicks, Barry Miller, Jim Carrey, Joan Allen, Kevin J. O'Connor, Barbara Harris, Don Murray, Maureen O'Sullivan, Leon Ames, John Carradine, Lisa Jane Persky, Helen Hunt.

Turner is superb in this time-travel fantasy (owing more to Frank Capra than Robert Zemeckis) about a middle-aged woman transported back in time after passing out at her twenty-five-year high school reunion. Once again a teenager, Turner must decide whether to follow the same course in life or change the future by taking a different path. Some found Cage's performance as Kathleen's boyfriend-husband very grating, but since he's supposed to be a jerk that's the point. A movie far more concerned with emotions than technology, this has no special FX and instead concentrates on characters and feelings; among the many perfect moments are when Turner encounters her long-dead grandparents and when she discovers her selfish beau Cage singing sad love ballads at an other-side-of-the-tracks black nightclub. Originally a Penny Marshall project to star Debra Winger, this remains the most underrated and most atypical film of Coppola's career.

PEOPLE, THE

★★☆ Star Classics, 1972, NR, 74 min. Dir: John Korty. Cast: Kim Darby, William Shatner, Dan Herlihy, Diane Varsi, Laurie Walters.

A rather flat made-for-TV version of a novel (by Zenna Henderson) I can remember reading in high school. A young teacher (Darby) comes to a small, Amish-like rural community and eventually discovers that the backward mountain folk are actually extraterrestrials . Some good atmosphere and on-target casting but the approach taken to the material is too vague to really work.

PEOPLE THAT TIME FORGOT, THE

★★☆ Embassy, 1977, PG, 90 min. Dir: Kevin Connor. Cast: Patrick Wayne, Doug McClure, Sarah Douglas, Dana Gillespie, Thorley Walters, Shane Rimmer.

This sequel to *The Land That Time Forgot* is actually better, with less fakey FX and funnier characters. The plot is a reworking of *Beneath the Planet of the Apes,* with Wayne (right after he did *Sinbad and the Eye of the Tiger*) leading an expedition to the lost prehistoric continent to rescue McClure from a city of volcano-worshipping savages. Oh, and there're some dinosaurs, too. This Edgar Rice Burroughs flick was the last movie produced by Britain's Amicus Productions. The title, by the way, is grammatically incorrect; it should be *The People Whom Time Forgot* or simply *The People Time Forgot*—oh, never mind.

PEOPLE WHO OWN THE DARK, THE

★★ Star Classics, 1975, R, 85 min. Dir: Leon Klimovsky. Cast: Paul Naschy, Maria Perschy, Alberto de Mendoza, Nadiuska, Teresa Gimpera, Julia Saly.

Prolific Spanish horror king Naschy's only science fiction film, this variation on *The Last Man on Earth* finds a group of wealthy Satanists trapped in a house after the Big One has been dropped and somehow transformed most of the population into blind homicidal maniacs. Some suspenseful moments and an unexpected ending along with all the usual bad dubbed dialogue, including this classic Naschy comeback line: "Yeah, and the Easter Bunny shits jelly beans!" Arnold, eat your heart out. Aka *Planeta Ciego (Blind Planet).*

PERSEUS AND THE GORGON'S HEAD
See: *Clash of the Titans.*

PERSEUS THE INVINCIBLE
See: *Medusa Against the Son of Hercules.*

PETER PAN

★★★ Goodtimes, 1960, NR, 100 min. Dir: Vincent J. Donehue. Cast: Mary Martin, Cyril Ritchard, Sondra Lee, Margalo Gilmore, Maureen Bailey.

This 1960 filmed-for-NBC-TV version of the Broadway hit became something of an annual TV classic much in the manner of *The Wizard of Oz,* though it's not quite as good. Once you get past the idea that it's a middle-aged woman in the role of Peter, the young boy who won't grow up, Martin is really good as the boisterous, magical Pan and Ritchard has flamboyant fun with the role of Captain Hook (originated on the stage by Boris Karloff). The musical numbers include "Never-Never Land," "I've Gotta Crow," and "I'm Flying."

PETE'S DRAGON
★★ Disney, 1977, G, 134 min. Dir: Don Chaffey. Cast: Helen Reddy, Jim Dale, Mickey Rooney, Shelley Winters, Red Buttons, Sean Marshall, Jim Backus, voice of Charlie Callas.

Overlong Disney fantasy that attempted, unsuccessfully, to recapture the *Mary Poppins* experience—it's not even up to *Bedknobs and Broomsticks*. An Irwin Allen-type cast mugs its way through the tale of a young boy (Marshall) whose best friend is a dragon (played by an animated cartoon and voiced by Callas) sought as a circus attraction by villains Dale, Rooney, and Winters. A few laughs and one good song ("Candle on the Water") but this is mostly for those who'll sit through *anything* Disney. Beware shorter prints—on second thought, that may help.

PHANTOM, THE
★★☆ Paramount, 1996, PG, 101 min. Dir: Simon Wincer. Cast: Billy Zane, Kristy Swanson, Treat Williams, Catherine Zeta Jones, Casey Siemaszko, James Remar, Patrick McGoohan, Samantha Eggar.

Zane looks great as the masked and purple-tighted superhero the Phantom in this lavish adaptation of the Lee Falk comic strip character, originally made for the screen as a serial with Tom Tyler in the '40s. Known as "The Ghost Who Walks," the Phantom seems immortal because a son follows in his father's footsteps in the role with each new generation. Here our hero battles villain Williams and his pirate gang, who are after some ancient skulls with mystical powers. Zane is first-rate but Williams overdoes it and the plot is needlessly confused and hard to follow. Great 1930s period atmosphere and special FX and a fine support cast (including McGoohan as the Phantom's dad), but a stronger script and more assured direction are definitely in order here.

PHANTOM CREEPS, THE
★★★ Sinister Cinema, 1939, NR, 180 min. Dirs: Ford Beebe, Saul A. Goodkind. Cast: Bela Lugosi, Robert Kent, Dorothy Arnold, Regis Toomey, Roy Barcroft, Edward Van Sloan.

This delirious twelve-chapter serial features Bela at his best. Possessing a huge, snarly-faced robot (that mostly just lumbers around for effect), mechanical spider-bombs, and an invisibility belt, Lugosi is a mad inventor who's out to conquer the world. He doesn't succeed, not so much from intervention from government agent Kent and reporter Arnold, but because of his own dumb luck. One of the reasons they invented the chapter play in the first place, I'm certain, is this is great, cheesy fun,

with stock footage from *The Invisible Ray* and stock music from *Bride of Frankenstein*. Aka *The Shadow Creeps* and also out in a shortened feature version, parts of this have played on *Mystery Science Theater 3000*. "How fortunate; this will simplify everything!"

PHANTOM EMPIRE, THE
★★★ Sinister Cinema, 1935, NR, 240 min. Dirs: Otto Bower, B. Reeves Eason. Cast: Gene Autry, Frankie Darro, Betsy King Ross, Dorothy Christy, Wheeler Oakman, Smiley Burnette.

Another great anything-goes serial, with Autry (as himself) discovering an underground civilization beneath his ranch. The empire is ruled by evil queen Christy and her tin-can robot guards and Gene finds the time for a song or two in between dare-doing. Total hilarity, also out in a feature version called *Radio Ranch*.

PHANTOM EMPIRE, THE
★☆ Prism, 1986, R, 90 min. Dir: Fred Olen Ray. Cast: Ross Hagen, Susan Stokey, Dawn Wildsmith, Sybil Danning, Jeffrey Combs, Robert Quarry, Michelle Bauer, Russ Tamblyn.

They share the same title and a few plot similarities but this is no remake of the old serial—for one thing, the Gene Autry version didn't include any topless Amazon women. Explorers searching for treasure in some underground caves encounter a monster, cannibals, dinosaur footage from *Planet of the Dinosaurs,* and warrior queen Danning. Worth seeing, maybe, for its cast (with Tamblyn in a brief, John Carradine-like cameo) but still pretty bad.

PHANTOM FROM SPACE
★☆ Goodtimes, 1953, NR, 72 min. Dir: W. Lee Wilder. Cast: Ted Cooper, Noreen Nash, James Seay, Rudolph Anders, Dick Sands.

Sands is the title phantom, a bald barbell boy in a deep-sea diving suit who can render himself invisible and spends a night terrorizing Los Angeles's Griffith Park. Dull low-budgeter with a few stray laughs (like the invisible phantom clumsily trying to carry off heroine Nash) amidst all the tedium. Director Wilder's fascination for mundane small talk might have worked for a drama about civil servants but here it just gives you an itchy fast-forward finger.

PHANTOM MEETS THE RETURN OF DR. MABUSE, THE
See: *The Return of Dr. Mabuse.*

PHANTOM PLANET, THE
★★ Sinister Cinema, 1961, NR, 82 min. Dir: William Marshall. Cast: Dean Fredericks, Coleen Gray, Tony

Dexter, Dolores Faith, Francis X. Bushman, Richard Kiel.

There's a lot going on in this complicated sci-fi quickie but it never really makes the most of all its disparate elements. Earth astronaut Fredericks lands on a planetoid, where he shrinks to twelve inches and aids the tiny inhabitants in their war against a race of dog-faced monsters. There's an awful lot of imagination on display here; too bad the direction, special FX, makeup, and set design are all thumbs.

PHANTOM TOLLBOOTH, THE
★★★ MGM/UA, 1970, G, 90 min. Dirs: Chuck Jones, David Monohan, Abe Levitow. Cast: Butch Patrick, voices of Hans Conreid, Mel Blanc, June Foray, Daws Butler, Candy Candido.

Bored kid Patrick (Eddie Munster himself) is whisked into an animated fantasy world where letters and numbers are at war. This sophisticated kid's picture, based on a book by Norton Juster, may be too heady for the very young but the thoughtful plot is rewarding and the animation and vocal acting first-rate.

PHASE IV
★★☆ Paramount, 1973, PG, 86 min. Dir: Saul Bass. Cast: Nigel Davenport, Lynne Frederick, Michael Murphy, Alan Gifford, Helen Horton, Robert Henderson.

Ants in the Arizona desert become superintelligent and begin plotting world conquest. Can entomologists Davenport and Murphy stop them? The only film directed by title designer Bass, this has striking visual qualities but is dramatically muddled and has an especially perplexing, *2001*-type ending.

PHILADELPHIA EXPERIMENT, THE
★★★ Starmaker, 1984, PG, 102 min. Dir: Stewart Raffill. Cast: Michael Paré, Nancy Allen, Bobby Di Cicco, Louise Latham, Eric Christmas, Kene Holliday.

In 1944 a mysterious experiment at the Philadelphia naval yard projects sailors Paré and Di Cicco ahead in time forty years. Paré and modern gal Allen fall in love while they try to save the world from the malfunctioning time warp. The original story, written by John Carpenter (who was also originally to direct), has its fair share of holes, but a likable cast and a nice concentration on emotion over pyrotechnics help make this one of the better '80s time-travel flicks.

PHILADELPHIA EXPERIMENT 2, THE
★★☆ Vidmark Entertainment, 1993, PG-13, 98 min. Dir: Stephen Cornwell. Cast: Brad Johnson, Marjean

Richard Kiel as the less-than-scary alien of The Phantom Planet *(1961).*

Holden, Gerrit Graham, John Christian Graas.

This overcomplicated sequel has some good ideas but is too muddled to really work. Square-jawed Johnson (in the Michael Paré role) discovers that time is still being altered; when a stealth bomber is sent back to the '40s and lands in Nazi hands, they win the war and take over the world! More like *Back to the Future II* than the original *Philly Experiment* but not without some merit.

PHOENIX THE WARRIOR
★☆ Sony, 1987, NR, 90 min. Dir: Robert Hayes. Cast: Persis Khambatta, Kathleen Kinmont, James Emery, Peggy Sands.

A feminist postnuke movie in which germ warfare kills off nearly all the males on the planet. Women—including title character Kin-

161

Judi Meredith and Florence Marley are ready to rumble in Planet of Blood *(1966).*

mont—train as warriors and one guy (Emery) is discovered alive and seen as the only hope to continue mankind. Lame stuff without the sense of humor to pull this sort of story off.

PLAGUE DOGS, THE

★★★ Nelson, 1982, NR, 86 min. Dir: Martin Rosen. Voices: John Hurt, Christopher Benjamin, James Bolam, Nigel Hawthorne, Warren Mitchell, Judy Geeson.

Unusual animation for adults and older kids based on a book by Richard Adams. Two dogs escape from a medical lab and find freedom until it is revealed that they've been exposed to the bubonic plague. Not exactly *Lady and the Tramp,* this beautifully animated followup to *Watership Down* isn't for everyone but is an intelligent, well-crafted antidote to stuff like *All Dogs Go to Heaven* and all those treacly *Benji* and *Beethoven* movies.

PLANETA BURG

★★★ Sinister Cinema, 1962, NR, 90 min. Dir: Pavel Klushantsev. Cast: Kyunna Ignatova, Gennadi Vernov, Georgi Zhonov.

This is that familiar-looking Russian sci-fi flick whose stock FX footage turned up in so many Roger Corman quickies like *Voyage to a Prehistoric Planet.* Russians land on Venus and search for life, though it isn't until after they leave that an eerily beautiful Venusian reveals itself. Slow but full of the sort of visual cleverness too few American sci-fi films possess. Aka *Planet of Storms* and *Cosmonauts on Venus.*

PLANET EARTH

★★ Unicorn, 1974, NR, 74 min. Dir: Marc Daniels. Cast: John Saxon, Diana Muldaur, Janet Margolin, Ted Cassidy, Johana DeWinter, Christopher Gary, Aaron Kincaid, Majel Barrett.

Another failed Gene Roddenberry series pilot, this is basically just a reworking of *Genesis II*—reworked again as *Strange New World*—with '70s guy Saxon awakening after decades of suspended animation to discover a future world where Amazonian women rule and men are slaves. The cast is good and there are some effective touches of humor but this is still pretty silly stuff.

PLANET OF BLOOD

★★ Sinister Cinema, 1966, NR, 78 min. Dir: Curtis Harrington. Cast: John Saxon, Basil Rathbone, Judi Meredith, Dennis Hopper, Florence Marley, Forrest J. Ackerman.

Another *Alien* antecedent, this one about a rescue mission to Mars that encounters a seductive, green-skinned alien (Marley) who turns out to be a bloodthirsty vampire. Harrington does a good job of blending his quickly shot U.S. footage with haunting scenes from the Russian space epic *Meshte Nastreshu (A Dream Come True)* (1963) and the cast is an exceptional one for such a cheapie. Too bad the pace is so slow and too many plot developments are advanced via dialogue rather than action. Aka *Queen of Blood.*

PLANET OF HORRORS

See: *Galaxy of Terror.*

PLANET OF STORMS

See: *Planeta Burg.*

PLANET OF THE APES

★★★★ Fox, 1968, PG, 111 min. Dir: Franklin J. Schaffner. Cast: Charlton Heston, Roddy McDowall, Kim Hunter, Maurice Evans, Linda Harrison, James Whitmore, James Daly, Woodrow Parfey.

Rod Serling coscripted this classic version of Pierre Boileau's novel *Monkey Planet*, featuring Heston (who's rarely been better) as an astronaut rocketed into a distant future where talking apes hunt and cage mute, animalistic humans. The *Star Wars* of its day, this became a phenomenon of late '60s pop culture and won a special Oscar for its outstanding John Chambers makeup design. Stunning photography by Leon Shamroy and eerie music by Jerry Goldsmith. Followed by four sequels—beginning with *Beneath the Planet of the Apes*—and a pair of television series—one live action and one animated. Currently a hot property for remake status with strange bedfellows Arnold Schwarzenegger and Oliver Stone involved.

"Who's the damn dirty ape now, huh, Chuck?" Charlton Heston and friends in Planet of the Apes *(1968).*

PLANET OF THE DINOSAURS
★★ Goodtimes, 1978, PG, 85 min. Dir: James K. Shea. Cast: James Whitworth, Pamela Bottaro, Chuck Pennington, Charlotte Speer, Louie Lawless, Harvey Shain.

If movies could be rated on special FX alone, this would be a four-star winner. Sadly, though, the great stop-motion work goes completely unsupported in the story, direction, and acting departments. Stranded on a distant planet inhabited by prehistoric beasts, a bunch of Earth astronauts realize they're there for the long haul and try to make a new life for themselves. The trick photography and model work, supervised by Doug Beswick, is terrific but the poorly handled story and amateurish acting make this almost as hard to endure as *The Crater Lake Monster.*

PLANET OF THE VAMPIRES
★★★ Orion, 1965, NR, 86 min. Dir: Mario Bava. Cast: Barry Sullivan, Norma Bengell, Angel Aranda, Evi Marandi.

Italian horror great Bava brings real pizzazz to this *very* low-budget Neapolitan space movie. Sullivan and crew are menaced by evil alien spirits who inhabit the bodies of the dead and turn them into vampires. Compensating for the poor dubbing and repetitive action, the commanding use of lighting and set design succeed in creating a truly alien atmosphere of colored mists and bizarre rock formations. Like *It! The Terror from Beyond Space* and *Planet of Blood,* this is one of the obvious inspirations for *Alien,* complete with a scene of the astronauts discovering a derelict alien spacecraft and the enormous skeletons of its dead crew. Aka *Terrore Nello Spazio (Terror in Space)* and *The Demon Planet.*

PLANET ON THE PROWL
★★ Monterey, 1964, NR, 80 min. Dir: Anthony Dawson [Antonio Margheriti]. Cast: Giacomo Rossi-Stuart, Ombretta Colli, Helina Zalewska, Peter Martell, Archie Savage, Renato Baldini.

Rossi-Stuart leads an expedition to investigate a rogue planet threatening the Earth only to discover that the "planet" is a huge, gaseous alien life form. A few interesting plot twists and visual touches help this run-of-the-mill Italian sci-fi flick. Aka *Missione Planeta Errante (Operation Wandering Planet)* and *War Between the Planets.*

PLANETS AGAINST US
★★ Sinister Cinema, 1961, NR, 85 min. Dir: Romano Ferrara. Cast: Jany Clair, Michel Lemoine, Maria Pia Luzi, Otello Toso.

French-Italian oddity about an alien with hypnotic powers constructing an army of robots to conquer the world. A few interesting visual flashes (like the villain reducing humans to dust with a touch) in the midst of a great deal of muddle. Aka *Le Monstre Aux Yeux Verts/Il Monstro Dagli Verdi (The Monster with Green Eyes)* and *Hands of a Killer.*

PLAN 9 FROM OUTER SPACE
★★★ Rhino, 1958, NR, 79 min. Dir: Edward D. Wood, Jr. Cast: Bela Lugosi, Vampira, Tor Johnson, Lyle Talbot, Gregory Walcott, Mona MacKinnon, Dudley Manlove, Joanna Lee, Duke Moore, Paul Marco, John "Bunny" Breckinridge, Criswell.

What more can be said of this classic of bad movie making about endlessly speechifying aliens who use a zombie army of three (the two-years-dead Bela, Vampira, and big Tor) in an attempt to take over the world. Easily the most famous Z movie of all time, this is made with just enough twisted talent, or something, to be a lot more fun and far more watchable than other, similar flicks like *The Creeping Terror* and *The Beast of Yucca Flats.* From the bombastic Criswell narration to the mismatched footage and classically stilted dialogue ("All you of Earth are stupid! Stupid!"), this is the Wood movie to catch. Aka *Grave Robbers from Outer Space.*

POPEYE
★★ Paramount, 1980, PG, 114 min. Dir: Robert Altman. Cast: Robin Williams, Shelley Duvall, Ray Walston, Paul Smith, Paul Dooley, Richard Libertini, Linda Hunt, Wesley Ivan Hurt.

The squinty sailor man searches for his missing dad in this big-bucks musical in which almost nothing works. Williams, in excellent makeup, mutters his way through the title role and Altman doesn't have a clue as how to stage a musical production number (which is just as well since none of Harry Nilsson's songs are especially memorable) but Duvall (as Olive Oyl), Smith (as Bluto), and Dooley (as Wimpy) are perfectly cast and the intricate production design often successfully recaptures the look of the old Max Fleischer cartoons on which this is based.

PORTRAIT OF JENNIE
★★★ CBS/Fox, 1948, NR, 86 min. Dir: William Dieterle. Cast: Jennifer Jones, Joseph Cotten, Ethel Barrymore, Lillian Gish, Cecil Kellaway, David Wayne, Henry Hull, Florence Bates.

Haunting love story about a failed artist (Cotten) inspired by his love for a ghost (Jones) doomed to relive her entire life and drowning death in the space of a year. Producer David O.

Selznick tried to bloat this gentle fantasy into another *Gone with the Wind* with an Oscar-winning special FX climax (tinted green in its original release) but this works best during its quieter moments, thanks to the excellent cast and Dieterle's sensitive direction. Aka *Tidal Wave*.

PRANCER

★★★ Nelson, 1989, G, 102 min. Dir: John Hancock. Cast: Sam Elliott, Rebecca Harrell, Cloris Leachman, Rutanya Alda, Abe Vigoda, Ariana Richards, John Joseph Duda, Michael Constantine.

Surprisingly tough-hearted Christmas fantasy, with Harrell as a motherless farm girl who becomes convinced that the wounded reindeer she's nursing back to health is the renowned flying Prancer of Santa's team fame. An interesting look at the loss of childhood innocence. Elliott gives a good account of himself in an atypical role as the girl's downtrodden father.

PREDATOR

★★☆ Fox, 1987, R, 107 min. Dir: John McTiernan. Cast: Arnold Schwarzenegger, Carl Weathers, Elpida Carrillo, Jesse Ventura, R. G. Armstrong, Kevin Peter Hall.

A muscles-in-the-jungle *Rambo* clone turns into an unacknowledged remake of *Without Warning* as Central American jungle mercenaries run into a vicious alien hunter after human prey. Popular *Alien* variation without much suspense (do you really think they'd kill Arnold off?) but good action highlights.

PREDATOR 2

★★☆ Fox, 1990, R, 108 min. Dir: Stephen Hopkins. Cast: Danny Glover, Gary Busey, Maria Conchita Alonso, Rueben Blades, Bill Paxton, Kevin Peter Hall.

This time the Predator is in L.A., where cop Glover (practically parodying his Lethal

Kevin Peter Hall takes L.A. by storm in Predator 2 *(1990).*

Weapon role) takes it on after the murder of partner Blades. Slightly better than the original, with an improved cast and some humor (including an *Alien* in-joke), but still too predictable to provide much honest tension.

PREHYSTERIA

★★☆ Paramount, 1992, PG, 86 min. Dirs: Albert Band, Charles Band. Cast: Austin O'Brien, Brett Cullen, Samantha Mills, Colleen Morris.

Six tiny dinosaurs hatch from eggs brought home by an archeologist (Cullen) and befriend his kids in this pretty enjoyable comic monster movie aimed at the young set. Dave Allen animated the dinos and O'Brien went on to the megaflop *Last Action Hero* while this proved a popular enough renter to inspire a couple of sequels.

PREHYSTERIA 2

★★ Paramount, 1994, PG, 81 min. Dir: Albert Band. Cast: Kevin R. Connors, Jennifer Harte, Dean Scofield, Owen Bush, Larry Hankin.

This quickie sequel mostly just rehashes situations from the first film, with an added *Hand That Rocks the Cradle/Addams Family Values* subplot about an evil nanny trying to pack our young hero off to military school. The special FX keep you watching.

PREHYSTERIA 3

★★ Paramount, 1995, PG, 85 min. Dir: Julian Breen. Cast: Fred Willard, Whitney Anderson, Pam Matteson, Dave Buzzotta, Matt Letscher, Bruce Weitz.

This time the dinos are at a miniature golf course, which they help the young heroes save from their greedy uncle. The offbeat setting helps, but this series ran out of creative juice with the conclusion of the first entry.

PREHISTORIC WOMEN

★ Rhino, 1950, NR, 70 min. Dir: Gregg Tallas. Cast: Laurette Luez, Mara Lynn, Allan Nixon, Joan Shawlee, Judy Landon, Johann Peturrson.

Cavegirls with perfect makeup and hair styles catch fish with their teeth and search for husbands in this campy low-budgeter set in 20,000 B.C. No dinosaurs per se, but the gals do fight a clunky-looking dragon and are menaced by Peturrson playing a hairy giant. Pretty awful, but it's still more fun than *Clan of the Cave Bear*.

PREHISTORIC WORLD

See: *Teenage Caveman*.

PRELUDE TO A KISS

★★ Fox, 1992, PG-13, 106 min. Dir: Norman René.

Cast: Alec Baldwin, Meg Ryan, Kathy Bates, Ned Beatty, Patty Duke, Sidney Walker, Stanley Tucci, Annie Golden.

Baldwin and Ryan fall in love and quickly marry, but on the honeymoon Alec is horrified to discover that Meg is possessed by the soul of a dying old man looking to be young again. This romantic fantasy may be the oddest of the myriad body switch movies that proliferated in the wake of *Big*. The actors (especially Walker as the old man) are first-rate but this AIDS allegory (based on a Tony-winning play by Craig Lucas and director René and also starring Baldwin and Walker) is too heavy-handed and contrived to really work.

PRESENCE, THE

★★ Vidmark Entertainment, 1992, PG-13, 90 min. Dir: Tommy Lee Wallace. Cast: Lisa Banes, Gary Graham, Kathy Ireland, Joe Lara, Richard Beymer, June Lockhart.

TV movie originally broadcast as *Danger Island* and probably meant to be a series pilot. An Irwin Allen-type group of plane crash survivors try to find their way off an uncharted island, where a deserted laboratory in an old house exposes the group to a disease that mutates several of them into monsters. This mild derivation of *Leviathan* has an interesting cast but the construction is too leisurely to build the required suspense or excitement.

PRINCESS BRIDE, THE

★★★ Nelson, 1987, PG, 98 min. Dir: Rob Reiner. Cast: Cary Elwes, Robin Wright, Mandy Patinkin, Chris Sarandon, Billy Crystal, Carol Kane, Peter Falk, Fred Savage, Wallace Shawn, Christopher Guest, Peter Cook, Andre the Giant.

A frustrated baby-sitting grandfather (Falk) tells his grandson (Savage) a revisionist fairy tale about a beautiful princess (Wright) who is rescued from her unhappy betrothal to a jerky prince (Sarandon) by a trio of pirates and her one true love (Elwes). William Goldman adapted his popular book into this funny, fast-paced comic fantasy, with spirited turns from Patinkin, Sarandon, Crystal, and Kane (the latter two in a hilarious cameo) and clever direction by Reiner.

PRINCESS WARRIOR, THE

★ Vista Street, 1990, R, 84 min. Dir: Lindsay Norgard. Cast: Sharon Lee Jones, Mark Pacific, Dana Fredsti.

Bum direct-to-video sci-fi comedy (I think it's a comedy) about a buxom alien woman (Jones) in L.A., where she is battled by her evil sister and her followers. Since its highlight is a wet T-shirt contest, you know exactly where this one is coming from.

PRISONERS OF THE LOST UNIVERSE

★★ VCL, 1982, PG, 94 min. Dir: Terry Marcel. Cast: Kay Lenz, Richard Hatch, John Saxon, Dawn Abraham, Peter O'Farrell, Ray Charleson.

Colorful but dumb made-for-cable pic, with Lenz and Hatch as earthlings accidentally transported to a hostile planet where sadistic warlord Saxon holds sway. Everything but the kitchen sink is chucked into the brew, but it's put together too pedestrianly to work.

PROGRAMMED TO KILL

★☆ Media, 1987, R, 91 min. Dir: Allan Holzman. Cast: Robert Ginty, Sandahl Bergman, James Booth, Louise Caire Clark.

A good cast tries to do what it can with this clichéd actioner about a murdered female terrorist (Bergman) reconstructed as a half-robot antiterrorist superweapon. This feminist *Robocop* had potential (and predates *Eve of Destruction* to a certain extent) but is defeated by its paltry budget and lack of imagination. Aka *Retaliator*.

PROJECT ALIEN

★☆ Vidmark Entertainment, 1989, R, 92 min. Dir: Frank Shields. Cast: Michael Nouri, Darlanne Fluegel, Maxwell Caulfield, Charles Durning.

Nouri, an American investigating a deadly meteor shower over Norway, discovers an alien visitation and subsequent cover-up. Dull nonthriller somewhat similar to the later Charlie Sheen vehicle *The Arrival*. Aka *Fatal Sky*.

PROJECT MOONBASE

★★ Sinister Cinema, 1953, NR, 63 min. Dir: Richard Talmadge. Cast: Donna Martell, Ross Ford, James Craven, Hayden Rourke, Barbara Morrison.

Robert A. Heinlein coscripted (though you'd never know it) this Robert Lippert quickie involving a space station on the moon in the distant future of 1970. This tries to make some headway by casting the moon base commander and U.S. president as women but is so otherwise condescending that the feminist subtext hardly matters. The first-wedding-on-the-moon climax is a highlight.

PROJECT: SHADOWCHASER

★★☆ Prism Entertainment, 1992, R, 97 min. Dir: John Eyres. Cast: Martin Kove, Meg Foster, Frank Zagarino, Paul Koslo, Joss Ackland.

Maybe my tolerance level is lowering drastically but I actually rather liked this opportunistic combination of *Die Hard, The Terminator,* and *Demolition Man*—which hadn't even been made yet! Kove is a cop brought out of cryogenic freezing to save president's daughter Foster from terrorists and a killer android (Zagarino) in a big-city high rise. Kove, whose career has included everything from soft core porn to costarring on the *Cagney and Lacey* TV show, is a likable hero and some of the action is good in this predictable but fun sci-fi action flick.

PROJECT X

★★ CBS/Fox, 1987, PG, 107 min. Dir: Jonathan Kaplan. Cast: Matthew Broderick, Helen Hunt, Bill Sadler, Johnny Ray McGhee, Jonathan Stark, Robin Gammell, Jean Smart, Dick Miller.

Curiously wrong-headed "message" movie about an air force smart ass (a well-cast Broderick) assigned to care for a group of superintelligent chimpanzees (who communicate via sign language), which he discovers are due to die in scientific experiments. This tries to mix its serious antivivisectional message with some cute comedy and romance and a touch of sci-fi/fantasy but never really seems to know what sort of movie it really wants to be. Hunt has appeal in an early leading role as the animal psychologist who tries to help Matt save the chimps.

PROTOTYPE

★★☆ King Bee, 1982, NR, 96 min. Dir: David Greene. Cast: Christopher Plummer, David Morse, Frances Sternhagen, Arthur Hill, James Sutorius, Stephen Elliott.

Richard Levinson and William Link (who created *Colombo* among other popular TV characters) scripted this well-intentioned if rather preachy TV movie. Plummer is good as a Nobel Prize-winning scientist who creates an artificial human being (Morse) that he eventually steals away from the U.S. government when he discovers that his creation is to be conditioned into the ultimate soldier. Low-key but maybe worth a look.

PROTOTYPE X29A

★★★ Vidmark Entertainment, 1992, R, 98 min. Dir: Phillip J. Roth. Cast: Lane Lenhart, Brenda Swanson, Robert Tossberg, Mitchell Cox.

An interestingly directed if somewhat oppressive and confusing futuristic thriller about a lady scientist who wants to re-create a guy in a wheelchair as a powerful cyborg, and a sad hooker who discovers that she too is a cyborg. This doesn't always work but has a lot of imagination and some impressive budget FX.

PULSE
★★ RCA/Columbia, 1987, PG-13, 91 min. Dir: Paul Golding. Cast: Cliff De Young, Roxanne Hart, Joey Lawrence, Charles Tyner.

A pre-*Tiger Beat* Lawrence is a kid trying to deal with his divorced dad's new marriage while being menaced by self-activating electrical appliances in this silly sci-fi/horror flick. Good special FX and photography help carry a weak, confusing storyline. Veteran character actor Tyner has a good role.

PUMA MAN, THE
★ Parade, 1979, R, 80 min. Dir: Alberto De Martino. Cast: Donald Pleasence, Sydne Rome, Walter George Alton.

Pathetic Italian superhero adventure in which the title character is given superpowers by an alien mask and battles evil monk Pleasence. Bottom-of-the-barrel thrills wasting the talents of Pleasence and the lovely Rome.

PUPPETMASTERS, THE
★★★☆ Hollywood Pictures, 1994, R, 108 min. Dir: Stuart Orme. Cast: Donald Sutherland, Eric Thal, Julie Warner, Yaphet Kotto, Richard Belzer, Andrew Robinson, Keith David, Will Patton, Marshall Bell, Tom Mason.

Top-flight adaptation of Robert A. Heinlein's classic, influential novel about an invasion of Iowa by alien slugs who ride the back and control the minds of human hosts they manipulate like puppets. Although this eschews the futuristic setting of the book, it still manages to stick remarkably close to the original work to good effect; it's up and running from the first scene on and almost never lets up. Colin Towns's piano-dominated musical score is nicely old-fashioned and the cast is nimble—particularly a spry Sutherland in one of his best roles in years. Originally filmed (more or less) as *The Brain Eaters* and aka *Robert A. Heinlein's The Puppetmasters*.

PURPLE MONSTER STRIKES!, THE
★★ Nostalgia Merchant, 1945, NR, 260 min. Dirs: Spencer Gordon Bennet, Fred C. Brannon. Cast: Dennis Moore, Linda Stirling, Roy Barcroft, James Craven, Emmett Vogan, Kenne Duncan.

Routine serial about an invading alien (Barcroft) out to take over the Earth with a destructive meteor. Despite the presence of serial heroine par excellence Stirling, there isn't much out of the ordinary to grab your attention here. Also available in an edited feature version called *D-Day on Mars*.

PURPLE PEOPLE EATER
★★ Media, 1988, PG, 87 min. Dir: Linda Shayne. Cast: Neil Patrick Harris, Ned Beatty, Shelley Winters, Peggy Lipton, James Houghton, Thora Birch, Molly Cheek, Little Richard, Chubby Checker, Sheb Wooley.

Veteran exploitation actress Shayne directs this silly kid's movie inspired by the old song (whose composer-performer Wooley appears in a cameo), with a pre-*Doogie Howser* Harris as a young teen befriended by a friendly alien (who sort of looks like an extraterrestrial Barney the dinosaur). Together they help oldsters Beatty and Winters and form their own rock band. For easy-to-please rugrats only.

PURPLE ROSE OF CAIRO, THE
★★★☆ Orion, 1985, PG, 82 min. Dir: Woody Allen. Cast: Mia Farrow, Jeff Daniels, Danny Aiello, Dianne Wiest, Van Johnson, Zoe Caldwell, Milo O'Shea, Edward Herrmann, John Wood, Glenne Headly.

One of the Woodman's best films, this Depression-era fantasy stars Farrow as an unhappily married '30s housewife who escapes her humdrum existence by daily trips to the movies. When movie hero Daniels actually walks off the screen and into her life, Mia learns a surprisingly harsh lesson on the consequences of living in a fantasy world. Farrow and Daniels are great and Aiello has a showy role as Mia's abusive husband, but some may find this film's mixture of comedy (the best scenes show the other characters in the movie Daniels escapes from trying to carry on the plot without him) and bittersweet drama somewhat off-putting.

QUANTUM LEAP
★★☆ MCA/Universal, 1989–93, NR, 46 min. per episode. Dirs: David Hemmings, Mike Vejar, Alan J. Levi, Donald P. Bellisario, others. Cast: Scott Bakula, Dean Stockwell, Jennifer Runyon, Janine Turner, Bruce McGill, John Cullum, Jason Priestley, Tia Carrere, John Allen Nelson, David Newson.

This well-intentioned but somewhat full-of-itself sci-fi TV series has a good premise (scientist Bakula travels through time, possessing various individuals—both men and women—in an effort to improve or save their lives) but was often too cute for its own good. Still, it became something of a cult hit (especially among female fans) and some of the episodes, especially the one where Scott becomes Lee Harvey Oswald, are clever and well done. Stockwell has a showy role as a helpful hologram who gives Bakula advice and tries to keep him from screwing up history too badly. The pilot episode runs 96 minutes; all others are 46 minutes long.

QUARANTINE

★★★ Republic, 1989, R, 92 min. Dir: Charles Wilkinson. Cast: Beatrice Boepple, Garwin Sanford, Jerry Wasserman.

Interesting AIDS allegory about a world of the future where a power-mad senator quarantines all those suffering from a deadly disease and creates two distinct societies of the oppressed and the oppressors. This above-average Canadian quickie is well worth the effort.

QUATERMASS

See: *The Quatermass Conclusion.*

QUATERMASS AND THE PIT

★★★☆ Sinister Cinema, 1958, NR, 180 min. Dir: Rudolph Cartier. Cast: Andre Morell, Cec Linder, Christine Finn, Anthony Bushell, Michael Ripper.

Nigel Kneale's brilliant BBC-TV serial (the third in the series) about an ancient Martian spaceship unearthed beneath the streets of London and the discovery by Professor Quatermass (Morell) that mankind owes its evolution to surgical intervention from the now long-dead Martian race. Marred somewhat by cheap videotape recording and some flat TV production values, but Kneale's thoughtful writing and the first-rate cast help make this one of the finest sci-fi pieces ever to come out of Great Britain. Remade by Hammer Films as a feature in 1967, which was retitled *Five Million Years to Earth* for U.S. release the following year.

QUATERMASS CONCLUSION, THE

★★ HBO, 1980, PG, 107 min. Dir: Piers Haggard. Cast: John Mills, Simon MacCorkindale, Barbara Kellerman, Margaret Tyzack, Brewster Mason.

Half-baked attempt to update Nigel Kneale's Quatermass series, with Mills in good form as the aging scientist out to stop an alien ray that's destroying the youth of the world. Mills and a halfway interesting premise are defeated by poor production values and a lack of decent special FX. Aka *Quatermass.*

QUATERMASS EXPERIMENT, THE

See: *The Quatermass Xperiment.*

QUATERMASS II

See: *Enemy From Space.*

QUATERMASS II: ENEMY FROM SPACE

See: *Enemy from Space.*

QUATERMASS XPERIMENT, THE

★★★ MGM/UA, 1955, NR, 81 min. Dir: Val Guest. Cast: Brian Donlevy, Jack Warner, Margia Dean, Richard Wordsworth, Lionel Jeffries, Howard Lang, Gordon Jackson, Thora Hird.

The first big international success for Britain's Hammer Films, this tense sci-fi/horror thriller (adapted by Nigel Kneale from his popular BBC television serial) involves a rocket crash and the lone survivor (Wordsworth) slowly mutating into a formless creature that absorbs the life from everything it touches. Donlevy is solid as the no-nonsense Professor Quatermass, tracking the monster throughout London until a final confrontation in St. Paul's Cathedral. Guest does a good job at imaginatively masking this film's tiny budget and Wordsworth is effective as the silent, doomed astronaut. Originally released in the states in a cut version called *The Creeping Unknown*, this video version restores three minutes of footage and the original British title. Look for Jane Asher (later a Paul McCartney girlfriend, and Vincent Price's costar in *The Masque of the Red Death*) as the little girl Wordsworth encounters at the shipyard. Aka *The Quatermass Experiment.* Sequels: *Enemy from Space, Five Million Years to Earth,* and *The Quatermass Conclusion.*

QUEEN OF BLOOD

See: *Planet of Blood.*

QUEEN OF OUTER SPACE

★★☆ Fox, 1958, NR, 79 min. Dir: Edward L. Bernds. Cast: Zsa Zsa Gabor, Eric Fleming, Laurie Mitchell, Paul Birch, Patrick Waltz, Dave Willock, Lisa Davis, Kathy Marlowe, Tania Velia, Lynn Cartwright.

A quintessential '50s camp classic has Fleming leading a team of astronauts to the planet Venus, where masked, disfigured man-hater Mitchell is opposed by Hungarian-accented dissident Gabor. Totally ridiculous fun, with astronauts who act like junior high school boys, hot-bodied alien babes played by a bevy of international beauty contest winners (a recurrent theme in '50s movie sci-fi), and the dahling Zsa Zsa looking great in rich Technicolor—everything efficiently held together by frequent Three Stooges helmer Bernds. Aka *Queen of the Universe*.

QUEEN OF SPADES
★★★ HBO, 1949, NR, 95 min. Dir: Thorold Dickinson. Cast: Edith Evans, Anton Walbrook, Yvonne Mitchell, Ronald Howard, Anthony Dawson, Mary Jerrold.

The best of several adaptations of Alexander Pushkin's famous tale about the determination of an impoverished army officer (Walbrook) to learn the secret behind aged countess Evans's success with cards. When he accidentally causes her death, the countess's ghost returns to haunt the young man. Eerie atmosphere and strong acting are the highlights of this British fantasy.

QUEEN OF THE UNIVERSE
See: *Queen of Outer Space*.

QUEST FOR FIRE
★★★ CBS/Fox, 1982, R, 97 min. Dir: Jean-Jacques Annaud. Cast: Everett McGill, Rae Dawn Chong, Ron Perlman, Nameer El Kadi, Gary Schwartz.

Uniquely realistic look at primitive man, with a trio of prehistoric cave guys searching for the fire that is essential to their tribe's survival. Along the way they meet the feral Chong, from a more advanced tribe, who becomes McGill's mate and eventually teaches him the secret of firemaking. Almost painfully earnest but also extremely well made and gruesomely believable. Anthony Burgess is credited with creating the cave folks' simplistic language; Desmond Morris choreographed the characters' body movements; and the costumes, what there are of them, earned an Oscar.

"Dahlings, vhen you take off da mask, let me slap her good!" Zsa Zsa Gabor et al. in Queen of Outer Space (1958).

QUEST FOR LOVE
★★★ IVE, 1971, PG, 90 min. Dir: Ralph Thomas. Cast: Tom Bell, Joan Collins, Denholm Elliott, Laurence Naismith, Neil McCallum, Simon Ward.

Solidly constructed British sci-fi based on a story by John Wyndham. Bell is accidentally transported to an alternate dimension where John F. Kennedy was never assassinated and Bell is unhappily married to unfaithful Collins. Tom falls in love with Joan and they are reconciled shortly before she dies unexpectedly. Finding himself back in his own world, Bell then desperately searches for Collins's counterpart. Good acting (especially Joan in a rare sympathetic role), writing, and direction distinguish this little-appreciated gem.

QUEST FOR THE MIGHTY SWORD
★ RCA/Columbia, 1989, PG-13, 94 min. Dir: David Hills [Aristide Massaccesi]. Cast: Eric Allen Kramer, Margaret Lenzey, Donald O'Brian, Laura Gemser, Melissa Mell.

The third, and I think last, in the Ator series finds the muscleman's son (Kramer, who makes Peter Lupus look like Peter O'Toole) searching for his missing mom and encountering a magical dwarf, a witch, a dragon, and other low-budget dangers along the way. Tenth-rate Conan clone, only for the most diehard fans of big pecs. Aka *Ator III: The Hobgoblin.*

QUIET EARTH, THE
★★★ CBS/Fox, 1985, R, 91 min. Dir: Geoff Murphy. Cast: Bruno Lawrence, Allison Routledge, Peter Smith.

Sharp, New Zealand-made end-of-the-world thriller. After the entire population of the Earth disappears, scientist Lawrence believes that he's the last person left until he encounters Routledge and Smith and the inevitable who's-gonna-date-whom problems arise. Something of an updated version of *The World, the Flesh, and the Devil,* directed with a nice eye by Murphy.

QUINTET
★★ CBS/Fox, 1979, R, 110 min. Dir: Robert Altman. Cast: Paul Newman, Bibi Andersson, Fernando Rey, Vittorio Gassman, Nina Van Pallandt, Brigitte Fossey.

A major box-office bomb for Altman and Newman, this arty drama set in some future ice age involves combatants in a life-or-death game called Quintet. Newman wants to be its master but must face various bloodthirsty challengers to achieve that status. This handsomely designed talkfest is literally too cold to warm up to but is well enough made and acted to be of passing interest to the curious.

RADAR MEN FROM THE MOON
★★★ Nostalgia Merchant, 1952, NR, 260 min. Dir: Fred C. Brannon. Cast: George Wallace, Aline Towne, Clayton Moore, Roy Barcroft, William Bakewell, Tom Steele.

Commando Cody, Sky Marshall of the Universe (Wallace, wearing the flying suit and helmet left over from *King of the Rocket Men*) battles an evil alien called Retik (Barcroft, also an evil alien in *The Purple Monster Strikes!*) who's out to destroy the Earth with his atomic weaponry. One of the best sci-fi serials, this is well-cast and fast-paced, with just enough little gimmicks and outrageous situations to keep you watching all the way to the end. The edited feature version is called *Retik, the Moon Menace.*

RADIOACTIVE DREAMS
★★☆ Vestron, 1986, R, 98 min. Dir: Albert Pyun. Cast: John Stockwell, Michael Dudikoff, Lisa Blount, George Kennedy, Don Murray, Michele Little.

Brothers Stockwell and Dudikoff have spent ten years in a bomb shelter reading Raymond Chandler novels. Eventually they emerge into postnuke 1996 to fight mutants, biker women, and monster rats. This semicomic end-of-the-world flick doesn't always come off but it's still one of Pyun's better movies, with a spirited cast and some good action.

RADIO RANCH
See: *The Phantom Empire* (1935).

RAIDERS OF ATLANTIS
★☆ Prism Entertainment, 1983, R, 90 min. Dir: Roger Franklin [Ruggero Deodato]. Cast: Christopher Connelly, Tony King, Marie Field, Ivan Rassimov, George Hilton.

The lost continent of Atlantis resurfaces after an atomic bomb blast. Scientist Field is accompanied by adventurers Connelly and King in an investigation that has them menaced by Atlantis's murderous inhabitants. Deodato tries to dress this tired adventure-fantasy with a lot of violence but it doesn't help much. Aka *I Predatori di Atlantide (Atlantis Interceptors).*

RAIDERS OF THE LOST ARK

★★★★ Paramount, 1981, PG, 115 min. Dir: Steven Spielberg. Cast: Harrison Ford, Karen Allen, Paul Freeman, Wolf Kahler, Ronald Lacey, Denholm Elliott, John Rhys-Davies, Anthony Higgins.

One of Spielberg's best movies, this tribute to old-time serials features Ford in his best-ever role as adventurer Indiana Jones. When Indy is hired on the brink of World War II by the American government to find the fabled Ark of the Covenant, our hero finds himself encountering a lost love (the sassy Allen), a sinister rival (Freeman), lots of snakes, and carloads of nasty Nazis out to claim the Ark for Der Führer. Everything works here: from the stunt work and special FX to the touches of humor to the relationship between Ford and Allen to John Williams's rousing music. And the ending has to be one of the most graphically violent scenes in any PG-rated movie in screen history. Followed by a couple of sequels (*Indiana Jones and the Temple of Doom* and *Indiana Jones and the Last Crusade*), a TV series (*The Young Indiana Jones Chronicles*), some sequels to the TV show, and lots of imitations.

RATBOY

★☆ Warner, 1986, PG-13, 104 min. Dir: Sondra Locke. Cast: Sondra Locke, Robert Townsend, Christopher Hewett, S. L. Baird, Gerrit Graham, Louie Anderson, Larry Hankin, Nina Blackwood.

Locke, the former Clint Eastwood gal pal, made her directorial debut with this well-cast but hopeless misfire. Sondra is a Hollywood loser who sees a last chance at fame by exploiting the half-human, half-rodent ratboy (Baird, actually a woman, in Rick Baker makeup) she encounters after he escapes from cruel keeper Townsend. A curious combination of screwball comedy and *E.T./Elephant Man*-type dramatics that never comes close to working in spite of a lot of sincerity on both sides of the camera.

RATS, THE

★ Video Treasures, 1983, NR, 97 min. Dir: Vincent Dawn [Bruno Mattei]. Cast: Richard Raymond, Alex McBride, Ann Gisel Glass, Janna Ryann.

More postnuke survivors find their hands full in a brave new world: this time it's mutant, flesh-eating rats causing all the problems. A gory Italian ripoff of the obscure camp classic *Chosen Survivors* (why isn't this one on home video, Columbia/TriStar?), with man-chewing rats subbing for the original's vampire bats.

REBEL STORM

★☆ Academy Entertainment, 1990, R, 99 min. Dir: Franky Schaeffer. Cast: Zach Galligan, Wayne Crawford, June Chadwick, John Rhys-Davies, Rod McCary, Elizabeth Kiefer.

Another fill-in-the-blanks postapocalyptic thriller, with a band of freedom fighters out to overthrow the usual totalitarian government. Nothing you haven't seen dozens of times before, right down to the usual-suspects exploitation movie cast.

RED DAWN

★★ MGM/UA, 1984, PG-13, 114 min. Dir: John Milius. Cast: Patrick Swayze, C. Thomas Howell, Lea Thompson, Charlie Sheen, Jennifer Grey, Powers Boothe, Ben Johnson, Harry Dean Stanton, Ron O'Neal, William Smith.

This popular anti-Communist movie could only have been made during the Reagan administration. When Commies invade Smalltown, U.S.A., ordinary teens (like Swayze, Sheen, and Thompson—you know, just plain folk) arm themselves and almost immediately become expert guerrilla fighters. Milius certainly knows how to push people's buttons, but this is too hoakily straightfaced even to begin to appreciate its own inherent ridiculousness—which could have turned a routine no-brain actioner into the *Mommie Dearest* of red-bashing fantasy flicks, something Jack Webb would have been proud of.

RED DWARF, THE

★★☆ CBS/Fox, 1988-1993, NR, 83–90 min per episode. Dirs: Ed Bye, Andy De Emmony, Juliet May, Grant Naylor. Cast: Chris Barrie, Craig Charles, Danny John-Jules, Robert Llewellyn, Hattie Hayridge, Norman Lovett.

Popular British cult sci-fi/comedy series about the rude, slobby crew of the intergalactic mining vessel *The Red Dwarf* and their misadventures with various alien life forms as they attempt to return to Earth. Very much an acquired taste—not unlike sushi or the music of Marilyn Manson—this can be very funny but also little more than a collection of flatulence jokes set in outer space, sort of like a sci-fi version of *The Young Ones*.

RED PLANET MARS

★★ MGM/UA, 1952, NR, 87 min. Dir: Harry Horner. Cast: Peter Graves, Andrea King, Bayard Veiller, Walter Sande, Marvin Miller, Morris Ankrum, Herbert Berghof, Gene Roth.

A good title and a good cast in one of the most outrageously ridiculous sci-fi dramas of the '50s. Scientist Graves and wife King establish radio contact with Mars and eventually discover that it's the voice of God himself warning them and the rest of the U.S. about an imminent Communist takeover. (I'm not making this up!) Technically competent and played with an absurdly straight face, an Ed Wood-like approach might have made this into a camp classic. As is, this is too dull and pompous to make it the great pro-God, anti-Commie epic it so desperately wants to be. Love that from-out-of-nowhere shock, downbeat ending, though.

RED SONJA

★☆ CBS/Fox, 1985, PG-13, 89 min. Dir: Richard Fleischer. Cast: Arnold Schwarzenegger, Brigitte Nielsen, Sandahl Bergman, Paul Smith, Ernie Reyes, Jr., Ronald Lacey, Janet Agren, Pat Roach.

Musclebound mercenary Arnie helps female warrior Brig retrieve a magical talisman from bitch queen Bergman. Based on stories by *Conan* creator Robert E. Howard, this mostly lame sword-and-sorcery pap plays very much like director Fleischer's *Conan the Destroyer,* only not as good. Some colorful action and a good Ennio Morricone score but the acting is awful, even by the standards of this bunch!

REGENERATED MAN, THE

★★ Arrow, 1994, R, 90 min. Dir: Ted A. Bohus. Cast: Arthur Lundquist, Cheryl Hendricks, Chris Kidd, Gregory Sullivan.

Vandals who break into his New Jersey laboratory force Dr. Robert Clarke (Lundquist) to drink his own experimental serum. Soon after the good doc begins transforming into a hideous monster with a throbbing skull who impales victims on bone fragments that burst out of his body. Cheap but ambitious sci-fi/horror, this has good makeup and a few clever plot twists.

REMOTE CONTROL

★★★ IVE, 1987, R, 88 min. Dir: Jeff Lieberman. Cast: Kevin Dillon, Deborah Goodrich, Christopher Wynne, Jennifer Tilly, Frank Beddor, Bert Remsen.

Video store employee Dillon discovers a videocassette developed by aliens that can turn viewers into homicidal maniacs. The police think Kev is responsible for all the killings around the area so he takes it on the lam with dreamy Goodrich in order to uncover the force behind the killer cassette. Lieberman, director of some exceptional low-budget horror movies including *Squirm,* brings a nice sense of style and energy to this slightly tongue-in-cheek sleeper, and there are good performances from Dillon, Goodrich, Tilly, and Remsen.

REMO WILLIAMS: THE ADVENTURE BEGINS

★★☆ HBO, 1985, PG-13, 121 min. Dir: Guy Hamilton. Cast: Fred Ward, Joel Grey, Kate Mulgrew, Wilford Brimley, J. A. Preston, George Coe, Charles Cioffi, William Hickey.

Based on the character from the popular *Destroyer* series of novels by Richard Sapir and Warren Murphy, this seriocomic actioner stars Ward in the title role: a New York cop recruited into a secret society of crimefighters out to bring justice to an unjust society. Grey, in heavy makeup, has a great character role as the aged Asian Sinanju master who trains Fred. There's a spectacular fight high atop the Statue of Liberty, but this is too long and uncertain of itself to work completely. Despite the title, no further big screen Remo adventures materialized.

REPO MAN

★★★ MCA/Universal, 1984, R, 92 min. Dir: Alex Cox. Cast: Harry Dean Stanton, Emilio Estevez, Olivia Barash, Tracey Walter, Vonetta McGee, Sy Richardson, Susan Barnes, Fox Harris.

New Wave teen punk Estevez takes a job as assistant to auto repossesser Stanton. When they get their hands on a valuable Chevy Malibu, Harry and Emilio are more than a little surprised to find a radioactive alien corpse in the trunk. Entertaining, anything-goes cult film with Stanton and Estevez in their best roles, a sharp supporting cast, clever direction, and a rockin' soundtrack featuring Iggy Pop, Black Flag, Suicidal Tendencies, and others. The Monkees' Mike Nesmith was executive producer.

REPTILICUS

★★ Orion, 1961, NR, 81 min. Dir: Sidney Pink. Cast: Carl Ottosen, Ann Smyrner, Mimi Heinrich, Asbjorn Andersen, Marla Behrens, Dirk Passer.

One of the funniest giant monster films ever made, this starts eerily enough, with workers drilling for oil dredging up a bloody piece of dinosaur tail. The tail is taken to a scientific complex in Copenhagen, where it reconstitutes into an entire creature that terrorizes the city. Gorgeous color photography and a modicum of suspense, but then the big puppet monster shows up and this becomes a total laugh. Interestingly, U.S. distributor American International cut out scenes of Reptilicus flying because they thought they were too ludicrous! Not as bad as *The Giant Claw* but a close second; shots of the monster turned up on a lot of '60s TV shows like *The Monkees.*

RESURRECTION OF ZACHARY WHEELER, THE

★★★ VCI, 1971, G, 100 min. Dir: Bob Wynn. Cast: Angie Dickinson, Bradford Dillman, Leslie Nielsen, James Daly, Jack Carter.

Investigating the remarkable recovery of U.S. senator Dillman after a catastrophic plane crash, reporter Nielsen uncovers a mysterious clinic where doctors are experimenting with cloning. First-rate sci-fi mystery with a solid cast (including Angie as a seductive doctor) and an intriguing storyline that only stumbles a bit at the end. Shot on video, this was a theatrical release in some quarters but had its main exposure on TV.

RETALIATOR

See: *Programmed to Kill.*

RETURN, THE

★☆ HBO, 1980, PG, 91 min. Dir: Greydon Clark. Cast: Cybill Shepherd, Jan-Michael Vincent, Raymond Burr, Martin Landau, Neville Brand, Vincent Schiavelli.

Years after having a close encounter as kids, Shepherd and Vincent are drawn to a New Mexico cave inhabited by hermit Schiavelli and a mysterious alien force. This dull quickie has a surprisingly upscale cast (including a post-Bogdanovich and pre-*Moonlighting* Cybill in the role I'll bet she'd most like to forget) but isn't nearly as much outrageous fun as Clark's next film, *Without Warning.* Aka *The Alien's Return.*

RETURN FROM WITCH MOUNTAIN

★★★ Disney, 1978, G, 95 min. Dir: John Hough. Cast: Bette Davis, Christopher Lee, Kim Richards, Ike Eisenman, Denver Pyle, Jack Soo.

Slick sequel to *Escape to Witch Mountain* has psychic alien kids Richards and Eisenman falling into the hands of evil Davis and Lee. Fun Disney fantasy that's just as enjoyable as the original, with the extra bonus of the great Bette and Chris adding a nicely sinister touch to the usual lightweight Disney proceedings.

RETURN OF CAPTAIN AMERICA, THE

See: *Captain America.* (1944)

RETURN OF CAPTAIN INVINCIBLE, THE

★★☆ Magnum, 1983, PG, 90 min. Dir: Phillipe Mora. Cast: Alan Arkin, Christopher Lee, Kate Fitzpatrick, Bill Hunter, Graham Kennedy, Michael Pate.

Moderately funny superhero spoof, with Arkin as a down-and-out Captain Invincible, hitting the bottle and living in Australia until called back in action by the U.S. president. Several

bizarre musical production numbers try to give this a *Rocky Horror* feel (and were written by Richard O'Brien and Richard Hartley of *Rocky Horror* fame) but this is mostly worth seeing for Lee's truly hilarious, image-trashing performance as the flamboyant bad guy. Aka *Legend in Leotards.*

RETURN OF CHANDU, THE

★★★ Sinister Cinema, 1934, NR, 180 min. Dir: Ray Taylor. Cast: Bela Lugosi, Maria Alba, Clara Kimball Young, Lucien Prival, Bryant Washburn, Phyllis Ludwig.

In the original *Chandu the Magician* feature film, Lugosi played the evil villain Roxar, but in this serial followup he plays the titular hero! Bela uses his mystical powers to save an innocent princess from a bloodthirsty cult and their female leader. Creaky but fun, with Bela in rare form and the great wall from *King Kong* turning up as a major set. Later cut into the features *The Return of Chandu* and *Chandu on the Magic Island.*

RETURN OF DR. MABUSE, THE

★★☆ Sinister Cinema, 1961, NR, 90 min. Dir: Harald Reinl. Cast: Lex Barker, Daliah Lavi, Gert Frobe, Wolfgang Priess, Ady Berber.

Entertaining sequel to *The Thousand Eyes of Dr. Mabuse* features police inspectors Barker and Frobe (the former Tarzan and future Goldfinger together) trying to stop Mabuse's mad plan to take over the world with an army of zombies and help from the Chicago Mafia. Colorful nonsense also released as *The Phantom Meets the Return of Dr. Mabuse.*

RETURN OF SWAMP THING, THE

★★ RCA/Columbia, 1989, PG-13, 86 min. Dir: Jim Wynorski. Cast: Louis Jourdan, Heather Locklear, Sarah Douglas, Dick Durock.

Cartoony sequel to Wes Craven's more serious-minded original, with returning villain Jourdan (who does a funny tribute to *Gigi* here) still going after Swampy's secret plant growth formula and creating mutant monsters that run wild through the swamp. Meanwhile, *Melrose Place* diva Heather shows up to help our mossy hero overcome memories of lost love Adrienne Barbeau. Forgettable but fun; followed by a brief TV series.

RETURN OF THE ALIENS: THE DEADLY SPAWN

See: *The Deadly Spawn.*

RETURN OF THE FLY

★★☆ CBS/Fox, 1959, NR, 80 min. Dir: Edward L.

Bernds. Cast: Vincent Price, Brett Halsey, David Frankham, Danielle De Metz, John Sutton, Dan Seymour.

Efficient like-father-like-son sequel to *The Fly* in which Price reluctantly helps nephew Halsey carry on dad's old experiments, with the expected result. Much more a horror film than the original, with spooky mood lighting and a couple of violent murders including the gory dispatching of the dreaded guinea pig man. More or less remade as *The Fly II*.

RETURN OF THE JEDI

★★☆ Fox, 1983, PG, 133 min. Dir: Richard Marquand. Cast: Mark Hamill, Harrison Ford, Carrie Fisher, Billy De Williams, Anthony Daniels, Peter Mayhew, Kenny Baker, David Prowse, Ian McDiarmid, Warwick Davis, voices of James Earl Jones, Frank Oz.

Last and weakest in the *Star Wars* trilogy starts out great with everybody in the clutches of evil Jabba the Hutt. Then things get really annoying and dumb, with the introduction of the cuddly Ewok tribe as they aid our heroes in the ultimate destruction of a new Death Star. Flat direction and performances (especially from Ford, who looks like he can't figure out what the hell he's doing surrounded by all those chirping teddy bears) but the FX are ILM at the top of their form (resulting in yet another Oscar), with many breathtaking moments to compensate for the many weaknesses. Shooting title: *Revenge of the Jedi*.

RETURN TO FANTASY ISLAND

★★ Video Treasures, 1978, NR, 96 min. Dir: George McCowan. Cast: Ricardo Montalban, Adrienne Barbeau, Joseph Campanella, Joseph Cotten, Cameron Mitchell, Karen Valentine, George Chakiris, Horst Buchholz, George Maharis, France Nuyen, Laraine Day, Herve Villechaize.

Second pilot for the series, with Mr. Roarke (Montalban) and little Tattoo (Villechaize) welcoming another group of wealthy losers to live out their fantasies, including Barbeau stranded on a desert island and Valentine trapped in a haunted house. Fans should enjoy this; everyone else will wonder how so many high-profile performers were suckered into appearing in both this and the subsequent series.

RETURN TO OZ

★★★ Disney, 1985, PG, 110 min. Dir: Walter Murch. Cast: Fairuza Balk, Nicol Williamson, Jean Marsh, Piper Laurie, Matt Clark.

A box-office flop, nobody seems to appreciate this belated nonmusical sequel to *The Wizard of Oz*. That's a shame, really, because this rather bleak, downbeat fantasy (based on *The Marvelous Land of Oz* and several others) is actually much closer to the spirit of the L. Frank Baum books than was the splashy MGM movie. Dorothy (Balk) is given psychiatric treatment when Aunt Em and Uncle Henry begin to fear for her sanity after she refuses to believe that her trip to Oz was only a dream. Eventually Dot ends up back in Oz, where the Emerald City is a ruin and the sinister Gnome King (Williamson) and an evil princess (Marsh, in a first run-through for her role in *Willow*) now rule. Great special FX bring to life new companions like Jack Pumpkinhead, Tik-Tok the mechanical man, and Billina the talking hen. This may lack the charm of the original but it's certainly one of the most complex and downright scary films aimed at children to be made since the '30s and, as such, is more recommended for adults than kids.

RETURN TO THE LOST WORLD

★☆ Worldvision, 1992, PG, 99 min. Dir: Timothy Bond. Cast: John Rhys-Davies, David Warner, Eric McCormack, Tamara Gorski, Nathania Stanford.

This direct follow-up to the 1992 *Lost World* remake is a little better (maybe) but the special FX are still awful. Most of the cast from the original return to discover that the prehistoric plateau is actually an incredible source for crude oil (an idea borrowed from the 1976 *King Kong*) and the dinosaurs are in danger of slaughter due to corporate development. Too ambitious for its own good.

REVENGE OF THE JEDI

See: *Return of the Jedi*.

REVENGE OF THE TEENAGE VIXENS FROM OUTER SPACE

☆ Continental, 1985, R, 83 min. Dir: Jeff Ferrell. Cast: Lisa Schwedop, Howard Scott, Amy Crumpacker, Sterling Ramberg.

Ultra-lame sci-fi sex comedy about a quartet of alien bimbos landing in a small town and seducing all the local high school horndogs until their outraged girlfriends decide to put a stop to all this extraterrestrial snuggling. Only for people who thought *Galactic Gigilo* should have won an Oscar.

RIFT, THE

See: *Endless Descent*.

ROAD WARRIOR, THE

★★★★ Warner, 1981, R, 94 min. Dir: George Miller. Cast: Mel Gibson, Bruce Spence, Vernon Wells, Virginia Hey, Mike Preston, Emil Minty.

One of the greatest action movies ever made, this first sequel to *Mad Max* finds his Melness defending a tiny desert community from a band of violent road punks, who are after the town's valuable oil supply. Breathtaking stunts and nonstop action put this Aussie actioner high on the list of best movies of the '80s; many Hollywood films have tried to copy it but no one has come close to recapturing its gritty realism and off-the-wall sense of violent fun. Even Gibson is good. Original title: *Mad Max 2*; sequel: *Mad Max: Beyond Thunderdome.*

ROBERT A. HEINLEIN'S THE PUPPETMASTERS

See: *The Puppetmasters.*

ROBO C.H.I.C.

See: *CYBER C.H.I.C.*

ROBOCOP

★★★★ Orion, 1987, R, 103 min. Dir: Paul Verhoeven. Cast: Peter Weller, Nancy Allen, Daniel O'Herlihy, Ronny Cox, Kurtwood Smith, Miguel Ferrer, Robert DoQui, Ray Wise.

Terrific, much imitated tale of a futuristic Detroit cop (Weller) who's killed in the line of duty and resurrected as a part-cyborg super-law enforcement machine. This is easily Dutch director Verhoeven's best film, mixing action, gore, great special FX (courtesy of Phil Tippett), and a wonderful eye for social satire (the corporate commercials are hilarious) into one of the best science fiction films of the modern age. Some felt this too grim but I think it hits all the right notes and never outstays its welcome. Followed by two sequels and a watered-down TV series; the director's cut laser disc restores some of the gore cut for the R rating.

ROBOCOP 2

★★☆ Orion, 1990, R, 118 min. Dir: Irvin Kerschner. Cast: Peter Weller, Nancy Allen, Daniel O'Herlihy, Belinda Bauer, Tom Noonan, Robert DoQui, Patricia Charbonneau, Gabriel Damon.

This okay sequel has Robo threatened this time by crazed drug dealer Noonan and returning corporate bigwig O'Herlihy, who wants to replace our hero with a bigger, badder robot law enforcer (a marvelous Phil Tippett creation). Louder, longer, and not nearly as effective as part one, this lacks the first film's wicked sense of humor but does have some good action highlights, including an excellent climactic fight sequence.

ROBOCOP 3

★★ Orion, 1991, PG-13, 104 min. Dir: Fred Dekker. Cast: Robert Burke, Nancy Allen, Rip Torn, Mako, C.C.H. Pounder, Jill Hennessy, Remy Ryan, Robert DoQui.

Peter Weller took a powder and was replaced by Burke for this toned-down third installment that wasn't released until 1993. This time Robo joins a band of rebel freedom fighters after his partner (an underused Allen) is killed. This ups the comedy and decreases the gore but the Japanese villains (including Mako) look like they'd be more at home in an episode of *McHale's Navy*. Slightly diverting but hardly a patch on the original.

ROBOCOP: THE SERIES—THE FUTURE OF LAW ENFORCEMENT

★★ Orion, 1994, NR, 89 min. Dir: Paul Lynch. Cast: Richard Eden, Yvette Nipar, Cliff De Young, Andrea Roth, David Garber.

The pilot film for the shot-in-Canada *Robocop* TV series, this pretty much sets the tone, with more laughs than action or thrills. Eden is Robo and Nipar is his partner, with De Young as a comic relief bad guy. Episodes of this costly flop series are also available; they all look great but it's obvious no one really knew where to go with the characters on a weekly basis.

ROBOJOX

See: *Robot Jox.*

ROBO MAN

See: *Who?*

ROBOT HOLOCAUST

★ Lightning, 1986, R, 90 min. Dir: Kim Kincaide. Cast: Norris Culf, Jennifer Delora, Angelika Jager, Joel Von Ornsteiner.

Manhattan-shot clinker about a robot vs. human war in the distant future. Ed French did the budget makeups, which sometimes work, but the dopey story and wooden acting got this an early berth on the fledgling *Mystery Science Theater 3000* show.

ROBOT JOX

★★ RCA/Columbia, 1987, PG, 85 min. Dir: Stuart Gordon. Cast: Gary Graham, Anne-Marie Johnson, Paul Koslo, Robert Sampson, Hilary Mason, Carolyn Purdey-Gordon.

The great Dave Allen FX are the real highlight of this often interesting but more often flaccid flick from *Re-Animator* man Gordon. Futuristic gladitorial battles are staged between huge robots for worldwide televised entertainment. When one of the robots stumbles and crushes a crown of fans, its pilot (Graham) quits and is replaced by a tough "synthetic" woman (Johnson). The "Transformer"-like robots are a crowd pleaser and the cast is fine, but everytime this thing tries to get dramatic on you—watch out! Filmed as *Robojox*; sequel: *Robot Wars*.

ROBOT MONSTER

★☆ Rhino, 1953, NR, 63 min. Dir: Phil Tucker. Cast: George Nader, Claudia Barrett, Selena Royale, John Mylong, Gregory Moffett, George Barrows.

Almost as popular as *Plan 9 from Outer Space* but not nearly as much fun, this is the tale of an alien gorilla with a diving helmet over his head who wipes out nearly all mankind with a short-wave radio and stock footage of dinosaurs and lightning bolts. The monster likes to give long-winded speeches on the meaning of existence and other pompous subjects but still knows how to act up around a babe in a tight dress. Still, you have to give this movie something for its fractured sense of self; no other movie from this era would kill off the cute little kids and studly hero and leave it up to the heroine to take on the Ro-Man herself by beaning him with a handy boulder. And then there's the playful Elmer Bernstein music, tacky 3-D FX, and "What the hell did all that mean, anyway?" twist ending. Aka *Monster from Mars* and *Monsters from the Moon*.

ROBOT NINJA

☆ Cinema Home, 1989, R, 80 min. Dir: J. R. Bookwalter. Cast: Michael Todd, Linnea Quigley, Burt Ward, Scott Spiegel.

Bookwalter's first film was an ambitious amateur gorefest called *The Dead Next Door* and was very good. This dumb, offensive superhero sci-fi comedy isn't. Title character Todd is out to stop a gang of vicious rapists (now there's a subject just brimming with humorous possibilities); lots of cheap gags and even cheaper special FX.

"I will pet her and keep her and call her George." Robot Monster *(1953).*

ROBOT WARS
★☆ Paramount, 1993, R, 106 min. Dir: Albert Band [Alfredo Antonini]. Cast: Don Michael Paul, Barbara Crampton, James Staley, Yuji Okumoto, Danny Kamekona.

Once again, some above-average Dave Allen stop-motion FX save a pretty bad movie. This is more or less a sequel to *Robot Jox,* with more gigantic battle robots (including an huge and impressive scorpion) going at it; Paul is the obnoxious hero and Crampton the sexy scientist heroine.

ROCKET ATTACK U.S.A.
★ Sinister Cinema, 1958, NR, 71 min. Dir: Barry Mahon. Cast: John McKay, Monica Davis, Daniel Kern, Art Metrano, Edward Czerniuk.

Exploitation king Mahon's take on the Cold War movie genre is one of the most depressing films you'll ever see. Undercover agents behind Soviet lines try to sabotage Russian nuclear weapons. Two star-crossed agents (a guy and a girl) fall in love, even though part of her job is to sleep with slobby Soviet officials. Amazingly, not only do they fail at their mission, but both the agents are killed and New York is nuked! There's so much stock footage that almost nothing else happens and when it does it's never good. See it to believe it.

ROCKETEER, THE
★★☆ Disney, 1991, PG, 108 min. Dir: Joe Johnston. Cast: Bill Campbell, Jennifer Connelly, Timothy Dalton, Alan Arkin, Paul Sorvino, Terry O'Quinn, Ed Lauter, Melora Hardin, Clint Howard, Tiny Ron.

A well-made and reasonably entertaining box-office flop based on the graphic novel by Dave Stevens and old Republic serials like *King of the Rocket Men.* Campbell is the handsome, forthright flyboy with a jetpack who battles Nazi spies (including a dashing Dalton as an Errol Flynn-like movie star) in 1938 Hollywood. Arkin is a bit much as the bumbling professor who develops the jetpack but Connelly is sweet as the love interest .(The original heroine was a nudie model based on classic cheesecake goddess Betty Page and originally intended as a showcase for Stevens's ex-wife Brinke Stevens. Brink Stevens in a Disney film? Not in this lifetime.) Tiny Ron is impressive in Rick Baker makeup as a Rondo Hatton-like henchman. Tighter editing would have helped this a lot.

ROCKETSHIP X-M
★★★ Fox Hills, 1950, NR, 77 min. Dir: Kurt Neumann. Cast: Lloyd Bridges, Osa Massen, Hugh O'Brian, John Emery, Noah Beery, Jr., Morris Ankrum.

Earth's first rocket to the moon is driven off course by an asteroid storm and ends up on Mars instead. Rushed into production to cash in on George Pal's *Destination Moon,* this managed to beat it into theaters and is actually more fun. Perfectly cast and full of the sort of action that would become a cliché within a couple of years of this film's release, this may be talky and scientifically inaccurate, to say the least, but is worth working with to get to the wholly unexpected downbeat ending. Some video prints have some additional special FX footage added to the film in the late '70s by distributor Wade Williams.

ROCKET TO THE MOON
See: *Cat Women of the Moon.*

ROCKY JONES, SPACE RANGER
★★ Video Yesteryear, 1954–55, NR, 78 min per tape. Dir: Hollingsworth Morse. Cast: Richard Crane, Sally Mansfield, Scotty Beckett, Maurice Cass.

These are unedited, original episodes of the early sci-fi series, many of which were recut into "features" released abroad and available from Sinister Cinema under titles like *Manhunt in Space* and *Forbidden Moon.* Full of hammy acting, cardboard sets, and cartoony special FX, this show's production values make *The Honeymooners* look like *Dynasty.* Another compilation of uncut episodes is *Rocky Jones, Space Ranger: Renegade Satellite.*

RODAN
★★☆ Paramount/Gateway, 1956, NR, 72 min. Dir: Inoshiro Honda. Cast: Kenji Sawara, Yumi Shirakawa, Akihiko Hirata, Akio Kobori.

Toho Productions' first color monster movie, this slow but fun hit starts out eerily when workers disappear from a flooded Japanese mine, but then things get downright silly as big rubber caterpillar creatures chase people around and enormous red pteradons with 500-foot wingspans break the sound barrier and reduce various Nipponese metropoli to rubble. The overserious narration (by an uncredited Keye Luke and Les Tremayne) is frequently at odds with the often goofy visuals but the rich color photography is effective and Rodan was popular enough to return in other films like *Ghidrah, The Three-Headed Monster* and *Destroy All Monsters.* Aka *Radon* and *Rodan, The Flying Monster.*

RODAN, THE FLYING MONSTER
See: *Rodan.*

ROLLERBALL
★★★ MGM/UA, 1975, R, 128 min. Dir: Norman Jewison. Cast: James Caan, Maud Adams, John

James Caan as the bloody but unbowed hero of Rollerball *(1975).*

Houseman, John Beck, Ralph Richardson, Moses Gunn, Pamela Hensley, Barbara Trentham.

An underrated, ahead-of-its-time sci-fi actioner set in the twenty-first century. Caan is well cast as the top player in the world-popular sport of Rollerball, a combination of roller derby, hockey, and human pinball where combatants are often killed. When the government agency that backs the game decides that Jimmy's rugged individualism is a bad image for the people and asks him to step down as champ, he defiantly refuses. This exciting if overlong version of William Harrison's *The Rollerball Murders* really needs to be seen on the big screen to be appreciated, but it's interesting to consider how this fictionally predated real-life TV shows like *American Gladiators*.

ROLLER BLADE

★ New World, 1976, R, 88 min. Dir: Donald Jackson. Cast: Suzanne Solari, Jeff Hutchinson, Shaun Michelle, Michelle Bauer.

This action fantasy is decidedly weird but pretty awful. Rollerskating Amazons of the future battle fascist warriors and sometimes skate nude. Not as interesting as you might

think, this junk was popular enough to inspire—if you can call it that—a couple of sequels.

ROLLER BLADE SEVEN, THE

★ York, 1992, R, 90 min. Dir: Donald Jackson. Cast: Scott Shaw, Allison Chase, Karen Black, Don Stroud, William Smith, Frank Stallone, Joe Estevez, Rhonda Shear.

This is actually the third and forth Roller Blade movies edited into one crummy final chapter. Talentless Shaw is the Mad Max-like hero fighting ninjas and Amazons and meeting up with nothing-to-lose guest stars like Karen, Don, and Big Bill. This is bad in ways it's best not even to contemplate. TV title: *Return of the Roller Blade Seven*.

ROLLER BLADE WARRIORS: TAKEN BY FORCE

★ Raedon, 1988, UR, 90 min. Dir: Donald Jackson. Cast: Kathleen Kinmont, Suzanne Solari, Rory Calhoun, Abby Dalton, Elizabeth Kaitan, Lisa Toothman.

You'd have to be forced to watch this second in a useless series. Kinmont is the roller derby

Amazon queen out to save the psychic Kaitan from sacrifice by an evil cult. A lot of pretty actresses (including veteran Dalton, Kinmont's mom) are the only reason to watch this inept action fantasy.

ROSWELL—THE U.F.O. COVER-UP

★★☆ Republic, 1994, PG-13, 91 min. Dir: Jeremy Kagan. Cast: Kyle MacLachlan, Martin Sheen, Kim Griest, Dwight Yokam, Doug Wert, Charles Martin Smith, Peter MacNichol, J. D. Daniels.

A good cast and restrained direction help this made-for-cable reenactment of the alleged true story of a government coverup of a UFO landing in the desert near Roswell, New Mexico, in 1947. Steve Johnson created the alien corpses for this sometimes eerie movie that was probably made to cash in on *The X-Files.*

R.O.T.O.R.

★ Imperial Entertainment, 1987, R, 91 min. Dir: Cullen Blaine. Cast: Richard Gesswein, Margaret Trigg, Jayne Smith.

Shot-in-Texas cheapie *Robocop/Terminator* rip about a part cyborg police officer going berserk and starting a violent killing spree. Too inexpensively put together to bring its story to life in any way, shape, or form.

RUNAWAY

★★ RCA/Columbia, 1984, PG, 100 min. Dir: Michael Crichton. Cast: Tom Selleck, Cynthia Rhodes, Kirstie Alley, Gene Simmons, Stan Shaw, G. W. Bailey, Joey Cramer, Cec Verrell.

One of several attempts in the mid-'80s at turning *Magnum* hunk Selleck into a movie star, this sci-fi thriller stars Tom as a cop of the future after out-of-control robots turned into murder weapons by madman Simmons (the Kiss star without his wild makeup and rude tongue). Sometimes diverting but ultimately too cold and unlikable to make anything out of its story premise, supporting cast, or special FX.

RUNNING AGAINST TIME

★★★ MCA/Universal, 1990, PG, 96 min. Dir: Bruce Seth Green. Cast: Robert Hays, Catherine Hicks, Sam Wanamaker, James DiStefano, Brian Smiar.

A first-rate time-travel movie, with Hays using professor Wanamaker's time-travel device to go back and prevent the JFK assassination- only to end up being accused of the crime himself! Girlfriend Hicks and Wanamaker himself also travel back to help, only to screw up history even more. An exciting, well-made cable flick adapted from Stanley Shapiro's novel *A Time to Remember.*

RUNNING DELILAH

★☆ Signet, 1992, PG-13, 85 min. Dir: Richard Franklin. Cast: Kim Cattrall, Billy Zane, Diana Rigg, Francois Guetary, Yorgo Voyagis.

Some interesting stars do what they can with this inept shot-in-France ripoff of *Robocop* and *La Femme Nikita* but it ain't easy. Cattrall is a nearly dead and badly mutilated female secret agent who is reconstructed as a bionic super- crime fighter. Zane is her pouty pretty-boy partner and Rigg is wasted as their boss. Watch a *Bionic Woman* rerun instead.

RUNNING MAN, THE

★★★ Avid Entertainment, 1987, R, 100 min. Dir: Paul Michael Glaser. Cast: Arnold Schwarzenegger, Maria Conchita Alonso, Yaphet Kotto, Jim Brown, Richard Dawson, Jesse Ventura, Mick Fleetwood, Dweezil Zappa, Erland van Lidth de Juede, Professor Toru Tanaka.

Even though this adaptation of a novel by "Richard Bachman" (Stephen King, of course) borrows a lot from *Rollerball* and *Death Race 2000* and even the obscure *Deathrow Game Show,* this has the right stars, the right look, and the right sense of humor to pull off its patently goofy story. After being framed for a series of murders, twenty-first-century police detective Arnold ends up fighting for his life on a nationally televised kill-or-be-killed game show hosted by none other than Mr. "Survey Said!" Dawson. Dumb as dirt but better than most recent Schwarzenegger vehicles, with lots of gratuitous violence, groan-inducing one- liners, and solid direction from Glaser (Starsky on *Starsky and Hutch*), who inherited this project from Andrew (*Under Siege*) Davis.

SADKO

See: *The Magic Voyage of Sinbad.*

SAMPO

See: *The Day the Earth Froze.*

SAMSON

★★ Sinister Cinema, 1960, NR, 99 min. Dir: Gianfranco Parloni. Cast: Brad Harris, Alan Steel,

Brigitte Corey, Walter Reeves, Serge Gainsbourg.

Harris is muscleman Samson and future Hercules Steel is his son. Together they help princess Corey regain her throne from an evil queen in this badly dubbed, especially confusing fantasy-beefcake epic from Italy. Several sequels followed, most of them retitled Maciste movies.

SAMSON AND THE SEVEN MIRACLES OF THE WORLD

★★☆ Sinister Cinema, 1961, NR, 90 min. Dir: Riccardo Freda. Cast: Gordon Scott, Yoko Tani, Helene Chanel.

Freda brings a nice sense of style to this slightly above average he-man hokum, with ex-Mr. Vera Miles Scott (also a former Tarzan) as a rechristened Maciste (now called Samson) who travels to the court of Ghenghis Khan, battles Tartars, loves a Chinese princess (the lovely Tani) and starts an earthquake after being buried alive. Good fun for muscle cultists. Originally titled *Maciste alla Conte del Ghan Khan (Maciste in the Court of Ghenghis Khan)*.

SANTA CLAUS

See: *Santa Claus: The Movie.*

SANTA CLAUS

★☆ Something Weird, 1959, NR, 80 min. Dir: Rene Cardona. Cast: José Elias Moreno, Cesare Quezadas, Nora Veryan, José Luis Aquirre.

Exported from Mexico to U.S. theaters at holiday time for years by K. Gordon Murray, this almost surreal kid's pic concerns a red-faced horned devil called Pitch, who tempts various little rugrats to do bad at Christmastime. Meanwhile Santa watches everything through a giant telescope from his castle in the clouds, where children from all around the world—even Russia!—help the Kringle man get ready for the big day. The best character is a sweet little girl called Lupita, who's almost tempted into stealing a doll. Cultural stereotypes are paraded shamelessly, including a pair of African youngsters with bones through their noses! Some prints cut out the Africans and the devil character completely—so what's left of interest to watch?

SANTA CLAUS CONQUERS THE MARTIANS

★ Rhino, 1964, NR, 80 min. Dir: Nicholas Webster. Cast: John Call, Leonard Hicks, Vincent Beck, Donna Conforti, Victor Stiles, Bill McCutcheon, Leila Martin, Pia Zadora.

"Hooray for Santy Claus!" I hated this New York-shot holiday "classic" when I was dragged to see it at some late '60s kiddie matinee, and I don't like it much now either. Claus and a couple of bad kid actors are kidnapped and carried off to Mars, where Santa tries to cheer up the green-skinned Martian youth (including little Pia in her movie debut) while villains plot against him and . . . oh, who cares! Maybe the creepiest Christmas movie this side of *Silent Night, Deadly Night*, it's easy to laugh at but leaves you feeling pretty weird all the same.

SANTA CLAUS, THE

★★☆ Disney, 1994, PG, 97 min. Dir: John Pasquin. Cast: Tim Allen, Judge Reinhold, Wendy Crewsen, Eric Lloyd, Peter Boyle, Mary Gross, David Krumholtz, Larry Brandenbury.

Home Improvement TV star Allen scored an unexpected smash hit with this Yuletide comedy about a divorced dad (Tim) who accidentally kills St. Nick (that's right, he kills Santa! In a Disney film, yet!) and finds himself pressed into service to take the big guy's place. At first reluctant, eventually Allen comes to embrace his new identity just in time for the feel-good finalé. One hundred percent predictable but also fairly funny, this avoids much of the usual comic crudity for laughs that grow out of the situation and characters. It's not great, but it's fun.

SANTA CLAUS: THE MOVIE

★ ☆ Video Treasures, 1985, PG, 112 min. Dir: Jeannot Szwarc. Cast: David Huddleston, Dudley Moore, John Lithgow, Burgess Meredith, Judy Cornwell, Jeffrey Kramer, Christian Fitzpatrick, Carrie Kei Heim.

Alexander and Ilya Salkind hoped to repeat the success of their first *Superman* epic with this big-budget holiday fantasy that turned out to be one of the biggest busts of the 1985–86 movie season. Telling the "true" story of Kris Kringle, the first half hour or so isn't bad and Huddleston and Cornwell (she from the popular Britcom *Keeping Up Appearances*) are well cast as Santa and his missus but the main plot involving the annoying Moore as a bumbling elf and Lithgow as a rich toy manufacturer who hates Christmas is pretty lame. Thank God the Salkinds didn't decide to do the life story of the Messiah next as *Jesus: The Movie*. Aka *Santa Claus*.

SATAN'S SATELLITES

See: *Zombies of the Stratosphere.*

SATELLITE OF BLOOD

See: *First Man into Space.*

SATURN 3
★★ Avid Entertainment, 1980, R, 88 min. Dir: Stanley Donan. Cast: Kirk Douglas, Farrah Fawcett, Harvey Keitel, Douglas Lambert.

Just what the codirector of *Singing in the Rain* is doing at the helm of this absurd sci-fi/horror rip of *Alien* is anyone's guess. Douglas and Fawcett are space lovers whose space station Eden is invaded by brutish Keitel and his killer robot and soon the clothes and body parts start to drop off with unimaginative frequency. Heavily cut before release, but it doesn't help much.

SCANNER COP
★★★ Republic, 1993, R, 94 min. Dir: Pierre David. Cast: Daniel Quinn, Richard Lynch, Darlanne Fleugel, Richard Grove, Mark Rolston, Brion James, Hilary Shepard, Cyndi Pass.

The *Scanners* series takes a clever side turn into the action adventure genre with Quinn as the likable adopted son of police official Grove, who becomes a patrolman with a mission as he uses his scanner powers to battle mad scientist Lynch, who's hypnotizing ordinary citizens into becoming cop killers. Lots of action and gory head explosions but with attention paid, too, to the characters and their relationships. Followed by *Scanners: The Showdown.*

SCANNER COP II
See: *Scanners: The Showdown.*

SCANNERS
★★★ Nelson, 1980, R, 103 min. Dir: David Cronenberg. Cast: Jennifer O'Neill, Patrick McGoohan, Stephen Lack, Michael Ironside, Lawrence Dane, Robert Silverman.

One of Canadian horror director Cronenberg's biggest hits, with Ironside as an evil Scanner—a psychic who can make your head explode through intense concentration—battling good Scanner Lack for world conquest. Uneven editing and a real limp performance from Lack notwithstanding, this is one of Cronenberg's most entertaining movies, with good acting from Ironside, McGoohan, and O'Neill (see how big clothes and the editor hide her real-life pregnancy) and jolting special FX, some of them supervised by Dick Smith.

SCANNERS 2: THE NEW ORDER
★★☆ Media, 1991, R, 104 min. Dir: Christian Duguay. Cast: Deborah Raffin, David Hewlett, Vlasta Varna, Yvan Pontoni, Isabelle Mejias, Tom Butler.

Pretty good second in the series. Hewlett is very good as the Scanner son of the original film's hero and heroine out to stop a new pack of evil Scanners. Predictable but well done, with the expected action and gory violence.

SCANNERS 3: THE TAKEOVER
★★ Republic, 1992, R, 100 min. Dir: Christian Duguay. Cast: Liliana Komorowska, Steve Parrish, Valerie Valos, Daniel Pilon, Collin Fox, Peter Wright.

Black comedy number three boasts an outrageous bit of acting by Komorowska as a nice Scanner girl turned into a crazed villainess by her father's experimental new drug meant to control a Scanner's destructive impulses. Although still pretty gory, it's obvious that no one was taking this very seriously. The final scene seems borrowed from both Cronenberg's *Videodrome* and Lamberto Bava's *Demons 2.*

SCANNERS: THE SHOWDOWN
★★ Republic, 1994, R, 94 min. Dir: Steve Barnett. Cast: Daniel Quinn, Patrick Kilpatrick, Robert Forster, Khrystyne Haje, Stephen Mendel, Brenda Swanson, Jewel Shepard, Kane Hodder.

Scanner cop Quinn returns to fight hulking Kilpatrick, who drains the power of Scanners vampire-style in order to make himself the ultimate Scanner and destroy Quinn, who sent him to prison. Routine sequel with good but repetitious FX and Quinn devolving from a likable misanthrope into just another foul-mouthed action hero. Aka *Scanner Cop II.*

SCARED TO DEATH
★★★ Video Treasures, 1980, R, 93 min. Dir: William Malone. Cast: John Stinson, Diana Davidson, Toni Janotta, Jonathan David Moses.

Filmed as *The Terror Factor,* this budget-conscious *Alien* concerns a genetically engineered monster called the Syngenor who lives off human spine fluid (just like the monsters in *Fiend Without a Face*). Stinson is good as the witty, self-deprecating private eye hired to find the creature when it escapes from the lab and there's a good ending where the Syngenor is crushed under a press (just like David Hedison in the original *The Fly*) and heroine Davidson has a last-minute nightmare (just like Amy Irving in *Carrie*). Director Malone also designed the fairly impressive monster costume. Sequel: *Syngenor.*

SCREAMERS
★★★ Columbia/TriStar, 1996, R, 108 min. Dir: Christian Duguay. Cast: Peter Weller, Jennifer Rubin, Roy Dupuis, Andy Lauer, Liliana Komorowska, Charles Powell.

Erstwhile *Scanners* sequel maven Duguay made his big-screen bow with this above-average sci-fi/action/horror flick. Weller stars as the leader of a small band of renegades at war on a distant planet with an army of government soldiers. Weller's team develops an attack squadron of decapitating robots called Screamers but the robots begin to develop an artificial intelligence of their own and the ability to copy the form of any living being they perceive as an enemy—including Weller and his crew. Overly complicated and sometimes derivative (even the title comes from a low-budget Italian horror film) but well enough acted and directed to rise above this, making this loose adaptation of Philip K. Dick's story *Second Variety* worth watching and hardly deserving of its box office failure.

SCROOGE

★★ Goodtimes, 1935, NR, 67 min. Dir: Henry Edwards. Cast: Sir Seymour Hicks, Donald Calthrop, Robert Cochran, Mary Glynne, Oscar Asche, Maurice Evans, Philip Frost, Eve Gray.

Static but watchable early British adaptation of Charles Dickens's *A Christmas Carol*. Hicks, who had a hand in the scripting, is good in the title role.

SCROOGE

★★★ Fox, 1970, G, 118 min. Dir: Ronald Neame. Cast: Albert Finney, Alec Guinness, Edith Evans, Kenneth More, Laurence Naismith, Suzanne Neve, David Collings, Gordon Jackson, Roy Kinnear, Kay Walsh, Michael Medwin, Mary Peach.

Delightful musical version of *A Christmas Carol*, with songs by Leslie Bricusse. Finney survives his offbeat casting to give a spirited turn as the legendary pennypincher. A top-drawer supporting cast of British theater folk play all the familiar Dickens characters. Guinness's turn as Marley's ghost seems to suggest that he and Scrooge were partners in more than one sense, a strange touch for a family-themed movie. The Scrooge-goes-to-Hell climax is sometimes cut on TV.

SCROOGED

★★★ Paramount, 1988, PG-13, 101 min. Dir: Richard Donner. Cast: Bill Murray, Karen Allen, John Forsythe, Carol Kane, John Glover, Robert Mitchum, Bobcat Goldthwaite, David Johansen, Alfre Woodard, Michael J. Pollard, Mabel King, John Houseman, Robert Goulet, Lee Majors, Jamie Farr, Buddy Hackett, Mary Lou Retton, Brian Doyle Murray.

Murray is perfectly cast as a snide, mean-spirited TV executive who learns the true meaning of Christmas in this updating of Dickens's *Christmas Carol*. When this tries to be sweet and sentimental it never works but whenever it lets its darker side loose (as in the hilarious opening parodying inane network Christmas specials) it always hits a bull's-eye, with Bill in top form and others like Forsythe, Kane, and Goldthwaite lending great support. Up until its sloppy ending, this is the perfect Christmas movie for those who hate Christmas movies.

SEA SERPENT, THE

★ Lightning, 1984, PG, 92 min. Dir: Gregory Greens [Amando de Ossorio]. Cast: Ray Milland, Timothy Bottoms, Taryn Power, Jared Martin.

Jaws and *Moby Dick* were the inspirations for this cheap Spanish monster film about a sea captain (Bottoms) obsessed with catching a gigantic eel terrorizing the coast. The cast and director have talent but the awful special FX make this very hard to take seriously. Milland is amazingly spry in his final role.

SECOND SIGHT

★☆ Warner, 1989, PG, 84 min. Dir: Joel Zwick. Cast: John Larroquette, Bronson Pinchot, Bess Armstrong, Stuart Pankin, John Schuck, James Tolkan, William Prince, Christine Estabrook.

Lame comedy-fantasy featuring Larroquette (who can save almost anything) as a private eye who uses spacey partner Pinchot's psychic abilities in his investigations. You know you're in trouble when the love interest (Armstrong) is a nun!

SECRET OF DR. MABUSE, THE

See: *The Death Ray of Dr. Mabuse*.

SECRET OF NIMH, THE

★★☆ MGM/UA, 1982, G, 82 min. Dir: Don Bluth. Voices: Elizabeth Hartman, Derek Jacobi, Dom DeLuise, John Carradine, Peter Strauss, Shannon Doherty.

Interesting but not always effective animated film (with sci-fi undertones) about a mother field mouse determined to find a new home for her brood with the help of a bunch of scientifically mind-altered lab rats. Based on a book by Robert C. O'Brien, this has fluid animation but may be a bit too cerebral for younger kids.

SECRET OF THE TELEGIAN

★★☆ Sinister cinema, 1960, NR, 86 min. Dir: Jun Fukuda. Cast: Koji Tsurata, Tadao Nakamura, Akihiko Hirata, Yumi Shirakawa.

Japanese variation on the *Fly* movies, about a maniac who uses a matter-transmitting machine to strike out at his victims no matter where they hide. Shallow drama but good special FX.

SEEDPEOPLE

★ Paramount, 1992, R, 82 min. Dir: Peter
Manoogian. Cast: Sam Hennings, Andrea Roth, Dane
Witherspoon, Holly Fields.

Laughably awful *Invasion of the Body Snatchers*
steal about aliens replacing the population of a
sleepy California valley community with evil
duplicates. One of the worst films Charles
Band ever produced, with special FX on the
level of the *Barney* TV show.

7 FACES OF DR. LAO

★★★ MGM/UA, 1964, NR, 100 min. Dir: George Pal.
Cast: Tony Randall, Barbara Eden, John Ericson,
Arthur O'Connell, Kevin Tate, Argentina Brunetti,
Noah Beery, Jr., Minerva Urecal, John Qualen, Lee
Patrick.

Good pal version of Charles Finney's *The Circus
of Dr. Lao,* with a heavily made-up Randall as
the proprietor of a mysterious circus that
arrives in a small turn-of-the-century western
town and teaches the populace harsh lessons
about life and themselves. Randall is great in
William Tuttle's Oscar-winning makeup (the
faces include a Yeti, the great god Pan, and the
gorgon Medusa, as well as a sea serpent animated by Jim Danforth). Good work from Eden
(as a sexually frustrated school marm) and
O'Connell (as a greedy land developer) and a
nice musical score by Leigh Harline. Flashbacks
of an ancient city's destruction are actually
stock footage from *Atlantis, the Lost Continent.*

7TH VOYAGE OF SINBAD, THE

★★★☆ Columbia/TriStar, 1958, NR, 88 min. Dir:
Nathan Juran. Cast: Kerwin Mathews, Kathryn Grant,
Torin Thatcher, Richard Eyer.

The first of Ray Harryhausen's *Sinbad* trilogy
has Mathews as the heroic sailor who saves
princess Grant from a spell of miniaturization
after he braves an island crawling with gigantic Cyclops, a huge two-headed bird called the
Roc, a sword-wielding skeleton, and a fire-

It's cyclops versus dragon at the climax of The 7th Voyage of Sinbad *(1958).*

breathing dragon. Thatcher is the flamboyant villain-magician and Eyer is a little kid genie who helps. Colorful photography and a grand Bernard Herrmann score back up some of Harryhausen's most memorable FX. Sequels: *The Golden Voyage of Sinbad* and *Sinbad and the Eye of the Tiger.*

SHADOW, THE

★★★ MCA/Universal, 1994, PG-13, 119 min. Dir: Russell Mulcahy. Cast: Alec Baldwin, Penelope Ann Miller, John Lone, Tim Curry, Peter Boyle, Ian McKellen, Jonathan Winters, Sab Simono.

This lavish updating of the popular old radio character—who can "cloud men's minds"—was a bust at the box office but is actually pretty good. Baldwin is an American ex-patriot in the 1930s Tibet who returns to New York City as dashing playboy Lamont Cranston and fights a supernatural Chinese warlord (Lone), who rises from a sarcophagus in a museum using the mystic techniques he learned in the Orient. Colorful casting and fun gimmicks (like an invisible building) make this underrated action fantasy worth seeing. Favorite scene: a guy is tossed off the top of the Empire State Building and falls screaming to his death in the background of another scene; no one even notices.

SHADOW CREEPS, THE

See: *The Phantom Creeps.*

SHADOWZONE

★★☆ Paramount, 1989, R, 88 min. Dir: J.S. Cardone. Cast: Louise Fletcher, David Beecroft, Shawn Weatherley, James Hong.

Scientific experiments with the dream state unleash a monster from some alternate reality to menace characters trapped in an underground complex. Sounds routine, with all the usual graphic gore and nudity of your usual direct-to-video yawner, but a clever premise and an out-of-control Fletcher make it better than you'd think.

SHAGGY D.A., THE

★★★ Disney, 1976, G, 91 min. Dir: Robert Stevenson. Cast: Dean Jones, Suzanne Pleshette, Tim Conway, Keenan Wynn, Jo Anne Worley, Dick Van Patten.

Good fun sequel to the Disney classic, with Jones as an older version of the Tommy Kirk character who starts turning into a sheepdog once again while running for local district attorney. The typically good Disney supporting cast includes Pleshette ("Hi, Bob") as Dean's wife, Tim, Wynn, and *Laugh-In* veteran Worley.

SHAGGY DOG, THE

★★★ Disney, 1959, NR, 104 min. Dir: Charles T. Barton. Cast: Fred MacMurray, Jean Hagen, Tommy Kirk, Annette Funicello, Tim Considine, Kevin Corcoran, Cecil Kellaway, Alexander Scourby.

Disney's first live-action comedy-fantasy was this mini-classic, a toned-down variation on *I Was a Teenage Werewolf* from the director of *Abbott and Costello Meet Frankenstein.* MacMurray only has two sons here, one of whom (Kirk) is placed under a spell by a magical ring and begins transforming into a sheepdog. With lots of slapstick, a silly subplot about a spy ring, and a busty young Annette at her hottest. Remade for TV in 1995; sequels: *The Shaggy D.A.* and *The Return of the Shaggy Dog.*

SHE

★★☆ Sinister Cinema, 1925, NR, 64 min. Dir: Leander Cordova. Cast: Betty Blythe, Carlyle Blackwell, Mary Odette.

Silent version of H. Rider Haggard's classic novel about an ageless queen (Blythe) of a mythical kingdom searching for the reincarnation of her long-lost love. Blythe is well cast in this diverting if slow fantasy.

SHE

★★★ Kino, 1935, NR, 94 min. Dirs: Irving Pichel, Lansing Holden. Cast: Helen Gahagan, Randolph Scott, Helen Mack, Nigel Bruce, Gustav von Seyffertitz, Samuel S. Hinds, Noble Johnson, Lumsden Hare.

King Kong producer-director Merian C. Cooper backed this absurd but fun version of Haggard's novel, in which Gahagan (in her only movie role before retiring from acting and entering politics and becoming a U.S. senator who once ran against Richard Nixon) as the immortal ice queen of a lost civilization (moved from Africa to Tibet) who sees in the sturdy Randolph the image of her murdered lover. Great settings and special FX (the avalanche and rock bridge scenes are real doozies) but indifferent direction spoils the effectiveness of some of the scenes (including the disintegration climax). Although this tape is advertised as complete and uncut, a 104-minute version is known to exist.

SHE

★★☆ MGM/UA, 1965, NR, 105 min. Dir: Robert Day. Cast: Ursula Andress, John Richardson, Peter Cushing, Christopher Lee, Rosenda Monteros, Bernard Cribbins, Andre Morell, John Maxim.

One of Hammer Films' biggest hits, this is really a rather dull adventure film, with Richardson as a soldier of fortune lured to a

John Richardson sees that Ursula Andress gets the point in She *(1965).*

mysterious desert city where the voluptuous Andress is Ayesha, She Who Must Be Obeyed. Cushing is good in the old Nigel Bruce role as Richardson's mentor but Lee looks ridiculous in his high priest threads and the final fate of spunky slave girl Monteros is needlessly cruel. Lavish production values (for Hammer, anyway), a good score by James Bernard, and a better handled ending than in the 1935 version make this okay but hardly compelling viewing. The much campier (and more fun) sequel is *The Vengeance of She*.

S*H*E*

★★ Prism Entertainment, 1980, NR, 96 min. Dir: Robert Lewis. Cast: Cornelia Sharpe, Omar Sharif, Anita Ekberg, Robert Lansing, Fabio Testi, Isabella Rye.

An ultra-campy cast highlights this made-for-TV feminist James Bond variant, with Sharpe as a female superspy up against international spy ring leader Sharif. Written by Bond veteran Richard Maibaum, most of the humor here is unintentional but it still helps.

SHE

★☆ Lightning, 1982, R, 106 min. Dir: Avi Nesher. Cast: Sandahl Bergman, David Goss, Quin Kessler, Harrison Muller, Elena Wiedermann, Gordon Mitchell.

This in-name-only "remake" does retain the idea of an ageless beauty (Bergman) who stays young by bathing in a magic fountain but for the most part is just another bad Italian *Conan* clone, with Bergman and her trio of warrior followers (named Tom, Dick, and Harry) battling various mutants, vampires, and other postapocalyptic stereotypes.

SHEENA

★☆ Columbia/TriStar, 1984, PG, 117 min. Dir: John Guillermin. Cast: Tanya Roberts, Ted Wass, Donovan Scott, Elizabeth Toro.

I'm a big fan of Tanya but even that's not enough to make me sit still through this mostly awful updating of *Sheena, Queen of the Jungle.* Roberts looks great as the blonde jungle girl who can psychically communicate with animals but the plot (involving Sheena with nature photographer Wass and their attempt to save the African veldt) has hardly enough development for 67 minutes, let alone 117. The real-life African princess Toro is a regal treat as Tanya's mentor.

SHE'S BACK

★ Vestron, 1988, R, 88 min. Dir: Tim Kincaid. Cast: Carrie Fisher, Robert Joy, Matthew Cowles, Sam Coppola, Donna Drake, Bobby Di Cicco.

Awful fantasy about a Bronx housewife (Fisher, a long way from that galaxy far, far away) who is murdered by a gang of street toughs and then urges her meek husband (Joy) to avenge her. Tries to be a comedy but is never the least bit funny; all of the humor is forced and the acting is terrible. Aka *Dead and Married.*

SHORT CIRCUIT

★★★ Fox, 1986, PG, 98 min. Dir: John Badham. Cast: Ally Sheedy, Steve Guttenberg, Fisher Stevens, G. W. Bailey, Austin Pendleton, voice of Tim Blaney.

Pleasant *E.T.* wannabe in which a robotic ultimate weapon (voiced by Blaney) escapes from a military complex and is befriended by kooky animal lover Sheedy and humanized by the experience. Totally formula-bound but still very entertaining and popular enough to spawn a mostly needless sequel. Is it my imagination or did Guttenberg float through the entire decade of the 1980s playing the same character in film after film?

SHORT CIRCUIT 2

★★ Fox, 1988, PG, 110 min. Dir: Kenneth Johnson. Cast: Fisher Stevens, Cynthia Gibb, Michael McKean, Jack Weston, Dee McCaffrey, voice of Tim Blaney.

You know a sequel is in trouble when the only actor who returns from the original is the third-billed comic relief (*Gone with the Wind II* starring Butterfly McQueen would be better), with Stevens as the clichéd malaprop-spouting Hindu who helps save our robot hero (now calling himself Johnny) from evil toy manufac- turer McKean (why are toy manufacturers in the movies always evil?). Gibb is the unlikely love interest in this overlong and underdeveloped followup that's not terrible but just terribly unimaginative.

SIEGFRIED

★★★★ Kino, 1924, NR, 186 min. Dir: Fritz Lang. Cast: Paul Richter, Margarete Schon, Throdor Loos, Hanna Ralph, Rudolf Klein-Rogge, Georg John.

Originally titled *Die Nibelungen,* this two-part epic fantasy is Lang's great achievement. The first half details the various battles of legendary hero Siegfried, who has a cloak of invisibility and bathes in the blood of the huge dragon he slays. After his death, the second half tells of Sig's widow Kriemhild and her revenge against Attila the Hun. This silent masterpiece is one of the greatest films ever made, with breathtaking atmosphere, complicated special FX, and surprising moments of violence and seminudity you don't normally associate with a film of this vintage. Often copied but never equaled, this German film has influenced everyone from Ray Harryhausen to George Lucas.

SILENCERS, THE

★★☆ RCA/Columbia, 1966, NR, 102 min. Dir: Phil Karlson. Cast: Dean Martin, Stella Stevens, Victor Buono, Daliah Lavi, Robert Webber, Cyd Charisse, Nancy Kovack, James Gregory, Beverly Adams, Arthur O'Connell, Roger C. Carmel, Richard Devon.

The first and best of the four Matt Helm adventures (based on the character created by Donald Hamilton) fashioned as vehicles for Martin. In this one, Dino is out to stop evil Buono (the head of the dreaded Big O organization) from destroying America's atomic testing sites. Good supporting cast, with Stevens stealing all her scenes as Dean's klutzy assistant.

SILENT RUNNING

★★★ MCA/Universal, 1971, G, 89 min. Dir: Douglas Trumbull. Cast: Bruce Dern, Cliff Potts, Ron Rifkin, Jesse Vint.

After nuclear war defoliates the entire Earth, the last vegetation is sent into space, where it is cared for by botanist Dern. When ordered to destroy the space garden by his superiors, Bruce, aided by a trio of "droids" played by paraplegic actors in robot costumes, goes nutso (big surprise) and murders his fellow crew members in order to save his beloved plants. The directorial debut of special FX ace Trumbull, this often has the look of *2001,* on which he worked, and has good work from Dern in his first starring role. Coscripted by

Bruce Dern takes a dip in Silent Running *(1971).*

Michael Cimino and Steven Bochco; turn down the sound during the awful pro-ecology Joan Baez songs.

SILVER NEEDLE IN THE SKY

★★ Sinister Cinema, 1953, NR, 70 min. Dir: Hollingsworth Morse. Cast: Richard Crane, Sally Mansfield, Scotty Beckett, Maurice Cass.

Rocky Jones and friends find intrigue on a spaceship full of alien diplomats on their way to an intergalactic peace conference. Okay reedited Rocky feature with some marked similarities to the classic *Star Trek* episode "Journey to Babel."

SIMON

★★ Warner, 1980, PG, 97 min. Dir: Marshall Brickman. Cast: Alan Arkin, Madeline Kahn, Austin Pendleton, Judy Graubart, William Finley, Wallace Shawn, Fred Gwynne, Adolph Green.

A good idea gets mostly mediocre handling in this comedy about a psychologist (Arkin) brainwashed into believing that he's a visitor from outer space. Scattershot laughs but often needlessly mean-spirited. Graubart (from the great '70s kid's TV program *The Electric Company*) steals this away from many of her better known costars in a sweet role as Arkin's ditzy girlfriend.

SINBAD AND THE EYE OF THE TIGER

★★ Columbia/TriStar, 1977, PG, 113 min. Dir: Sam Wanamaker. Cast: Patrick Wayne, Jane Seymour, Taryn Power, Margaret Whiting, Patrick Troughton, Kurt Christian, Damien Thomas, Bernard Kay.

Ray Harryhausen's third and final *Sinbad* movie (a *Sinbad Goes to Mars* project was abandoned in the mid-'80s) has some of his best FX but also one of his worst plots. An evil sorceress (Whiting, coming on like Akim Tamiroff in drag) turns a handsome prince into a baboon so his beautiful sister (the ravishing Seymour) asks Sinbad (Wayne, making John Phillip Law look good) to take them to a magical temple at the top of the world where the spell may be broken. Seymour and Power (as a helpful magician's daughter) have appeal (and their near-nude scene is shocking to find here) and many of the animated critters (including the baboon, a horned troglodyte, a gigantic walrus, and the brozen statue Minoton) are first-rate but this is way too long, with a story that could have been resolved in half the time and isn't helped at all by the flat direction and bland musical score. A must for Harryhausen fans but everyone else might want to pass on it. Filmed as *Sinbad at the Edge of the World.*

SINBAD AT THE EDGE OF THE WORLD
See: *Sinbad and the Eye of the Tiger.*

SINBAD OF THE SEVEN SEAS
★ Warner, 1986, PG-13, 95 min. Dirs: Enzo Castellari, Luigi Cozzi. Cast: Lou Ferrigno, Teagan Clive, John Steiner, Daria Nicolodi.

Not released until 1989, this Italian Harry-hausen wannabe is of the same paltry school as Ferrigno's *Hercules* epics. Nicolodi relates the tale of how Sinbad (Lou) once battled an evil king (Steiner) on an island inhabited by ghosts, demons, and the requisite Amazon women. Cozzi was mostly responsible for the colorful but mediocre special FX sequences.

SINBAD'S GOLDEN VOYAGE
See: *The Golden Voyage of Sinbad.*

SINBAD THE SAILOR
★★☆ Turner, 1947, NR, 117 min. Dir: Richard Wallace. Cast: Douglas Fairbanks, Jr., Maureen O'Hara, Anthony Quinn, Walter Slezak, George Tobias, Jane Greer, Mike Mazurki, Sheldon Leonard.

Richly Technicolored bauble with the dashing Fairbanks in the title role, searching evil Quinn's island for the legendary treasure of Alexander the Great and finding love with luscious O'Hara. This entertainingly tongue-in-cheek fantasy never takes itself seriously, which would explain some rather odd casting and silly plotting.

SISTERHOOD, THE
★★ Media, 1988, R, 76 min. Dir: Cirio H. Santiago. Cast: Rebecca Holden, Lynn-Holly Johnson, Chuck Wagner, Barbara Hooper.

Mediocre *Mad Max* clone with an alleged feminist edge—I say alleged because for all the female heroics, half the female cast run around with their breasts hanging out. Holden leads a band of lady rebels in the nuclear aftermath who help Johnson avenge the death of her brother at the hands of brutal male warriors. Not the worst of this genre but not all that great either. Lynn-Holly psychically communicates with her pet hawk à la *Ladyhawke* and there are lots of girl-guy fisticuffs.

SKY PIRATES
★☆ CBS/Fox, 1986, PG-13, 88 min. Dir: Colin Eggleston. Cast: John Hargreaves, Meredith Phillips, Max Phipps, Bill Hunter, Simon Chilvers, Alex Scott.

Confused Australian action-fantasy set at the end of World War II. Hargreaves is a pilot who discovers a magical talisman on Easter Island he believes was left there by aliens and battles villain Phipps for its possession. An interesting idea gets muddled handling, with way too many plot loopholes and an uncharismatic cast.

SLAPSTICK OF ANOTHER KIND
★★ Vestron, 1982, PG, 82 min. Dir: Steven Paul. Cast: Jerry Lewis, Madeline Kahn, Marty Feldman, Jim Backus, John Abbott, Pat Morita, Samuel Fuller, Merv Griffin, Virginia Graham, voice of Orson Welles.

Say what you will but this very strange adaptation of a book by Kurt Vonnegut is nothing if not different. Lewis and Kahn are half-alien superintelligent kids who become morons when separated from one another. Jerry and Madeline also play the kid's human parents and both they and a very offbeat support cast do what they can with this disjointed, confusing comic fantasy that's marred mostly by the inadequate direction of young Paul, who was barely out of his teens at the time.

SLAUGHTERHOUSE FIVE
★★★ MCA/Universal, 1972, R, 104 min. Dir: George Roy Hill. Cast: Michael Sacks, Ron Leibman, Valerie Perrine, Eugene Roche, Sharon Gans, Perry King, Holly Near, John Dehner.

Overlong but mostly on-the-money film version of Kurt Vonnegut's novel about Billy Pilgrim (Sacks) who becomes "unstuck" in time and relives a life that cumulates in his being abducted by aliens, along with luscious starlet Montana Wildhack (Perrine in her topless debut). Full of wonderful moments and performances, with Leibman especially good as Sacks's lifelong mortal enemy.

SLAVE GIRLS FROM BEYOND INFINITY
★★ Tempe, 1987, R, 72 min. Dir: Ken Dixon. Cast: Elizabeth Kaitan, Cindy Beal, Brinke Stevens, Don Scribner, Carl Horner, Kirk Graves.

Our lovely lasses are hunted by a madman *Most Dangerous Game*-style on a lost planet in this watchable T&A cheapie. Of course, its watchability is entirely dependent on your tolerance for large breasts being paraded by at regular intervals. Hey, if it works for you. . . .

SLEEPER
★★★☆ MGM/UA, 1973, PG, 88 min. Dir: Woody Allen. Cast: Woody Allen, Diane Keaton, John Beck, Mary Gregory, Don Keefer, John McLiam.

One of Woody's best early films is this sci-fi spoof in which Allen is revived after two hundred years in suspended animation to discover a world where smoking and junk food are good for you, sex is provided by machines, and an assassination attempt has left the U.S. president reduced to nothing but a nose! Woody targets everything from *1984* to the Gene Roddenberry TV movie *Genesis II* and almost all the gags work (I particularly like the moment where Allen identifies a photo of Bela Lugosi as a past mayor of New York), especially the Buster Keaton-like sequence of Allen disguised as a robot—who gets purchased first by a gay guy and ultimately by goofy heroine Keaton. Love the scene with Woody and the orb, too.

SLIME PEOPLE, THE

★ Rhino, 1963, NR, 76 min. Dir: Robert Hutton. Cast: Robert Hutton, Les Tremayne, Susan Hart, Robert Burton, Judee Morton, William Boyce.

Rubber monsters from the Earth's core terrorize Los Angeles and a very small cast in this cheap creature feature starring and directed by familiar B-movie leading man Hutton. Some scenes predate *Night of the Living Dead,* with characters trapped in a deserted meat market by the slimy beasts but the thrills are few and the laughs are many—it's just too drawn out to be funny in a way that would make it fun to watch.

SLIPSTREAM

★★☆ Virgin Vision, 1989, PG-13, 92 min. Dir: Steven M. Lisberger. Cast: Bill Paxton, Mark Hamill, Kitty Aldridge, Bob Peck, Eleanor David, Ben Kingsley, F. Murray Abraham, Robbie Coltrane.

In a future world where atmospheric changes have caused ceaseless winds that have devastated much of the Earth, Paxton and Hamill are battling bounty hunters both after the same quarry. This big-scale British movie (partly filmed in Turkey) has ambition and a sense of style and features Hamill in one of his best roles as a bad guy, but after a serious start it eventually turns into something of a satire, a change in tone that doesn't work at all. Peck plays Paxton's robot partner while Oscar winners Kingsley and Abraham are wasted in small roles.

SNOW CREATURE, THE

★☆ Goodtimes, 1954, NR, 70 min. Dir: W. Lee Wilder. Cast: Paul Langton, Leslie Denison, Teru Shimada, Darlene Fields.

A Himalayan expedition captures a tall Yeti (whose face is never clearly seen) and transports it to Los Angeles, where government officials argue about what to do with it until it escapes and goes on a budget-conscious rampage. The first of several '50s Abominable Snowman movies, this has some interesting direction and photography but pages of dull dialogue and flat acting, much in the manner of the same director's *Phantom from Space.*

SNOW WHITE AND THE THREE STOOGES

★☆ Fox, 1961, NR, 117 min. Dir: Walter Lang. Cast: Moe Howard, Larry Fine, Joe DeRita, Carol Heiss, Edson Stroll, Patricia Medina, Guy Rolfe, Edgar Barrier, Buddy Baer, Blossom Rock.

Wide-screen Technicolor fantasy, with Olympic skating star Heiss as Snow White, Medina well cast as the evil queen, and the Stooges as, well, the Stooges—in incredibly watered down form, that is. The biggest-budgeted of the many Stooges features made in the early '60s but also the worst; Moe, Larry, and Curly Joe take a back seat to all that skating and romance. Moe should have eye-gouged the whole lot of them. Hero Stroll later played a seaman on *McHale's Navy,* while Rock was Grandmama on *The Addams Family.*

SOLARBABIES

★ MGM/UA, 1986, PG-13, 94 min. Dir: Alan Johnson. Cast: Richard Jordan, Jami Gertz, Jason Patric, Lukas Haas, Charles Durning, Sarah Douglas, Peter DeLuise, Frank Converse, Adrian Pasdar, Terrence Mann, Kelly Bishop, James LeGros.

Mel Brooks backed this appalling tripe about teens (led by Gertz) after an alien sphere called "Bohdi" that will help them escape from villain Jordan and evil lady scientist Douglas. A huge box-office flop, although set in the future on another planet, everyone acts just like your typical '80s California kids. Don't even let the promise of this above-average cast tempt you into watching—you'll hate yourself if you do.

SOLAR CRISIS

★★ Vidmark Entertainment, 1990, PG-13, 111 min. Dir: Alan Smithee [Richard C. Sarafian]. Cast: Tim Matheson, Charlton Heston, Corin Nemec, Peter Boyle, Jack Palance, Annabel Schofield, Brenda Bakke, Tetsuya Bessho, Dan Shor, Paul Koslo, Michael Berryman, voice of Paul Williams.

A slow, all-star sci-fi disaster film backed by a Japanese production company but shot in America. In the year 2050, a solar flare causes concern that the sun may explode and destroy the Earth. Matheson is the commander of the spaceship carrying a robotic explosive device (voiced by Williams!) that will hopefully prevent the sun's destruction; Heston is his estranged father; Schofield is a beautiful British-accented lady android; Boyle is a villain; and Palance a grizzled desert bum who rides a motorcycle. Something of a hit in Japan, this TV movie-style epic was released directly to tape in the U.S. Aka *Star Fire.*

SOLARIS
★★★☆ Fox/Lorber, 1972, NR, 165 min. Dir: Andrei Tarkovsky. Cast: Natalya Bondarchuk, Donatas Banionis, Yuri Yarvet, Anatoly Solonitsin.

Epic Russian sci-fi (with touches of horror) about a psychologist sent to a space station where the crew has been suffering from strange dreams and hallucinations and several have died under mysterious circumstances. A long, mind-boggling metaphysical journey with some similarity to *2001* but enough unique identity of its own to make it a rewarding viewing experience.

SOME CALL IT LOVING
★★☆ Monterey, 1973, R, 103 min. Dir: James B. Harris. Cast: Zalman King, Tisa Farrow, Carol White, Richard Pryor.

Odd fantasy (based on a story by John Collier) with King as a sullen rich guy who buys carnival "Sleeping Beauty" Farrow and awakens her with a kiss. In the end, though, he discovers that reality doesn't always measure up to the fantasies we create for ourselves. Pryor has a small, somewhat out of place role as a foul-mouthed graffiti artist.

SOMEWHERE IN TIME
★★★ MCA/Universal, 1980, PG, 103 min. Dir: Jeannot Szwarc. Cast: Christopher Reeve, Jane Seymour, Christopher Plummer, Teresa Wright, Bill Erwin, George Voskovec.

Gentle adaptation of Richard Matheson's romantic fantasy *Bid Time Return* about a lonely young playwright (Reeve) who falls in love with the eighty-year-old photograph of a beautiful actress (Seymour). Through intense mental concentration, Reeve projects himself into the past, where he and Seymour meet and briefly find love together before his inevitable return to the present. A box-office failure when first released, this film has seen its reputation grow over the years and now is something of a cult hit. Reeve and Seymour are at their most personable, the John Barry music (with some select classical themes) is beautiful, and the ending—downbeat yet in a sense happy—finishes this on just the right note.

SOMEWHERE TOMORROW
★★★ Media, 1983, PG, 87 min. Dir: Robert Wiemer. Cast: Sarah Jessica Parker, Nancy Addison, Tom Shea, Rick Weber, Paul Bates, James Congdon.

Appealing fantasy with Parker (during her *Square Pegs* period) as a teen who meets a cute boy (Shea) she discovers to be the ghost of a plane crash victim. Or is she just imagining it all after bumping her head? Good performances and moments of real drama to offset the comic elements in this underrated kids' movie that deserves to be better known.

SON OF BLOB
★★ Video Gems, 1972, PG, 88 min. Dir: Larry Hagman. Cast: Robert Walker, Jr., Gwynne Gilford, Carol Lynley, Burgess Meredith, Godfrey Cambridge, Dick Van Patten, Marlene Clark, Cindy Williams.

In a very '70s sequel, Alaskan Pipeline worker Cambridge brings a piece of frozen Blob back home to Southern California, where it defrosts and gobbles up much of the all-star cast. Look for director Hagman's cameo as a street bum in this tongue-in-cheek (or is that Blob-in-cheek?) followup. Aka *Beware! The Blob.*

SON OF FLUBBER
★★☆ Disney, 1963, NR, 100 min. Dir: Robert Stevenson. Cast: Fred MacMurray, Nancy Olson, Keenan Wynn, Tommy Kirk, Elliot Reid, Joanna Moore, Leon Ames, Ed Wynn, Charlie Ruggles, Paul Lynde.

Everybody's back from *The Absent Minded Professor* when prof MacMurray creates a new invention called Dry Rain while the school uses his Flubbergas to win the big football game. Predictable sequel with lots of pratfalls and FX, though it's the cast that really makes this worth watching.

SON OF GODZILLA
★★ Interglobal, 1967, NR, 84 min. Dir: Jun Fukuda. Cast: Tadao Takashima, Akira Kubo, Beverly Maeda, Akihiko Hirata.

Zilla becomes a proud papa when a huge egg on an island being used for weather experiments hatches out a pug-nosed little (relatively speaking) critter called Minya. The big G and his boy then take on some huge praying mantises and a giant spider before going into frozen hibernation—an oddly touching and poetic final shot. Not the best of the series, thanks mostly to the awful Godzilla suit and cheesier-than-usual FX, but adequate filler for Ziller fans. Aka *Gojira no Musuko (Godzilla and Son).*

SON OF KONG
★★☆ Turner, 1933, NR, 69 min. Dir: Ernest B. Schoedsack. Cast: Robert Armstrong, Helen Mack, Frank Reicher, John Marston, Victor Wong, Noble Johnson.

Weak puppy sequel, with Armstrong and company returning to Kong's Island looking for treasure but meeting his friendly twelve-foot son instead. After a slow first half, this practically runs screaming toward its spectacu-

Robert Armstrong and Helen Mack have ringside seats in Son of Kong *(1933).*

lar, emotional climax as the island is destroyed by an earthquake and little Kong dies saving Armstrong—the final image of the huge ape hand, one of its fingers bandaged, slipping beneath the waves is unforgettable. Too bad the rest of this quickly slapped together followup really doesn't measure up.

SON OF SAMSON

★★ Sinister Cinema, 1960, NR, 90 min. Dir: Carlo Campogalliani. Cast: Mark Forest, Chelo Alonso, Angelo Zanolli, Vira Silenti.

Samson's son Maciste (Forest) tries to save ancient Egypt from an evil queen with hypnotic powers. Some good photography helps this routine peblum originally titled *Maciste nella Valle dei Re (Maciste in the Valley of the Kings)* and aka Maciste—The Mighty.

SON OF SINBAD

★★ VCI, 1953, NR, 88 min. Dir: Ted Tetzlaff. Cast: Dale Robertson, Sally Forrest, Vincent Price, Mari Blanchard, Lili St. Cyr, Leon Askin.

The legendary sailorman's son (Robertson) and his buddy Omar Khayyam (Price) dally with damsels and try to gain control of a power source called "Greek Fire" in this colorfully absurd fantasy. Not released until 1955, allegedly due to St. Cyr's sexy dance numbers, this is typical of the sort of Arabian Nights movies Hollywood turned out before they

were reinvented by Ray Harryhausen. Kim Novak has a bit part. Aka *Nights in a Harem.*

SORCERESS

★☆ Thorn/EMI, 1982, R, 83 min. Dir: Brian Stuart [Jack Hill]. Cast: Lynette Harris, Leigh Anne Harris, Robert Ballesteros, Martin LaSalle.

Pretty awful New World sword-and-sorcery quickie about twin girl warriors (the Harris sisters) avenging their parents' deaths at the hands of an evil warlock. Based on a story by Jim Wynorski, this shot-in-Mexico fantasy has lots of cut-rate monsters but surprisingly little eroticism. After producer Roger Corman reedited the film without Hill's input, Hill had his name removed; it was replaced by the bogus Brian Stuart—actually the first names of Corman's two sons.

SOYLENT GREEN

★★☆ MGM/UA, 1973, PG, 97 min. Dir: Richard Fleischer. Cast: Charlton Heston, Leigh Taylor-Young, Edward G. Robinson, Joseph Cotten, Chuck Connors, Paula Kelly, Brock Peters, Whit Bissell, Mike Henry, Dick Van Patten.

Well-cast but somewhat flat version of Harry Harrison's classic story *Make Room! Make Room!* about a future Earth society's rather gruesome and sickening answer to overpopulation. Heston is his usual stoic self as a New York cop investigating the reasons behind a political assassination, but Robinson is the one to watch in his last role as Heston's elderly roommate who decides to kill himself and whose death leads Charlton to the discovery that "Soylent Green is . . ." See it and find out.

SPACEBALLS

★★☆ MGM/UA, 1987, PG, 96 min. Dir: Mel Brooks. Cast: Mel Brooks, John Candy, Rick Moranis, Bill Pullman, Daphne Zuniga, Dick Van Patten, George Wyner, John Hurt, voices of Joan Rivers, Dom DeLuise.

Scattershot Brooks parody of *Star Wars* and several other popular modern sci-fi films. Pullman is the Han Solo clone reluctantly trying to save bitchy princess Zuniga from the clutches of diminutive Darth Vader wannabe Moranis. The best moments are provided by Brooks as the mystical Yogurt, DeLuise as icky Pizza the Hut, and funny nods to both *Alien* and *Planet of the Apes*.

SPACE CAMP

★★☆ Vestron, 1986, PG, 107 min. Dir: Harry Winer. Cast: Kate Capshaw, Lea Thompson, Kelly Preston, Larry B. Scott, Leaf Phoenix, Tate Donovan, Tom Skerritt, Barry Primus, Terry O'Quinn, Mitchell Anderson.

A group of teens and younger kids are chosen for a NASA summer camp for future astronauts and—guess what?—are accidentally launched into space. Enjoyable hokum with all the expected clichés (including a cute robot), buoyed by a good cast.

SPACED INVADERS

★☆ Touchstone, 1990, PG, 102 min. Dir: Patrick Read Johnson. Cast: Doug Barr, Royal Dano, Arianna Richards, J. J. Anderson, Greg Berger, Debbie Lee Carrington.

"Cute" comedy about a group of slapstick Martians who come to Earth on Halloween night after intercepting a rebroadcast of Orson Welles's *War of the Worlds* program and mistaking it for a real attack. Feeble sci-fi spoof that's thoroughly convinced it's totally hilarious—but isn't. Aka *Martians*.

SPACED OUT

★☆ Thorn/EMI, 1979, R, 84 min. Dir: Norman J. Warren. Cast: Barry Stokes, Tony Maiden, Glory Annen, Ava Cadell, Michael Rowlatt, Kate Ferguson.

Originally titled *Outer Touch,* this British sci-fi sex comedy is pretty weak tea. Alien ladies arrive on Earth and after capturing a couple of locals are turned on to the joys of sex. The American release version spiced things up a bit by adding a bit more nudity and redubbing a computer to crack dirty jokes.

Michael Ironside is the evil Overdog in Spacehunter: Adventures in the Forbidden Zone *(1983).*

SPACEHUNTER: ADVENTURES IN THE FORBIDDEN ZONE

★★ Columbia/TriStar, 1983, PG, 89 min. Dir: Lamont Johnson. Cast: Peter Strauss, Molly Ringwald, Ernie Hudson, Andrea Marcovicci, Michael Ironside, Beeson Carroll.

Smarmy Strauss is the title character who finds himself saddled with bratty teen Ringwald while trying to rescue a trio of beautiful damsels in the clutches of an evil character called Overdog—no relation to Underdog, I guess. Released to theaters in 3-D, this has some good FX and makeup but wastes the contributions of talents like Marcovicci (as an android) and Ironside (as Overdog).

SPACE MEN

See: *Assignment: Outer Space.*

SPACE MONSTER DAGORA
See: *Dagora, the Space Monster.*

SPACE MUTINY
★ AIP, 1987, R, 90 min. Dir: David Winters. Cast: Reb Brown, Cameron Mitchell, John Phillip Law, Cissy Mitchell, James Ryan.

Laughable video drek about trouble on a spaceship captained by a bearded Mitchell. Brown is the hero who helps Cam and his daughter (real-life daughter Cissy) put down a crew uprising spearheaded by Law. Almost hypnotic in its awfulness, sharp-eyed viewers will notice that all the special FX footage is stock shots from *Battlestar Gallactica.*

SPACE PATROL
★★ Rhino, 1951–55, NR, 90 min. per tape. Dir: Dick Darley. Cast: Ed Kemmer, Lyn Osborn, Virginia Hewitt, Nina Bara, Rudolph Anders, Marvin Miller.

A low-budget early '50s sci-fi television series about the thirtieth-century outer space adventures of Commander Buzz Corey (Kemmer) and his crew. Nostalgic older Baby Boomers may want to check out this *Rocky Jones*-like show.

SPACE RAGE
★☆ Vestron, 1985, R, 77 min. Dir: Conrad E. Palmisano. Cast: Richard Farnsworth, Michael Paré, John Laughlin, Lee Purcell, William Windom, Lewis Van Bergen.

Cheap sci-fi Western about bounty hunters stalking their prey on a distant planet. Worth it only for some of the cast, especially Farnsworth as an aging ex-cop who becomes the hero.

SPACE RAIDERS
★★ Warner, 1983, PG, 82 min. Dir: Howard R. Cohen. Cast: Vince Edwards, David Mendenhall, Patsy Pease, Thom Christopher, Luca Bercovici, Dick Miller.

Mild Roger Corman production about a kid stowaway on a spaceship (commanded by Edwards) that also has an alien on board. Miller enlivens things briefly but this is mostly for fans of stock special FX footage and music from *Battle Beyond the Stars.* Aka *Star Child.*

SPACESHIP
See: *Naked Space.*

SPACESHIP TO THE UNKNOWN
See: *Flash Gordon: Rocketship.*

SPACE RANGERS
★★☆ Cabin Fever, 1993, NR, 100 min. per tape. Dir: Ben Bolt. Cast: Jeff Kaake, Linda Hunt, Marjorie Monaghan, Cary-Hiroyuki Tagawa, Jack McGee, Clint Howard.

This short-lived TV series was made to cash in on all those new *Star Trek* shows and isn't bad. Hunt is the commander of an intergalactic police force (headed by Kaake) who battles various space villains. Something like a '90s version of the old *Rocky Jones* show (with better FX), this is silly and often clichéd but still fun.

SPACEWAYS
★★ Sinister Cinema, 1953, NR, 76 min. Dir: Terence Fisher. Cast: Howard Duff, Eva Bartok, Alan Wheatley, Andrew Osborn, Michael Medwin, Cecil Chevreau.

Odd mixture of sci-fi and murder mystery, with Duff as an American scientist in England who's suspected of murdering girlfriend Bartok's husband and hiding the body in a recently launched rocket. Not as interesting as it sounds, this early Hammer Film has too much talk and too little action.

SPECIES
★★☆ MGM/UA, 1995, R, 108 min. Dir: Roger Donaldson. Cast: Ben Kingsley, Michael Madsen, Marg Helgenberger, Forest Whitaker, Alfred Molina, Natasha Henstridge, Whip Hubley, Michelle Williams.

It's *Alien* on Earth as a shape-shifting, fast-maturing female monster (the sexy Henstridge) spawned from otherworldly DNA rampages through L.A. looking for some helpless guy with whom to procreate—so why does she keep stopping off at gay bars? The H. R. Giger-designed monster is impressive (like some extraterrestrial *Bride of Frankenstein*) but the story rushes on so quickly it never bothers to answer many of the (often intriguing) questions it poses. There's a good cast (with Madsen and Helgenberger making a pleasantly mature romantic couple) and some tense scenes, but the climax is ripped off from producer Frank Mancuso, Jr.'s earlier hit *Friday the 13th Part V.*

SPIRIT OF '76
★★★ RCA/Columbia, 1990, PG, 82 min. Dir: Lucas Reiner. Cast: David Cassidy, Olivia D'Abo, Leif Garrett, Barbara Bain, Julie Brown, Tommy Chong, Carl Reiner, Rob Reiner, Moon Zappa, Don Novello, Geoff Hoyle, Iron Eyes Cody, Jeff McDonald, Steve McDonald.

A pretty funny sleeper directed by the son of Rob (Meathead) Reiner and the grandson of Carl (Alan Brady on the *The Dick Van Dyke Show*). In the year 2176, Cassidy, D'Abo, and

Hoyle take a time machine back to 1776 to learn about the U.S. Constitution. Instead, they end up in 1976, where they're confronted with the horrors of disco music, platform shoes, polyester leisure suits, and smile buttons. A clever idea well executed on a budget, with lots of guest stars and cultural references to keep track of and plenty of period music on the soundtrack.

SPLASH

★★★ 1984, Disney, PG, 111 min. Dir: Ron Howard. Cast: Daryl Hannah, Tom Hanks, John Candy, Eugene Levy, Dody Goodman, Richard B. Shull, Shecky Greene, Howard Morris.

Hannah, in her most appealing role, is a beautiful mermaid who can grow legs when she leaves the water. She falls in love with unhappily engaged New York businessman Hanks, whom she had saved from drowning as a child. Overlong and predictable but still brightly entertaining, this comic fantasy was hardly a new idea (remember *Mr. Peabody and the Mermaid*?) but has been copied many times since and has Hanks and Candy at their best. Made-for-TV sequel: *Splash Too.*

SPLIT SECOND

★★ HBO, 1992, R, 90 min. Dirs: Tony Maylam, Ian Sharp. Cast: Rutger Hauer, Kim Cattrall, Neil Duncan, Michael J. Pollard.

In a dreary future London, a violent serial killer stalked by Hauer seems to be an alien but turns out to be a heart-ripping demon. Routine sci-fi/horror thriller (begun by Maylam and finished by Sharp) with Hauer and Cattrall in good form, but Duncan steals it as Rutger's nerdy police partner who becomes tougher (and funnier) as the story goes along.

SPY SMASHER

★★★ Republic, 1942, NR, 185 min. Dir: William Witney. Cast: Kane Richmond, Marguerite Chapman, Hans Schumm, Sam Flint, Tristram Coffin, Georges Renavent.

A great serial with Richman as the title character, a costumed superhero (originating in *Whiz Comics*) who uses his supersonic Batplane (hey, didn't Batman come up with that idea first?) to battle Nazi supercriminal the Mask (Schumm). Well-paced action highlights from serial kingpin Witney help make this one of the most enjoyable serials currently available on tape. The reedited feature version is called *Spy Smasher Returns.*

SPY SMASHER RETURNS

See: *Spy Smasher.*

STALKER

★★★ Fox/Lorber, 1979, NR, 160 min. Dir: Andrei Tarkovsky. Cast: Alexander Kaidanovsky, Nikolai Grinko, Anatoli Solonitsin, Alice Friendlich.

Solaris director Tarkovsky returns with this long, intelligent Russian sci-fi drama filmed in both color and black-and-white. Kaidanovsky guides Grinko and Solonitsin through a forbidden wasteland in a bleak future. Not for everyone but well worth it for those willing to work with it.

STAR CHILD

See: *Space Raiders.*

STARCRASH

★★ Embassy, 1979, PG, 92 min. Dir: Lewis Coates [Luigi Cozzi]. Cast: Caroline Munro, Marjoe Gortner, Christopher Plummer, David Hasselhoff, Joe Spinell, Robert Tessier, Judd Hamilton, voice of Hamilton Camp.

Filmed as *The Adventures of Stella Starr,* this Italian imitation of *Star Wars* and *Barbarella* is awful but still fun to watch. Munro, in one of her few leading roles, is the outer space heroine who tries to save the universe from evil emperor Spinell (in a delirious bit of miscasting) with the help of comrades Gortner, a pre-*Baywatch* Hasselhoff, and a comic relief robot embodied by her ex-husband Hamilton but voiced by Camp. Everything about this—from the plotting to the direction to the special FX—is second-rate, but with a cast like this it's hard to hate.

STAR CRYSTAL

★☆ Starmaker, 1985, R, 93 min. Dir: Lance Lindsay. Cast: Juston Campbell, Faye Bolt, John W. Smith.

Another bad *Alien* ripoff. This time astronauts find a rocklike egg containing a murderous creature with tentacles that kills off most of the cast until a friendly, *E.T.* type shows up at the end to help. Cheap and dreary with bad acting and mediocre FX.

STAR FIRE

See: *Solar Crisis.*

STARFLIGHT ONE

★★ Vestron, 1983, NR, 155 min. Dir: Jerry Jameson. Cast: Lee Majors, Lauren Hutton, Hal Linden, Ray Milland, Gail Strickland, Robert Webber, Tess Harper, George Di Cenzo, Pat Corley, Terry Kiser, Kirk Cameron, Michael Sacks, Jocelyn Brando, Robert Englund.

I find it difficult to believe that neither Irwin Allen nor Jennings Lang were involved in this TV movie since it copies a lot from their various disaster movies. A supersonic passenger jet ends up trapped in space and various rescue attempts are tried while several supporting characters are killed off. John Dykstra supervised the FX and the cast is fun but this is way too long and obvious to generate much excitement. Jameson also directed the much better airplane disaster pic *Airport '77*, while the executive producer here was none other than Henry Winkler. Aka *Starfight: The Plane That Couldn't Land*.

STARFLIGHT: THE PLANE THAT COULDN'T LAND

See: *Starflight One*.

STARGATE

★★★★ LIVE, 1994, PG-13, 120 min. Dir: Roland Emmerich. Cast: Kurt Russell, James Spader, Jaye Richardson, Alexis Cruz, John Diehl, Viveca Lindfors.

One of the best sci-fi epics in years, this stars Spader in one of his best roles as an Egyptologist who helps reactivate an ancient gateway to another dimension. Spader and grim, suicidal marine commander Russell (in one of *his* best roles) travel through the gate into an alternate desert universe where aliens—who were behind the building of the pyramids and were the inspiration for ancient Egyptian mythology—are mistreating their slaves. Inevitably Jim and Kurt lead a revolt and overthrow the aliens' leader (androgynous Richardson from *The Crying Game*). A surprise big box-office hit, this seventy-million-dollar U.S.-French coproduction is a lot more complex and intelligent than most modern sci-fi. It makes up for occasional confusing parts through the sheer strength of its fine acting, imaginative direction, and special FX. David Arnold composed the beautiful score; Emmerich directed *Independence Day* next.

STAR KNIGHT

★★ Vidmark Entertainment, 1985, R, 92 min. Dir: Fernando Colombo. Cast: Klaus Kinski, Harvey Keitel, Fernando Rey, Marie Lamour.

A very strange sci-fi/fantasy with a badly dubbed Kinski as an medieval alchemist who befriends a visiting alien. Keitel is a knight who thinks that the alien's spacecraft is actually a dragon he must face in battle to win the hand of princess Lamour. So absurd that it's actually enjoyable, in a perverse sort of way; Keitel even contributes a totally out of place *Taxi Driver* in-joke! Aka *Knight of the Dragon*.

STARMAN

★★★ Goodtimes, 1984, PG 115 min. Dir: John Carpenter. Cast: Jeff Bridges, Karen Allen, Richard Jaeckel, Charles Martin Smith, Robert Phalen, Lu Leonard.

A stranded alien in Wisconsin takes the form of Allen's late husband Bridges and forces her to help him get to the rendezvous spot where a spaceship will pick him up. Along the way they are pursued by nice NASA scientist Smith and bad FBI agent Jaeckel and, not unexpectedly, fall in love. Carpenter (who wasn't the first choice as director) proves that he is just as capable of making romantic fantasy as he is horror and action films. Despite the myriad clichés this is highly entertaining and fun, with excellent performances by Jeff and Karen; Dick Smith supervised the makeup FX. Very little violence (for Carpenter) but a surprising nude scene for Bridges. Best line: "Red means stop; green means go; yellow means go very fast!"

STARSHIP INVASIONS

★☆ Warner, 1977, PG, 87 min. Dir: Ed Hunt. Cast: Robert Vaughn, Christopher Lee, Helen Shaver, Daniel Pilon, Henry Ramer, Victoria Johnson.

Laughable Canadian sci-fi with Vaughn as a UFO expert abducted by good aliens who need his help in battling bad aliens headed by Lee. It's always fun watching good actors trying to make something out of total crap but even Vaughn and Lee—not to mention Shaver—are defeated by this corny tripe. The plot is inane, the makeup sloppy, and the starships look like balloons from a Thanksgiving Day parade. The late '70s was clearly a rough time for B-movie actors.

STAR SLAMMER

★★ Vidmark Entertainment, 1994, R, 90 min. Dir: Fred Olen Ray. Cast: Aldo Ray, Sandy Brooke, Ross Hagen, Mayra Gant, Bobbie Bresee, Susan Stokey, Dawn Wildsmith, Erick Caiden, Johnny Legend, John Carradine.

The world's first women-in-prison sci-fi movie, this is surprisingly entertaining and fun. Ray is livelier than usual as a mutant bad guy who tortures female prisoners on a space station prison run by eye-patched female warden Gant. Brooke is the usual railroaded innocent heroine who mounts an escape, while Carradine appears briefly in what seems to be stock footage from another movie. The familiar set is left over from *Battle Beyond the Stars*. Aka *Prison Ship* and *The Adventures of Tara Part 1*.

STAR TREK: DEEP SPACE NINE

★★★ Paramount, 1992–96, NR, 46 min. per tape. Dirs: David Carson, Paul Lynch, Winrich Kolbe, others. Cast: Avery Brooks, René Auberjonois, Terry Farrell, Nana Visitor, Colm Meaney, Siddig El El Fadil, Cirroc Lofton, Armin Shimerman.

The third *Star Trek* series (or fourth if you count the animated series) is darker and more serious in tone than *The Next Generation,* from which it spun off, taking with it the characters played by Farrell and Meaney. Brooks is good as embittered Commander Sisto, who's in charge of a space station orbiting the war-torn planet of Bajor. The 96-minute pilot ("Emissary") sets the tone as Sisto encounters the man he holds responsible for his wife's death—Captain Jean-Luc Picard (guest star Patrick Stewart). Most of the regular characters are various sorts of aliens and the series' harder edge often makes it a lot more interesting than many episodes of the kinder, gentler *Next Gen.*

STAR TREK: FIRST CONTACT

★★★ Paramount, 1996, PG-13, 110 min. Dir: Jonathan Frakes. Cast: Patrick Stewart, Jonathan Frakes, Gates McFadden, LeVar Burton, Brent Spiner, Marina Sirtis, Michael Dorn, Alice Krige, James Cromwell, Alfre Woodard.

Totally without expectation, the eighth in the big-screen *Star Trek* adventures (and the second for the crew of *The Next Generation*) turns out to be one of the best. As the evil Borg (first seen in the *Next Gen* episode "The Best of Both Worlds") devastate the galaxy, the *Enterprise* and her crew are called into action. When several Borg escape the destruction of their mother ship via time warp, they end up in the twenty-first century, where inventor Zefram Cochrane (*Babe's* Cromwell in a role first played by Glenn Corbett in the original *Star Trek* episode "Metamorphosis") has just perfected his new warp drive to be first tested on the newly commissioned *Enterprise.* Can Picard and company follow the Borg and stop them from changing history as well as the *Enterprise* crew, who are slowly being replicated into Borgs themselves? Frakes's direction is strong and confident, bringing a nice, creepy touch of horror to the *Trek* universe, following in the tradition of the second-in-command becoming the one to truly know and understand how a good *Star Trek* movie should play. Nearly everything works, from the atmosphere to the FX to the humor to the cast—with Krige a standout as the slimy, Cenobite-like Borg queen.

STAR TREK: GENERATIONS

★★☆ Paramount, 1994, PG, 118 min. Dir: David Carson. Cast: Patrick Stewart, William Shatner, Malcolm McDowell, Jonathan Frakes, Gates McFadden, Brent Spiner, LeVar Burton, Marina Sirtis, Michael Dorn, Whoopi Goldberg, Alan Ruck, James Doohan, Walter Koenig, Gwyneth Walsh.

The seventh big screen *Trek* adventure tries to mix the past with the future with uneven results. McDowell really goes over the top (and for Malcolm, that's saying plenty) as a scientist obsessed with gaining control of an alternate universe known as the Nexus (isn't that a brand of shampoo?). A time warp allows Captains Picard and Kirk (Stewart and Shatner, an interesting contrast in acting styles if ever there was one) to team up and defeat him. Less humor-driven than many of the other *Trek* features, this wastes the contribution of Doohan and Koenig but is still worth seeing even with the plot holes large enough to pilot a starship through. Followed by *Star Trek: First Contact.*

STAR TREK: THE ANIMATED SERIES

★★★ Paramount, 1973–75, NR, 50 min. per tape. Dir: Hal Sutherland. Voices: William Shatner, Leonard Nimoy, DeForest Kelley, James Doohan, Nichelle Nichols, George Takei, Majel Barrett, Mark Lenard, Roger C. Carmel, Stanley Adams.

While the original *Star Trek* series was breaking syndication records on UHF stations around the country, Paramount and Filmation decided to team for this limited animation Saturday morning half-hour series. It was cheaper to do than the long-rumored prime-time revival and, despite the often flat animation, had some very well-written episodes, many of them surprisingly deep for Saturday morning TV. Most of the classic cast returned to voice their old characters (some of them voicing other characters as well) and many of the show's writing staff returned to pen some episodes (several of them sequels to old *Trek* shows), including D. C. Fontana, David Gerrold, and even actor Walter Koenig (whose Chekov character—as well as Grace Lee Whitney's Janice Rand—was not included here). My favorite of the shows include "Yesteryear" (written by Fontana), in which Spock uses the Guardian of Forever gateway first seen in "The City on the Edge of Forever" to return to his own childhood; "The Jihad," in which Kirk and Spock join a host of aliens from around the galaxy to stop a religious war; "The Slaver Weapon," somewhat reminiscent of "The Galileo Seven," with Spock, Uhura, and Sulu searching for a powerful alien device on a distant planetoid; and the comic "Mudd's Passion," in which old friend Harry Mudd gives Christine Chapel a mysterious drug he promises will win her Spock's love.

STAR TREK—THE MOTION PICTURE

★★☆ Paramount, 1979, PG, 142 min. Dir: Robert Wise. Cast: William Shatner, Leonard Nimoy, DeForest Kelley, Persis Khambatta, Stephen Collins, James Doohan, Nichelle Nichols, George Takei, Walter Koenig, Majel Barrett, Grace Lee Whitney, Mark Lenard, Marcy Lafferty, Jon Raschid Kamal, David Gautreaux.

The first *Trek* movie has the advantages of a still reasonably youthful cast, a grand musical score by Jerry Goldsmith (whose main theme would subsequently become the title music for the *ST—The Next Generation* TV show), and the best special FX money ($40 million, they say) could buy. But then there's the screenplay, a pretentious and obvious affair—with the *Enterprise* out to thwart a destructive entity called V'ger on a collision course with Earth—originally meant for the first episode of a proposed but abandoned new *Trek* series and clearly derived from such classic episodes as "The Changeling" and "The Doomsday Machine." Like the *King Kong* remake of a couple of years earlier, this was committed to a locked-in release date and was consequently rushed into theaters so fast the prints barely had time to dry. As a result, the editing isn't the best (though the ten minutes of footage added for the TV and video versions help make things more coherent), and with the story's concentration on newcomers Khambatta and Collins—whom nobody came to see—most of the classic supporting cast is reduced to staring awestruck at an endless parade of Douglas Trumbull-John Dykstra special FX. Despite this, though, Kelley, Doohan, Koenig, and Whitney all have their little moments to shine and Nimoy gives his best performance of the movie series as he takes Spock from the moment of total emotional abandonment to the final realization that it is our emotions that separate living beings from machines and that these emotions must be dealt with and not ignored. Not the worst of the series but far from the best.

STAR TREK II: THE WRATH OF KHAN

★★★ Paramount, 1982, PG, 113 min. Dir: Nicholas Meyer. Cast: William Shatner, Leonard Nimoy, DeForest Kelley, Ricardo Montalban, Kirstie Alley, James Doohan, Nichelle Nichols, George Takei, Walter Koenig, Bibi Besch, Merritt Butrick, Paul Winfield, Judson Scott, Ike Eisenmann, John Winston.

The *Enterprise*'s second big-screen adventure is something of an improvement over the first. On a training mission for young recruits—including the fetching Alley as the half—Vulcan/half-Romulan Lt. Saavik-Kirk and company run afoul of old "Space Seed" nemesis Khan (Montalban), who's out to avenge the death of his wife and steal a priceless invention called the Genesis Device that can create artificial environments including entire planets. Shatner gives the best performance as Kirk he ever would or ever will give—playing off his advancing years and coming face to face with his errant past in the form of lost love Besch and grown son Butrick. There are a few faux pas (like Chekhov being recognized by Khan even though they never met before) and Montalban's robust playing falls just short of self-parody, but the sardonic edge Meyer brings to this sequel helps make it click right up until the hollow ending with Spock's "death" having about as much dramatic impact as all the supposed deaths of Jason Voorhees in every *Friday the 13th* movie. Filmed as *Star Trek: The Vengeance of Khan* and originally released as *Star Trek: The Wrath of Khan.*

STAR TREK III: THE SEARCH FOR SPOCK

★★★☆ Paramount, 1984, PG, 105 min. Dir: Leonard Nimoy. Cast: William Shatner, DeForest Kelley, Christopher Lloyd, Robin Curtis, James Doohan, Nichelle Nichols, George Takei, Walter Koenig, Merritt Butrick, Mark Lenard, Judith Anderson, John Larroquette, James B. Sikking, Miguel Ferrer, Robert Hooks, Cathie Shirriff, Grace Lee Whitney, Leonard Nimoy.

My favorite of the film series, this picks up just after the ending of *II* with the battered *Enterprise* returning to Earth, where Kirk discovers that Spock has placed his spirit into McCoy! Meanwhile, things aren't going too well back on the Genesis planet, either, as it begins to self-destruct and Lt. Saavik (now played by Curtis) and Kirk's son David discover a young Vulcan who just may be Spock reborn. Apart from a hammy turn from Lloyd as a Klingon baddie, this is the one film that comes the closest to recapturing the style and feel of the old show, with an ending full of all the sort of shock and emotional upheaval the second film strived for but never really attained. Leave it to Nimoy to finally get this series on track. Look for Whitney's cameo during the docking sequence.

STAR TREK IV: THE VOYAGE HOME

★★★ Paramount, 1986, PG, 119 min. Dir: Leonard Nimoy. Cast: William Shatner, Leonard Nimoy, DeForest Kelley, Catherine Hicks, James Doohan, Nichelle Nichols, George Takei, Walter Koenig, Majel Barrett, Grace Lee Whitney, Robin Curtis, Jane Wyatt, Mark Lenard, John Schuck, Brock Peters, Robert Ellenstein, Jane Weidlin, Michael Berryman.

The most popular (both critically and at the box office) of the *Trek* movies, this replaces the darkness of *III* with light comedy and social satire. To save the Earth from destruction, the *Enterprise* crew—manning the Klingon bird of prey warship left over from the previous adventure—must travel back in time to the twentieth century. There they capture a pair of humpback whales—extinct in their own time—in order to use their whale song as a signal to deflect a deadly alien probe. Though this leaves way too many loose ends dangling it's still a great deal of fun, with roguish acting, good lines ("Ah, the giants," "I've come millions of miles—eh, *thousands* of miles to be here . . ."), and a nice love interest for Kirk in Hicks—playing a role originally intended for Eddie Murphy!

STAR TREK V: THE FINAL FRONTIER

★★ Paramount, 1989, PG, 106 min. Dir: William Shatner. Cast: William Shatner, Leonard Nimoy, DeForest Kelley, Laurence Luckinbill, David Warner, James Doohan, Nichelle Nichols, George Takei, Walter Kornig, Charles Cooper, Cynthia Gouw, Todd Bryant.

A renegade Vulcan scientist (Luckinbill, giving this movie's best performance), who turns out to be Spock's long-lost half-brother, engineers a hostage situation on a distant planet in order to lure the *Enterprise* there. He then hijacks the starship and pilots it to the end of the known universe for an encounter with God—who should have used divine intervention and asked for a rewrite. It's nice to hear Jerry Goldsmith's theme from the first movie again but Shatner's (debut) direction is all thumbs. The film shucks the gentle humor of *IV* in favor of the ham-fisted hilarity of a Benny Hill skit: Shatner, Nimoy, and Kelley are made to look totally ridiculous and there're embarrassments aplenty for Doohan and Nichols, too. Easily the weakest of the movie series.

STAR TREK VI: THE UNDISCOVERED COUNTRY

★★★ Paramount, 1991, PG, 109 min. Dir: Nicholas Meyer. Cast: William Shatner, Leonard Nimoy, DeForest Kelley, Christopher Plummer, Kim Cattrall, David Warner, James Doohan, Nichelle Nichols, George Takei, Walter Koenig, Grace Lee Whitney, Mark Lenard, Brock Peters, John Schuck, Michael Dorn, Iman, Kurtwood Smith, Christian Slater.

When a Klingon ambassador (Warner, in a different role from the one he played in *Trek V*) is assassinated, Kirk is accused and he and McCoy (who tried to save the guy but failed) are sent to an icy prison planet while more sabotage and assassination are planned for an upcoming peace conference. After the debacle of the last entry, Meyer manages to get things rolling once again with a nice mixture of laughs and suspense. Cattrall is good as Spock's Vulcan protégé (originally Kirstie Alley was to have returned as Saavik but things didn't pan out) and although Plummer overdoes it as the eye-patched, Shakespeare-spouting Klingon villain, he's a study in subtlety when compared to Christopher Lloyd in *Trek III*. Good roles for Takei and Whitney in a nice send-off for the classic cast—most of whom look in better shape and spirits than they did in part five. The video prints contain two additional scenes vital to the plot that were cut from the theatrical version.

STAR TREK: THE VENGEANCE OF KHAN

See: *Star Trek II: The Wrath of Khan*.

STAR TREK: THE WRATH OF KHAN

See: *Star Trek II: The Wrath of Khan*.

STAR WARS

★★★ Fox, 1977, PG, 121 min. Dir: George Lucas. Cast: Mark Hamill, Harrison Ford, Carrie Fisher, Alec Guinness, Peter Cushing, Anthony Daniels, Kenny Baker, Peter Mayhew, David Prowse, voice of James Earl Jones.

A long time ago in a galaxy far, far away, callow farmboy Luke Skywalker (Hamill) joins forces with cocky smuggler Han Solo (Ford) and retired Jedi Knight Ben (Obi-Wan) Kenobi (Guinness) to rescue kidnapped Princess Leia (Fisher) from the clutches of evil Grand Moff Tarkin (Cushing) and his right-hand man Darth Vader (Prowse in the costume, Jones doing the voice) holding her on the dreaded Death Star. Lucas revolutionized moviemaking with this sci-fi fantasy (this was the first movie ever to make almost as much from various toy and merchandise sales as it did in ticket sales). Although never one of my favorites, this still has a lot to recommend it, from John Dykstra's intricate special FX to John Williams's sweeping music, and it possesses an honest,

Carrie Fisher and Mark Hamill watch their post-Luke and -Leia careers take a plunge in Star Wars *(1977).*

genuinely refreshing innocence that's missing from most of today's mass-produced, audience-tested, big-studio tripe. A multiple Oscar winner with homages to everything from *Flash Gordon* to *The Wizard of Oz,* it was followed by *The Empire Strikes Back* and *Return of the Jedi,* has been spoofed and copied many times, and is due to be prequelled by another trilogy that producer-director Lucas has been talking about doing for over a decade now.

STAY TUNED

★★ Warner, 1992, PG, 87 min. Dir: Peter Hyams. Cast: John Ritter, Pam Dawber, Jeffrey Jones, Eugene Levy, David Tom, Heather McComb, Bob Dishy, Joyce Gordon, Fred Blassie, Salt n' Pepa.

A satanic cable hookup sends TV addict Ritter and wife Dawber into their television, where they spend twenty-four hours trapped in various programs and commercials. This one-joke fantasy (borrowing its premise from the climax of the horror film *Shocker*) is mildly funny but works only sporadically—like when Ritter and Dawber end up in a Chuck Jones animated cartoon or John lands on a familiar-looking *Three's Company*-like sitcom.

STEEL AND LACE

★★★ Fries, 1990, R, 92 min. Dir: Ernest Farino. Cast: Bruce Davison, Clare Wren, David Naughton, Stacy Haiduk, William Prince, David L. Lander, Brian Backer, Michael Cerveris.

Gory and absurd, this sci-fi variation on your usual run-of-the-mill rape-revenge movie is surprisingly enjoyable. Davison, looking especially crazed, is the scientist brother of classical pianist Wren, who commits suicide after being gang raped. He resurrects her as a powerful cyborg who disguises herself and tracks down the rapists to castrate and kill them. The image of twirling drills emerging from the robotrix's breasts to impale a victim is especially memorable. Director Farino is a former special FX man who worked on TV commercials featuring Mrs. Butterworth and the Pillsbury Doughboy.

STEEL DAWN

★★ Vestron, 1987, R, 100 min. Dir: Lance Hool. Cast: Patrick Swayze, Lisa Niemi, Christopher Neame, Brion James, Anthony Zerbe, John Fujioka.

Swayze followed up his big success in *Dirty Dancing* with this *Mad Max* clone that did little to enhance the former ballet dancer's tough-guy image. Actually a disguised remake of *Shane*, this has Pat as your standard-issue post-nuke hero who protects a young widow (real life wife Niemi) and her son from bad guy Zerbe. Filmed in South Africa, this has some well-choreographed sword fights but little else.

STEPHEN KING'S GOLDEN YEARS
See: *Golden Years*.

ST. GEORGE AND THE SEVEN CURSES
See: *The Magic Sword*.

STORMQUEST
★★ Media, 1987, R, 90 min. Dir: Alex Sessa. Cast: Brent Huff, Kai Baker, Christina Whitaker, Linda Lutz.

In this comic book-style fantasy shot in Argentina, Hunky Huff is a male resistance fighter and Lutz is the statuesque "Stormqueen" of a feminist kingdom called Kimba. All the usual breasts and bad jokes appear in this boneheadedly likable quickie.

STRANDED
★★ RCA/Columbia, 1987, PG-13, 80 min. Dir: Tex Fuller. Cast: Ione Skye, Maureen O'Sullivan, Joe Morton, Cameron Dye, Susan Barnes, Brendan Hughes, Spice Williams, Flea.

A decidedly odd sci-fi/drama about a pretty teen and her feisty grandma (Skye and O'Sullivan) held hostage in their remote farmhouse by aliens. *Brother from Another Planet* star Morton is the sheriff who has more problems with the local rednecks than he does with the extraterrestrials. Well acted but mostly pretty boring.

STRANDED IN SPACE
See: *The Stranger*.

STRANGE DAYS
★★☆ Fox, 1995, R, 145 min. Dir: Kathryn Bigelow. Cast: Ralph Fiennes, Angela Bassett, Juliette Lewis, Tome Sizemore, Michael Wincott, Vincent D'Onofrio, Glenn Plummer, Brigitte Bako.

Set in the final hours of the year 1999, this frentic, flashy sci-fi thriller concerns the misadventures of Lenny Nero (Fiennes), a conman dealing in virtual reality; selling sound bites of other peoples' lives to drug addicts and thrill seekers after the ultimate sex-and-violence highs. A box office dud, this Generation X variation on David Cronenberg's *Videodrome* really isn't bad, just unfocused and without discipline, not unlike several members of its cast. Fiennes and Bassett are good and Lewis is, well, Lewis—if you know Juliette, then you'll know what I mean. There's enough in the way of flashy sights and sounds to keep you sufficiently diverted from the not terribly coherent plot.

STRANGE INVADERS
★★★ Vestron, 1983, PG, 94 min. Dir: Michael Laughlin. Cast: Paul LeMat, Nancy Allen, Diana Scarwid, Louise Fletcher, Fiona Lewis, Michael Lerner, Wallace Shawn, June Lockhart, Kenneth Tobey, Lulu Sylbert.

Laughlin followed up his clever slasher film *Strange Behavior* with this fun semispoof of '50s sci-fi films. Insectoid aliens take on human form and settle into small-town America in the 1950s. Thirty years later they still behave like Eisenhower is in the White House and *Leave It to Beaver* is in its first run, prompting an investigation from tabloid reporter Allen. Meanwhile, divorced dad LeMat arrives to gain custody of half-alien daughter Sylbert from spacey ex-wife Scarwid. A well-made, knowing little film with a marvelous cast, including Lerner as a nut who insists he was once abducted by extraterrestrials and Lewis as an intergalactic Avon Lady—no, seriously.

STRANGE NEW WORLD
★★ Unicorn, 1975, NR, 74 min. Dir: Robert Butler. Cast: John Saxon, Kathleen Miller, Keene Curtis, Martine Beswick, James Olson, Ford Rainey, Catherine Bach, Richard Farnsworth.

Gene Roddenberry dusts off his old *Genesis II* concept yet again with Saxon, Miller, and Curtis as space explorers who return to Earth after two centuries in suspended animation to discover some radical changes. The two-part plot looks for all the world like a pair of TV show episodes edited together and probably was. Good cast, though, with Saxon more or less playing the same character he did in *Planet Earth*.

STRANGER, THE
★★ King of Video, 1973, NR, 96 min. Dir: Lee H. Katzin. Cast: Glenn Corbett, Sharon Acker, Cameron Mitchell, Lew Ayres, Dean Jagger, George Coulouris.

Drab TV movie ripoff of *Journey to the Far Side of the Sun*, this pilot for an unsold, *Fugitive*-style series has Corbett as an astronaut stranded on a planet that's the mirror image of the Earth, except that it's run by a totalitarian government that wants our hero dead. There's a good supporting cast of veteran character actors but this is remarkably depressing. *Mystery Science Theater 3000* has shown this as *Stranded in Space*.

STRANGER FROM VENUS

★★ Nostalgia Merchant, 1954, NR, 76 min. Dir: Burt Balaban. Cast: Patricia Neal, Helmut Dantine, Derek Bond.

Neal went to England to star in this unofficial remake of her classic *The Day the Earth Stood Still* with Dantine as the alien who comes to Earth to warn us about our nuclear testing. The actors are good but this is too dry and unimaginatively directed to have much impact. Aka *Immediate Disaster*.

STRANGE WORLD OF PLANET X, THE

See: *The Cosmic Monsters.*

STREET FIGHTER

★★ MCA/Universal, 1994, PG-13, 95 min. Dir: Stephen de Souza. Cast: Jean-Claude Van Damme, Raul Julia, Ming-Na Wen, Wes Studi, Kylie Minogue, Damien Chapa.

Die Hard scripter de Souza made his directorial debut with this loud fantasy-actioner based on the video game. Van Damme (who has a lot of charisma but not much acting ability) is the hero trying to rescue hostages held by Nazi-like dictator Julia (who died shortly after completing filming). Beautifully photographed by William A. Fraker, this has lots of martial arts action (which is good) but lots of rap music too (which is bad).

STRYKER

★☆ Starmaker, 1983, R, 86 min. Dir: Cirio H. Santiago. Cast: Steve Sandor, Andria Savio, William Osteander, Julie Gray, Ken Metcalf, Monique St. Pierre.

No, its not about a well-endowed porno star, though that might've helped. Actually, this is just another low-brow *Mad Max* clone (shot in the Philippines by junk movie veteran Santiago) about warrior men battling Amazon women over a dwindling water supply in a postholocaust world. Yawn. Aka *Savage Dawn.*

SUPER FORCE

★★ MCA/Universal, 1990, NR, 92 min. Dir: Richard Compton. Cast: Ken Olandt, Lisa Niemi, Larry B. Scott, G. Gordon Liddy, Marshall Teague, voice of Patrick Macnee.

Two episodes of a short-lived *Robocop*-like TV show edited together. Olandt is the twenty-first-century former astronaut turned supercop with a hopped-up motorcycle and an indestructible suit of body armor. The bad guys he bests in the predictable storylines include former Watergate scandal figure and talk show host Liddy. Pretty much what you'd expect.

SUPER FUZZ

★ Embassy, 1981, PG, 94 min. Dir: Sergio Corbucci. Cast: Terence Hill, Ernest Borgnine, Joanne Dru, March Lawrence, Julie Gordon, Lee Sandman.

Awful "comedy" with spaghetti Western star Hill (whose "charm" has always escaped me) as a rookie cop who becomes a flying superman after exposure to radiation. Borgnine is his long-suffering partner and Lawrence is the stereotypical gangster Hill pursues. Nothing about this tepid Italian fantasy (shot in Miami) works. Aka *Supersnooper.*

SUPERGIRL

★★☆ Avid Entertainment, 1984, PG, 104 min. Dir: Jeannot Szwarc. Cast: Helen Slater, Faye Dunaway, Peter O'Toole, Hart Bochner, Peter Cook, Brenda Vaccaro, Mia Farrow, Simon Ward, Marc McClure, Maureen Teefy.

Nobody much likes this spinoff from the Christopher Reeve *Superman* series but I think it's kinda fun. Supe's cousin Kara (Slater, living with mom Farrow and dad Ward with a small band of Krypton survivors at the center of the Earth) battles evil witch Dunaway (whose acting here makes her *Mommie Dearest* turn seem a study in subtlety) for a powerful runestone called the Omega Hedron. The special FX are a bit wobbly and too much of the plot is devoted to Slater's would-be relationship with handsome dope Bochner, but this is still better than *Superman III.* McClure guest stars as Jimmy Olsen and Slater is very appealing in the title role. Foreign prints run 124 minutes.

SUPERMAN (1948)

See: *Superman—The Serial.*

SUPERMAN

★★★☆ Warner, 1978, PG, 143 min. Dir: Richard Donner. Cast: Christopher Reeve, Margot Kidder, Marlon Brando, Gene Hackman, Glenn Ford, Valerie Perrine, Ned Beatty, Susannah York, Phyllis Thaxter, Jackie Cooper, Terence Stamp, Sarah Douglas, Jack O'Halloran, Marc McClure, Jeff East, Larry Hagman.

The Man of Steel's first big-screen adventure since the '50s was this $50-million-plus super production scripted by Mario Puzo and directed by Donner, who had just scored a big hit with *The Omen.* An unknown Reeve is great as both Superman and Clark Kent (for the first time you can actually accept the fact that those around him really think that Supe and Clark are two different people) as our hero's life story is traced from his babyhood escape from the exploding planet Krypton to his growing up with adoptive parents Ford and Thaxter in

Christopher Reeve and Margot Kidder soar in Superman *(1978).*

Smallville, U.S.A. (the best part of the movie), to his arrival in Metropolis and his fight against dastardly Lex Luthor (Hackman), who wants to destroy California with an earthquake to increase his Nevada property values. This too often veers unevenly between parody and sincerity and some of the elaborate special FX fail to convince, but the high spirits of the cast (though Brando is glum in his multimillion-dollar cameo as Superman's true father) and John Williams's soaring score make this a must and the best of the superhero films. The network TV version added back much cut footage, some of it good, most of it not, including an extended cameo by TV Lois Lane Noel Neill and serial Superman Kirk Alyn.

SUPERMAN II

★★★ Warner, 1980, PG, 127 min. Dirs: Richard Lester, Richard Donner. Cast: Christopher Reeve, Margot Kidder, Gene Hackman, Terence Stamp, Sarah Douglas, Jack O'Halloran, Valerie Perrine, Ned Beatty, Susannah York, Jackie Cooper, Marc McClure, E. G. Marshall, Clifton James, Pepper Martin.

This troubled first sequel was mostly filmed back to back with part one but much of it was reshot by Lester after a dispute between original director Donner and producers Alexander and Ilya Salkind. Marlon Brando was also written out and comedy was played up even more as a trio of Kryptonian criminals led by evil General Zod (Stamp) arrive on Earth just as Superman decides to forsake his powers for the love of Lois Lane. Like the original, this is full of ups and downs but is well served by its cast and has a surprisingly mean-spirited streak that makes for some surprising plot twists. Not released in the U.S. until 1981.

SUPERMAN III

★★ Warner, 1983, PG, 123 min. Dir: Richard Lester. Cast: Christopher Reeve, Richard Pryor, Annette O'Toole, Robert Vaughn, Margot Kidder, Pamela Stevenson, Annie Ross, Jackie Cooper, Marc McClure, Gavin O'Herlihy.

Whoever had the bright idea of turning the third in the *Superman* series into an out-and-out comic vehicle for Pryor should be horse whipped. Not that he isn't talented and funny—just check out *Bustin' Loose* or *Stir Crazy*—but what the hell is he doing here? Anyway, Richard plays a bumbling computer whiz hired by bad guy Vaughn to create a supercomputer that will defeat Superman. Meanwhile, the Man of Steel heads home to Smallville for his high school reunion, where he encounters old flame Lana Lang (the appealing O'Toole) before being transformed into a loutish bad Superman by some synthetic kryptonite. Kidder was originally written out as Lois Lane since she was feuding with the Salkinds; she came back for a few scenes at Pryor's insistence but she's not in it enough to help. Like the other *Superman* movies, this was heavily padded with outtakes for its network TV showings.

SUPERMAN IV: THE QUEST FOR PEACE

★★☆ Warner, 1987, PG, 90 min. Dir: Sidney H. Furie. Cast: Christopher Reeve, Margot Kidder, Gene Hackman, Mariel Hemingway, Jon Cryer, Jackie Cooper, Marc McClure, Sam Wanamaker, Mark Pillow, Damian McLawhorn.

It took a while, but this fourth (and I suppose last) installment finally came out to poor reviews and indifferent box office. Yet, it's better than *III* and is actually improved by its padded TV version, where some vital footage is restored. This time Supe is out to dispose of all the world's nuclear weapons (an idea contributed by star Reeve). Old nemesis Luthor is back (Hackman, in fine form) too; creating the superpowerful baddie Nuclear Man (Pillow, in blonde bouffant hair and Lee press-on nails) who fights our hero from the Statue of Liberty to the Great Wall of China. The FX aren't especially good (lots of bleeding matte lines) but the actors carry the ball in high style—especially Kidder in the heartbreaking scene where she tells Clark Kent how much Superman means to her.

SUPERMAN AND THE MOLE MEN

★★ Warner, 1951, NR, 58 min. Dir: Lee Sholem. Cast: George Reeves, Phyllis Coates, Jeff Corey, Walter Reed, J. Farrell MacDonald, Billy Curtis.

This short B&W feature was actually the pilot for the *Adventures of Superman* TV series (later cut into the two-part episode *Unknown People*) with Clark Kent and Lois Lane (Reeves and Coates) investigating a small town that's been invaded by big-headed midgets from the center of the Earth. Cheap and overly serious but worth seeing for fans of Reeves in his classic role. Aka *Superman and the Strange People*.

SUPERMAN AND THE STRANGE PEOPLE

See: *Superman and the Mole Men*.

SUPERMAN—THE SERIAL

★★★ RCA/Columbia, 1948, NR, 180 min. Dirs: Spencer Gordon Bennet, Thomas Carr. Cast: Kirk Alyn, Noel Neill, Tommy Bond, Carol Foreman, Pierre Watkin, George Meeker, Jack Ingram, Terry Frost.

A big hit in its day, this chapter play was the first live-action version of the exploits of the Man of Steel (played with wholesome innocence by Alyn). Here he battles the evil Spider Lady (Foreman) while helping Lois Lane (Neill, who later created the role in the *Superman* TV series) get out of all manner of scrapes. Try to ignore the cheesy special FX and you should enjoy this as much as I did. Originally titled just plain *Superman* and also released in a condensed feature version.

SUPER MARIO BROTHERS

★★ Hollywood Pictures, 1993, PG 118 min. Dirs: Rocky Morton, Annabel Jankel. Cast: Bob Hoskins, John Leguizamo, Dennis Hopper, Samantha Mathis, Fiona Shaw, Lance Henriksen, Fisher Steven, Richard Edson.

Another bloated fantasy aimed at kids and based on a popular video game. Hoskins and Leguizamo are the titular siblings, plumbers who end up in some alternate universe where they must save princess Mathis from evil, dinosaur-headed King Koopa (Hopper, in maybe the most embarrassing role since his well-publicized mid-'80s comeback). Lots of heavy-duty makeup and special FX and lots of loud music but something like a plot would have been appreciated too.

SURVIVALIST, THE

★☆ TWE, 1987, R, 96 min. Dir: Sig Shore. Cast: Steve Railsback, Susan Blakely, Marjoe Gortner, Cliff De Young, David Wayne, Jason Healy.

Various characters (notably Railsback in the title role) try to survive in Texas after the U.S. and U.S.S.R. drop the big ones. There's little suspense or interest here—except in wondering how many semi-name stars were coerced into appearing in this low-octane postnuke drek.

SURVIVAL ZONE

★☆ Prism Entertainment, 1983, R, 90 min. Dir: Percival Rubens. Cast: Gary Lockwood, Camilla Sparv, Morgan Stevens.

More postnuke boredom set in Texas, with Lockwood and Sparv trying to save their family from a world gone mad. The main menace here is a gang of cannibal rapists on motorcycles (!)—just so you'll know exactly what to expect.

SURVIVOR

★☆ Vestron, 1987, R, 97 min. Dir: Michael Shackleton. Cast: Chip Mayer, Sue Kiel, Richard Moll, Richard Haines, John Carson, Rex Garner.

Painfully talkative *Road Warrior* wannabe shot in South Africa. Title character Mayer travels the nuked-out wasteland of the future until he stumbles across villain Moll's stronghold, where the last fertile women on Earth (including Kiel) are being held. This could have been a contender but is ultimately undone by its own pretentiousness.

SWAMP THING

★★☆ Embassy, 1981, PG, 91 min. Dir: Wes Craven. Cast: Louis Jourdan, Adrienne Barbeau, Ray Wise, David Hess, Nicholas Worth, Dick Durock.

This lightweight film version of the dark-hued DC Comics character is a pretty atypical vehicle for Craven and isn't bad, but could have been much better. It pulls punches for its PG rating and the makeup FX are uneven and often downright sloppy, but the acting hits just the right notes, with Jourdan avoiding the self-parodying, camp approach he would adopt for (the admittedly more cartoonlike) sequel and Barbeau in top form as the tough but tender

CIA agent heroine (who looks great wearing a clingy evening gown in the middle of the swamps).

SWITCH

★☆ Warner, 1991, R, 114 min. Dir: Blake Edwards. Cast: Ellen Barkin, Jimmy Smits, JoBeth Williams, Lorraine Bracco, Tony Roberts, Perry King, Lysette Anthony, Victoria Mahoney.

A poor copy of the '60s comedy *Goodbye Charlie* (which wasn't all that great to begin with) about a philandering creep who's murdered by several of the women he's cheated on and is reincarnated as a woman (Barkin) as punishment for his sins. A typically smug and pandering Edwards sex comedy (with Bracco included as a lesbian for cheap titillation purposes) that was obviously intended as a vehicle for Smits (as the confused detective investigating the murder) but is nearly saved by Barkin in a funny, ballsy performance that deserves a much better film surrounding it.

SWITCH IN TIME, A

See: *Norman's Awesome Experience.*

SWORD AND THE DRAGON, THE

★★★ Sinister Cinema, 1956, NR, 95 min. Dir: Alexander Prushko. Cast: Boris Andreyev, Natalie Medvedeva, Andrei Abrikosov, Alexei Shvorin.

Imaginative slice of Russian fantasy (originally filmed in 3-D) with Andreyev as legendary hero Ilya Mourometz who uses his magical sword to defeat various devils, a wind demon (great effect), and a three-headed, fire-breathing dragon (a not so great one) threatening his kingdom. Once you get past the lunk-headed dubbing there's a lot to enjoy in this richly textured import. Aka *Ilya Mourometz* and *The Hero and the Beast.*

SWORD AND THE SORCERER, THE

★★★ MCA/Universal, 1982, R, 100 min. Dir: Albert Pyun. Cast: Lee Horsley, Kathleen Beller, Simon MacCorkindale, George Maharis, Richard Lynch, Nina Van Pallandt, Richard Moll, Jeff Corey, Robert Tessier, Anna Bjorn.

My favorite entry in the overcrowded sword-and-sorcery field of the early '80s, this borrows from *Excalibur* and *Conan* but adds more fantasy and gruesome horror touches. Horsley (who starred in the *Matt Houston* TV series right after this) is the hero with the triple-blade supersword who helps feisty princess Beller (who starred on *Dynasty* right after this) rescue her brother the prince from evil Lynch's torture dungeon. In a standout scene, Maharis (formerly of *Route 66* and a *Playgirl* centerfold)

transforms into a slimy demon played by Moll. This was the twenty-six-year-old Pyun's first feature and he hasn't done anything nearly as good since.

SWORD OF THE VALIANT

★★ MGM/UA, 1984, PG, 101 min. Dir: Stephen Weeks. Cast: Miles O'Keeffe, Cyrielle Claire, Sean Connery, Leigh Lawson, Peter Cushing, Trevor Howard, Lila Kedrova, John Rhys-Davies.

O'Keeffe is a young knight put under a spell by magician Connery, whom he kills; within one year the knight must solve a magical riddle or die. O'Keefe is awful but Connery (on scene for all of ten minutes) and the veteran British supporting cast add stature to this minor Brit fantasy, a remake of Weeks's 1973 film *Gawain and the Green Knight.*

SYNGENOR

★★ Southgate, 1990, R, 98 min. Dir: George Elanjian, Jr. Cast: Starr Andreeff, Mitchell Laurence, David Gale, Riva Spier, Charles Lucia, Melanie Shatner.

An *Alien*-like creature terrorizes people trapped in a high-rise in this in-name-only sequel to *Scared to Death.* A hilarious performance by the *Re-Animator* star as an out-of-control, drug-addicted corporate executive makes watching this predictable monster flick worthwhile.

TALES OF TOMORROW

★★★ Rhino, 1951–53, NR, 90 min. per tape. Dir: Leonard Valenta. Cast: Boris Karloff, Lon Chaney, Jr., Paul Newman, James Dean, Henry Jones, Mary Alice Moore, Mercedes McCambridge, Leslie Nielsen.

A number of episodes of this early sci-fi/horror anthology series are available on tape and despite their primitive technical quality are pretty interesting. Among the better segments are a Jekyll-and-Hyde-type thriller starring Dean; a robot-in-love story featuring McCambridge; and an infamous version of *Frankenstein* with an obviously inebriated Chaney in impressive makeup as the monster.

TANK GIRL

★★ MGM/UA, 1995, R, 104 min. Dir: Rachel Talalay.
Cast: Lori Petty, Malcolm McDowell, Ice-T, Naomi
Watts, Don Harvey, Jeff Kober.

This flashy film version of the Alan Martin-
Jamie Hewlett comic character really tanked at
the B.O. but it's not that bad. In the year 2033
our feisty heroine (an abrasive but well-cast
Petty, coming on like Cyndi Lauper after a
spell of basic training) finds herself at odds
with the evil Kessler (McDowell in his usual
psychovillain spot), who controls the world's
water supply—an overworked plot device in
the last couple of years if ever there was one.
The direction of Talalay (*Freddy's Dead, Ghost
in the Machine*) lacks the light touch this sort of
thing requires but the cast does its best to hold
your interest. Favorite exchange: McDowell:
"How does it feel knowing you're about to
die?" Petty: "You tell me!"

TARANTULA

★★★ MCA/Universal, 1955, NR, 80 min. Dir: Jack
Arnold. Cast: John Agar, Mara Corday, Leo G. Carroll,
Nestor Paiva, Ross Elliott, Raymond Bailey.

One of the best of the giant insect movies to
follow in the wake of *Them!* this atmospherically directed thriller stars Carroll as a scientist
whose experiments with a growth hormone
taint him with acromegalyand create a huge
spider that terrorizes the Arizona desert. Low-
key acting and top-notch special photography
by Clifford Stine still keep this genuinely
scary, even after more than forty years. Clint
Eastwood has an important role at the very

end. Based on an episode of *Science Fiction Theater*, sans giant spider, called *No Food for
Thought.*

TEENAGE CAVEMAN

★★ RCA/Columbia, 1958, NR, 66 min. Dir: Roger
Corman. Cast: Robert Vaughn, Darrah Marshall, Leslie
Bradley, Frank De Kova, Robert Shayne, Jonathan
Haze.

The anything-but-a-teenager Vaughn stars in
this silly prehistoric saga as a hotheaded
young tribesman, a sort of neanderthal-with-
out-a-cause who trespasses on forbidden
ground and encounters a weird monster (left
over from *Night of the Blood Beast*) in his quest
for the meaning of life. Surprisingly earnest
and noncampy but also pretty boring; worth
seeing, though, for the double-twist ending.
The nude swim scene featuring nudie model
Marshall (and featured prominently on the
posters) was pretty daring for the time. Filmed
as *Prehistoric World* and aka *Out of the Darkness.*

TEENAGE MONSTER

See: *Meteor Monster.*

TEENAGE MUTANT NINJA TURTLES

★★☆ IVE, 1990, PG, 93 min. Dir: Steve Barton. Cast:
Judith Hoag, Elias Koteas, voices of Corey Feldman,
Robbie Rist, Brian Tochi, Kevin Clash, David
McCharen.

This mammothly successful kids' picture was
a live-action spinoff of the animated TV series
based on the comics created by Kevin Eastman
and Peter Laird, the biggest kid-oriented phe-

*An angry arachnid on the
march in* Tarantula *(1955).*

nomenon before *Mighty Morphin' Power Rangers*. The pizza-lovin' turtles—once-real terrapins exposed to radioactivity—are martial-arts-trained superheroes living in the sewers of New York; they help TV reporter Hoag investigate a crimewave sweeping the city. Nothing special, but the Jim Henson Creature Shop FX are good and some of the action surprisingly intense for a movie aimed at the small fry.

TEENAGE MUTANT NINJA TURTLES II: SECRET OF THE OOZE
★★ RCA/Columbia, 1991, PG, 88 min. Dir: Michael Pressman. Cast: Paige Turco, David Warner, Ernie Reyes, Jr., Michelan Sista, Toshishiro Obata, Raymond Serra, Vanilla Ice, voices of Leif Tilden, Kenn Troum, Mark Caso, Kevin Clash, François Chav.

The second in the Turtle trilogy was bigger budgeted but clearly rushed into production to strike while the iron was still hot. The evil Shredder is after the last container of radioactive ooze that created the Ninja Turtles in order to create a horde of monsters under his control. Fans might enjoy it but it's a shame to see a fine actor like Warner in silly stuff like this; the Vanilla Ice rap song is a low point in '90s cinema.

TEENAGE MUTANT NINJA TURTLES III
★★☆ Columbia/TriStar, 1993, PG, 96 min. Dir: Stuart Gillard. Cast: Elias Koteas, Paige Turco, Stuart Wilson, Sab Shimono, Vivian Wu, voices of Marco Caso, Matt Hill, Jim Raposs, David Fraser, James Murray.

The third Turtle adventure is an improvement on *II* and in some ways is better than the first, too. The turtles and their friends April and Casey are transported into the distant past and end up in feudal Japan, where they help a village against an evil warlord, *Seven Samurai* style. The violence-isn't-the-answer-to-everything concept seems pretty hollow considering all the martial arts fighting this series showcases.

TEENAGERS FROM OUTER SPACE
★★ Sinister Cinema, 1959, NR, 85 min. Dir: Tom Graeff. Cast: David Love, Dawn Anderson, Harvey B. Dunn, Bryant Grant, Tom Lockyear [Tom Graeff], Robert King Moody, Sonia Torgenson, Gene Sterling.

An alien race arrives on Earth to farm huge lobsters called Gargon. Young Love breaks from his fellows and ends up boarding with pretty Anderson and dotty granddad Dunn, all the while being pursued by assassin Grant, who's armed with a ray gun that can reduce a victim to bones. Graeff produced, directed, wrote, photographed, and edited this dopey but ambitious cheapie that's more technically credible than most Ed Wood movies but is just as dramatically and philosophically bent. For years people thought that do-it-all-yourself Graeff was starring, too, under the alias David Love but Love was actually Tom's boyfriend, while *he* costarred under a pseudonym as the *heroine's* boyfriend! It's a silly business, isn't it? Originally released by Warner Brothers on a double bill with *Gigantis, the Fire Monster*. British title: *The Gargon Terror*.

TEKWAR: THE MOVIE
★★☆ MCA/Universal, 1994, NR, 92 min. Dir: William Shatner. Cast: Greg Evigan, William Shatner, Sheena Easton, Eugene Clark, Torri Higginson, Barry Morse.

This made-for-cable movie, based on the first of Shatner's series of successful *Tekwar* novels, stars Evigan as a cop awakened from fifty years in cryogenic freezing to a future world where he must help stop the influx of a powerful virtual reality drug called Tek. Not bad, but the series that followed was better thanks to the briefer, less padded plots used for the one-hour episodes. Aka *William Shatner's Tekwar*.

TENTH VICTIM, THE
★★★ Nelson, 1965, NR, 90 min. Dir: Elio Petri. Cast: Marcello Mastroianni, Ursula Andress, Elsa Martinelli, Massimo Serato, Salvo Randone.

Great pop art '60s Italian sci-fi about a future society where citizens hunt each other for sport and sexy huntress Andress (whose arsenal of weaponry includes a lethal bra!) targets Mastroianni as her tenth victim. A tongue-in-cheek adaptation of Robert Sheckley's story *The Seventh Victim*, this has imaginative sets, costumes, and photography and is surprisingly lighthearted, considering the plot.

TERMINAL ENTRY
★★ Celebrity, 1987, R, 95 min. Dir: John Kincade. Cast: Edward Albert, Paul Smith, Yaphet Kotto, Patrick Laborteaux, Kabi Bedi, Jill Terashita, Tracy Brooks Swope, Barbara Edwards.

A group of teenage computer hackers accidentally tap into a national defense computer and discover a foreign plot to destroy our defense and overthrow the government. A predictable *War Games* clone with the added, and highly unnecessary, attraction of nude sex scenes to distract you from the familiar main plot.

TERMINAL MAN, THE
★★☆ Warner, 1974, PG, 107 min. Dir: Mike Hodges. Cast: George Segal, Joan Hackett, Jill Clayburgh,

Richard Dysart, Michael C. Gwynne, Donald Moffatt, Matt Clark, James B. Sikking, Steve Kanaly, Ian Wolfe.

A cold but well-acted version of Michael Crichton's book about a man (Segal, in a good dramatic performance) who receives a computer implant in his brain that turns him into a violent killer. An interesting white-on-white visual look contrasts sharply with the often bloody violence but the classical music used in place of a regular film score makes this seem even slower and more languid than it actually is.

TERMINATOR, THE
★★★★ HBO, 1984, R, 108 min. Dir: James Cameron. Cast: Arnold Schwarzenegger, Linda Hamilton, Michael Biehn, Lance Henricksen, Paul Winfield, Rick Rossovich, Dick Miller, Bill Paxton.

Cameron, whose previous film was the less than memorable *Piranha II: The Spawning*, really hit the big time with this runaway train of a movie, a mixture of elements from several old *Outer Limits* episodes with the structure of a *Friday the 13th* movie. Schwarzenegger has his greatest role as an unstoppable android from the future, sent (naked) back to the 1980s to kill the future mother (Hamilton) of a future rebel leader who will overthrow the totalitarian government responsible for the android's manufacture. Biehn is on hand as a rebel who also arrives from the twenty-first century; *his* mission is to protect Hamilton from Arnie. Some balked at this film's violence but its grand sense of dark humor never lets the violence become too grim or off-putting. Cameron stages the action with the sort of skill and relish few of this movie's many imitators would ever attain. Funny cameos by Miller (as an arms-dealing hock shop owner) and Paxton (as a smart-ass punk whose clothes Arnold steals) in one of the great sci-fi action movies of the '80s.

TERMINATOR 2: JUDGMENT DAY
★★★ LIVE, 1991, R, 136 min. Dir: James Cameron. Cast: Arnold Schwarzenegger, Linda Hamilton, Edward Furlong, Robert Patrick, Joe Morton, Earl Boen, Jenette Goldstein, Xander Berkeley.

Fifteen or so years after the events in the original *Terminator,* a new improved cyborg (Patrick) is sent back from the future to eliminate Hamilton's son Furlong before he can grow into the rebel who'll save the world. Luckily another android cast in the form of the original Terminator (you-know-who) arrives to protect mother and son from the shape-shifting killer. Some prefer this to the original and I can see their point (that $100-million-dollar

budget can buy a lot of state-of-the-art FX) but this is too retooled to fit Arnold's new image as kid-loving nice guy to have the sort of gutsy impact as the first film—I find it funny, too, that this new Terminator doesn't kill any innocent bystanders this time, he just maims them by shooting them in the knees! Still, there are some great moments, including the pumped-up Hamilton's unforgettable apocalyptic dream sequence. The longer, director's cut laser disc has much additional footage including a cameo by Michael Biehn.

TERROR AT HALFDAY
See: *Monster a Go-Go.*

TERROR BENEATH THE SEA
★★ Sinister Cinema, 1966, NR, 85 min. Dir: Hajimo Sato. Cast: Peggy Neal, Shinichi [Sonny] Chiba, Mike Daneen, Andrew Hughes, Erick Nielson.

A mad scientist creates a race of fishmen in an underwater laboratory in this routine Japanese sci-fi. Notable mostly for an early appearance of martial arts movie hero Chiba but not much else. From the makers of *The X from Outer Space.* Aka *Kaitei dai Senso (Battle Beneath the Sea).*

TERROR FROM THE YEAR 5000
★★ Sinister Cinema, 1958, NR, 70 min. Dir: Robert J. Gurney. Cast: Ward Costello, Joyce Holden, Frederic Downs, Salome Jens.

A scientist's time machine brings a disfigured female killer with hypnotic fingernails back from the distant future. A low-low-budget sci-fi/horror that finally kicks in with the arrival of Jens (the distinguished character actress making her screen debut) in the title role. Aka *Cage of Doom.*

TERROR IN SPACE
See: *Planet of the Vampires.*

TERROR IN THE MIDNIGHT SUN
See: *Invasion of the Animal People.*

TERRORNAUTS, THE
★★☆ Nelson, 1966, NR, 75 min. Dir: Montgomery Tully. Cast: Simon Oates, Zena Marshall, Charles Hawtry, Patricia Hayes, Stanley Meadows, Max Adrian.

Cheap but fun version of Murray Leinster's story *The Wailing Asteroid* about a scientific complex and its staff—not to mention charwoman—transported by aliens to a distant asteroid for study. This Amicus production hasn't the budget for its ambitions but makes up for it by being short and funny.

"I'll be back—but first I have to touch up my makeup." *Arnold Schwarzenegger in* The Terminator *(1984).*

TERROR OF GODZILLA
See: *Terror of Mechagodzilla.*

TERROR OF MECHAGODZILLA
★★ Paramount/Gateway, 1975, PG, 80 min. Dir: Inoshiro Honda. Cast: Katushiko Sasaki, Tomoko Ai, Akihiko Hirata, Tado Nakamura.

Aliens reconstruct Mechagodzilla using its severed head and then send it and another creature called Titanosaurus (controlled by sonic waves) after Godzilla. The last *Godzilla* movie for nearly a decade, this is needlessly grim and violent and is further marred in this video edition by being the (badly) cut TV print. Aka *Mechagoira no Gyakusyu (Revenge of Mechagodzilla)*, *Terror of Godzilla*, and *Monsters of a Prehistoric Planet.*

TERROR OF THE MAD DOCTOR
See: *The Testament of Dr. Mabuse.*

TERRORVISION
★★ Avid Entertainment, 1986, R, 82 min. Dir: Ted Nicholaou. Cast: Gerrit Grahame, Mary Woronov, Diane Franklin, Chad Allen, Bert Remsen, Alejandro Rey.

Dumb but enjoyable monster comedy about an alien that's accidentally sucked into a suburban home via a powerful cable TV hookup and devours most of the pseudo-hip Putterman family (headed by the winning combo of Grahame and Woronov—just think of the gene pool). This Empire Pictures hack job should suck but ends up working almost in spite of itself.

TERROR WITHIN, THE
★★ MGM/UA, 1989, R, 88 min. Dir: Thierry Notz. Cast: George Kennedy, Andrew Stevens, Starr Andreeff, Terri Treas.

In the nuclear-devastated future, a woman raped by a mutant gives birth to a killer monster that terrorizes scientists in an underground bunker. A Roger Corman-produced *Alien* rip that's short on logic and originality but still manages, in its own modest way, to be entertaining. Kennedy's always-garrulous presence helps as well.

TERROR WITHIN II, THE
★☆ Vestron, 1991, R, 85 min. Dir: Andrew Stevens. Cast: Andrew Stevens, Stella Stevens, R. Lee Ermey, Clare Hoak.

Stevens directs himself in this nobody-asked-for-it vanity production sequel with Andy coming on like a poor man's Mel Gibson as our futuristic hero fights another icky monster while trying to find the cure for a globe-deci-mating plague. Your appreciation level for this one is based solely on how much Andrew Stevens you can handle in one sitting. Mom Stella is always welcome, though.

TESTAMENT
★★★★ Paramount, 1983, PG, 89 min. Dir: Lynne Littman. Cast: Jane Alexander, William Devane, Roxana Zal, Ross Harris, Lukas Haas, Philip Anglim, Rebecca DeMorney, Kevin Costner, Leon Ames, Mako.

Originally a production for PBS's *American Playhouse* this end-of-the-world drama is similar to *The Day After* (which appeared at about the same time) but is much better. Alexander gives an unforgettable performance as a woman trying to hold her family together after husband Devane is killed in the nuclear strike that destroys much of the U.S. A beautifully acted and heartbreakingly sad movie that deals with human emotions rather than special FX, this pulls no punches yet is amazingly life-affirming for a movie about the annihilation of mankind.

TESTAMENT OF DR. MABUSE, THE
★★☆ Sinister Cinema, 1962, NR, 88 min. Dir: Werner Klinger. Cast: Gert Frobe, Senta Berger, Helmut Schmid, Charles Regnier, Walter Rilla, Wolfgang Preiss, Ann Savo, Harald Juhnke.

A loose remake of the 1932 Fritz Lang film, this concerns an asylum head who is possessed by Mabuse's spirit after being hypnotized by the bad doctor before his death. Another *Mabuse* flick mixing espionage, sci-fi, and horror elements to good effect, this West German production was originally released in the States as *Terror of the Mad Doctor.*

TEST TUBE TEENS FROM THE YEAR 2000
★★ Paramount, 1993, R, 74 min. Dir: Ellen Cabot [David DeCoteau]. Cast: Morgan Fairchild, Brian Bremer, Christopher Wolf, Michele Matheson, Ian Abercrombie, Sara Suzanne Brown.

A movie *must* be bad if a guy like DeCoteau takes his name off it, right? Actually, this sci-fi sex comedy is funnier than you'd expect even though it doesn't have an original bone in its body. Two nerds from the future are pursued by a buff *Terminator* wannabe back in time to Fairchild's girls' school, where our heroes try to alter their destiny by loosing their virginity to a couple of hot coeds. Originally titled *Virgin Hunters*, this was changed to please a certain video chain even though it's the *guys* and not the girls who are the hunted virgins. Morgan shows untapped comic potential in a role tailor-made for Mary Woronov.

TETSUO
See: *Tetsuo: The Iron Man.*

TETSUO: THE IRON MAN
★★★ Fox/Lorber, 1989, UR, 67 min. Dir: Shinya Tsukamoto. Cast: Tomoroh Taguchi, Kei Fujiwara, Shinya Tsukamoto.

This virtually plotless but gripping Japanese cyberpunk thriller details the grotesque transformation our hero Tetsuo undergoes as he becomes a literal iron man with a wicked rotating drill for a penis. Often looking like a live-action Anime as directed by David Lynch or David Cronenberg, the film mixes sex, gore, and technology into a highly disturbing brew that uses black-and-white photography with a creative texture rarely seen in American films today. Aka *Tetsuo.*

THEM!
★★★★ Warner, 1954, NR, 92 min. Dir: Gordon Douglas. Cast: James Whitmore, Joan Weldon, Edmund Gwenn, James Arness, Onslow Stevens, Sean McClory.

The original Big Bug movie, this tense thriller details the strange deaths and disappearances that plague the New Mexico desert and turn out to be the work of a horde of gigantic ants. Solid acting and direction and mature scripting make the difference in this top-notch monster film. Shot for color but released only in

black and white, some early prints actually featured a color title card. Leonard Nimoy has a brief bit as an army telegraph operator.

THEY CAME FROM BEYOND SPACE
★★ Nelson, 1966, NR, 85 min. Dir: Freddie Francis. Cast: Robert Hutton, Jennifer Jayne, Zia Mohyeddin, Michael Gough, Bernard Kay, Geoffrey Wallace, Maurice Good, Katy Wild.

Alien invaders arrive in Britain in a meteorite shower and possess the bodies of Earthlings, all except Yank Hutton, who has a metal plate in his head and can't be controlled. Cheap Amicus sci-fi film, based on the story *The Gods Hate Kansas* by Joseph Millard, flatly directed by the usually reliable Francis. Good Cast, though a prominently billed Gough is wasted in a silly cameo as the "Master of the Moon."

THEY LIVE!
★★ MCA/Universal, 1988, R, 95 min. Dir: John Carpenter. Cast: Roddy Piper, Meg Foster, Keith David, Raymond St. Jacques.

Piper is an unemployed steel worker who accidentally gets his hands on a pair of glasses that allow him to see the true ghoulish nature of alien invaders (not to mention their subliminal messages used to control the populace) who've infiltrated high government and industrial positions. A politically minded reworking of *Invasion of the Body Snatchers*

"I'll give you such a pinch!" James Whitmore in Them! *(1954).*

released during the '88 presidential campaign, this is amusing but shallow, with way too many logic loopholes to make it work. Carpenter scripted under the pseudonym Frank Armitage.

THIEF OF BAGDAD, THE
★★★ HBO, 1924, NR, 140 min. Dir: Raoul Walsh. Cast: Douglas Fairbanks, Julanne Johnston, Anna May Wong, Sojin, Snitz Edwards, Brandon Hurst, Charles Belcher, Etta Lee.

Classic silent fantasy (coscripted by Fairbanks as "Elton Thomas") with Doug at his swashbuckling best as the thief who proves his worth to Caliph's daughter Johnston through a series of fabulous adventures. Its incredible length (even longer in the original release) works against it, but this Arabian Nights adventure has magnificent William Cameron Menzies sets and some still impressive special FX including a flying horse, a magic carpet, and a giant spider.

THIEF OF BAGDAD, THE
★★★★ Embassy, 1940, NR, 106 min. Dirs: Michael Powell, Ludwig Berger, Tim Whalen. Cast: Sabu, Conrad Veidt, June Duprez, John Justin, Rex Ingram, Miles Malleson, Mary Morris, Hay Petrie.

Sabu is the thief who helps commoner Justin win the heart of princess Duprez. Veidt is the colorful villain and Ingram steals it as a huge genie freed from his bottle by Sabu. One of the great fantasy films of all time, this British film began production in London but was later moved to Hollywood for completion when World War II broke out in Europe. The vivid Technicolor widescreen photography (beautifully showcasing the marvelous sets and clever special FX) won an Oscar and the Miklos Rozsa score is one of his best.

James Arness as the killer carrot from outer space in The Thing *(1951).*

THIEF OF BAGDAD, THE
★★ Video Gems, 1978, G, 96 min. Dir: Clive Donner. Cast: Roddy McDowall, Peter Ustinov, Terence Stamp, Kabir Bedi, Marina Vlady, Frank Finlay, Ian Holm, Pavla Ustinov.

Fourth filming of the Arabian Nights tale (the third starred Steve Reeves, of all people), this was made for TV and looks it. The better actors are all wasted in cameo or guest star parts but the John Stears special FX are good.

THING, THE
★★★★ Turner, 1951, NR, 79 min. Dirs: Christian Nyby, Howard Hawks. Cast: Kenneth Tobey, Margaret Sheridan, Robert Cornthwaite, Douglas Spencer, Dewey Martin, James Arness.

One of the greatest sci-fi/horror films ever made, this taut filmization of John W. Campbell's story *Who Goes There?* was ostensibly directed by Nyby but actually helmed by Hawks, who brings to it all the toughness and grit of his best work. At an arctic military base a blood-drinking alien (Arness in effective Frankensteinian makeup by Lee Greenway) goes on a rampage as army hero Tobey (in the role of a lifetime) tries to stop it and

egghead scientist Cornthwaite tries foolishly to communicate with it. Still quite scary, with a spooky electronic score by Dimitri Tiomkin (before this sort of music became a sci-fi cliché) and tight editing adding to the overall effect. Most current prints are missing seven minutes of footage, cut for a reissue version, including the infamous "bondage" date scene. Aka *The Thing from Another World.*

THING, THE
★★★ MCA/Universal, 1982, R, 108 min. Dir: John Carpenter. Cast: Kurt Russell, Wilford Brimley, Richard Dysart, Donald Moffatt, Keith David, David Clennon.

Released shortly after *E.T.,* this gory remake was blasted by critics and ignored by audiences but, in retrospect, emerges as one of the better remakes of a classic film to come along in quite a while. An Antarctic military base is invaded by an alien lifeform that can take over and duplicate any living thing; the base's personnel quickly come to realize that any one of their fellows could be the Thing. Rob Bottin's state-of-the-art FX are still pretty unsettling even after more than a decade and there are enough in the way of homages to the original *Thing* to keep the buffs busy. Too bad the characters are so uninteresting and interchangeable, lacking the distinct personalities of those in the original film. The widescreen location photography (somewhat marred by panning-and-scanning) imparts a real feeling of icy isolation and loneliness in the viewer.

THING FROM ANOTHER WORLD, THE
See: *The Thing.* (1951)

THINGS TO COME
★★★ Goodtimes, 1936, NR, 92 min. Dir: William Cameron Menzies. Cast: Raymond Massey, Sir Cedric Hardwicke, Ralph Richardson, Pearl Argyle, Edward Chapman, Allan Jeayes, Maurice Braddell, Ann Todd, Derrick de Marney, Margaretta Scott.

Lavish adaptation of H. G. Wells's *The Shape of Things to Come* about a devastating global war (instigated by Richardson) and the subsequent rebuilding of civilization (spearheaded by Massey). This early British sci-fi movie is something of a classic with its elaborate sets (designed by director Menzies) and studied acting from a great cast but suffers from a disjointed, episodic feel, due in part to being cut down from an original 113 minutes. The 1979 *The Shape of Things to Come* (starring Jack Palance and Carol Lynley) is a remake in name only.

30 FOOT BRIDE OF CANDY ROCK, THE
★★ Columbia/TriStar, 1958, NR, 75 min. Dir: Sidney Miller. Cast: Lou Costello, Dorothy Provine, Gale Gordon, Charles Lane, Jimmy Conlan, Peter Leeds, Robert Burton, Doodles Weaver.

Lou is a would-be inventor whose latest device causes girlfriend Provine to grow into a giant. Costello's only film without partner Bud Abbott, this mild spoof of *Attack of the 50-Foot Woman* (which is much funnier) has a few laughs and a seasoned supporting cast but is nothing special. Completed in '58, this wasn't generally released until about the time of Costello's death in 1959.

THIS ISLAND EARTH
★★★ MCA/Universal, 1955, NR, 85 min. Dirs: Joseph Newman, Jack Arnold. Cast: Jeff Morrow, Faith Domergue, Rex Reason, Russell Johnson, Lance Fuller, Robert Nichols, Douglas Spencer, Regis Parton [Edwin Parker].

Scientist Reason is lured to a Georgia think tank by strange genius Morrow, who turns out to be an alien from the planet Metaluna, sent to Earth to recruit our finest minds to find the answer that could save the alien's dying world. The only really A-budgeted Universal sci-fi film from this period, this has gorgeous color and flashy special FX but is terribly slow and drawn-out. Arnold reportedly stepped in at the eleventh hour and directed all the scenes on Metaluna, which explains why they're so tense and exciting when compared to the rest of the film. Morrow is good as the kindly alien Exeter, making up for the general flatness of the rest of the cast, and the last-minute inclusion of the big-brained, Faith Domergue-fondling Metalunan mutant brings a nice, campy feel to this film's closing moments. Based on a much more serious novel by Raymond F. Jones.

THOUSAND AND ONE NIGHTS, A
★★★ Columbia/TriStar, 1945, NR, 93 min. Dir: Alfred E. Green. Cast: Cornel Wilde, Evelyn Keyes, Phil Silvers, Adele Jergens, Rex Ingram, Dusty Anderson, Dennis Hoey, Nestor Paiva.

Aladdin (Wilde) finds a bottle containing a sultry female genie (Keyes) who involves him in various comic adventures. Ingram repeats his own genie role from *The Thief of Bagdad* and Shelley Winters has a bit part as a harem girl in this fun Technicolor fantasy.

THOUSAND EYES OF DR. MABUSE, THE
★★★ Sinister Cinema, 1960, NR, 103 min. Dir: Fritz Lang. Cast: Peter Van Eyck, Dawn Addams, Gert Frobe, Wolfgang Preiss, Andrea Checci, Howard Vernon, Werner Peters, Linda Sini.

Lang's last film was this exciting thriller that revived his old Dr. Mabuse character for an entire series of films shot in West Germany in the '60s. Mabuse's latest plans involve hypnotism, mind control, and world conquest; his activities are investigated by cops Van Eyck and Frobe; and everything leads to a genuinely thrilling climax. Aka *The Secret of Dr. Mabuse* and *The Diabolical Dr. Mabuse*; sequels: *The Return of Dr. Mabuse, The Invisible Dr. Mabuse, Dr. Mabuse vs. Scotland Yard,* and *The Death Ray of Dr. Mabuse.*

THREADS

★★★ New World, 1984, NR, 110 min. Dir: Mick Jackson. Cast: Karen Meagher, Reece Dinsdale, Rita May, Nicholas Lane, Victoria O'Keefe, David Brierly.

British TV's answer to *The Day After,* this tells of a nuclear disaster on the eve of a young couple's wedding in Sheffield, England, and how the subsequent fallout destroys the community and those who live there. Maybe the grimmest and most disturbing film of its kind, this suffers from overlength but is exceedingly well acted and realistic to a fault—like a cross between *Testament* and *East Enders.*

THREE STOOGES IN ORBIT, THE

★★☆ Columbia/TriStar, 1962, NR, 87 min. Dir: Edward L. Bernds. Cast: Moe Howard, Larry Fine, Joe DeRita, Carol Christensen, Edson Stroll, Emil Sitka, George Neise, Nestor Paiva.

Martians (who look like outer space versions of Frankenstein's Monster) come to Earth to steal goofball scientist Sitka's ("Hold hands, you love birds") experimental flying submarine but find their plans complicated by kiddie show hosts the Stooges. Pretty entertaining, with all the tried-and-true gags and silly low-budget special FX and makeup.

THREE STOOGES MEET HERCULES, THE

★★ Columbia/TriStar, 1962, NR, 89 min. Dir: Edward L. Bernds. Cast: Moe Howard, Larry Fine, Joe De Rita, Vicki Trickett, Quinn Redeker, Samson Burke, Emil Sitka, George Neise, Gregg Martell, Gene Roth.

The boys, along with inventor Redecker and girlfriend Trickett, are transported a thousand years into the past by a time machine that lands them in ancient Greece. Moe, Larry, and Curly Joe try to pass the timid Quinn off as Hercules until the real muscleman appears. There's also a two-headed Cyclops and a spoof of the *Ben Hur* chariot race in this mild Stooges comedy.

THREE WORLDS OF GULLIVER, THE

★★☆ Columbia/TriStar, 1960, NR, 99 min. Dir: Jack Sher. Cast: Kerwin Mathews, Jo Morrow, June Thorburn, Lee Patterson, Gregoire Aslan, Basil Sydney.

Columbia hoped to repeat the success of *The Seventh Voyage of Sinbad* by reteaming star Mathews with more Ray Harryhausen special FX but the results aren't nearly as good. Most of the FX in this watered-down version of Jonathan Swift's tale (not a kid's story, anyway) involve the tiny people of Lilliput and the giants of Brobdingnag but there's a stop-motion giant alligator and squirrel, too, and a typically rousing score by Bernard Herrmann.

THRESHOLD

★★★ CBS/Fox, 1981, PG, 97 min. Dir: Richard Pearce. Cast: Donald Sutherland, Jeff Goldblum, Mare Willingham, Sharon Acker, John Marley, Michael Lerner, Paul Hecht, Robert Joy.

Doctor Sutherland and biologist Goldblum team up to create the first artificial heart, which is eventually transplanted into dying teen Winningham. This Canadian drama (more science fact than science fiction these days) rises above its formula disease-of-the-week framework thanks to strong acting by the three leads (with Goldblum in a dry run for his quirky scientist roles in *The Fly* and *Jurassic Park*) and to director Pearce's concentration on medical accuracy over melodrama.

THX-1138

★★★ Warner, 1971, PG, 88 min. Dir: George Lucas. Cast: Robert Duvall, Donald Pleasence, Maggie McOmie, Don Pedro Colley, Ian Wolfe, Sid Haig.

Based on a short film he made while attending USC, Lucas's first feature is a grim but interesting drama in the *1984* mold about a future subterranean society where love and sex are forbidden. A shaven-headed Duvall enters into a relationship with McOmie and tragedy results. Good acting and interesting visual qualities help make up for a somewhat dry and pretentious storyline. Years later, Lucas would name his film remastering and preservation division after this movie.

TIDAL WAVE

See: *Portrait of Jennie.*

TIME AFTER TIME

★★★ Warner, 1979, PG, 112 min. Dir: Nicholas Meyer. Cast: Malcolm McDowell, David Warner, Mary Steenburgen, Charles Cioffi, Kent Williams, Patti D'Arbanville.

In 1988, Jack the Ripper (Warner) steals a time machine manufactured by H. G. Wells (McDowell) and takes it to '70s San Francisco. Wells pursues and while stalking the Ripper meets and falls in love with a pretty bank officer (Steenburgen) who's fated to become

The Morlocks whip things into shape in The Time Machine *(1960).*

one of the Ripper's victims. This delightful genre-bender (it has sci-fi, horror, comedy, drama, romance—everything but songs!) made a star of Steenbergen and showcased McDowell in one of his few "normal" roles (of course, *Caligula* was next up). It holds up much better than a lot of other late '70s fantasies and the romantic Miklos Rozsa music is especially good; some of the slashings are surprisingly brutal for a PG-rated movie. Look for Corey Feldman and Shelly Hack in bits.

TIME BANDITS

★★★ Paramount, 1981, PG, 110 min. Dir: Terry Gilliam. Cast: Sean Connery, Shelley Duvall, John Cleese, Katherine Helmond, Ian Holm, Michael Palin, Ralph Richardson, David Warner, Peter Vaughn, Craig Warnock, Kenny Baker, David Rappaport.

Six dwarves kidnap a young English lad (Warnock) and take him on a trip through time while being pursued by the devil (Warner) and assisted by the Supreme Being (Richardson). Along the way they meet giants (Helmond and Vaughn), an obtuse Robin Hood (Cleese), and a friendly King Agamemnon (Connery, with charisma to spare). The first in Gilliam's fantasy trilogy (followed by *Brazil* and *The Adventures of Baron Munchausen*), this has a spirited cast and lots of coy special FX (like Warner's sinister stronghold being made up of thousands of Lego blocks) but overall it lacks the sort of charm (and is often too loud and strident) that would have made it a classic.

TIME COP

★★★ MCA/Universal, 1994, R, 98 min. Dir: Peter Hyams. Cast: Jean-Claude Van Damme, Mia Sara, Ron Silver, Bruce McGill, Gloria Reuben, Scott Bellis.

A surprisingly imaginative adaptation of a Dark Horse comic about twenty-first-century villains who use a time machine to travel to different time periods and steal valuable objects. Van Damme is the cop who is sent to stop them and ends up in 1994, where he tries to change history and save the life of murdered wife Sara. One of the best vehicles for the "Muscles from Brussels," this keeps the gratuitous martial arts action to a minimum and instead just tells a good story.

TIME GUARDIAN, THE

★★ New Line, 1987, PG, 105 min. Dir: Brian Hannant. Cast: Tom Burlinson, Nikki Coghill, Carrie Fisher, Dean Stockwell, Tim Robertson, Peter Merrill.

Confusion reigns in this Australian film about a city of the distant future sent into the past (our present) by title character Burlinson to evade invasion by an army of killer cyborgs. Burlinson and Fisher wind up in the outback, where geologist Coghill helps them battle some cyborgs who have followed them. A lot of interesting ideas that go nowhere fast.

TIME MACHINE, THE

★★★★ MGM/UA, 1960, NR, 103 min. Dir: George Pal. Cast: Rod Taylor, Yvette Mimieux, Alan Young, Sebastian Cabot, Tom Helmore, Whit Bissell, Doris Lloyd, voice of Paul Frees.

Pal's greatest triumph was this beautifully crafted version of the H. G. Wells novel about a young inventor (Taylor) who builds a time-travel device that takes him from the year 1899 into a postatomic war future. There the gentle, childlike Eloi (including a radiant Mimieux in her debut) are bred like cattle for the hideous, underground-dwelling mutants called Morlocks. Everything about this movie clicks, from the acting to the story to the music to the Oscar-winning special FX. A must.

TIME MACHINE, THE

★☆ VCI, 1978, G, 99 min. Dir: Henning Schellerup. Cast: John Beck, Priscilla Barnes, Andrew Duggen, Rosemary DeCamp, Jack Kruschen, Whit Bissell.

Painfully inept remake (made for theaters but seen mostly on TV) with Beck as a computer genius who develops a time machine that eventually transports him to the world of the Eloi (including Barnes) and the Morlocks. This cheapjack *Classics Illustrated* movie, shot in Utah, is notable only for the fact that Bissell appears here playing the same character he did in the 1960 version.

TIME OF THE BEAST

See: *Mutator.*

TIME OF THEIR LIVES, THE

★★★ MCA/Universal, 1946, NR, 82 min. Dir: Charles T. Barton. Cast: Bud Abbott, Lou Costello, Marjorie Reynolds, Binnie Barnes, Gale Sondergaard, John Shelton, Ann Gillis, Donald MacBride.

In one of A&C's most offbeat films, Costello and Reynolds are mistaken for British spies during the Revolutionary War and killed. One hundred seventy years later psychiatrist Abbott (a descendant of the man who betrayed Lou and Marjorie) buys the house their spirits haunt and is comically tormented by the ghosts. A little slow, but good special FX and a lack of the usual patter routines make this worthwhile even for non-A&C fans.

TIMERIDER

See: *Timerider: The Adventures of Lyle Swan.*

TIMERIDER: THE ADVENTURES LYLE SWAN

★★ Pacific Arts, 1983, PG, 93 min. Dir: William Dear. Cast: Fred Ward, Belinda Bauer, Peter Coyote, Ed Lauter, Richard Masur, Tracey Walter, L. Q. Jones, voice of Nick Nolte.

Ex-Monkee Mike Nesmith produced and co-wrote this time-travel fantasy with Ward as a motorcyclist sent by a time warp back to the old West, circa 1877. This has some similarities to the later *Back to the Future III* but once it

establishes its premise it has absolutely no idea what to do with it and wastes a good cast. Aka *Timerider.*

TIME RUNNER

★☆ New Line, 1992, R, 90 min. Dir: Michael Mazo. Cast: Mark Hamill, Rae Dawn Chong, Brion James, Marc Bauer.

Hamill is simply awful as a time traveler from the year 2022 who arrives in 1992 to try to prevent a future war with aliens; Chong is a '90s scientist who tries to help him. This plodding, derivative Canadian movie borrows from a lot of better films and tries to cover for its lack of coherent plot with a lot of explosions.

TIMESTALKERS

★★☆ Fries, 1987, NR, 96 min. Dir: Michael Schuktz. Cast: Klaus Kinski, Lauren Hutton, William Devane, Forrest Tucker, John Ratzenberger, Gail Youngs, John Considine, Tracey Walter.

Brain Clemens adapted the script for this TV movie (based on an unpublished novel by Ray Brown called *The Tintype*) with Kinski (in his American telemovie debut) as a mad scientist who steals a rival's time-travel device and flees to the old West (that plot again). Devane is a contemporary college professor who helps future woman Hutton track Klaus down. Imaginative, but hampered by its TV-movie structuring. Tucker's last film.

TIME TRACKERS

★★ MGM/UA, 1989, PG, 87 min. Dir: Howard R. Cohen. Cast: Wil Shriner, Kathleen Beller, Ned Beatty, Lee Bergere, Alex Hyde-White, Bridget Hoffman.

Futuristic evil genius Bergere decides to use his new time machine to alter history to his benefit and is tracked back to medieval England by Beller (daughter of the time machine's true inventor), Shriner, and twentieth-century cop Beatty, whom they meet on the way. This comic fantasy never really makes up its mind whether to play for laughs or thrills; after a funny beginning it settles down into just one more gimmicky time-travel movie and never recovers. Beatty has some amusing moments. Heroine Beller and bad guy Bergere once played father and daughter on TV's *Dynasty.*

TIME TRAVELERS, THE

★★★ HBO, 1964, NR, 82 MIN. Dir: Ib Melchior. Cast: Preston Foster, Philip Carey, Merry Anders, Steve Franken, John Hoyt, Joan Woodbury, Dennis Patrick, Forrest J. Ackerman.

Imaginative low-budgeter with scientist Foster and assistants Carey and Anders inventing a "time window" that can see into the future.

The doctor and his crew then climb through the window and end up in a world where nuclear holocaust survivors are forever menaced by hostile mutants and hope to escape the radiation-ravaged Earth in a rocket ship. Good acting and creative scripting make this inexpensive little flick more fun than you might imagine; love that time-bending ending. More or less remade as *Journey to the Center of Time* and an obvious inspiration for the *Time Tunnel* TV series.

TIME WALKER

★☆ Charter, 1982, PG, 85 min. Dir: Tom Kennedy. Cast: Ben Murphy, Nina Axelrod, Kevin Brophy, Shari Belafonte, James Karen, Antoinette Bower, Darwin Jostin, Austin Stoker.

A mummy rampaging on a college campus turns out to be an alien with a lethal touch. Stupid horror/sci-fi with a solid cast wasted on dumb characters who keep doing absurd things to keep the plot a-boiling. Is this Tom Kennedy the same guy who hosted TV game shows in the '70s and '80s? Shown on *Mystery Science Theater 3000* as *Being from Another Planet*.

TIME WARP

See: *Journey to the Center of Time.*

TOBOR THE GREAT

★☆ Republic, 1954, NR, 77 min. Dir: Lee Sholem. Cast: Charles Drake, Karin Booth, Billy Chapin, Taylor Holmes, Steven Geray, Robert Shayne, Lyle Talbot, Henry Kulky.

There's nothing especially great about this clichéd boy-and-his-robot story. Chapin is an annoying brat who befriends his scientist grandpa's newest experiment and helps save it from foreign spies. The script and acting are as clunky as the robot suit.

TOMCAT

★☆ Republic, 1993, R, 96 min. Dir: Paul Donovan. Cast: Richard Grieco, Maryam D'Abo, Natalie Radford.

Silly blending of horror, sci-fi, and erotic thriller elements with (an often shirtless) Grieco as the subject of an experiment with feline DNA. He becomes a strong, seductive killer who slinks about like a cat and beds most of the female cast members. For fans of the star's musculature only. Aka *Tomcat: Dangerous Desires* and *Dangerous Desires.*

TOMCAT: DANGEROUS DESIRES

See: *Tomcat.*

TOMMYKNOCKERS, THE

★★ Vidmark Entertainment, 1993, NR, 125 min. Dir: John Power. Cast: Jimmy Smits, Marg Helgenberger, Joanna Cassidy, E. G. Marshall, Traci Lords, Robert Carradine, Cliff De Young, Allyce Beasley.

A truncated feature-length version of the Stephen King miniseries about people in a small town being taken over by a glowing green force emanating from a long-buried alien spacecraft. A poor man's *Invasion of the Body Snatchers* with a top-flight cast (especially Smits, Helgenberger, and Cassidy) but not much else.

TOM THUMB

★★★ MGM/UA, 1958, G, 98 MIN. Dir: George Pal. Cast: Russ Tamblyn, June Thorburn, Peter Sellers, Terry-Thomas, Alan Young, Jessie Matthews.

Exuberant musical-fantasy with Tamblyn as the diminutive hero, beloved by adoptive parents Young and Matthews and sought by villain Terry-Thomas and henchman Sellers (great in an early role). One of Pal's best, with Oscar-winning special FX and Tamblyn practically leaping off the screen and dancing in your lap.

TOPPER

★★★☆ Hal Roach, 1937, NR, 97 min. Dir: Norman Z. McLeod. Cast: Cary Grant, Constance Bennett, Roland Young, Billie Burke, Alan Mowbray, Eugene Pallette, Arthur Lake, Hedda Hopper.

Bubbly adaptation of Thorne Smith's novel about milquetoast Cosmo Topper (Young) and the way his life is endlessly complicated by the ghosts of high-living Grant and Bennett. A great mixture of screwball comedy and ghostly fantasy with a perfect cast. Followed by two sequels, a TV series, and a TV movie remake (with Kate Jackson and Andrew Stevens); avoid the ugly colorized version.

TOPPER RETURNS

★★★ Video Treasures, 1941, NR, 88 min. Dir: Roy Del Ruth. Cast: Joan Blondell, Roland Young, Carole Landis, Billie Burke, Dennis O'Keefe, Patsy Kelly, George Zucco, Eddie "Rochester" Anderson.

Third and last in the original *Topper* series is the second best with Blondell taking over for Constance Bennett and helping Cosmo (Young) to solve her own murder and save Landis from a similar fate. Crackling blend of comedy, murder mystery, and even a touch of horror; the fine support cast includes longtime Jack Benny sidekick Anderson in a funny scene with a trained seal.

TOPPER TAKES A TRIP
★★☆ Video Treasures, 1939, NR, 85 min. Dir: Norman Z. McLeod. Cast: Constance Bennett, Roland Young, Billie Burke, Alan Mowbray, Verree Teasdale, Franklin Pangborn, Irving Pichel, Alex D'Arcy.

Cary Grant is featured only in flashback footage in this first *Topper* followup, in which the ghostly Bennett tries to help stop Burke from filing for divorce from seemingly crazy, ghost-seeing hubby Young. Not as good as the first and third in the series but still fun and a lot better than what passes for fantasy-comedy today, let me tell you.

TOTAL RECALL
★★★ Avid Entertainment, 1990, R, 109 min. Dir: Paul Verhoeven. Cast: Arnold Schwarzenegger, Rachel Ticotin, Sharon Stone, Ronny Cox, Michael Ironside, Marshall Bell.

This very expensive ($70 million) film version of Philip K. Dick's *We Can Remember It for You Wholesale* doesn't succeed as an adaptation of the author's work; retooled into a vehicle for Arnold it comes off fine, though it really wasn't the box-office success its makers hoped. Schwarzenegger is a construction worker who discovers that he is the victim of twenty-first-century mind control. He travels with Ticotin to the Earth colonies of Mars, where he has a violent run-in with estranged wife Stone and discovers his true destiny. Lots of typically flashy Verhoeven action and violence and some interesting (if not always believable) Rob Bottin special makeup FX successfully pave over some glaring story holes.

TRANCERS
★★★ Vestron, 1985, PG-13, 76 min. Dir: Charles Band. Cast: Tim Thomerson, Helen Hunt, Art La Fleur, Biff Manard, Anne Seymour, Richard Herd, Michael Stefani, Telma Hopkins.

Stand-up comic Thomerson is great in his first starring role, as Jack Deth, a cop from three hundred years in the future who travels back to '80s Los Angeles to stop villain Stefani from taking over the city with his army of "Trancers"—hypnotized, zombielike slaves. Fast-paced and funny, with a good cast (including Hunt years before her *Mad About You* success) and solidly constructed script. Original title: *Future Cop*.

TRANCERS II: THE RETURN OF JACK DETH
★★ Paramount, 1991, R, 86 min. Dir: Charles Band. Cast: Tim Thomerson, Helen Hunt, Megan Ward, Richard Lynch, Martine Beswick, Jeffrey Combs, Barbara Crampton, Art La Fleur.

Now it's Lynch who's turning victims (mostly homeless people) into zombies. Thomerson returns to the past to battle him and be reunited with Hunt—much to the chagrin of wife-from-the-future Ward. Originally part of an aborted Empire Pictures anthology of horror and sci-fi tales called *Pulse Pounders* (shot in 1987) and later expanded to feature length, this routine sequel is worth it mainly for the cast.

TRANCERS III: DETH LIVES
★★☆ Paramount, 1992, R, 83 min. Dir: C. Courtney Joyner. Cast: Tim Thomerson, Melanie Smith, Andrew Robinson, Helen Hunt, Megan Ward, Stephen Macht.

Deth returns again, this time to battle an alien called the Shark and evil renegade army colonel Robinson, who's creating more Trancers out of soldiers. Part III is pretty good, thanks mainly to Thomerson's off-the-cuff performance, but Hunt and Ward are wasted in token guest appearances.

TRANCERS 4: JACK OF SWORDS
★★ Paramount, 1993, R, 74 min. Dir: David Nutter. Cast: Tim Thomerson, Stacie Randall, Ty Miller, Stephen Macht, Alan Oppenheimer.

This time Deth ends up in a medieval parallel dimension, where he battles more Trancers and a vampire nobleman who breeds peasants as food. Talky and confusing, not up to earlier entries in the series.

TRANCERS 5: SUDDEN DETH
★☆ Paramount, 1994, R, 73 min. Dir: David Nutter. Cast: Tim Thomerson, Stacie Randall, Ty Miller, Stephen Macht, Terri Ivens, Mark Arnold.

Shot back to back with part four, this alleged final entry continues Jack's adventures in that other dimension where there are more damsels to rescue and more Trancers to fight. Fans of Thomerson's witty line delivery might like it but I really think this franchise has reached the end of its tether.

TRANSATLANTIC TUNNEL
★★ Budget, 1935, NR, 70 min. Dir: Maurice Elvey. Cast: Richard Dix, Leslie Banks, Madge Evans, Helen Vinson, George Arliss, Walter Huston, C. Aubrey Smith, Basil Sydney.

A potentially interesting story—about the construction of a tunnel beneath the ocean from Great Britain to the U.S.—gets bogged down by enough melodramatic subplots for three Irwin Allen movies. The great sets and cast are still its main distinction. Originally called *The Tunnel*, running 94 minutes.

TRAPPED IN SPACE
★★☆ Paramount, 1994, PG, 87 min. Dir: Arthur

Allan Seidelman. Cast: Jack Wagner, Kay Lenz, Jack Coleman, Craig Wasson, Sigrid Thornton, Kevin Colson.

Speaking of Irwin Allen, this made-for-cable version (debuting on the Sci-Fi channel) of Arthur C. Clarke's story "Breaking Strain" is very much in the tradition of the Master of Disaster's all-star spectacles like *The Poseidon Adventure* et cetera. Space travelers discover that a ruptured oxygen tank has destroyed most of their air supply, allowing only one of them to make it back to Earth—but which one? Surprisingly suspenseful and acted with a nice sense of sweaty paranoia by its terminally goofed-out cast of familiar faces.

TREASURE OF THE FOUR CROWNS
★☆ MGM/UA, 1982, PG, 97 min. Dir: Ferdinando Balbi. Cast: Tony Anthony, Ana Obregon, Gene Quintano, Francisco Rabal, Jerry Lazarus, Marshall Lupo.

A 3-D rip of *Raiders of the Lost Ark* about a band of adventurers trying to retrieve four magical crowns from an evil cult leader (from Brooklyn!) who wants to rule the world. This Spanish quickie (from the makers of the 3-D Western *Comin' at Ya!* whose success sparked a brief early '80s 3-D revival) has some nice locations but very pathetic FX and copies scenes from *Raiders, Topkapi,* and others.

TREMORS
★★☆ MCA/Universal, 1990, PG-13, 96 min. Dir: Ron Underwood. Cast: Kevin Bacon, Fred Ward, Finn Carter, Michael Gross, Reba McIntire, Charlotte Stewart.

This big-studio tribute to the '50s monster films of Jack Arnold (most notably *Tarantula*) has become something of a cult movie. Giant worms terrorize a tiny desert community, with handymen Bacon and Ward and survivalists Gross and McIntire giving them the most trouble. So-so special FX (which look somewhat like leftovers from *Dune*), but the tongue-in-cheek approach is well sustained and the cast is fun.

TREMORS 2: AFTERSHOCKS
★★ MCA/Universal, 1995, PG-13, 100 min. Dir: S. S. Wilson. Cast: Fred Ward, Christopher Gartin, Helen Shaver, Michael Gross.

This belated sequel to the popular original was actually made for theaters but released straight to video instead. Ward returns as the giant worm hunter who's hired by an oil company to get rid of the underground monsters terrorizing a desert drill site. Pretty predictable and unadventurous; Shaver (as a lady scientist) and a returning Ward and Gross hit all the right notes, but Gartin, standing in for I'm-much-too-big-a-star-for-this-sort-of-nonsense Kevin Bacon, is an annoying pretty boy without an ounce of talent or charisma.

TRIAL OF THE INCREDIBLE HULK
★★ Goodtimes, 1989, NR, 93 min. Dir: Bill Bixby. Cast: Bill Bixby, Lou Ferrigno, Rex Smith, Marta DuBois, Nancy Everhard, John Rhys-Davies, Joseph Mascolo.

I want the truth, the whole truth, and nothing but the truth. Why did they keep making these well-after-the-fact *Hulk* TV movies? I know there's no reasonable answer so I'll just conclude by saying that this one teams the green guy with another Marvel superhero called Daredevil (who's blind, no less) for more slow-motion supershenanigans.

TRIPODS
★★☆ Sony, 1984–85, NR, 150 min. Dir: Graham Theakston. Cast: John Shackley, Jim Baker, Ceri Seel, Richard Wordsworth.

A compilation of episodes of the cultish BBC-TV series (aimed at kids) based on books by John Christopher. Aliens in tall, three-legged war machines invade England and take over the populace with mind-controlling skull caps. A small band of children fight back. Not bad, though the series was canceled before the story could be wrapped up.

TRIUMPH OF THE SON OF HERCULES
★★ Sinister Cinema, 1963, NR, 87 min. Dir: Amergio Anton. Cast: Kirk Morris, Cathia Caro, Carla Colo, Ljuba Bodin.

Herc's offspring (Morris) is given the usual set of challenges and at one point takes on a band of apelike temple guards. More muscle madness for undiscriminating peblum fans. Aka *Il Trionfo di Maciste (Triumph of Maciste)*.

TRON
★★☆ Disney, 1982, PG, 96 min. Dir: Steven Lisberger. Cast: Jeff Bridges, Bruce Boxleitner, Cindy Morgan, David Warner, Barnard Hughes, Dan Shor.

Computer whiz Bridges gets sucked into a computer and ends up in a strange alternate reality where he has to fight for survival in a series of gladiatorial-type video competitions. The first feature film with computer-generated special FX, this is great looking but rather slackly plotted. Most of the supporting cast play dual roles; Jeff is in fine form as the quick-witted hero.

TUNNEL, THE
See: *Transatlantic Tunnel.*

TURKEY SHOOT
See: *Escape 2000.*

12 MONKEYS
★★★ MCA/Universal, 1995, R, 130 min. Dir: Terry Gilliam. Cast: Bruce Willis, Madeleine Stowe, Brad Pitt, Christopher Plummer, David Morse, Frank Gorshin.

Gilliam's twisty tribute to Chris Marker's classic 1962 French short *La Jetée,* this features (the ubiquitously nude) Willis as an inmate in a Philadelphia asylum who raves about the destruction of the world and turns out to be a man from the future who's come back to prevent the outbreak of a plague that will decimate the Earth's population. This surprisingly downbeat mainstream sci-fi thriller has good work from Willis and Stowe (as a helpful scientist) and an effectively bleak wintry look, helping to make up for some convoluted plotting and Pitt's overacting in an Oscar-nominated supporting role as one of Bruce's fellow nutcases who also may be more than he seems.

12:01
★★★☆ New Line, 1993, PG-13, 96 min. Dir: Jack Sholder. Cast: Jonathan Silverman, Helen Slater, Martin Landau, Jeremy Piven, Nicolas Surovy, Robin Bartlett.

Good made-for-cable flick derived from a student film directed by screenwriter Philip Morton and somewhat anticipating the better-known *Groundhog Day.* Office worker Silverman finds himself trapped in a time warp and reliving the same day over and over, trying to save the life of pretty Slater, whom he secretly loves. Consistently clever and imaginative and deserving of a far wider reputation.

20 MILLION MILES TO EARTH
★★★ Columbia/TriStar, 1957, NR, 82 min. Dir: Nathan Juran. Cast: William Hopper, Joan Taylor, Frank Puglia, John Zaremba, Thomas B. Henry, Bart Bradley [Bart Braverman].

The last and best of Ray Harryhausen's trilogy of globe-hopping monster-on-the-loose films from the '50s (the others being *The Beast from 20,000 Fathoms* and *It Came From Beneath the Sea*), this one features a Venusian creature called a Ymir (though not named in the film

Seems like unused scenes from Dumbo *make a cool ending for* 20 Million Miles to Earth *(1957).*

itself) hatching from a gelatinous egg salvaged from a crashed rocket on return flight. The creature doubles in size every day, until its climactic tear through Rome and last stand high atop the Colosseum. Flavorful backgrounds and moody cinematography help make up for a rather colorless cast (little kid actor Bradley reverted to his true name as an adult to appear in the *Vega$* TV series). The special FX, on the other hand, are among Harryhausen's most accomplished. Note in passing: Either the Ymir is a female or more possibly the first gay monster in movie history—check out that effeminate walk and the scene where it grabs a guy off the streets of Rome.

27TH DAY, THE
★★☆ Columbia/TriStar, 1957, NR, 75 min. Dir: William Asher. Cast: Gene Barry, Valerie French, George Voskovec, Arnold Moss, Paul Birch, Marie Tsien, Azemat Janti, Friedrich Ledebur.

An erudite alien (Moss) arrives on Earth in a flying saucer (stock footage from *Earth vs. the Flying Saucers*) and kidnaps five men and women of different nationalities. Each of the five is gifted with a tiny time capsule capable destroying the world, then the alien sits back and watches human nature take its course. A surprisingly sober, even somber film for its time, this is sometimes reminiscent of *Red Planet Mars* (once again, the Russians are the ultimate evil and of all the peoples of the world, only they come to a bad end) but is more intelligent, with solid acting and a thoughtful script written by John Mantley.

20,000 LEAGUES UNDER THE SEA
★★★★ Disney, 1954, G, 127 min. Dir: Richard Fleischer. Cast: James Mason, Kirk Douglas, Peter Lorre, Paul Lukas, Robert J. Wilke, Carleton Young.

Easily Walt Disney's best live-action feature, this adaptation of the Jules Verne book stars Mason in his best role as Captain Nemo, the nineteenth-century inventor of the futuristic submarine Nautilus, who glides under the Atlantic in the guise of a legendary sea monster sinking warships. Sailor Douglas (just overflowing with energy and charm), scientist Lukas, and government envoy Lorre are captured and eventually lead a mutiny to stop the misguided Nemo's plans to eliminate all war through death and destruction. Many Disney films tend to be overrated by audiences and critics (thinking they must be good simply because they are Disney films) but this is richly deserving of its classic status, with top-flight sets, photography, acting, and special FX. The legendary giant squid scene is the standout. Sequel: *Mysterious Island*.

TWILIGHT ZONE—THE MOVIE
★★☆ Warner, 1983, PG, 101 min. Dirs: John Landis, Steven Spielberg, Joe Dante, George Miller. Cast: Dan Aykroyd, Albert Brooks, Scatman Crothers, John Lithgow, Vic Morrow, Kathleen Quinlan, Jeremy Licht, Kevin McCarthy, Abbe Lane, Donna Dixon, Patricia Barry, William Schallert, Bill Lane, Murray Matheson, Selma Diamond, John Larroquette, Dick Miller, voice of Burgess Meredith.

This big-screen reincarnation of the classic show is made up of four segments and a wraparound; three of the four tales are remakes of old shows. Landis's framing story (with Aykroyd and Brooks) is both very funny and very scary (and employs an unused make-up effect from *Poltergeist*) but his main segment is pretentious and obvious and will probably be remembered only for the on-set accidental death of star Morrow. Spielberg's story ("Kick the Can") is so sweet it hurts (too bad he abandoned his original idea to do a Richard Matheson-scripted horror story instead), but Dante's "It's a Good Life" is a clever and funny updating of the original (despite a dumb ending) and Miller's "Nightmare at 20,000 Feet" actually improves on the old episode, with a scarier monster and an enjoyably edgy performance from Lithgow. Jerry Goldsmith's music, both light and airy and broody and intense, adds just the right touch to hold things together. This film's (moderate) success led to a new *TZ* series that aired on CBS from 1985 to 1987.

2001: A SPACE ODYSSEY
★★★★ MGM/UA, 1968, PG, 139 min. Dir: Stanley Kubrick. Cast: Keir Dullea, Gary Lockwood, William Sylvester, Daniel Richter, Margaret Tyzack, Leonard Rossiter, Robert Beatty, voice of Douglas Rain.

This lavish film version of Arthur C. Clarke's story *The Sentinel* became an instant classic upon its release in the psychedelic '60s and still looks great today. When a mysterious alien slab is discovered on the moon, a spaceship is dispatched to Jupiter to investigate its origin. The ship's on-board computer HAL, however, has other plans. The Douglas Trumbull special FX won a well-deserved Oscar and the futuristic images are beautifully married to the sounds of classical music (most notably Strauss's "Thus Spake Zarathustra"); the actors may be secondary to the story and settings but Rain gives an unforgettable vocal performance as the voice of HAL. Originally released at 160 minutes, Kubrick recut the film himself shortly after the premiere to its current length. Sequel: *2010: The Year We Make Contact*.

2010: THE YEAR WE MAKE CONTACT

★★★ MGM/UA, 1984, PG, 114 min. Dir: Peter Hyams. Cast: Roy Scheider, John Lithgow, Helen Mirren, Keir Dullea, Bob Balaban, Madolyn Smith, Elya Baskin, voice of Douglas Rain.

A well-cast Scheider commands a U.S.-Russian investigation into what happened to those who traveled to Jupiter in the original *2001*. HAL is reactivated to cause more trouble and Dullea shows up at the end for an interesting but frankly silly cameo. This long-after-the-fact sequel is surprisingly low-key and intellectual for a sci-fi film produced in the wake of the *Star Wars* series (Arthur C. Clarke had a hand in the scripting), with a more personable supporting cast this time out (including the lovely Smith in an early role as a cosmonaut) and first rate FX by Richard Edlund. The overly literal ending, however, really doesn't come off.

2020: NEW BARBARIANS

See: *The New Gladiators*.

2020 TEXAS GLADIATORS

★☆ Media, 1982, R, 91 min. Dir: Kevin Mancusco [Aristede Massaccessi]. Cast: Harrison Muller, Sabrina Siani, Peter Hoote, Al Cliver.

More Italian *Mad Max* droppings from the unstoppable Massaccessi (aka Joe D'Amato). This time it's a postnuke reworking of *Hannie Caulder*, with Siani in the old Raquel Welch role as a violated widow who teams up with Muller to take revenge for the murder of husband Cliver. You've seen it all too many times before.

TWO LOST WORLDS

★☆ Sony, 1950, NR, 62 min. Dir: Norman Dawn. Cast: James Arness, Laura Elliott, Bill Kennedy, Gloria Petroff, Tom Hubbard, Jane Harlan.

A boring period pirate movie unexpectedly becomes a lost-world and dinosaurs pic as the heroes escape from their swashbuckling captors onto an island overrunning with stock footage from *One Million B.C.* Some of the editing is clever but this low-budget gobbler really isn't worth sitting through to admire it.

TWO WORLDS OF JENNIE LOGAN, THE

★★☆ Fries, 1979, NR, 99 min. Dir: Frank DeFelitta. Cast: Lindsay Wagner, Marc Singer, Linda Gray, Alan Feinstein, Irene Tedrow, Henry Wilcoxon.

Wagner discovers an antique lace dress in the attic of her newly purchased old mansion and after donning it is transported into the past, where she falls in love with an artist fated soon to die in a duel. Lindsay's sensitive, sincere acting elevates this made-for-TV *Somewhere in Time* cash-in (actually broadcast before the release of that film), which might have worked better had it played its situation for horror and suspense rather than syrupy romance.

UFO

★★☆ Today, 1972–73, NR, 50 min. per tape. Dirs: David Lane, Ken Turner. Cast: Ed Bishop, George Sewell, Wanda Ventham, Michael Billington, Gabrielle Drake, Antonia Ellis.

After years of producing marionette sci-fi shows like *Thunderbirds* and *Captain Scarlet,* British TV producers Gerry and Sylvia Anderson tried their hand at a live-action sci-fi series. Trouble was, everybody acted like puppets anyway and, although it lasted two seasons, the series never really caught on. Bishop is the head of SHADO (Supreme Headquarters Alien Defense Organization), which operates from bases in England and on the moon and deals with the usual crew of alien invaders and the like. Although this series tended to be a bit dry, there were some memorable stories and characters (my favorite is Drake as moonbase operative Gay, who wears a metallic miniskirt, vinyl go-go boots, and white eyeliner).

UFORIA

★★☆ MCA/Universal, 1980, PG, 94 min. Dir: John Binder. Cast: Cindy Williams, Harry Dean Stanton, Fred Ward, Beverly Hope Atkinson, Harry Carey, Jr., Diane Deifendorf.

Eccentric blend of sci-fi and quirky comedy with former Shirley Feeney Williams as a born-again supermarket checkout gal who believes that she's been chosen as the new Noah to lead a band of survivors to an alien spacecraft to escape Earth's imminent destruction. Evangelist Stanton tries to exploit Cindy to his own ends but she finds true love with drifter Ward. Unreleased until 1986, this not always successful marriage of Steven Spielberg and Frank Capra has good acting and interesting insights into what people need to believe in order to be happy, but it's ultimately too uneven and unsure of itself to work completely.

ULTIMATE WARRIOR, THE

★★ Warner, 1975, R, 94 min. Dir: Robert Clouse.
Cast: Yul Brynner, Max von Sydow, Joanna Miles,
William Smith, Stephen McHattie, Lane Bradbury.

Routine end-of-the-world flick with Brynner
trying to survive in the ruins of Manhattan,
helping pregnant Miles and fighting villains
von Sydow and Smith. Well cast and with
good production design, but uninspired writing and direction keep it strictly second rate.

UNDERSEA KINGDOM, THE

★★☆ Nostalgia Merchant, 1936, NR, 260 min. Dirs:
B. Reeves Eason, Joseph Kane. Cast: Ray "Crash"
Corrigan, Lois Wilde, Monte Blue, William Farnum,
Boothe Howard, C. Montague Shaw, Smiley
Burnette, Lon Chaney, Jr.

This serial is something of a flawed camp masterpiece. Corrigan (more or less playing himself) leads an expedition by submarine to an
underwater continent where survivors of
Atlantis are at war and our heroes are menaced by robots, laser cannons, and the like.
Too cheap for its ambitions, this waterlogged
Flash Gordon wannabe plays well as comedy,
with boat-in-a-bathtub special FX, villains in
caftans and funny hats, and muscular henchmen in miniskirts. The feature version is called
Sharad of Atlantis.

UNDERSEA ODYSSEY

See: *The Neptune Factor.*

UNEARTHLY STRANGER, THE

★★★ Sinister Cinema, 1963, NR, 74 min. Dir: John
Krish. Cast: John Neville, Gabriella Licudi, Philip
Stone, Patrick Newell, Jean Marsh.

Eerie British role-reversal of *I Married a Monster from Outer Space,* with Neville (later an
excellent Sherlock Holmes in *A Study in Terror*)
as a scientist who discovers that beautiful
bride Licudi is actually an alien spy. All the
women, in fact, in this moody little movie are
revealed to be extraterrestrials whose tears
scald their faces like acid. Made by the same
production team responsible for the *Avengers*
TV show (note the presence of Newell, who
played "Mother" on the series), this is downbeat and spooky; well worth checking out for
those seeking a good sci-fi film without a lot of
gratuitous special FX.

UNIDENTIFIED FLYING ODDBALL

★★ Disney, 1979, G, 93 min. Dir: Russ Mayberry.
Cast: Dennis Dugan, Ron Moody, Jim Dale, Kenneth
More, Sheila White, John LeMesurier.

Unmemorable Disney bastardization of *A Connecticut Yankee in King Arthur's Court* with

TERRIFYING
WEIRD...MACABRE!
Unseen things out of
Time and Space!

UNEARTHLY STRANGER

AN AMERICAN INTERNATIONAL PICTURE

JOHN NEVILLE · GABRIELLA LICUDI · PHILIP STONE

ALBERT FENNELL JOHN KRISH REX CARLTON & JULIAN WINTLE LESLIE PARKYN PRODUCTION

*Great monster—too bad it isn't in the movie!
Original ad art for* The Unearthly Stranger
(1963).

Dugan as a bumbling astronaut accidentally
sent back in time to Camelot, where he
encounters Arthur, Merlin the magician, and
the rest of the gang. The cast tries hard but
they really shouldn't have bothered. Disney
bothered us again with another reworking of
the same idea in *A Kid in King Arthur's Court.*

UNIVERSAL SOLDIER

★★☆ LIVE, 1992, R, 104 min. Dir: Roland Emmerich.
Cast: Jean-Claude Van Damme, Dolph Lundgren, Ally
Walker, Ed O'Ross, Jerry Orbach, Leon Rippy.

Van Damme and Lundgren, admittedly no
Gielgud and Olivier, are well matched in this
sci-fi/action/horror thriller. JC and Dolph are
bitter enemies who die in a Vietnam massacre
in 1969; some twenty-three years later they are
revived from cryogenic freezing as unstoppable zombie warriors who are supposed to
put a stop to terroristic activities but keep trying to bump each other off. The guys look
good (male nudity fans will like the cryogenics
scene) and Emmerich (*Independence Day*) gives
this some much-needed energy and humor,
but in the end it's all too standard a Holly-

wood product ever to be as interesting as it could have been.

UNKNOWN ISLAND

★★ Nostalgia, 1948, NR, 76 min. Dir: Jack Bernhard. Cast: Virginia Grey, Richard Denning, Barton MacLane, Philip Reed.

Third-rate lost-world saga about an expedition to an uncharted Pacific island inhabited by dinosaurs and a giant sloth—which looks suspiciously like a guy in an ape suit with tusks added. This gains a point or two for being one of the few films of its kind up to that time to be shot in color and has a *very* colorful bit of overacting from MacLane (coming on like he thinks he's still in one of those old Warner Brothers Big House melodramas), but the dull plot and fakey special FX (the dinosaurs are mostly played by guys in stiff costumes) make this hard to endure.

UNKNOWN ORIGIN

★★ New Horizons, 1995, R, 75 min. Dir: Scott Levy. Cast: Roddy McDowall, Melanie Shatner, Don Stroud, Alex Hyde-White.

Shown on cable as *The Alien Within,* this passable Roger Corman-produced flick is like a cut-rate rehash of *Leviathan.* Workers in an undersea science research lab are killed off by a slimy, serpentlike mutant spawned from a germ culture found aboard a derelict Russian submarine. Viewable enough, with an unexpected surprise ending and a solid B cast (including Bill's daughter Melanie in the Sigourney Weaver role) making forgivable this production's overall cheapness.

UNKNOWN WORLD

★★ Sinister Cinema, 1951, NR, 74 min. Dir: Terrell O. [Terry] Morse. Cast: Bruce Kellogg, Marilyn Nash, Jim Bannon, Victor Kilian, Otto Waldis, Dick Cogan.

Hoping to find a new world to inhabit in case of a devastating atomic war, six scientists invent a huge drill-like contraption called the cyclotram, which bores its way under the Earth's crust and takes them on a journey to the center of the Earth. Some colorful photography shot at Carlsbad Caverns, but overall this is too boring (ha, ha) to garner much excitement.

UNTAMED WOMEN

★★☆ J&J, 1952, NR, 70 min. Dir: W. Merle Connell. Cast: Mikel Conrad, Doris Merrick, Richard Monahan, Mark Lowell, Midge Ware, Carol Brester, Morgan Jones, Lyle Talbot.

Conrad and three air force colleagues find themselves on an uncharted island inhabited

by a cult of gorgeous female Druids, some ape men, and the odd dinosaur or two. Professionally enough made to outclass the films of Ed Wood or Phil Tucker but just as ridiculous in the story, acting, and dialogue departments, this is a quintessential '50s camp classic. The incredibly arbitrary and callous ending has to be seen to be believed. Sort of remade as *Dinosaur Island.* Classic line: "Shoot anything with hair that moves!"

UNTIL THE END OF THE WORLD

★★★ Warner, 1991, R, 157 min. Dir: Wim Wenders. Cast: William Hurt, Sam Neill, Solveig Dommartin, Max von Sydow, Jeanne Moreau. Lois Chiles, Allen Garfield, Rudiger Vogler, David Gulpilil, Ernie Dinog.

Wenders pays tribute to *On the Beach* with this jumbled but never less than fascinating sci-fi road movie. A falling satellite threatens the world with destruction in 1999; party girl Dommartin begins an obsessive trek after criminal Hurt, following him around the globe and eventually arriving in Australia, where a new invention allows the blind to see. Takes a while to get going but once it does is worth the effort, with good work from Neill (as Dommartin's boyfriend) and von Sydow (as her dad) and plenty of fascinating touches in both visuals and music.

V

★★★☆ Warner, 1983, NR, 205 min. Dir: Kenneth Johnson. Cast: Marc Singer, Faye Grant, Jane Badler, Richard Herd, Andrew Prine, Michael Durrell, Neva Patterson, Robert Englund, Jennifer Cooke, Peter Nelson, Penelope Windust, Rafael Campos.

Benevolent alien visitors arrive on Earth spreading peace, love, and fellowship, becoming popular both socially and politically and basically setting the future agenda for mankind. Luckily, though, heroes Singer and Grant discover that the visitors are actually lizardlike monsters in human guise who are here to harvest us as food. Sold to the non-sci-fi crowd as a Nazi allegory for our times, this is actually one of the best made-for-TV sci-fi films ever produced, with solid FX, great makeup work, and a powerhouse cast (Badler and Englund stand out as bad and good aliens, respectively). Best scene: Grant unmasking alien leader Herd on national TV. Exceedingly well written by director Johnson, this was followed by *V—The Final Battle* and a short-lived TV series and was clearly a major inspiration behind the not-quite-as-satisfying blockbuster *Independence Day*.

VALLEY OF GWANGI, THE

★★★ Warner, 1969, G, 95 min. Dir: Jim O'Connolly. Cast: James Franciscus, Gila Golan, Richard Carlson, Laurence Naismith, Freda Jackson, Curtis Arden.

Originating as a script treatment prepared by Willis O'Brien in the 1940s, this entertaining monster movie in a western setting is one of Ray Harryhausen's best. A traveling Wild West show in turn-of-the-century Mexico (actually Spain) discovers a lost valley of prehistoric creatures and makes one of them—a vicious allosaurus dubbed Gwangi by local gypsies—part of their troupe. You can pretty much guess the rest but Harryhausen's great stop-motion FX and a stirring score by Jerome Moross make even the most predictable situations (including an elephant-monster fight scene right out of *20 Million Miles to Earth*) seem fresh.

VAMPIRE MEN OF THE LOST PLANET

See: *Horror of the Blood Monsters*.

VARAN THE UNBELIEVABLE

★☆ VCI, 1958, NR, 70 min. Dirs: Inoshiro Honda, Jerry A. Barewitz. Cast: Myron Healey, Ysuruko Kobayashi, Clifford Kawada, Derick Simatsu.

Possibly Toho Studios worst monster movie, this cheeseball of a film had much of its original footage (including the title monster, a sort of reptilian flying squirrel) cut and boring new stuff with Healy added. Either way this is still a mess, with substandard FX and photography and a storyline that's nothing but clichés. Aka *Daikaiju: Baran (The Monster Baran)*.

VENGEANCE

See: *The Brain* (1962).

VENUS AGAINST THE SON OF HERCULES

★★ Sinister Cinema, 1962, NR, 92 min. Dir: Marcello Baldi. Cast: Massimo Serato, Jackie Lane, Roger Browne, Linda Sini.

The Italian muscle express rolls on with this typical entry. Herc's kid finds love and terror in the clutches of an evil, spell-casting witch queen and her man-eating plants. Aka *Marte, Dio Della Guerra (Mars, God of War)*.

VIBES

★★ RCA/Columbia, 1988, PG, 99 min. Dir: Ken Kwapis. Cast: Cyndi Lauper, Jeff Goldblum, Peter Falk, Julian Sands, Googy Gress, Michael Lerner, Ramon Bieri, Elizabeth Peña.

Psychics Lauper and Goldblum meet at an ESP seminar and soon end up searching for Falk's missing son and a lost city of gold in the wilds of Ecuador. Pop singer Lauper is cute in her film debut but this comic-fantasy-adventure lacks the sense of humor and excitement to put it over in spite of everyone's best efforts.

VICE VERSA

★★★ Sinister Cinema, 1948, NR, 111 min. Dir: Peter Ustinov. Cast: Roger Livesey, Kay Walsh, David Hutcheson, Anthony Newley, James Robertson Justice, Petula Clark.

Actor Ustinov wrote and directed this fantasy about a London stockbroker and his son (Livesey and Newley) who wish on a magic stone and suddenly find themselves occupying each other's bodies. Lively if somewhat dated comedy that predates all those body-switch movies of the '80s (and is generally a lot better); it was itself remade in 1988. Interesting to see future musical performers Newley and Clark appearing together as kid actors in the same film.

VICE VERSA

★★★ RCA/Columbia, 1988, PG, 100 min. Dir: Brian Gilbert. Cast: Judge Reinhold, Fred Savage, Corinne Bohrer, Swoosie Kurtz, Jane Kaczmarek, David Proval, William Prince, Gloria Gifford.

An ancient skull with mystical powers allows dad Reinhold and son Savage to exchange bodies, eventually learning to understand each other better and improve each other's lives. Obviously made to cash in on the success of *Big*, this remake of the 1948 British film is surprisingly good; it's never laugh-out-loud funny but its genial tone and the good performances from Reinhold and Savage make it superior to most others of its kind.

VIDEODROME

★★★ MCA/Universal, 1982, R, 88 min. Dir: David Cronenberg. Cast: James Woods, Deborah Harry, Sonja Smits, Les Carlson.

Cable TV station programmer Woods discovers a bizarre program called *Videodrome* with the power to addict and then kill a viewer by creating in him a deadly, hallucination-causing brain tumor. One of Cronenberg's most outrageous and personal movies, this flopped at the box office (where it was released cut by Universal) but is worthy of rediscovery thanks to

Woods's intense acting in one of his best roles and some simply amazing Rick Baker special FX.

VIEW TO A KILL, A

★★ MGM/UA, 1985, PG, 131 min. Dir: John Glen. Cast: Roger Moore, Tanya Roberts, Christopher Walken, Grace Jones, Patrick Macnee, Patrick Bauchau, Lois Maxwell, Desmond Llewelyn, Robert Brown, Fiona Fullerton, Alison Doody, Dolph Lundgren.

Moore's last go as James Bond involves 007 in a grand-scale plot by genetically engineered madman Walken to destroy California's Silicon Valley with an artificial earthquake (shades of the original *Superman* movie) so that he can corner the world's software market. More cartoony than ever, this Bond adventure is overlong and only occasionally entertaining. Tanya is ill served in a badly written role as the dippy heroine (who looks more like Rog's daughter than his lady friend), Macnee and Fullerton are wasted in too-brief supporting parts, Maxwell does more than usual in her swansong as Moneypenny, and Jones steals it as Walken's right-hand girl May Day (her bedroom scene with Moore makes you fear for the poor guy's safety). Best scene: The Hitchcockian climax high atop the Golden Gate Bridge. The catchy Duran-Duran theme song became the most successful single in the series' history.

VIKING WOMEN AND THE SEA SERPENT, THE

★★ RCA/Columbia, 1957, NR, 66 min. Dir: Roger Corman. Cast: Abby Dalton, Susan Cabot, Brad Jackson, June Kenney, Betsy Jones-Moreland, Richard Devon, Jonathan Haze, Gary Conway, Michael Forest, Jay Sayer.

One Corman's dopiest movies, this poor man's version of *The Vikings* stars the lovely Dalton as the ringleader of a group of statuesque Norse gals who travel by long boat to a distant land, where their men are being held prisoner and the waters are guarded by a badly matted-in giant eel. Awful, but funny enough to be gotten through; it'll keep you wondering what was going through the actors' minds while mouthing their incredible dialogue. Aka *The Saga of the Viking Women and Their Voyage to the Waters of the Great Sea Serpent*. Talk about a mouthful!

VILLAGE OF THE DAMNED

★★★☆ MGM/UA, 1960, NR, 77 min. Dir: Wolf Rilla. Cast: George Sanders, Barbara Shelley, Michael Gwynne, Laurence Naismith, Martin Stephens, John Phillips.

Chilling version of John Wyndham's *The Midwich Cukoos* about an alien invasion by proxy as the women of a sleepy English village are impregnated by a mysterious force and give birth to platinum blonde babies with glowing eyes and supernormal powers over the minds and wills of others. Almost everything about this subtle sci-fi/horror classic works, from its low-key presentation to its nicely understated acting to its sharp photography and spooky music. Remade in 1995; sequel: *Children of the Damned*.

VILLAGE OF THE DAMNED

★★ MCA/Universal, 1995, R, 95 min. Dir: John Carpenter. Cast: Christopher Reeve, Kirstie Alley, Linda Kozlowski, Mark Hamill, Michael Paré, Meredith Salenger, Lindsay Hahn, Thomas Dekker, Peter Jason, Karen Kahn.

Carpenter's sleek but decidedly unneeded remake effectively relocates the action to a dreamy northern California town, which provides much atmosphere. Unfortunately, even with a number of changes to the original story (some not for the best), this remains too predictable for its own good. Reeve (in his last role before his well-publicized horse riding accident) has the old George Sanders part of the teacher who tries to deal with a band of supernaturally powered half-alien kids with white hair and fiery eyes who've taken over the town. Alley is badly miscast as a villainous operative from NASA out to exploit the otherworldly brats; Kozwolski is underused in a rough approximation of the old Barbara Shelley role; and Hamill goes way over the top as a crazed minister. Pretty disappointing but there is an exceptional use of sound FX and music, especially in Dolby.

VILLAGE OF THE GIANTS

★☆ Embassy, 1965, NR, 82 min. Dir: Bert I. Gordon. Cast: Tommy Kirk, Beau Bridges, Ronny Howard, Charla Dougherty, Johnny Crawford, Tim Rooney, Tisha Sterling, Joy Harmon.

Gordon's first adaptation of H. G. Wells's *The Food of the Gods* (if H. G. hated *Island of Lost Souls*, I wonder what he would have made of this!) stars future director Howard as a brat called Genius who invents a growth substance that looks like purple play-dough and turns a pack of overaged juvenile delinquents into curtain-draped giants who demand an adult curfew and scarf bucket after bucket of Kentucky Fried Chicken. Ya gotta love this cast and scenes like Crawford riding on giantess Harmon's do-it-yourself bra or a rumble on a familiar-looking suburban street where you can glimpse both Samatha's house from

Bleach blonde brats from beyond in Village of the Damned *(1960).*

Bewitched and Major Nelson's digs from *I Dream of Jeannie* in the background, but this still takes real dedication to sit through.

VINDICATOR, THE

★★☆ CBS/Fox, 1986, R, 88 min. Dir: Jean-Claude Lord. Cast: Teri Austin, Richard Cox, Pam Grier, David MacIlwraith.

Stan Winston designed the impressive full-body cyborg suit for this not bad sci-fi/horror hybrid in which murdered scientist Cox's brain is used to activate the unstoppable android that goes on a vengeful rampage while still loving girlfriend Austin. Original title: *Frankenstein '88.*

VIRTUAL ASSASSIN

★★ Turner, 1995, R, 99 min. Dir: Robert Lee. Cast: Michael Dudikoff, Suki Kaiser, Brion James, Jon Cuthbert.

It's the same old stuff as tough guy Dudikoff protects scientist Kaiser from high-tech hoodlums who want to bump her off for inventing a powerful computer antivirus that could innoculate the entire internet. Run-of-the-cassette direct-to-video fodder recommended only for Dudikoff completists.

VIRTUOSITY

★★☆ Paramount, 1995, R, 105 min. Dir: Brett Leonard. Cast: Denzel Washington, Kelly Lynch, Russell Crowe, Stephen Spinella, William Forsythe, Louise Fletcher.

In 1999, jailed ex-cop Washington is sprung to hunt down the diabolical Crowe, actually a composite being created from the profiles of hundreds of serial killers who's escaped from cyberspace into the real world. A sci-fi variation on the thriller *Copycat*, this is slick but oh-so-pat and obvious with its routine plot (and annoying mugging from Crowe), somewhat redeemed by fancy direction and good work from Denzel.

VIRUS

★★ Media, 1980, PG, 155 min. Dir: Kinji Fukasaku. Cast: Glenn Ford, Chuck Connors, Bo Svenson, Olivia Hussey, George Kennedy, Sonny Chiba, Robert Vaughn, Henry Silva, Stephanie Faulkner, Isao Natsuki.

This bloated Japanese-American coproduction is about the accidental unleashing of a worldwide plague that decimates the entire world population except for a few hundred people (mostly men) at an Antarctic military base.

Beautifully photographed but fatally overextended and unintentionally funny, this sci-fi/disaster movie mixes sweeping panoramas of icy nature and human destruction with the usual Irwin Allen-type melodramatics and just-in-it-for-the-bucks all-star cast.

VISITOR, THE

★ Samuel Goldwyn, 1978, R, 90 min. Dir: Michael J. Paradise [Guilio Paradisi]. Cast: John Huston, Shelley Winters, Glenn Ford, Mel Ferrer, Joanne Nail, Lance Hendriksen, Sam Peckinpah, Paige Conner.

This is one of the damnedest things I've ever seen: an Italian-backed horror/sci-fi/religious drama filmed in Atlanta with a down-at-the-heels name cast and scenes stolen from just about any '60s or '70s horror/sci-fi movie you can name. Huston and Winters (fresh off the same producers' *Jaws* rip *Tentacles*) are the alien guardian and nanny for a bratty little girl (Connor) who mouths off at, abuses, and even kills those around her until the ludicrous, *Exorcist II: The Heretic*-inspired finalé, where our seemingly possessed little miss is set upon by a flock of pigeons (!) before she can kill her mom. She ends up with a bald head, living in Heaven with Jesus! I'd be interested to know just what the director, stars, or screenwriter were on when they made this thing; I actually paid to see it in a theater and was sorely tempted to walk several times but hung in there just to see if it could get any worse. Let me save you the trouble: it always does.

VISIT TO A SMALL PLANET

★★ Paramount, 1960, NR, 85 min. Dir: Norman Taurog. Cast: Jerry Lewis, Joan Blackman, Earl Holliman, Fred Clark, Lee Patrick, Gale Gordon, John Williams, Barbara Lawson.

Jerry Lewis starring in a sci-fi comedy based on a play by Gore Vidal sounds almost too weird to be true (even in Hollywood concept hell) but here's the evidence. Jerry is a bumbling alien sent to Earth to observe mankind and ends up falling for Blackman. More talk than the usual Lewis physical hijinks and it suffers accordingly. One bright moment, when Jerry ends up dancing with beat gal Lawson. Sort of remade as *Pajama Party*.

VOYAGE OF THE ROCK ALIENS

★☆ Vestron, 1984, PG, 90 min. Dirs: James Fargo, Bob Giraldi. Cast: Pia Zadora, Craig Sheffer, Tom Nolan, Ruth Gordon, Michael Berryman, Jermaine Jackson.

An interesting cast flounders in this dumb Zadora vehicle, with Pia as a rock singer (an idea that seems less unlikely in these Courtney Love days) who forms a band with alien Nolan. Any movie with the wherewithal to cast Gordon as a sheriff must have something going for it, but that's still not enough to make you want to waste your time watching this badly dated vanity epic.

VOYAGE TO THE BOTTOM OF THE SEA

★★★☆ Fox, 1961, NR, 105 min. Dir: Irwin Allen. Cast: Walter Pidgeon, Joan Fontaine, Barbara Eden, Peter Lorre, Robert Sterling, Frankie Avalon, Michael Ansara, Henry Daniell, Howard McNear, Regis Toomey.

Okay, I admit it, I'm a real sucker for an Irwin Allen movie. I love his hackneyed plots, splashy budget FX, and all-star casts that have graced the big and small screens from 1959's *The Big Circus* to 1979's *Cave-In*. This is probably his second-best film (after *The Poseidon Adventure*) and is a lot more serious than the subsequent TV series—of course it doesn't have any werewolves or Yetis on a submarine, either, but you can't have everything. When the radioactive Van Allen belt that circles the Earth bursts into flame, Admiral Nelson (Pidgeon) decides to use his experimental new sub, the *Seaview*, as a launching pad for atomic missiles he hopes will extinguish the fire before the planet is fried. Favorite moments: the *Seaview* bursts up out of the water like an enormous dolphin (everybody inside must have been knocked about like ping pong balls); Fontaine taking an impromptu swim in a shark tank; and Walt slapping Frankie in the kisser for being a weasly little goldbrick. I'll bet Annette Funicello *really* liked that part.

VOYAGE TO THE PLANET OF PREHISTORIC WOMEN

★☆ Sinister Cinema, 1966, NR, 80 min. Dir: Derek Thomas [Peter Bogdanovich]. Cast: Mamie Van Doran, Mary Marr, Paige Lee, Aldo Roman, Margot Hartman, voice of Peter Bogdanovich.

A pseudonymous Bogdanovich made his directing debut shooting laughable new footage of Mamie at Malibu to splice into the Russian epic *Planeta Berg* for this quickie AIP rehashing of some familiar footage. This time Earth explorers encounter telepathic gill woman (well, almost encounter) with clamshell bras who worship a floppy pterodactyl in scenes vaguely related to the main plot. Makes *Voyage to the Prehistoric Planet* look like *Planet of the Apes*. Aka *Gill-Women of Venus*.

VOYAGE TO THE PREHISTORIC PLANET

★★ Sinister Cinema, 1965, NR, 74 min. Dir: John Sebastian [Curtis Harrington]. Cast: Basil Rathbone,

Faith Domergue, Marc Shannon, Christopher Brand.

Harrington followed up his Americanization of the Russian film *Meshte Nastreshu* with this reworking of *Planeta Berg* and including new footage of Rathbone and Domergue shot on sets left over from *Planet of Blood*. The new footage is static and talky but doesn't detract too much from the majesty of the original material, though this doesn't work quite as well as *Planet of Blood*.

V—THE FINAL BATTLE
★★☆ Warner, 1984, NR, 270 min. Dir: Richard T. Heffron. Cast: Marc Singer, Faye Grant, Jane Badler, Richard Herd, Neva Patterson, Andrew Prine, Michael Ironside, Robert Englund, Sarah Douglas, Dick Miller.

This three-part followup to the original two-part TV movie is even more involved but a lot less satisfying. Singer and Grant continue their battle with the sinister visitors led by Badler and Herd. There's a subplot about an Earth girl impregnated with a half-alien baby and some fun actors in small roles to help you through this overlong epic. Most of the unresolved plot threads here were picked up in the brief TV series that followed.

VULCAN, SON OF JUPITER
★★☆ Sinister Cinema, 1962, NR, 75 min. Dir: Emmimo Salvi. Cast: Gordon Mitchell, Bella Cortez, Furio Meniconi.

Hero Mitchell battles mutants and lizard men and flexes his pecs in this slightly better than the norm Italian muscleman fantasy. Good score and lots of fantasy touches.

WAR BETWEEN THE PLANETS
See: *Planet on the Prowl.*

WARGAMES
★★★ MGM/UA, 1983, PG, 110 min. Dir: John Badham. Cast: Matthew Broderick, Ally Sheedy, Dabney Coleman, John Wood, Barry Corbin, Juanin Clay.

Likable bit of high-tech fluff with Broderick as a teen computer whizz who nearly starts

World War III by breaking into the U.S. military's secret computer banks. Excellent performances from Broderick and the lovely Sheedy and a well-calculated screenplay that gets the maximum mileage out of its far-fetched (but not entirely improbable) premise help make this a lot more fun than some more recent teen-oriented cyber-thrillers I could name.

WARLORDS
★★ Vidmark Entertainment, 1988, R, 87 min. Dir: Fred Olen Ray. Cast: David Carradine, Dawn Wildsmith, Ross Hagen, Fox Harris, Brinke Stevens, Robert Quarry, Michelle Bauer, Debra Lamb.

Ray's contribution to the *Mad Max* postnuke cycle is pretty lame but at least it's well cast and funny. Carradine teams up with femme warrior Wildsmith to rescue wife Stevens and there's lots of gratuitous topless scenes, laughable action scenes, and cheesy FX. Fred's done a lot worse.

WARLORDS OF THE 21ST CENTURY
★☆ Nelson, 1982, PG, 91 min. Dir: Harley Corkliss. Cast: Michael Beck, Annie McEnroe, James Wainwright, John Ratzenberger, Randolph Powell, Bruno Lawrence.

Shot in New Zealand under the title *Battletruck*, this tiresome *Mad Max* reworking stars Beck as the hero trying to protect a community's valuable oil supply from vicious hijackers. The cast struggles in this inadequate, inconsequential actioner with a dull PG rating.

WARNING FROM SPACE
★★ Something Weird, 1956, NR, 90 min. Dir: Koiji Shima. Cast: Keizo Kawasaki, Toyomi Karita, Shozo Nanbu.

Friendly aliens, who look like giant one-eyed starfish, arrive on Earth to warn us about an upcoming collision between our planet and an errant asteroid. This bizarre Japanese sci-fi is certainly different from their usual offerings, but with its carloads of witless dubbed dialogue it still isn't all that good. Aka *Uchujin Tokyo ni Arawaru (The Cosmic Man Appears in Tokyo)* and *The Mysterious Satellite.*

WARNING SIGN
★★ CBS/Fox, 1985, R, 99 min. Dir: Hal Barwood. Cast: Sam Waterston, Kathleen Quinlan, Yaphet Kotto, Jeffrey DeMunn, Richard Dysart, G. W. Bailey.

Pregnant security guard Quinlan is the sole survivor when the staff of the medical research lab she works at is wiped out by a deadly new virus. Then the victims begin returning to life as zombies. A big-budget ripoff of any number of cheap exploitation films with a predictable plot but good acting from a top cast. Filmed as *Biohazard*.

WAR OF THE COLOSSAL BEAST

★★☆ Columbia/TriStar, 1958, NR, 68 min. Dir: Bert I. Gordon. Cast: Sally Fraser, Roger Pace, Russ Bender, Dean Parkin.

Parkin (in effective scar makeup) takes over the role of colossal man Glenn Manning in this okay sequel to *The Amazing Colossal Man* with the big boy now sporting a grotesquely disfigured face as he rampages through rural Mexico and downtown Los Angeles. Strained in places but helped a lot by some above average (for him) Gordon FX. Casual observation: Glenn must have been working out between films (probably to help take his mind off his face), as he now sports a younger-looking, leaner build than in the original. Aka *Revenge of the Colossal Man* and *The Terror Strikes!*

WAR OF THE GARGANTUAS

★★☆ Paramount/Gateway, 1967, G, 93 min. Dir: Inoshiro Honda. Cast: Russ Tamblyn, Kumi Mizuno, Kenji Sahara, Kipp Hamilton.

Gigantic, Yeti-like creatures (one brown and one green; one good and one evil; one friendly and one . . . well, you get the picture) duke it out all over Japan in this agreeably absurd Toho monster mash originally titled *Sanda tai Gailah (Sanda vs. Gailah)* and originally a sequel to *Frankenstein Conquers the World* before extensive reediting. Ludicrous as all get out, with some really sick moments for a film rated G by the MPAA, but well worth seeing for the better-than-usual FX work and the vocal stylings of Miss Kipp Hamilton.

WAR OF THE MONSTERS

See: *Gamera vs. Barugon*.

WAR OF THE PLANETS

See: *Cosmos—War of the Planets*.

WAR OF THE WORLDS

★★★☆ Paramount, 1953, G, 85 min. Dir: Byron Haskin. Cast: Gene Barry, Ann Robinson, Les Tremayne, Lewis Martin, Robert Cornthwaite, Jack Kruschen, Henry Brandon, Paul Birch, Alvy Moore, Edgar Barrier, Ann Codee, voice of Sir Cedric Hardwicke.

An exciting, well-cast, and well-paced version of the H. G. Wells book about Martian invaders arriving on Earth in unstoppable war machines and creating destruction across the globe in their bid to conquer our planet and eradicate mankind. The *Independence Day* of its generation, this George Pal production is one of his best, with gorgeous color, Oscar-winning special FX (the climactic destruction of Los Angeles is a showstopper), good acting (even if most of the characters are strictly from stock), and effectively sonorous narration from the redoubtable Hardwicke. The scene in the smashed farmhouse where heroine Robinson comes face to face with a Martian (played by veteran gorilla impersonator Charles Gemora) is still legitimately scary. Followed years later by a brief TV series in which Robinson made an occasional appearance; look fast for a brief bit by Carolyn Jones.

WARRIOR AND THE SORCERESS, THE

★★ Vestron, 1984, R, 76 min. Dir: John Broderick. Cast: David Carradine, Luke Askew, Maria Socas, Anthony DeLongis, Harry Townes, William Marin.

A cheapo Roger Corman reworking of *Yojimbo* with Carradine as a double-crossing warrior on a distant planet with two suns (where one woman has four breasts!), where he gets involved in a war between two kingdoms. Fans of gratuitous female nudity will be pleased to know that sultry leading lady Socas goes through the whole movie topless, but everyone else will probably find this to be just one more routine sword-and-sorcery move of its era.

WARRIOR OF THE LOST WORLD

★☆ HBO, 1983, R, 90 min. Dir: David Worth. Cast: Robert Ginty, Persis Khambatta, Donald Pleasence, Fred Williamson, Harrison Muller.

Another poor man's *Mad Max* with a slightly better cast than usual. In a postnuke future hero Ginty travels about on a talking, computerized motorcycle (that never shuts up) and helps Khambatta and her scientist dad Muller in their struggles against despotic leader Pleasence and towering henchman Williamson. The plot makes little sense but there's much unintended humor (played up big time when this was shown on *Mystery Science Theater 3000*) to help you get through it.

WARRIORS OF THE WASTELAND

★☆ HBO, 1982, R, 87 min. Dir: Enzio G. Castellari. Cast: Timothy Brent [Giancarlo Preté], Fred Williamson, Anna Kanakis, Venantino Venantini, George Eastman, Enzo G. Castellari.

This earns an extra half star for being the only Italian *Mad Max* wannabe to feature a gang of rapist homosexual thugs (the politically correct squad should definitely bypass this one) but is otherwise thouroughly routine and had to be cut to get an R rating in the States. Brent and the always reliable Williamson (as Nadir) are

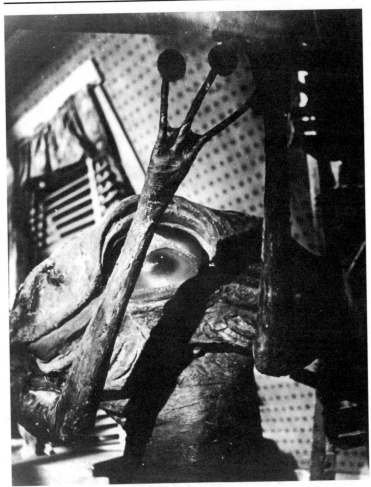

Charles Gemora as one of the invaders from The War of the Worlds *(1953).*

the heroes who team to stop our graphic-violence-prone pack of thugs. Aka *I Nuovi Barbari (The New Barbarians).*

WATCHERS

★☆ IVE, 1988, R, 92 min. Dir: Jon Hess. Cast: Corey Haim, Michael Ironside, Barbara Williams, Lala Sloatman.

Pretty awful adaptation of a portion of the Dean Koontz book reworked into a vehicle for heartthrob Haim. A superintelligent golden retriever is psychically linked to a murderous monster. When Corey and mom Williams adopt the doggie (recently escaped from some government lab) they are pursued by both the monster and a totally out-of-control Ironside (who's the best thing about the movie). This sci-fi/horror mess has a terrible monster design but was somehow popular enough to be followed by a pair of totally bogus sequels.

WATCHERS II

★★ IVE, 1990, R, 97 min. Dir: Thierry Notz. Cast: Marc Singer, Tracy Scoggins, Irene Miracle, Mary Woronov.

More of a slightly improved remake than a sequel, this time we get Singer instead of Corey Haim (a fair trade I'd say) who teams with Scoggins and another superdog to stop the rampage of another monstrous watcher. This solid but unexceptional B movie is your best bet if you simply *have* to see a *Watchers* movie.

WATCHERS III

★ New Horizons, 1994, R, 80 min. Dir: Jeremy

Stanford. Cast: Wings Hauser, Gregory Scott Cummins, Daryl Roach, Lolita Ronalds, John K. Linton, Ider Cifuentes Martin.

Roger Corman's legendary cost-cutting strikes again in this *Predator*-inspired "sequel" that's actually just a slight rewrite of the script for *Carnosaur II*. Hauser leads a band of mercenaries through the jungles of Central America where yet another golden retriever-with-a-degree and goo-encrusted monster lurk. The plot of this totally predictable junk could have been scribbled out on a couple of Post-it notes while Dean Koontz sued Corman for reusing his title without permission—and who would blame him?

WATERSHIP DOWN
★★★☆ Warner, 1978, PG, 92 min. Dir: Martin Rosen. Voices: John Hurt, Ralph Richardson, Denholm Elliott, Harry Andrews, Zero Mostel, Richard Briers, Joss Ackland, Michael Hordern.

An incredible animated film (not at all for kids) about a psychic female rabbit called Hazel who leads her family through various perils to reach an idyllic new home called Watership Down. This adaptation of Richard Adams's allegorical novel is beautifully animated and solidly voiced by a fine cast of veteran (mostly British) character actors.

WATERWORLD
★★ MCA/Universal, 1995, PG-13, 136 min. Dir: Kevin Reynolds. Cast: Kevin Costner, Dennis Hopper, Jeanne Tripplehorn, Tina Majorino, Michael Jeter, Robert Joy.

In a flooded future world, people cling to manmade islands while the villanous Hopper travels about in a huge tanker searching for the last bit of dry land to control. When Tripplehorn and daughter Majorino are threatened for their property, Costner (as the web-footed "Mariner") comes to the rescue. Intended as a sort of sci-fi updating of *Shane*, this overpriced Costner vehicle emerges instead as a water-logged *Mad Max* clone. It's not good by any means but really isn't as awful as its detractors hoped either. Visually interesting but long and meandering; being a big fan of Kevin's squint or Dennis's ranting is definitely a plus in trying to navigate these waters.

WAVELENGTH
★★ Nelson, 1983, PG, 87 min. Dir: Mike Gray. Cast: Robert Carradine, Cherie Currie, Keenan Wynn, Cal Bowman, James Hess, Terry Burns.

Rock musician Carradine and psychic girl-friend Currie are drawn to the desert site where the U.S. government is secretly experi-menting with captured extraterrestrials. This cheap but thoughtful *Close Encounters*-inspired flick has good acting and a musical score by Tangerine Dream but is too laconic for its own good. Writer-director Gray also coscripted *The China Syndrome*.

WEDLOCK
See: *Deadlock*.

WEIRD SCIENCE
★★★ MCA/Universal, 1985, PG-13, 94 min. Dir: John Hughes. Cast: Kelly LeBrock, Anthony Michael Hall, Ilan Mitchell-Smith, Bill Paxton, Suzanne Snyder, Judie Aronson, Robert Downey, Jr., Robert Rusler, Jill Whitlow, Michael Berryman, Vernon Wells, Kym Malin.

A pair of nerdy high school losers (Hall and Mitchell-Smith) use a computer to create their ideal woman (LeBrock), who turns their lives upside down in no time. This fantasy-comedy is dumb (and often tasteless) but also pretty funny and watchable. Paxton steals it as Hall's abusive older brother who gets turned into a huge toad monster. Too bad writer-director Hughes's script (written in between more "serious" teen-oriented films) never really develops its premise in any truly interesting ways. LeBrock, though, never looked sexier.

WELCOME TO BLOOD CITY
★☆ Thorn/EMI, 1977, NR, 96 min. Dir: Peter Sasdy. Cast: Jack Palance, Keir Dullea, Samantha Eggar, Barry Morse, Hollis McLaren, Chris Wiggins.

Pretty pathetic British-Canadian imitation of *Westworld* about a computer-controlled west-ern town-resort. Dullea is a vacationer up against Palance as the black-clad sheriff; scientist Eggar creates a robotic double of herself so she can sleep with Keir. Dullea calls this his worst film and he's not far wrong; it's barely saved by its talented cast. Never released theatrically in the U.S., and no wonder.

WESTWORLD
★★★ MGM/UA, 1973, PG, 88 min. Dir: Michael Crichton. Cast: Richard Benjamin, James Brolin, Yul Brynner, Norman Bartold, Alan Oppenheimer, Victoria Shaw, Linda Gaye Scott, Majel Barrett, Dick Van Patten, Steve Franken.

Crichton gives his *Jurassic Park* premise an ini-tial run-through with this fun sci-fi thriller about Delos, an adult amusement park where patrons live out their fantasies (including sexu-al ones) with lifelike robots. When something goes wrong with the park's computer system, the robots (including Brynner in a parody of his *Magnificent Seven* role) go on a murderous spree. Well done on an obviously tight budget, with Brynner great as a prototype of Schwarzenegger's *Terminator* character: an android who keeps coming back again and again everytime it's "killed." Followed by *Futureworld* and the short-lived TV series *Beyond Westworld*.

WHAT WAITS BELOW

★☆ Vestron, 1983, PG, 82 min. Dir: Don Sharp. Cast: Robert Powell, Lisa Blount, Timothy Bottoms, Richard Johnson, Anne Heywood, Liam Sullivan.

Bland reworking of *The Mole People* in which explorers discover an underground race of

Yul Brynner blows his top in Westworld *(1973).*

Is it Bambi Meets Godzilla? *No, it's* When Dinosaurs Ruled the Earth *(1969).*

Sumerians. A superior cast and director but cheap production values and a poor script. Filmed as *Secret of the Phantom Caverns.*

WHEN DINOSAURS RULED THE EARTH
★★★ Warner, 1969, PG, 96 min. Dir: Val Guest. Cast: Victoria Vetri, Robin Hawdon, Patrick Allen, Imogen Hassall.

Marked for sacrifice because of her blonde hair, cave girl Vetri escapes from her mountain tribe and later hooks up with nice fisherman Hawdon and is adopted by a mother dinosaur who mistakes Vic for one of her offspring. Great silliness with Oscar-nominated FX by Jim Danforth; though cut for a PG rating in the States (removing some nudity and violence)

this is still plenty sexy, with everybody (including the men) in costumes so tiny you almost forget to notice the dinosaurs. A sequel of sorts to *One Million Years B.C.*, this was followed by *Creatures the World Forgot.*

WHEN WOMEN HAD TAILS
★★ Sinister Cinema, 1970, R, 110 min. Dir: Pasquale Festa Campanile. Cast: Senta Berger, Giuliano Gemma, Frank Wolff, Lando Buzzance.

An Italian knockoff of *When Dinosaurs Ruled the Earth* (sans dinosaurs) played for laughs. Berger is stunning as the cavebabe with lengthy hair and tail who's sought by various male cast members stranded on her island home. Not very funny (maybe something was lost in the translation) but Senta's considerable charms may make it worth a look. Followed by two sequels.

WHEN WOMEN LOST THEIR TAILS

★☆ Sinister Cinema, 1971, R, 94 min. Dir: Pasquale Festa Campanile. Cast: Senta Berger, Giuliano Gemma, Frank Wolff, Francesco Mule.

When Women Had Tails must have made a few bucks somewhere in the world because the same director and stars returned for this sequel for more *Flintstones*-era battle of the sexes. If you're a Senta fan you may want to check this out; everyone else should skip it. Sequel: *When Women Played Ding Dong.*

WHEN WORLDS COLLIDE

★★★ Paramount, 1951, NR, 81 min. Dir: Rudolph Maté. Cast: Richard Derr, Barbara Rush, Peter Hanson, Larry Keating, John Hoyt, Frank Cady, Hayden Rourke, Judith Ames.

Colorful (if rather flatly acted) version of the Edwin Balmer-Philip Wylie novel about Earth's imminent destruction from collision with the rogue star Bellus and how a handful of survivors try to escape to Bellus's one habitable planet called Zyra. This George Pal-produced protodisaster movie has Oscar-winning FX (including the flooding of Manhattan) but the final scenes depicting the survivors' escape rocket's safe landing on Zyra are frustratingly abrupt and undramatic. Still it's generally entertaining, with some breathtaking matte painting (except for the one depicting Zyra's landscape, which looks like something out of a Walt Disney animated feature) and a good performance from Hoyt as a mean old bastard in a wheelchair who finances the escape solely as a means to save his own weasly little hide. Someone really should look into remaking this—today's computer-generated special FX would really do it proud. Stuart Whitman has a bit part.

WHERE HAVE ALL THE PEOPLE GONE?

★★ Lorimar, 1974, NR, 74 min. Dir: John Llewellyn Moxey. Cast: Peter Graves, Verna Bloom, Kathleen Quinlan, George O'Hanlon, Jr., Michael James Wixted.

A solar flare decimates most of the world's population and Graves tries to hold his family together as what's left of society falls apart around them. The good cast helps this indifferent TV movie rehashing of themes better explored in *Panic in Year Zero.*

WHERE TIME BEGAN

★★ Nelson, 1978, G, 86 min. Dir: Juan Piquer Simon. Cast: Kenneth More, Pep Munne, Jack Taylor, Yvonne Sennis, Frank Brana.

Bland retelling of *Journey to the Center of the Earth* with More in the old James Mason role of the professor who leads a band of explorers down a volcanic crater that takes them to a primordial world at the center of the Earth. Cheap sets and special FX but the story still holds interest and More is good.

WHITE LIGHT

★★ Academy Entertainment, 1990, R, 96 min. Dir: Al Waxman. Cast: Martin Kove, Martha Henry, Allison Hossack, Heidi von Palleske, James Purcell, Bruce Boa.

Cop Kove is killed but then restored to life. After his recovery he becomes obsessed with finding the woman (Henry) he met while on the "Other Side" in this *Ghost*-inspired romantic fantasy directed by Kove's old *Cagney and Lacy* costar Waxman.

WHO?

★★ Ace, 1974, PG, 93 min. Dir: Jack Gold. Cast: Elliott Gould, Trevor Howard, Joseph Bova, Ed Grover, James Noble, John Lehne.

Odd, unsatisfying mix of spies and sci-fi, with Gould as an FBI agent investigating the death of German scientist Bova and his subsequent reappearance as a bionic-like automation with a metal mask face. A good cast flounders with uncertain material. Aka *Robo Man.*

WHO FRAMED ROGER RABBIT?

★★★ Disney, 1988, PG, 103 min. Dirs: Robert Zmeckis, Richard Williams. Cast: Bob Hoskins, Christopher Lloyd, Joanna Cassidy, Stubby Kaye, voices of Kathleen Turner, Charles Fleischer, Mel Blanc, Mae Questel, June Foray, Amy Irving.

Hoskins (in a role originally offered to Harrison Ford) is a private eye in 1940s Hollywood (where cartoon characters are actually living beings) who helps popular toon star Roger Rabbit (voiced by Fleischer) beat a wrongful murder rap. The plot is thin and Roger really isn't a very likable or interesting character but his sexy wife Jessica (voiced by both Turner and Irving—the latter does the singing) is memorable and this is probably the only chance you'll ever have to see cartoon characters from Walt Disney, Warner Brothers, and others (like Popeye and Betty Boop) mix it up on the same screen. The special FX and animation director Williams both won Oscars.

WILDER NAPALM

★★ Columbia/TriStar, 1993, PG-13, 110 min. Dir: Glenn Gordon Caron. Cast: Dennis Quaid, Debra Winger, Arliss Howard, Jim Varney, M. Emmet Walsh, Glenn Gordon Caron.

This romantic-fantasy-comedy—which steals

ideas from the Stephen King horror film *Firestarter* and Ron Howard's *Backdraft*—casts Winger as a pyromaniac loved by brothers Quaid and Howard, both of whom can start fires at will. Shelved for a while, mostly because TriStar hadn't a clue as how to market it, this has good acting from the leads but is hopelessly muddled and unfunny.

WILD IN THE STREETS
★★★ HBO, 1968, PG, 97 min. Dir: Barry Shear. Cast: Christopher Jones, Shelley Winters, Diane Varsi, Hal Holbrook, Millie Perkins, Ed Begley, Richard Pryor, Bert Freed.

Campy late '60s time capsule stars Jones as a singing idol who's elected president when the voting age is lowered to fourteen. He begins his administration by imprisoning everyone over thirty, including overbearing mom Winters, in detention camps. This dark-hued satire seems less dated now then it did a few years ago (thanks mainly to the current nostalgic interest in the '60s) but is still a bit too silly to take seriously. The cast is great, though, with Pryor especially good in an early role, as one of Jones's devoted followers.

WILD PALMS
★★☆ ABC, 1993, NR, 100-150 min. per tape. Dirs: Keith Gordon, Phil Joanou, Kathryn Bigelow, Peter Hewitt. Cast: James Belushi, Dana Delaney, Kim Cattrall, Angie Dickinson, Robert Loggia, David Warner, Ben Savage, Brad Dourif, Ernie Hudson, Nick Mancuso, Bebe Neuwirth, Robert Morse, Robert Cornthwaite, William Schallert.

A sci-fi-slanted *Twin Peaks* imitation that's a bit more coherent than its inspiration but overall not as good. In the year 2007, lawyer Belushi gets involved with senator Loggia, who also happens to be the L. Ron Hubbard-like leader of a religious cult who practices mind control on his followers. The impressive supporting cast includes Dickinson in one of her best roles in years as Loggia's zealot sister and there are lots of virtual reality scenes and interesting invented postmodern slang and epigrams for the characters to spew at one another. The plot, though, just seems to trail off after the first couple of hours.

WILD, WILD PLANET
★★★ Sinister Cinema, 1964, NR, 93 min. Dir: Anthony Dawson [Antonio Margheriti]. Cast: Tony Russell, Lisa Gastoni, Franco Nero, Michel Lemoine, Umberto Raho, Linda Sini, Moa Thai, Massimo Serato.

The first and best of a quartet of quickie sci-fi flicks directed by Italian mainstay Margheriti in 1964 (the others were *War of the Planets,*

Planet on the Prowl, and *Snow Devils*) about beautiful alien women, aided by bald androids, who abduct prominent Earth scientists after shrinking them to doll size and carting them away in a suitcase! Full of truly wild and weird touches including a closet full of mutants, a pair of disembodied breathing lungs (a prop that would later reemerge in *Andy Warhol's Frankenstein*), and karate-kicking alien babes in bikinis, this enjoyable hokum has to be seen to be appreciated. Aka *I Criminali della Gallassia (Criminals of the Galaxy).*

WILD WOMEN OF WONGO, THE
★ Amvest, 1958, NR, 72 min. Dir: James Wolcott. Cast: Adrienne Bourbeau, Jean Hawkshaw, Ed Fury, Johnny Walsh, Pat Crowley.

Almost unwatchable shot-in-Florida prehistoric quickie about the women of Wongo, beauties with ugly husbands, and the men of Goona, hunks with ugly brides, who eventually find true love. Not really campy enough to be funny, this is mostly just a lot of muddy color footage of native girls dancing (badly) and people squinting into the camera as they mouth their inane caveman talk. Star Bourbeau is not to be confused with *Maude* actress and later ex-Mrs. John Carpenter Adrienne Barbeau. Male lead Fury was a popular male nude model who later found a modicum of fame in various Italian muscleman epics.

WILD WORLD OF BATWOMAN, THE
☆ Sinister Cinema, 1966, NR, 70 min. Dir: Jerry Warren. Cast: Katherine Victor, Steve Brodie, George Andre, Lloyd Nelson, Bruno Ve Sota, Richard Banks.

Maybe Warren's worst movie (I know, I know), this was held up for release for years because Jerry was afraid of being sued by the *Batman* TV show producers (like maybe Jerry had something they wanted) and really should never have been allowed to escape the studio vault. Warren regular Victor does what she can to maintain her dignity while wearing an absurd, ill-fitting costume as Batwoman, a superheroine in constant war against evil villains Dr. Neon and Ratfink—who turn out to be the same guy, though that's not very hard to guess. With lots of just-point-the-camera-and-shoot scenes of people sitting around and talking, girls in bikinis doing the twist by a pool, and from-out-of-nowhere stock footage from *The Mole People* (maybe Warren was afraid of being sued over that, too), this stands proudly as maybe one of the dozen or so worst movies ever made—and it isn't even funny! Aka *She Was a Hippy Vampire.*

WILLIAM SHATNER'S TEKWAR

See: *Tekwar: The Movie.*

WILLOW

★★☆ Columbia/TriStar, 1988, PG, 125 min. Dir: Ron Howard. Cast: Val Kilmer, Joanne Whalley, Warwick Davis, Jean Marsh, Patricia Hayes, Billy Barty, Gavin O'Herlihy, Kevin Pollak.

Dwarf Davis teams up with soldier-of-fortune Kilmer and princess Whalley to save an innocent baby from the clutches of evil queen Marsh, who wants the baby dead because of a prophecy that says the child will one day grow into a warrior who will unseat her from power. Howard hoped for another fantasy hit along the lines of *Splash* and *Cocoon* but this flopped badly at the box office. It really isn't all that bad but seems at constant odds with itself about what audience it wants to address, with lots of cutesy comedy but some pretty dark, intense moments as well. The ILM FX are excellent but they tend to overshadow the cast—all save Davis and Marsh.

WILLY WONKA AND THE CHOCOLATE FACTORY

★★★☆ Warner, 1971, G, 98 min. Dir: Mel Stuart. Cast: Gene Wilder, Jack Albertson, Peter Ostrum, Roy Kinnear, Aubrey Woods, Michael Bollner, Ursula Reit, Denise Nickerson.

Based on Roald Dahl's book *Charlie and the Chocolate Factory,* this musical fantasy is one of the most delightfully frightening and subversive kids' films ever made. Wilder is perfectly cast as the title character, the smarmy owner of a fabulous candy factory who invites a select group of children and their parents to tour with the promise that one of the youngsters will some day inherit the establishment as their own. Most of the kids turn out to be greedy dolts or snobs who come to bad ends, falling into machinery and the like, until only nice kid Ostrum and grandpa Albertson are left. The settings are great and some of the songs (including "The Candyman," later an anthem for both Anthony Newley and Sammy Davis, Jr.) are memorable but the true reasons to watch this film are Wilder's creepy performance (he even manages subtly to suggest that Willy Wonka is a child molester with a taste for young boys) and the awful fates of the bad kids (including *Dark Shadows* regular Nickerson, who turns into a giant blueberry). Of course, we're told at the end that everyone was restored to life and/or normalcy and everything is fine—but you never do see them again, do you?

WINGS OF DESIRE

★★★☆ Orion, 1987, PG-13, 130 min. Dir: Wim Wenders. Cast: Bruno Ganz, Solveig Dommartin, Otto Sander, Curt Boris, Nick Cave, Peter Falk.

One of Wenders's best films, this haunting fantasy, shot in West Berlin, is about a sad, lonely angel (Ganz) who falls in love with a circus performer (Dommartin) and wishes to be human again to win her. This imaginatively shot movie uses black-and-white photography for the angel's point of view and color for everything else. The film is far grimmer and more thoughtful (though a bit too long) than any of the myriad angel fantasies churned out by Hollywood over the years. Amusing cameo by Falk. Aka *Der Himmel Uber Berlin (Heaven over Berlin)*; sequel: *Faraway, So Close.*

WIRED TO KILL

★★ Lightning, 1986, R, 96 min. Dir: Franky Schaeffer. Cast: Emily Longstreth, Deven Holescher, Merritt Butrick, Frank Collison, Garth Gardner, Kristina David.

This earns an extra point for curiosity value because it's one of the few action pictures you'll ever see with a hero in a wheelchair, but otherwise it's not worth much. In the plague-ravaged Los Angeles of 1998, Holescher is crippled by evil Butrick and his gang of mutant savages. With the aid of sister Longstreth, our hero seeks a bloody revenge from his wheelchair with the help of a killer robot. This had to be cut for an R but is still pretty gory. Aka *Booby Trap.*

WISHMAN

★★ Monarch, 1991, PG, 90 min. Dir: Michael Marvin. Cast: Paul LeMat, Geoffrey Lewis, Quin Kessler, Brion James, Nancy Parsons, Paul Gleason, Gloria Leonard, Liz Sheradin.

Lewis is an Irish genie (!) who presses Beverly Hills junkman LeMat into service to retrieve his missing bottle. This odd comic fantasy seems aimed at kids but really isn't and works best as an (admittedly odd) showcase for the untapped comic talents of character actors Lewis, James, and Parsons.

WITCHES, THE

★★★ Warner, 1989, PG, 91 min. Dir: Nicolas Roeg. Cast: Angelica Huston, Mai Zetterling, Jason Fisher, Rowan Atkinson, Bill Paterson, Jenny Runacre.

Another creepy Roald Dahl book for kids gets turned into another bent little fantasy for kids of all ages. Young Fisher discovers a witch convention at a British seaside hotel managed by Atkinson (Mr. Bean himself). The witches plan to destroy the children of the world with poisoned chocolate and turn Jason into a mouse before he can warn anyone but with the help of grandma Zetterling our young mouse boy saves the day just the same. The great witch makeup FX created by Jim Henson's Creature Shop were considered too scary by some (all the more reason to see this). To please the distributor the U.S. version tacked on a last-minute happy ending, where the kid is restored to human form, but don't let that keep you from watching.

WITCH'S CURSE, THE

★★ Sinister Cinema, 1961, NR, 78 min. Dir: Riccardo Freda. Cast: Kirk Morris, Helene Chanel, Vera Silenti, Andrea Bosic.

A very strange Italian peblum mixing muscles and fantasy with touches of horror borrowed from Mario Bava's classic *Black Sunday*. A witch's curse terrorizes a Scottish village and threatens a beautiful girl so Maciste (don't ask what he's doing in Scotland) travels back in time to relieve the spell. Really dumb but some of the scenes have good atmosphere, reminiscent of some of Freda's horror films. Aka *Maciste All'Inferno (Maciste in Hell)*.

WITHIN THE ROCK

★★ A-Pix, 1996, R, 91 min. Dir: Gary Tunnicliffe. Cast: Xander Berkeley, Brian Krause, Caroline Barclay, Michael Zelniker, Duane Whitaker, Barbara Patrick, Bradford Tatum, Michael Jay.

Routine made-for-cable *Alien* rip (with a little of *The Green Slime* thrown in as well, never a good sign) about astronauts landing on an asteroid that's on a collision course with Earth, with the intention of blowing it to smithereens. But a monster (looking like the *Predator* covered in dry mud) lies in wait to bump them off one by one. Just the same old song, originally played on the Sci-Fi Channel.

WITHOUT WARNING

★☆ HBO, 1980, R, 89 min. Dir: Greydon Clark. Cast: Jack Palance, Martin Landau, Cameron Mitchell, Neville Brand, Tarah Nutter, Ralph Meeker, Sue Ane Langdon, Larry Storch, David Caruso, Kevin Peter Hall.

This cheap exploitation combination of *Alien* and *Friday the 13th* has a dynamite cast but is too murky and dumb to be as enjoyable as it should have been. Hall plays a bald, big-headed alien hunter who seeks human prey in some desolate woods, striking down various old character actors and teen types with his weapon of choice: a hairy, blood-sucking frisbee with teeth! Just the thought that the two top-billed stars of this film would eventually go on to win Oscars in the best supporting actor category is enough to make your head spin. Aka *It Came Without Warning*.

WIZ, THE

★★ MCA/Universal, 1978, G, 133 min. Dir: Sidney Lumet. Cast: Diana Ross, Michael Jackson, Nipsey Russell, Ted Ross, Mabel King, Richard Pryor, Lena Horne, Theresa Merritt.

Based on the 1975 Broadway hit, this all-black reworking of *The Wizard of Oz* has the best casting and production values you could imagine and is still dull, dreary, and a real trial to sit through. Casting the undeniably talented (but undeniably too old) Ross as Dorothy was a big mistake and Jackson (presurgery and prescandal) doesn't do much with the role of the Scarecrow, but Russell and Ross are better cast as the Tin Man and Lion and King steals it in an all-too-brief appearance as a sassy Wicked Witch of the West. Much of the photography is too dark to see any of the elaborate production design and special FX but a couple of the songs (especially "Ease on Down the Road") will get your toes a-tappin'. Quincey Jones arranged the score.

WIZARD OF MARS, THE

★★ Academy Entertainment, 1964, NR, 81 min. Dir: David L. Hewitt. Cast: John Carradine, Roger Gentry, Vic McGee, Eve Bernhardt, Jerry Rannow.

The people who brought you *Journey to the Center of Time* first went the sci-fi route with this sci-fi reworking of *The Wizard of Oz*. Four astronauts (a woman and three men) land on Mars and follow a yellow road across the barren red landscape to an Emerald City-type palace where they're confronted by "wizard" Carradine. Very, very cheap looking but not without its flashes of imagination. Aka *Horrors of the Red Planet*.

WIZARD OF OZ, THE

★★★★ MGM/UA, 1939, NR, 101 min. Dir: Mervyn LeRoy. Cast: Judy Garland, Ray Bolger, Bert Lahr, Jack Haley, Frank Morgan, Billie Burke, Margaret Hamilton, Charley Grapewin, Clara Blandick, the Singer Midgets.

What more could anyone say about this beloved musical fantasy that hasn't already been said? Well, for starters I could mention that this was one of my very favorite movies as a kid and I eagerly awaited its yearly showing on TV each Easter. Now that I can see it any time I want on video, I must say that it holds up beautifully, though it's a shame no one will ever be able to restore the missing musical numbers ("The Jitterbug" and "The Rainbow

Bridge") to the latter half. Garland became a legendary star thanks to her rendition of the almost-cut "Over the Rainbow" (though the seventeen-year-old actress didn't look like a twelve-year-old to me as a kid and still doesn't now). The rest of the cast is perfect, too, and I often wonder if this would have become as big a classic if original-choice stars Shirley Temple, W. C. Fields, Gale Sondergaard, and Buddy Ebsen had actually been in it (Ebsen did film a few scenes as the Tin Man but was replaced by Haley after an allergic reaction to the silvery makeup). L. Frank Baum's original book is longer and more complicated (not to mention more Freudian) but this retains much of its spirit and the irony of characters vainly in search of something they already have. Favorite moments: Glinda the Good (Burke) reacting to a puff of sulphuric smoke that gets a little too close to her pert little nose; the talking apple trees; Morgan's multiple roles as Professor Marvel, the Guardian of the Gates, the doorkeeper of the Emerald City, the cockney cabbie, and the Wizard; and Dorothy watching in horror as the calm, reassuring face of Aunt Em (Blandick) reflected in a crystal ball suddenly transforms into the cackling, mocking face of Hamilton ("I'll give you Auntie Em, my little pretty!"). There, doesn't that make you want to watch it all over again?

WIZARD OF SPEED AND TIME, THE

★★☆ Southgate, 1988, PG, 95 min. Dir: Mike Jittlov. Cast: Mike Jittlov, Paige Moore, Richard Kaye, David Conrad, John Massari, Steve Brodie, Angelique Pettyjohn, Philip Michael Thomas, Arnetia Walker, Frank LaLoggia, Jim Danforth, Forrest J. Ackerman.

Expanded from a student short film, this clever fantasy about a young special FX technician (Jittlov) who wants to make his own movie is sweet and well intended, if a bit rough around the edges. The many guest stars help but the real reason to see it are Jittlov's incredible, imaginative special FX sequences.

WIZARDS

★★ Fox, 1977, PG, 80 min. Dir: Ralph Bakshi. Voices: Bob Holt, Jesse Welles, Richard Romanus, Mark Hamill.

Uneven Bakshi animated fantasy set in a postnuclear world where survivors have been transformed into supernatural creatures like gnomes and fairies and an evil wizard tries to raise an undead army of Nazi soldiers to conquer all. Some really spooky moments in another animated feature that tries to play to a kid audience that's really too young to understand it.

WIZARDS OF THE DEMON SWORD

★☆ Troma, 1990, R, 90 min. Dir: Fred Olen Ray Cast: Lyle Waggoner, Russ Tamblyn, Heidi Payne, Blake Bahner, Dawn Wildsmith, Lawrence Tierney, Michael Berryman, Jay Richardson.

Some of the casting here takes honors but everything else about this comic fantasy is strictly last class, even for Ray! A young couple search for a magical sword coveted by evil lord Waggoner (whose curious career has taken him from *Carol Burnett Show* hunk to *Playgirl* centerfold to B movie acting to great wealth as a renter of movie set trailer dressing rooms). Lots of guest stars, stock footage, and bad special FX. Aka *Demon Sword*.

WIZARDS OF THE LOST KINGDOM

★★ Media, 1983, PG, 76 min. Dir: Hector Olivera. Cast: Bo Svenson, Vidal Peterson, Thom Christopher, Barbara Stock, Maria Socas, Dolores Michaels.

In this Roger Corman fantasy aimed at kids, Svenson is a warrior who helps young wizard Peterson battle various monsters and bad guy wizard Christopher to protect his late father's kingdom. Mediocre special FX and little sense of wonder sink this sword-and-scorcery flick that was somehow popular enough to inspire a sequel.

WIZARDS OF THE LOST KINGDOM II

★☆ Media, 1988, PG, 80 min. Dir: Charles B. Griffith. Cast: David Carradine, Bobby Jacoby, Lana Clarkson, Mel Welles, Sid Haig.

Jacoby takes over the role of the boy wizard in this needless followup that sees him pitted against Carradine as the sinister "Dark One." Not even the promise of a supporting cast like this makes this cheesy fantasy worth tuning in.

WOMAN IN THE MOON

★★☆ Video Yesteryear, 1929, NR, 112 min. Dir: Fritz Lang. Cast: Gerda Maurus, Willy Fritsch, Fritz Rasp, Gustav von Wagenheim.

Lang's last silent movie was this prophetic but dull sci-fier about the first trip to the moon. The four astronauts who land there (including Maurus as the title character) discover the place to be encrusted with gold and diamonds and soon greed begins to tear the explorers apart. Some impressive special FX and settings but this isn't nearly as good as Lang's masterpiece *Metropolis*. Some prints run as long as 156 minutes. Aka *Girl in the Moon*.

WOMEN OF THE PREHISTORIC PLANET

★☆ Paragon, 1966, NR, 87 min. Dir: Arthur C. Pierce. Cast: Wendell Corey, John Agar, Keith Larsen,

Irene Tsu, Merry Anders, Robert Ito, Adam Roarke, Stuart Margolin, Paul Gilbert, Lyle Waggoner.

A spacecraft lands on a swamp planet where a female crew member (Tsu) falls in love with a loin-clothed caveguy (Ito). When the ship departs, leaving the lovers behind, the commander (Corey) decides to christen this new Eden the planet Earth. This set-bound cheapie (typical of the sort of low-rent sci-fi that proliferated in the early to mid-'60s) has an interesting budget cast (with veteran Agar giving the best performance) but is done in by its cardboard sets, dull plot, and tacky FX (though a young Jim Danforth contributed a not-bad matte painting). Even the title is a cheat—the women in the movie aren't from the prehistoric planet at all, but I guess *The Guy from the Prehistoric Planet* just doesn't have the same ring.

WONDERFUL WORLD OF THE BROTHERS GRIMM, THE

★★★ MGM/UA, 1962, G, 129 min. Dirs: Henry Levin, George Pal. Cast: Laurence Harvey, Claire Bloom, Barbara Eden, Russ Tamblyn, Yvette Mimieux, Karl Boehm, Buddy Hackett, Terry-Thomas, Jim Backus, Oscar Homolka, Martita Hunt, Walter Slezak, Beulah Bondi, Otto Kruger, Ian Wolfe, Arnold Stang.

The (alleged) true story of fairy tale mavens Wilhelm and Jacob Grimm (Harvey and Boehm) is used to bridge three of their tales. "The Dancing Princess," about a youth (Tamblyn) who uses a cloak of invisibility to spy on the princess (Mimieux) he loves, and "The Shoemaker and the Elves," about a tired cobbler (also played by Harvey) who gets the unexpected help of a band of pixies to complete his work, are routine. The one to see, however, is "The Singing Bone,"I> in which a cowardly knight (Terry-Thomas) murders the serf (Hackett) who actually killed the dragon (a great Jim Danforth effect) the knight was hired to slay and is undone by his victim's talking bone. There's a great cast and lush production values but the stories take too long to get going and the framing story is contrived in the extreme, making this a fun but lesser Pal fantasy.

WONDERS OF ALADDIN, THE

★★ Charter, 1961, NR, 93 min. Dirs: Henry Levin, Mario Bava. Cast: Donald O'Connor, Noelle Adam, Vittorio DeSica, Aldo Fabrizi, Michele Mercier, Terence Hill.

Bava did second-unit work and eventually took over directing this minor fantasy with an overaged O'Connor as the hero who finds a magic lamp. The genie who pops out is played

by DeSica but, despite Bava's usual imaginative visual touches, there's not much wonder on display in this slow Italian-American coproduction.

WORLD GONE WILD

★★☆ Media, 1988, R, 95 min. Dir: Lee H. Katzin. Cast: Bruce Dern, Michael Paré, Catherine Mary Stewart, Adam Ant, Rick Podwell, Anthony James.

The Seventh Samurai, or maybe *The Magnificent Seven*, gets reworked in a sci-fi context yet again as aging hippie Dern gathers together a group of warriors to protect a peaceful twenty-first-century settlement (in a postnuke landscape, natch) from a band of scavengers (led by Ant) who use the literary works of Charles Manson as inspiration. Not as bleak as most of these apocalyptic freak shows thanks to some tongue-in-cheek humor and Dern's actor-gone-wild histrionics as the world's most out-of-control flower child.

WRECKING CREW, THE

★★ RCA/Columbia, 1969, PG, 105 min. Dir: Phil Karlson. Cast: Dean Martin, Sharon Tate, Elke Sommer, Nancy Kwan, Tina Louise, Nigel Green.

You have to hand it to Dino for sticking it out through four of these dumb Matt Helm pictures. This last of the quartet is basically just a ripoff of *Goldfinger*, with Green as the madman after the world's gold supply. Tate has a good comic role as Helm's bumbling female partner and Louise (fresh off *Gilligan's Island*) gets killed by a bomb in a whiskey bottle.

XANADU

★★ MCA/Universal, 1980, PG, 96 min. Dir: Robert Greenwald. Cast: Olivia Newton-John, Gene Kelly, Michael Beck, James Sloyan, Dimitra Arliss, Sandahl Bergman, voices of Wilfrid Hyde White, Coral Browne.

Flat disco-era remake of the musical fantasy *Down to Earth*, with Newton-John as a muse who steps out of a graffiti mural and brings love and hope to the life of down-and-out roller-boogie artist Beck (I doubt there ever was a roller-boogie artist who *wasn't* down and out, but I digress). A couple of the songs (especially the ballad "Suddenly") aren't bad and Kelly tries to give this a boost but Olivia lacks the screen presence to put this over—something Rita Hayworth did effortlessly in the original. Originally released to theatres at 88 minutes, 12 additional minutes were added to the TV and video prints.

X FROM OUTER SPACE, THE

★ Orion, 1967, NR, 89 min. Dir: Kazui Nihonmatsu. Cast: Peggy Neal, Eiji Okada, Itoko Harada, Franz Gruber.

The world's first (and so far only) movie about a gigantic rubber chicken from the stars, this below-standard Japanese monster flick may have the most jaw-droppingly awful menace since *Reptilicus.* Even the most diehard fan of the Japanese monster genre will want to give this a pass. Aka *Uchu Daikaiju Guilala (The Monster Guilala).*

X—THE MAN WITH X-RAY EYES

★★★ Orion, 1963, NR, 79 min. Dir: Roger Corman. Cast: Ray Milland, Diana van der Vlis, Harold J. Stone, Don Rickles, John Hoyt, John Dierkes.

Maybe Oscar-winner Milland's last good role, this sees him as eye specialist Dr. Xavier, whose experimental eyedrops give him superior vision and eventually drive him to murder and madness. Although somewhat held back by its budget and limited special FX, this well-written little movie is intelligent and understated (except maybe for the music, which sounds like something out of *House on Haunted Hill*), with a solid support cast (look for lots of Corman regulars in minor roles) and a legendarily grim shock ending. Aka *The Man with the X-Ray Eyes.*

XTRO

★★ New Line, 1982, R, 81 min. Dir: Harry Bromley Davenport. Cast: Bernice Stegers, Philip Sayer, Danny Brainin, Maryam D'Abo.

A man who was abducted by aliens returns to his wife and son as a strange half-human half-alien mutant who wants the son to become a monster as well. This cheesy British ripoff of *Alien* is a weird mixture of domestic drama and sci-fi/horror. It really doesn't satisfy on any of these levels but sticks in the mind thanks to a couple of outrageous scenes (including a shocking moment when our transformed-into-an-alien hero rapes a girl whose belly balloons up and bursts open to reveal Sayer in his original human form). The same director returned years later with a pair

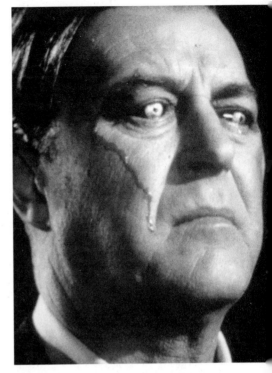

"Extended Wear, my eye!" Ray Milland in X—The Man with X-Ray Eyes (1963).

of direct-to-video in-name-only sequels.

XTRO II: THE SECOND ENCOUNTER

★★ New Line, 1991, R, 89 min. Dir: Harry Bromley Davenport. Cast: Jan-Michael Vincent, Paul Koslo, Tara Buckman, Jano Frandsen.

Whiny scientists and stud-puppy military men battle a deadly monster from another dimension in this "sequel" that's actually yet another variation on *Aliens* crossed with *Shadowzone.* Slick but unremarkable.

XTRO 3: WATCH THE SKIES

★★ Triboro Entertainment, 1995, R, 90 min. Dir: Harry Bromley Davenport. Cast: Robert Culp, Sal Landi, Karen Moncrieff, Andrew Devoff, Jim Hanks.

Practically a remake of *Xtro II*, this has yet another squadron of marines menaced by yet another monster from an alternate universe at a scientific complex on an island. Totally suspenseless and lacking in excitement, Davenport really needs to get his hands on another franchise.

YEAR 2889

See: *In the Year 2889.*

YESTERDAY MACHINE, THE

★ Video City, 1963, NR, 85 min. Dir: Russ Marker. Cast: Tim Holt, Robert Britton, Anne Pellegrino, Jack Herman, Bill Thurman.

A jaw-droppingly absurd shot-in-Texas cheapster about a Nazi mad scientist who kidnaps a cheerleader to use as a subject in his experiments in time travel. This makes Larry Buchanan's Texas quickies look like MGM product with a just-when-you-think-it-can't-get-any-weirder plot, just-point-the-camera-and-start-talking direction, and a brief appearance by hard-up former Western star Holt as a detective investigating the cheerleader's disappearance. Don't say you weren't warned.

YOG, MONSTER FROM SPACE

★★ IMA, 1970, G, 84 min. Dir: Inoshiro Honda. Cast: Akira Kubo, Atsuko Takahasi, Yoshio Tsuchiya, Kenji Sahara.

Offbeat but decidedly minor Toho monster flick about an alien lifeform possessing various South Seas Island creatures and transforming them into gigantic monsters. The island setting makes for a nice change from the usual city stomping but the monsters, including a huge squid, are kind of silly looking. Aka *Nankai no Daikajiju (Monster Amoeba from Space)* and *Space Amoeba.*

YONGARY, MONSTER FROM THE DEEP

★☆ Orion, 1967, NR, 79 min. Dir: Kiduck Kim. Cast: Yungil Oh, Chungin Nam, Soonjai Lee, Moon Kang.

An earthquake in mainland China awakens a huge horned dinosaur from centuries of slumber and sends it on a city-stomping mission to Seoul, South Korea. The Korean film industry tries to get in on the Japanese monster act but prove that they're nearly as inept at it as were the Danish with *Reptilicus.* Sometimes funny but mostly a bore. Aka *Dai Koesu Yongkari (The Monster Yonkari).*

YOR, THE HUNTER FROM THE FUTURE

★☆ RCA/Columbia, 1983, PG, 88 min. Dir: Anthony

M. Dawson [Antonio Margheriti]. Cast: Reb Brown, Corinne Clery, John Steiner, Carole Andre, Alan Collins.

Reedited from a four-part Italian miniseries called *Il Mondo de Yor (The World of Yor),* this absurd feature is good for a few laughs but not much else. Brown isn't much of an actor but he sure looks good in a loincloth as our hero Yor, who saves cavebabe Clery (in a bad prehistoric perm) from a badly constructed dinosaur before they are both magically projected into a postnuke future for the same old *Mad Max* clichés. Director Margheriti made some good movies in the '60s but by this point had pretty much run out of creative steam. Strange but awful; for beefcake fans only.

YOUNG SHERLOCK HOLMES

★★ Paramount, 1985, PG-13, 109 min. Dir: Barry Levinson. Cast: Nicholas Rowe, Alan Cox, Sophie Ward, Anthony Higgins, Susan Fleetwood, Freddie Jones, Nigel Stock, Michael Hordern.

Steven Spielberg was the executive producer of this "what if?" speculative fantasy of the teen years of Sherlock Holmes and Dr. Watson, so no wonder it often looks (rather inappropriately) like another Indiana Jones action-fantasy. The young detective-to-be investigates a murder at his prep school and uncovers a bloodthirsty Egyptian cult who kill via a hallucination-causing drug—the most impressive scene shows a stained-glass figure come to murderous life. If you know anything about the Holmes canon you'll realize just how annoyingly dishonest most of this is (for one thing, Holmes and Watson didn't first meet until both were well into their middle years), but on a purely physical level (acting, Victorian set design, ILM FX) this film can't be faulted, even though it ends on a terribly sour note. Actor Higgins, by the way, first got his start in Hammer horror movies under the name Anthony Corlan. Aka *Young Sherlock Holmes and the Pyramid of Fear.*

YOUNG SHERLOCK HOLMES AND THE PYRAMID OF FEAR

See: *Young Sherlock Holmes.*

YOU ONLY LIVE TWICE

★★☆ MGM/UA, 1967, PG, 116 min. Dir: Lewis Gilbert. Cast: Sean Connery, Mie Hama, Donald Pleasence, Akiko Wakabayashi, Karin Dor, Tetsuro Tamba, Teru Shimada, Bernard Lee, Lois Maxwell, Desmond Llewelyn, Charles Gray, Tsai Chin.

Although it's readily apparent that Connery was fast becoming tired of the James Bond series by this point, this colorful adventure is

What more is there to say? Yog, Monster from Space *(1970).*

far from the worst in the group. In Japan searching for the whereabouts of missing U.S. and Soviet spacecraft, Bond fakes his own death, disguises himself as a Japanese (the dumbest part of the movie), marries lovely agent Hama (all in the line of duty), and discovers that archnemisis Blofeld (seen on screen for the first time in the creepy persona of Pleasence) has hidden the space capsules and their crew in his volcano crater hideaway. Scripted by Roald Dahl (huh?!), this is even more episodic than usual but is worth seeing for the great (and vastly underrated) Nancy Sinatra theme song and outstanding support-

"No, Mr. Bond, I expect you to . . . " Oh, that was Goldfinger. *Donald Pleasence as Blofeld in* You Only Live Twice *(1967).*

ing cast. Lovely costars Hama and Wakabayashi originally appeared together in *King Kong vs. Godzilla*; villainess Dor (who gets fed to a tank of piranhas) was a big star in her German homeland, where she appeared in many horror and Edgar Wallace mystery films; and Gray (as a friendly informant killed off early on) would play Blofeld in *Diamonds Are Forever* and is probably best known as the narrator of *The Rocky Horror Picture Show*.

Z

ZARDOZ

★★☆ Fox, 1974, R, 105 min. Dir: John Boorman.
Cast: Sean Connery, Charlotte Rampling, Sara
Kestelman, John Alderton, Sally Anne Newton, Niall
Buggy.

Like most of Boorman's more controversial
films (like *Excalibur* and *Exorcist II: The Heretic*)
there seems to be no middle ground on this
oddball futuristic adventure: People either
love it or hate it. Actually, though, like *Exorcist
II*, this is a wild mixture of the truly imaginative and visionary with some of the goofiest
scripting around. It's the year 2293 and Connery (sans his usual toupee and much of his
clothing) is an exterminator charged by the
ruling class of intellectuals who live in a paradise called the Vortex to constantly rout the
brutish denizens of Earth's now barren landscape. Sean and other exterminators are lorded
over by a godlike flying stone head called

Zardoz, which distributes guns and good
advice, but involvements with both Rampling
and Kestleman lead Connery to the truth—or
something—about his world and his god. Full
of amazing visual bits and funny references
(including the origin of Zardoz's name) but
kind of hard to warm up to.

ZELIG

★★★☆ Warner, 1983, PG, 79 min. Dir: Woody Allen.
Cast: Woody Allen, Mia Farrow, Garrett Brown,
Stephanie Farrow, Will Holt, Sol Lomita, Mary Louise
Wilson, Michael Jeter.

One of Allen's best (and most underrated)
films is this near-brilliant "mockumentary"
about Leonard Zelig (Woody), a 1920s
phenomenon known as the "Chameleon Man"
who can alter his appearance at will to resemble
anyone he meets—all a psychological result of
his incredible shyness. Years before *Forrest
Gump*, Allen placed both himself and other
cast members on the screen right alongside
various famous historical figures through an
adroit use of editing, treated film stock, lighting, and doubles. Allen has never been more
appealing as the childlike Zelig and there are
many hilarious highlights, perhaps the best
being the fistfight that breaks out on the Papal
balcony during the Pope's address.

*From the looks of
things, I'll bet he
wasn't the only guy
who was stoned on
the set of* Zardoz
(1974).

ZERAM
★★★ Fox/Lorber, 1991, Dir: Keita Amemiya. Cast: Yuko Moriyama, Yukihiro Hotaru, Kunihiko Ida.

This impressive Japanese sci-fi thriller is very much in the spirit of a live action anime. Moriyama is an alien bounty hunter on Earth who's after a great-looking robot death-machine with a blank face and a snakelike appendage that emerges from its forehead. Very much influenced by the *Alien* movies but still very much an original work, this has incredible production design and special FX and almost nonstop action. The one debit: some incredibly misjudged comic relief. Original title: *Zeriam*; followed by *Zeram 2*.

ZERO POPULATION GROWTH
See: *Z.P.G.*

ZETA ONE
See: *The Love Factor.*

ZOMBIES OF THE STRATOSPHERE
★★ Republic, 1952, NR, 260 min. Dir: Fred C. Brannon. Cast: Judd Holdren, Aline Towne, Wilson Wood, Lane Bradbury, John Crawford, Leonard Nimoy, Tom Steele, Gayle Kellogg.

It's got a great title and the historical value of featuring Nimoy in his first alien role but this second and last Commando Cody serial, following *Radar Men from the Moon,* still isn't very good. Badly dressed alien invaders hide out in a cave and make Earth gangsters an offer they can't refuse. Luckily Holdren and his amazing flying jetpack are there to save us all from alien conquest. Recycled costumes, props, and special FX footage will make this seem familiar even if you never saw it before. The feature version, which plays somewhat better, is called *Satan's Satellites.* Like almost all of Republic's serial releases, they also offer this in a (surprisingly good-looking) colorized version.

ZONE TROOPERS
★★ Lightning, 1985, PG, 88 min. Dir: Danny Bilson. Cast: Tim Thomerson, Timothy Van Patten, Biff Manard, Art La Fleur, William Paulson.

One of Empire Pictures' oddest releases was this mixup of *The Dirty Dozen* and *E.T.* featuring Thomerson, leading a small squadron of WWII soldiers, and journalist Manard (once a *Playgirl* centerfold) against Nazi troops who've discovered a crashed spaceship somewhere in Italy. The Americans then decide to rescue the friendly alien pilot (makeup by John Buechler), who in turn helps them win the battle. This Steven Spielberg-Sam Fuller hybrid had a lot of promise but botched nearly everything thanks

to Empire's usual refusal to try anything different beyond the actual premise, with undeveloped characters, cheesy FX, and every war movie cliché in the book trotted out to take the place of any real use of imagination.

ZONTAR, THE THING FROM VENUS
+ Sinister Cinema, 1966, NR, 80 min. Dir: Larry Buchanan. Cast: John Agar, Anthony Houston, Susan Bjurman, Pat Delaney.

Buchanan's most (in)famous movie, this cheapjack remake of Roger Corman's *It Conquered the World* is amazingly bad, even for Larry. The Corman original was hardly Roger's finest hour but it at least had a great Beverly Garland performance and·a nice sense of the absurd. *Zontar,* on the other hand, just goes through the motions of the same plot with drab settings, poor performances (Houston, in the old Lee Van Cleef role, does some of the broadest, most annoying acting it's ever been my displeasure to endure), and a batlike monster design that makes the original carrot creature look like it sprung from the mind of H. R. Giger. If you want to see a Buchanan film that's at least *fun* trash, watch *In the Year 2889* instead.

ZOTZ!
★★ RCA/Columbia, 1962, NR, 87 min. Dir: William Castle. Cast: Tom Poston, Julia Meade, Jim Backus, Fred Clark, Cecil Kellaway, Margaret Dumont.

College professor Poston uncovers an ancient coin that can freeze people in place or even kill them if you point it directly at them and say "Zotz!" Russian agents wishing to possess the coin kidnap Tom's beautiful girlfriend Meade to that end. One of gimmick horror king Castle's weirdest and least satisfying films; obviously an attempt to emulate Disney comedies like *The Absent Minded Professor,* it's flat and not especially funny, and wastes a great cast of supporting character actors.

Z.P.G.
★★☆ Paramount, 1971, PG, 95 min. Dir: Michael Campus. Cast: Oliver Reed, Geraldine Chaplin, Diane Cilento, Don Gordon, Bill Nagy.

Grim futuristic drama about a couple (Reed and Chaplin) in an overcrowded, polluted future world where childbearing is forbidden. Why Ollie and Gerry would ever want to bring a child into this unhappy world remains a mystery but they do and defy all odds, and threats of extermination, to conceive. The unexpected happy ending is about the only surprise in this well-acted but oh-so-typically-early-'70s sci-fi scripted by novelists Max Erlich and Frank DeFelitta. Aka *Zero Population Growth.*

EPISODE GUIDES

DOCTOR WHO
CBS/Fox, 1963–89, NR, running times vary per tape.

The world's longest-running science fiction television series, this British series debuted on the BBC the day after the JFK assassination and was still running when *People* magazine voted his son the "Sexiest Man Alive." A cult hit in its home country for years, it didn't turn up in the United States until the early '70s, when a few PBS stations began running some of the serialized episodes. By the end of the decade *Who* had managed to become something of a success in this country as well.

The Doctor (the title derives from the fact that people keep asking, "Doctor Who?") is a Time Lord from the planet Gallifrey who arrives on Earth in his time-and-space machine the Tardis (which looks like a British police call box) to battle various alien invaders, including the robotic Daleks, the Cyborg-like Cybermen, and his own archnemesis, the evil Time Lord known as the Master. Originally played with grandfatherly élan by William Hartnell, the Doctor has the power to "regenerate" himself, allowing the lead actor to be replaced every few years. As time passed, Hartnell (1963–68) was followed by Patrick Troughton (1968–70), Jon Pertwee (my favorite *Who*, 1970–74), Tom Baker (the most popular *Who*, 1974–81) Peter Davison (1981–84), Colin Baker (1984–87), and Sylvester McCoy (1987–89). Through the years the Doc had a variety of assistants and companions, such as pert Jo Grant (Katy Manning), spunky Sarah Jane Smith (Elisabeth Sladen), sexy warrior gal Leela (Louise Jameson), the unflappable Brigadier Lethbridge Stewart (Nicholas Courtney), and stalwart Sergeant Benton (John Levine). Roger Delgado was the best of the actors to play the stylish villain the Master. Like the U.S. series *Dark Shadows*, *Doctor Who* was cheap and often naive (even innocent), but it had lots of imagination and a nice line in self-deprecation that always made it worth watching.

ARC OF INFINITY
★★☆ 1983, 98 min. Dir: Ron Jones.

An alien entity looking to bond with a Time Lord in order to cross into another dimension via the arc of infinity chooses our Time Lord as his victim. Look for Colin Baker in an early role as Security Commander Maxil.

ARK IN SPACE, THE
★★★ 1974, 90 min. Dir: Rodney Bennett.

The Doctor, Sara, and Harry (Ian Marter) end up in the distant future, where the last survivors of the human race are threatened by antlike aliens on a space station.

ANDROID INVASION, THE
★★★ 1975, 96 min. Dir: Barry Letts.

The Doctor and Sarah meet the evil Thraal and their *Body Snatchers*-type plan to repopulate the Earth with humanoid robots.

ANDROIDS OF TARA, THE
★★☆ 1978, 98 min. Dir: Michael Hays.

The Doctor and Romana (Mary Tamm) holiday on the planet Tara, where they become pawns in a plot by a wicked count to steal the planet from the benevolent Prince Reynart.

ARMAGEDDON FACTOR, THE
★★★ 1979, 148 min. Dir: Michael Hayes.

The Doctor, Romana (Lalla Ward), and robot dog K–9 conclude their search for the Key to Time as they become entangled in a war between planets. Can they stop the evil Shadow, a servant of the Black Guardian, from destroying everything with his Armageddon Device? A fitting end for a not always alluring saga.

BLACK ORCHID
★★☆ 1982, 73 min. Dir: Ron Jones.

A *Who*-dunnit in which the Doctor and Nyssa

(Sarah Sutton) visit the manor of an English lord who sees in Nyssa the reincarnation of his dead fiancée. Meanwhile, the estate is stalked by a mysterious killer.

BRAIN OF MORBIUS, THE
★★★ 1976, 98 min. Dir: Christopher Barry.

The Doctor and Sarah land on a spooky planet where an alien mad scientist has transplanted the brain of an evil Time Lord into a composite creature of his own design. An entertaining *Who* variation on an old *Frankenstein* movie. The video has now been reissued at the original 98-minute length.

CARNIVAL OF MONSTERS
★★☆ 1973, 101 min. Dir: Barry Letts.

A really weird one, with an omnipotent alien life-form transforming the Doctor and Jo—along with a variety of strange monsters—into miniaturized playthings.

CAVES OF ANDROZANI, THE
★★☆ 1984, 101 min. Dir: Graeme Harper.

Peter Davison's last stand as Doctor number four has him going up against the evil Sharaz Jek, a creator of androids after a mysterious, powerful new drug.

CLAWS OF AXOS, THE
★★★ 1971, 98 min. Dir: Michael Ferguson.

A spaceship that looks like a huge slinky covered in muslin lands in rural England one wintry morning. The Doctor and his UNIT friends investigate and meet the golden-eyed people of Axos, who gift the Earth men with a powerful element called axonite, which will eventually help the Axons take over the world. The Master also figures in this above-average Pertwee adventure featuring some especially surrealistic special FX.

CURSE OF FENRIC, THE
★★ 1989, 104 min. Dir: Alan Wareing.

The Doctor ends up in World War II Britain, where he comes up against the ravenous wolves of Fenric. Routine.

CURSE OF PELADON, THE
★★★ 1972, 97 min. Dir: Lennie Mayne.

The Doctor and Jo accidentally land on a stormswept planet where an intergalactic space conference is underway. Mistaken for the ambassadors from Earth, our heroes try to avert an assassination. Pretty good Pertwee stuff and nonsense.

DAEMONS, THE
★★★★ 1971, 122 min. Dir: Christopher Barry.

Possibly the best written and most imaginative *Who* (and certainly the best of the Pertwee shows) has the Doctor and Jo trying to thwart the Master's plan to resurrect an ancient demon called Azal in a quaint little English village. Often reminiscent of Nigel Kneale's *Quatermass* serials, this sports some genuinely chilling moments.

DAY OF THE DALEKS
★★☆ 1972, 90 min. Dir: Paul Bernard.

The Doctor tries to stop his old nemeses the Daleks from invading the Earth. One of the lesser Dalek adventures.

DEADLY ASSASSIN, THE
★★★☆ 1976, 90 min. Dir: David Maloney.

In a more serious than usual Baker story, the Doctor returns to Gallifrey, where his attempt to save the Grand Master of the Time Lords results in him being accused of the latter's assassination. The change in tone from some of the other, campier Baker shows is striking and there's a special guest appearance by a rather crisp-looking Master.

DEAD PLANET, THE
★★★☆ 1963, 101 min. Dir: Christopher Barry.

One of the first *Who* adventures finds the Doctor, Susan (Carole Ann Ford), Ian (William Russell), and Barbara (Jacqueline Hill) meeting for the first time and traveling to a distant planet ruled by the Daleks—hateful, withered aliens in tanklike protective body armor. A historically important episode partly remade as the feature *Dr. Who and the Daleks* and followed by the immediate sequel *The Expedition*.

DEATH TO THE DALEKS
★★★ 1973, 90 min. Dir: Michael E. Briant.

Trying to stop a deadly plague from sweeping across the galaxy, an illness to which Sarah has already fallen victim, the Doctor runs into his dreaded enemies the Daleks. Are they behind it all? A solid Pertwee *Who* with a few unexpected twists.

DOCTOR WHO AND THE SILURIANS
★★★ 1970, 167 min. Dir: Timothy Combe.

UNIT sends the Doctor and Liz (Caroline John) to investigate a power leakage at a nuclear reactor. In a nearby cave, the Doc and his companion discover a race of lizardlike monsters called Silurians who are behind it all. First-rate adventure originally titled *The Silurians*.

EARTHSHOCK
★★☆ 1982, 99 min. Dir: Peter Grimwade.

In this okay Davison entry, the Doctor encounters his old enemies the Cybermen while investigating a murder in the twenty-sixth century.

ENLIGHTENMENT
★★☆ 1983, 97 min. Dir: Fiona Cumming.

The Black Guardian makes plans to dispose of the Doctor during an intergalactic race. Fun but forgettable, like a live action sci-fi version of a *Tom Slick* cartoon.

EXPEDITION, THE
★★★ 1963, 73 min. Dir: Richard Martin.

This followup to *The Dead Planet* finds the Doctor and his companions trying to free the gentle Thals from the domination of the evil Daleks.

FIVE DOCTORS, THE
★★★★ 1983, 90 min. Dir: Peter Moffatt.

This wonderful reunion episode celebrated the Doctor's twentieth anniversary by involving then-current Doc Davison with his past four incarnations (Richard Hurndall subbed for the late William Hartnell) as well as many of the best companions and even the Master. A real delight for any fan of the long-running series.

FRONTIER IN SPACE
★★☆ 1973, 144 min. Dir: Paul Bernard.

The Doctor and Jo travel to the twenty-sixth century, where Earth is at war with the planet Draconia. Tension mounts as they encounter the Master and the Tardis is stolen by the ape-like Ofrons.

GENESIS OF THE DALEKS
★★★☆ 1975, 143 min. Dir: David Maloney.

One of the best Baker adventures pits the Doctor, Sarah, and Harry against a savage army of Daleks and Davros, their sinister, crippled creator.

GHOST LIGHT
★★★ 1989, 72 min. Dir: Alan Wareing.

The Doctor takes Ace (Sophie Aldred) to an allegedly haunted Victorian mansion where they encounter not ghosts but a powerful alien entity living in an ancient spaceship beneath the house. H. P. Lovecraft meets *Upstairs, Downstairs* in this enjoyable horror tale featuring such nice touches as a neanderthal butler called Nimrod and a shrouded female thing-in-the-attic.

IMAGE OF THE FENDAHL
★★★☆ 1977, 94 min. Dir: George Spenton-Foster.

The Doctor and Leela encounter a group of archeologists in an old English manor. When one member of the group (Wanda Ventham) is possessed by an ancient skull, the Doc fears that the Fendahl, creatures of ancient Gallifrian myth, are about to return. A great horror *Who* with just the right blend of suspense and laughs, and one of the best, most exciting endings in the entire series.

INFERNO
★★★☆ 1970, 167 min. Dir: Douglas Camfield.

Another outstanding Pertwee adventure with the Doctor and Liz involved in an experiment to pierce the Earth's crust, which results in an outbreak of werewolfism due to a strange substance brought up by the drill. Then there's a dimensional time shift and things really start to drift off into *Dark Shadows* land as the Doctor bounces back and forth from one world to another. See it to believe it.

INVASION, THE
★★☆ 1968, 146 min. Dir: Douglas Camfield.

The Doctor and friends Zoe (Wendy Padbury) and Jamie (Frazer Hines) join forces with UNIT and Brigadier Lethbridge Stewart to do battle with an army of Cybermen in the sewers of London. A not bad entry from the rarely seen (in the U.S.) Troughton years.

KEEPER OF THE TRAKEN, THE
★★ 1981, 98 min. Dir: John Black.

When the sinister Melkur plots to annihilate the whole Traken society their ruler, the Keeper, calls in the Doctor and Nyssa to stop the fiend.

KINDA
★★☆ 1982, 98 min. Dir: Peter Grimwade.

On the idyllic planet of Deva Loka, the mind of Tegan (Janet Fielding) is taken over by a malevolent force called the Mara. Can the Doctor save her?

KROTONS, THE
★★ 1968, 91 min. Dir: David Maloney.

Released from centuries of suspended animation, the evil Krotons use their mind-bending powers to steal the thoughts of a gentle alien race known as the Gonds.

LOGOPOLIS
★★★ 1981, 99 min. Dir: Peter Grimwade.

Baker's last adventure pits the Doctor and the

Master against each other on the planet Logopolis. Can the Doctor stop his nemesis from unraveling the very essence of time and destroying the universe? Of course he can.

MASQUE OF MANDRAGORA, THE
★★☆ 1976, 99 min. Dir: Rodney Bennett.

The Doctor and Sarah travel to the Middle Ages, where they attend a grand ball and battle an evil cult. Sort of like a *Who* remake of the Vincent Price classic *The Masque of the Red Death.*

PIRATE PLANET, THE
★★☆ 1978, 101 min. Dir: Pennant Roberts.

In their continual search for the Key to Time, the Doctor, Romana, and K-9 end up on the planet Zanak, where the people are being controlled by an evil Cyborg pirate called the Captain. Funniest scene: K-9 taking on the Captain's robotic parrot.

PLANET OF EVIL
★★☆ 1975, 94 min. Dir: David Maloney.

The Doctor and Sarah follow a distress signal to the farthest planet in the universe, where a group of scientists were murdered by a monstrous force. Will the Doc and Sarah be next?

PLANET OF THE SPIDERS
★★★★ 1974, 180 min. Dir: Barry Letts.

Pertwee's last bow as the Doctor is one of his best. A rural think tank for international scientists turns out to be a cover for an invasion by mind-controlling, spiderlike aliens. Some nice creepy moments of various folk (including Sarah) being menaced by the obviously puppet spiders are reminiscent of some old *Outer Limits* episodes.

POWER OF KROLL, THE
★★☆ 1978, 91 min. Dir: Norman Stewart.

On the third moon of the planet Delta Magna, the Doctor and Romana continue their Key to Time search and Romana is nearly sacrificed by the locals to their god Kroll.

PYRAMIDS OF MARS
★★ 1975, 91 min. Dir: Paddy Russell.

The Doctor and Sarah versus a professor of Egyptology possessed by an evil alien. Wait till you see the lumbering, robotlike mummies; you'll think you accidentally tuned into an episode of *Ultraman* by mistake.

RESCUE, THE
★★★ 1965, 73 min. Dir: Christopher Barry.

The Doctor, Ian, and Barbara find stranded Earthlings terrorized by the hostile Didonians of the planet Dido. But as far as the Doc knows, the Didonians are a peaceful race. So what gives? Don't judge by appearances in this adventure introducing new companion Vicki (Maureen O'Brien).

RESURRECTION OF THE DALEKS
★★★☆ 1984, 97 min. Dir: Matthew Robinson.

My favorite Davison *Who* adventure has the Doctor and his friends in contemporary London, where the Daleks are about to go back into action with their resurrected leader Davros back for revenge. The unexpected final scene and farewell for Tegan is genuinely shocking and moving.

REVENGE OF THE CYBERMEN
★★☆ 1974, 92 min. Dir: Michael E. Briant.

The Doctor, Sarah, and Harry battle the newly reactivated Cybermen who are trying to take over a space station.

RIBOS OPERATION, THE
★★★ 1978, 99 min. Dir: George Spenton-Foster.

The Doctor and K-9 embark on their search for the Key to Time. Accompanied by female Time Lord Lady Romana, they end up on the planet Ribos, where intergalactic con men are trying to sell the planet—and two pieces of the fabulous key. A seriocomic beginning to the Doctor's greatest quest.

ROBOT
★★★★ 1974, 99 min. Dir: Christopher Barry.

Baker's first go at the Doctor gets him up and running as he tries to stop a clunking military robot from going berserk. In the climax, it grows to King Kong proportions and even carries off Sarah, Fay Wray style. This also features the first appearance of Dr. Harry Sullivan, one of the Doc's more likable companions.

ROBOTS OF DEATH
★★☆ 1977, 91 min. Dir: Michael E. Briant.

The Doctor and new companion Leela solve a series of murders on a planet inhabited by out-of-control robots.

ROMANS, THE
★★★ 1965, 73 min. Dir: Christopher Barry.

In Italy, A.D. 64, the Doctor and his companions become witness to the great fire that destroyed Rome. One of the most ambitious of the Hartnell episodes, hampered slightly by the usual lack of budget.

SEEDS OF DEATH
★★☆ 1969, 137 min. Dir: Michael Ferguson.

Ice Warriors from Mars attempt to take over Earth with fungus-spawning seed pods. Routine and somewhat overlong Troughton entry.

SEEDS OF DOOM, THE
★★★☆ 1976, 144 min. Dir: Douglas Camfield.

A *Doctor Who* version of *Day of the Triffids* has monster plants attempting to take over England. One of the best of the Bakers, with Tony Beckley giving an outstandingly weird performance as the mad, plant-loving millionaire who helps the invasion along.

SHADA
★★ 1980, 110 min. Dir: Pennant Roberts.

Never aired on television due to a BBC strike, this video version is linked by Tom Baker to smooth over unshot footage. The Doctor, Romana, and K–9 seek help from another earthbound Time Lord.

SILVER NEMESIS
★★☆ 1988, 139 min. Dir: Chris Clough.

The Doctor and Ace battle an invading Cyberman army. The video contains much footage cut from the original broadcast.

SNAKEDANCE
★★☆ 1983, 98 min. Dir: Fiona Cumming.

On the planet of Manussa, Tegan is taken over by a personified evil force known as the Mara. Can the Doctor save her before Tegan's destiny is altered forever? A not bad Davison entry.

SONTARIAN EXPERIMENT, THE
★★☆ 1974, 50 min. Dir: Rodney Bennett.

One of the Doctor's shortest adventures, this two-parter pits him against a potato-headed Sontarian scientist out to conquer the Earth.

SPEARHEAD FROM SPACE
★★☆ 1970, 92 min. Dir: Derek Martinus.

The Doctor and Liz battle living mannequins in the control of invading aliens.

STONES OF BLOOD, THE
★★☆ 1978, 96 min. Dir: Darrol Blake.

The Doctor and Romana run afoul of an ancient Druid cult in this okay horror-themed story, originally broadcast at Halloween.

SURVIVAL
★★☆ 1989, 72 min. Dir: Alan Wareing.

The Doctor takes Ace home to West London, where they discover that aliens called Cheetahs are hunting humans as prey after teleporting them back to their home world. An old foe of the Doc's, the Master, tries to help our heroes—but why? A pretty good McCoy entry.

TALONS OF WANG CHIANG, THE
★★☆ 1977, 140 min. Dir: Michael E. Briant.

Dr. Who meets Fu Manchu in Victorian London as the Doc and Leela become involved in a tong war started by an evil Asian magician.

TERROR OF THE AUTONS
★★☆ 1971, 95 min. Dir: Barry Letts.

The Doctor and new assistant Jo Grant confront the Master's latest scheme to defeat the Doctor, this time with the aid of faceless automations called Autons.

THREE DOCTORS, THE
★★★ 1973, 99 min. Dir: Lennie Mayne.

The Doctor's tenth-anniversary celebration episode—the first of the reunion shows—has current Doc Pertwee calling on previous incarnations Hartell and Troughton to fight a renegade Time Lord known as Omega. Some of the interplay between the three leads is priceless.

TOMB OF THE CYBERMEN
★★☆ 1967, 100 min. Dir: Morris Barry.

Archeologists on the planet Talos uncover an ancient crypt harboring the remains of the Doctor's old nemesis, the Cybermen.

TWO DOCTORS, THE
★★★ 1985, 132 min. Dir: Peter Moffatt.

Probably Colin Baker's most enjoyable *Who* story finds him involved with his second incarnation and his old companion Jamie, as Who 2 (Patrick Troughton in his final performance) is about to be operated on by the sinister Sontarians. Solidly imaginative and fun.

UNEARTHLY CHILD, AN
★★★★ 1963, 98 min. Dir: Waris Hussein.

The series' very first episode finds the Doctor and granddaughter Susan arriving on Earth and traveling back to prehistoric times. A genuine classic undimmed even by the cheap sets and primitive special FX.

VENGEANCE ON VAROS
★★ 1985, 89 min. Dir: Waris Hussein.

On the planet Varos, the Doctor and Peri (Nicola Bryant) end up in the dreaded Punishment Dome, where prisoners are tortured and executed as live TV entertainment. A somewhat heavy-handed Whovian variation on the film *Videodrome*.

VISITATION, THE
★★☆ 1982, 73 min. Dir: Ron Jones.

The Doctor and friends visit the seventeenth century, where aliens prey on superstitious peasants by pretending to be ancient demons.

WAR GAMES, THE
★★★ 1969, 124 min. Dir: David Maloney.

One of the best of the Troughtons finds the Doctor, Zoe, and Jamie forced to take part in a series of war-simulation games put on by an alien society who frequently abduct the people of different worlds as warriors. Well done.

WEB PLANET, THE
★★★ 1965, 148 min. Dir: Richard Martin.

The Doctor and his companions land the Tardis on a planet called Vortis, where the antlike Zarbi try to wrest power from the butterflylike Menophera. Slow, but the eerie, stagebound atmosphere often makes this—like many Hartnell episodes—look like the British version of *Dark Shadows*.

THE INVADERS
Goodtimes, 1967–68, NR, 50 min. per episode.

Larry Cohen, who carved an impressive niche for himself as the master of quirky horror and exploitation movies in the '70s, created this scary Quinn Martin-produced series. A variation on the *Invasion of the Body Snatchers* theme, it starred the ever-twitchy Roy Thinnes (previously a regular on *General Hospital*) as David Vincent, an architect who witnesses a late-night UFO landing. Naturally no one believes him and the increasingly paranoid Vincent begins to realize that the invaders are taking human form and infiltrating high government positions. The invaders can be told apart from ordinary humans by their bent pinkie fingers and bad habit of dissolving in red flame when they die, but few people catch on to the truth.

Premiering as a midseason replacement show on ABC-TV in January 1967, this quickly built a minor cult reputation thanks to its spooky concept, intelligent scripting, and solid playing from Thinnes and a bevy of top guest stars, but seemed to lose some of its edge during the second season when veteran actor Kent Smith was added to the cast as another believer who aids Thinnes. Like *Kolchak—The Night Stalker*, this is an obvious forerunner to

The X-Files and remains one of the best shows of its type. A pilot for a new series with Scott Bakula and Thinnes returning in a guest role was aired in 1994 but lacked the edgy fear and unbridled paranoia of the original series.

BEACHHEAD
★★★★ 1967. Dir: Joseph Sargent. Guest cast: Diane Baker, J. D. Cannon, James Daly, Bonnie Beecher, Ellen Corby, Vaughn Taylor.

The series pilot is a beautifully sustained bit of tension and terror, with David Vincent sighting one of the invaders' flying saucers and then finding himself disbelieved at every turn. Eventually Baker becomes sympathetic to Vincent's plight—but is she one of the aliens?

BELIEVERS, THE
★★★ 1967. Dir: Paul Wendkos. Guest cast: Carol Lynley, Kent Smith, Anthony Eisley, Rhys Williams.

Wendkos's direction and Lynley's loveliness add distinction to this later episode in which Vincent joins forces with others who have caught on to the invaders. Soon the aliens have marked everyone for death.

CONDEMNED, THE
★★☆ 1967. Dir: Richard Benedict. Guest cast: Ralph Bellamy, Marilyn Mason, Murray Hamilton, Larry Ward.

The last show of the first season finds Vincent framed for murder by the invaders. Routine mix of sci-fi and crime melodrama.

EXPERIMENT, THE
★★★ 1967. Dir: Joseph Sargent. Guest cast: Roddy McDowall, Laurence Naismith, Harold Gould, Dabbs Greer.

Continuing the high standards set by the first episode, the second finds Vincent out to save a scientist marked for assassination by the invaders after he discovers their existence.

IVY CURTAIN, THE
★★☆ 1967. Dir: Joseph Sargent. Guest cast: Jack Warden, Susan Oliver, Murray Matheson, Byron Morrow.

Vincent discovers that the invaders are using a children's school as an alien indoctrination center in this okay episode.

LABYRINTH
★★☆ 1967. Dir: Murray Golden. Guest cast: Sally Kellerman, Ed Begley, James Callahan, John Zaremba, Virginia Christine.

Armed with an alien X-ray, Vincent travels to Washington, D.C., thinking he at last has the proof he needs to convince the authorities of the invaders' existence in this not-bad later show.

MOONSHOT

★★☆ 1967. Dir: Paul Wendkos. Guest cast: Peter Graves, John Ericson, Joanne Linville, Kent Smith, Anthony Eisley, Strother Martin.

Vincent and NASA security man Graves investigate the mysterious deaths of two astronauts; David believes the aliens are involved. Above-average episode with an especially good cast.

MUTATION, THE

★★★☆ 1967. Dir: George Eckstein. Guest cast: Suzanne Pleshette, Edward Andrews, Lin McCarthy, Roy Jenson.

Pleshette's excellent acting makes this the second best of the series as Vincent is aided in his quest by a stripper who turns out to be an alien-human halfbreed.

QUANTITY UNKNOWN

★★★ 1967. Dir: Sutton Roley. Guest cast: James Whitmore, Susan Strasberg, William Talman, Milton Selzer.

Vincent himself is mistaken for an invader when he investigates a mysterious plane crash. Some good twists in this offbeat episode.

SAUCER, THE

★★☆ 1967. Dir: Jesse Hibbs. Guest cast: Anne Francis, Charles Drake, Dabney Coleman, Kelly Thordsen.

Vincent captures an alien spacecraft in this routine entry highlighted by an appearance by sexy *Forbidden Planet* heroine Francis.

SPORES, THE

★★★☆ 1967. Dir: William Hale. Guest cast: Gene Hackman, John Randolph, Judee Morton, James Gammon, Mark Miller, Patricia Smith.

Year two's best episode is the one most blatantly styled after *Invasion of the Body Snatchers*, with alien invaders now being spawned fully grown from other worldly seed pods. A good guest cast and direction make this a winner.

WALL OF CRYSTAL

★★★ 1967. Dir: Joseph Sargent. Guest cast: Burgess Meredith, Linden Chiles, Julie Sommers, Edward Asner, Russ Conway, Peggy Lipton.

The invaders kidnap Vincent's brother and pregnant sister-in-law to stop his vendetta against them. Another fine episode from director Sargent, with a top cast including future TV stars Sommers (*The Governor and J.J.*), Asner (*The Mary Tyler Moore Show*), and Lipton (*The Mod Squad*).

LOST IN SPACE

Columbia House, 1965–68, NR, 50 min. per tape.

Following the success of the TV incarnation of his movie Voyage to the Bottom of the Sea, producer Irwin Allen decided to try a second sci-fi series, this one set in outer space. The Space Family Robinson was the result, a straightforward adventure show loosely derived from Johann Wyss's The Swiss Family Robinson. Former Zorro Guy Williams was patriarch Professor John Robinson; Lassie mom June Lockhart was cast to type as wife and mother Maureen Robinson; and the Robinson kids were teenager Judy (lovely Marta Kristen), twelve-year-old Penny (Angela Cartwright), and ten-year-old Will (Bill Mumy). Mark Goddard was Major Don West, the handsome pilot of the spacecraft Jupiter 2, sent into space in 1997 on a colonization mission to the star system of Alpha Centauri.

The serialized pilot featured impressive photography and special effects but the CBS executives found the show too dry and serious for its intended kiddie audience. As a result, the show was revamped with the addition of two new characters: Dr. Zachary Smith (Jonathan Harris), a NASA psychiatrist and double agent for some unnamed foreign power, and the Robinson's robot (voiced by Dick Tufeld), whom Dr. Smith sabotages, thereby ending up trapped on the *Jupiter 2* at takeoff. The first black-and-white episodes are still reasonably serious in tone but as time passed Dr. Smith and the robot became more and more popular as comic relief characters. (With each subsequent episode, Smith became more cowardly and the robot funnier and more human.) The show was restructured to feature their antics prominently in nearly every episode, making them the series' main stars, much in the way Barnabas Collins came to dominate *Dark Shadows* and Fonzie *Happy Days*.

Many fans are rather unkind to *Lost in Space* because it lacks the "sophistication" of *Star Trek* and usually reduces the sci-fi genre to the stereotypical ray gun shootouts and bug-eyed monster clichés. Actually, time has been a lot kinder to *Lost* than it has to the original *Trek*. *Lost in Space* was silly in the '60s and it remains consistently silly when seen today, while *Trek* looked a lot more intellectual thirty years ago and now often comes off pompous and forced. I loved *Lost in Space* as a kid and still have a soft spot for it now; it's certainly Irwin's best sci-fi TV series and even at its worst has a lovable cheesiness that always makes it fun to watch, you bubble-headed boobies. "Oh, the pain, the pain!"

ALL THAT GLITTERS

★★☆ 1966. Dir: Harry Harris. Guest cast: Werner Klemperer, Larry Ward.

A runaway space criminal (Ward) gifts Dr. Smith with a mysterious necklace that gives him a platinum touch. Routine episode enlivened by Klemperer (Colonel Klink on *Hogan's Heroes*) as a bounty hunter after the fugitive, as well as by an emphasis on the friendship between Smith and Penny rather than the usual Smith-Will-Robot triangle.

ANDROID MACHINE, THE

★★★ 1966. Dir: Don Richardson. Guest cast: Dee Hartford, Fritz Feld, Tiger Joe Marsh.

Hartford is great as Verda the android, accidentally ordered up from an intergalactic vending machine by Dr. Smith. One of season two's most enjoyable shows, this was popular enough to be followed by a sequel, *Revolt of the Androids*. The first of several appearances by mouth-popping veteran character actor Feld as Mr. Zumdish.

ANTI-MATTER MAN, THE

★★★★ 1967. Dir: Sutton Roley.

One of the highlights of the third season, this episode was an obvious attempt to give star Williams something new and different to do. An accidental dimensional shift between the matter and antimatter worlds brings an evil double of Professor Robinson to menace the family. Imaginative direction and a nicely shaded performance from Williams—in his best work since the season one ender "Follow the Leader"—make this a winner.

ASTRAL TRAVELER, THE

★★ 1967. Dir: Don Richardson. Guest cast: Sean McClory, Dawson Palmer.

Will and Dr. Smith discover a dimensional revolving door that transports them to a haunted Scottish castle. A subpar episode helped a bit by McClory's robust acting as the bagpipe-playing ghost.

ATTACK OF THE MONSTER PLANTS

★★☆ 1966. Dir: Justus Addiss.

A sequel to *The Space Croppers*, though actually broadcast first, finds the Robinsons' planet overrun by mutant plants—one of which creates an evil double for Judy. Kristen gets a rare chance to shine as the bad Judy, whose final fate isn't even explained in this sometimes creepy story resembling *Invasion of the Body Snatchers* and *Day of the Triffids*.

BLAST OFF INTO SPACE

★★★☆ 1966. Dir: Nathan Juran. Guest cast: Strother Martin, Dawson Palmer.

The first show of the second season starts things off with a bang as the Robinsons' planet is destroyed by a series of natural catastrophes and the family has to escape—too bad Dr. Smith sold some of their fuel to a space miner (a great role for guest star Martin) for some life-giving substance called cosmonium. The apocalyptic climax is most impressive.

CASTLES IN SPACE

★★ 1967. Dir: Sobey Martin. Guest cast: Alberto Monte, Corinna Tsopei.

An odd, mostly actionless episode about outer space bandito Monte trying to claim from the Robinson party the frozen-in-suspended-animation body of princess Tsopei. Monte's spirited performance (he calls the robot "El Toro") saves this otherwise bland concoction.

CAVE OF THE WIZARDS

★★★ 1967. Dir: Don Richardson.

A weird but memorable episode in which Dr. Smith is taken over and mutated by an alien power that wants him as the new leader for an alien society. The ending, where Will Robinson cries when he thinks he's lost his friend forever, is surprisingly moving—surprising when you consider that the kid is bawling over a guy in blue face makeup and glitter mascara.

CHALLENGE, THE

★★★ 1966. Dir: Don Richardson. Guest cast: Michael Ansara, Kurt Russell.

Ansara and Russell are father and son aliens who challenge Professor Robinson and Will to a series of mental and physical competitions. A solid first-season episode highlighted with the rarely explored relationship between father John and son Will.

CHANGE OF SPACE, A

★☆ 1966. Dir: Sobey Martin. Guest cast: Frank Graham.

At Dr. Smith's urging, Will takes a ride in an alien spacecraft (looking much like the diving bell from *Voyage to the Bottom of the Sea*) and returns from the trip an intellectual giant. When Smith takes the sojourn himself, he becomes a decrepit old man. One of season one's weakest shows, with little to recommend.

COLLISION OF THE PLANETS

★ 1967. Dir: Don Richardson. Guest cast: Dan Travanti, Linda Gaye Scott, Joey Tata.

A bunch of antisocial alien bikers must redeem themselves in their society by destroying a planetoid on a collision course with their home world. Unfortunately, said planetoid is now the home of the Robinsons. Only an early appearance by *Hill Street Blues* star Travanti as the lead biker makes this abysmal episode worth a look.

COLONISTS, THE

★★ 1967. Dir: Ezra Stone. Guest cast: Francine York.

Equal rights are pushed back to the Stone Age in this early women's lib show about a race of man-hating Amazons enslaving the Robinson men. Naturally, Dr. Smith does everything he can to kiss up to tough-talking Amazon queen York (coming on like Laurie Mitchell in *Queen of Outer Space*). Often amusing, but I don't think Gloria Steinem would find it very funny.

CONDEMNED OF SPACE, THE

★★☆ 1967. Dir: Nathan Juran . Guest cast: Marcel Hillaire.

In the premiere episode of season three, *Jupiter 2* stops off at a space station that turns out to be a prison for the most dangerous criminals in the galaxy, who are kept in suspended animation. Hillaire gives a bravura performance as a French-accented baddie with a deadly cat's cradle.

CURSE OF COUSIN SMITH, THE

★★ 1966. Dir: Justus Addiss. Guest cast: Henry Jones.

One of season two's dopiest shows has veteran character actor Jones turning up as Dr. Smith's crooked cousin. In a series of contrivances worthy of Irwin Allen at his best, cousin Smith tries to deal Zach out of a valuable inheritance.

DAY AT THE ZOO, A

★★☆ 1967. Dir: Irving J. Moore. Guest cast: Leonard Stone, Gary Tigerman.

Stone makes the first of two appearances as intergalactic showman Farnum-B, who imprisons several of the Robinson party in his space zoo. Another showcase for Cartwright as Penny Robinson, who develops a nice friendship with the rascally Farnum.

DEADLIEST OF THE SPECIES, THE

★★★ 1967. Dir: Don Richardson. Guest cast: Ronald Gans, Sue England, Lyle Waggoner, Ralph Lee.

The robot falls in love with a female alien robot—who happens to be bent on the Robinson's destruction. As corny as it sounds, this mechanical love story comes off surprisingly well—though you never find out what happens to the reprogrammed lady robot at the end.

DEADLY GAMES OF GAMMA 6, THE

★★☆ 1966. Dir: Nathan Juran. Guest cast: Mike Kellin, Peter Brocco, Harry Monty, Ronald Weber.

Dr. Smith is tricked into entering the boxing arena with an invisible alien. If Smith loses the match, Earth will be destroyed. Kellin is good as the sinister alien promoter and there are some well-staged fight scenes in this fun episode.

DERELICT, THE

★★★ 1965. Dir: Alex Singer. Guest cast: Dawson Palmer, Don Forbes.

Driven far off course, the *Jupiter 2* stops off at a huge alien spacecraft inhabited by hibernating bloblike creatures. This second episode to air has Dr. Smith still a hard-hearted villain and the robot still little more than a prop, but the aliens are pretty creepy and the model of their ship pretty impressive.

DREAM MONSTER, THE

★★☆ 1967. Dir: Don Richardson. Guest cast: John Abbott, Dawson Palmer.

Abbott is a Dr. Frankenstein-like alien scientist who drains the Robinsons' emotions to make his android creation more human. Of course, this process leaves the Robinsons less human. Likable performance from veteran character actor Abbott.

FLAMING PLANET, THE

★★ 1968. Dir: Don Richardson. Guest cast: Abraham Sofaer.

No, it's not *Priscilla, Queen of the Desert*, but a world inhabited by the last member of a warrior race (well played by Sofaer), who wants the Robinsons as partners in an endless series of war games. The subplot about Dr. Smith's houseplant becoming a monster is dumb, but it has a good payoff.

FLIGHT INTO THE FUTURE

★★☆ 1967. Dir: Sobey Martin. Guest cast: Lew Gallo, Don Einer.

Dr. Smith, Will, and the robot end up on a planet where illusions of the future are manufactured. The robot sees himself replicated as a heroic statue; Smith is branded a coward by a surly descendant; and Will encounters sister Judy's great granddaughter. Eerie scenes of a derelict *Jupiter 2* make this episode interesting.

FOLLOW THE LEADER

★★★☆ 1966. Dir: Don Richardson. Guest cast: Gregory Morton.

Professor Robinson is trapped in an underground crypt, where he is possessed by the spirit of an evil alien entity (voiced by Morton) and plots to kill his entire family after manufacturing enough fuel for a successful takeoff. Williams is in good form as the possessed professor and young Mumy outstanding in his final scene—pleading for the return of his true dad as the bewitched Robinson tries to kill him. Ironically, the machine manufactured by the possessed Robinson led to the castaways obtaining enough detronium for a successful blastoff at the start of the next season.

FORBIDDEN WORLD, THE

★★★ 1966. Dir: Don Richardson. Guest cast: Wally Cox, Janos Prohaska.

The Robinsons crash on another alien planet, this one inhabited by a lonely alien (Cox) and his birdlike companion (Prohaska in a monster suit that originally appeared on the *Outer Limits* episode *The Duplicate Man*). Dr. Smith foolishly drinks what he thinks is alien wine but is actually a powerful liquid explosive. This episode sets the stage for the rest of the second season; it's funny and imaginative and has just the right touch of dark humor to make it work.

FUGITIVES IN SPACE

★★★★ 1968. Dir: Ezra Stone. Guest cast: Michael Conrad, Tol Avery, Charles Horvath.

One of the very best from year three has Don and Dr. Smith imprisoned for allegedly helping a werewolflike alien criminal (*Hill Street Blues'* Conrad ["Be Careful Out There"] in great makeup). Later everyone escapes and is pursued by the authorities. Good fun and genuinely exciting in places, with some nice touches: the robot bakes an explosives-containing cake for the prisoners, and Smith saves Don's life!

GALAXY GIFT, THE

★★★☆ 1967. Dir: Ezra Stone. Guest cast: John Carradine, Jim Mills.

A friendly alien called Arcon (a bald-pated Carradine, looking like a skinny Tor Johnson) gives Penny a magical amulet sought by the Saticons, aliens first seen in the *Wreck of the Robot* episode. The Saticons convince Dr. Smith that they will return him to Earth if he gives them the amulet but he, Penny, the robot, and Debbie the Bloop end up in a facsimile of San Francisco's Chinatown instead. One of year two's best shows, with Carradine bringing a nice sense of theatricality to his role, and a nice role for Penny.

GHOST IN SPACE

★★★ 1966. Dir: Don Richardson. Guest cast: Dawson Palmer.

An effectively atmospheric horror episode has Dr. Smith convinced that the invisible creature terrorizing the Robinsons is actually the ghost of his Uncle Thaddeus. Everyone gets to change their clothes in this episode and the creature, when it materializes, is pretty creepy, but as ever this belongs to the wonderful Jonathan Harris.

GHOST PLANET, THE

★★★ 1966. Dir: Nathan Juran. Guest cast: Michael Fox, Sue England.

Dr. Smith is tricked into landing the *Jupiter 2* on a misty, cyborg-inhabited planet, believing it to be Earth. An exciting episode with some nice set design; the missile that strikes the *Jupiter* at the climax effectively crippled the ship for the rest of the second season.

GIRL FROM THE GREEN DIMENSION, THE

★★☆ 1967. Dir: Nathan Juran. Guest cast: Vitina Marcus, Harry Raybould.

Athena the green girl from *Wild Adventure* returns to renew her crush on Dr. Smith, while her brutish green boyfriend just wants to crush Smith—period. Another comic episode with Marcus lighter-than-air as Athena.

GOLDEN MAN, THE

★★★★ 1966. Dir: Don Richardson. Guest cast: Dennis Patrick, Ronald Gans, Bill Troy.

One of the best episodes from year two, this parable about prejudice stars a smiling Patrick (later a regular on both *Dark Shadows* and *Dallas*) as a charming golden-skinned alien who easily charms Dr. Smith into handing over the Robinsons' weaponry to help him in his war against a hostile and rude froglike creature. Of course, Patrick is really a hideous monster with a face like a dried-up turnip and Penny discovers that the frog guy is really quite a nice chap. Great moments include Smith and Penny climbing under barbed wire made of sparkling Christmas tree lights and Patrick rescuing Judy from a mine field with the "mines" played by colorful beach balls.

GREAT VEGETABLE REBELLION, THE

★ 1968. Dir: Don Richardson. Guest cast: Stanley Adams, Jim Millholin.

In *Lost's* most infamous episode, the Robinsons are trapped on a planet overrun with vegetation. A big carrot man (Adams) tries to turn Dr. Smith into a stalk of celery and Penny into a bouquet of flowers. It's bad, all right, but at least it's funny.

HAUNTED LIGHTHOUSE, THE

★★☆ 1967. Dir: Sobey Martin. Guest cast: Woodrow

Parfey, Lou Wagner, Kenya Coburn.

Penny befriends an alien teen called J5 (Wagner), who, unbeknownst to the Robinsons, has the power to create illusions and has an invisible cat as a pet. J5 joins the Robinsons on their journey, which takes them to a derelict space lighthouse commanded by a befuddled Parfey. Wagner is annoying but Parfey touching as the lonely lighthouse keeper; both turned up the next year in *Planet of the Apes*.

HIS MAJESTY SMITH
★★ 1966. Dir: Harry Harris. Guest cast: Liam Sullivan, Kevin Hagen.

Minor but often funny episode with Dr. Smith chosen as the new leader of an alien race—little realizing that he is being set up as a sacrifice to their gods.

HUNGRY SEA, THE
★★★ 1965. Dir: Sobey Martin.

Continuing their journey across their new planet in the Chariot, the Robinsons are beset by earthquakes, floods, and wild temperature changes. A solid early episode, with Dr. Smith showing a first sign of humanity when he sends the robot after the Robinsons to warn them about the planet's strange orbit pattern.

HUNTER'S MOON
★★ 1967. Dir: Don Richardson. Guest cast: Vincent Beck.

The Most Dangerous Game, Irwin Allen style, as Professor Robinson is stalked by an alien hunter called Megazor (Beck). Beck also played a surly alien in the camp classic *Santa Claus Conquers the Martians*.

INVADERS FROM THE FIFTH DIMENSION
★★★☆ 1965. Dir: Leonard Horn. Guest cast: Joe Ryan, Ted Lehmann.

Creepy, mouthless aliens needing a human brain to pilot their ship force Dr. Smith to get them one by encasing his neck in a glowing ring that will tighten and strangle him if he does not obey. One of the best shows from year one, with plentiful atmosphere courtesy of director Horn.

ISLAND IN THE SKY
★★★★ 1965. Dirs: Tony Leader, Irwin Allen.

Professor Robinson investigates a planet via jet-pack to see if it is habitable and disappears. Major West then crash lands the *Jupiter 2* on the planet, where they would remain for the rest of the first season. An effective reworking of elements from the original pilot, this has action

and suspense and a great scene of the *Jupiter* swooping low over the desert canyon before it crashes. This episode also introduces Debbie the Bloop—an alien chimp with antenna.

JUNKYARD IN SPACE
★★ 1968. Dir: Ezra Stone. Guest cast: Marcel Hillaire.

The final episode lands the *Jupiter 2* on a junk planet, where Dr. Smith sells the robot for scrap in return for food when the Robinsons' supplies run low. Hillaire, seen before in *The Condemned of Space*, plays the robotic junkman who commandeers the *Jupiter* for his own purposes.

KEEPER, THE
★★★★ 1966. Dir: Sobey Martin. Guest cast: Michael Rennie, Wilbur Evans.

Lost's only two-parter guest stars the sublime Rennie as the title character who travels the universe gathering specimens of all life-forms. Of course Dr. Smith is easily talked into handing over Will and Penny with a promise of a return trip to Earth. The mass escape of monsters from the Keeper's ship is a great scene (even though it seems like it's the same four monsters trundling by over and over) but the climactic attack on the Chariot by a gigantic spider is too silly for words. Rennie earlier appeared with Harris on the *Third Man* TV series.

KIDNAPPED IN SPACE
★★ 1967. Dir: Don Richardson. Guest cast: Grant Sullivan, Carol Williams, Joey Russo.

The Robinson party is kidnapped by time-manipulating aliens who want the robot to repair their damaged mechanical leader. Routine but for a scene where Dr. Smith, tinkering with an alien time device, accidentally transforms himself into a little kid.

LOST CIVILIZATION, THE
★★☆ 1966. Dir: Don Richardson. Guest cast: Royal Dano, Kym Karath.

Although there are several episodes in which the Robinson women and Dr. Smith are left on their own, this is the only time the Robinson men have an adventure without the ladies. Will discovers a lost underground kingdom where he awakens a young princess with a kiss and an evil Major Domo plans to conquer the planet with an army of frozen soldiers. An offbeat show with touches of fairy tales and old serials.

MAGIC MIRROR, THE
★★★ 1966. Dir: Nathan Juran. Guest cast: Michael J. Pollard, Dawson Palmer.

A sort of intergalactic Peter Pan (Pollard)—an ageless boy living in an alternate universe behind an ornate old mirror—pursues Penny to join him as a companion. Another good Penny show, with Pollard his usual spacey self.

MECHANICAL MEN, THE
★★ 1967. Dir: Seymour Robbie.

This totally goofed out segment features dozens of tiny mechanical men (looking for all the world like toy versions of the Robinson robot—and most likely they were) who switch the personalities (and voices) of the robot and Dr. Smith to create the perfect leader. See this one and you still won't believe it.

MUTINY IN SPACE
★☆ 1967. Dir: Don Richardson. Guest cast: Ronald Long.

Will, Dr. Smith, and the robot are shanghaied by the crazed Admiral Zahrk, (Long) who forces them to pilot his spacecraft in search of his mutinous crew. Exceptionally dumber than usual apart from an enjoyably over-the-top turn by Long.

MY FRIEND, MR. NOBODY
★★★★ 1965. Dir: Paul Stanley.

A true classic, this is highlighted by a sensitive Angela Cartwright performance as Penny befriends an invisible alien entity she calls Mr. Nobody. Meanwhile, Dr. Smith tricks Don into blasting for dutronium in an area he knows is actually encrusted with diamonds. The climax, where Mr. Nobody goes on a destructive rampage after Penny has been injured by an explosion, is especially exciting.

OASIS, THE
★★ 1965. Dir: Sutton Roley.

Kicked out of the Robinson encampment after one screwup too many, Dr. Smith sets up his own camp in an area where some alien fruit transforms him into a giant. Mediocre first-season episode with only Jon Harrison's acting to recommend.

ONE OF OUR DOGS IS MISSING
★★★☆ 1965. Dir: Sutton Roley. Guest cast: Dawson Palmer.

Another great Dr. Smith and the ladies episode. While Will and the other men are away, Smith and the Robinson women discover a crashed space capsule containing a NASA lab dog. Meanwhile, an apelike monster with designs on Judy (it's lonely out there in space,

you see) is on the prowl. Lots of fun, with a terrific action climax, but just one question: whatever happened to the dog?

PHANTOM FAMILY, THE
★★☆ 1967. Dir: Ezra Stone. Guest cast: Alan Hewitt.

An alien scientist with a face like a crusty lobster (Hewitt) constructs duplicates of Don, Dr. Smith, Judy, and Penny and instructs a reluctant Will to train them to be human.

PRINCESS OF SPACE
★★☆ 1968. Dir: Don Richardson. Guest cast: Robert Foulk, Arte Johnson, Sheila Mathews.

It's *Anastasia, Lost in Space* style as an alien (Foulk) tries to pass Penny off as a missing princess she resembles. An okay Penny show, with good work from future *Laugh-In* star Johnson and future Mrs. Irwin Allen Mathews.

PRISONERS OF SPACE
★★★ 1966. Dir: Nathan Juran. Guest cast: Dawson Palmer.

The Robinsons are held by an intergalactic tribunal for crimes they've allegedly committed against various alien life-forms. A good, economic episode reusing much footage and monsters from earlier shows. And the capper is legitimately funny.

PROMISED PLANET, THE
★★ 1968. Dir: Ezra Stone. Guest cast: Gil Rogers, Keith Taylor.

This really weird one has the Robinsons finally arriving at what they believe to be Alpha Centauri. It's really an alien base, however, populated by go-go dancing teens whose effeminate leader (Rogers) wants Will and Penny to join them. Dr. Smith in a Beatle wig is not a sight easily forgotten.

QUESTING BEAST, THE
★★ 1967. Dir: Don Richardson. Guest cast: Hans Conreid, Jeff County, Sue England.

A decent idea gets cheesy handling as Will befriends an aging outer space knight (Conreid) who talks of valor, bravery, and honor. But Will loses his faith when the knight turns out to be a phony coward, while the talking female dragon he's after seems to embody all the qualities the knight espouses. The crummy dragon suit really hurts.

RAFT, THE
★☆ 1965. Dir: Sobey Martin. Guest cast: Dawson Palmer.

The Robinsons build an escape vessel stolen by

Dr. Smith, who ends up stranded with Will on the other side of the planet, where they're menaced by a raggy vegetable monster. The silly monster suit returned several times and later turned up on the *Night Gallery* episode "Brenda."

RELUCTANT STOWAWAY, THE
★★★★ 1965. Dirs: Tony Leader, Irwin Allen. Guest cast: Fred Crane, Tom Allen, Don Forbes, Hal Torey.

The first episode is actually the second pilot, using much of the original material (directed by Allen) along with new stuff introducing Dr. Smith and the robot. When Smith programs the robot to destroy the *Jupiter 2* soon after liftoff, he's trapped on board and his added weight drives the ship off course. Full of tension and drama, it's genuinely surprising, in light of later shows, to see Smith karate chop a security guard and then cold-bloodedly dump his body out an escape hatch.

RETURN FROM OUTER SPACE
★★★ 1965. Dir: Nathan Juran. Guest cast: Reta Shaw, Donald Loseby, Walter Sande, Sheila Mathews, Keith Taylor, Robert Easton.

The first *Lost in Space* Christmas show (though actually broadcast several days after the holiday) has Will using the matter transmitter left behind by the aliens from "The Sky is Falling" to transport himself back to Earth. He ends up in a small New England town (looking like something out of *It's a Wonderful Life*) where no one, save one other kid (Loseby) will believe Will when he tells them who he is and where he came from. A nice showcase for Billy Mumy and the first of several appearances (in a variety of roles) of later Irwin Allen wife Mathews.

REVOLT OF THE ANDROIDS
★★★★ 1967. Dir: Don Richardson. Guest cast: Dee Hartford, Don Matheson, Dawson Palmer.

In this excellent sequel to "The Android Machine," a more human Verda (Hartford) returns to the Robinsons, pursued by another android called IDAK (Matheson, later a regular on Irwin Allen's *Land of the Giants*) sent to return her to the Celestial Department Store. One of the second season's finest hours, with a wonderful performance from Hartford and some terrific dialogue (IDAK: "Crush, kill, destroy!" Smith to Verda: "Whisper sweet, oily little nothings into his ear. Lure him away with promises of delicious diodes.").

ROCKET TO EARTH
★☆ 1967. Dir: Don Richardson. Guest cast: Al Lewis.

Even the presence of the always-good-for-a-laugh Lewis can't help this silly trifle about an alien magician with a living ventriloquist's dummy who tries to help Dr. Smith return home.

SKY IS FALLING, THE
★★★ 1965. Dir: Sobey Martin. Guest cast: Don Matheson, Francoise Ruggieri, Eddie Rosson.

Another solid episode about prejudice and not judging a book by its cover. In this case, Dr. Smith automatically assumes that a visiting alien family called Taurons are a menace even after Will befriends their young son.

SKY PIRATE, THE
★★☆ 1966. Dir: Sobey Martin. Guest cast: Albert Salmi.

Salmi gives a rascally performance as space scoundrel Alonzo P. Tucker, who impresses Will with his stories of adventure and Dr. Smith with the hope that his ship may be a way back to Earth. Salmi would return as Tucker in "Treasure of the Lost Planet".

SPACE BEAUTY
★★★★ 1968. Dir: Irving J. Moore. Guest cast: Leonard Stone, Dee Hartford, Miriam Schiller.

A must for fans of Judy Robinson—and who isn't? Farnum-B (Stone) returns with a beauty contest scam and Judy is soon signed up. Naturally she wins, but discovers almost too late that her prize is to spend eternity as the bride of the contest's sponsor—a satanic figure who's little more than a suit of armor filled with fire. One of my favorites, with Hartford making a welcome return, this time playing Farnum's right-hand-girl Nancy Pi Squared. Look for the dragon from "The Questing Beast" as one of the contestants!

SPACE CIRCUS
★★★ 1966. Dir: Harry Harris. Guest cast: James Westerfield, Melinda Fee, Michael Greene, Harry Vartresian, Dawson Palmer.

The Robinsons are visiting by an intergalactic one-ring show that wants to take Will away with them when he demonstrates heretofore unknown psychic abilities. A colorful second-season show with good roles for the blustery Westerfield and pretty Fee.

SPACE CREATURE, THE
★★★☆ 1967. Dir: Sobey Martin.

A very scary episode inspired by Agatha Christie's *Ten Little Indians*. One by one the Robinson party vanish from the in-flight *Jupiter*

2 until only Will and a ghostly figure that lives off fear are left. The first and only appearance of the *Jupiter*'s power core is featured.

SPACE CROPPERS, THE
★★★ 1966. Dir: Sobey Martin. Guest cast: Mercedes McCambridge, Sherry Jackson, Dawson Palmer.

Alien hillbillies arrive to plant a crop of monster plants. The mother (*Exorcist* demon voice McCambridge) is romanced by Dr. Smith (who sees her as a way off the planet); the sexy daughter (Jackson) makes a play for Don; and the son (Palmer, for once without heavy make-up—most of the time) is a werewolf! Odd to see the distinguished McCambridge in this silly but fun combo of *Lil' Abner* and *The Wolf Man*.

SPACE DESTRUCTORS, THE
★★★★ 1967. Dir: Don Richardson. Guest cast: Tommy Farrell.

The classic Dr. Smith android episode features the good doctor uncovering a machine that manufactures cyborgs, all of which he programs to sport his own face. One of the series' most memorable episodes; the scenes of Will transformed into a Smith look-alike are positively horrifying and Jonathan Harris's final speech is genuinely touching.

SPACE FAMILY ROBINSON, THE
★★★★ 1965. Dir: Irwin Allen.

Never seen publicly until the advent of video and cable TV, this is the original, unaired pilot, sans Dr. Smith, the robot, and much of the humor of the later episodes. In 1997, the Robinson family and Major West are put into suspended animation for a five-year trip to the star system of Alpha Centauri. A malfunction in the *Jupiter 2*'s guidance system forces the party to crash land on a hostile alien planet inhabited by strange animals and cyclopean giants. The seriousness of the approach used here is almost shocking when contrasted to the foolishness of some of the broadcast episodes. Much of the background music is taken from Bernard Herrmann's score for *The Day the Earth Stood Still*.

SPACE PRIMEVALS, THE
★★ 1967. Dir: Nathan Juran. Guest cast: Arthur Batanides.

The Robinsons set down on yet another uncharted planet, this one inhabited by primitives ruled by an omnipotent computer (an idea often used on *Star Trek*, which may have inspired this episode). Forgettable apart from a great scene where Dr. Smith saves Don's life and as the hostilities melt away they reveal a surprising mutual affection—no wonder Don and Judy never got married!

SPACE TRADER, THE
★★★ 1966. Dir: Nathan Juran. Guest cast: Torin Thatcher.

Juran favorite Thatcher (*The Seventh Voyage of Sinbad*) gives a flamboyant performance as the title character, an alien dealer in goods of all kinds. What he wants from the Robinsons is just one thing—Dr. Smith!

SPACE VIKINGS, THE
★★☆ 1967. Dir: Ezra Stone. Guest cast: Sheila Mathews, Bern Hoffman.

Another over-the-top second seasoner with plenty of laughs as Will, Dr. Smith, and the robot encounter the Norse god Thor (Hoffman) and a singing Valkyrie (Mathews) who rides a winged horse.

TARGET: EARTH
★★★ 1968. Dir: Nathan Juran. Guest cast: James Gosa, Brent Davis.

Bloblike aliens duplicate the Robinsons as part of a plot to invade Earth. Will and Dr. Smith thwart the plan and finally make it back to Earth—for about ten seconds. A good year-three show, with a subtle *Invaders* in-joke for the observant.

THERE WERE GIANTS IN THE EARTH
★★★★ 1965. Dirs: Leo Penn, Irwin Allen. Guest cast: Dawson Palmer.

The Robinsons discover that their new home planet is about to be plunged into a deadly winter season. Fleeing south (all but Dr. Smith and the robot), our heroes find the way of their land rover, the Chariot, blocked by huge Cyclops monsters. Great special FX in this classic show made up in part from footage from the original pilot.

THIEF FROM OUTER SPACE, THE
★★☆ 1966. Dir: Sobey Martin. Guest cast: Malachi Throne, Ted Cassidy, Maxine Gates.

Will encounters an outer space Ali Baba (a flashy Throne turn) out to discover the whereabouts of a missing princess. This started the *Lost* trend away from sci-fi into pure fantasy and is more enjoyable than most, with a good role for Cassidy (the erstwhile Lurch) as Throne's put-upon slave.

TIME MERCHANT, THE
★★★★ 1968. Dir: Ezra Stone. Guest cast: John Crawford, Byron Morrow, Hoke Howell.

Another classic, with Crawford as an alien tinkerer in time who returns Dr. Smith to Earth just before the launch of the *Jupiter 2*. When it is discovered that Smith's extra weight actually saved the *Jupiter* from destruction by collision with an asteroid, the robot follows Smith to persuade him to let history repeat itself and once again become a reluctant stowaway. A clever, well-written later episode; Crawford has fun as the sarcastic time merchant.

TOYMAKER, THE

★☆ 1967. Dir: Robert Douglas. Guest cast: Walter Burke, Fritz Feld, Tiger Joe Marsh, Larry Dean, Dawson Palmer.

Dr. Smith, Will, and the robot end up as prisoners in the Celestial Department Store's toy department. Bland Christmas episode actually not shown until January 1967.

TREASURE OF THE LOST PLANET

★★★ 1967. Dir: Harry Harris. Guest cast: Albert Salmi, Jim Boles, Craig Duncan, Dawson Palmer.

Tucker the pirate (Salmi) returns and persuades Will and Dr. Smith to join him and a trio of mutant cutthroats in search of a buried treasure, guided on their way by a talking severed head in a box. Weird but fun, with a high alien body count and influences from the B movie *The Thing that Couldn't Die*.

TRIP THROUGH THE ROBOT

★★★★ 1967. Dir: Don Richardson.

Fantastic Voyage was an obvious inspiration for this one, in which a strange gas renders the robot gigantic and Will and Dr. Smith climb inside him to effect repairs and return him to normal. Totally unlike any other *Lost* episode and all the better for it, with a full array of gadgets to represent the robot's interior.

TWO WEEKS IN SPACE

★★☆ 1967. Dir: Don Richardson. Guest cast: Fritz Feld, Edy Williams, Richard Kirshner, Eric Matthews, Carroll Roebke, Ronald Gans.

One of the goofiest ever, with Dr. Smith turning the *Jupiter* into a hotel for shape-shifting alien tourists who are actually a band of escaped criminals. Feld returns for the last time as Mr. Zumdish; you haven't lived until you've seen Jonathan Harris making nice with busty veteran Russ Meyer starlet Williams.

VISIT TO A HOSTILE PLANET

★★☆ 1967. Dir: Sobey Martin. Guest cast: Robert Foulke, Pitt Herbert, Claire Wilcox, Robert Pine.

The Robinsons finally make it back to Earth, but a time warp has thrown them back in time fifty years and they're mistaken for a UFO. Pretty silly stuff, obviously inspired by a couple of *Star Trek* episodes, with Dr. Smith trying to pass himself off as a visiting fire chief from Chickasaw Falls.

VISIT TO HADES, A

★★★☆ 1966. Dir: Don Richardson. Guest cast: Gerald Mohr.

One of the most memorable *Lost* shows, this has a great performance from Mohr as an alien whom Dr. Smith mistakes for Satan. Mohr traps Smith, Judy, and Don in an underground world the doc thinks is hell, while the devilish alien and Don fight over the lovely Miss Robinson.

WAR OF THE ROBOTS

★★★ 1966. Dir: Sobey Martin.

Robby the robot from *Forbidden Planet* guests as an alien robotoid Will finds and repairs. The robotoid proves to be a helpful companion and even makes the Robinsons' robot jealous but in the end reveals his true evil nature. A good show for robot fans.

WELCOME STRANGER

★★★ 1965. Dir: Alvin Ganzer. Guest cast: Warren Oates.

Oates gives his usual fine performance, as a cowboy-hatted astronaut who lands on the Robinsons' planet; he sees through Dr. Smith almost at once and takes an understandable shine to Miss Judy. Although he prefers bumming around in space, the would-be cowpoke agrees to return Will and Penny to Earth. A good dramatic episode; great Smith line: "Zack? Indeed!"

WEST OF MARS

★★ 1966. Dir: Nathan Juran. Cast: Allan Melvin, Mickey Manners, Ken Mayer, Eddie Quillan.

Jonathan Harris in a dual role and a guest appearance by Melvin (Sam the butcher on *The Brady Bunch*) help this otherwise typically inane genre-bender, with Dr. Smith mistaken for a vicious outer space outlaw by Marshall Melvin.

WILD ADVENTURE

★★☆ 1966. Dir: Don Richardson. Guest cast: Vitina Marcus.

Dr. Smith is nearly lured away from an inflight *Jupiter 2* by Athena (Marcus), a green-skinned space siren who takes nourishment from dutronium. Marcus's sprightly acting sparks this slight installment.

WISH UPON A STAR

★★★★ 1965. Dir: Sutton Roley. Guest cast: Dawson Palmer.

Dr. Smith discovers an alien thought-reading device in the ruins of a strange spacecraft. The machine grants every wish and the good doctor is in heaven—until the device's grotesque, stone-faced owner shows up. Often sighted as one of the series' finest hours; eerily directed and smartly written (by Barney Slater). Jonathan Harris rises to the occasion with one of his best performances.

WRECK OF THE ROBOT

★★ 1966. Dir: Nathan Juran. Guest cast: Jim Mills.

The Saticons—masked aliens wearing long black cloaks and bowler hats—are after the Robinson robot (or "Me-can-i-cal Man" as they call him) as a blueprint for their own destructive robot army. The evil Saticons, who walk like they're always drunk, would return in "The Galaxy Gift."

OUTER LIMITS

MGM/UA, 1963–65. NR, 50 min. per tape.

The Outer Limits has always been one of my favorite TV shows, the result, no doubt, of half-remembered childhood encounters with life-altering episodes like "The Zanti Misfits" with its foot-long, human faced alien ants or "The Mutant" with Warren Oates as the sunnyside-up-eyed title character. The combined effort of executive producer Leslie Stevens and producer Joseph Stefano (the scriptwriter of Alfred Hitchcock's *Psycho*), *Limits* is unique in that it was a mixture of science fiction and gothic horror; its aliens, robots, and space men rubbed shoulders with spooky old houses, misty forests, and dark shadows. The imaginative photography—often the work of Conrad Hall or Kenneth Peach—coupled with literate scripts, solid actors, and intelligent direction, helped make this a rare mix of thoughtfulness and horror; like many anthologies its stories run the gamut from the sublime to the just plain silly but it's never less than interesting and has handily held its own against a high-touted but far less satisfying modern cable incarnation.

ARCHITECTS OF FEAR, THE

★★★ 1963. Dir: Byron Haskin. Cast: Robert Culp, Geraldine Brooks, Leonard Stone, Hal Bokar.

Realizing that the warring factions of the world will never voluntarily come together in peace, scientists decide to unite them via a common enemy by surgically transforming Culp into a hideous creature from space. Though slightly heavy-handed in its message,

this is well acted and directed and the bizarre-looking monster is handled with surprising restraint.

BEHOLD, ECK!

★★ 1964. Dir: Byron Haskin. Cast: Peter Lind Hayes, Joan Freeman, Parley Baer, Jack Wilson.

Silly comic segment with Hayes as an eye specialist who develops a pair of glasses that allow him to see a seemingly friendly race of invisible aliens. This inconsequential number looks like a bad episode of *The Twilight Zone* rather than a *Limits* segment.

BELLERO SHIELD, THE

★★★☆ 1964. Dir: John Brahm. Cast: Martin Landau, Sally Kellerman, Chita Rivera, Neil Hamilton, John Hoyt.

This imaginatively directed episode is like a sci-fi variation on *Macbeth*. Landau is an earnest scientist who creates a lightbridge into space that brings to Earth a glowing alien (Hoyt). The alien's indestructible shield of protection is stolen by Landau's grasping, greedy wife (Kellerman). The talented cast makes the most of their finely drawn characters and intelligent dialogue in one of the series' very best shows.

BORDERLAND, THE

★★ 1963. Dir: Leslie Stevens. Cast: Nina Foch, Peter Mark Richman, Phillip Abbott, Gladys Cooper, Alfred Ryder.

Wealthy Foch and Abbott finance scientist Richman's experiments with a parallel universe where everything is the mirror image of its counterpoint in our world. An uneventful but sometimes interesting story salvaged by its talented cast and the odd good moment-like Richman sticking his left hand into the other dimension and pulling out a right one!

BRAIN OF COLONEL BARHAM, THE

★★ 1965. Dir: Charles Haas. Cast: Grant Williams, Anthony Eisley, Elizabeth Perry, Martin Kosleck.

Routine, uncredited rewrite of Curt Siodmak's novel *Donovan's Brain*, with scientists using an army officer's disembodied brain to pilot an experimental spacecraft and discovering almost too late the officer's psychotic tendencies. A fair later episode of the series.

CHAMELEON, THE

★★★ 1964. Dir: Gerd Oswald. Cast: Robert Duvall, Howard Caine, Henry Brandon, Douglas Henderson.

In a typically fine performance, Duvall is a hardened criminal given one last chance to redeem himself by being physically altered into the replica of aliens who've recently arrived on the Earth. The purpose: to discover if the invaders are friend or foe. Solid segment with an unexpectedly touching ending.

CHILDREN OF SPIDER COUNTRY, THE

★★ 1964. Dir: Leonard Horn. Cast: Lee Kinsolving, Kent Smith, Dabbs Greer, Bennye Gatteys.

Limits goes the Angry Young Man route in this tale of a restless youth (Kinsolving) who turns out to be an alien half breed whose other-worldly dad (Smith) comes to claim him. An intriguing idea that's not especially well handled; the insect-headed, business-suit-wearing Smith is one of the shows silliest "bears"—the term used by the producers for each episode's resident monster.

COLD HANDS, WARM HEART

★★ 1964. Dir: Charles Haas. Cast: William Shatner, Geraldine Brooks, Lloyd Gough, Malachi Throne.

Overacting champ Shatner stars as an astronaut who returns from an orbital flight around Venus and now can't seem to get warm. A dull story with a spooky but superfluous monster and Brooks practically reprising her concerned wife bit from "Architects of Fear."

CONTROLLED EXPERIMENT

★★★ 1963. Dir: Leslie Stevens. Cast: Barry Morse, Carroll O'Connor, Grace Lee Whitney, Robert Fortier.

Sparkling comedy with Morse and O'Connor as Martians who come to Earth to investigate that human phenomenon called murder. Clever writing coupled with a great cast make this a wonderfully entertaining if most atypical episode.

CORPUS EARTHLING

★★★☆ 1963. Dir: Gerd Oswald. Cast: Robert Culp, Salome Jens, Barry Atwater, Ken Renard.

In one of the best, creepiest *Limits*, Culp is a doctor with a metal plate in his head that allows him to overhear a conversation between a pair of icky, rocklike monsters who are plotting to take over the world by possessing human beings. Sounds silly, but the scenes of these "rocks" slithering onto people's hands or faces is real nightmare stuff.

COUNTERWEIGHT

★★☆ 1964. Dir: Paul Stanley. Cast: Michael Constantine, Jacqueline Scott, Larry Ward, Sandy Kenyon, Shary Marshall, Crahan Denton.

A group of people taking part in a simulated space flight are menaced by an alien out to stop man from spreading his corruption to the stars. Well acted but talky; this plays like a sci-fi version of an *Airport* movie with a Jim Danforth-animated monster turning up for the climax.

CRY OF SILENCE

★★☆ 1964. Dir: Charles Haas. Cast: Eddie Albert, June Havoc, Arthur Hunnicutt.

An adequately atmospheric tale about a middle-aged couple (Albert and Havoc) terrorized by an invisible alien life-form that can possess everything from frogs to tumbleweeds. Silly but not without merit.

DEMON WITH A GLASS HAND

★★★★ 1964. Dir: Byron Haskin. Cast: Robert Culp, Arline Martel, Abraham Sofaer, Steve Harris, Rex Holman, Robert Fortier.

Harlan Ellison penned this absorbing tale about a man from the future (Culp) with a robotic glass hand fighting aliens out to interfere with Earth history. One of *Limits'* best; acted with strength and conviction and intricately plotted and thought out—the twist ending may be a bit obvious but that still doesn't detract from its poignancy.

DON'T OPEN TILL DOOMSDAY

★★★☆ 1964. Dir: Gerd Oswald. Cast: Miriam Hopkins, Buck Taylor, Melinda Plowman, John Hoyt, David Frankham, Russell Collins.

Eloping college sweethearts spend the night in the dilapidated bridal suite of the crazed Mrs. Kry (screen veteran Hopkins), who hopes to trap them in a box with an alien blob creature looking for help in blowing up the world. More horror than sci-fi (the plot has all the sense of a really bad dream), this plays like a cross between *Whatever Happened to Baby Jane?* and *The Rocky Horror Picture Show*, with a heavy dose of sexual symbolism and a nuttier-by-the-minute performance from Hopkins.

DUPLICATE MAN, THE

★★☆ 1964. Dir: Gerd Oswald. Cast: Ron Randell, Constance Towers, Sean McClory, Konstantin Shayne, Steven Geray, Mike Lane.

A scientist (Randell) clones himself so that his double can hunt down an escaped alien monster called a Megazoid that the scientist has brought to Earth. Some thoughtful moments about the loss of identity are lost themselves in the middle of a contrived but well-acted storyline, with the Megazoid standing out as one of the series' feeblest "bears." The futuristic hillside house seen here was also prominently featured in the Brian De Palma horror film *Body Double*.

EXPANDING HUMAN, THE

★☆ 1964. Dir: Gerd Oswald. Cast: Skip Homeier, Keith Andes, James Doohan, Barbara Wilkin, Vaughn Taylor, Peter Duryea.

A superdull *Jekyll and Hyde* variant about a murder on a college campus committed by the superstrong, superintelligent alter ego of a professor (Homier) working on a mind-expanding new drug. Homeier does the best he can with a clichéd role and *Star Trek*'s own Scotty (Doohan) turns up as an investigating cop, but this is still one of *Limits'* worst.

FEASIBILITY STUDY, A

★★★ 1964. Dir: Byron Haskin. Cast: Sam Wanamaker, Phyllis Love, David Opatoshu, Joyce Van Patten.

Several city blocks are teleported to a misty alien world for study. Unfortunately, contact with the aliens contaminates the abducted humans and turns them into gooey monsters. One of *Limits'* scariest and most relentlessly downbeat episodes, with great atmosphere and creepy monsters, let down slightly by its pious, unrealistic characters who talk like no one you ever met in your life.

FORMS OF THINGS UNKNOWN, THE

★★★ 1964. Dir: Gerd Oswald. Cast: Vera Miles, Barbara Rush, David McCallum, Sir Cedric Hardwicke, Scott Marlowe.

This offbeat gothic horror tale was actually the pilot for a proposed supernatural spinoff series to be called *The Unknown*. In the *Diabolique*-like opening, two women (Miles and Rush) murder their abusive lover (Marlowe), then stumble into the weird house of an inventor (the spacey McCallum) tinkering with time. All of the acting is good but Hardwicke steals it in one of his last roles, as McCallum's blind but all-seeing old butler.

FUN AND GAMES

★★★☆ 1964. Dir: Gerd Oswald. Cast: Nick Adams, Nancy Malone, Ray Kellogg, Robert Johnson.

One of the series' most memorable episodes, this deals with a chuckling, malevolent alien master of ceremonies (a supremely smarmy Johnson, all big head and long, tapering talons) who stages games of death between the people of different planets. Adams and Malone are the earthlings transported to a swampy planetoid, where they face off against a pair of apelike creatures with razor-tipped boomerangs. If the humans survive, they escape with their lives; if they lose, the Earth will be destroyed. After a talky start this really kicks into gear, with solid performances and some unexpected plot twists.

GALAXY BEING, THE

★★★★ 1963. Dir: Leslie Stevens. Cast: Cliff Robertson, Jacqueline Scott, Lee Phillips, Allyson Ames, William O. Douglas, Jr.

The series' pilot, originally called "Please Stand By," features Robertson as the first of many *Limits'* idealistic loners. Radio station operator Robertson accidentally contacts a light-emitting alien of a similarly curious nature; the basically gentle creature is inadvertently transported to Earth by a power surge. Like many of the series' best shows, this combines philosophical science with gothic-style horror—the alien's climactic stroll down main street is right out of an old Frankenstein or Mummy movie—with imaginative FX and fine acting from Robertson.

GUESTS, THE

★★☆ 1964. Dir: Paul Stanley. Cast: Gloria Grahame, Geoffrey Horne, Luana Anders, Vaughn Taylor, Nellie Burt, Burt Mustin.

Another horror episode, from a story by Charles Beaumont, about a young drifter (Horne) trapped in a Victorian mansion with a group of ageless malcontents and a brain from outer space seeking knowledge of human emotions. Too farfetched to work as anything but fantasy, the confusing story gets by mostly on its supporting players and some dreamy dialogue. Unlike the other episodes in the series, this contains no opening or closing narration.

HUMAN FACTOR, THE

★★☆ 1963. Dir: Abner Biberman. Cast: Harry Guardino, Gary Merrill, Sally Kellerman, Joe de Santis, Ivan Dixon, James B. Sikking.

Good performances propel this somewhat contrived story about the experimental exchange of brainwaves between a psychiatrist and a psychotic army officer, the mind-switch nearly leading to a nuclear catastrophe. Often very much like *The Thing* with its snowbound military base setting but there's more talk than action.

INHERITORS, THE

★★★ 1964. Dir: James Goldstone. Cast: Robert Duvall, Steve Ihnat, Ivan Dixon, Donald Harron, Dee Pollack, James Frawley, Jan Shutan, James Shigeta, Suzanne Cupito [Morgan Brittany], Charles Herbert.

Limits' only two-parter, this concerns four Vietnam vets, altered genetically when struck by bullets containing alien DNA, who band together to take a group of physically and emotionally impaired youngsters to a distant planet. Duvall is excellent as the government agent out to stop them; he assumes that the altered men's motivations must be evil because they are alien. A highlight of the mostly deadweight second season, this *Twilight Zone*-type story has nary a monster in sight.

INVISIBLE ENEMY, THE
★★ 1964. Dir: Byron Haskin. Cast: Adam West, Rudy Solari, Peter Marko, Robert DoQui, Joe Maross, Ted Knight.

An Earth ship investigates the disappearance of the first manned mission to Mars that fell victim to sharklike monsters living beneath the planet's sandy surface. A modestly suspenseful but poorly realized story with some nifty Jim Danforth animation, an opening FX shot lifted from *It! The Terror from Beyond Space,* and West in his last pre-*Batman* role.

INVISIBLES, THE
★★★ 1964. Dir: Gerd Oswald. Cast: Don Gordon, Tony Mordente, George Macready, Neil Hamilton, Dee Hartford, Richard Dawson.

Alien parasites control government officials and military leaders in this well-written (by Joseph Stefano) mix of spy versus spy and sci-fi/horror. Exemplary casting and direction in this tale that resembles *Invasion of the Body Snatchers* and *Puppetmasters.*

I, ROBOT
★★☆ 1964. Dir: Leon Benson. Cast: Howard DaSilva, Leonard Nimoy, Marianna Hill, Read Morgan, Ford Rainey, John Hoyt, Peter Brocco, Robert Sorrells.

Based on the first of Otto Binder's famous *Adam Link* stories, this reasonably well done segment concerns a robot (Morgan in an amazingly clunky costume) on trial for the murder of its creator. A sci-fi *Inherit the Wind* with blatant *Frankenstein* references, this has a good cast but talks your ear off. The only episode of the original series, thus far, to be remade for the new *Outer Limits* show, with Nimoy returning and his son directing.

IT CRAWLED OUT OF THE WOODWORK
★★★ 1963. Dir: Gerd Oswald. Cast: Scott Marlowe, Michael Forest, Kent Smith, Barbara Luna, Edward Asner, Joan Camden.

Scientists at a research institute create a powerful creature of pure, shapeless energy with the ability to revive the dead as electric zombies. A Stephen King favorite, this doesn't make much dramatic sense but has a great cast—Asner (pre-*Mary Tyler Moore Show*) is best as a no-nonsense cop—and some truly frightening moments.

KEEPER OF THE PURPLE TWILIGHT
★★☆ 1964. Dir: Charles Haas. Cast: Warren Stevens, Robert Webber, Gail Kobe, Curt Conway, Edward C. Platt, Mike Lane.

An extraterrestrial in human form steals the emotions of an earth scientist in order to better understand the human race—as a prelude to invasion. Good acting from Webber as the alien and some effective makeup make this one of the more watchable second-season shows.

MAN WHO WAS NEVER BORN, THE
★★★★ 1963. Dir: Leonard Horn. Cast: Martin Landau, Shirley Knight, John Considine, Karl Held, Maxine Stuart.

An astronaut is accidentally projected into the future where a hideously deformed mutant called Andro (Landau) tells of a devastating nuclear war that will befall mankind at the end of the twentieth century. Andro travels back in time to prevent the inevitable, unexpectedly falling in love with the mother (Knight) of the yet-to-be-born scientist who triggers the apocalypse. *Limits'* finest hour, this intricately—if not always believably—crafted mixture of sci-fi, horror, and fairy tale is beautifully acted, directed, photographed, and scored, with many quotable lines of dialogue and a haunting downbeat ending. An obvious inspiration for the original *Terminator.*

MAN WITH THE POWER, THE
★★☆ 1963. Dir: Laslo Benedek. Cast: Donald Pleasence, Priscilla Morrill, Edward C. Platt, Fred Bier, John Marley, Frank Maxwell.

Halloween veteran Pleasence is well cast as a middle-aged milquetoast given destructive tele-kinetic powers by a NASA experiment in mind control. Not unexpectedly, Don's hidden resentments against his wife, boss, and others soon take their disastrous toll. Routine episode enlivened by its cast and an interesting, unspoken gay subtext in Pleasance's relationship with a handsome, friendly young astronaut (Bier) also scheduled for a telekinetic brain implant.

MICE, THE
★★ 1964. Dir: Alan Crosland, Jr. Cast: Henry Silva, Diana Sands, Ronald Foster, Don Ross, Gene Tyburn, Hugh Langtry.

An experimental life-form exchange between the Earth and the planet Chromo masks an insidious alien invasion plot. An especially icky monster and top-drawer performance from Silva as a convicted murderer chosen for the life-form exchange—is it any wonder they're sending us monsters when we're sending them murderers?—enhance this otherwise unexceptional episode. Sands as a black heroine was another nice touch for the time but she's too underused to make much of an impact.

MOONSTONE

★★ 1964. Dir: Robert Florey. Cast: Ruth Roman, Alex Nicol, Tim O'Connor, Curt Conway, Hari Rhodes.

Earth scientists and military men stationed at a research lab on the moon discover a glowing globe containing benevolent aliens being pursued by larger, deadlier life-forms. A remarkably atmospheric but dramatically flat episode saved by its striking moonscapes and a good performance from Roman.

MUTANT, THE

★★☆ 1964. Dir: Alan Crosland, Jr. Cast: Warren Oates, Larry Pennell, Betsy Jones-Moreland, Walter Burke, Robert Sampson, Richard Derr.

Oates is the infamous guy with the fried egg eyes in this middling adventure. On an outpost on a distant world where there is no night, Oates is mutated by a strange, silvery rain that gives him mind-reading abilities, a lethal touch, and really big peepers. Awkward but well acted by Oates (who brings nice shadings of humor and pathos to his monster role) and Burke; look for a cameoing "Zanti Misfit" in the cave scene.

NIGHTMARE

★★★☆ 1963. Dir: John Erman. Cast: Ed Nelson, Martin Sheen, James Shigeta, David Frankham, John Anderson, Whit Bissell.

The perfect title for one of *Limits'* most frightening shows. Earth is at war with a race of Satanic-looking aliens called Ebonites who capture a group of soldiers and play torturous mind games on them. A harrowing, well-acted, and intelligently written (by Joseph Stefano) and directed drama marred only by a rather difficult to swallow third-act twist. The Ebonites are among the most-literally-hellish creatures ever conceived for TV.

O.B.I.T.

★★★ 1963. Dir: Gerd Oswald. Cast: Peter Breck, Jeff Corey, Alan Baxter, Harry Townes, Joanne Gilbert, Konstantin Shayne.

A newly developed military observation device accidentally spies on a scientist being murdered—by a one-eyed alien monster! But who's manipulating whom—and for what purpose? An undeservedly underrated episode with good work from Corey and a memorable cyclopean monster that later turned up on an episode of *The Munsters*.

ONE HUNDRED DAYS OF THE DRAGON, THE

★★☆ 1963. Dir: Byron Haskin. Cast: Sidney Blackmer, Phillip Pine, Nancy Rennick, Joan Camden, Richard Loo, Mark Roberts.

The newly elected president of the United States turns out to be a Chinese Communist agent whose face and body have been altered by an experimental new drug. A silly but entertaining early episode echoing everything from *The Manchurian Candidate* to *Black Dragons*.

PREMONITION, THE

★☆ 1965. Dir: Gerd Oswald. Cast: Dewey Martin, Mary Murphy, William Bramley, Emma Tyson, Kay Kuter.

A test pilot and his wife become trapped outside time in some sort of limbo world; taking advantage of the situation they manage to rescue their young daughter, who is fated to die in a street accident. The penultimate *Limits* show, this isn't the worst but is close enough, with little action and a silly "Limbo Being" (a guy in a business suit projected in negative) conveniently turning up to explain this most inexplicable situation.

PROBE, THE

★ 1965. Dir: Felix Feist. Cast: Peter Mark Richman, Peggy Ann Garner, Ron Hayes, William Stevens, William Boyett, Janos Prohaska.

The last and least episode of the series finds four plane crash survivors held captive in an alien spacecraft. Almost devoid of any excitement or production dress, with a bland cast and chintzy set design. Even the introduction of a token monster—a bloblike, man-sized microbe played by Prohaska—doesn't do much to enliven things.

PRODUCTION AND DECAY OF STRANGE PARTICLES, THE

★★ 1964. Dir: Leslie Stevens. Cast: George Macready, Signe Hasso, Robert Fortier, Allyson Ames, Rudy Solari, Leonard Nimoy.

Atomic testing at a cyclotron unleashes a force that kills most of the personnel and fills their radiation suits with pulsating energy creatures. An interestingly directed but patently unbelievable story with remarkably similarities to later horror films like *Night of the Zombies* and *Warning Sign*; it just runs in place until a slam-bang ending that's one of the series' most exciting. Ames was then the wife of producer-director Stevens; Nimoy makes the first of two *Limits* appearances as an ill-fated technician.

SECOND CHANCE

★★★ 1964. Dir: Paul Stanley. Cast: Simon Oakland, Don Gordon, Janet DeGore, John McLiam, Angela

Clark, Mimsy Farmer, Yale Summers, Arnold Merritt.

An amusement park spaceship ride turns out to be the real thing as a benevolent alien called an Empyrean (well played by Oakland) abducts seven people for a trip to the stars. If you can get past the utter illogic of its premise, this episode (originally titled "Joyride") is fast-paced fun. Oakland's alien provides some especially pointed moralistic dialogue: he chides a failed, middle-aged businessman for "wearing out his wife's soul," a female artist for a love affair that had "no moral right to begin" with a married man, and a smarmy college jock for throwing a game, cheating on tests, and betraying his cheerleader girlfriend (presumably with his gofer best pal, who cries, "You meant something to me!" before being swept into space). Gordon is typically good as the spaceship's human "pilot"; veteran exploitation actress Farmer has an early role as the cheerleader.

SIXTH FINGER, THE

★★★☆ 1963. Dir: James Goldstone. Cast: David McCallum, Jill Haworth, Edward Mulhare, Nora Marlowe, Constance Cavendish, Robert Doyle.

Welsh scientist Mulhare finds a way to advance evolution and experiments on simple coal miner McCallum—transforming him into a psychic, bald-domed, six-fingered man of the future. Excellent acting and intelligent scripting help make this one of the best and best-remembered episodes of the series—though the happy ending added at the last minute rings a bit false. Mulhare would find his greatest fame on later TV shows like *The Ghost and Mrs. Muir* and *Knightrider*.

SOLDIER

★★★ 1964. Dir: Gerd Oswald. Cast: Michael Ansara, Lloyd Nolan, Tim O'Connor, Catherine MacLeod, Ralph Hart, Jill Hill.

Harlan Ellison scripted this strong second-season opener about a soldier from the future sent via time warp to the twentieth century, where a scientist hired to unscramble the soldier's weird language tries to befriend him. Outstanding direction and a powerful performance from Ansara help make up for some simplified concepts and flat acting from Nolan as the linguist.

SPECIAL ONE, THE

★★ 1964. Dir: Gerd Oswald. Cast: Richard Ney, Flip Mark, MacDonald Carey, Marion Ross, Edward C. Platt, Jason Wingreen.

An alien called Mr. Zeno becomes tutor for a gifted young boy called Kenny. Mom and, especially Dad, become jealous of Zeno's hold on the boy but, as things begin to take on distinct pedophilic connotations, the alien is undone by the genius of the boy he is trying to exploit. A rather bland concoction and very much a product of its time (the squeaky clean family could have stepped whole out of an early '60s sitcom), notable mostly for the great alien materialization effect and Ross getting an early runthrough for her Mrs. C role on TV's *Happy Days.*

SPECIMEN: UNKNOWN

★★ 1964. Dirs: Gerd Oswald, Robert H. Justman. Cast: Stephen McNally, Richard Jaeckal, Russell Johnson, Arthur Batanides, Gail Kobe, Peter Baldwin, Dabney Coleman, John Kellogg.

More weak tea about alien sunflowers that shoot deadly spores attacking both the crew of a spacecraft and the rescue team that tries to save them when the ship crashes. This tries to recapture the mood of the sci-fi/horror classic *The Day of the Triffids* but isn't very successful; the cast of characters is uninteresting and the menace is more foolish than frightening.

TOURIST ATTRACTION

★★ 1963. Dir: Lasio Benedek. Cast: Ralph Meeker, Janet Blair, Jerry Douglas, Henry Silva, Jay Novello.

An American mercenary tries to exploit a form of huge, prehistoric fish creatures found in the waters off a small South American dictatorship. The monsters—looking like something from *The Creature from the Black Lagoon*—are memorable but everything else about this well-cast but ponderous show is strictly second rate.

WOLF 359

★★☆ 1964. Dir: Laslo Benedek. Cast: Patrick O'Neal, Sara Shane, Peter Haskell, Ben Wright, Dabney Coleman.

Experimenting with a miniaturized alien landscape in a glass tank, a scientist (O'Neal) is brought under the control of a ghostly life-form. One of the better season-two shows, this is predictable but has good acting and atmospheric direction and photography, though much of the original script's concept of the scientist wanting to be a god to his self-contained alien world was removed by network censors.

ZANTI MISFITS, THE

★★★★ 1963. Dir: Leonard Horn. Cast: Michael Tolan, Olive Deering, Robert F. Simon, Bruce Dern, Claude Woolman.

Anyone who ever first saw this episode as a little kid—myself included—will never shake it off. A prison ship from the planet Zanti disgorges a horde of twelve-inch human-featured insectoid aliens who attack military personnel in a desert ghost town called Morgue. An eerie, horrific classic with excellent—and familiar—desert locations, effective stop-motion animated aliens, and a wonderfully outré cast, including Dern as a twitchy bank robber and Deering as his neurotic accomplice.

ZZZZ

★★☆ 1964. Dir: John Brahm. Cast: Joanna Frank, Phillip Abbott, Marsha Hunt, Booth Coleman.

A straightforwardly earnest but unreedemably oddball tale about a queen bee who takes human form (the very well-formed Frank) to seduce an entomologist (Abbott) and create a genetically superior offspring. Though well directed by Brahm and definitively enacted by Frank, Abbott's overall woodenness makes him an unlikely candidate for any cross breeding (his holier-than-thou final speech brings new meaning to the phrase "heavy handed") and the slim plot barely holds interest for fifty minutes.

THE PRISONER

MPI, 1968, NR, 50 min. per episode.

One of the oddest television programs ever aired, *The Prisoner* was a pet project of its star, Patrick McGoohan, who saw in it a chance to air his views on personal freedom in modern society. A sort of sequel to McGoohan's popular *Secret Agent* series (remember the great "Secret Agent Man" theme song?), this starred the actor as a retiring British agent whisked away to a mysterious, futuristic resort known as "The Village." Called "Number 6" by everyone he encounters, our hero discovers that he is under constant observation via television cameras and all attempted escapes are thwarted by huge rolling white balls called Rovers that force would-be escapees back to the Village, where mind-control experiments are performed at the local hospital. What is the purpose of the Village and why is McGoohan being held there? And by whom? These questions are only vaguely answered in this Kafkaesque nightmare world filled with role playing and duplicity, fascinating some viewers but frustrating others.

I must admit that this surreal series takes a while to warm up to but McGoohan's personal magnetism as an actor makes you feel for his predicament and keeps you watching. The final two episodes tried to clear up a few questions about Number 6 and his captors but in the end the true strength of *The Prisoner* is that no explanations are really necessary. The loss of freedom, for whatever reason, is the main issue here. It doesn't matter whether it's by friend or foe; what matters is that repression of any sort can only end in the crushing of the human spirit.

A, B, AND C

★★★☆ Dir: Pat Jackson [Patrick McGoohan]. Guest cast: Katherine Kath, Sheila Allen, Colin Gordon, Peter Bowles.

In one of *The Prisoner*'s most imaginative episodes, Number 6 becomes the subject of experiments for a process that can control and manipulate dreams. A powerful entry whose themes anticipate later films like *Exorcist II: The Heretic, Dreamscape,* and *A Nightmare on Elm Street.*

ARRIVAL, THE

★★★★ Dir: Don Chaffey. Guest cast: Virginia Maskell, Guy Doleman, Paul Eddington, George Baker.

The classic first episode sets up the series premise. Ex-government agent McGoohan is gassed in his London apartment and transported to the mysterious "Village." Eerie and intriguing; highlighted, like so many episodes, by the architecturally interesting Village itself—actually a real resort in north Wales.

CHANGE OF MIND, A

★★☆ Dir: Joseph Serf. Guest cast: Angela Browne, John Sharpe, George Pravda, Angelo Muscat.

Village authorities try again to learn Number 6's secrets through a process that can transfer thoughts from one person to another. A routine rehashing of some familiar *Prisoner* themes.

CHECKMATE

★★★ Dir: Don Chaffey. Guest cast: Peter Wyngarde, Patricia Jessel, Ronald Radd, Rosalie Crutchley.

Number 6 decides to filter out the prisoners from the jailers among his fellow Village inhabitants in this above average show. Good performance by Wyngarde (*The Innocents; Burn, Witch, Burn*) as the devilish Number 2.

CHIMES OF BIG BEN, THE

★★★ Dir: Don Chaffey. Guest cast: Nadia Gray, Leo McKern, Finlay Currie, Richard Wattis.

The second episode, this features the first of McGoohan's many escape attempts, this one involving another ex-agent brought to the Village and enlisted by our hero in his plans. Solid entry with especially well-written dialogue in the scenes featuring McGoohan and Gray.

DANCE OF THE DEAD

★★★ Dir: Don Chaffey. Guest cast: Mary Morris, Duncan MacRae, Norma West, Angelo Muscat.

When Number 6 meets an old friend from his past he discovers that his captors are involved in a plot to make the outside world think that he is dead. The climactic masked ball scene is impressive.

DO NOT FORSAKE ME OH MY DARLING

★★★☆ Dir: Pat Jackson [Patrick McGoohan]. Guest cast: Zena Walker, Nigel Stock, Clifford Evans, Angelo Muscat.

One of the series' most interesting episodes transfers Number 6's mind to a man outside the Village who searches for Number 6's fiancée to find out if she knows of his whereabouts. Almost too imaginative for its own good, this leads to some confusion in the scenes depicting Stock as the free agent "possessed" by McGoohan's character.

FALL OUT

★★★★ Dir: Patrick McGoohan. Guest cast: Leo McKern, Kenneth Griffith, Alexis Kanner, Angelo Muscat.

The final episode is nearly all allegory and no plot as Number 6 is put on trial and eventually wins his freedom from the Village—but not himself. Somewhat oblique but still a must.

FREE FOR ALL

★★★ Dir: Patrick McGoohan. Guest cast: Erick Portman, Rachel Herbert, George Benson, Angelo Muscat.

A well-founded spoof of the political process as Number 6 finds himself pressed into running for the position of Number 2.

GENERAL, THE

★★ Dir: Peter Graham Scott. Guest cast: Colin Gordon, John Castle, Peter Howell, Betty McDowall.

Easily the weakest link in the series; a tired rumination on mind control involving a form of "education" used on villagers via TV signals beamed directly into their eyes.

GIRL WHO WAS DEATH, THE

★★★ Dir: David Tomblin. Guest cast: Justine Lord, Kenneth Griffith, Christopher Benjamin, Michael Brennan.

Number 6 narrates a Village fairy tale where he finds himself involved with a beautiful assassin known as "Death." A refreshingly offbeat entry in the series.

HAMMER INTO ANVIL

★★★ Dir: Pat Jackson [Patrick McGoohan]. Guest cast: Patrick Cargill, Victor Maddern, Basil Hoskins, Hilary Dwyer.

Number 6 tries all-out psychological warfare against an increasingly unstable Number 2 (well played by Cargill) in this exceptional black comedy episode.

IT'S YOUR FUNERAL

★★☆ Dir: Robert Asher. Guest cast: Darren Nesbitt, Annette Andre, Mark Eden, Wanda Ventham.

The Prisoner is manipulated with misinformation about an assassination in the Village to prevent his interference in his captor's true plans. A fair entry; somewhat overplotted.

LIVING IN HARMONY

★★★★ Dir: David Tomblin. Guest cast: Alexis Kanner, Valerie French, David Bauer, Gordon Tanner.

Infamous as the one episode of The Prisoner ABC-TV would not run because of its violence, this Western parody has Number 6 taking on the role of an Old West Marshall—one who refuses to carry a gun. Richly detailed and extremely well thought out, this is The Prisoner at its very best.

MANY HAPPY RETURNS

★★★★ Dir: Joseph Serf. Guest cast: Patrick Cargill, Georgina Cookson, Donald Sinden, Brian Worth.

Without doubt the series' finest hour, this has the Prisoner awakening one morning to find the Village deserted and deciding to take advantage of this unexpected situation by mounting an escape. A brilliantly visual premise bolstered by one of McGoohan's most intuitive performances.

ONCE UPON A TIME

★★★★ Dir: Patrick McGoohan. Guest cast: Leo McKern, Angelo Muscat, Peter Swanwick, John Cazabon.

A mind probe used to discover the reasons behind the Prisoner's resignation from government service leads to a psychological battle to the death between Numbers 6 and 2. Another dynamite episode, with top performances from McGoohan and the always reliable McKern (The Omen, Ladyhawke) as Number 2.

SCHIZOID MAN, THE

★★★☆ Dir: Pat Jackson [Patrick McGoohan]. Guest cast: Janne Merrow, Anton Rodgers, Earl Cameron, Angelo Muscat.

Number 6 begins to doubt both his sanity and his very identity when confronted by an exact double. Another winner, with Merrow adding some good moments as a psychic neighbor with a mental link to our hero's mind.

SPACE: 1999

Image Entertainment, 1975–77, NR, 48 min. per tape.

Gerry and Sylvia Anderson followed up their very odd *UFO* series with this elaborate, somewhat confused, but always watchable attempt at grabbing a little of *Star Trek*'s thunder. Filmed in England but clearly aimed at the U.S. market, *Space* was reasonably successful in syndication until it ran out of steam toward the end of its second and last season. Plots tended to be either too simple-minded or too verbose and usually fell back on the overworked evil alien invader cliché. Still, it was a good-looking series with elaborate Brian Johnson special effects, slinky Rudi Gernreich costumes, and a full roster of distinguished British guest stars.

Martin Landau and Barbara Bain (then husband and wife) star as Commander John Koenig and Dr. Helena Russell of Moonbase Alpha. An interplanetary disaster sends the moon out of orbit and off into space (an impossible scenario but still fun); the Alpha crew encounters various strange life-forms while trying to find a way home. Other regulars include Barry Morse as Professor Howard Bergman, Nick Tate as Lt. Alan Carter, Zienia Merton as Sandra Benes, and Prentis Hancock as Paul Morrow. During the second season, Morse was dropped and two new characters added— Catherine Schell as the shape-shifting alien Maya (an obvious homage to *Trek*'s Mr. Spock) and Tony Anholt as macho Tony Verdeshi—but they did little to save the show from cancellation. Few of *Space*'s episodes are up to the standards of the best of *Star Trek* but it has a fun, pulpy feel that makes it a lot more enjoyable than many of the plastic post-*Star Wars* series to follow, like *Battlestar Gallactica* and *Buck Rogers*.

ALL THAT GLISTERS

☆ 1976. Dir: Ray Austin. Guest cast: Patrick Mower.

An *Outer Limits*-like episode with the Alphans menaced by hostile, living rocks.

ALPHA CHILD

★★☆ 1975. Dir: Ray Austin. Guest cast: Julian Glover, Cyd Hayman, Wayne Brooks.

A *Space: 1999* version of *Rosemary's Baby*. Hayman plays an Alphan woman who gives birth to a baby possessed by an evil alien entity. Not bad.

ANOTHER TIME, ANOTHER PLACE

★★★ 1975. Dir: David Tomblin. Guest cast: Judy Geeson.

Geeson is excellent in this downbeat tale of a woman who envisions disaster for Moonbase Alpha and her crew.

BLACK SUN, THE

★★☆ 1975. Dir: Lee H. Katzin. Guest cast: Paul Jones, Jon Laurimore.

Professor Bergman desperately tries to create a protective force field when the Moonbase is endangered by a deadly space phenomenon called a Black Sun.

BREAKAWAY

★★★ 1975. Dir: Lee H. Katzin. Guest cast: Roy Dotrice, Philip Madoc, Lou Sutton.

A series of explosions on the moon blow it out of Earth's orbit , sending the personnel of Moonbase Alpha on a perilous journey. The premiere episode is full of drama and '70s disaster movie-type excitement; it's about as scientifically accurate as an episode of *Mork and Mindy* but it's still one of the series' best hours.

COLLISION COURSE

★★☆ 1976. Dir: Ray Austin. Guest cast: Margaret Leighton.

Veteran actress Leighton excels in this dreamy episode in which Commander Koenig has visions of a strange alien woman, as Moonbase Alpha heads for collision with an unknown planet.

DEATH'S OTHER DOMINION

★★☆ 1975. Dir: Charles Crichton. Guest cast: Brian Blessed, John Shrapnel, Mary Miller.

Immortal space explorers offer the gift of eternity to the Alphans. Good direction by Crichton elevates this standard show.

DRAGON'S DOMAIN

★★★☆ 1975. Dir: Charles Crichton. Guest cast: Gianni Garko, Douglas Wilmer, Barbara Kellerman.

No one believes an astronaut (Garko), who claims to have discovered a graveyard of alien spacecraft guarded by a deadly monster. My favorite episode, with solid storyline and some nice, scary moments.

EARTHBOUND

★★★ 1975. Dir: Charles Crichton. Guest cast: Christopher Lee, Roy Dotrice.

Horror legend Lee adds stature to this one, about an alien spacecraft crashing near Moonbase Alpha on its way to conquer Earth. Even with the silly face-paint makeup, Lee makes this worth watching.

END OF ETERNITY

★★ 1975. Dir: Ray Austin. Guest cast: Peter Bowles, Jim Smilie.

Routine tale of another evil alien on the prowl that Koenig must dispose of.

EXILES, THE

★★☆ 1976. Dir: Ray Austin. Guest cast: Peter Duncan, Stacy Dornig, Margaret Inglis.

That old sci-fi staple of not judging by appearances is trotted out yet again as a pair of angelic-looking aliens turn out to be deadly killers.

FORCE OF LIFE

★★☆ 1975. Dir: David Tomblin. Guest cast: Ian McShane, Gay Hamilton, John Hamill.

Another *Outer Limits*-inspired show, with McShane as an Alphan who endangers everyone by his sudden, unexplained need for intense heat.

FULL CIRCLE, THE

★☆ 1976. Dir: Bob Kellett. Guest cast: Oliver Cotton.

Total absurdity as a time warp sends the Alphans back to the Cro Magnon era. An easy-to-ridicule mess.

GUARDIAN OF PIRI

★★ 1975. Dir: Charles Crichton. Guest cast: Catherine Schell, Michael Culver.

Schell has an early *1999* role as a seductive alien woman who promises the Alphans the perfect life on her computer-controlled world. Predictably, things aren't quire as they seem in this *Star Trek*-like entry.

INTERNAL MACHINE, THE

★★☆ 1976. Dir: David Tomblin. Guest cast: Leo McKern.

McKern is typically good in this okay tale of a lonely alien machine seeking human companionship and picking Koenig and Russell as its new "friends."

JOURNEY TO WHERE

★★★ 1976. Dir: Tom Clegg. Guest cast: Freddie Jones, Isla Blair, Laurence Harrington.

In one of *1999*'s best episodes, Koenig, Russell, and Carter are sent back in time to the fourteenth century and witness the spread of the Black Plague.

LAST ENEMY, THE

★★ 1975. Dir: Bob Kellett. Guest cast: Caroline Mortimer, Maxine Audley, Kevin Stoney, Carolyn Courage.

Fair entry in which Koenig attempts to bring peace to warring alien cultures whose fighting threatens Moonbase Alpha and its population.

LAST SUNSET, THE

★★ 1975. Dir: Charles Crichton.

The Alphans must decide whether to give up their quest for Earth when they find a inhabitable planet they could make their new home.

MARK OF ARCHANON, THE

★★ 1976. Dir: Charles Crichton. Guest cast: John Standing, Michael Gallagher.

Routine stuff with a pair of aliens released from suspended animation and infesting the Alphans with a deadly disease.

MATTER OF LIFE AND DEATH

★★☆ 1975. Dir: Charles Crichton. Guest cast: Richard Johnson, Stuart Damon.

The discovery of Dr. Russell's long-missing husband (Johnson) leads to terror when it is found that he is now composed of dangerous antimatter. Silly, but Johnson, as always, is first rate and there's an appearance by a pre-*General Hospital* Damon.

METAMORPH, THE

★★★ 1976. Dir: Charles Crichton. Guest cast: Brian Blessed, Anoushka Hempel.

The second-season opener introduces new regular Maya, who rescues the Alphans from her devious scientist-father. More action-packed and less cerebral than many year-one shows and much better than most that followed.

MISSING LINK

★★★ 1976. Dir: Ray Austin. Guest cast: Peter Cushing, Joanna Lumley.

Cushing is an alien scientist from the future who abducts Koenig, in whom he sees the "missing link" in his experiments. Above average for the series, with good roles for Hammer Films great Cushing and future *Absolutely Fabulous* star Lumley.

MISSION OF THE DARIANS

★★☆ 1976. Dir: Ray Austin. Guest cast: Joan Collins, Aubrey Morris, Dennis Burgess.

The Alphans discover the last survivors of an alien race who stay alive via cannibalism. Collins and the somewhat gruesome subject matter help this one stand out from the pack.

ONE MOMENT OF HUMANITY

★★☆ 1976. Dir: Charles Crichton. Guest cast: Billie Whitelaw, Leigh Lawson.

Whitelaw is good as an alien scientist who wants to use Russell and Verdeshi as the emotional blueprint for her android creations.

RING AROUND THE MOON
★★ 1976. Dir: Ray Austin. Guest cast: Max Faulkner.

The Alphans battle an alien who's absorbing Moonbase information as a prelude to invading Earth.

RULES OF LUTON, THE
★★☆ 1976. Dir: Val Guest. Guest cast: David Jackson, Godfrey James, Roy Marsden.

Guest's direction enlivens this one, with Koenig and Maya kidnapped by a trio of plantlike alien creatures.

SPACE BRAIN
★★ 1976. Dir: Charles Crichton. Guest cast: Shane Rimmer, Carla Romanelli, Derek Anders.

A huge alien entity steals the mind of an Eagle pilot in order to communicate with the Alphans. Some good atmosphere in this otherwise fair segment.

TAYBOR, THE
★★1976. Dir: Bob Brooks. Guest cast: Willoughby Goddard.

A very *Lost in Space*-like episode has Goddard as a space trader who offers the Alphans a way back to Earth—in exchange for Maya.

TESTAMENT OF ARKADIA, THE
★★ 1975. Dir: David Tomblin. Guest cast: Lisa Harrow.

Koenig tries to free Moonbase Alpha from the power-draining influence of the ancient planet Arkadia.

TROUBLED SPIRIT, THE
★★☆ 1975. Dir: Ray Austin. Guest cast: Giancarlo Prette, Hilary Dwyer, Anthony Nicholls.

A confused but interesting horror-themed segment, with Prette as a botanist who spirit terrorizes the Alphans—even though he isn't even dead yet! Prette's wife is played by British horror veteran Dwyer (*The Oblong Box, Cry of the Banshee*).

VOYAGER'S RETURN
★★ 1976. Dir: Bob Kellett. Guest cast: Jeremy Kemp, Barry Stokes, Alex Scott.

A scientist tries to cover up the fact that he was responsible for the creation of a killer machine terrorizing the Alphans.

WAR GAMES
★★ 1976. Dir: Charles Crichton. Guest cast: Anthony Valentine, Isla Blair.

Another tired evil alien show in which the Alphans are forced to settle on a planet whose inhabitants make them somewhat less than welcome.

STAR TREK
Paramount, 1966–69, NR, 50 min. per tape.

The brainchild of producer Gene Roddenberry, *Star Trek* was conceived as a *Wagon Train* to the stars, a multicharacter sci-fi/drama series dealing each week with the adventures of the twenty-third-century starship *Enterprise* and her crew as they boldly go where no man has gone before. After two pilot episodes, Roddenberry finally got his vision on the air on NBC-TV. Never that popular with critics or the general public, *Trek* struggled through two seasons and was near cancellation when a letter-writing campaign brought it back for a mostly mediocre third and final year. A big hit in syndication in the '70s, *Trek* inspired a Saturday morning animated series, a string of big-budget movies, and a whole new series: *Star Trek: The Next Generation.*

Unlike many of today's TV shows and movies, it's not the special effects or contrivances of *Trek* that involve you but the characters. William Shatner is all hammy aplomb as Captain James T. Kirk, the cocky womanizing commander, and he is ably supported by the coolness (in all senses of the word) of Leonard Nimoy as the pointy-eared half-human, half-Vulcan science officer Mr. Spock, and by the delightful DeForest Kelley as good ol' boy ship's surgeon Dr. Leonard McCoy. Other regulars are Grace Lee Whitney as the beautiful, dutiful Yeoman Janice Rand; James Doohan as that eternal optimist, Chief Engineer Montgomery Scott; Nichelle Nichols as sensual Communications Officer Uhura; George Takei, a bundle of untapped energy as Helmsman Sulu; Majel Barrett (who also provides the voice of the *Enterprise's* computer) as lovesick-for-Spock Nurse Christine Chapel; Walter Koenig as the proudly Russian Ensign Paaval Checkov; and the rarely mentioned John Winston as stalwart British Lt. Kyle.

At its best, *Trek* can be thought-provoking and fun, stuck in a '60s sensibility that's at once forward-thinking and hopelessly dated. At its worst, it's like *Lost in Space* with a B.A. in political science, all hoaky monsters and self-conscious messages about our life and times. I'm not a Trekker by any means but I've always found the original *Star Trek* to be thoroughly entertaining; some of the episodes are great, many of them corny fun, and a few are positively painful, but on the whole it's still a milestone in television science fiction and will remain so for years to come.

"Hey, where's Grace Lee Whitney?" The Enterprise *crew gathers for a portrait in* Star Trek *(1968).*

ALL OUR YESTERDAYS

★★★ 1969. Dir: Marvin Chomsky. Guest cast: Mariette Hartley, Ian Wolfe.

One of the best episodes from the generally unimpressive third season finds Captain Kirk, Mr. Spock, and Dr. McCoy lost in the past of an alien world on the brink of destruction. Kirk is nearly tried for witchcraft while Spock and McCoy end up in an ice age cave with political exile Hartley. An exceptional performance by Nimoy (who experiences the emotional dawn of the Vulcan's evolution into their present nonemotional form) and good support from Kelley and Hartley make this next-to-last broadcast segment exceptional.

ALTERNATIVE FACTOR, THE

☆ 1967. Dir: Gerd Oswald. Guest cast: Robert Brown, Janet MacLachlan, Richard Derr.

The absolutely worst episode of the series, this features Brown as a seemingly insane alien scientist who actually has an evil twin from some weird alternate universe. A total waste of time.

AMOK TIME

★★★★ 1967. Dir: Joseph Pevney. Guest cast: Arlene Martel, Celia Lovsky, Lawrence Montaigne, Byron Morrow.

The premiere episode of the second season, this takes us for the first time to the planet Vulcan, where Spock takes part in a native mating ritual. Another good Nimoy performance is matched by Martel (as Spock's cold-hearted betrothed) and Lovsky (as a Vulcan high priestess) and there's a nice, prominent role for Nurse Chapel, too.

AND THE CHILDREN SHALL LEAD

★ 1968. Dir: Marvin Chomsky. Guest cast: Melvin Belli, Craig Hundley, Pamelyn Ferdin.

A very silly segment in which an alien called the Gorgon (former Attorney General Belli) controls the minds of a group of children (whose parents were killed by the monster) and is transported by the *Enterprise*. Ferdin later starred in the live-action Saturday morning series *Space Academy*.

APPLE, THE

★★ 1967. Dir: Joseph Pevney. Guest cast: Celeste Yarnall, Keith Andes, David Soul, Shari Nims, Jay Jones.

An *Enterprise* landing party is stranded on an idyllic planet where the gentle inhabitants (who act like the Eloi in *The Time Machine*) are lorded over by a Godzilla-headed stone god called Vol. This dumb but watchable segment must set the record for the number of red-shirted security guards who get offed. A pre-*Starsky and Hutch* Soul has an early role as one of the white-haired natives.

ARENA

★★★ 1967. Dir: Joseph Pevney. Guest cast: Carole Shelyne, Vic Perrin.

Kirk and a lizardlike alien commander are sent by a powerful alien race to a desert planet, where the two of them are forced to battle it out. Another solid first-season show (that lizard guy really scared me when I was a little kid), this is based (without credit) on a classic short story by Fredric Brown.

ASSIGNMENT: EARTH

★★ 1968. Dir: Marc Daniels. Guest cast: Robert Lansing, Teri Garr.

The *Enterprise* goes back in time (again) to 1960s Earth, where the crew encounters a man called Gary Seven (Lansing), who's been given powerful abilities by an alien race. The pilot for a proposed spinoff series, this is moderately entertaining, with Garr in an early role as Lansing's clichéd ditzy blonde secretary.

BALANCE OF TERROR

★★★★ 1966. Dir: Vincent McEveety. Guest cast: Mark Lenard, Paul Comi, Barbara Baldwin, John Warburton, Stephen Mines.

One of the all-time best *Trek* episodes, this plays like an updated World War II submarine chase story. The *Enterprise* races a Romulan ship—which has just destroyed an Earth outpost—back to the infamous "Neutral Zone," which they are forbidden to cross. Tension-packed, this uses all the regular cast to good effect and has a good role for Lenard (who would go on to play Spock's dad Sarek) as the conscience-driven Romulan commander. And opening the show at the wedding of two of the *Enterprise* crew members was a nice touch.

BREAD AND CIRCUSES

★★ 1968. Dir: Ralph Senensky. Guest cast: William Smithers, Logan Ramsey, Rhodes Reason, Lois Jewell, Ian Wolfe.

The *Enterprise* arrives at a planet that conveniently looks like an ancient Roman setting on the Paramount backlot. There they search for a stranded Federation officer who's become—big surprise—the despotic ruler of the empire. Routine, but the idea of televised *American Gladiators*-like combat, with real weapons, was an effective accouterment.

BY ANY OTHER NAME

★★ 1968. Dir: Marc Daniels. Guest cast: Warren Stevens, Barbara Bouchet, Julie Cobb, Carl Byrd.

Another of those "aliens take over the *Enterprise*" episodes that's basically remembered for reducing most of the crew to little white styrofoam blocks. This *does*, however, pull an unexpected gag involving the fates of the usual landing party yeoman and red shirt and features *Forbidden Planet* star Stevens and Euro-horror regular Bouchet as the aliens.

CAGE, THE

★★★★ 1965. Dir: Robert Butler. Cast: Jeffrey Hunter, Leonard Nimoy, Susan Oliver, John Hoyt, Majel Barrett, Laurel Goodwin.

The original *Trek* pilot, rejected by the network and later refashioned into the two-parter *The Menagerie*, is presented here uncut and without the tacked on new footage. Original *Enterprise* commander Christopher Pike (Hunter) and his crew (including a very young-looking Mr. Spock) search for Earth castaways on an alien planet whose inhabitants can materialize any thought, any dream, any desire. Intelligently written and directed with later Nurse Chapel Barrett cast as the tough female first officer Number One (the network brass allegedly had a very hard time dealing with her) and Oliver as a castaway who hides a terrible disfigurement behind an illusion of beauty. Available in both black-and-white and colorized versions.

CATSPAW

★★☆ 1967. Dir: Joseph Pevney. Guest cast: Antoinette Bower, Theo Marcuse, Michael Barrier.

Psycho author Robert Bloch scripted this fun Halloween episode with Kirk and company imprisoned in a spooky castle by a pair of devilish aliens in human guise. Kirk's best line, to a skeleton: "Bones?"

CHANGELING, THE

★★★ 1967. Dir: Marc Daniels. Guest cast: Barbara Gates, Arnold Lessing, voice of Vic Perrin.

The *Enterprise* encounters Nomad, a twentieth-century Earth probe transformed by an alien race into a powerful, independently thinking being. One of the obvious models for the plot of the first *Star Trek* movie, this well-crafted segment is particularly well thought out, though the subplot where Nomad wipes away Uhura's knowledge and memory and her retraining by Dr. McCoy and Nurse Chapel (and emerging none the worse for the experience) is a bit hard to swallow.

CHARLIE X

★★★★ 1966. Dir: Lawrence Dobkin. Guest cast: Robert Walker, Jr., Patricia McNulty, voice of Abraham Sofaer.

The *Enterprise* rescues teenage space castaway Charlie Evans (Walker) who has, unbeknownst to the crew, been given supernormal mental powers by unseen alien guardians. Charlie uses these powers to impress father-figure Captain Kirk and win the heart of Janice Rand. The best treatment of the familiar *Trek* plot about an ordinary human given godlike abilities, this is well written (by Dorothy Fontana as a vehicle for Whitney as Yeoman Rand) and sensitively acted by Walker. There's also a nice, and rarely explored, feeling of comradeship between various crew members—especially in the delightful rec room scene where Rand prods Uhura into singing a song about Spock. And Spock smiles!

CITY ON THE EDGE OF FOREVER, THE
★★★★ 1967. Dir: Gene Roddenberry. Guest cast: Joan Collins, David L. Ross, John Harmon.

Kirk and Spock follow a chemically deranged McCoy (who accidentally received an injection meant for an injured crewman) through a time portal back to the Earth of the 1930s, where the captain falls in love with a forward-thinking soup kitchen worker (Collins) destined to a tragic fate. Many consider this Harlan Ellison-penned segment the original series' finest hour and with its overwhelming sense of sadness and emotion it's certainly a contender. Kirk's parting shot ("Let's get the hell out of here") was one of the first instances of a four-letter word being used on prime-time TV.

CLOUD MINDERS, THE
★☆ 1969. Dir: Judd Taylor. Guest cast: Jeff Corey, Diana Ewing, Charlene Polite, Fred Williamson.

David Gerrold (*The Trouble with Tribbles*) wrote the original story on which this subpar episode is based. Kirk and the gang get involved with a slave uprising in an alien city that hovers in the clouds above its world. The usual third-season heavy-handedness.

CONSCIENCE OF THE KING, THE
★★★ 1966. Dir: Gerd Oswald. Guest cast: Arnold Moss, Barbara Anderson, Bruce Hyde, William Sargent.

A floridly acted whodunit with Kirk attempting to ascertain whether a distinguished Shakespearean actor (Moss) is really an infamous dictator known as Kodos the Executioner. This solid show is noteworthy for a number of reasons: Hyde's second and last appearance as the likable Lt. Riley; Uhura singing a pretty ballad called "Beyond Antares"; and the final filmed appearance of Yeoman Rand—though her big scene was ultimately cut when the show ran into overtime, reducing her to a brief but effective walk-on.

CORBOMITE MANEUVER, THE
★★★ 1966. Dir: Joseph Sargent. Guest cast: Anthony Call, Clint Howard, voice of Ted Cassidy.

The *Enterprise* runs afoul of an enormous, powerful alien spacecraft whose commander orders the starship destroyed. The first episode of the show filmed for its first season (though actually the tenth broadcast), you can see the cast starting to get into their characters as this episode explores the popular *Trek* themes of aggression and power not being everything and that things aren't always as they seem.

COURT MARTIAL
★★ 1967. Dir: Marc Daniels. Guest cast: Elisha Cook, Joan Marshall. Percy Rodriguez, Richard Webb, Alice Rawlings.

Contrived story in which Kirk is brought up on charges for an order he gave that resulted in the death of a crewman who was also an old friend. Pretty mediocre for the usually fine first season with unlikely occurrences galore (like a former love of Kirk's—one of the many—being appointed prosecuting attorney!), though casting perennial loser Cook as James T.'s lawyer was an effective touch.

DAGGER OF THE MIND
★★☆ 1966. Dir: Vincent McEveety. Guest cast: Marianna Hill, James Gregory, Morgan Woodward, Susanne Wasson.

When an inmate escapes from an insane asylum and manages to get aboard the *Enterprise*, Kirk and psychiatrist Hill investigate conditions at the place and uncover a dastardly mind-control device. An okay first-year episode that's notable mainly for the first use of the patented Vulcan mind meld. Veteran exploitation actress Hill seems a nice gal but her character is such a dippy bimbo that it's hard to take her seriously as a dedicated medical professional.

DAY OF THE DOVE
★ 1968. Dir: Marvin Chomsky. Guest cast: Michael Ansara, Susan Howard.

An evil entity that draws its strength from the violence and hatred of others forces the crew of the *Enterprise* into battle with Klingons commanded by veteran movie bad guy—and former Barbara Eden hubby—Ansara. One of the weakest *Trek* segments, this has a nice touch in that Ansara is accompanied on his mission by wife Howard but otherwise is a real bummer.

DEADLY YEARS, THE
★★ 1967. Dir: Joseph Pevney. Guest cast: Charles Drake, Sarah Marshall, Beverly Washburn, Felix Locher.

A landing party—including Kirk, Spock, McCoy, and Scotty—is exposed to a disease that ages them prematurely; Shatner goes without his usual hairpiece. A sometimes amusing segment with a fair share of unintended laughs.

DEVIL IN THE DARK, THE

★★☆ 1967. Dir: Joseph Pevney. Guest cast: Ken Lynch, Barry Russo, Janos Prohaska.

Miners on a distant planet are being killed by a monster (played by Prohaska) that looks like a big rock and is really only protecting its cache of eggs. A well-remembered but fairly routine episode made memorable by a classic McCoy line: "I'm a doctor, not a bricklayer!"

DOOMSDAY MACHINE, THE

★★☆ 1967. Dir: Marc Daniels. Guest cast: William Windom, John Copage, Richard Compton, Elizabeth Rogers.

Moby Dick, Star Trek style, with a crazed Star Fleet captain (Windom, one of the best actors to work continually in '60s and '70s TV) taking over the *Enterprise* to stalk the enormous monstrosity that crippled his own ship and killed his crew. Incidentally, Windom's character was supposed to be the father of the character played by Stephen Collins in *ST—The Motion Picture*.

ELAAN OF TROYIUS

★★☆ 1968. Dir: John Meredyth Lucas. Guest cast: France Nuyen, Jay Robinson, Tony Young.

An alien princess (Nuyen) whose tears can enslave men is being transported by the *Enterprise* to an arranged marriage that is expected to end the war between the bride's and groom's civilizations. Naturally things become complicated when Kirk becomes the girl's willing slave. Silly stuff highlighted by a great campy performance by Robinson as a mincing alien ambassador.

EMPATH, THE

★★★ 1968. Dir: John Erman. Guest cast: Kathryn Hays, Alan Bergman, Willard Sage, Jason Wingreen.

One of the better year-three shows finds Kirk, Spock, and McCoy imprisoned by aliens who are experimenting on a woman (Hays) with the ability to absorb the injuries and illnesses of others. An intelligently written script (by Joyce Muscat) and Hays's marvelous performance make this a winner.

ENEMY WITHIN, THE

★★★☆ 1966. Dir: Leo Penn. Guest cast: Jim Goodwin, Edward Madden, Garland Thompson.

Shatner goes above and beyond the campy call of duty in this Richard Matheson-scripted story about a transporter malfunction splitting Kirk into two beings: one good, the other not so good. Bill as the bad Kirk is a sight to behold (all heavy eye makeup and swaggering bravura) and McCoy gets to say "He's dead, Jim" for the first time, but the real highlights of this Jekyll and Hyde tale are Shatner's amazingly understated work as the good Kirk and an incredibly brutal-for-its-time scene where the evil captain attempts to rape Janice Rand.

ENTERPRISE INCIDENT, THE

★★☆ 1968. Dir: John Meredyth Lucas. Guest cast: Joanne Linville.

A very good performance by Linville as a no-nonsense Romulan commander is the best thing about this Dorothy Fontana-scripted trifle in which the *Enterprise* violates the Neutral Zone as part of a plot to steal the Romulan cloaking device. Some tense moments, but the scenes of Kirk in Romulan disguise are legendary in their foolishness.

ERRAND OF MERCY

★★★ 1967. Dir: John Newland. Guest cast: John Colicos, John Abbott, Peter Brocco.

The Klingons get their first *Trek* exposure in this understated tale of the Federation and the Klingon Empire's struggle over the possession of a vitally positioned world inhabited by primitive pacifists. One of the few *Trek* shows with a surprise ending that truly surprises, this has good work from Colicos as the Klingon commander and a tight script that concentrates on the dynamics of the Kirk-Spock relationship with no other regulars to be seen.

FOR THE WORLD IS HOLLOW AND I HAVE TOUCHED THE SKY

★ 1968. Dir: Tony Leader. Guest cast: Kate Woodville, Jon Lormer.

For this story is hollow and its writer truly touched—in the head. McCoy, mistakenly believing that he has a terminal disease, becomes the willing consort of the queen (Woodville) of an underground civilization its people think is actually on its planet's surface —the sky is really a painted cave roof. *Star Trek* at its flimsiest.

FRIDAY'S CHILD

★☆ 1967. Dir: Joseph Pevney. Guest cast: Julie Newmar, Tige Andrews, Michael Dante, Cal Bolder.

Another of those shows in which Kirk and company violate the Prime Directive. Newmar (Catwoman herself!) is a pregnant alien princess who must never be touched by outsiders. Guess who gets hands-on with our untouchable heroine? Not very good at all.

GALILEO SEVEN, THE

★★★☆ 1967. Dir: Robert Gist. Guest cast: John Crawford, Don Marshall, Phyllis Douglas, Peter Marko.

An effectively offbeat segment with Spock and six others—including McCoy, Scotty, and a Yeoman Rand substitute (Douglas)—crash landing in a shuttlecraft on a doomed planetoid inhabited by sumo wrestlers in fur coats. Will Spock's logical mind be enough to save them? A good showcase for Nimoy, Kelley, and Doohan, with a modicum of suspense and even a few scares—that is, if you can take those mink-coated mountain men seriously.

GAMESTERS OF TRISKELION, THE

★☆ 1968. Dir: Gene Nelson. Guest cast: Angelique Pettyjohn, Joseph Ruskin, Steven Sandor, Victoria George.

The quintessential campy Star Trek episode. Kirk, Uhura, and Chekov are captured by alien brain creatures and pitted against other intergalactic captives in a series of life and death contests. Absurd to the nth degree with Ruskin as a glow-eyed referee, busty Pettyjohn—aka porno star Heaven St. John—as an alien babe with really big hair and a Reynolds Wrap bikini, and Shatner (who goes shirtless through much of this) shouting, "What's happening to Lt. Chuchora!" when it looks like some apeman is puttin' the moves on our lovely communications officer. Priceless.

IMMUNITY SYNDROME, THE

★★☆ 1968. Dir: Joseph Pevney.

The Enterprise becomes a dangerous antibody in a huge, amoebalike life-form in this slightly above average second-season show. The special FX are pretty good too.

I, MUDD

★★ 1967. Dir: Marc Daniels. Guest cast: Roger C. Carmel, Kay Elliot, Richard Tatro.

Harry Mudd (Carmel, blustery as ever) returns for this somewhat strained comedy in which Mudd trys to take over the Enterprise with an army of androids. Roger C. sparkles, but this is too contrived to be fun and too self-conscious to be really funny.

IS THERE IN TRUTH NO BEAUTY?

★★★☆ 1968. Dir: Ralph Senensky. Guest cast: Diana Muldaur, David Frankham.

Easily the best episode of the mostly wasteful third season, this thoughtful rumination on beauty and ugliness is almost unbelievably good. Muldaur (in her second Trek assignment) is the blind go-between escorting an alien ambassador called a Medusian—a creature so ugly that to look upon him will drive you mad. Frankham, as one of the original designers of the Enterprise and a former suitor of Muldaur, gives Shatner a run for his money in the overacting stakes as he goes insane and pilots the ship beyond the edge of the known universe, but Muldaur is good and Nimoy great in the concluding scenes where Spock mind-melds with the Medusian so that Spock can bring the Enterprise back to safety.

JOURNEY TO BABEL

★★★☆ 1967. Dir: Joseph Pevney. Guest cast: Jane Wyatt, Mark Lenard, Reggie Nalder, William O'Connell.

Dorothy Fontana (who else?) scripted this first-rate segment in which the Enterprise transports ambassadors—including Spock's mother and father—to a peace conference. Along the way the journey is disrupted by sabotage, assassination attempts, and tensions between Spock and dad Sarek. Solid acting, direction, and scripting marred only by some hoaky alien makeups and a major military faux pas, typically imposed on the show by sexist network executives, where Kirk passes command onto Ensign Checkov over of Lieutenant Uhura. We all know women can't handle the pressures of command—just ask Kate Mulgrew.

LET THAT BE YOUR LAST BATTLEFIELD

★★ 1969. Dir: Judd Taylor. Guest cast: Frank Gorshin, Lou Antonio.

Another episode well remembered for its campy absurdity, this has Gorshin and Antonio as warring aliens driven by racial prejudice—one is black on the left side and white on the right, the other white on the left and black on the right. Lead-footed but well intentioned, like most of Trek's statement shows, this is dumb but nicely acted by Gorshin (Batman's Riddler) and Antonio.

LIGHTS OF ZETAR, THE

★★ 1969. Dir: Herbert Kenwith. Guest cast: Jan Shutan, Libby Erwin.

Scotty makes the mistake of falling in love with a pretty-eyed, husky-voiced female officer (Shutan) just as she's possessed by a disembodied alien life-form. It's Star Trek meets The Exorcist; silly but passably entertaining, with Shutan appealing and a nice-sized role for Mr. Scott. Coauthored by Lamb Chop's best friend, Shari Lewis!

MAN TRAP, THE

★★★☆ 1966. Dir: Marc Daniels. Guest cast: Jeanne Bal, Alfred Ryder, Bruce Watson.

The first aired episode of *Trek,* featuring the infamous salt vampire, a shape-shifting monster that mostly disguises itself as a lost love of Dr. McCoy. Like many of the early shows, this does a good job of highlighting all the regulars—especially McCoy, Sulu, and Rand—and Uhura is given a nice moment when she encounters the vampire in the guise of a handsome technician who speaks Swahili.

MARK OF GIDEON, THE

★☆ 1969. Dir: Judd Taylor. Guest cast: Sharon Acker, David Hurst, Gene Dynarski, Richard Derr.

Kirk is trapped by aliens on a fake *Enterprise* by the people of the planet Gideon as part of plan to contain an alien infestation. More talk—very little of it interesting—than action in a story cowritten by Stanley Adams (the trader from *The Trouble with Tribbles*).

MENAGERIE, THE

★★★ 1966. Dirs: Marc Daniels, Robert Butler. Guest cast: Jeffrey Hunter, Susan Oliver, Malachi Throne, Julie Parrish, John Hoyt, Laurel Goodwin.

"The Cage" is cleverly reedited into the series' only two-parter. Spock is courtmartialed when he commandeers the *Enterprise* to return his disabled, disfigured former commander Pike (played in the original footage by Hunter) to the planet of illusions they had visited years before. A smartly written, economic use of seemingly unusable material and another nice showcase for Nimoy.

METAMORPHOSIS

★★☆ 1967. Dir: Ralph Senensky. Guest cast: Glenn Corbett, Elinor Donahue.

Kirk, Spock, McCoy, and a lady ambassador (Donahue—Princess, or was it Kitten? on *Father Knows Best*) crash a shuttlecraft on a planet inhabited by a stranded Earthman (Corbett) and the disembodied alien entity that has fallen in love with him. A flawed but not ineffectual dissertation on alternate forms of love with too pat an ending but some nice moments.

MIRI

★★★ 1966. Dir: Vincent McEveety. Guest cast: Kim Darby, Michael J. Pollard, Jim Goodwin, Ed Macready.

Kirk, Spock, McCoy, and Rand land on an Earthlike planet where botched generic engineering has killed all the adults and left the children near-immortals—until they reach puberty. A solid year-one episode with good roles for a pre-*True Grit* Darby and a pre-*Bonnie and Clyde* Pollard. The sexual tension between Kirk and Rand really comes to a boil here. Some of the kids are actually played by the real-life children of Shatner and Whitney.

MIRROR, MIRROR

★★★★ 1967. Dir: Marc Daniels. Guest cast: Barbara Luna, Vic Perrin, Ben Andrews.

Maybe year two's best and best-remembered episode, written by Jerome Bixby. An ion storm sweeps Kirk, McCoy, Scotty, and Uhura into a parallel universe where the *Enterprise* is run like a prison ship, advancement is obtained by assassination, and a female officer (the sultry Luna) does double duty as the captain's mistress. Less talky and more action-oriented than most *Trek* shows, the highlight is a free-for-all battle in sickbay between our heroes and the bearded alternate Spock—check out how he sends Uhura crashing into a wall! "Your agonizer, please!"

MUDD'S WOMEN

★★☆ 1966. Dir: Harvey Hart. Guest cast: Roger C. Carmel, Karen Steele, Susan Denberg, Maggie Thrett, Jim Goodwin, Gene Dynarski.

Harry Mudd (Carmel) is an intergalactic con man who arrives on the *Enterprise* with a trio of chemically enhanced beauties he hopes to sell as mail-order brides to miners on a lonely, sand-swept planet. A modest first-season show grounded more in '60s ideas about men and women, beauty and sexual attractiveness, than in any futuristic ideals of same—the *Enterprise* men act like they haven't seen a woman in months. No wonder Uhura, Rand, and Chapel are nowhere to be found here. Carmel is his typically garrulous self; costar Denberg went on to star in *Frankenstein Created Woman* before her accidental death due to drug use.

NAKED TIME, THE

★★★★ 1966. Dir: Marc Daniels. Guest cast: Bruce Hyde, Stewart Moss.

In my personal favorite Trek episode, an alien disease, passed by perspiration, brings out the hidden thoughts and desires of the *Enterprise* personnel. Best moments: Lt. Riley (Hyde) croaking out the Irish ditty "Kathleen" over the *Enterprise* P.A. system; Uhura's annoyed expression when Riley comments, "Women shouldn't look made up"; Christine Chapel confessing her love for Spock while lovingly kissing his fingers and Spock's confused reaction; and Kirk barking to Janice Rand, arriving on the bridge after just beating off an accosting crewman, "Yeoman, take the helm!" A great episode, well written by John D. F. Black and remade as the *Next Generation* segment "The Naked Now."

OBSESSION
★★★ 1967. Dir: Ralph Senensky. Guest cast: Stephen Brooks, Jerry Ayres.

Is Kirk losing it? Spock and McCoy think so when he keeps endangering everybody in his single-minded pursuit of a gaseous creature he once encountered years ago on his first mission. A nicely atypical episode, scripted by one-time *Dark Shadows* head writer Art Wallace, with some suspense and humor.

OMEGA GLORY, THE
★ 1968. Dir: Vincent McEveety. Guest cast: Morgan Woodward, Roy Jensen, Irene Kelly, David L. Ross.

Another renegade Starfleet captain has to be taken to task, this time for the selfish manipulation of the innocent people of the planet Omega. Written by Gene Roddenberry, this episode is rife with anti-Vietnam War sentiments, not-so-subtle subtleties, and lead-footed pacifist statements, highlighting *Trek*'s greatest failing—the sacrifice of entertainment value to pretentious self-importance.

OPERATION: ANNIHILATE!
★★ 1967. Dir: Herschel Daugherty. Guest cast: Joan Swift, Craig Hundley, Fred Carson, Maurishka.

Alien blob monsters that attach themselves to the human nervous system attack the *Enterprise* crew when Kirk visits his brother's family at an outpost on the planet Devena. The icky creatures, which look like leftovers from *The Outer Limits,* provide a few frissons in this otherwise silly chiller.

PARADISE SYNDROME, THE
★ 1968. Dir: Judd Taylor. Guest cast: Sabrina Scharf, Rudy Solari.

One of the all-time worst episodes finds Kirk suffering from amnesia while visiting a planet doomed to be destroyed by an asteroid. He marries a maiden of an American Indian-type tribe whose simple people believe him to be a healer called Kirock. Almost painfully bad.

PATTERNS OF FORCE
★★ 1968. Dir: Vincent McEveety. Guest cast: Richard Evans, Valora Noland, Skip Homeier, David Brian.

Alien Nazis battle *Enterprise* officers in an episode that looks like it was shot on sets leftover from *Hogan's Heroes.* But where's Colonel Klink when you really need him? Another outing on the tired theme of "renegade Federation officer interferes with the natural development of an alien culture," making economic use of the Paramount backlot.

PIECE OF THE ACTION, A
★★★ 1968. Dir: James Komack. Guest cast: Anthony Caruso, Vic Tayback, Lee Delano, John Harmon.

This is starting to sound familiar, but the *Enterprise* crew discovers a planet resembling an era of Earth's past—in this case the Roaring Twenties—while searching for a missing starship. Unlike some other *Trek* episodes stuck in this rut, this one plays up the inherent humor of the situation thanks to the light touch of sitcom director Komack, who makes this the best of *Trek*'s comic segments. Besides, how could you get mad at any show with Tayback in the cast? You could? Well, kiss my grits!

PLATO'S STEPCHILDREN
★★ 1968. Dir: David Alexander. Guest cast: Michael Dunn, Liam Sullivan, Barbara Babcock.

"The Squire of Gothos" meets "Who Mourns for Adonis?" in this most foolish of *Trek* shows. Telekinetic aliens who admire ancient Greek culture use the *Enterprise* officers—Kirk, Spock, McCoy, Uhura, and Chapel—as playthings. This is seriously goofy stuff that wastes a tender performance from gifted dwarf actor Dunn. Worth watching mainly for Kirk's attire (he's nearly naked in a mostly topless micromini); Spock serenading Uhura and Christine; and the kiss between Kirk and Uhura, seriously bungled due to network interference.

PRIVATE LITTLE WAR, A
★★ 1968. Dir: Marc Daniels. Guest cast: Nancy Kovack, Michael Whitney, Ned Romero, Janos Prohaska.

Klingons interfere with the natural evolution of a planet's people so, once more, Kirk must try to balance things out, this time by arming a tribe whose leader's wife (Kovack, pulling out all the stops) wants total power. Routine stuff worth seeing for Kirk's fight with a white gorillalike monster (played by veteran monkey man Prohaska) and a healing plant that looks like a joke shop novelty item.

REQUIEM FOR METHUSELAH
★☆ 1969. Dir: Murray Golden. Guest cast: James Daly, Louise Sorel.

Talky, drawn-out tale of an ageless alien (Daly, father of Tyne and Tim) who claims to have lived on Earth in various guises including DaVinci and Solomon and whose "daughter" (Sorel) turns out to be an android. A dull rehashing of familiar themes from the usually talented Jerome Bixby ("Mirror, Mirror").

RETURN OF THE ARCHONS
★★ 1967. Dir: Joseph Pevney. Guest cast: Harry Townes, Jon Lormer, Torin Thatcher, Charles Macauley, Brioni Farrell, Christopher Held.

Kirk et al. land upon a computer-controlled world where the robotic inhabitants occasionally let go with wild "festivals." Another show where we're shown the folly of folks letting a machine do all the thinking for them and Spock learns that a little illogic can be a good thing.

RETURN TO TOMORROW
★★★☆ 1968. Dir: Ralph Senensky. Guest Star: Diana Muldaur.

Well above average episode for the latter part of the second season. Kirk, Spock, and a lady scientist (Muldaur, later of *Next Generation*) willingly allow themselves to be possessed by disembodied alien intelligences until android bodies can be constructed for them. Trouble begins when Spock's visitor starts liking his body a little *too* much. A nicely emotional episode with good dialogue and a clever trick ending. Favorite scene: the possessed Spock dishing out discipline to an uncooperative Uhura.

SAVAGE CURTAIN, THE
★★☆ 1969. Dir: Herschel Daugherty. Guest cast: Lee Bergere, Barry Atwater, Philip Pine, Robert Herren, Carol Daniels Dement.

Kirk and Spock join with resurrected historical figures like Abe Lincoln (a well-cast Bergere) and a Vulcan leader called Surak (Atwater, also good) in battling the most evil villains in history—all part of the machinations of a rock-like alien. A not-bad third-season show with potential but somewhat indifferent handling.

SHORE LEAVE
★★★ 1967. Dir: Robert Spear. Guest cast: Emily Banks, Bruce Mars, Shirley Bonne, Barbara Baldwin, Perry Lopez.

A well-loved and well-executed episode about the *Enterprise*'s stopoff at a planet on which the ruling omnipotent computer grants one's every wish—both good and bad. Lots of nice bits (McCoy spotting Alice in Wonderland and the White Rabbit; Kirk brawling with old academy foe Finnegan) and a nice sense of humor make this one of the first season's highlights. With Banks as the Janice Rand substitute yeoman (many later year-one scripts had to be rewritten for other actresses after the depar-ture of Whitney from the cast) and Baldwin returning as Angela Martine, the young widow from "Balance of Terror."

SPACE SEED
★★★★ 1967. Dir: Marc Daniels. Guest cast: Ricardo Montalban, Madlyn Rhue, Mark Tobin, Kathy Ahart.

Montalban is outstanding as Khan, a genetically engineered superman from Earth's past who is revived from suspended animation and quickly takes over the *Enterprise*. One of the series' ten best, with great dialogue (Khan to Marla MacGiver [Rhue]: "Go—or stay, but do it because it is what you *want* to do!"), a well-utilized premise, and a surprisingly upbeat conclusion—somewhat negated, however, in the big-screen sequel *Star Trek II: The Wrath of Khan*.

SPECTRE OF THE GUN
★☆ 1968. Dir: Vincent McEveety. Guest cast: Rex Homan, Bill Zuckert, Sam Gilman, Bonnie Beecher.

Kirk and his men are trapped by aliens in a reenactment of the gunfight at O.K. Corral. One of the dumbest *Trek* shows; it's directed and designed in a fairly interesting manner but the storyline is too goofy for words. Kelley appeared in the actual movie version of *Gunfight at the O.K. Corral*, and that's Doohan, sans the Scots burr, as the voice of the alien being.

SPOCK'S BRAIN
★★ 1968. Dir: Marc Daniels. Guest cast: Marj Dusay, Sheila Leighton.

Alien bimbos steal the brain of the *Enterprise*'s second officer to run their ruler-computer in the silly third-season premiere. A cross between *Donovan's Brain* and *Fire Maidens of Outer Space* that's good for a few laughs—intentional, I think.

SQUIRE OF GOTHOS, THE
★★★☆ 1967. Dir: Donald McDougall. Guest cast: William Campbell, Venita Wolf, Michael Barrier, Richard Carlyle.

Campbell (whose character here must surely have been the inspiration for *Next Generation*'s Q) gives an outstanding performance as Tre-lane—a foppish alien life-form with supernatural powers and a love for the past cultures of Earth—who captures the *Enterprise* bridge crew as companions. A well-done variation on "Charlie X" (itself rehashed as "Plato's Stepchildren" among others) accomplished with action, humor, and intelligence. That's an uncredited Doohan and Barbara Babcock as the voices of Trelane's parents.

TASTE OF ARMAGEDDON, A

★★☆ 1967. Dir: Joseph Pevney. Guest cast: David Opatoshu, Barbara Babcock, Sean Kenny, Miko Mayama, Robert Sampson.

Kirk and crew end up on a planet, at war with a neighbor, where computers deal theoretical missile strikes and "casualties" report to disintegration chambers for execution. One of *Trek's* better variations on the evil computer storyline, with a predictable but satisfying ending.

THAT WHICH SURVIVES

★★☆ 1969. Dir: Herb Wallerstein. Guest cast: Lee Meriwether, Arthur Batanides, Naomi Pollack.

Former Miss America Meriwether is an effectively mournful presence as an android (made in its female creator's image) whose deadly touch does away with members of a landing party on a barren world a thousand light years from the *Enterprise*. It's a *Trek Ten Little Indians* minus the suspense (you know none of the regular characters will die) but well done nonetheless.

THIS SIDE OF PARADISE

★★☆ 1967. Dir: Ralph Senensky. Guest cast: Jill Ireland, Frank Overton, Grant Woods, Michael Barrier.

Spores from alien plants—another *Outer Limits* holdover—drug the *Enterprise* crew and turn them into passive knuckleheads. Spock even falls in love with lovely guest star Ireland. An okay episode that's the most fun when everybody starts acting like drugged-out goofballs and McCoy's southern accent really starts to get out of hand.

THOULIAN WEB, THE

★★★ 1968. Dir: Ralph Senensky.

Kirk disappears in an uncharted area of the galaxy where the *Enterprise* is emeshed in an energy web and various crew members—like Uhura in one memorable scene—see visions of their supposedly dead commander. One of the best third-season shows, this doesn't always work but is at least different enough to stand out from the rest of its uninspired pack.

TOMORROW IS YESTERDAY

★★☆ 1967. Dir: Michael O'Herlihy. Guest cast: Roger Perry, Sherri Townsend, Jim Spencer, Ed Peck.

Originally intended as a direct sequel to "The Naked Time," this has the *Enterprise* thrust back in time to 1960s Earth, where it's mistaken for a UFO by an air force pilot (Perry) whom Kirk is forced to take aboard when his jet is accidentally destroyed. An entertaining but fairly run-of-the-mill segment.

TROUBLE WITH TRIBBLES, THE

★★★ 1967. Dir: Joseph Pevney. Guest cast: William Campbell, Stanley Adams, William Schallert, Whit Bissell, Michael Pataki.

The *Enterprise* docks at a space station overrun with Klingons and alien fuzzballs called tribbles. One of *Trek's* best-remembered if more overrated episodes, this is more enjoyable for the seriocomic tensions between the *Enterprise* crew and the Klingons (writer David Gerrold constructed some fine moments for Scotty and the uptight Klingon commander, played to the hilt by Campbell) than for all the slapstick involving the purring tribbles.

TURNABOUT INTRUDER, THE

★★☆ 1969. Dir: Herb Wallerstein. Guest cast: Sandra Smith, Harry Landers.

An evil lady scientist (Smith), jealous of Kirk's career, uses an alien device to switch bodies with him. *Trek's* answer to *Dr. Jekyll and Sister Hyde,* this last broadcast episode isn't great but is certainly amusing. Shatner, in female mode, camps it up even worse than he did as the evil Kirk in "The Enemy Within," and Smith gives a far stronger performance than the silly material really warrants.

ULTIMATE COMPUTER, THE

★★★ 1968. Dir: John Meredyth Lucas. Guest cast: William Marshall, Barry Russo.

An electronics genius (Marshall of *Blacula* fame) invents an all-powerful computer that's installed in the *Enterprise* as part of an experiment to see if a starship can be run without a crew. Things go predictably awry when the computer takes out other starships during supposedly harmless war games. A solid second-season show all around, with especially strong acting from Marshall.

WAY TO EDEN, THE

★☆ 1969. Dir: David Alexander. Guest cast: Skip Homeier, Charles Napier, Mary Linda Rapelye, Deborah Downey, Phyllis Douglas, Victor Brandt.

Another third-season camp-fest, with the *Enterprise* picking up a commune of futuristic hippies and their scientist guru (Homeier). Laughs galore as *Trek* goes hip in the manner of a *Monkees* episode, though the downbeat ending in which the Edenic planet is revealed to be riddled with acid-laced grass and plants (the sulfuric kind of acid, that is) and poisoned fruit is a stunner. Douglas, the yeoman from "The Galileo Seven," plays one of the hippies.

WHAT ARE LITTLE GIRLS MADE OF?

★★★☆ 1966. Dir: James Goldstone. Guest cast: Michael Strong, Sherry Jackson, Ted Cassidy, Harry Basch.

Robert Block penned this fine episode in which Nurse Chapel (one of the few *Trek* regulars to get a back story) discovers that her long-missing scientist fiancé (Strong) is living on a planet also inhabited by androids that can be manufactured in any form—like Captain Kirk's! Full of great performances (Cassidy, Lurch from *The Addams Family* is excellent as mountainous android Ruk) and nice little touches (like Uhura giving Christine a kiss on the cheek as Chapel leaves the bridge to join her fiancé), making this one of the first season's best. Look for Shatner's underpants during the duplication sequence.

WHERE NO MAN HAS GONE BEFORE

★★★ 1966. Dir: James Goldstone. Guest cast: Gary Lockwood, Sally Kellerman, Paul Fix, Andrea Dromm, Paul Carr, Lloyd Haynes.

The second *Trek* pilot, and the first to star Shatner, is an intelligent handling of a familiar theme: an ordinary human given extraordinary powers he uses to his advantage. Lockwood and Kellerman are good as the crew members possessed by dark forces as the *Enterprise* skirts the edge of the universe, and the ending is nicely dark and uncompromising. Too bad the big fight scene between Shatner and Lockwood is played mostly by obvious doubles. The characters played by Fix, Dromm, and Haynes would later be rewritten for DeForest Kelly, Grace Lee Whitney, and Nichelle Nichols, while Haynes would later find fame on *Room 222.*

WHOM GODS DESTROY

★★ 1969. Dir: Herb Wallerstein. Guest cast: Steve Ihnat, Yvonne Craig, Keye Luke.

Kirk, Spock, and McCoy are captured by Garth (Ihnat), a shape-shifting madman who wants to commandeer the *Enterprise* as part of his plan to take over the galaxy. Routine episode notable mainly for Craig (TV's Batgirl) as a sexy green-skinned alien babe who comes to a messy end.

WHO MOURNS FOR ADONIS?

★★☆ 1967. Dir: Marc Daniels. Guest cast: Michael Forest, Leslie Parrish.

The *Enterprise* runs afoul of an omnipotent alien (Forest) who claims to be the Greek god Apollo. Nothing special but far from the sort of repetitive nonsense the series would eventually decline to, with a committed bit of acting by Forest as Apollo. Girl watchers will like the lovely Parrish in her gravity-defying Greek gown, while guy watchers should enjoy the muscular Michael in his revealing mini skirt.

WINK OF AN EYE

★★ 1968. Dir: Judd Taylor. Guest cast: Kathie Browne, Jason Evers, Eric Holland, Geoffrey Binney.

Kirk again finds himself trapped on a seemingly deserted *Enterprise,* only to discover that his metabolism has been sped up to match that of the Scalosians (who appear to humans as little more than buzzing shadows) by their queen (Browne), who wants Jimbo for her mate. It's the same old stuff, distinguished by a shot of Kirk pulling on his boots after he and the queen do the nasty—the most blatant display of the captain's hotbloodedness ever shown.

WOLF IN THE FOLD

★★★ 1967. Dir: Joseph Pevney. Guest cast: John Fielder, Charles Macauley, Pilar Seurat, Joseph Bernard, Tania Lemani, Virginia Ladridge.

Another episode written by Robert Bloch, this one makes use of one of the horror master's favorite concepts: that Jack the Ripper is really a form of deathless psychotic energy with its current string of murders blamed on poor Scotty. A surprisingly high female body count and a nicely written part for Doohan make this a more-interesting-than-usual show.

STAR TREK: THE NEXT GENERATION

Paramount, 1987–94, NR, 46 min. per episode.

The success of the *Star Trek* movies led Gene Roddenberry to create a whole new *Trek* TV series with new characters. Set in the twenty-fourth century—some years after events in the original *Star Trek* and the films that followed it—it would run more than twice as long as the original series, helped the new Fox Network establish itself as a contender against the big three networks, and was followed by spinoffs (*Star Trek: Deep Space Nine* and *Star Trek: Voyager*) and ripoffs (*Babylon 5*) of its own. This new, improved Starship *Enterprise* is captained by Patrick Stewart as Jean-Luc Picard. The bald-pated Shakespearean actor was an excellent choice for the role, bringing a sense of calm dignity to the *Enterprise* bridge. Other regulars are Jonathan Frakes as "Number One," William Riker; Gates McFadden as Dr. Beverly Crusher; Wil Wheaton as her teenage son Wesley; Mirina Sirtis as the empathic half-Betazoid Deanna Troi; Denise Crosby as Tasha Yar; Brent Spiner as the android Data; LaVar Burton as the blind Geordi Laforge, who can "see" via a wraparound eyewear device; and Michael

Dorn as the Klingon Worf—Klingons and the Federation are now part of the same alliance.

Contrary to the original series, which peaked early on in its first season and then became increasingly silly, *Next Generation*, after a shaky first year and a mostly misguided second, really hit its stride in its third year on the air with some bold storylines and fine ensemble acting. Some complained about the show's overt political correctness and all-inclusiveness of every race, sex, creed, and the like, but this "kinder, gentler" approach obviously had appeal and worked well for the series. Crosby left the show near the end of the first season and Wheaton dropped out during the fourth, though both made later return appearances; in year two McFadden was temporarily replaced by Diana Muldaur as Dr. Katherine Pulaski and Whoopi Goldberg was added to the cast as lounge hostess Guinan. John de Lancie made frequent guest appearances as the malevolent but playful alien Q, while classic *Trek* actors Leonard Nimoy, DeForest Kelley, James Doohan, and Mark Lenard appeared in their old roles.

One of the biggest-budgeted television shows ever aired, the average *Next Generation* episode cost $1,000,000 to produce, with ILM FX much improved over the special effects of the original show and the Jerry Goldsmith theme music from the first *Star Trek* movie. After seven years on the air, the *Next Generation* crew followed their classic predecessors onto the big screen where, undoubtedly, they'll continue to boldly go where no one has gone before for sometime yet to come.

ALL GOOD THINGS

★★★ 1994. Dir: Winrich Kolbe. Guest cast: John de Lancie, Denise Crosby, Colm Meaney, Clyde Kusatsu.

Picard is sent bouncing back and forth in time from the present to the future to the past in this well-plotted and -acted final episode. Lots of old friends appear; as ever the sparring between Picard and de Lancie's Q is a highlight, though the "end of time and space as we know it" theme gets to be a bit heavy.

ALLEGIANCE

★★★ 1990. Dir: Winrich Kolbe. Guest cast: Stephen Markel, Reiner Schone, Jocelyn O'Brien.

A hackneyed concept—Picard kidnapped by aliens and replaced with a double—is given a new lease on life thanks to Patrick Stewart's marvelous performance as the false Picard.

ANGEL ONE

★★☆ 1988. Dir: Michael Rhodes. Guest cast: Karen Montgomery, Sam Hennings, Patricia McPherson.

A dated battle of the sexes story with Riker, Troi, and Yar landing on a planet where the men are weak and passive and the women strong and aggressive. Silly, but worth seeing for Jonathan Frakes in his slave boy costume.

ARSENAL OF FREEDOM, THE

★★☆ 1988. Dir: Les Landau. Guest cast: Vincent Schiarelli, Marco Rodriguez, Julia Nickson.

An okay ensemble show in which the *Enterprise* crew searches for a missing Starship on a planet run by an automated defense device.

BATTLE, THE

★★☆ 1987. Dir: Rob Bowman. Guest cast: Frank Corsentino, Doug Warhit, Robert Towers.

The second Ferengi episode, a slight improvement on the first ("The Last Outpost"), still no great shakes. A Ferengi commander (Warhit) gifts Picard with the derelict ship he once commanded in battle that ended in the death of the Ferengi's son. Soon Picard begins to relive the battle in his mind—or is it in his mind?

BEST OF BOTH WORLDS, THE

★★★★ 1990. Dir: Cliff Bole. Guest cast: Elizabeth Dennehy, George Murdock, Whoopi Goldberg, Colm Meaney, Todd Merrill.

The Next Generation's best and best-remembered episodes, this two-part top-quality outing has Picard kidnapped and "assimilated" by the biomechanical Borg race who need the captain's knowledge of Starfleet in their plans for universal dominance. Meanwhile, Riker takes command while at constant loggerheads with his ambitious female "Number One" (Dennehy, daughter of Brian). The second half is a bit of an anticlimax but this is still the new *Trek*'s finest hour.

BIG GOODBYE, THE

★★★☆ 1988. Dir: Joseph L. Scanlon. Guest cast: Lawrence Tierney, Harvey Jason, William Boyett, Dick Miller.

A minor classic, this first of the holodeck episodes traps Picard, Crusher, and Data in the captain's hard-boiled *Maltese Falcon*-like fantasy. A clever variation on the classic *Trek* episode "A Piece of the Action," this is exceptionally well written by Tracy Torme, son of Mel.

BONDING, THE

★★★ 1989. Dir: Winrich Kolbe. Guest cast: Susan Powell, Gabriel Damon, Colm Meaney.

An above-average, emotional episode about the loss of a parent. Picard and Troi try to comfort a young boy who's recently lost his mother. Soon a ghostly entity comes to the boy, who believes it to be his mom's friendly spirit. Isn't it?

BOOBY TRAP

★★☆ 1989. Dir: Gabrielle Beaumont. Guest cast: Susan Gibney, Whoopi Goldberg, Colm Meaney.

Picard leads an away team to investigate an ancient alien vessel, only to discover that the ship is a lure used to trap various spaceships and drain them of all energy. Routine apart from some nice insights into the character of Guinan (Goldberg).

BROTHERS

★★☆ 1990. Dir: Rob Bowman. Guest cast: Cory Danziger, Colm Meaney, Adam Ryen.

On a mission to save a young boy's life, Data suddenly malfunctions and forces the *Enterprise* back to the home world of his creator, Dr. Noonien Soong. Data's "brother" Lore also turns up in this vehicle for Brent Spiner as Data/Lore/Soong.

CAPTAIN'S HOLIDAY

★★☆ 1990. Dir: Chip Chalmers. Guest cast: Jennifer Hetrick, Karen Landry, Michael Champion.

Picard's vacation is anything but restful as he becomes involved with a femme fatale (Hetrick) and the search for an ancient artifact.

CHILD, THE

★☆ 1988. Dir: Rob Bowman. Guest cast: Seymour Cassel, Whoopi Goldberg, Colm Meaney, R. J. Williams.

A writer's strike forced the *Next Generation* producers to use this old script for the unfilmed *Star Trek II* series. Troi is impregnated by an alien force and gives birth to a rapidly aging child. Nice to see Marina Sirtis in an expanded role but this is still one of the silliest *Next Generation* episodes.

CLUES

★★ 1991. Dir: Les Landau. Guest cast: Pamela Winslow, Colm Meaney, Whoopi Goldberg, Rhonda Aldrich.

Investigating a mysterious planet, the *Enterprise* personnel discover that a wormhole—or was it?—has caused them to lose an entire day of their lives. The most interesting aspect of this episode is that it's based on a script submitted by a series fan, Bruce D. Arthurs.

CODE OF HONOR

★★★ 1987. Dir: Russ Mayberry. Guest cast: Jessie Lawrence Ferguson, Karole Selman, James Louis Watkins.

Negotiations for a cure for a deadly plague stall when an alien chief involved in them falls for Yar. An amusing vehicle for Denise Crosby highlighted by a memorable cat fight between Crosby and Selman.

COMING OF AGE

★★ 1988. Dir: Michael Vejar: Guest cast: Ward Costello, Robert Schenkkar, John Putch, Robert Ito.

A modest vehicle for the usually fan-reviled Wesley, who prepares to take the Starfleet Academy exam while Picard's loyalty is tested by an old friend.

CONSPIRACY

★★★☆ 1988. Dir: Cliff Bole. Guest cast: Henry Darrow, Ward Costello, Robert Schenkkar, Ursaline Bryant, Ray Reinhardt, Michael Berryman.

One of season one's best (and darkest) episodes is a variation on *The Puppet Masters* in which Starfleet is nearly toppled by alien parasites who possess various command personnel. Scary and gripping, with a gory exploding head scene that offended some namby-pamby fans.

CONTAGION

★★ 1989. Dir: Joseph L. Scanlon. Guest cast: Thalmus Resulala, Carolyn Seymour, Colm Meaney.

A computer virus from an ancient alien civilization cripples both the *Enterprise* and an attacking Romulan vessel. Mediocre show from the mostly uninspired second season.

DARMOK

★★★☆ 1991. Dir: Winrich Kolbe. Guest cast: Richard James, Ashley Judd, Paul Winfield, Colm Meaney.

A very good variation on the original *Trek*'s "Arena" finds Picard and an alien called a Tamarian—whose language is indecipherable—trapped on a hostile planet with a deadly monster. Youngest Judd sister Ashley makes her acting debut as a pretty ensign.

DATALORE

★★★ 1988. Dir: Rob Bowman. Guest cast: Biff Yeager.

The first Data back story has the android returning to the lab where he was created. There his lookalike "brother" Lore shuts him down and tries to take his place aboard the *Enterprise*. The first episode in the series that really delved into a character's psyche and a harbinger of things to come.

DATA'S DAY

★★★ 1991. Dir: Robert Wiemer. Guest cast: Rosalind Chao, Colm Meaney, Sierra Pecheur.

A sweet episode depicting a day in the life of

the *Enterprise*'s resident android—on this particular day Data's friend Keiko (Chao) is having second thoughts about her upcoming marriage to O'Brien (Meaney). Another nice Brent Spiner showcase.

DAUPHIN, THE
★★☆ 1989. Dir: Rob Bowman. Guest cast: Paddi Edwards, Jamie Hubbard, Colm Meaney, Madchen Amick.

Simple story of Wesley's first romance. Trouble arises when it turns out that the alien princess (Hubbard) he loves is a shape-shifter.

DEFECTOR, THE
★★★ 1989. Dir: Robert Scheerer. Guest cast: James Sloyan, Andreas Katsulas, John Hancock.

A Romulan defector (Sloyan) is picked up by the *Enterprise* and reveals that his people are plotting to retake the Neutral Zone as their own. But can he be trusted? Solid dramatics with an unexpectedly downbeat ending. Look for Patrick Stewart (in heavy make-up) in a surprise cameo as a soldier.

DEJA Q
★★★☆ 1990. Dir: Les Landau. Guest cast: John de Lancie, Whoopi Goldberg, Corbin Bernsen.

A powerless Q (de Lancie) turns up on the *Enterprise,* trailed by a formless creature that nearly destroys Data, who is assigned to protect Q from danger. A top episode with a sparkling deLancie and a nice sense of humor. *L.A. Law* star Bernsen appears at episode's end as the Q who restores de Lancie's power.

DEVIL'S DUE
★★ 1991. Dir: Tom Benko. Guest cast: Marta Dubois, Paul Lambert, Marcello Tubert.

Another unfilmed *Star Trek II* script was dusted off for this routine outing about a seductive female devil trying to corrupt the *Enterprise* crew. You can almost see William Shatner swaggering through this one.

DISASTER
★★★ 1991. Dir: Gabrielle Beaumont. Guest cast: Rosalind Chao, Colm Meaney, Michelle Forbes, Erika Flores.

Catastrophe befalls the *Enterprise* when power failures trap various characters in various parts of the ship, leaving Troi in command of the bridge. This homage to the disaster films of Irwin Allen leaves no cliché unturned (my favorite bit is Worf delivering Keiko's baby) and, against all odds, turns out to be one of the highlights of the fifth season.

DRUMHEAD, THE
★★★☆ 1991. Dir: Jonathan Frakes. Guest cast: Jean Simmons, Bruce French, Henry Woronicz, Spencer Garrett.

An explosion of the *Enterprise*'s dilithium chamber leads to a charge of sabotage and treason against a young Klingon officer (Woronicz). Veteran actress Simmons (just off the *Dark Shadows* revival) is excellent as an admiral who comes out of retirement to head the investigation and eventually accuse Picard himself. Exceptionally well directed by Frakes.

ELEMENTARY, DEAR DATA
★★☆ 1988. Dir: Rob Bowman. Guest cast: Daniel Davis, Alan Shearmann, Anne Elizabeth Ramsay, Biff Manard.

A somewhat contrived second-season episode in which Data's fascination with Sherlock Holmes leads to his, Laforge 's, and Pulaski's holodeck encounter with a professor Moriarty (Davis) who wishes to take over the *Enterprise.* Nice Victorian atmosphere but many of the later holodeck episodes come off better.

11,001,001
★★★☆ 1988. Dir: Paul Lynch. Guest cast: Carolyn McCormick, Gene Dynarski.

One of year one's best written shows (by Maurice Hurley and Robert Lewin). A strange race called the Bynars is called in to overhaul the *Enterprise*'s computer system—leading to holodeck images (including the lovely McCormick) that are a little too real. The melancholy ending is a nice touch.

EMISSARY, THE
★★★ 1989. Dir: Cliff Bole. Guest cast: Suzie Piakson, Lance LeGault, Georgann Johnson, Colm Meaney, Anne Elizabeth Ramsay.

In a good showcase for Michael Dorn's Worf, a half-human, half-Klingon emissary (Piakson)—sent to smooth things over when the crew of a Klingon ship (in suspended animation since before the Klingon-Federation alliance) is awakened—turns out to be his old girlfriend. Good chemistry between Dorn and Piakson makes this work.

ENCOUNTER AT FARPOINT
★★★ 1987. Dir: Corey Allen. Guest cast: John de Lancie, Michael Bell, Colm Meaney, DeForest Kelley.

On its first mission, the newly commissioned *Enterprise* encounters the omnipotent alien being Q (de Lancie) investigating an advanced research lab allegedly built by the low-tech Bandi race. *Trek* veteran D. C. Fontana scripted the series' two-part opener; it does a good job of setting up the characters and their relationships but tends toward talkiness. The Kelley cameo is warmly effective.

ENEMY, THE

★★★ 1989. Dir: David Carson. Guest cast: John Snyder, Andreas Karsulas, Colm Meaney, Steve Rankin.

Laforge and a Romulan shuttle crash survivor are forced to join forces to survive in a hostile, stormswept world. A solid show constructed around a familiar theme with some nicely harsh moments—especially when Worf refuses to donate blood to another injured Romulan, who subsequently dies.

ENSIGN RO

★★★☆ 1991. Dir: Les Landau. Guest cast: Michelle Forbes, Scott Marlowe, Cliff Potts, Whoopi Goldberg.

Forbes makes a strong first impression as Ensign Ro Laren, a young Bajoran who was once courtmartialed following a botched away-team mission. When Bajoran extremists attack, Ro is suspected of being a traitor when her away team is taken hostage. A strong, character-driven show with an especially nice bit where Ro is befriended by Guinan.

ENSIGNS OF COMMAND

★★★ 1989. Dir: Cliff Bole. Guest cast: Eileen Seeley, Mark L Taylor, Grainger Hines, Colm Meaney, Richard Allen.

Data is sent to head the evacuation of a planet that has been recently treatied to a corporation that demands it to be cleared of all inhabitants. Trouble is, the settlers refuse to leave. A solid Data show; Seeley is good as the woman who helps the android with his task.

EVOLUTION

★★ 1989. Dir: Winrich Kolbe. Guest cast: Ken Jenkins, Whoopi Goldberg.

Wesley's new science project inadvertently causes a malfunction in an inventor's space probe, set to be launched from the *Enterprise*. This third-season opener is notable for the return of Dr. Crusher but little else.

FAMILY

★★★★ 1990. Dir: Les Landau. Guest cast: Samantha Eggar, Jeremy Kemp, Theodore Bikel, Georgia Brown, Colm Meaney, Doug Wart, David Tristin Birkin.

One of my favorites, this wasn't particularly well received when first aired but has become an acknowledged classic since. With almost no scenes aboard the *Enterprise* (in dry dock after the Borg attack), this deals with the family ties of Picard (who visits his brother in France); Worf (who is visited by his human foster parents); and Wesley (who gets to view a holographic message from his late father). A powerhouse actor's episode with a great guest cast.

FINAL MISSION

★★☆ 1990. Dir: Corey Allen. Guest cast: Nick Tate, Kim Hamilton, Mary Kohnert.

Wesley's swansong sees him and Picard stranded on an alien world where our young hero must (of course) save the wounded captain's life. Predictable all the way but still watchable. Tate is probably best known for his role of Alan Carter on *Space: 1999*.

FIRST CONTACT

★★★ 1991. Dir: Cliff Bole. Guest cast: George Coe, Carolyn Seymour, George Hearn, Bebe Neuwirth.

A clever variation on *The Day the Earth Stood Still* in which an undercover Riker is injured while exploring the unknown world of Malcoria III. Picard and Troi beam down to help but their offer of peace is mistrusted by the Malcorian people, who see the *Enterprise* crew as alien monsters. An effective look at space exploration from another point of view, with our heroes viewed in the same light as the Earth-invading bug-eyed monsters of some 1950s B movie.

FUTURE IMPERFECT

★★★ 1990. Dir: Les Landau. Guest cast: Andreas Katsulas, Chris Demetral, Carolyn McCormick, Patti Yasutake, Todd Merrill.

After blacking out in battle, Riker awakens to discover that nearly two decades have passed: he is now the commander of the *Enterprise* with a teenage son and a dead wife who was actually a holodeck illusion from the "11,001,001" episode. An interesting showcase for Jonathan Frakes marred only by a silly ending.

GALAXY'S CHILD

★★☆ 1991. Dir: Winrich Kolbe. Guest cast: Susan Gibney, Whoopi Goldberg, April Grace.

The offspring of an alien killed by the *Enterprise* crew attaches itself to the ship and begins to drain it of all energy. Meanwhile, Laforge meets the woman (Gibney) with whose holodecked image he has fallen in love. A good idea—about the loss of a fantasy when you meet an idealized person in the flesh—gets lost in the background of yet another monster story.

GAME, THE

★★★ 1991. Dir: Corey Allen. Guest cast: Wil Wheaton, Ashley Judd, Colm Meaney, Patti Yasutake.

Wesley's return visit to the *Enterprise* coincides with the latest onboard rage: a virtual reality video game that actually induces mind control in the player. A *Trek* version of David Cronenberg's *Videodrome*, this comes off pretty well though the romantic subplot involving Wes and Ensign Lefler (Judd) I just couldn't buy.

HALF A LIFE

★★★☆ 1991. Dir: Les Landau. Guest cast: Majel Barrett, David Ogden Stiers, Michelle Forbes, Colm Meaney, Carel Struycken, Terrence E. McNally.

An especially moving episode, with Troi's mother Lwaxana (Barrett) played for seriousness for once. When Lwaxana becomes interested in an alien scientist (Stiers, Major Charles Emerson Winchester on *M*A*S*H*), she is horrified that he must soon die a ritual suicide—the fate of all those in his society when they reach the age of sixty. Forbes was so impressive in her role as Stiers's daughter that she was soon rewarded with the semi-regular role of Ensign Ro.

HAVEN

★★☆ 1987. Dir: Richard Compton. Guest cast: Majel Barrett, Rob Knepper, Nan Martin, Robert Ellenstein, Carel Strycken.

Troi's mom Lwaxana (Barrett) arrives with the young man with whom Deanna was pledged to "bond" with when they both were children. The first vehicle for Miss Majel as Lwaxana, this reworking of the original *Trek*'s "Amok Time" has moments but its comedy is often forced and its emotions hollow.

HEART OF GLORY

★★★☆ 1988. Dir: Rob Bowman. Guest cast: Vaughn Armstrong, Charles H. Hyman, David Froman.

Worf's loyalties are tested when the *Enterprise* picks up a trio of Klingon dissidents who oppose the Federation-Klingon alliance. A near-classic *Next Generation* episode; Michael Dorn gets his first chance in the spotlight, as Worf is torn between his friends and his heritage.

HIDE & Q

★★☆ 1987. Dir: Cliff Bole. Guest cast: John de Lancie, Elaine Nalee, William A. Wallace.

Q (de Lancie, nimble as ever) returns with a test for Riker, whom he tempts with the power of life and death and the ability to grant his friend's greatest wishes. A fun but lesser Q adventure.

HIGH GROUND, THE

★★★ 1990. Dir: Gabrielle Beaumont. Guest cast: Kerrie Keane, Richard Cox, Marc Buckland.

The *Enterprise* is threatened by terrorists who kidnap Crusher when they arrive at the deunified world of Rutin IV. A solidly constructed allegory on the conflict in Northern Ireland, this is a nice attempt to bring more action to the series. Choice moment: Picard clocking a terrorist on the *Enterprise* bridge.

HOLLOW PURSUITS

★★☆ 1990. Dir: Cliff Bole. Guest cast: Dwight Shultz, Colm Meaney.

Shultz has a good role in this otherwise routine show about a nerdy engineer who can't handle life and continually escapes into a holodeck fantasy world. Some fun touches but rather contrived.

HOME SOIL

★ 1988. Dir: Corey Allen. Guest cast: Walter Gotell, Elizabeth Lindsay, Gerard Pendergast.

Maybe the *Next Generation*'s worst episode, a sad rehash of the original *Trek*'s "Devil in the Dark" about a Federation terraforming station on a hostile planet terrorized by a microscopic lifeform whose territory is threatened. Gotell is best known for playing Russian General Gogol in several James Bond movies.

HOST, THE

★★☆ 1991. Dir: Marvin V. Rush. Guest cast: Barbara Tarbuck, Franc Luz, Nicole Orth-Pallavicini, Patti Yasutake.

Dr. Crusher falls in love with an alien mediator (Luz) who turns out to be only the human host body for the alien within. This episode stirred a bit of controversy because of the ending where the alien chooses a new female host yet still loves Crusher—raising the spectre of lesbianism—but is too routine to be very memorable otherwise.

HUNTED, THE

★★☆ 1990. Dir: Cliff Bole. Guest cast: Jeff McCarthy, James Cromwell, Colm Meaney.

Another allegory, this one about the treatment of Vietnam vets. The *Enterprise* encounters a new alien society willing to join the Federation but ultimately refused because of the way it treats its genetically engineered warriors after their usefullness in battle is at an end. Flawed but not without interest.

I, BORG

★★★ 1992. Dir: Robert Lederman. Guest cast:

Jonathan Del Arco, Whoopi Goldberg.

The *Enterprise* rescues a spacecraft crash survivor who turns out to be a young Borg (Del Arco) who begins to show signs of humanity once he is cut off from his fellows. Another good Borg show about how even the most hated of enemies can become a friend under the proper circumstances.

ICARUS FACTOR, THE
★★ 1989. Dir: Robert Iscove. Guest cast: Mitchell Ryan, Colm Meaney, Lance Spellberg.

Riker reencounters his estranged father (Ryan), whom he hasn't seen in years, while Worf is out of sorts after missing an important Klingon ritual. Separately either one of these plots would have made for a good episode, but mixed together neither is given the time to develop properly, leaving this otherwise very well-acted segment feeling very unsatisfying.

IDENTITY CRISIS
★★★ 1991. Dir: Winrich Kolbe. Guest cast: Maryann Plunkett, Patti Yasutake, Amick Byram.

Laforge and the only other survivor of an away team to a strange planet discover themselves infected with alien DNA that transforms them into a new species. Unique special effects compliment this suspenseful entry.

IN THEORY
★★ 1991. Dir: Patrick Stewart. Guest cast: Michele Scarabelli, Rosalind Chao, Colm Meaney, Whoopi Goldberg.

Stewart made his directorial bow with this well-intentioned but mediocre story about a female Enterprise officer (Scarebelli) who falls in love with Data.

JUSTICE
★★ 1987. Dir: James L. Conway. Guest cast: Brenda Bakke, Jay Louden, Josh Clark.

The *Enterprise* stops off for a little R and R at the idyllic planet Rubicon, where young Wesley accidentally breaks one of their laws and is marked for death.

LAST OUTPOST, THE
★★ 1987. Dir: Richard Colla. Guest cast: Armin Shimerman, Jake Dengel, Tracey Walter.

The Federation's first contact with the Ferengi involve them in a joint mission to investigate the long-dead Tkon Empire. Mediocre introduction to the mostly miscalculated comic-relief villains, who usually come off as Borscht Belt Klingons.

LEGACY
★★★ 1990. Dir: Robert Scheerer. Guest cast: Beth Toussaint, Don Mirault, Colm Meaney.

On a rescue mission to the late Tasha Yar's planet Turkana IV, the *Enterprise* officers encounter her younger sister Ishara (Toussaint), who is involved in a local civil war. Yar's legacy truly lives on in this well-done episode, and the trusting Data learns a nicely bitter lesson when he befriends the duplicitous Ishara.

LONELY AMONG US
★☆ 1987. Dir: Cliff Bole. Guest cast: John Durbin, Colm Meaney, Kavi Raz.

Murder occurs while the *Enterprise* is transporting ambassadors to a peace conference. A weak imitation of the original *Trek*'s classic "Journey to Babel."

LOSS, THE
★★ 1990. Dir: Chip Chalmers. Guest cast: Whoopi Goldberg, Kim Braden, Mary Kohnert.

When Troi's empathic powers mysteriously vanish, she begins to doubt her usefulness to her fellow crew members. Once again Troi is spotlighted in a sadly underwritten and routine episode. The scene where Deanna talks with Guinan (Goldberg) is the best, and shows both Mirina Sirtis and Whoopi at their most sympathetic.

LOUD AS A WHISPER
★☆ 1989. Dir: Larry Shaw. Guest cast: Howie Seago, Leo Damian, Marnie Mosiman, Thomas Oglesby, Colm Meaney.

A well-meant but heavy-handed message show about a deaf alien mediator (played by real-life hearing-impaired Seago) who "hears" via a chorus of telepathic assistants. When the chorus is killed by terrorists, the mediator must find a new way to communicate. Actress Mosiman is married to Q himself, John de Lancie.

MANHUNT
★ 1989. Dir: Rob Bowman. Guest cast: Majel Barrett, Robert Costanza, Carel Struycken, Rod Arrants, Colm Meaney, Mick Fleetwood, Rhonda Aldrich, Robert O'Reilly.

Lwaxana Troi (Barrett) is back again, with Picard escaping her affections into his favorite holodeck fantasy as private eye Dixon Hill. The worst of the Lwaxana episodes, this dire melange of unconnected elements was originally scripted by Tracy Torme, who took a pseudonym after it was extensively (and badly) rewritten by other hands.

MATTER OF HONOR, A

★★★☆ 1989. Dir: Rob Bowman. Guest cast: John Putch, Christopher Collins, Brad Thompson, Colm Meaney.

One of the few highlights of season two, this extraordinary episode is *Next Generation* at its near-best. An exchange program between the Federation and the Klingon Empire reassigns Riker to a Klingon vessel and a young Klingon ensign (Putch, son of *All in the Family*'s Jean Stapleton) is sent aboard the *Enterprise*. Sharply written, with Jonathan Frakes making the most of his biggest role to date with some of Riker's best scenes.

MATTER OF PERSPECTIVE, A

★★ 1990. Dir: Cliff Bole. Guest cast: Craig Richard Nelson, Gina Hecht, Colm Meaney.

When a scientist's wife (Hecht) accuses Riker of her husband's murder, Picard suggests using the holodeck to recreate the crime and get at the truth. The use of the holodeck is about the only noteworthy aspect of this rehashing of the classic *Trek*'s "Wolf in the Fold."

MATTER OF TIME, A

★★☆ 1991. Dir: Paul Lynch. Guest cast: Matt Frewer, Stefan Gierash, Sheila Franklin.

An ebullient time traveler (Frewer, of *Max Headroom* fame) arrives on the *Enterprise* with a hidden agenda in this pleasant enough segment with a few effective twists.

MEASURE OF A MAN, THE

★★★★ 1989. Dir: Robert Scheerer. Guest cast: Amanda McBroom, Clyde Kusatsu, Brian Brophy, Colm Meaney, Whoopi Goldberg.

Year two's best episode is this beautifully written story (by Melinda Snodgrass) of whether the android Data is a being in his own right or merely the property of Starfleet to be done with as they see fit. A fine rumination on personal freedom with the entire cast in top form.

MÉNAGE À TROI

★★ 1990. Dir: Robert Legato. Guest cast: Majel Barrett, Frank Corsentino, Ethan Phillips, Carel Struycken.

Picard helps Lwaxana Troi (Barrett, as ever), who finds herself saddled with an unwanted lovesick Ferengi suitor (Corsentino). Mediocre comedy with a funny ending; the Lwaxana-Deanna "nude" scene is a series low point, an embarrassing bid to be controversial.

MIND'S EYE, THE

★★★ 1991. Dir: David Livingston. Guest cast: Larry Dobkin, John Fleck, Colm Meaney.

Laforge is kidnapped and given brainwashing implants as part of a Romulan plot to disrupt the Klingon-Federation alliance. Nicely suspenseful; Geordi given a welcome central role.

MOST TOYS, THE

★★ 1990. Dir: Timothy Bond. Guest cast: Saul Rubinek, Nehemiah Persoff, Jane Daly, Colm Meaney.

Data's destruction is faked by a collector of strange artifacts (Rubinek), who wants to add the android to his collection. There are a few echoes of *The Measure of a Man*, but mostly this comes off more like an episode of *Lost in Space*.

NAKED NOW, THE

★★ 1987. Dir: Paul Lynch. Guest cast: Brooke Bundey, Benjamin W. S. Lum, Michael Rider.

Contact with a dead research vessel unleashes a disease that brings out all the hidden desires and feelings in the *Enterprise* crew. The second episode of the series, this mediocre remake of the classic *Trek* episode "The Naked Time" has little of the original's emotional impact. Director Lynch is probably best known for the Jamie Lee Curtis vehicle "Prom Night.

NEUTRAL ZONE, THE

★★★ 1988. Dir: James L. Conway. Guest cast: Marc Alaimo, Peter Mark Richman, Grace Harrison, Leon Rippy, Anthony James.

The *Enterprise* must contend with both an invisibly cloaked Romulan ship and three humans awakened from cryogenic freezing after three centuries of hibernation. The final show of the first season, this is good fun, with echoes of the original *Trek* episodes "Space Seed" and "Balance of Terror." Conway also directed the cult horror film *The Boogens*.

NEW GROUND

★★☆ 1992. Dir: Robert Scheerer. Guest cast: Georgia Brown, Brian Bonsall, Jennifer Edwards, Sheila Franklin, Richard McGonagle.

Worf's son Alexander (Bonsall) is brought aboard the *Enterprise* by Worf's foster mom (Brown) for a little fatherly discipline. After the usual father-son misunderstandings, Worf and the boy find common ground. An okay episode spotlighting the *Enterprise*'s resident Klingon hothead; nice scene of Troi counciling Worf on how to raise the brat.

NIGHT TERRORS

★☆ 1991. Dir: Les Landau. Guest cast: Rosalind Chao, John Vickery, Colm Meaney, Whoopi Goldberg, Craig Hurley, Brian Tochi.

After discovering a starship adrift with only its

Betazoid counselor (Vickery) still alive, Troi is tormented by a series of distrubing nightmares. A *Next Generation* version of *A Nightmare on Elm Street,* this is yet another case where the lovely Deanna is showcased in an otherwise bad episode.

THE NTH DEGREE

★★ 1991. Dir: Robert Legato. Guest cast: Dwight Shultz, Jim Norton, Kay E. Kuter, Page Leong.

An alien probe turns the nerdy Barclay (Shultz) into a superintelligent advanced form of human life who pilots the *Enterprise* to the end of the universe. A followup to "Hollow Pursuits," this brought back Shultz, which is good, but emulates too many other sources, like *The Lawnmower Man,* which isn't.

OFFSPRING, THE

★★☆ 1990. Dir: Jonathan Frakes. Guest cast: Hallie Todd, Nicolas Coster, Judyanne Elder.

Data builds for himself a "daughter" called Lal (Todd) but Starfleet insists that a laboratory and not a starship is the place she should be raised. Frakes made his directorial debut with this episode, which merely rehashes issues from *"The Measure of a Man"* but is made worthwhile by the performances of Todd and Brent Spiner.

OUTRAGEOUS OKANA, THE

★★ 1988. Dir: Robert Becker. Guest cast: Bill Campbell, Teri Hatcher, Joe Piscopo, Whoopi Goldberg, Douglas Rowe, Albert Stratton.

A rather forced comic episode with Campbell (later the star of *The Rocketeer*) as a charming vagabond who is suspected of stealing a valuable jewel and making an alien leader's daughter pregnant. The best scenes occur in a holodeck comedy club, with Piscopo well cast as an obnoxious comic.

PEAK PERFORMANCE

★★★ 1989. Dir: Robert Scheerer. Guest cast: Roy Brocksmith, Armin Shimerman, David L. Lander.

The Ferengi and the Federation join forces to prepare against the Borg. The *Enterprise* and another starship, the *Hathaway* (a tribute to Nancy Kulp, perhaps?), commanded by Riker, engage in war games that become only too real. A uniquely good Ferengi show with many effective twists; Lander is best known as Squiggy on *Laverne and Shirley.*

PEN PALS

★★☆ 1989. Dir: Winrich Kolbe. Guest cast: Nikki Cox, Nicholas Cascone, Colm Meaney.

Data fears he may have violated the Prime Directive when he begins a radio correspondence with a frightened alien orphan (Cox) whom he is forced to bring aboard the *Enterprise* to save from her unstable planet.

PRICE, THE

★★★ 1989. Dir: Robert Scheerer. Guest cast: Matt McCoy, Elizabeth Hoffman, Dan Shor, Scott Thompson, Colm Meaney, Kevin Peter Hall.

At last—a good Troi episode! Deanna falls for a handsome negotiator at a conference where various parties bid for the ownership of a seemingly stable wormhole. Even the Ferengi are good in this better-than-usual outing.

Q-PID

★★★☆ 1991. Dir: Cliff Bole. Guest cast: John de Lancie, Jennifer Hetrick, Clive Revill.

Q (de Lancie) plays matchmaker, or something, when he creates a Robin Hood fantasy for Picard as Robin and Vash (Hetrick, returning from "Captain's Holiday") as Maid Marian, hoping that they will admit their feelings for each other. One of the series' most renowned and funniest episodes, featuring a disgruntled Worf's classic "I am *not* a merry man!" line.

Q WHO?

★★★☆ 1989. Dir: Rob Bowman. Guest cast: John de Lancie, Whoopi Goldberg, Colm Meaney, Lycia Naff.

The Borg make their first, formidable appearance here with Q (de Lancie) peevishly sending the *Enterprise* off into unknown reaches of space, where they encounter the half-humanoid, half-android Borg, who possess a group mind and a relentless need to assimilate all technology. Although Q is kept on the sidelines for the most part, his encounter with Guinan (Goldberg) is one of season two's finest moments.

REDEMPTION

★★☆ 1991. Dirs: Cliff Bole, David Carson. Guest cast: Denise Crosby, Tony Todd, Whoopi Goldberg, Colm Meaney, Robert O'Reilly, Gwyneth Walsh, Barbara March, J. D. Callum.

In this two-part episode, Worf resigns from the *Enterprise* to take part in a Klingon civil war, where he discovers that one of the warriors is the half-Romulan daughter of Tasha Yar (Crosby). *Next Generation*'s second cliffhanger isn't nearly as effective as "The Best of Both Worlds." Michael Dorn is in good form but the Tasha's daughter subplot is a lot more preposterous a plot twist to get Crosby back on the show than had they merely resurrected her character of Yar à la Spock in the third *Star Trek* movie.

REMEMBER ME

★★☆ 1990. Dir: Cliff Bole. Guest cast: Eric Menyuk, Bill Erwin, Colm Meaney.

Wesley's failed experiment with a warp-field accidentally sends his mother into an alternate universe where all those she knows and loves begin disappearing. Despite a fine Gates McFadden performance and some standout special effects, this segment remains too over-complicated to work fully.

REUNION

★★★★ 1990. Dir: Jonathan Frakes. Guest cast: Suzie Plakson, Robert O'Reilly, Jon Steuer, Charles Cooper, Patrick Massett, Michael Rider.

Frakes scores another bullseye with this classic Klingon-themed episode where Worf's ex (Plakson) and heretofore unknown son (Steuer) visit the *Enterprise* along with several contenders to replace the Klingon's recently assassinated leader. A real actor's tour-de-force for Michael Dorn and guest stars Plakson and Cooper.

ROYALE, THE

★★ 1989. Dir: Cliff Bole. Guest cast: Noble Willingham, Sam Anderson, Jill Jacobson, Colm Meaney.

Investigating some wreckage from a twenty-first-century spacecraft, Riker, Data, and Worf become trapped in a weird, otherworldly casino created by aliens from a pulp novel in the spacecraft. An interesting idea gets flat handling; writer Tracy Torme took another pseudonym for this one.

SAMARITAN SNARE

★★☆ 1989. Dir: Les Landau. Guest cast: Christopher Collins, Leslie Morris, Lycia Naff.

While Picard is away on a shuttle ride with Wesley, Riker underestimates the intentions of a pair of dumpy, harmless-seeming aliens called Pakleds who ultimately kidnap Laforge when he beams aboard their ship. A slight reworking of the original *Trek*'s "The Corbomite Maneuver," with a nice role for LeVar Burton's Geordi.

SAREK

★★★ 1990. Dir: Les Landau. Guest cast: Mark Lenard, Joanna Miles, Rocco Sisto, Colm Meaney.

The legendary Vulcan ambassador Sarek (Lenard) is being transported by the *Enterprise* to a peace conference when he begins showing signs of a debilitating, Alzheimer's type of disease. Great performances from Lenard and Patrick Stewart (Picard mind-melds with Sarek at one point to experience all of the Vulcan's long-repressed emotions) in this well-crafted homage to one of the original series' best remembered characters.

SCHIZOID MAN, THE

★★★ 1989. Dir: Les Landau. Guest cast: W. Morgan Sheppard, Suzie Plakson, Barbara Alyn Woods.

Dr. Ira Graves (Sheppard), the mentor of Data's creator, dies, but before he does he finds a way to place his consciousness in the android's body. A better than usual second-season segment, with the usual good work from Brent Spiner and the classic "beard" scene.

SHADES OF GRAY

★ 1989. Dir: Rob Bowman. Guest cast: Colm Meaney.

The final episode of the mostly dire second season may be the worst of the lot. Riker is stricken with a deadly microorganism and lies near death while Troi tries desperately to rid him of the negative thoughts and memories the disease lives off. Lots of hand wringing and film clips.

SILICONE AVATAR

★★☆ 1991. Dir: Cliff Bole. Guest cast: Ellen Geer, Susan Diol.

A twenty-fourth-century sex-change retelling of *Moby Dick*, with Geer as a scientist out to destroy the dreaded Crystalline Entity (first seen in the episode "Datalore") after it kills her son. A subplot where Data shares the dead son's consciousness adds emotional weight to this otherwise routine story.

SINS OF THE FATHER

★★★☆ 1990. Dir: Les Landau. Guest cast: Tony Todd, Charles Cooper, Patrick Massett, Themla Lee.

When a Klingon exchange officer (Todd, best known as the *Candyman*) arrives aboard the *Enterprise* and turns out to be Worf's younger brother, Worf and Picard head to Klingon to clear the name of the brother's father, branded a traitor. Emmy-winning art direction and high-caliber dramatics in one of season three's richest shows.

SKIN OF EVIL

★★☆ 1988. Dir: Joseph L. Scanlon. Guest cast: Walker Boone, Mart McChesney, voice of Ronald Gans.

The infamous final episode for Tasha Yar, this finds the security chief dispatched by an oozing black monster called Armus, created from the cast-off sins of an alien race. Coscripted by *Outer Limits* veteran Joseph Stefano, this is often downright silly, but the final "farewell" scene still packs an emotional wallop.

SUDDENLY HUMAN

★★☆ 1990. Dir: Gabrielle Beaumont. Guest cast: Chad Allen, Sherman Howard, Barbara Townsend.

The *Enterprise* rescues a human teenager (Allen) raised as a Talarian who ends up at the center of a custody battle between his human grandmother and adoptive Talarian father. Originally intended as a story about child abuse (both sexual and otherwise), this evolved instead into a semi-remake of the classic *Trek* episode "Charlie X" with a soupçon of *Kramer vs. Kramer*. Well acted, but mostly a missed opportunity.

SURVIVORS, THE

★★★ 1989. Dir: Les Landau. Guest cast: John Anderson, Anne Haney.

An away team encounters the two lone human survivors of a colony ravaged by alien attack—but neither survivor turns out to be what they seem. An interesting, rather downbeat story with good acting from Anderson and Haney and echoes of the original *Trek*'s "Man Trap" episode.

SYMBIOSIS

★★ 1988. Dir: Win Phelps. Guest cast: Merritt Butrick, Judson Scott, Kenneth Tigar.

A heavy-handed antidrug message show, with the *Enterprise* rescuing crew members and a miracle cure from a disabled freighter. The "cure," however, turns out to be an addictive narcotic used to control an entire race. Butrick, who played Kirk's son in *Star Trek*'s II and III, died of AIDS not long after this was shot.

TIME SQUARED

★★☆ 1989. Dir: Joseph L. Scanlon. Guest cast: Colm Meaney.

A distortion in time forces Picard to confront his own future self. An interesting but somewhat confusing show that was "dumbed down" considerably from a more sophisticated (and coherent) storyline devised by scripter Maurice Hurley.

TIN MAN

★★ 1990. Dir: Robert Scheerer. Guest cast: Michael Cavanaugh, Harry Groener, Colm Meaney.

The *Enterprise* transports a powerful telepath (Groener) to a rendezvous with an omnipotent, machinelike alien nicknamed "Tin Man"—also being sought by the Romulans. An emotional but too predictable adaptation of the novel *Tin Woodsman* by Dennis Putnam Bailey and David Bischoff.

TOO SHORT A SEASON

★★ 1988. Dir: Rob Bowman. Guest cast: Clayton Rohner, Marsha Hunt, Michael Pataki.

An aged Starfleet admiral is given a de-aging drug by an alien race and startles both his wife and the *Enterprise* crew by growing forty years younger overnight. The guest cast is great, but this effort, co-scripted by D. C. Fontana, is a bit thin dramatically.

TRANSFIGURATIONS

★★★ 1991. Dir: Tom Benko. Guest cast: Mark La Mura, Charles Dennis, Julie Warner, Colm Meaney.

An amnesic alien (La Mura) with incredible healing powers is brought aboard the *Enterprise*. A simple, well-acted story with a nice subplot where the shy Laforge romances pretty Warner.

UNIFICATION

★★★☆ 1991. Dirs: Les Landau, Cliff Bole. Guest cast: Leonard Nimoy, Mark Lenard, Denise Crosby, Malachi Throne, Graham Jarvis, Vidal Peterson.

In this two-part episode featuring a special appearance by the original *Trek*'s favorite son, Picard seeks out fabled Vulcan scientist and former Starfleet officer Spock (Nimoy) to inform him of the death of his father, Sarek (Lenard). Spock is heavily involved in negotiations to reunite the Vulcan and Romulan peoples but various factions, one headed by the evil Selena (Crosby), are out to sabotage his efforts. A *Next Generation* high-watermark, the richly structured drama full of action and emotion does get a bit goofy and contrived in part two but is still a classic.

UNNATURAL SELECTION

★☆ 1989. Dir: Paul Lynch. Guest cast: Patricia Smith, J. Patrick McNamara, Colm Meaney.

Dr. Pulaski is infected with a lethal premature aging disease in this reworking of the old "Deadly Years" classic *Trek* episode conceived as a showcase for Diana Muldar. One of the weakest of all *Next Generation* shows, with an especially absurd ending.

UP THE LONG LADDER

★★ 1989. Dir: Winrich Kolbe. Guest cast: Barrie Ingham, Rosalyn Landor, John deVries, Colm Meaney.

The *Enterprise* rescues two groups of alien colonists, one of which was cloned from the other. When the clones need fresh DNA to survive, they kidnap Riker and Pulaski to that end. A fascinating idea marred by mediocre treatment.

VENGEANCE FACTOR, THE
★★★ 1989. Dir: Timothy Bond. Guest cast: Lisa Wilcox, Nancy Parsons, Joey Aresco, Stephen Lee, Marc Lawrence.

Picard's attempt to bring peace to warring alien races is complicated when Riker falls for a female assassin (Wilcox, of *Nightmare on Elm Street*, parts 4 and 5) determined to kill off all members of the enemy tribe. An exceptional guest cast (including Parsons—from *Motel Hell* and *Porky's*—and veteran character actor Lawrence) sparks this one.

WE'LL ALWAYS HAVE PARIS
★★ 1988. Dir: Robert Becker. Guest cast: Michelle Phillips, Rod Loomis, Isabel Lorca, Jean Paul Vignon.

When the *Enterprise* rescues a scientist experimenting with time, Picard is shocked to learn that the man's wife (former Mamas and Papas singer Phillips) is his long lost love. This rather sappy romance is a throwback to all those original *Trek* Kirk's women shows (where virtually every female guest star played an old conquest), made palatable by sincere acting.

WHEN THE BOUGH BREAKS
★★☆ 1988. Dir: Kim Manners. Guest cast: Jerry Hardin, Branda Strong, Jandi Swanson, Paul Lambert, Ivy Bethune.

Modest first-season show that attempts to deal with the families stationed aboard the *Enterprise*. A dying alien race steals the Starship's children—including Wesley—to perpetuate their race.

WHERE NO MAN HAS GONE BEFORE
★★★☆ 1987. Dir: Rob Bowman. Guest cast: Stanley Kamel, Eric Menyuk, Herta Ware, Biff Yeager.

A brilliant Starfleet scientific consultant plunges the *Enterprise* into a different dimension when his new warp drive malfunctions. The first truly great *Next Generation* episode, full of fascinating plot twists and excellent special effects.

WHERE SILENCE HAS LEASE
★★ 1988. Dir: Winrich Kolbe. Guest cast: Earl Boen, Charles Douglass, Colm Meaney.

Prolific *Next Generation* director Kolbe's first episode was this intriguing but not really successful tale of the *Enterprise* trapped in an endless void by an alien superpower studying the crew's reaction to death.

WHO WATCHES THE WATCHERS?
★★★ 1989. Dir: Robert Wiemer. Guest cast: Kathryn Leigh Scott, Ray Wise, Pamela Seagall, James Greene, John McLiam.

A Prime Directive violation leads to the *Enterprise* crew being mistaken for ancient gods on a primitive planet. A thoughtful, well-acted show whose impressive guest cast includes Scott (Maggie Evans on the original *Dark Shadows*) and Wise (Leland Palmer on *Twin Peaks*).

WOUNDED, THE
★★★ 1991. Dir: Chip Chalmers. Guest cast: Rosalind Chao, Bob Gunton, Colm Meaney, Marc Alaimo.

Solidly dramatic segment puts a welcome spotlight on semi-regular O'Brien (Meaney). A renegade starship destroying ships of the Cardassian race turns out to be commanded by a captain (Gunton) under whom O'Brien once served.

YESTERDAY'S ENTERPRISE
★★★★ 1990. Dir: David Carson. Guest cast: Denise Crosby, Whoopi Goldberg, Tricia O'Neill, Christopher McDonald.

Classic episode in which a time rift sends the original starship *Enterprise* into the twenty-fourth century. With history changed, the Klingon-Federation alliance has never occurred and Tasha Yar is still alive. Only Guinan realizes that something's amiss until she convinces Picard and Yar that time and history must be restored to normalcy. A beautifully complicated, beautifully acted "what if" episode with pleasing echoes of the classic *Trek's* great "Mirror, Mirror" segment.

THE TWILIGHT ZONE
CBS/Fox, 1959–64, NR, 50 min. per tape.

Introduced each week in the sharp, clipped manner of creator, writer, and guiding force Rod Serling, *The Twilight Zone* is unique among TV anthology shows for a number of reasons. For one thing, Serling, whose previous TV work included the Emmy-winning *Patterns* and *Requiem for a Heavyweight,* used the framework of science fiction, fantasy, and horror to tell the sort of stories he wanted to tell about ordinary people in extraordinary circumstances. It's the *humanity* of Serling's characters and their predicaments that sets the show apart from the tongue-in-cheek *Alfred Hitchcock Presents* and the gimmicky *One Step Beyond.* Premiering in 1959 and quickly becoming both a critical and popular favorite (the phrase *Twilight Zone* soon became part of the pop lexicon and the eerie theme music one of the most imitated in TV history), the half-hour show (with one season going a full hour) showcased top talent on both sides of the camera, including directors like John Brahm, Robert Florey, and Ida Lupino, and writers such as Richard Matheson, Charles Beaumont, and George Clayton Johnson. Guest stars included Jack Klugman, Agnes Moorehead, William Shatner, Cliff Robertson, Inger Stevens, Dennis Hopper, Robert Duvall, Anne Francis, Buster Keaton, Telly Savalas, Martin Landau, Robert Redford, Carol Burnett, Lee Marvin, Burt Reynolds, Vera Miles, Hazel Court, Julie Newmar, Lois Nettleton, and the ubiquitous Burgess Meredith.

After the three-time Emmy-winning show was canceled in 1964, Serling wrote several screenplays, including coscripting the classic *Planet of the Apes*, and in 1969 he wrote a TV horror film called *Night Gallery*. Later spun off into the weekly series *Rod Serling's Night Gallery*, Serling's actual involvement with the show was minimal; he basically appeared as on-camera narrator (à la *Zone*) and wrote some of the more thoughtful episodes, later lamenting the fact that NBC was more interested in action and gimmicks than in creating a well-acted and -written anthology horror show. Though Serling died of cancer at the young age of fifty in 1976, his legacy lived on. *Twilight Zone—The Movie*, directed by Steven Spielberg, Joe Dante, George Miller, and John Landis and made up of remakes and/or homages of classic episodes, was a box-office hit in 1983 and two years later CBS launched a new series of *The Twilight Zone* in September 1985. Although it lasted two seasons and contained several notable episodes (as well as remakes of several classic *Zones*), its main accomplishment was in showing just how individual and special Serling's vision for the original *Twilight Zone* was—and will remain.

DEATH'S HEAD REVISITED

★★★☆ 1961. Dir: Don Medford. Cast: Joseph Schildkraut, Oscar Beregi, Karen Verne, Ben Wright.

One of Serling's favorite themes—the sins of the past catching up with the sinner—is perfectly showcased in this ghost story about a former German SS officer (Beregi) tormented by the spirits of concentration camp victims at the ruins of Dachau.

DUMMY, THE

★★★★ 1962. Dir: Abner Biberman. Cast: Cliff Robertson, Frank Sutton, George Murdock, Sandra Warner.

Classic episode, similar in theme to the movie *Magic* and the final story in the anthology film *Dead of Night*, with Robertson as a ventriloquist dominated by his dummy. A familiar story is given a lift via stylish direction, intense acting (Robertson and Sutton—the latter best known as Sergeant Carter on *Gomer Pyle, USMC*—are superb), and a chilling surprise ending.

ENCOUNTER, THE

★★☆ 1964. Dir: Robert Butler. Cast: Neville Brand, George Takei.

When a mysterious force traps a prejudiced World War II veteran and a young Japanese gardener in an attic, old resentments come into play. The strong acting of the two players (including future *Star Trek* star Takei) elevate this hard-to-swallow scenario that has been little seen since its original broadcast.

EYE OF THE BEHOLDER, THE

★★★★ 1960. Dir: Douglas Heyes. Cast: Maxine Stuart, Donna Douglas, William Gordon, Joanna Heyes, Edson Stroll, Jennifer Howard.

A horribly disfigured young woman is given one last chance at life through radical plastic surgery—but things aren't quite as they seem. Another classic, beautifully directed by Heyes and with a punchline that's still effective after all these years. Stuart plays the bandaged heroine and future *Beverly Hillbillies* star Douglas is the girl revealed at the end. Some prints bear the title *A Private World of Darkness*.

FEVER, THE

★★☆ 1960. Dir: John Brahm. Cast: Harry Townes, Ross Martin, Philip Pine, Don Gordon, Beverly Garland, Peter Brocco.

A man with the ability to alter his face to resemble anyone he wishes makes the fatal mistake of impersonating the wrong man. An absurd premise is given some weight via good direction and a strong cast.

FUGITIVE, THE

★★☆ 1962. Dir: Richard L. Bare. Cast: H. Pat O'Malley, Susan Gordon, Nancy Kulp, Wesley Lau, Russ Bender.

Sweet fantasy about a kindly old man (O'Malley) who turns out to be a shape-shifting visitor from space who uses his otherworldly powers to cure a crippled young girl (Gordon, daughter of veteran schlock movie director Bert I. Gordon).

GAME OF POOL, A

★★★ 1961. Dir: Buzz Kulick. Cast: Jack Klugman, Jonathan Winters.

A dramatic tour-de-force for Klugman and Winters as a billiard hall hustler calls upon the ghost of the greatest pool player who ever lived for one final game. The stakes: the hustler's life.

GRAVE, THE

★★★ 1961. Dir: Montgomery Pittman. Cast: Lee Marvin, Strother Martin, James Best, Lee Van Cleef, Ellen Willard, Stafford Repp.

Spooky story of the Old West with Marvin perfectly cast as a braggadocio gunslinger, marked for death by a murdered gunman who promised to reach out from the grave for revenge. The impressive supporting cast of character actors includes Repp, later to play Chief O'Hara on the *Batman* TV show.

HITCH-HIKER, THE

★★★ 1960. Dir: Alvin Genzer. Cast: Inger Stevens, Leonard Strong, Adam Williams, Russ Bender, Mitzi McCall, Eleanor Audley.

A radio play by Lucille Fletcher (*Sorry, Wrong Number*) formed the basis for this eerie show about a motorist (an edgy Stevens) haunted by the recurrent figure of a menacing hitchhiker (Strong). The surprise ending is quite similar to that of the horror classic *Carnival of Souls*.

HOWLING MAN, THE

★★★★ 1960. Dir: Douglas Heyes. Cast: John Carradine, H. M. Wynant, Robin Hughes, Frederic Ledubur, Ezelle Poule.

A young traveler stumbles upon a European monastery where the brothers claim that a man imprisoned in a cell is actually the devil. Another classic, with top performances from horror great Carradine and character actor Hughes (the latter probably best known for the title role of *The Thing That Couldn't Die*), totally over-the-top direction (the camera work will make you seasick), and a great ending.

INVADERS, THE

★★★☆ 1961. Dir: Douglas Heyes. Cast: Agnes Moorehead, voice of Douglas Heyes.

Moorehead is a mute farm woman menaced by miniature spacemen in this well-remembered episode sparked by an emphatic star performance. Written by Richard Matheson, this is something of a first runthrough for many ideas that would later resurface in the famous Zuni doll segment of the TV movie *Trilogy of Terror*.

I SING THE BODY ELECTRIC

★★☆ 1962. Dirs: James Sheldon, William Claxton. Cast: Josephine Hutchinson, David White, Veronica Cartwright, Charles Herbert, Dana Dillaway, Vaughn Taylor.

Ray Bradbury adapted his own story for this one, about a trio of motherless kids whose father buys for them a robot grandmother as a caretaker. Hutchinson (as the grandma) and Cartwright (as the eldest child) shine in this otherwise ordinary episode, remade to better effect in 1982 as the TV special *The Electric Grandmother* starring Maureen Stapleton. Codirector Claxton later helmed the giant bunny classic *Night of the Lepus*.

JUDGMENT NIGHT

★★★ 1959. Dir: John Brahm. Cast: Nehemiah Persoff, Ben Wright, Patrick Macnee, James Franciscus, Deidre Owen, Hugh Sanders.

On a fog-bound luxury liner, an increasingly hysterical passenger (Persoff) is convinced that the ship will sink—and that he's experienced all this before. A creepy *Flying Dutchman* variant directed with an atmospheric eye by Brahm. Partly reworked as the *Night Gallery* episode "Lone Survivor."

KICK THE CAN

★★★ 1962. Dir: Lamont Johnson. Cast: Ernest Truex, Russell Collins, John Marley, Marjorie Bennett, Burt Mustin, Hank Patterson.

A magical game of kick the can turns a group of retirement home residents into children. George Clayton Johnson wrote this nicely moving piece that was remade by Steven Spielberg for *Twilight Zone—The Movie* with a slightly different and much more conventional ending.

KING NINE WILL NOT RETURN

★★☆ 1960. Dir: Buzz Kulik. Cast: Robert Cummings, Paul Lambert, Gene Lyons, Jenna McMahon.

Cummings is excellent in this otherwise predictable story about a man who discovers that he is the sole survivor of a military plane crash—but has no memory of who he is or what his life was prior to the crash.

LAST FLIGHT, THE

★★☆ 1960. Dir: William Claxton. Cast: Kenneth Haigh, Simon Scott, Alexander Scourby, Robert Warwick.

A cowardly World War I flyer passes through a strange cloud and suddenly finds himself at a 1960s air base. A well-acted if somewhat obvious fantasy, scripted by Richard Matheson, that was the first non-Serling teleplay of the series aired.

LAST RITES OF JEFF MYRTLEBANK, THE

★★☆ 1962. Dir: Montgomery Pittman. Cast: James Best, Sherry Jackson, Lance Fuller, Dub Taylor, Edgar Buchanan, Jon Lormer.

Pleasant backwoods comedy about a country bumpkin (Best) who suddenly comes back to life at his own funeral. Now possessing strange powers, Jeff's superstitious neighbors believe him to be inhabited by the devil.

LATENESS OF THE HOUR, THE

★★★ 1960. Dir: Jack Smight. Cast: Inger Stevens, John Hoyt, Irene Tedrow, Mary Gregory.

The first of a half dozen *Zones* experimentally shot on videotape rather than film stock, this well-acted melodrama stars the always effective Stevens as a scientist's beautiful daughter who discovers that she is actually an android.

LONELY, THE

★★★☆ 1959. Dir: Jack Smight. Cast: Jack Warden, Jean Marsh, John Dehner, Ted Knight.

One of *Zone's* most notable early episodes concerns a convicted murderer stranded on a hostile desert planet with only a female-shaped robot for a companion. Warden and Marsh are excellent in this offbeat love story given an air of stifling authenticity by its boiling Desert Valley location work. Marsh later cocreated and starred in *Upstairs, Downstairs,* while Knight would find fame as Ted Baxter on *The Mary Tyler Moore Show.*

LONG DISTANCE CALL

★★☆ 1961. Dir: James Sheldon. Cast: Billy Mumy, Philip Abbott, Patricia Smith, Lili Darvas.

There's good acting in this ghost story about a young boy (a pre-*Lost in Space* Mumy) who communicates with his dead grandmother with a toy telephone—an idea later stolen by the movie *Poltergeist II.* Another videotaped episode.

MASKS, THE

★★★★ 1964. Dir: Ida Lupino. Cast: Robert Keith, Virginia Gregg, Milton Selzer, Alan Sues, Brooke Hayward.

Genuinely scary story of a dying millionaire (Keith) who forces his nasty relatives to don a set of grotesque Mardi Gras masks if they expect to inherit his fortune—with horrifying results. Veteran actress-director Lupino brings a real sense of unease to this creepy study of petty, greedy people and their tragic comeuppance. The cast includes future *Laugh-In* star Sues and Dennis Hopper's first wife Hayward.

MONSTERS ARE DUE ON MAPLE STREET, THE

★★★☆ 1960. Dir: Ron Winston. Cast: Claude Akins, Jack Weston, Barry Atwater, Mary Gregory, Anne Barton.

Paranoia and fear pits neighbor against neighbor when a power failure convinces the residents of a quiet suburban street that they are about to be invaded. This episode effectively captures the dark side of the all-American neighborhood, with an outstanding cast and an amusing tag scene.

MR. DENTON ON DOOMSDAY

★★☆ 1959. Dir: Alan Reisner. Cast: Dan Duryea, Martin Landau, Doug McClure, Jeanne Cooper, Malcolm Atterbury, Ken Lynch.

The first of several Western-themed episodes features Duryea as a drunken former gunslinger who buys what he believes to be a magic potion that will restore his former shooting ability for one last gunfight. The casting is perfection in this otherwise rather heavy-handed morality play.

MR. DINGLE, THE STRONG

★★ 1961. Dir: John Brahm. Cast: Burgess Meredith, Don Rickles, James Westerfield, Douglas Spencer, Michael Fox.

Meredith shines, as usual, in this otherwise silly comedy about a vacuum cleaner salesman given incredible strength by a two-headed Martian invader (played by Spencer and Fox).

NICK OF TIME

★★★★ 1960. Dir: Richard L. Bare. Cast: William Shatner, Patricia Breslin, Guy Wilkerson, Stafford Repp.

Classic horror episode stars Shatner in good form as a young husband who becomes obsessed with the predictions of a devil-headed fortune telling machine in a small-town cafe. Richard Matheson wrote this low-key, underplayed spooker that scares through implication rather than blatant shock tactics.

NIGHTMARE AT 20,000 FEET

★★★☆ 1963. Dir: Richard Donner. Cast: William Shatner, Christine White, Ed Kemmer, Asa Maynor, Nick Cravat.

Another Shatner classic. Bill pulls out all the stops as a hysterical airline passenger who keeps seeing a destructive gremlin on the wing of his storm-lashed plane. Apart from the silly makeup for the gremlin (played by Cravat, longtime friend and former aerialist partner of Burt Lancaster) this show holds up well, though it was probably improved on by the George Miller remake in the *Twilight Zone* movie.

NIGHT OF THE MEEK

★★★☆ 1960. Dir: Jack Smight. Cast: Art Carney, John Fiedler, Burt Mustin, Val Avery, Meg Wyllie, Robert Lieb.

Timeless holiday episode finds Carney at his best as a drunken department store Santa Claus who becomes the real thing through the power of faith. Another videotaped episode; remade for the '80s *Zone* incarnation with Richard Mulligan in the Carney role.

NOTHING IN THE DARK

★★★ 1962. Dir: Lamont Johnson. Cast: Gladys Cooper, Robert Redford, R. G. Armstrong.

An old woman (Cooper), living alone and frightened of death, allows a wounded young cop (Redford, quite wooden in an early role) into her apartment—little realizing who the young man really is. Good dialogue and sterling performances by Cooper and Armstrong highlight this segment scripted by George Clayton Johnson.

OBSOLETE MAN, THE

★★☆ 1961. Dir: Eliot Silverstein. Cast: Burgess Meredith, Fritz Weaver, Joseph Elic, Harry Fleer.

Powerfully acted—if rather one-note—drama about a totalitarian future where a condemned prisoner (Meredith) turns the tables on his prosecutor (Weaver) to prove that the will of the individual is greater than the will of the state.

OCCURRENCE AT OWL CREEK BRIDGE, AN

★★★★ 1962. Dir: Robert Enrico. Cast: Roger Jacquet, Anne Cornaly, Anker Larsen, Stephane Fey.

Originally a French short film picked up by *Zone* producers to save a few production bucks, this turns out to be one of the best and eeriest stories ever aired. Based on the Ambrose Bierce tale, it stars Jacquet as a southern spy captured by northern troops during the Civil War and sentenced to hang. Luckily, our hero manages to escape his hanging and run home to his loving wife—doesn't he? Rarely seen and truly classic.

ODYSSEY OF FLIGHT 33, THE

★★☆ 1961. Dir: Justus Addiss. Cast: John Anderson, Paul Comi, Sandy Kenyon, Nancy Rennick.

An airliner is projected back through time to the prehistoric era. A famous if rather ordinary episode, with a good cast, some clever twists, and stock dinosaur footage from *Dinosaurus!*

ONCE UPON A TIME

★★ 1961. Dirs: Norman Z. McLeod, Leslie Goodwins.

Cast: Buster Keaton, Stanley Adams, Jesse White, Milton Parsons.

Conceived by writer Richard Matheson as a vehicle for silent screen great Keaton, this comic episode hardly comes off at all. In 1890, a janitor (Buster) steals an inventor's time travel helmet and travels ahead in time seventy years—only to discover that the 1960s aren't at all the utopia he'd envisioned. Keaton tries, but this isn't the least bit funny.

PASSAGE FOR TRUMPET, A

★★★☆ 1960. Dir: Don Medford. Cast: Jack Klugman, John Anderson, Mary Webster, Frank Wolff.

Klugman is superb on this variation of *It's a Wonderful Life,* about a down-and-out, suicidal trumpet player given a second chance at life after being trapped in a limbo between the living and the dead. A bit predictable, perhaps, but still a winner.

PASSERBY, THE

★★ 1961. Dir: Elliot Silverstein. Cast: Joanne Linville, James Gregory, Austin Green, Warren Kemmerling.

While waiting for her husband to return home from the Civil War, a southern woman (Linville) soon comes to realize that all those passing along the road in front of her house are really dead. Good acting helps this passable, obvious *Gone with the Wind* with ghosts.

PERCHANCE TO DREAM

★★★ 1959. Dir: Robert Florey. Cast: Richard Conte, John Larch, Suzanne Lloyd, Eddie Marr.

A man with a heart condition (Conte) seeks psychiatric help due to a recurring nightmare of a beautiful girl (Lloyd) he fears will kill him. Charles Beaumont wrote this taut segment, well acted by Conte and atmospherically directed by veteran Florey (*The Beast with Five Fingers*).

PRIME MOVER, THE

★★☆ 1961. Dir: Richard L. Bare. Cast: Buddy Ebsen, Dane Clark, Christine White, Jane Burgess.

Amusing tidbit featuring Ebsen as a country bumpkin with telekinesis (picture Jed Clampett crossed with *Carrie*) who uses his abilities to help his friend (Clark) win at gambling in Las Vegas.

PROBE 7—OVER AND OUT

★☆ 1963. Dir: Ted Post. Cast: Richard Basehart, Antoinette Bower, Barton Heyman, Harold Gould.

Fine actors Basehart and Bower are stranded in this hoary chestnut about two space travelers from different worlds forced to survive together on a hostile planet. The "surprise" ending's a real groaner.

PURPLE TESTAMENT, THE

★★★ 1960. Dir: Richard L. Bare. Cast: William Reynolds, Dick York, Barney Phillips, Warren Oates.

Reynolds is excellent in this eerie story about a soldier with the ability to predict which of his comrades will die in battle.

QUALITY OF MERCY, THE

★★☆ 1961. Dir: Buzz Kulik. Cast: Dean Stockwell, Albert Salmi, Jerry Fujikawa, Dale Ishimoto, Leonard Nimoy, Michael Pataki.

An overzealous young army officer (Stockwell) gets to see World War II from another perspective when he suddenly finds his mind occupying the body of a Japanese soldier. A very good cast highlights this thoughtful but talky entry.

SHADOW PLAY

★★★ 1961. Dir: John Brahm. Cast: Dennis Weaver, Harry Townes, Wright King, Anne Barton, Bernie Hamilton, Gene Roth.

Weaver is first rate in this suspenseful tale of a convicted murderer who tries to prevent his upcoming execution by claiming that the entire world and everyone in it is merely a figment of his imagination that will cease to exist when he dies.

SHELTER, THE

★★☆ 1961. Dir: Lamont Johnson. Cast: Larry Gates, Jack Albertson, Peggy Stewart, Sandy Kenyon, John McLiam, Joseph Bernard.

UFO reports cause a man to lock his family away in a bomb shelter also coveted by his less well-prepared neighbors. The acting is good but most of this was better handled in "The Monsters Are Due on Maple Street."

SIXTEEN MILLIMETER SHRINE, THE

★★★ 1959. Dir: Mitchell Leisen. Cast: Ida Lupino, Martin Balsam, Jerome Cowan, Alice Frost.

A *Zone* version of *Sunset Boulevard*, with Lupino in good form as an aging actress who now feels more alive in her old movies than in real life; eventually she literally retreats into the movies. Balsam is equally good as Ida's devoted agent in this first-class show.

STEEL

★★★ 1963. Dir: Don Weis. Cast: Lee Marvin, Joe Mantell, Chuck Hicks, Tipp McClure.

Marvin is at the top of his game as the manag-er of a robot boxer who steps into the ring himself to win the money needed to effect repairs on his beloved mechanical pugilist. Another solid, Richard Matheson-scripted entry.

THIRD FROM THE SUN

★★☆ 1960. Dir: Richard L. Bare. Cast: Fritz Weaver, Joe Maross, Edward Andrews, Lori March, Denise Alexander, Jeanne Evans.

A scientist plots to escape via spaceship with his family when nuclear war seems imminent. Another episode that probably played a lot better when it first aired, due to the pre-dictability of its "shock" ending, this Serling adaptation of a Richard Matheson story still has fine acting and imaginative direction in its favor.

TIME ENOUGH AT LAST

★★★★ 1959. Dir: John Brahm. Cast: Burgess Meredith, Vaughn Taylor, Jacqueline DeWit, Lela Bliss.

Unforgettable tale of a book-loving bank teller (Meredith) who just wants to be left alone to read—and feels that he's at last found his chance when seemingly everyone else in the world is killed by nuclear devastation. Everything works in this quintessential episode, from the performing of Meredith to the devastating last-minute twist. Maybe the most famous of *Zone* episodes.

TO SERVE MAN

★★★ 1962. Dir: Richard L. Bare. Cast: Lloyd Bochner, Richard Kiel, Susan Cummings, Theo Marcuse.

One of the series' most memorable punchlines tops this story about huge alien invaders (all of them played by Kiel, the future Jaws from *The Spy Who Loved Me* and *Moonraker*) who invite a shipload of gullible Earthlings back to their homeworld for dinner. Bochner hilariously spoofed this episode in a throwaway gag in *Naked Gun* 2+.

TRADE INS, THE

★★★ 1962. Dir: Elliot Silverstein. Cast: Joseph Schildkraut, Alam Platt, Noah Keen, Theo Marcuse, Edson Stroll.

Schildkraut is great in this sensitive study about the value of the elderly in society. Old and sick, he is convinced by loving wife Platt that he should have his mind transferred to the studly younger body of Stroll, only to discover that there's more to the quality of life than a full head of hair and a killer bod—sentiments that surely wouldn't pass muster today!

TWO
★★★☆ 1961. Dir: Montgomery Pittman. Cast: Charles Bronson, Elizabeth Montgomery.

Another sci-fi-tinged Adam and Eve story, and better done than most, featuring Bronson and Montgomery as nuclear war survivors from opposite sides of the conflict who try to come together in the ruins of modern society. The stars are top notch and the atmosphere compelling in this memorable show.

WALKING DISTANCE
★★★ 1959. Dir: Robert Stevens. Cast: Gig Young, Frank Overton, Irene Tedrow, Michael Montgomery, Byron Foulger, Ronnie Howard.

Another favorite Serling theme—a man trying to reach into the past to recapture the goodness he's lost—is well served in this episode, with Young as a burnt-out advertising man who returns to his boyhood home, where he finds himself projected into his own past and encountering himself as a child. Young has rarely been better.

WHERE IS EVERYBODY?
★★★ 1959. Dir: Robert Stevens. Cast: Earl Holliman, James Gregory, Paul Langton, Gary Walberg.

The pilot episode, with Holliman as an amnesiac air force pilot who finds himself stumbling about a completely deserted landscape devoid of all other people—though things aren't quite what they seem. A good, if not great, starting point for the classic series; the ultimate truth of the plot still packs a bit of a punch.

THE X-FILES
FOX, 1993–94, NR, 92 min. per tape.

Intended by creator Chris Carter as a tribute to one of his favorite TV shows, Kolchak: The Night Stalker, The X-Files has quickly established itself as one of the most popular cult shows of the last few years. Gillian Anderson plays Dana Scully, a special agent for the FBI assigned by her superiors to work with agent Fox Mulder (David Duchovny). Mulder, nicknamed "Spooky" by his colleagues, is intensely obsessed by the bureau's so-called "X-Files," unsolved or ongoing cases involving aspects of the supernatural and the unexplained, and it is these sorts of cases in which the agents now find themselves continually involved.

Unlike Kolchak, which played its horrors with broad, tongue-in-cheek strokes, The X-Files has a serious, melancholy tone that often makes it heavy going, relieved by the on-target casting of the likable, slightly goofy Duchovny and the pretty, hard-faced Anderson. Also frequently featured are Mitch Pileggi as assistant FBI director Walter Skinner and William B. Davis as the "cigarette smoking man," a shadowy figure often seen guiding Mulder's actions from the sidelines. Various plots involve everything from UFO abductions (Mulder's own sister was supposedly the victim of such a kidnapping) to evil tree spirits to alien parasites to werewolves and more. Filmed in Vancouver, British Columbia, the bleak Canadian locales offer a moody background to the often overfamiliar plots. I like The X-Files, but more for its sly winks at classic horror and science fiction movies and television than for its "The truth is out there!" superserious paranoia stuff. A bit more humor and a little less self-reverence could help this become a true classic of its kind.

ASCENSION
★★ 1994. Dir: Michael Lange. Guest cast: Steve Railsback, Nicholas Lea, Sheila Larkin, Steven Williams.

In this followup to "Duane Barry," Mulder is removed from the case of the deranged agent Barry (Railsback) after Scully is kidnapped. Like too many Files episodes, this sets up some great ideas then spoils them by overkill, like the flashbacks to the abduction of Mulder's sister, a plot device that worked better via the suggestion that it may have all been a figment of Mulder's overactive imagination.

BEYOND THE SEA
★★★★ 1994. Dir: David Nutter. Guest cast: Brad Dourif, Don Davis, Sheila Larkin, Fred Henderson.

One of the series' best and most offbeat episodes. After being visited by the spirit of her late father (Davis), Scully comes to believe in the possibility of the supernatural while Mulder has his doubts about a mass-murdering death row inmate (Dourif, the voice of Chucky in the Child's Play movies) who claims to be in contact with the restless spirits of his victims. The role-reversal plotting and wigged out Dourif performance make this a classic.

CONDUIT
★★★ 1993. Dir: Daniel Sackheim. Guest cast: Carrie Snodgress, Joel Palmer, Charles Cioffi, Taunya Dee.

The agents investigate the alleged alien abduction of a teeage girl, a case that revives in Mulder memories of his own sister's disappearance long ago. A solid, well directed episode that effectively fleshes out the Mulder back story without revealing too much—a mistake often made in later segments.

David Duchovny shines a light on the unknown in
The X-Files *(1994).*

DARKNESS FALLS

★★★☆ 1994. Dir: Joe Napolitano. Guest cast: Jason Beghe, Tom O'Rourke, Titus Welliver, Barry Greene.

When an ancient tree is felled in the northwest woods, primordial demons are unleashed on the area. One of the series' scariest shows, with an environmental stance that's both evenhanded and unforced.

DEEP THROAT

★★★☆ 1993. Dir: Daniel Sackheim. Guest cast: Jerry Hardin, Charles Cioffi, Seth Green, Michael Bryan French, Andrew Johnston, Lalainia Lindejerg.

After an ex-air force test pilot goes berserk, Scully and Mulder investigate his background, with the aid of the mysterious Deep Throat (Hardin), and discover that he was once stationed at a military base that may be the site of a captured UFO. The second episode, this improves on the pilot by being unburdened by situational setups and simply gets on with it. A great touch is that the only witnesses to a UFO appearance are a couple of stoned grungers.

DUANE BARRY

★★☆ 1994. Dir: Chris Carter. Guest cast: Steve Railsback, C.C.H. Pounder, Nicholas Lea, Frank C. Turner, Stephen E. Miller, Barbara Pollard.

The first half of an awkward two-parter has Mulder reteamed with Lea after Scully is taken hostage by a crazed FBI agent (a well-cast Railsback) who claims to have been abducted by aliens. An interesting idea that just doesn't come off and really sputters out during the protracted conclusion.

E.B.E.

★★☆ 1994. Dir: William Graham. Guest cast: Jerry Hardin, Allan Lysell, Peter La Croix, Bruce Harwood.

Mulder becomes obsessed—again—with the coverup of a downed Iraqi jet he is sure was the victim of a close encounter. The usual stuff, familiar but well enough handled.

ERLENMEYER FLASK, THE

★★★ 1994. Dir: R. W. Goodwin. Guest cast: Simon Webb, Jerry Hardin, Ken Kramer, Anne DeSalvo, Lindsay Ginter.

The discovery of an alien corpse may finally provide the proof Mulder needs to convince his superiors, and the world, of the existence of extraterrestrials—or has he finally lost his mind? A solid episode with a good role for Hardin's Deep Throat and some really bizarre twists.

EVE

★★★☆ 1993. Dir: Fred Gerber. Guest cast: Harriet Harris, Jerry Hardin, Erika Krievins, Sabrina Krievins.

When two loving fathers are murdered, vampire-style, on opposite coasts of the United States at precisely the same moment, the agents are shocked to discover that the victims have identical eight-year-old daughters. A marvelously confusing tale of genetics and cloning, vampirism and bad seeds that keeps you guessing and provocatively never fully answers all the questions it raises.

FALLEN ANGEL

★★★ 1993. Dir: Larry Shaw. Guest cast: Frederick Coffin, Jerry Hardin, Marshall Bell, Scott Bellis.

Mulder is in more hot water than usual when he investigates an alleged toxic waste spill in Wisconsin he believes is a coverup for a UFO crash. A strong show with a great character in Bellis's long-haired UFO groupie (who knows more than he is aware of), but the climax is more than a little unlikely.

HOST, THE
★★★ 1994. Dir: Daniel Sackheim. Guest cast: Darin Morgan, Marc Bauer, Freddy Andreiuci, Gabrielle Rose.

Mulder considers leaving the bureau after a string of "meaningless" cases until his latest assignment brings him and Scully face to face with a murderous, sewer-dwelling worm monster. A good, old-fashioned monster story that really kicks into gear after a rather contrived beginning.

ICE
★★★ 1993. Dir: David Nutter. Guest cast: Xander Berkeley, Felicity Huffman, Steve Hytner, Jeff Kober.

In a *Files* version of *The Thing*, scientists at an Alaskin geological dig are taken over by a mind-controlling, brain-burrowing slug. An economically constructed entry with some creepy special FX.

LITTLE GREEN MEN
★★ 1994. Dir: David Nutter. Guest cast: Raymond J. Barry, Mike Gomez, Vanessa Morley, Marcus Turner, Les Carlson.

The second-season opener is a disappointing, aimed-at-the-fans affair in which the X-Files operation is closed down and the reassigned Scully and Mulder examine their lives and relationship until Mulder discovers yet another military alien coverup. The germ of a good idea spoiled by too much coy soap opera.

ONE BREATH
★★ 1994. Dir: R. W. Goodwin. Guest cast: Sheila Larkin, Don Davis, Melinda McGraw, Steven Williams, Bruce Harwood, Nicola Cavendish.

Scully is found in a coma and a concerned Mulder investigates in this back story episode necessitated by Gillian Anderson's real-life pregnancy (she was also conspicuously absent from several other episodes from this period as well). This has a good character in Scully's New Age sister (McGraw) and an eerie scene with Scully in a boat and a ghostly, beckoning nurse (reminiscent of the film *The Innocents*) but not much else.

PILOT
★★★ 1993. Dir: Robert Mandel. Guest cast: Charles Cioffi, Cliff DeYoung, Sarah Koskoff, Leon Russom.

FBI agent Dana Scully is partnered with obsessive Fox Mulder to investigate a series of murders in an Oregon town where the victims are all members of the same high school graduating class. This first episode neatly sets up the series: Mulder is the intense believer in all things unnatural while Scully refuses to be taken in by any of this foolishness, even when faced with the evidence of a grotesque, otherworldly corpse found in a victim's grave. Well directed by Mandel, full of all the brooding atmosphere that's so much a part of the show's mystique.

SLEEPLESS
★★☆ 1994. Dir: Rob Bowman. Guest cast: Nicholas Lea, Tony Todd, Steven Williams, Jonathan Gries.

Mulder is now partnered with hunkling Lea while investigating a scientist's sleep disorder experiments and a Vietnam vet patient with amazing phycic powers. The first episode in which Gillian Anderson had to be more or less written out due to her pregnancy, this keeps threatening to be different only to retreat into the same old "evil conspiracy" stock plot overused during the first season.

SQUEEZE
★★★ 1993. Dir: Harry Longstreet. Guest cast: Doug Hutchinson, Donal Logue, Henry Beckman, Kevin McNulty.

The agents investigate a series of gruesome murders where the victims' livers are torn out and eaten. The most *Kolchak*-like of the early episodes, with a solid dose of creepiness and a strangely sympathetic antagonist. Followed by the sequel "Tooms."

TOOMS
★★★ 1994. Dir: David Nutter. Guest cast: Doug Hutchinson, Paul Ben Victor, Timothy Webber, Gillian Carfra.

This sequel to "Squeeze" is equally good, with the cannibalistic Tooms (Hutchinson) released by the authorities despite Mulder's protests. Meanwhile, Scully is reprimanded by her supervisors for not debunking her partner's claims more often. A worthy followup.

BillboardBooks

THANK YOU FOR BUYING A BILLBOARD BOOK.
IF YOU ENJOYED THIS TITLE, YOU MIGHT WANT
TO CHECK OUT OTHER BOOKS IN OUR CATALOG.

THE BILLBOARD BOOK OF AMERICAN SINGING GROUPS:
A History, 1940–1990 by Jay Warner
The definitive history of pop vocal groups, from the doo wop of Dion and the Belmonts, to the Motown hits of the Supremes, to the surf sound of the Beach Boys, to the country rock of Crosby, Stills and Nash. More than 350 classic acts spanning five decades are profiled here, with fascinating information about each group's career, key members, and musical impact as well as extensive discographies and rare photos. A one-of-a-kind reference for vocal group fans and record collectors alike. 544 pages. 80 photos. Paperback. $21.95. 0-8230-8264-4.

THE BILLBOARD BOOK OF NUMBER ONE ALBUMS:
The Inside Story Behind Pop Music's Blockbuster Records
by Craig Rosen
A behind-the-scenes look at the people and stories involved in the enormously popular records that achieved Number One album status in the Billboard charts. Inside information on over 400 albums that have topped the chart since 1956, plus new interviews with hundreds of superstar record artists as well as a wealth of trivia statistics and other facts. 448 pages. 425 photos. Paperback. $21.95. 0-8230-7586-9.

THE BILLBOARD BOOK OF NUMBER ONE HITS,
Third Edition, Revised and Enlarged
by Fred Bronson
The inside story behind the top of the charts. An indispensable listing of every single to appear in the top spot on the Billboard Hot 100 chart from 1955 through 1991, along with anecdotes, interviews, and chart data. 848 pages. 800 photos. Paperback. $21.95. 0-8230-8297-0.

THE BILLBOARD BOOK OF TOP 40 ALBUMS,
Third Edition, Revised and Enlarged by Joel Whitburn
The complete guide to every Top 40 album from 1955 to 1994. Comprehensive information on the most successful rock, jazz, comedy, country, classical, Christmas, Broadway, and film soundtrack albums ever to reach the top of the Billboard charts. Includes chart positions, number of weeks on the chart, and label and catalog number for every album listed. 416 pages. 150 photos. Paperback. $21.95. 0-8230-7631-8.

THE BILLBOARD BOOK OF TOP 40 COUNTRY HITS:
Country Music's Hottest Records, 1944 to the Present
by Joel Whitburn

From the classic recordings of Hank Williams and Bob Wills, to enduring artists Patsy Cline and Tammy Wynette, to today's young superstars Garth Brooks and Shania Twain, the rich history of country music is documented in this comprehensive compilation of Billboard's Country Singles charts. Provides exhaustive data on every record to score at least one Top 40 hit. 562 pages. 96 photos. Paperback. $21.95. 0-8230-8289-X.

THE BILLBOARD BOOK OF TOP 40 HITS,
Sixth Edition, Revised and Enlarged
by Joel Whitburn

A perennial favorite, listing every single to reach the Top 40 of Billboard's weekly Hot 100 charts since 1955. Includes new chart data and expanded biographical information and trivia on artists listed. 800 pages. 300 photos. Paperback. $21.95. 0-8230-7632-6.

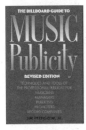

THE BILLBOARD GUIDE TO MUSIC PUBLICITY,
Revised Edition by Jim Pettigrew, Jr.

A clear-headed reference providing career-minded musicians and their representatives with key information about such vital activities as getting media exposure, preparing effective publicity materials, and developing short-term and long-range publicity. New to the revised edition is coverage of desktop publishing, compact disks, basic copy-editing tips, and a recommended reading list. 176 pages. 16 illustrations. Paperback. $18.95. 0-8230-7626-1.

THE REAL DEAL:
How to Get Signed to a Record Label From A to Z
by Daylle Deanna Schwartz

A new music industry primer offering crucial information and advice that any musician playing popular music and desiring a record deal needs to have. Also contains advice from top creative and business professionals and a resource section. 256 pages. Paperback. $16.95. 0-8230-7611-3.

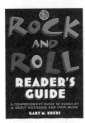

THE ROCK AND ROLL READER'S GUIDE
by Gary M. Krebs

An indispensable consumer guide for book collectors and music fans alike. The first comprehensive bibliography of books about, and by, rock and pop stars in addition to works written about the music scene itself. Focuses on both selected general reference works—such as artist profiles, chart data, pictorials, concert events, women and rock, and magazines—and all publications on artists A-Z. 464 pages. Paperback. $21.95. 0-8230-7602-4.

THIS BUSINESS OF ARTIST MANAGEMENT,
Revised and Enlarged Third Edition
by Xavier M. Frascogna, Jr. and H. Lee Hetherington

Firmly established as the standard reference work in the field of artist management in music, this new edition of the title formerly known as Successful Artist Management offers the wise guidance and authoritative professional information required to develop an artist's career. Now revised and updated to include interviews with top record executives, coverage of new forms of business, and updates on the legal framework of the music business. 304 pages. Hardcover. $21.95. 0-8230-7705-5.

THIS BUSINESS OF MUSIC,
Seventh Edition by M. William Krasilovsky
and Sidney Shemel

The bible of the music business, with over 250,000 copies sold. A practical guide to the music industry for publishers, writers, record companies, producers, artists, and agents. Provides detailed information on virtually every economic, legal, and financial aspect of the complex business of music. 736 pages. Hardcover. $29.95. 0-8230-7755-1.

KISS AND SELL:
The Making of A Supergroup by C.K. Lendt

A riveting expose of the machinations and manipulations of what's involved in making it to the top of the rock world, written by the man who traveled with Kiss for 12 years as their business manager. Both a case study of the harsh realities of how the business of music works and a unique perspective on the lives, lifestyles, and indulgences of rock stars. 352 pages. 18 photos. Paperback. $18.95. 0-8230-7551-6.

TERROR ON TAPE
by James O'Neill

The ultimate connoisseur's resource to horror movies on video. A complete, comprehensive guide to over 2,000 horror films from the past 75 years, from mainstream masterpieces like Psycho to cheesy exploitation flicks like Werewolf vs. the Vampire Woman, from cult classics like Night of the Living Dead to deservedly unknown bombs like The Worm Eaters. 400pp. 75 photos. Paperback. $16.95. 0-8230-7612-1.

The above titles should all be available from your neighborhood bookseller. If you don't find a copy on the shelf, books can also be ordered either through the store or directly from Watson-Guptill Publications. To order copies by phone or to request information on any of these titles, please call our toll-free number: 1-800-278-8477. To order copies by mail, send a check or money order for the cost of the book, with $2.00 postage and handling for one book and $.50 for each additional book, plus applicable sales tax in the states of CA, DC, IL, OH, MA, NJ, NY, PA, TN, and VA, to:

Watson Guptill Publications
PO Box 2013
Lakewood, NJ 08701-9913